HISTORICAL INTERSECTIONS OF INTERCULTURAL STUDIES (1): TRACING GENEALOGIES, TRAJECTORIES, DIVERSIFICATIONS

史学视角下的跨文化研究（一）：追踪谱系、轨迹与多样性

主　编：*Michael Steppat*
　　　　Steve J. Kulich（顾力行）

上海外语教育出版社
外教社 SHANGHAI FOREIGN LANGUAGE EDUCATION PRESS

图书在版编目(CIP)数据

史学视角下的跨文化研究.一,追踪谱系、轨迹与多
样性:英文/(德)迈克尔·斯代帕
(Michael Steppat),(美)顾力行(Steve J. Kulich)
主编.--上海:上海外语教育出版社,2024.--(跨文
化研究).-- ISBN 978-7-5446-8339-5

Ⅰ.K0-53

中国国家版本馆CIP数据核字第20241X7T00号

出版发行:**上海外语教育出版社**

（上海外国语大学内）邮编：200083

电　　话：021-65425300（总机）

电子邮箱：bookinfo@sflep.com.cn

网　　址：http://www.sflep.com

责任编辑：杨　洋

印　　刷：启东市人民印刷有限公司

开　　本：635×965　1/16　印张 30.25　字数 593 千字

版　　次：2024 年 12 月第 1 版　2024 年 12 月第 1 次印刷

书　　号：ISBN 978-7-5446-8339-5

定　　价：95.00 元

本版图书如有印装质量问题，可向本社调换

质量服务热线：4008-213-263

跨文化研究系列编委会

主　编

顾力行（上海外国语大学，上外跨文化研究中心）

Michael Steppat（德国拜罗伊特大学）

顾问编委

Dharm Bhawuk（美国夏威夷大学马诺阿分校）

陈国明（美国罗得岛大学）

陈　凌（香港浸会大学）

Kenneth Cushner　（美国肯特州立大学）

戴晓东（上海师范大学）

Darla Deardorff（南非斯坦陵布什大学）

窦卫霖（华东师范大学）

高一虹（北京大学）

关世杰（北京大学）

韩友耿（Jürgen Henze　德国柏林洪堡大学）

胡礼忠（上海外国语大学）

胡文仲（北京外国语大学）

贾文山（美国查普曼大学）

贾玉新（哈尔滨工业大学）

姜　飞（中国社会科学院大学）

陆建非（上海师范大学）

单　波（武汉大学）

宋　莉（哈尔滨工业大学）

孙有中（北京外国语大学）

孙　玉（上海外语教育出版社）

魏　明（Cooper Wakefield　美国玛丽安大学）
徐欣吾（Danny Hsu　美国深河学院）
颜静兰（华东理工大学）
严文华（华东师范大学）
张惠晶（美国奥尔巴尼大学）
张　睿（美国狄金森学院）
张雁冰（美国堪萨斯大学）
郑　萱（北京大学）
庄恩平（上海大学）

上外跨文化研究中心执行编委

张红玲（上外跨文化研究中心主任）
邓一恒（上外跨文化研究中心教授）
翁立平（上外跨文化研究中心副研究员）
迟若冰（上外跨文化研究中心副研究员）
张晓佳（上外跨文化研究中心副研究员）

Contents

Conceptual and Thematic Developments 2:
From African Interactions to "Where We're Going"

Cross-Cultural Encounter

Countries — Nations — Nation-States

Intercultural Research
Series Foreword

Michael H. Prosser
Chair of the SII International Advisory Board

Ancient Athens served as an intercultural and intellectual crossroads
for Asia and Europe. The Greek philosopher, Socrates' famous
statement "I am neither a citizen of Athens, nor of Greece, but of the
world" speaks eloquently of the impact of intercultural communication,
comparative analysis, and the importance of identity clarification
both in his and contemporary society. Greek philosophers Socrates,
Plato, and Aristotle all looked outward from their own culture,
identifying or debating major world value orientations such as goodness,
justice, truth, and happiness. For East Asia, multiple schools of thought
developed during the Spring and Autumn Period, shaping China's cross-
state communication. Confucius' *Analects* articulated the role of *ren*
(benevolence and kindness), *li* (propriety and right living through
ritual), *de* (moral power), *dao* (internalized moral direction),
and *mianzi* or *lian* (externalized social image and harmony). These
Confucian orientations were integrated into what became the fabric
of not only the Chinese state, but the educational and philosophical
orientation of much of East and South-Eastern Asia.

All of these early cultural conceptualizations of identities and values
strongly support the potentially positive intercultural, multicultural,
and global world orientations that have enhanced a dialogue of
civilizations and cultures, and stress factors that are unifying rather than
divisive. The challenge continues to be substantial since intercultural,
multicultural, and global communication might just as easily be highly
negative with increasing war, poverty, crime, and pandemics. The goal
of all those interested in promoting a better local and global society vastly
prefers the former.

The location from which this series originates shows some of these dynamics and contradictions. Just as each nation and people must deal with highs and lows, China is grappling both with some of the positive dialogues of modernization and internationalization, and with the challenges of divergent cultural or global discourses. From the depths of the Wenchuan earthquake in Sichuan that rallied not only the nation's, but the world's sympathy, engagement and commitment to rebuild, to the heights of the spectacularly well-orchestrated and successful 2008 Beijing Olympics; from the ongoing challenges of natural disasters like floods or human tragedies like accidents or the global financial crisis, to the futuristic development of Shanghai and its visionary and record-breaking participation and cooperation at the 2010 Shanghai Expo, we see these human and intercultural dynamics at work.

I would suggest that intercultural communication as a field has emerged to embody and embrace both these challenges of human clashes and the dialogues across cultures and civilizations. The anthropologists Edward T. Hall and Ruth Benedict serve as the symbolic grandparents of intercultural communication in North America, though neither set out to begin a new field. Others in North America in the 1960s and 1970s and coming from various viewpoints (see Vol. 2 for the complete list of influencing scholars) and I sought early to develop an intercultural communication discipline or sub-discipline, which has now spread broadly through much of the academic world.

When the field of intercultural communication began to develop rapidly in China during the 1980s and 1990s, Chinese scholars each brought and Sinocized many of these western intercultural theories and practical implications for China. Concerned international scholars have also sought to indigenize social and cultural psychology and the humanities to strengthen Chinese scholarship on intercultural communication. Currently many Chinese scholars, either in China itself, in North America, or other regions around the world, have developed robust theories and models or have postulated newer ones, as documented in the premier volume of this series, *Intercultural Perspectives on Chinese Communication* (2007).

The SISU Intercultural Institute (SII) of Shanghai International Studies University's (SISU), under Steve J. Kulich (Gu Lixing 顾力行), has accepted a mandate to undertake an *Intercultural Research* series of volumes which seeks to publish "cutting edge and seminal articles on the state of the intercultural field" in a variety of areas. As formulated in the establishment of the series, Kulich emphasized that "Each volume will focus on one primary domain and will include diverse theoretical and applied research from cultural, intercultural or cross-cultural approaches for that area, seeking to present and frame a 'state-of-the-art' or an extended development summary on the topic."

The SII is committed to close cooperation with both Chinese and international scholars, and that was reflected since the first, where domestic scholars of the CAFIC were joined by international scholars from various disciplinary or research perspectives to contribute IC research from their respective areas of focus. SII is also committed to highlight and bring some integration to the diverse disciplines that influence, contribute to or are informed by intercultural scholarship. This is illustrated particularly by efforts in that first and subsequent volumes to invite contributions from communication studies at both the interpersonal (*jiaoji*) as well as mass communication (*chuanbo*) levels and also to include the perspectives of cultural psychology, cultural anthropology and other related fields. The interdisciplinary nature of IC motivates the SII team to identify and integrate those aspects that contribute to shared foundations for the field, especially as these reflect intercultural, multicultural human development, or in short, to "develop a discipline to develop people."

This focus on cooperation continued first with disciplinary assessment and development seminars (in 2006, 2010, 2014, 2016, a continuing hallmark of the institute), the biennial thematic IC conferences held by Shanghai Normal University, dynamic cooperation among CAFIC Shanghai Branch institutions (which also includes regular cross-city scholar forums and the annual IC outstanding MA thesis conference) and international partners like the University of Bayreuth, Bavaria, Germany (from which the collaboration for this volume has emerged). Each volume has highlighted interdisciplinary and multi-perspective scholarship on *Identity and Intercultural Communication*, focusing on *I: Theoretical and Contextual Construction* (Vol. 2), and *II: Conceptual and Contextual Applications* (Vol. 3). Other volumes in the series take up the important topic of IC values — *Value Frameworks at the Theoretical Crossroads of Culture* (Vol. 4) and *Value Dimensions and Their Contextual Dynamics Across Cultures* (Vol. 5). Later volumes focus on subsequent themes, like IC and acculturation (Vols. 6 and 7), IC and comparative literature, which now has nationally listed disciplinary status (Vols. 8, 9, and 10), historical trajectories, and other topics for IC disciplinary development.

Naturally, since Shanghai Foreign Language Education Press is publishing the series, Chinese academic contributions are especially encouraged, as well as those from the wider international academic community. In his foreword for the first volume, *Intercultural Perspectives on Chinese Communication* (2007), Shijie Guan noted that three features characterize the series: (1) It serves as an interdisciplinary platform for China's IC research; (2) It emphasizes the importance of scientific methodology in IC research; (3) It focuses on the localization of IC research. He concludes his remarks by saying that "The publication of this series is an occasion to celebrate for the entire Chinese community: My hope is that it develops into a series that is interdisciplinary, methodology-promoting, indigenized into the Chinese settings and blend well theories with practice (p. xvi)." As he also notes in that foreword, "In today's world, communication between various cultures have become an important task for human beings. Just as Lourdes Arizpe, chair of the Scientific Committee of the *World Culture Report, 2000*, says, 'Cultural exchanges are in fact the axis of the new phenomena' as global cultures develop and change (p. ix)."

Since the initial books by Edward T. Hall, *The Silent Language, The Hidden Dimension, Beyond Culture,* and *The Dance of Life* began to shape the early study of intercultural communication theoretically and practically, so too, it is reasonable to assume that these volumes might provide new impetus for the academic study of various cultural contexts. The historical development, frameworks and research approaches presented both by well-established and emerging scholars in these volumes will surely move the academic understanding of key intercultural topic areas ahead. Each volume's contribution toward highlighting theoretical constructs, clarifying the "state-of-the-art" and presenting cutting edge research and practical applications will hopefully contribute to a new apex in the field of intercultural communication. To the ongoing development of the intercultural communication discipline both in China and abroad this series is dedicated.

International Academy for Intercultural Research (IAIR)
2015 Lifetime Achievement Award Winner

Charlottesville, Virginia

Volume Foreword

Why Interculturality is Problematic

Wim M. J. Van Binsbergen
African Studies Centre, University of Leiden;
Erasmus University, Rotterdam

The concept of *interculturality* has presented itself to the world as a program characterized by clarity and hope. It has often suggested that the constituent parts into which humankind seems to be divided are on the one hand unmistakably defined, internally integrated in themselves, and unequivocally marked within their own neat boundaries — but on the other hand, that between these parts constructive interaction and mutual understanding are possible, even on what is commended as a basis of equality — so that we may at long last be on our way *Zum ewigen Frieden*, to peace eternal (Kant, 1959). In light of the promises of interculturality as a collective representation, many of the historical ills of humanity — our divisiveness, group hatred, mutual exclusion, exploitation, mutual violence, historical inequality as in slavery and class formation, anomia (given the recent destruction — under the onslaught of globalization and of the technological innovations that made it possible — of long-established religious beliefs and cultural values) may appear to be ephemeral and epiphenomenal. Against the background of this lofty (even though patently unrealistic) prospect, it is little wonder that the concept of interculturality has conquered not only the media but also the world of scholarship over the last quarter of a century[1] — a trend to which

---

[1] Not to be confused with the older "cross-cultural" (in established anthropological usage since the mid-20th century; cf. Whiting & Child, 1953), the term "intercultural" constitutes a fairly recent neologism. It is not yet included in the authoritative *Shorter Oxford Dictionary* (Little et al., 1978), nor in *The Advanced Learner's Dictionary of Current English* (Hornby et al., 1963). Nonetheless, we may be surprised to see academic texts with "intercultural" in the title appear already before (see next page)

the present *Intercultural Research* book bears witness.

The present composite argument, which I am offering here and then at greater length in the chapter "The Shadow Play," consists of several parts.

In that chapter contribution, I shall explore interculturality theoretically, trace some of its historical and disciplinary antecedents, and point out some of the limitations which have sprung from that origin. Here a major contradiction becomes apparent, whose negotiation causes considerable effort. As an anthropologist, I have been steeped in a dominant paradigm that, ever since the 1960s, has sought to deconstruct the self-evidence with which the actors themselves perceive their social world as composed of tribes, nations, cultures, and ethnic groups. But if such collectivities, in the hands of social scientists, may be reduced to nostalgic and even ideological figments of the imagination that have no real, tangible existence, does not that also mean that interculturality, as (presumably) the interaction between cultures, can only exist as a form of similarly ideological wishful thinking? We should try to free ourselves from deceptive elements that have cluttered around interculturality, and yet retain the concept in order to put it to some better use. Within the limited allotted space I shall cursorily take a sobering look at culture, identity, ethnicity, national and international political space, and at inequality — and seek to peer through the smoke-screen that interculturality has oftentimes entailed as an intellectual and even political perspective.

We cannot give up the concept of interculturality: not only because humanity's future seems to largely depend on it, but also because practically and personally our experience with possible and even realized interculturality has clearly been extensive. For me it has formed the backbone of my adult life as a person (offering some of the most valuable and instructive episodes of my life) and as an intellectual (pressing me to develop my thinking beyond the complacency of Eurocentric hegemony). This highly selective exploration (and our present scope does not allow for more — a series of books would be more appropriate format) will be frustrated by limitations of

---

(continued) World War Ⅱ (Brown, 1939; Joshi, 1934). In selected privileged fields, such as educational studies, art studies, religious studies, the history of science, and marketing, treatises on interculturality already appeared from the 1940s onward. *The Journal of Intercultural Relations* began to appear in 1976, just like the *Journal of Intercultural Studies*. However, as late as 1993 the Dutch anthropologist Shadid could still speak of intercultural communication in medical care as "an unexplored terrain."

publication space and also by the inevitable personal constraints (disciplinary, theoretical, regional, paradigmatic, bibliographic, and linguistic) informing any intellectual product. The greatest handicap, however, may be that, in the course of this discussion, I seem to reject some assumptions of modern societal ideology, and to resist what some fellow scholars consider as a meaningful perspective toward a better world. ② Deconstructing ideas that for the people who hold them are a source of hope and an inspiration for political action, but that if ill-understood may invite anger, rejection, ridicule, even aggression: in such an endeavor, one may seem to deny — for the sake of some abstract, theoretical, uninspiring, lifeless truth — to specific and newly emancipating sections of humanity (nations that in the recent past still sighed under colonial rule; women; sexual minorities; people of color; recent intercontinental migrants) the very dignity, self-esteem, and pride they are struggling for or may have recently won, usually at the cost of long and painful historical battles. Can we still take seriously the promise — a basic tenet of critical intellectual life throughout the centuries and the continents — that grounded insight, gained as the result of painstaking critical reflection and the broadest empirical inspection, not only feeds intellectual life but also leads to a lasting, liberating insight changing the future for the better of humankind as a whole?

In extending this argument in the chapter "The Shadow Play," a focus on Africa there as well as in a few other chapters in Volume 11 will turn out to be both timely and felicitous, alongside a concern with other global regions. In our world's cultural heritage, this

---

② This applies *a fortiori* in the African context. Already in 1983 the leading Afrocentrist writer Molefi Asante wrote on "The Ideological Significance of Afrocentricity in Intercultural Communication." Having been repeatedly and vocally identified as a (moderate) Afrocentrist myself (2000a, 2000b, 2011), how can I doubt the possibility, the existence, and the liberating force of interculturality? Yet I reject the idea of humankind being composed of numerous identifiable, named, bounded, and internally integrated culture*s* (plural); what I see are myriad interlocking, superimposed, cultural orientations governing partial aspects of the lives of individuals and of groups — but in such a way that from the cradle to the grave, or even from the morning to the evening, one will always take recourse to various different cultural orientations. One may share some of these with most modern people (use of the cell phone, motor car, plastic or even virtual money) or with all fellow-citizens of one's nation-state (an official national language, the national anthem, allegiance to the flag and the national sport teams), but many are peculiar to much smaller and far more situational contexts, such as a profession, a creed, a hobby, or an extended family with its own little customs and scraps of private language.

continent has functioned not only as the labor reserve from which slaves and migrants have left for an often deplorable transcontinental future, but also as a laboratory for the dynamics of identity, ethnicity (especially in the post-Independence African context, intercultural is often an ill-analyzed synonym for merely interethnic: cf. Kom, 1995), inequality, the national and international political spaces in which these dynamics situate themselves, and the economic, ideological, and religious processes informing the transcontinental development.

On that continent are the scenes of several prolonged spells of my own fieldwork, in more than a handful of African countries between 1968 and 2011. Here also is the continent of my social-scientific and intercultural-philosophical competence as brought out in publications, extensive teaching, and decades of supervision of the research of others. I have been speaking six African languages, am conversant with a similar number of local African socio-cultural settings, am at home in at least two African villages whose inhabitants are my close kin. I have been an ethnic activist for the Nkoya people of Zambia, and have attained recognition as an African philosopher (cf. van Binsbergen, 2008). Transcontinentally, but also in my private personal life (when it comes to world-view, the continuity of generations, the place of humans in nature, the scope and limits of our ability to know and act) I often identify myself as an African — in line with the definition which the South African freedom fighter Robert Sobukwe would give of that identity: "any person who considers Africa, home." This in itself, given my origin in a Northwest European urban neighborhood, should already be enough to believe in the possibility and actual existence of interculturality, following from the African context. But my parallel identities as a North Atlantic anthropologist and philosopher have rendered me self-conscious, and lured me into an argument involving some critical reflections on interculturality, as well as on historical methodology.

Perhaps most important in the African part of my discourse is my claim that, while interethnic relations largely make up the socio-political space in Africa, this in itself does not mean interculturality. That is because African cultural orientations, especially in Niger-Congo-(>Bantu)-speaking Africa, tend to apply to huge geographic extensions, far from being neatly confined within the commonly recognized, and named, boundaries of ethnic groups such as exist in the locals' consciousness.[3] On the contrary, interculturality in Africa in the first place has come to involve evidence of (including but not limited to actors' conscious reference to) transcontinental exchanges, and these I aim to illustrate in a few descriptive vignettes in the chapter I am also contributing.

We might let ourselves be inspired, then, to a critical scrutiny of the words of philosopher Kwasi Wiredu:

> philosophical insight is not exclusive to any one race, culture, or creed. A corollary of this is that such insights can be shared across cultures. Of course, the same applies to philosophical errors. [...] Philosophical dialogue is possible among the inhabitants of all cultures, and can be fruitful both intellectually and practically. (Wiredu, 1998, pp. 154-155)

References

Appiah, K. A. (1992). *In my father's house: Africa in the philosophy of culture*. Oxford University Press.

Asante, M. K. (1983). The ideological significance of Afrocentricity in intercultural communication. *Journal of Black Studies*, *14*(1), 3-19.

Brown, F. J. (1939). Sociology and intercultural understanding. *Journal of Educational Sociology*, *12*(6), 328-331.

Hornby, A. S., Gatenby, E. V., & Wakefield, H. (1963). *The advanced learner's dictionary of current English* (2nd ed.). Oxford University Press.

Joshi, S. L. (1934). Hinduism and intercultural contacts. *The Journal of Religion*, *14*(1), 62-76.

Kant, I. (1959). Zum ewigen Frieden: Ein philosophischer Entwurf. In K. Vorlinder (Ed.), *I. Kant, Kleinere Schriften zur Geschichtsphilosophie, Ethik*

---

[3] Here I am turning against a popular conception of Africa as a patchwork-quilt of cultures (as distinct from ethnic groups), which today holds captive not only common Africans, politicians, missionaries, ethnic brokers, journalists, and development workers world-wide, but also the widely acclaimed North Atlantic philosopher of part-African descent, Kwami Anthony Appiah. In his best-known book, *In My Father's House*, already in the title Appiah affirms both his Africanness and his automatic assumption of Africa's cultural diversity, and he claims (without claiming any authoritative privileged knowledge concerning the African precolonial past and its identities):

> If we could have traveled through Africa's many cultures [in precolonial times] from the small groups of Bushman hunter-gatherers, with their stone-age materials, to the Hausa kingdoms, rich in worked metal — we should have felt in every place profoundly different impulses, ideas, and forms of life. (Appiah, 1992, p. 174)

und Politik (pp. 115–169). Felix Meiner. (Originally published 1795)

Kom, A. (1995). Conflits interculturels et tentative séparatiste au Cameroun. *Cahiers Francophone d'Europe Centre-Orientale*, *5–6*, 143–152.

Little, W., Fowler, H. W., & Coulson, J. (Eds.). (1978). *The shorter Oxford English dictionary: On historical principles* (revised and edited by C. T. Onions, etymologies revised by G. W. S. Friedrichsen, 3rd reset ed., 2 vols.). Clarendon Press.

Shadid, W. A. (1993). Intercultural communication in the medical care sector. In W. A. Shadid & P. J. M. Nas (Eds.), *Cultures, development and communication: Essays in honour of J. D. Speckmann* (pp. 70–91). Centre of Non-western Studies.

Van Binsbergen, W. M. J. (2000a). Dans le troisième millénaire avec Black Athena? In F.-X. Fauvelle-Aymar, J.-P. Chrétien, & C.-H. Perrot (Eds.), *Afrocentrismes: L'histoire des Africains entre Égypte et Amérique* (pp. 127–150). Karthala.

Van Binsbergen, W. M. J. (2000b, Oct.). Le point de vue de Wim van Binsbergen. *Politique africaine*, *79*, 175–180.

Van Binsbergen, W. M. J. (2008). The eclectic scientism of Félix Guattari: Africanist anthropology as both critic and potential beneficiary of his thought. *Quest: An African Journal of Philosophy/Revue Africaine de Philosophie*, *21* (1–2), 155–228, Special issue on "Lines and rhizomes: The transcontinental element in African philosophies."

Van Binsbergen, W. M. J. (Ed.). (2011). *Black Athena comes of age*. LIT.

Whiting, J. W. M., & Child, I. L. (1953). *Child training and personality: A cross-cultural study*. Yale University Press.

Wiredu, K. (1998). Can philosophy be intercultural?: An African viewpoint. *Diogenes*, *46*(184), 147–167.

Tracing Developments of Intercultural Research and Practice

Michael STEPPAT & Steve J. KULICH

"[W]e must study the history of our own disciplinary traditions and assumptions. [...] [W]e must be willing to spend at least a little time examining the history of our assumptions, and how they have developed over time. [...] Modern scholars can benefit from studying the past because it will help to reveal why we study what we do, and why we use the methods that we do." (Leeds-Hurwitz, 2010, p.30)

"[...] [R]ather than a single history of intercultural communication research, there are concurrent, confluent traditions: Much like the murky backwaters of the Amazon river, we sense currents of all approaches in each of the others, but each has separate origins, separate histories. [...]" (Baldwin, 2017, p.36)

1. Our Main Tasks

These influential thoughts on the evolution of intercultural communication and interaction study encourage us to explore their implications. Accordingly, the present volume is dedicated to investigating the historical dimensions of this research and practice domain, and especially to doing so from a variety of complementary perspectives.

It is not the first time this is happening. From its inception, the *Intercultural Research* series has called attention to historical processes. That begins with chapters in the very first volume by Michael Prosser, Changyuan Liu together with Song Wang, and Kwang-Kuo Hwang; the fourth volume, discussing value frameworks, includes an extensive focus on "reviewing history." Our concern in the present book is not to offer a general history of intercultural encounters, of the production of culture and how "the presence of otherness causes change" (Rozbicki & Ndege, 2012, p.1). We devote attention rather to the matter of intercultural thought and study. Certainly the authors quoted at the outset are not the only ones who have traced the field's growth and development, with the impulses from major contributing disciplines. In due course we will take note also of others. Among these is an emphasis on how history is vital for shaping communication practices: that means studying "History *as* Intercultural Communication" (Drzewiecka, 2010, p.288, with emphasis added). The idea of fluid traditions described so vividly by John Baldwin evokes the diversity of temporal cultures: it was already found by Michel de Certeau among a people in Dahomey for whom history is "*remuho*, 'the speech of these past times' — speech (*ho*), or presence, which comes from upriver and carries downstream" (1988, p.4).

This is suggestive. We will not want to underestimate the importance of the stream of speech and its immediacy in creating or shaping the past: rather than being a given quality, the past is actually "a product"; historical operations transform their milieux (De Certeau, 1988, p.72). Indeed, concurrent traditions are actually more than that, they are "competing interpretations" which tend to be partial and contested (Drzewiecka, 2010, p.289). This is where a genealogical inquiry, as pursued for instance by Michel Foucault, is suited to revealing the "erratic and discontinuous process" in which the past emerges into the present, an "aleatory path" alerting us to "the contingency of the present" (Garland, 2014, p.372); any knowledge that we wish to gain should seek to investigate the procedures of its production (Tamboukou, 1999). Consequently, knowing the past enables us to make "changes to our current assumptions and practices" (Leeds-Hurwitz, 2010, p.31). Or: interdisciplinary history enables intercultural scholars as well as practitioners to "(re)consider their own assumptions about what IC is" and "what its inherent purposes/trajectories are" (Kulich et al., 2020, p.91). These remarks highlighting the vital present/past relationship give us an opportunity to step back for a moment from our immediate concern with intercultural research concepts and practices. As we do so, it should be clear that our study object is not simply the range of directions of intercultural communication or interaction, as such. Rather it is the specific dimension of their evolution, supported by history of practice. Thus our concern shares in a more comprehensive need to consider how to account for the ontology and epistemology of historical study objects; our field is not in some singular way detached from these.

This means: we should think about what we *are* doing, and what we *should be* doing, if possible even *why* we are doing it, when we trace the research field's diversified growth. Without claiming for a moment that we qualify as historians, we think it appropriate to ask:

What are the **tasks**, in a larger sense, when we are examining or more likely creating histories? For this "foundational question," we can consult philosopher Daniel Little (2020, section 1).

- We learn that our *first* task is "providing conceptualizations and factual descriptions of events and circumstances in the past" — this suggests that their factual nature is subject to what the researcher provides or renders, a matter that will deserve more attention. Thus the historian fits evidence into "a coherent and truthful story." Yet surely this form of representation, both the coherence and the apparent narrative singularity, is not something we should take for granted.

- The *second* main task, at any rate, is trying to answer "why" questions: "conditions and forces" that brought about an event, so that a researcher will attempt to explain past events and patterns. Connected with this is the "how" question about processes "through which the outcome occurred," i.e., how it became possible.

- And a *further* task is then to probe "the human meanings and intentions" underlying actions, requiring a hermeneutic and interpretive line of investigation.

Perhaps needless to say, a historical account dealing with the past has to be based on "evidence in the present" (Little, 2020, section 1). How, then, are these time dimensions related? As we proceed, we shall look into this.

2. Objects of Inquiry

We need to deal with a further differentiation emerging from the tasks just described. We are now examining the **ontology** of the field's histories, its objects of inquiry. These are mutually empowering in a dynamic circularity, rather than being detached units, and the object constellations of individual projects form a gliding scale.

• Clearly, the "forces" just spoken of are a fairly comprehensive major object: they direct our attention to the macro-level of social structures and systems, including power hierarchies, whose impact on individual action and indeed *all* other objects is what we need to understand better (see also Kulich & Zhang, 2012, p. 889; Martin et al., 2020).

• Are human intentions significant to conditions and forces? Building on Zahle and Collin (2014), Little calls this the "microfoundation" of an "actor-centered" concept, one that focuses on individual actions and interactions (for which see also Kulich & Zhang, 2012, pp. 889–890). A simple numbering in the sequence of objects of inquiry (thus describing this as the *first*) is not meant to imply that there is necessarily any order of precedence. In historiography, the orientation toward human intentions goes back to the 19th century, providing impulses that have enabled Marc Bloch to identify the object of history as individual persons: "it is men that history seeks to grasp" (Bloch, 1954, pp. 21–22).

Yet in our context we need to modify this emphasis. In foregrounding actors, we should ask about the origin of action, which means asking whether an actor isn't rather "the moving target of a vast array of entities swarming toward it": action emerges as "dislocated" (Latour, 2005, p. 46). The focus on micro practices has (mis)led researchers to ignore how "structural constraints push and pull such practices," seeing that intercultural communication developed during World War II "as a tool of imperialism" (Moon, 2010, p. 35).

• What then requires attention is *secondly* the "institutional and situational environment" (Little, 2020, 1.1), which includes organizational forms, associations, and also patterns of norms, rules, or expectations that obtain in each environment and are relevant to the intercultural field. We might expect these components to be especially liable to the macro-level, while that is not automatically the case. Organizations and associations often operate by arranging publications as well as formats of meeting and exchange of viewpoints, expertise, and research results, and these are embedded in the category.

• Since the intercultural domain is not (so often) institutionalized as a discipline, we need to consider, *thirdly*, the influence and lines of questioning brought to bear by the range of contributing disciplines. For communication studies, there are surrounding and competing disciplines (see Löblich & Scheu, 2011, p. 9); this is not quite the case in the intercultural field. Currently a majority of scholars involved come from communication studies, psychology, sociology, and anthropology, but there are a number of further disciplines as well (see Kim, 2017, p. xliv): these range from cultural studies and linguistics to comparative literature (see Kulich, 2007, p. 4), especially considering that our perspective is not exhausted by or in the present. In this context, we should certainly not neglect the significance of philosophy (as duly cited in Kulich et al., 2020). In many cases the disciplines become integral parts of the intercultural field, so that their interplay emerges as an object of inquiry.

• A closer view shows, *fourthly*, that a further object is at stake. Little's account bypasses intellectual developments and the growth of ideas (for which see also Kulich et al., 2020, p. 65, and Leeds-Hurwitz, 2010). This is a research domain's "cognitive identity" — to which Löblich and Scheu, for the neighboring discipline of communication study, even grant the first place (2011, p. 3). It is apposite for the intercultural field too.

• Seeing that the individual microfoundation is especially complemented by institutional arrangements (as well as comprehensively influential sociopolitical forces), intellectual developments, too, are likely to have a special counterpart. That is (*fifthly*) indeed the case: in the intercultural field theoretical ideas are balanced by involvement in culturally coded and interactional practices, in such areas as competence training and education (see for instance Martin et al., 2020, pp. 22, 23, 32), where we can associate practices with cultures (also featured in Little, 2020, 1.1). While this nexus has no direct correspondence in history concepts of communication studies, we cannot sever the links between theory and practice (see Kulich et al., 2020, p. 91).

Each of the objects (possibly further ones could be added for particular contexts) is connected to all others by conceptual lines that operate by analogy to electric wires or cables transporting power where it is needed. A centralized node would be misleading and somewhat inaccurate. As a whole, the above considerations suggest a possible model for the core objects of inquiry, without introducing further particularizations at this stage and thus allowing for the incompleteness inherent in all models (Figure 1):

The discussion so far should allow us to grow aware of the requirement and especially the practice of selectivity, in making decisions about historical ontology and about methodology. A history of our field will include some matters as "appropriate" and will omit "other types of work" (Leeds-Hurwitz, 1990, p. 262). If a selection

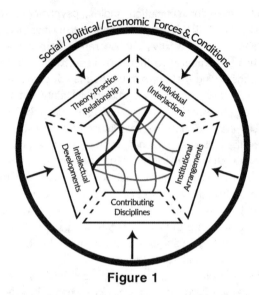

Figure 1

Core objects of inquiry for the histories of the
intercultural communication research and practice field

of topics and concepts is inevitable, we need to acknowledge that it
rests on "the scholar's *values*" — we share the awareness that
approaches are "selective and value-guided" (Little, 2020, 1.2). An
earlier volume of our *Intercultural Research* series has explained that
values represent "the desirable" (with the accompanying attitudes
and preferences) as well as "that which is desired" so that the objects
themselves gain differential value (Kulich, 2014, 5: 31). This
interrelation is subtle, but it becomes decisive for the composition
and consequently the reception of historical accounts. How, then,
are we to come to terms with the expectation and claim of objectivity,
as against subjectivity? Little, too, asks whether historical knowledge
can possibly represent the past objectively (2020, 3.2).

These aspects deserve discussion. What particularly need our
attention are (1) the manner and form of rendering a history,
(2) the past in relation to other time dimensions, and (3) the
question of research objectivity. They are not entirely separate from
each other, as the following remarks will show, and they are not
exhaustive. It is in their mutual effects that they represent the major
concerns involved in what we are undertaking.

3. The Challenges of Intercultural Histories

3.1 Representation

As a form of shorthand, we often speak of "the history" (as in the opening quotation). But we should take note of "concurrent" traditions. The form of representation itself subtly points our attention toward a characteristic quality: no existing account will suggest that intercultural communication's development is linear or unidirectional. Nonetheless, the usual mode of tracing it is what philosopher of history Louis Mink calls "configurational comprehension" or "the ability to hold together a number of elements in nice balance" (1987, p.39). This takes the shape of narrative as "primary cognitive instrument," which is "an irreducible form of understanding" (Mink, 1987, p.185). It traces a development which emerges only in looking back, with hindsight (Roth, 2017, p. 404). Unsurprisingly, this is the form of most representations of intercultural communication's history, enabling what Little calls a "coherent" story. Using narrative for studying social phenomena is a well-established intercultural communication approach as described by Anna De Fina, who cites among others the research by historian Hayden White (see De Fina, 2016, pp. 541 – 565). It is clearly suited to studying the research field's histories.

Yet there are exceptions to the prevailing use of narrative: Kulich et al. (2020) use both the classic narrative genre and an extensive and interrelated set of tables, demonstrating that more than one representational form is adequate for re-examining a complex interdisciplinary history. Each, as it were, tells its own story. We find that the world is "full of partial stories that run parallel to one another, beginning and ending at odd times. They mutually interlace and interfere at points, but we cannot unify them completely in our minds" (James, 2003, Lecture Ⅳ, p. 63). Thus when we go through any single representational form, however well crafted, it should not mislead us into thinking that there is "a single story" embracing the ensemble of processes; there are "many stories, not only different stories about different events, but even different stories about the same events" (Mink, 1987, p.193). What is more, "[t]he same event, under the same description or different descriptions, may belong to different stories" and accordingly assume a variable significance in more than one narrative (Mink, 1987, p.198). This means that histories cannot actually "aggregate" into "some one narrative, an implied unifying perspective," since we cannot realistically expect them to cohere (Roth, 2017, p.402).

With this in mind, we believe it is time for a plurality of perspectives to represent the development of intercultural thinking. We can go beyond the classic form of presenting one narrative, and listening to one history author. Here we are guided by Friedrich Nietzsche's insight in *Genealogy of Morality*: "There is only a perspectival seeing, only a perspectival 'knowing'; and the more affects we allow to speak about a matter, the more eyes, different eyes, we know how to bring to bear on one and the same matter, that much more complete will our 'concept' of this matter, our 'objectivity' be" (1998, p.85). Accordingly, in this volume we offer space for a range of experiences and conceptual perspectives (for which cf. Park & Pooley, 2008). This format will extend the scope of the narratives of intercultural communication's history.

3.2 Temporality

Past/Present/...

Looking at the past raises the question of its relationship to other temporal dimensions. The historian's efforts, especially in narrative, are aimed toward understanding any complex historical event "in time" (Little, 2020, 1.3). Intuitively we tend to think of past events in dictionary terms, as "having existed or taken place in a period before the present" (*Merriam-Webster*, 2021). And yes, for many practical purposes a common-sense distinction between past and present may seem quite adequate. Yet in order to *study* the past we should look again. We might make use of a pertinent distinction: wherever the past is just "that which preceded the present, that from which the present has grown," it is "a practical" rather than historical past, and it is one which generally serves the present's political interests (Oakeshott, 1933, p.103). From a similar consideration, a few voices urge us not to go so far as to make the past "immediately relevant and useful," in serving "to empower people in the present, to help them develop self-identity" (Wood, 2008, p.8). Such a restraint cannot but be controversial, and we will not commit ourselves to it, at least not consistently.

Generally, however, we need to bear in mind that we are tracing genealogies. Ideas are rooted in "concerns generated by certain facts about us and our situation," and an idea persists because it evidently fills a need; genealogical inquiry enables what could be called "reverse-engineering the points of ideas, [...] revealing what they do for us when they function well" (Queloz, 2021, pp. 2-3). Correspondingly, what the past *is* depends wholly upon "how we think of it" (Oakeshott, 1933, p. 103), even upon the individual researcher's "psychology" (Spiegel, 2007, p. 6). Would it not be possible, in some contexts, to approach the historical (unlike the practical) past as being "independent of the present," differing from it (Oakeshott, 1933, p. 106)? Yet it is more accurate to consider it in light of a concept of experience. One can then assume that, "[i]f the historical past be knowable, it must belong to the present world of experience" and thus "rests upon the present," as "a special organization" of present experience (Oakeshott, 1933, pp. 107, 111). This is a form of objective idealism, and it results in an acknowledged paradox which should be easy to discern. It is one which cannot be resolved in any one direction without becoming unduly reductive (see also Thompson, 2019, p. 49). The same paradox is negotiated also by later researchers (see Fasolt, 2013, and Gorman, 2013).

Other authorities, too, speak of temporal interdependence. Writing in 1940, cultural critic Walter Benjamin maintains that "it is an irretrievable image of the past which threatens to disappear in any present that does not recognize itself as intended in that image" (2003, 4:391). More simply, we would agree that knowing the past "can have a profound effect on our own consciousness, on our sense of ourselves," which is why it is "natural" for us to desire to find origins of our circumstances at the present time (Wood, 2008, pp. 6, 10). This "identity continuity" in a context of group dynamics is a significant object of research (see Smeekes & Verkuyten, 2015). Thus, on the one hand, we can achieve our "understanding" of the past "only through the eyes of the present" (Carr, 1987, p. 24). Yet on the other hand we do *not* need to see history just in terms of the past/present relationship. Re-reading Alexis de Tocqueville's preface to *Democracy in America*, E. H. Carr thinks of history rather as "a dialogue between the events of the past and progressively emerging future ends" because "[o]nly the future can provide the key to the interpretation of the past" (1987, p. 123).

Widening the temporal relations in this way is useful. It can help us to avoid overestimating the fleetingly evanescent moment of any *now*. Here, we can come back to philosophy. Interpreting Husserl, Jacques Derrida declares that "the presence of the perceived present can appear as such only inasmuch as it is continuously compounded with a nonpresence and nonperception, with primary memory and expectation (retention and protention)" (Derrida, 1973, p. 64). Hence a trace of earlier experience *as well as* an anticipation, both being apparent absences, shape what we think of as the present. There is "no purity of the living present" because the present in general is "reconstituted" (Derrida, 1978, p. 212). There is an adjacent aspect, which we can only touch on: a politics of time. It becomes visible when one attempts to come to terms with "non-coevalness" as the situation of subalterns and of numerous refugees and migrants; the notion of a single historical time for all, referring also to all cultures, has been analyzed as colonialist and imperialist (Bevernage, 2016, pp. 354, 372). Accordingly, conceptions of the so-called present time conceal elements of ideology (see Bevernage, 2016, p. 370).

Are we then right in thinking that we need a "sense of ourselves" (Wood), or the *present* experience, to understand history? We would agree that

> [t]he whole truth concerning an event can only be known after, and sometimes only *long* after the event itself has taken place. And this part of the story historians alone can tell. It is not something which even the best sort of witness can know. [...] [N]ot being witness to the event is not so bad a thing if our interests are historical. (Danto, 1962, pp. 154, 155; see also Carr, 1987, p. 24)

We might ask, what would the alternative be? Philosopher Arthur Danto's answer depicts a notion of the Ideal Chronicler. One would imagine this person capable of producing a "*full description* of an event *E*":

> He knows whatever happens the moment it happens, even in other minds. And he is to have the gift of instantaneous transcription: everything that happens across the whole forward rim of the Past is set down by him, as it happens, the *way* it happens,

like an Ideal Witness, with "isomorphism" between the chronicle and *E* (Danto, 1962, pp. 151, 152). It should be obvious that such a chronicle and such a chronicler have never existed. Nor would we expect one for studies of intercultural communication and interaction. On balance, we agree with Thomas Kuhn's assessment that the science historian's task is rather to "trace different, and often less than cumulative, developmental lines for the sciences. Rather than seeking the permanent contributions of an older science to our present vantage, they attempt to display the historical integrity of that science *in its own time"* (1970, p. 3, emphasis added; see also Rogers & Hart, 2002, p. 2). This temporal dimension embraces the "developmental lines" of intercultural initiatives, concepts, and practices: duration, after-effect or influence, discontinuities, and the (non-) parallelism of lines that may be partly related. With all this in mind, we want to remain wary of a reductive presentism.

Co-Existence

Let us dig a little deeper. As we have heard, we should aim to understand any complex historical event "in time" (Little, 2020, 1.3). But what does this mean? While we are focused mainly on historical time, for our purposes, we cannot systematically and consistently detach it from cosmological and planetary time (see for instance Chakrabarty, 2009). From there, it's not far to research in quantum physics — or is that too remote from the development of intercultural communication? One can, however, argue in favor of its relevance for cross-cultural contact (see Bennett, 2012 and 2021). And indeed, physics is able to illuminate the widening time perspective for us in helpful ways. A quantum theory of time has been finding a method to correspond to the idea of the universe as a four-dimensional spacetime block. In this view, "events at all times coexist as one entity" (Vaccaro, 2018, p. 2; also Hristova et al., 2020, p. 778). The quantum theory operates initially with describing a galaxy's internal clock time, with a given value, and hence with a conditional state of that galaxy. In this concept, significantly for us, "no one conditional state can be singled out as representing the present, and divide other conditional states into sets representing the past and the future" (Vaccaro, 2018, p. 10).

Though we might not expect it, the concept embraces the idea that a conditional state with a particular clock time "can represent a human having the subjective perception of the present moment" — the conditional state contains evidence of "past evolution," and thus it "supports the subjective perception of being able to recall the past and contemplate the future" (Vaccaro, p. 10). Recalling, of course, activates the significance of memory, which we have encountered above in Derrida's thinking and which challenges traditional history's concern with temporal linearity in that memory studies focuses on "the coexistence of different time layers" (Hristova et al., 2020, p. 778).

Here we should take note of the finding that a particle of matter can co-exist at multiple times. It allows us to realize that "temporalities are specifically entangled and threaded through one another," that we cannot have a "determinate time" (Barad, 2017, p. 67). Thus "temporal diffraction is the manifestation of an ontological indeterminacy of time: there is no fact of the matter to when it is taking place" (Barad, 2017, p. 68). If Mink as a historian speaks of "configurational comprehension," physics calls attention to the "taking account of all possible histories" in "spacetimemattering configurings" — each history, that is, "coexists with the others" (Barad, 2017, p. 68).

Accordingly, as a physicist and also historian of consciousness, Karen Barad speaks of "a past that has yet to come. It is not merely that the future and the past are not 'there' and never sit still, but that the present is not simply here-now" (2010, p. 244). In a sense close to Derrida, Barad explains that "the past was never simply there to begin with and the future is not simply what will unfold; the 'past' and the 'future' are iteratively reworked and enfolded" (2010, p. 260). This occurs in a process of intra-activity (as described in the concept of what is called agential realism): entities that seem to be distinct are actually relational in that they only "emerge from/ through their intra-action," which consists of a "mutual constitution" between objects and agencies of observation (Barad, 2010, p. 267; 2007, p. 202). Perhaps all this seems somewhat removed from our intercultural concerns? It isn't: our field's metatheory is capable of exploring a "Present-Future/History-Past" dialectic, as it urges us to acknowledge the "interdependent and complementary" aspects of what seem to be temporal opposites (Martin & Nakayama, 1999, pp. 14, 17).

We might remember that the historian is called upon to create a "coherent" story (Little, 2020). Nonetheless, the notion of coherence should not be reduced to an illusion of continuity or linearity. We will need to bear in mind that time has "loosened" into what emerges as "a network of relations that no longer holds together as a coherent canvas" (Rovelli, 2018, p. 80). What we can gain from this apparent negativity is "heterogeneous history," diffracted, hence "marked by patterns of difference" (Barad, 2007, p. 71).

It seems advisable, then, to start "Looking Back to Look Forward" (Kulich et al., 2020, p. 93). In this volume, we too believe that, in coexistence or entanglement, the past/present/future relationship as such can be reduced neither to succession nor to discrete and discontinuous elements.

Supplement and Iteration

It is futile to separate the matter of time from that of culturally differentiated historical discourse. The represented object, in our case, is the reported and interpreted past, which may look different to diverse cultures. Edward T. Hall, of course, called attention to the diversity of cultural "voices of time" (1959, Chapter 1). By the same token, intercultural communication and interaction studies have developed differently in various world regions (see Martin et al., 2020, p.30). In each case, the past is ontologically dependent above all on representation: "No representation, no past"; since different temporal cultures have differing representational practices, the past emerges as "a cultural construction" with variables (Ankersmit, 2006, pp.328, 329). When the past in each case is conveyed into the present by means of historical writing, is it a submerged presence, becoming (as it were) a "stowaway" (Eelco Runia, qtd. in Ankersmit, 2006, p. 329)? Actually it remains inevitably absent — while its representation is what becomes a part of the culturally specific present. This can remind us of Derrida's tenet that the signifying structure is a *supplement*: it takes the place of the absent Other in that it is, paradoxically, "neither a presence nor an absence. No ontology can think its operation" (Derrida, 1997, p.314).

How, then, does representation relate to its object? As one can understand from analyzing the *raison d'être* of picture frames (Schapiro, 1969), we can observe that the very existence of a frame serves to demarcate the object, viz. the painting, from the observer. By contrast, the absence of a frame evokes "a *continuum* between the representation and what is represented" so that both of these "now flowed over into each other" (Ankersmit, 2006, p.332). What is represented will then repeat itself, as and when it is represented. But isn't this what happens in a writing process, which we can understand as the "graphic order" where "representation is reproduction; it repeats the signifying and signified masses en bloc" suggesting that any actual analysis is elided (Derrida, 1997, p.299)? A written sign, after all, is not tied to the subject: it "can give rise to an iteration both in the absence of and beyond the presence of the empirically determined subject who, in a given context, has emitted or produced it," so that "the unity of the signifying form is constituted only by its iterability" (Derrida, 1982, pp.317, 318).

Without referring to Derrida, however, historical theorist Frank Ankersmit calls attention to situations in which "actions represented

will continuously repeat themselves in the action of representation, "
resulting in a form of myth, here with negative connotations, which
an "institution never succeeds in properly objectifying when thinking
about itself and its past" (Ankersmit, 2006, p. 335). Hence we
ought to ask: Is this a risk for our project? Whether intercultural
communication operates loosely as a form of what used to be called
"invisible college" (Crane, 1972) or becomes institutionalized, will
it find itself subject to the same manner of interrogation about its
representational continuum? What can we then learn from the
historical pathways that we did not already know? After all, and
valuably enough, we learn that a proposition by Margaret Mead in
1951 "is still one of the goals of much intercultural communication
research today, " and that assumptions of the 1930s were "similar or
identical to those held by scholars of intercultural communication
today" (Leeds-Hurwitz, 2010, p. 28). It thus seems natural enough
to speak of "[k]nowing *our* own history" (Leeds-Hurwitz, 2010, p.
30), of encouraging intercultural experts to understand "the diverse
lines of *our* history, " and of noting the "interactive sources of *our*
work" (Kulich et al., 2020, p. 62, emphases added). This can
be motivated by a Heraclitean desire to "know oneself, " now as
product of a historical process — a process which "has deposited in
you an infinity of traces, without leaving an inventory" (Gramsci,
1971, p. 324). Finding the elements of that inventory has appeared
imperative to Gramsci; one can even regard it as "the most
interesting" human task (Said, 2005, p. 13). Yet it is no less
important for us to realize that a continuum lacks safeguards against
overflow or iteration. Let's not lose sight of this — in each case we
should scrutinize whether it can amount to a drawback, in light of
the purpose of the account (the supplement, as it were) that is
offered as representing a research field's history.

3.3 Objectivity

Detachment

So we have heard about the conditions for a subjective perception of
time. We have heard about Oakeshott's stress on "how we think of"
the past, and about Nietzsche's argument for different eyes to enable
objectivity. We then need to ask, is objectivity desirable, and is it
achievable?

We do not mean the distinction between orientations of sociological
research, whether "more objective (cause-driven behavior, predictability,

reality external to observer)" or "more subjective (choice-making behavior, rule-following, reality as individual perspective)," nor do we mean Young Yun Kim's distinction between objective or "analytic-reductionistic-mechanistic-behavioral-quantitative" and subjective or "synthetic-holistic-ideographic-contextual" theories (see Baldwin, 2017, p.28). Our focus is rather on what Louis Mink has described as an ideal of being objective in the sense of being "impersonal and free of judgment and interpretation" (1987, p.177).

This raises the query whether it should be an ideal at all. We can hardly help recalling Nietzsche's scathing description of the historian's "affectation of tranquillity," with an "incisive coldness and detachment": "What is then preferred is that which produces no emotion at all and the driest phrase is the right phrase. One goes so far, indeed, as to believe that he to whom a moment of the past means nothing at all is the proper man to describe it" (Nietzsche, 1997, p.93). More recently, Pierre Bourdieu's study of *habitus* shows that objectivity comes about in "a commonsense world" which features general agreement on "the meaning (*sens*) of practices and the world" (Bourdieu, 2005, p.179). Happily, the "impersonal" ideal has disappeared, at least concerning historical narrative. It has been replaced by being objective as meaning "subject to both empirical and conceptual criticism" (Mink, 1987, p.177).

How, then, do facts matter? In very general terms, it is probably easy to recognize that we should not reduce objectivity to factuality. In the metatheatrical play *Six Characters in Search of an Author*, Luigi Pirandello's "Father" figure memorably declares: "But a fact is like a sack which won't stand up when it is empty. In order that it may stand up, one has to put into it the reason and sentiment which have caused it to exist" (Pirandello, 1922, Act 1, p.22). Judgment and interpretation then provide the filling. Facts, as it were, "speak only when the historian calls on them: it is he who decides to which facts to give the floor, and in what order or context" (Carr, 1987, p.11). Abstractly, we tend to think of a fact as a real occurrence or a piece of information, in a dictionary sense. Yet that is not quite the same when we think of a historical fact: this is understood as "a conclusion, a result, an inference, a judgment" belonging to "the world of present experience" (Oakeshott, 1933, p.111) — which is where the historical past is to be found. We can learn something of value from Roland Barthes, in this context. What seems to be a factual system is likely to be or to conceal a myth, which is here understood as a "semiological system" of signification: it not only activates "an unlimited mass of signifiers" for any signified but (especially) makes it appear as though there were "a natural relationship" between a signifier and a signified; by this means it "transforms history into nature" (Barthes, 1972, pp. 118, 128, 130; see also Bourdieu, 2005, p. 178).

Situated Claims

But we cannot go very far before we sense the need for greater precision. And here we come back to the concerns of intercultural communication. Its critical paradigm, which is one of its main pillars, rightly queries the truthfulness of notions of an objective reality: they fail to do justice to people and ethnicities "whose cultural truths (and very existences)" are not acknowledged as analytically relevant; it is tempting to assume that "their truths needed only to be adjusted to our own" (Cooks, 2010, p. 114). Thus the pioneering work of Edward T. Hall "addressed those with the mobility and privilege to travel to and from 'other' spaces/people" (Cooks, p. 114). While that has brought valuable insights to pass, it cannot be the whole (hi)story.

We should take note of the composition of *The International Encyclopedia of Intercultural Communication* (2017): it features 57% US-based authors and 22.5% based in Europe (see Kim, 2017, p. xlv). Shall we gather, in keeping with this preponderance, that "[h]istory is a story Western culture buffs tell each other" (Haraway, 1988, p. 577)? And that the same goes for "IC"? We should be wary of perpetuating existing dominance relations in letting the buffs tell their stories. It is inevitable that a history of Intercultural Communication, as a modern research and practice field, should focus strongly on the USA. That does not have to be the case for the wider fields of intercultural studies. At the same time we should be wary of critical schools that, with a non-Western focus, "provide a single narrative to describe people of a particular descent" (Baldwin, 2017, p. 35). In each of these ways history can be a form of exercising temporal power, intervening in the research and practice landscape to act on and modify perceptions.

Feminist thought has contributed the awareness that knowledge is always situated and embodied, with "limited location" rather than a "splitting of subject and object" (Haraway, 1988, p. 583; see also Halualani & Nakayama, 2010, p. 3). The implications have gone far beyond feminism. They enable us to acknowledge that, whether oriented toward feminism or otherwise, scholarship should not ignore the insight that "[k]nowledge claims are always socially situated": the failure of dominant groups to "interrogate their advantaged social situation and the effect of such advantages on their beliefs" impair their epistemological objectivity (Harding, 1992, p. 442). We can infer, accordingly, that historical time is likely to be "inherently ethical and political" (Bevernage & Lorenz, 2013, p. 11), seeing that it operates within a discursive framing of chronopolitics.

Bracketing

It may not be amiss at this stage to call attention to the need for "bracketing." Perhaps nourished by our specific socialization, for each of us, our intellectually informed worldview shapes what is interesting for us as well as, we assume, for the audience we want to address, and what can "register as variables for analysis" (Cooks, 2010, p. 113). Supra-individually, while often embracing individual habituation, we can think of it as a paradigm in the shape of hidden assumptions (see Clarke, 2017, p. 2). In phenomenological thinking, the first stage of analysis consists of "'horizontalizing' the phenomena under investigation," which means "striving to describe them without privileging any particular perspective or imposing theoretical assumptions. [...] This requires, first, a reflexive process of bracketing, or invoking the epoché, by carefully articulating one's own perspectives and assumptions" (DeTurk, 2010, p. 570).

This goes back to propositions by Edmund Husserl in 1929. According to these, my life in which I pursue scientific inquiries proceeds in the sense that, by means of my experiencing and my activity of valuing, the spatiotemporal world I enter gains its sense and status "in and from me, myself," hence in and from my judging it. I need to "refrain from doing any believing that takes 'the' world straightforwardly as existing"; instead, my scientific questioning requires an "inhibiting" or "putting out of play" all "positions taken toward the already-given Objective world" (Husserl, 1960, pp. 21, 20). In his Ideas (First Book), Husserl had earlier, in 1913, explained the need for a process of "annulment of positing": we have convictions, a natural attitude, which have been shaped by our developing experiential consciousness.

We are not called upon, however, to give up or to alter our positing (our conviction), rather we "put it out of action," we "exclude it," and thus "parenthesize it" (Husserl, 1982, pp. 58, 59). This results in a specific mode of consciousness. It is added to our original positing, our original assumptions, and then "changes its value" (1982, p.59). Accordingly, I must not accept any proposition about the world's actualities "until after I have put parenthesis around it" (1982, p. 62). We need to "make cognized" the "complete system of fashionings of consciousness which constitute the originary givenness of all such Objectivenesses" (1982, p.365). The prose may sound tortuous. Does it mean we should place our own assumptions and convictions in some drawer and then forget about them, in the course of our historical research? On the contrary: it rather means growing aware and taking note of them, a process which (and for Husserl this is essential) changes the value of our assumptions, and thus amounts to a "radical alteration of the natural positing" (1982, p.57). Seen in this way, it's an opportunity that we do not want to cast aside when we embark on any stage of our historical inquiries.

4. Conclusion: Dynamic History

From various angles, then, we keep coming back to the question of how histories are presented. Can historical reality possibly be independent of its later textual representation, or is it "intrinsically 'constructed'" within its representations (Little, 2020, 3.2)? Supported by the views we have considered, we take the latter to be likely. Constructionist thinkers in the manner of the so-called linguistic turn would embrace the assessment that historians "*constitute* their subjects" as objects of a narrative, by means of the descriptive language they use (White, 1978, p. 95; see also Roth, 2017, p. 399). At least intermittently, that language of historians features what Danto has analyzed as a "narrative sentence": it refers to "a time-ordered pair of events *E-1* and *E-2*," and it is predictive until any particular and variable second E or E-at-t[ime]-2 occurs (Danto, 1962, pp. 170, 172). It can even extend its scope by featuring sentences that include a reference to the narrator's future (see Day, 2008, p. 227). Narrative sentences play a key role for instance in such topics as "IC Scholars before Their Time" (DuBois et al., 2017, p.54), when we hear that, as a "prescient" academic, Rachel Davis-DuBois in 1939 among other achievements "conceptualized the fore-runner of the later Peace Education programs" (DuBois et al., 2017, p.75).

By being epistemically capable of generating such utterances, the process of writing histories and consequently our reception will always be strongly "dynamic and not static" (Roth, 2017, p. 400). The rich polyvocality of views and experiences we are offering in the present volume confirms this, throughout. It opens a number of pathways for fresh inquiry into timespaces of intercultural exploration. Far from remaining distinct, these get continuously "threaded through one another" (Barad, 2017). With the outstanding contributions we have succeeded in recruiting, this volume's contents should push us onward to new areas of temporally conscious research.

The Scope and Contents of This Volume

An interplay of explorations, and of timespaces, should become evident in the inquiries featured in this volume. A range of inter- and transcultural developments, with manifestations of cultural variance, needs to be studied. We hope that this book will prompt those of us undertaking intercultural research to think earnestly about the opportunities which complementary disciplinary perspectives will enable. As previous volumes in the series have devoted attention to matters of communication, intercultural identity, value frameworks and dimensions, adaptation, and literature, they have on many occasions glanced at research objects in a historical context. We now intend to build on these precedents, and investigate historical processes in a more comprehensive way.

Without attempting to avoid intersecting earlier volumes' focal areas entirely, we have recruited contributions highlighting historical perspectives with reference to the following specific themes: for Historical Perspectives (I), Volume 11 includes (1) Conceptual and Thematic Developments in two major sections, (2) Cross-Cultural Encounter, and (3) Countries — Nations — Nation-States. The companion Volume 12, for Historical Perspectives (II), will call attention to (1) Education and Pedagogy, (2) East Asian Intercultural Dynamics with reference to China as well as Japan, and (3) Foundations and Pioneers.

The volumes are independent of each other, and each can be taken without recourse to the other. The sections move from theoretical reflections to specific and practically oriented studies, to show the range of relevant dimensions. We now offer a brief introduction to the chapters and the research issues that are presented in the volume. This is what awaits you.

Conceptual and Thematic Developments 1:
From Constructivism to Relational Traditions

This first main section focuses especially on histories of ideas and concepts that have shaped intercultural domains in significant ways. Important concepts occur likewise in the second segment of this main section, as well as in further sections. Accordingly, reflecting the complex interconnections of our historically nourished reality, the chapters dovetail to some extent with approaches in other sections that trace divergent contexts. The section concentrates on re-thinking forms of constructivism; the relevance of the theory of sociocultural models, including a synopsis; the underlying power of Whiteness in the construction of communication; and the tradition of Descartesian universalism and rationalism as against culture-relative or relational thinking. All these represent key issues in the developing field of intercultural communication.

In Chapter 1, Milton Bennett comments on "Constructivism," the epistemological position that knowledge and experience of the world are constructed, not discovered. Events that are selected as representative of intercultural communication are construed in a constructivist paradigm, to explain how intercultural theory has been able to address issues of cross-cultural relations more successfully than theories based in other paradigms. The chapter reviews how modern forms of constructivism have been incorporated into human communication theory and thence into intercultural communication theory, and considers how constructivist intercultural theory has been implemented in developmental forms of training and education. Especially pertinent is a quantum form of constructivism. Hitherto this is less discussed outside of physics, but is fast becoming an important idea for social science. Constructivist intercultural theory is clearly represented in intercultural training and education, but in many other areas the constructivist quality of intercultural communication theory has largely been replaced by the prevailing theory of the respective host field. This tendency has led to specific disadvantages, most seriously in domestic multicultural relations.

Valery Chirkov in Chapter 2 addresses the historical and conceptual origins of the theory of sociocultural models (TSCM), a theory that aims at explaining mechanisms of intracultural relations and communication. Chirkov treats these relations as a baseline from which the examination of intercultural relations should start, and hence as strongly relevant to the latter. The chapter examines contributions of social philosophers and scholars from Germany, France, and the USA since the end of the 19th century to understanding the psycho-socio-cultural regulation of people's intracultural relations: the regulatory processes that exist within the communal space; the corresponding mental correlates in the minds of members of the community; the interactions of these processes; and functions of the emergent synthesis and the modes of their execution.

Added to the chapter is a synopsis that highlights the consilience of the reviewed ideas. The TSCM invites intercultural relation researchers to study sociocultural models that exist in different cultural communities and regulate relations of their members. This theory also encourages scholars to consider how discrepancies among these models may generate barriers for intercultural communication and provides directions to examine these barriers and develop interventions for their minimization.

Chapter 3, by Thomas Nakayama and Judith Martin, responds to recent calls for interrogating the history and development of research and theory in intercultural communication. There is an underlying power of Whiteness in the construction of communication itself. Because of this legacy, the authors interrogate the absence of Whiteness theory/studies in the intercultural field, seeing that attention to absences in the development of a field of study can be instructive in clarifying the frequent invocation of "we," as well as how intercultural communication has been shaped in whose interests and goals. The chapter thus examines the political and social contexts in which the field of intercultural communication was established, to demonstrate how these contexts impacted the field to serve primarily the interests of Whiteness in various roles. The examination concludes with some challenges facing the future of intercultural communication.

From another angle, in Chapter 4 Gesine Lenore Schiewer traces concepts that are common in intercultural communication research and practice back to two general paradigms. One of the two can be found in prominent approaches of the so-called "dialogue of cultures," but it is also found in intercultural education research. It refers to approaches of philosophy in the tradition of Descartesian *universalism* and rationalism. The other, alternative paradigm is associated with the *culture-relative* or relational thinking of Johann Gottfried Herder, Wilhelm von Humboldt, and others. Both of these paradigms were taken up in the 20th century in communication studies, which was now forming as an independent research field.

Because of their importance, the chapter offers an overview of the strengths and weaknesses of the two paradigms.

Conceptual and Thematic Developments 2:
From African Interactions to "Where We're Going"

Complementing the historical dimensions thematized in the first segment, this segment extends the reach of the above considerations of theme and concept with attention to a diversity of global regions. Prominent among these is Africa, in keeping with the continent's significance in our world.

In Chapter 5, Wim van Binsbergen observes that the concept of interculturality has often been used to denote the encounter or combination of more than one culture. Much of the anthropology of social organization since the 1960s has been preoccupied with a form of deconstruction of identity and ethnicity, "tribe," or "nation." For anthropologists African tribes, although dominating the societal thought of African actors, are recently invented traditions, impositions by bureaucrats, White entrepreneurs, missionaries, and European researchers. For analysts who bring to their work a different regional perspective than that of the North Atlantic region, however, such an approach often amounts to a self-sacrifice. The chapter argues that cultural patterning typically addresses specific facets and spheres of a person's total life, while each of these orientations may have a different history and provenance. In Western thought, it is only recently that such post-structuralist concepts as *différance* and *differend*, and the elaboration of ternary and multi-value logics, have created a context where we can affirm interpersonal encounter despite different cultural orientations — where we can bring about interculturality.

Africa is a central subject again in Chapter 6, by Keyan Tomaselli and Paul Tembe, who study communitarianism between three different societies. They offer a comparative analysis of *ubuntu* (Southern Africa), Confucianism (China), and *jantelagen* (Sweden), mapping the respective contours of these concepts in relation to their host societies. This involves questioning the societies' claims to exceptionalism, while the authors seek to explain why communitarianism works in some societies but less so in some others (mostly African). The comparative approach opens the door to a more sophisticated analysis of *ubuntu* than has been the case to date. It becomes evident how communitarianism can benefit national economies and distribution of social resources, when it moves from being simply ethnic rhetoric to actual implementation through social structures.

Africa and China are focal areas, too, in Chapter 7 by Richard Harris, as well as Japan and other regions. As Harris reminds us, in 1963 Edward T. Hall coined the term *proxemics* to describe the human use of space as an "elaboration of culture." Hall's approach inspired scholars to look more closely at the ways in which people perceive and interact with each other and with the physical environments, natural and built, in which they find themselves. Yet as the world globalized, people from different cultural backgrounds came more frequently and significantly into contact with each other, particularly in urban environments, and as a result other aspects of proxemics have become more salient. One tends to assume that two or more people in a certain setting will tend to perceive their surroundings in similar ways, sharing similar cognitive and emotional experiences. But this assumption neglects crucial aspects. This chapter accordingly expands Hall's insights by suggesting a model that considers a wider range of intercultural perceptions and responses.

Stephen Croucher in Chapter 8 includes a focus on South Africa and China as well as other major regions in a review of the evolution of research literature on intercultural communication. The review has four purposes: it summarizes the development of the discipline from the traditional United States perspective, with a focus on the work of Edward T. Hall, while also recognizing the work of others; it discusses the discipline's theorizing period of expansion; it briefly explores the discipline's growth outside of the traditional U.S. perspective, focusing on other global regions; and it offers a perception of opportunities, issues, and directions for development of the discipline.

Cross-Cultural Encounter

The encounter between cultures can be both a concept and a genuine experience, and both of these are already thematized at times in the initial sections as described above. This section devotes more immediate attention to such encounters, in theory and practice.

In Chapter 9, Rolf Elberfeld reminds us that it was only a little more than a century after the uncountable noun "culture" played an important role in Herder's new version of the history of humanity that the plural form "cultures" was first introduced into the language of the humanities by Jacob Burckhardt, then being picked up and disseminated by Friedrich Nietzsche. This plural form has permanently changed the manner in which the present as well as the past is described. We can now speak of a "culture of cultural encounter." The chapter accordingly recalls the concepts of culture (and cultures) offered by Johann Gottfried Herder, Wilhelm von Humboldt, Jacob Burckhardt, and Friedrich Nietzsche, because it is through these that such a perspective has become possible. Building on this historical inquiry, the chapter interprets the creative work of two composers, one Japanese and one German, as a "culture of cultural encounter": it appears to be high time to develop such a culture.

With a different approach, but an equally strong individual commitment, Clifford H. Clarke in Chapter 10 presents a diversified theory grounding to trace the history of an intercultural management training firm. This enterprise worked with dozens of professionals serving dozens of global clients in long-term contracts throughout thirty years (1980–2010). They shifted intercultural training paradigms by collaboratively engaging corporate leaders, selected researchers from universities, and managers of foreign subsidiaries anticipating new assignees. The firm approached clients seeking collaboration in (a) assessing the individual assignees and the sending and receiving organizations, (b) designing training that integrated assessment data with theories that could guide intercultural learning processes, (c) creating multicultural and interactive team-training approaches, and (d) assessing the performance of new skills, as demonstrated in training and in the workplace, that met corporate standards of function-specific performance in the workplace. The integration of researcher-consultant-trainer roles into corporate subsidiaries in long-term embedded positions was one of the unique elements of this history.

Countries — Nations — Nation-States

Questions concerning historical perspectives on nations as distinct entities, and nationhood, have played a role in several of the chapter contributions thus far. Such entities may seem to be naturally related to the study of cultural values, or they may seem to be less suited or of lower priority for intercultural inquiries. This complex topic deserves a separate discussion, and the section offers two approaches for a closer analysis. In our companion Volume 12, the chapter by Naoki Sakai also presents important contributions to this topic area.

In a U.S. context, Robert E. Park's study of foreign-language newspapers in the earlier 20th century needs consideration and recognition in this context. Filipa Subtil, José Luís Garcia, and Wendy Leeds-Hurwitz devote an important study to it (Chapter 11). Park was studying newspapers in urban centers hosting multiple immigrant groups, and emerges as an important precursor to several current assumptions within intercultural communication, especially the move away from equating cultures with nations, and the possibility of simultaneously holding multiple identities. Park's research on the media's influence on identity construction contains theoretical contributions that remain highly relevant to a world increasingly configured by global media: in particular, on accepting complexity and the fact that individuals may and do simultaneously hold multiple and conflicting identities. Hence, beyond the nation-state, the appropriate unit of analysis became the ethnic group.

From a wide perspective, Rongtian Tong in Chapter 12 discusses the way in which the nation-state as a form of polity has achieved global dominance. Yet within the scope of human history, the polity as well as its dominance are relatively recent phenomena. Prior to its ascendency, the world was filled with a plethora of distinct and unique form of polities. The chapter asks how and why the sweeping transition into a homogeneous system of nation-states has occurred? It reviews some seminal theories, classical and contemporary, that dissect the rationale behind the formation of the nation-state. It thus explores the historical, philosophical, political, and cultural factors that ultimately led to the arrival of the nation-state as the dominant form of polity. Understanding the underpinnings of the nation-state appears critical to Intercultural Communication, as the field finds its origins in a time and place where the concept of culture both constructed the nation-state and emerged out of it. Elucidating the pretenses on which the nation-state is built may enable us to re-think our ideas of culture and how it should be measured and analyzed.

Acknowledgments

In concluding these introductory statements, we would like to express our thanks and appreciation to all those who have supported the endeavor and helped us to bring about this volume. We wish to give our strong appreciation to Prof. Zha Mingjian, Vice President of SISU, for his personal initiative in furtherance of our work. The Intercultural Institute staff at SISU has contributed very helpful service to us all along. Colloquia as well as research conducted at the John W. Kluge Center of the Library of Congress, enabled by Director Dr. John R. Haskell during Michael Steppat's recurrent Fellowships, have contributed especially valuable stimuli and ideas to our inquiry. We are indebted to this scholarly environment.

This publication project is part of a commitment to contribute to the internationalization and interdisciplinary cooperation of the Intercultural Institute and of SISU itself, by linking the cooperating and interculturally oriented researchers on interdisciplinary research and writing projects, selecting and editing the best new work, and publishing continuing topical volumes in this monograph series of *Intercultural Research*. Our volumes seek to highlight benchmarks of international scholarship, in an effort to move the enterprise of our disciplinary cooperation forward. From the outset, this series has aimed to provide a set of monographs in which each volume is focused on one important topic area. Each chapter is meant to be a specially invited "state-of-the-art" analysis of a key topic in intercultural communication studies and its disciplinary partners. Like its companions, this volume attempts to fulfill the high goals we have for this series, having both international and Chinese scholars providing their best work as a reference or benchmark on which to further the research agenda. Researchers in several countries have helped us progressively clarify our ideas and approaches. Michael Steppat has benefited from national research support at the cluster level (Exc 2052/1-390713894).

We owe great thanks, moreover, to Shanghai Foreign Language Education Press for its professional excellence in the printing and publishing of the volume.

We wish to take this opportunity to express our profound gratitude to each of the contributors to this book, for having prepared excellent scholarly essays and engaging with us in fruitful discussion. Building on this experience, we feel strongly encouraged in looking forward to further explorations together. We will be grateful to all who are stimulated to build on the chapters put forward here.

References

Ankersmit, F. R. (2006). "Presence" and myth. *History and Theory*, 45, 328-336.
Baldwin, J. (2017). Murky waters: Histories of intercultural communication research. In Ling Chen (Ed.), *Intercultural communication* (pp.19-44). De

Gruyter.

Barad, K. (2007). *Meeting the universe halfway: Quantum physics and the entanglement of matter and meaning*. Duke University Press.

Barad, K. (2010). Quantum entanglements and hauntological relations of inheritance: Dis/continuities, spacetime enfoldings, and justice-to-come. *Derrida Today*, *3*(2), 240–268. doi: 10.3366/E1754850010000813

Barad, K. (2017). Troubling time/s and ecologies of nothingness: Re-turning, re-membering, and facing the incalculable. *New Formations*, *92*, 56–86. doi: 10.3898/NewF:92.05.2017

Barthes, R. (1972). *Mythologies* (A. Lavers, Trans.). The Noonday Press. (Originally published 1957)

Benjamin, W. (2003). On the concept of history. In H. Eiland & M. W. Jennings (Eds.), E. Jephcott et al. (Trans.), *Walter Benjamin: Selected writings* (Vol. 4: 1938 – 1940, pp. 389 – 400). Harvard University Press. (Originally published 1942)

Bennett, M. J. (2012). Paradigmatic assumptions and a developmental approach to intercultural learning. In M. Vande Berg, R. M. Paige, K. H. Lou (Eds.), *Student learning abroad: What our students are learning, what they're not, and what we can do about it* (pp.90–114). Stylus Publishing.

Bennett, M. J. (2021). The Intercultural Viability Indicator: Constructivist assessment of organizational intercultural competence. *Journal of Intercultural Communication & Interactions Research*, *1*(1), 55–81.

Bevernage, B. (2016). Tales of pastness and contemporaneity: On the politics of time in history and anthropology. *Rethinking History*, *20* (3), 352 – 374. https://doi.org/10.1080/13642529.2016.1192257

Bevernage, B., & Lorenz, C. (2013). Introduction. In C. Lorenz & B. Bevernage (Eds.), *Breaking up time: Negotiating the borders between present, past and future* (pp.7–37). Vandenhoeck & Ruprecht.

Bloch, M. (1954). *The historian's craft* (P. Putnam, Trans.). Alfred A. Knopf/ Manchester University Press.

Bourdieu, P. (2005). Outline of the theory of practice: Structures and the habitus. In G. M. Spiegel (Ed.), *Practicing history: New directions in historical writing after the linguistic turn* (pp.174–194). Routledge. (Originally published 1972)

Carr, E. H. (1987). *What is history?* The George Macaulay Trevelyan Lectures (2nd ed.). Penguin Books. (Originally published 1961)

Chakrabarty, D. (2009). The climate of history: Four theses. *Critical Inquiry*, *35*(2), 197–222.

Clarke, C. (2017). Reflections from history: How shifting paradigms created intercultural innovations. *Journal of Intercultural Communication*, *20*, 1–26.

Cooks, L. (2010). Revisiting the borderlands of critical intercultural communication. In T. K. Nakayama & R. T. Halualani (Eds.), *The handbook of intercultural communication* (pp.112–129). Wiley-Blackwell.

Crane, D. (1972). *Invisible colleges: Diffusion of knowledge in scientific communities*. The University of Chicago Press.

Danto, A. N. (1962). Narrative sentences. *History and Theory*, *2*(2), 146–179.

Day, M. (2008). *The philosophy of history*. Continuum.

De Certeau, M. (1988). *The writing of history* (T. Conley, Trans.). Cornell

University Press. (Originally published 1975)

De Fina, A. (2016). Narrative analysis. In Zhu Hua (Ed.), *Research methods in intercultural communication* (pp.541–565). Wiley Blackwell.

DeTurk, S. (2010). "Quit whining and tell me about your experiences!": (In) Tolerance, pragmatism, and muting in intergroup dialogue. In T. K. Nakayama & R. T. Halualani (Eds.), *The handbook of intercultural communication* (pp.565–584). Wiley-Blackwell.

Derrida, J. (1973). *Speech and phenomena: And other essays on Husserl's theory of signs* (D. B. Allison & N. Garver, Trans.). Northwestern University Press.

Derrida, J. (1978). *Writing and difference* (A. Bass, Trans.). The University of Chicago Press.

Derrida, J. (1982). *Margins of philosophy* (A. Bass, Trans.). The University of Chicago Press.

Derrida, J. (1997). *Of grammatology* (G. C. Spivak, Trans.). The Johns Hopkins University Press.

Drzewiecka, J. A. (2010). Public memories in the shadow of the other: Divided memories and national identity. In T. K. Nakayama & R. T. Halualani (Eds.), *The handbook of intercultural communication* (pp. 286–310). Wiley-Blackwell.

DuBois, G., Potts, L. B., & Kulich, S. J. (2017). IC scholars before their time: Rachel Davis-DuBois and the IC Education Movement. In S. J. Kulich & A. S. English (Eds.), *China Intercultural Communication Annual*, 2, 54–79.

Fasolt, C. (2013). Breaking up time — Escaping from time: Self-assertion and knowledge of the past. In C. Lorenz & B. Bevernage (Eds.), *Breaking up time: Negotiating the borders between present, past and future* (pp.176–197). Vandenhoeck & Ruprecht.

Garland, D. (2014). What is a "history of the present"? On Foucault's genealogies and their critical preconditions. *Punishment & Society*, *16*(4), 365–384.

Gorman, J. (2013). The limits of historiographical choice in temporal distinctions. In C. Lorenz & B. Bevernage (Eds.), *Breaking up time: Negotiating the borders between present, past and future* (pp. 155–175). Vandenhoeck & Ruprecht.

Gramsci, A. (1971). *Selections from the prison notebooks* (Q. Hoare & G. N. Smith, Trans.). International Publishers.

Hall, E. T. (1959). *The silent language*. Doubleday.

Halualani, R. T., & Nakayama, T. K. (2010). Critical intercultural communication: At a crossroads. In T. K. Nakayama & R. T. Halualani (Eds.), *The handbook of intercultural communication* (pp. 1–16). Wiley-Blackwell.

Haraway, D. (1988). Situated knowledges: The science question in feminism and the privilege of partial perspective. *Feminist Studies*, *14*(3), 575–599.

Harding, S. (1992). Rethinking standpoint epistemology: What is "strong objectivity"? *The Centennial Review*, *36*(3), 437–470.

Hristova, M., Ferrándiz, F., & Vollmeyer, J. (2020). Memory worlds: Reframing time and the past — an introduction. *Memory Studies*, *13*(5), 777–791.

Husserl, E. (1960). *Cartesian meditations: An introduction to phenomenology* (D. Cairns, Trans.). Martinus Nijhoff. (Originally published 1929)

Husserl, E. (1982). *Ideas pertaining to a pure phenomenology and to a phenomenological philosophy, First book* (F. Kersten, Trans.). Collected Works Vol. 2. Martinus Nijhoff. (Originally published 1913)

Hwang, K.-K. (2007). The development of indigenous social psychology in Confucian society. In SISU Intercultural Institute (Ed.), *Intercultural perspectives on Chinese communication* (pp. 252–287). Intercultural Research Vol. 1. Shanghai Foreign Language Education Press.

James, W. (2003). *Pragmatism: A new name for some old ways of thinking* (B. Vescio, Introd.). Barnes & Noble. (Originally published 1907)

Kim, Y. Y. (Ed.). (2017). *The international encyclopedia of intercultural communication*. John Wiley.

Kuhn, T. S. (1970). *The structure of scientific revolutions* (2nd ed.). The University of Chicago Press. (Originally published 1962)

Kulich, S. J. (2007). Linking intercultural communication with China studies — language and relationship perspectives. In SISU Intercultural Institute (Ed.), *Intercultural perspectives on Chinese communication* (pp. 3–21). Intercultural Research Vol. 1. Shanghai Foreign Language Education Press.

Kulich, S. J. (2014). Reviews, definitions, and approaches to values studies. In S. J. Kulich, Weng, L., & M. H. Prosser (Eds.), *Value dimensions and their contextual dynamics across cultures* (pp. 27–60). Intercultural Research Vol. 5. Shanghai Foreign Language Education Press.

Kulich, S. J., Weng, L., Tong, R., & DuBois, G. (2020). Interdisciplinary history of intercultural communication studies. In D. Landis & D. P. S. Bhawuk (Eds.), *The Cambridge handbook of intercultural training* (pp. 60–163). Cambridge University Press.

Kulich, S. J., & Zhang, X. (2012). Profiling people in multiple domains: Toward a sociology of science for intercultural disciplines. *International Journal of Intercultural Relations*, *36*, 885–901.

Latour, B. (2005). *Reassembling the social: An introduction to actor-network-theory*. Oxford University Press.

Leeds-Hurwitz, W. (1990). Notes in the history of intercultural communication: The Foreign Service Institute and the mandate for intercultural training. *Quarterly Journal of Speech*, *76*, 262–281.

Leeds-Hurwitz, W. (2010). Writing the intellectual history of intercultural communication. In T. K. Nakayama & R. T. Halualani (Eds.), *The handbook of intercultural communication* (pp. 21–33). Wiley-Blackwell.

Little, D. (2020). Philosophy of history. In E. N. Zalta (Ed.), *The Stanford encyclopedia of philosophy* (Winter 2020 Edition).

Liu, C-Y., & Wang, S. (2007). Who are we and where are we going? — Cultural transformation in the past twenty-five years in China in the global context. In SISU Intercultural Institute (Ed.), *Intercultural perspectives on Chinese communication* (pp. 175–192). Intercultural Research Vol. 1. Shanghai Foreign Language Education Press.

Löblich, M., & Scheu, A. M. (2011). Writing the history of communication studies: A sociology of science approach. *Communication Theory*, *21*, 1–22.

Martin, J. N., & Nakayama, T. K. (1999). Thinking dialectically about culture and communication. *Communication Theory*, *9*(1), 1–25.

Martin, J. N., Nakayama, T. K., & Carbaugh, D. (2020). A global look at the history and development of language and intercultural communication studies. In J. Jackson (Ed.), *The Routledge handbook of language and intercultural communication* (2nd ed., pp. 19–38). Routledge. (First ed. 2012.)

Merriam-Webster (2021). An Encyclopaedia Britannica Company.

Mink, L. O. (1987). *Historical understanding* (B. Fay, E. O. Golob, & R. T. Vann, Eds.). Cornell University Press.

Moon, D. G. (2010). Critical reflections on culture and critical intercultural communication. In T. K. Nakayama & R. T. Halualani (Eds.), *The handbook of intercultural communication* (pp. 34–52). Wiley-Blackwell.

Nietzsche, F. (1997). *Untimely meditations* (D. Breazeale, Ed.; R. J. Hollingdale, Trans.). Cambridge University Press. ("On the uses and disadvantages of history for life," pp. 57–124, originally published 1874)

Nietzsche, F. (1998). *On the genealogy of morality* (M. Clark & A. J. Swensen, Trans.). Hackett. (Originally published 1887)

Oakeshott, M. (1933). *Experience and its modes*. Cambridge University Press.

Park, D. W., & Pooley, J. (Eds.). (2008). *The history of media and communication research: Contested memories*. Peter Lang.

Pirandello, L. (1922). *Three plays*. E. P. Dutton.

Prosser, M. H. (2007). One world, one dream: Harmonizing society through intercultural communication: A prelude to China intercultural communication studies. In SISU Intercultural Institute (Ed.), *Intercultural perspectives on Chinese communication* (pp. 22–91). Intercultural Research Vol. 1. Shanghai Foreign Language Education Press.

Queloz, M. (2021). *The practical origins of ideas: Genealogy as conceptual reverse-engineering*. Oxford University Press.

Rogers, E. M., & Hart, W. B. (2002). The histories of intercultural, international, and development communication. In W. B. Gudykunst & B. Mody (Eds.), *Handbook of international and intercultural communication* (2nd ed., pp. 1–18). Sage.

Roth, P. A. (2017). Philosophy of history. In L. McIntyre & A. Rosenberg (Eds.), *The Routledge companion to philosophy of social science* (pp. 397–407). Routledge.

Rovelli, C. (2018). *The order of time* (E. Segre & S. Carnell, Trans.). Allen Lane.

Rozbicki, M. J., & Ndege, G. O. (Eds.). (2012). *Cross-cultural history and the domestication of otherness*. Palgrave Macmillan.

Said, E. (2005). *On 'Orientalism.'* Media Education Foundation (Northampton, MA).

Schapiro, M. (1972–1973). On some problems in the semiotics of visual art: Field and vehicle in image-signs. *Simiolus*, *6*(1), 9–19. (Originally published 1969)

Smeekes, A., & Verkuyten, M. (2015). The presence of the past: Identity continuity and group dynamics. *European Review of Social Psychology*, *26*(1), 162–202. doi: 10.1080/10463283.2015.1112653

Spiegel, G. M. (2007). Revising the past/revisiting the present: How change happens in historiography. *History and Theory*, *46*(4), 1-19. (Theme issue Revision in History)

Tamboukou, M. (1999). Writing genealogies: An exploration of Foucault's strategies for doing research. *Discourse Studies in the Cultural Politics of Education*, *20*(2), 201-217.

Thompson, M. P. (2019). *Michael Oakeshott and the Cambridge school on the history of political thought*. Routledge.

Vaccaro, J. A. (2018). The quantum theory of time, the block universe, and human experience. *Philosophical Transactions of the Royal Society (A)*, 1-13. https://doi.org/10.1098/rsta.2017.0316

White, H. (1978). *Tropics of discourse: Essays in cultural criticism*. The Johns Hopkins University Press.

Wood, G. (2008). *The purpose of the past: Reflections on the uses of history*. The Penguin Press.

Zahle, J. & Collin, F. (Eds.). (2014). *Rethinking the individualism-holism debate: Essays in the philosophy of social science*. Springer.

Conceptual and Thematic
Developments 1:

From Constructivism to
Relational Traditions

1

A Brief History and Commentary on Constructivism in Intercultural Communication Theory

Milton J. Bennett

Intercultural Development Research Institute, Milan

Summary: "Constructivism" is the epistemological position that knowledge and experience of the world is constructed, not discovered. That position pervades this chapter, including the chapter's approach to history as a construction, albeit one constrained by our previous experience with past events (Rovelli, 2018). Events selected as representative of intercultural communication are construed in a constructivist paradigm, with the purpose of explaining how intercultural theory has been able to address some issues of cross-cultural relations more successfully than theory based in other paradigms. The chapter's scope is (1) to review how modern forms of constructivism have been incorporated into human communication theory and thence into intercultural communication theory, and (2) to consider how constructivist intercultural theory has been implemented in developmental forms of training and education.

The four modern forms of constructivism considered are: developmental, radical, perceptual, and quantum. The first two are well represented in social science literature. The third refers to the perceptual flexibility that is commonly discussed in intercultural communication, while the fourth, so far less discussed outside of physics, is fast becoming an important idea for social science. Constructivist intercultural theory is clearly represented in intercultural training and education, but in applied linguistics, economics and business, cross-cultural psychology, and equity/inclusion, the constructivist quality of intercultural communication theory has largely been replaced by the prevailing theory of the host field. This development has led to specific disadvantages, most seriously in domestic multicultural relations.

1. Introduction

1.1 Short Definition of Constructivism

Pending a more precise definition in the following section, "constructivism" is the epistemological position that knowledge and experience of the world is constructed, not discovered. The position does not consider events less real; it simply holds that the reality of events is not because they have an independent or *a priori* existence. Instead, the reality of specific events emerges from the interaction of a probability of existence with an observation of that probability. In the case of social events such as human communication, which is the concern of this chapter, human perception interacts with various probabilities of behavior, yielding particular behavior that is taken as meaningful. Intercultural communication is the specific case of human communication wherein constructions of meaning interact with constructions of cultural context, yielding the potential of various kinds of bridging behavior.

"History" is no exception to this epistemological principle. Rather than being the discovery of existing past events, a constructivist history emerges from the relationship of an observer and the probability of past events. While historical probability is more limited than that of potential future events because of previous relationships (Rovelli, 2018), it is not absolute; otherwise, there would never be arguments about the interpretation, importance, and even existence of historical events. So, the brief history presented in this chapter relies on the author's interpretation of certain past events in the field of intercultural communication as representing "constructivism," and it credits that condition with the success of intercultural communication in addressing issues that cannot be adequately explained with less constructivist epistemology.

1.2 Range of Convenience

Another caveat for undertaking this task is summed up in the *range of convenience corollary* from George Kelly's *Personal Construct Theory* (1963): "a construct is convenient for a finite range of events only" (p. 69). He explicates this by stating that a concept occupies a finite semantic space, and outside of that space the concept becomes impossibly vague, begging for a new concept to fit the new space. The limitation of a concept to a particular semantic and relational space does not make it less useful. On the contrary, recognizing its range of convenience can make a concept act more like a laser than like a flashlight, illuminating its subject brightly and narrowly rather than broadly but dimly.

Kelly comes to mind when people argue that intercultural communication has been around since ancient times, for instance in describing Mesopotamian trade practices, or when people complain that intercultural communication is a Western concept. In terms of Kelly's corollary, the fact that Mesopotamians were interacting with people outside their group did not mean they were engaging in intercultural communication, since the semantic space wherein the concepts of "culture" and "interaction" reside did not exist then. And intercultural communication is a Western concept; it dwells in a time and semantic space populated by all sorts of other Western concepts. Neither of these facts makes intercultural communication less useful; in fact, it allows the concept to illuminate a finite range of events with greater clarity. This can be true without belittling the importance of identifying historical threads that inevitably form the zeitgeist for any new construct (e. g., Kulich et al., 2020).

In this chapter, I will assume a similar stance regarding the epistemological concept of "constructivism." If we take that concept in its most general sense, that human beings are actively engaged in constructing their view of the world, then its history in Western thought dates back to at least the early-18th-century writings of Giambattista Vico and George Berkeley (von Glasersfeld, 2007), and arguably it should extend to the ancient Greek philosopher Heraclitus. However, since this chapter focuses on constructivist currents in the relatively recent concept of human communication theory, the range of convenience is restricted to those forms of constructivism that existed in the latter part of the 20th century. This would include, notably, the thinking of Piaget (1957), Mead (1968), Bateson (1972), von Foerster (1979), and von Glasersfeld

(1984).

The limited scope of this chapter, therefore, is (1) to review how modern forms of constructivism have been incorporated into human communication theory and thence into intercultural communication theory, and (2) to consider how constructivist intercultural theory has been implemented in developmental forms of training and education.

2. Constructivism

The term "constructivism" is used in a wide range of disciplines, only some of which are relevant to communication theory. Here the term refers to an epistemological position that contrasts with "positivism" and "relativism." As I have argued elsewhere (Bennett, 2013a), referencing the work of Kuhn (1967) and Briggs and Peat (1984), the three epistemological positions of positivism, relativism, and constructivism are implementations in social science of three basic paradigms in physics: Newtonian, Einsteinian, and quantum. The relevant difference among the paradigms is how observation operates. In the Newtonian/positivist paradigm, objective observers are assumed to be capable of representing an independently existing reality. In the Einsteinian/relativist paradigm, observers are necessarily restrained by context, so they can only represent existing reality from their "point of view." In the quantum/constructivist paradigm, observers are both the producers and products of reality, so their observations are constructions rather than representations.

Variations on the idea of constructivism include "constructionism," a position associated with symbolic interactionism in sociology (Blumer, 1969; Goffman, 1974; Mead, 1934/2015) and experiential learning in education (Papert & Harel, 1991). While constructionists share with constructivists the assumption that "self" and "other" are dynamic constructs, they usually don't take an ontological position on whether there is an absolute reality underlying this and other interpretative distinctions. Instead, they focus on the social construction of knowledge, sometimes with the political agenda of deconstructing the power dynamics of such constructions (e.g., Derrida, 2007; Foucault, 1984). Constructivist writers, on the other hand, tend to treat reality itself as a construction of human perceptual discrimination and its metaphorical elaboration in shared language (Bennett, 2013b; Phillips, 1995).

For the purposes of this chapter, it is useful to consider four forms of constructivism: developmental, radical, perceptual, and quantum. Of these four, the first two are well represented in social science literature. The third, "perceptual constructivism," is a term I have coined to refer to the kind of perceptual flexibility that is commonly discussed in the field of intercultural communication. The fourth is, so far, less discussed outside of physics, but this chapter will suggest that it is fast becoming an important idea for social science in general and particularly for intercultural communication.

2.1 Developmental Constructivism

Piaget's hugely influential work, exemplified in *The Construction of Reality in the Child* (1957), extended John Dewey's idea that perceptual construct formation was central to human development (Dewey, 1960; Vanterstraeten & Biesta, 1998). Piaget argued that children begin perceiving the world in relatively undifferentiated ways — what he called "egocentrism" — and progressively develop more complex schemata that enable them to construe the world in increasingly sophisticated ways. While alternative explanations have been argued for exactly how and when children construct particular kinds of perceptual categories (e.g., Thelen & Smith, 1994; Vygotsky, 1986), those criticisms have largely maintained Piaget's original developmental conceptualization. That conceptualization subsequently became foundational in developmental psychology (Butterworth & Harris, 1994), and it is consistent with various subsequent movements in psychology such as that of "intelligent perception" in cognitive psychology (Gregory, 1966) and "psychological adaptation" in evolutionary psychology (Gould, 2002).

Piaget's theory of adaptive development was a major departure from the prevailing Darwinian theory of natural selection, here described by von Glasersfeld (2002):

> In the theory of evolution, the biological living space of each organism is hemmed in by the limits entailed by its physiological make-up and by the obstacles presented by its environment. Both these are given conditions over which neither the individual nor the species has control. In contrast, in Piaget's theory of cognition, a relative, labile equilibrium is possible only in the space generated by the active avoidance of, or continual compensation for, perturbations. The conceptual difference between the two essentially parallel theories resides in the source of the restraints. On the biological

> level the factors that limit survival are in no way determined by the
> organism itself. On the cognitive level, however, perturbations that
> impede equilibrium spring from the mutual incompatibility of goals
> the organism has chosen and/or of the means used to attain them.
> (p.10)

2.2   Radical Constructivism

The reason for differentiating radical from developmental forms of
constructivism is to acknowledge the different practical applications
that are made of the positions. Piaget (and Dewey before him) were
both interested in the practical question of how human beings who lacked
complete genetic conditioning were able to become accomplished in
adapting to their environments; in other words, how they learned to
learn (McLeod, 2018). This emphasis has led to largely educational
applications of developmental constructivism, usually in the form of
support for learner-centered experiential methods.

In contrast to an emphasis on learning, radical constructivism is
focused squarely on the cognitive aspect of adaptation (von Glasersfeld,
1995). That ontological focus is also found in the related forms of
"cybernetic constructivism" (von Foerster, 1984) and "autopoiesis"
(Maturana & Varela, 1992). Von Glasersfeld uses the term "radical"
in its sense of "root" to stress the ontogenic aspect of the view, while
von Foerster uses the term "cybernetic" for the operation of self-
reflexive control of systems. Using a more biological metaphor,
Maturana and Varela use the term "autopoiesis" to refer to the self-
organizing capability of organisms and "co-ontogenesis" to indicate
the generative interaction between organism and environment. What
all these ideas have in common is the epistemological assumption of
dialectic genesis moderated by conscious intentionality. In other
words, radical constructivism focuses on how both ourselves and our
environments are co-created in the process of actively seeking viable
ways of being in the world.

One important implication of active construction is that, since
they are creating each other, observers cannot be separated from
their observations. All explanations must therefore be to some extent
recursive, or self-reflexive; that is, they must include the act of
explaining as part of the observation. Here is the idea stated by
Maturana (1988):

> The praxis of living, the experience of the observer as such, just
> happens. [...] Because of this, explanations are essentially

superfluous; we as observers do not need them to happen; but when it happens to us that we explain, it turns out that between language and bodyhood the praxis of living of the observer changes as he or she generates explanations of his or her praxis of living. This is why everything that we say or think has consequences in the way we live. [...] (p. 27)

In paraphrase, Maturana is saying that we can act without self-consciousness, but if we do exercise that kind of consciousness, our self-observations become part of the reality in which we are acting.

The cognitive focus of radical constructivism is not opposed to *experience*. In fact, what Maturana calls the "praxis of living" is just that — experience. This necessary relationship of construction and experience is stated explicitly by Kelly in his theory of personal constructs (1963):

A person can be a witness to a tremendous parade of episodes and yet, if he [*sic*] fails to keep making something out of them, or if he waits until they have all occurred before he attempts to re-construe them, he gains little in the way of experience from having been around when they happened. (p. 73)

In a later talk published more recently, Kelly (2017) elaborated on that idea:

Keeping in mind that events do not actually repeat themselves [...] it begins to be clear that the succession we call experience is based on the constructions we place on what goes on. If those constructions are never altered, all that happens during a man's [*sic*] years is a sequence of parallel events having no psychological impact on his life. But if he invests himself — the most intimate event of all — in the enterprise, the outcome, to the extent that it differs from his expectation or enlarges upon it, dislodges the man's construction of himself. [...] A succession of such investments and dislodgments constitutes the human experience. (p. 6)

This idea of constructed experience will be a central influence in communication theory.

2.3 Perceptual Constructivism

In my recent work (e. g. Bennett, 2020, 2021) I have been using the term " perceptual constructivism " to refer to those aspects of constructivism that are most closely related to human perception and communication. The main mechanism of perceptual constructivism is *boundary formation*, a process described by G. Spenser Brown (1972) as "making a distinction." According to Brown, to indicate the existence of anything demands that a distinction be made that distinguishes the thing (figure) from all that it is not (ground). The boundary of the distinction is both ephemeral and mutable, meaning that the existence of events depends on their continuously being indicated, and the particular form of the event can change according to location of the boundary.

An example of perceptual constructivism in action is the event of a nation-state. A country depends first on its being indicated (perceived) as a particular grouping of people different than other groupings. Then, a boundary needs to be drawn that defines the location of that grouping. Of course, many wars have been fought about exactly how the boundary is drawn, and the position of the boundary usually changes over time, including disappearing entirely as particular groupings are no longer perceived. Thus, the nation-state is not an independent thing at all; it is an event co-created by groups of people who are indicating their difference from one another. The construction of all other events involving human perception follows the same pattern. (According to quantum mechanics, non-human interactions also generate events, but that is outside the range of convenience of this concept.)

Perceptual constructivism is meant to include aspects of categorical or cognitive complexity (Delia et al., 1970) and the general principle of linguistic relativity (Whorf, 1956), but it focuses more on the complexity of perceptual discrimination itself. So, for instance, specialized conceptual categories such as "terroir" and "vintage" help sommeliers focus their attention toward vinous events, but they are additionally able to make fine distinctions in taste, color, aroma, etc., that enable them to discriminate complex differences within the categories. Stated in constructivist terms, categorical and perceptual discrimination are co-ontogenically related.

2.4 Quantum Constructivism

I have long held that current ideas of constructivism are themselves reflections in social science of the thinking underlying quantum mechanics in physical science. That contention has been supported by a smattering of literature, largely in business (e.g., Lord et al., 2015; Wheatley, 2006; Zohar, 2016) and consciousness studies (e.g., Penrose et al., 2009/2017; Wolinsky, 1993). Now the quantum physicist Carlo Rovelli (2017, 2018, 2021) has undertaken the task of articulating the connection between the epistemology of quantum mechanics and the ontology of everyday experience. The theme that runs through all his lay-audience books is that events exist only in relationship to their observation. For instance, "time" is not a thing — it is how we describe our different experiences of events that are relatively known compared to those that are relatively unknown. As I mentioned earlier in this chapter, events that we locate in an historical "past" are those that we have already related to in some way — that is, they have been observed — and therefore the probability of them having some particular existence is relatively high (although not absolute). In contrast, events in the "future" have not yet been observed and therefore have no particular existence. Rovelli argues that all events behave this way, because observation is not just the act of perceiving; it is the interrelating of any two events such that one is arbitrarily the observer and the other the observed. Rovelli makes the same case for "here" — the description is only meaningful in relationship to a positioned observer; it can't exist as an autonomous concept.

Rovelli's rendering of quantum epistemology is profoundly constructivist; or perhaps we should say that constructivism is profoundly "quantum." The necessary relationship of events in quantum thinking is a parallel to the co-ontogenesis of Maturana, the dialectical constructivism of Piaget, and the constructive alternativism of Kelly. Quantum epistemology reminds us that the construing of events is not the same as the interpreting of events. "Interpretation" implies that the events exist apart from that interpretation, while "construing" events means that the events themselves are being constructed in relationship to the observer. It is this latter idea, not the relativity of perception, that underlies constructivist communication theory, as we will see in the upcoming sections.

3. Communication Theory

This chapter will refer to communication theory in the way proposed by Robert Craig (1999) in his influential article "Communication Theory as a Field" and incorporated in the popular textbook *Theories of Human Communication* (Littlejohn et al., 2021). Craig suggests two principles of second-order coherence that pervade a taxonomy of seven contexts of first-order application. Although he does not use the term "constructivism," the principles reflect that epistemological paradigm.

3.1 Second-Order Principles

The first principle holds that communication theory is "constitutive," meaning that it is constructed at a second-order metalevel to organize various first-order models and approaches into a coherent field of inquiry. In terms of perceptual constructivism, this is exactly like forming the boundaries of a nation-state, where the boundary both reflects commonalities in the territory and simultaneously generates bridges among different constituents that allow them to co-exist coherently in the territory. In other words, communication theory is a kind of autopoiesis, or second-order, self-reflexive, self-organizing system.

The second of Craig's principles — "metadiscourse" — also refers to the second-order aspect of communication theory. It assumes that human communication in its first-order sense is what people naturally do — they seek to coordinate action with one another. In this sense, they are not dissimilar to all other organisms that we know of. The fact that humans use highly developed languages to perform that coordination just allows them to do it in particularly ornate ways. So, communication theory is not about why we communicate, which could be (and is) equally the legitimate interest of anthropology, sociology, psychology, economics, politics, philosophy, and every other social science and humanities field. What makes human communication theory (and the field of communication studies in general) unique is its ability to model and explicate how communication occurs in various contexts. And that focus is what makes this approach to human interaction constructivist; it does not claim to establish a priori conditions or causality, but rather it specifies the relationships among defined elements that manifest in the behavior.

3.2 Language Logic: Wittgenstein

An important proponent of this epistemological position is Ludwig Wittgenstein, who argued that meaning does not exist in language, but only in its use (Wittgenstein, 2009). In other words, the event of meaning only comes into existence in the relationship of language and speakers. This position has been influential in supporting the pragmatic focus of communication theory. At the time of its original publication in 1953, Wittgenstein's position on language constituted a notable departure from the then-popular essentialist views of language. Those views included both the behaviorist theory of language acquisition through operant conditioning (Skinner, 1957) and the generative grammar position of Chomsky (1957). Despite the fact that Chomsky was famously critical of Skinner's dependence on instinctual structures (Chomsky, 1959), his own position was similarly essentialist, albeit more Platonic than Skinner's Aristotelian empiricism. Those two positions continue to be influential in linguistic theory, which I think explains why human communication theory — especially intercultural communication — has never had a very comfortable theoretical relationship with linguistic programs.

Wittgenstein was making an altogether different case for language — a constructivist case, I would argue. As he had previously written in *Tractatus* (1922, 6.432-7.0), language indeed had a logical structure, but logic itself was not an eternal aspect of reality. By this, I think Wittgenstein meant that language was constructed for the purpose of communication, and that it did not have any *a priori* existence. Language could logically describe all that was describable, he said, but there were indescribable aspects to the world that were "mystical." Whatever was eternal belonged only to the feeling of the mystical — it could not be described: "Whereof one cannot speak, thereof one should remain silent." With this last sentence, Wittgenstein affirms from a metalevel that every statement of logic is constructed, and, once realizing this, there is nothing left to say about logic and language other than to describe its usage (Bennett, 1977; Bennett & Castiglioni, 2004).

3.3 Cybernetics: Watzlawick

One of Craig's (1999) descriptions of first-order communication usage is cybernetics — the control of systems. An early example of cybernetic communication was the Shannon-Weaver (1948) SMCR (sender-message-channel-receiver) model of information transfer. The cybernetic tradition of communication theory is explicit in disavowing complex psychological processes underlying (causing) communication, preferring to focus on the already complex relationship among the sender's intention, the ability of a code to symbolize that intention, the ability of a channel or medium to convey the code, the interpretation of the receiver, cycles of feedback and feedforward between sender and receiver, and various unintended consequences of the process. A more recent example of this communication theory tradition applied to the interpersonal context is found in Watzlawick et al., *Pragmatics of Human Communication* (1967). One of their axioms, the "punctuation of a series of events," outlines how individuals in a couple attribute causality to each other by each of them saying, "it all started when he (or she or they) did [...]" (pp. 37-38). The analysis of such an interaction is constructivist in that it does not assume any actual cause of the conflict outside the relationship of the couple's perception of their own behavior; it describes a cybernetic process, and insofar as the analysis also implies that it could be used by the couple as an intervention in their own behavior, it becomes an example of the "cybernetics of cybernetics" à la Mead (1968) and von Foerster (1979). Or in Maturana's (1988) terms, the explanation of their behavior becomes part of their behavior.

3.4 Social Coordination and Empathy

Two other traditions of general communication theory as defined by Craig (1999) are important precursors to intercultural communication theory. One is "sociocultural — communication as the (re)-production of social order" (p. 144) and the other is "phenomenological — communication as the experience of otherness" (p. 138). In the sociocultural context, communication is the mechanism whereby groups of people coordinate meaning and action (Bennett, 2013a, p. 54). One way this happens at the macrolevel is the maintenance of cultural institutions through a dialectical process of socialization (internalization) and appropriate role-behavior (externalization), as described by the constructivist sociologists Berger & Luckmann (1967). At the microlevel, sociocultural coordination is described well by *Coordinated Management of Meaning* (Pearce, 2005). CMM posits that coordination of meaning occurs through rule structures that are internalized by interactants. By applying the relevant rules, people can, more or less, clarify ambiguity and resolve conflicts. The second-order concern of CMM is to describe how certain rules emerge in certain contexts, with the underlying assumption that all rules are simply consistencies in the way people relate to certain events, and their purpose is exactly to perpetuate that consistency.

The phenomenological tradition in communication theory concerns how people relate to each other through feeling rather than logical language — phenomena Wittgenstein referred to as "mystical." Specifically, the tradition focuses on the idea of "empathy" as a mechanism in human relationships. As is the case in other contexts of communication, second-order communication theory in this tradition is mainly concerned with how the mechanism — in this case, empathy — works to help coordinate meaning and action; less important are speculations by psychologists (e.g., Rogers, 1961) or philosophers (e.g., Buber, 1970) on the purpose of empathy (such as authenticity or self-transcendence). The essential thing is to have some way of bridging the gap that is created by distinguishing self and other, without obviating that distinction. Writ large, this is the primary issue of intercultural communication, as discussed in the next sections.

4. Intercultural Communication Theory

In response to increasing globalization and human migration, intercultural communication was defined as a context of application within communication studies in the late 1960's (for details of this inclusion, see Bennett, 2022; Kulich et al., 2020; Pusch, 2004). While intercultural communication had been defined at least a decade earlier, the late 1960's corresponds with the inclusion of cross-cultural and intercultural relations within the established field of communication studies (or speech communication, as it was sometimes called then). That, in turn, set the conditions for intercultural relations to be understood in terms of constructivist human communication theory.

4.1 Culture Relativity and Etic Observational Categories

Although he was not the first to use the term "intercultural communication" (Kulich et al., 2020), Edward T. Hall in *The Silent Language* and his colleague George Trager were largely responsible for locating intercultural relations in a communication context. By defining "culture" as communication, they formalized the idea that cultural members were actively engaged in coordinating meaning and action amongst themselves, and further, that participating in another culture demanded that visitors master some aspects of the host culture's coordinating process.

Hall had worked with Boas, Benedict, and Mead — central figures in the construction of cultural relativity — and, although he was a solid proponent of that position, he was aware that cultural relativity meant that different cultural groups could no longer be understood in terms of universal concepts. His attempt to use standard anthropological techniques that were based on permutations of universal categories of human behavior were therefore not appropriate for his teaching task, which was to prepare diplomats and business people to be more effective during short-term sojourns. To meet this need, he and Trager created a set of "etic observational categories" that allowed comparison among cultures without invoking a universal standard. Such etic categories had been created before to support general cross-cultural understanding, for instance by Ruth Benedict in *Patterns of Culture* in 1934, but their purpose was not specifically to guide intercultural communication. With categories such as high-context/low-context and monochronic/polychronic, the purpose was exactly to provide trainees with ways to broaden their ability to interpret messages and to generate appropriate alternative communication behavior that would fit better into a target culture's coordinating system.

In my conversations with Edward Hall when he was a lecturer at the Summer Institute of Intercultural Communication in the mid-1990s, he was explicit about the constructivist roots of his work. The comparative categories he generated were not "discoveries" of existing cultural differences; they were categories constructed for the express purpose of observing and contrasting communication behavior. He felt that the categories were often misused to describe the "traits" of people or cultures, when in fact they were simply devices to focus people's attention on ways to make their communication more effective in a different coordinating system. With this focus, Hall was incorporating Wittgenstein's constructivist idea of language as a pragmatic organizer of experience. Further, Hall was intentionally using the idea of communication as an organizer of social reality — a theme that pervades *The Silent Language*.

4.2 Linguistic Constructivism

Hall's linguist colleague Trager had worked with Edward Sapir and his student Benjamin Lee Whorf, sharing their interest in the relationship of language and culture (Whorf, 1956) — an idea now known as the Sapir/Whorf hypothesis. Hall incorporated this idea into his work. I remember comparing notes with him on the way Trukese, a Micronesian language that both of us knew, organized time and space differently from English, and how that was manifested in different cultural experience. Since my early graduate work in psycholinguistics, I have thought that Whorf and to some extent Sapir, as well, were misunderstood constructivists. The major criticism of their work came from universalists like Chomsky (1957) and Pinker (1994), who dismissed what they considered "linguistic determinism" as unsupported by empirical research (and which, by the way, disagreed with their ideas of innate linguistic structure). But when the hypothesis is considered in a constructivist context (e.g., Lakoff, 1987), it is clear that Sapir and Whorf were usually not making statements of causality, but rather were commenting on how the habits of language channeled the habits of thought and action in particular ways. People <u>could</u> think and act differently, but they habitually did not. This was my personal experience of teaching color terms to 5th grade students in Truk (now called Chuuk). The young students did not normally distinguish the colors "green" and "blue" in their everyday use of Trukese language, but they could easily do so in English after being taught to make the distinction (Stewart & Bennett, 1972/1991).

Language is not just a passive tool of human consciousness; it is an active part of our construction of the world, including consciousness itself. This is the point of Maturana's (1988) comment quoted earlier, here paraphrased as "explanations are not necessary, but when they occur, they become part of our praxis of living." A similar constructivist treatment of language is found in cognitive linguistics, for instance by George Lakoff and Mark Johnson in *Metaphors We Live By* (Lakoff & Johnson, 1980) and their later work, *Philosophy in the Flesh* (1999), and in a publication that pre-dates that work, *The Origin of Consciousness in the Breakdown of the Bicameral Mind* (Jaynes, 1976). The author of that opus, Julian Jaynes, argues that self-consciousness is a kind of epigenic evolutionary development that was originally stimulated by the need for groups of sapiens to interact with alien groups in a growing human population. In other words, according to Jaynes, we humans are not *a priori* self-conscious beings adapting to the world — we are beings that have become (to some degree) conscious as an adaptation to the multicultural world that we have created (cf. Bennett, 2016a, 2016b).

4.3 Metacultural Coordination

Remembering the Berger and Luckmann (1967) description of culture as a dialectic of internalized objective institutions and externalized worldviews, we can visualize intercultural communication as a meta-level — the coordination of coordinating systems. This, of course, parallels the constructivist idea of "cybernetics of cybernetics" discussed by Mead (1968) and von Foerster (1979). Intercultural communication is not a first-order activity like other everyday communication; it is inherently second-order, like meta-discourse or other forms of self-reflexive communication. As such, most intercultural communication theory is also inherently constructivist.

The inherent constructivist nature of intercultural communication is not recognized by all practitioners. When intercultural communication is naïvely approached as if it were just like other forms of first-order communication — but with outsiders — it creates a paradox. A logical paradox occurs when a class of events is considered as a member of its own class (Russell, 1948). In this case, the class (or conceptual category) of events is "culture," referring to different ways that human groups coordinate themselves. When that meta-level is ignored, groups can easily be treated as if they have an *a priori* existence in the world; they become *reified*, whereby the meta-level of observing groups of people in cultural terms is confused with groups actually having different cultures. At least two problems emerge from this confusion. One is that culture is treated like personality — a set of traits that underlie behavior in some causative way. This leads to descriptions of cultures as if they possessed qualities such as "style" or "values" that influenced culture members' behavior in predictable ways. That view of culture as a kind of group personality drove some "psychological anthropology" efforts during World War II to understand the psyche of the enemy, notably represented in Ruth Benedict's *The Chrysanthemum and the Sword* (1946).

Another paradoxical problem caused by confusing the second-order meta-level with first-order communication is a reified polarization of "similarity" and "difference." Most first-order communication is similarity-based for the purpose of basic coordination of meaning and action; people need to have similar schemata in order to match sender interpretations with receiver intentions, even with the addition of feedback and feedforward mechanisms. This everyday need for similarity generates an assimilationist pressure in multicultural societies; there is little natural tolerance for people whose schemata do not allow for relatively effortless coordination of meaning and action. And, of course, nearly all immigrants and even some visitors assimilate language and customs sufficiently for basic communication. However, as cultural differences pervade societies through immigration of new cultures and through stronger identity claims to the existing ones, there are more and more situations where first-order communication is insufficient. Among them are multicultural workplaces that deem cultural diversity to be an important asset, and communities that seek a climate of respect for cultural diversity. In these and many other familiar multicultural situations, the first-order demand for similarity runs counter to the desire for maintaining diversity.

To address the importance of acknowledging diversity, some intercultural practitioners are tempted to exalt cultural differences and reject similarities. But diversity cannot be a simple opposite to similarity as a basis for first-order communication. To assume so would mean that diverse peoples do not share the same meaning schemata, and therefore could not communicate with one another. This creates the paradoxical form of "political correctness," wherein people are being asked to acknowledge and respect the unique identities of people with whom they cannot communicate; that is, if similar schemata are necessary for communication, but others must avoid assimilating to a dominant culture schema for fear of losing their identity, while the dominant culture cannot use any other schema because of its inherent imperialism, then intercultural communication is paradoxically both demanded and precluded.

This paradox of political correctness is maintained by an assumption of reified cultural difference — the idea that different cultural groups have certain qualities and people have certain identities. Approaching cross-cultural encounters with these reifications generates simplistic descriptions of first-order cultural differences and stereotyped notions of cultural identity. When naïve intercultural practitioners conduct programs at this level, they justify the criticism leveled against intercultural communication that it ignores the "dynamic" nature of culture (e. g., Bjerregaard et al., 2009). But the flexibility of cultural boundaries is not the main problem here; more seriously, the problem is a failure to position intercultural communication as a second-order meta-communication from which distinctions of both similarity and difference are made.

From a constructivist perspective, "culture" is neither inherently dynamic nor is it inherently static. Culture is a cognitive category that allows us to contrast groups of people for some reason — in this case, for the purpose of intercultural communication. Similarity and difference are two interconnected poles of a perceptual dialectic that we create for the purpose of generating comparisons. Neither similarity nor difference exists independently in groups of people that we categorize by culture; both are products of our "etic observation" of the groups. For example, while it might be useful to say that Western cultures are more individualistic compared to more collectivist Eastern cultures, such a statement necessarily generates the broad distinction of East/West and applies the perceptual schema of individualism/collectivism to generate an observation of difference. It is equally valid to generate generational boundaries in both Western and Eastern groupings, and, applying the same etic observation, state that all cultures are changing in terms of individualism/collectivism. Or, of course, we can differentiate cultures in terms other than national boundary or geographical region. The point for intercultural communication is that information about cultural differences is really incidental to the main purpose of the theory, which is to define second-order communication competencies.

As it was intended by its constructivist founders, intercultural communication avoids ethnocentrism by operating in liminal space at a meta-level or in the intersection between self and other. By contrast, our everyday communication generally demands only something like "theory of mind" for assuming that interlocutors are also capable of intending and interpreting meaning. After that, the goal of most communication is to be as unconscious of it as possible. This is probably why being "self-conscious" is seen as a detriment, rather than an asset, in everyday parlance. For second-order intercultural communication, self-consciousness is a constant necessity. Below is a familiar list of competencies that could be referenced to virtually all sophisticated textbooks of intercultural communication. The point of listing them here is to emphasize their divergence from typical monocultural first-order communication.

Intercultural communicators need to be:

- Culturally self-aware, meaning that they can easily reference their own cultural schemata and compare them to differing cultural schemata of interlocutors without stereotyping either self or other
- Intentionally non-evaluative of cultural differences for the purpose of interpretation
- Empathic for the purpose of understanding value differences, while maintaining ethical commitment to their own values
- Able to choose from an expanded repertoire of cultural behaviors that are appropriate in a range of cultural contexts
- Able to generate third-culture solutions or other means of coordinating joint action without suppressing cultural difference.

4.4 Intercultural Training and Education

The goal of intercultural training is fundamentally to create transferable second-order communication skills such as those listed above, while the goal of other cross-cultural approaches is often to acquire knowledge about specific other cultures. The implicit assumption of culture-specific approaches is that knowledge and skills, perhaps combined with the right attitude, will generate adaptive behavior in another culture. The more explicit assumption of a culture-general intercultural approach is that only shifting one's experience into a different worldview (intercultural empathy) will allow authentic adaptation. The assumption that people can intentionally shift into a different worldview experience is, of course, constructivist.

Hall and Trager were motivated by the need to prepare sojourners, and training applications have continued a practical focus on increasing intercultural skills in international exchange, global business, multicultural workforces, and diversity/inclusion/equity. The pedagogical theory underlying most intercultural development derives from the philosophy of John Dewey and the constructivist models of Piaget and Vygotsky. An exemplar of this experiential approach, the Experiment in Living Abroad, was established in 1934 (before Hall and Trager's work at the Foreign Service Institute), but the Experiment's experiential approach to intercultural learning was institutionalized in the 1964 founding of the School of International Training to provide programming for the U.S. Peace Corps (SIT website, 2021). SIT programs have always made explicit reference to Hall and other founders of intercultural communication. Although it is not documented, it seems likely that the conduit of constructivist education into the work of Hall and Trager at the Foreign Service Institute was Vygotsky's association with linguistic relativity, and Trager's close association with Whorf. Hall and Trager pioneered the systematic use of theory-based experiential methods in their FSI training, using simulations and other exercises that demanded action and reflection (Rogers et al., 2002). These methods were continued in early intercultural training work of the Intercultural Communication Network and the Stanford Institute for Intercultural Communication (Pusch, 2004). All these efforts were geared towards second-order communication skills, a focus commonly known as "culture-general."

The most complete incorporation of constructivist intercultural training methods occurred in the Intercultural Communication Workshop, a program that began at the University of Pittsburgh and that migrated in various forms to many other universities (Bennett, 2022). Beginning in the late 1970's, I began developing a theoretical model of intercultural development based, among other grounded research, on my experience teaching the ICW. The result was the *Developmental Model of Intercultural Sensitivity* (Bennett, 1986, 2017b), which specified a movement along a continuum defined by increasing amounts of perceptual complexity vis-à-vis cultural difference. The DMIS combined the constructivist development ideas of Piaget and Vygotsky with the radical constructivism of Maturana and von Glasersfeld to suggest that intercultural training was guiding the reconstruction of an ethnocentric experience of alterity into a more ethnorelative experience. Additionally, the model specified that the second-order skill that enabled such a shift was that of perceptual boundary formation — an application of ideas from G. Spencer Brown and George Kelly. Insofar as the DMIS and other related and derivative developmental models continue to influence intercultural training with the goal of increasing second-order communication competence, it is fair to say that intercultural communication is fundamentally constructivist.

5. Conclusion

Recognizing the constructivist quality of communication theory in general and intercultural communication theory in particular may be more important than simply highlighting an historical trend in the field. For various reasons that are outside the scope of this discussion, work on intercultural relations is increasingly being separated from its communication theory roots. This has allowed the term "intercultural" to be applied to various other approaches to cross-cultural and intergroup relations, including that of applied linguistics (e. g ., Lange & Paige, 2003), economics and business (e. g., Hofstede & Hofstede, 2005), cross-cultural psychology (e. g., Matsumoto, 2010), and equity/inclusion (e. g ., Aman, 2018). In these and other applications, the constructivist, second-order quality of intercultural communication has largely been replaced by the prevailing theory of the host field.

While each of the following instances deserves another full-length chapter, I will mention a few implications of losing the constructivist focus of intercultural communication in alternative fields. For instance, language educators who focus on the linguistic aspects of intercultural communication (e. g., Fantini, 2012) do not usually treat it as a second-order phenomenon. This has led to intercultural competence being considered as an extension of linguistic competence, or simply becoming an alternative term for the pragmatic (as opposed to syntactic and semantic) dimension of language (e. g., Tannen, 1990). This leads to the simple idea that intercultural communication is a kind of code-shifting of nonverbal and communication-style behavior — a useful concomitant to syntactic and semantic shifts in exercising linguistic competence. While that is, in my experience, certainly true, it nevertheless does not address any of the second-order concerns of using appropriate cultural generalizations or coordinating third-culture mutual adaptation.

A condition similar to that of applied linguistics occurs in business applications, where models such as Hofstede's "cultural orientations" allow for contrasting cultures in ways that certainly increase the awareness of potential misunderstanding, but which do not provide the theoretical grounding for generating appropriate new behavior in alternative cultures. As such, intercultural communication becomes a kind of problem-solving technique rather than becoming part of a strategic vision for organizational development. Cross-cultural psychology probably makes the most valid claim on intercultural communication, since the roots of communication theory certainly include strong tendrils into psychology. But, as I have argued elsewhere (Bennett, 2020), traditional psychology tends to use an individual level of analysis, while intercultural work is firmly located at a group level where the unit of analysis is not personality, but manifestations of worldview. Aspects of social psychology (e. g., Zimbardo, 2007) are located more at the group level of analysis, but research methodology in all of psychology tends to keep the individual as the dependent variable — a limitation that can only be countered by using more constructivist research methods (Bennett, 2020, 2021).

To my mind, the most serious implication of losing the constructivist communication focus of intercultural work is in the general area of domestic multicultural relations, including a growing spectrum of diversity in ethnic, racial, gender, sexual orientation, and various role identities. I am concerned that these categories into which we ascribe ourselves and to which we ascribe others are being reified and treated as *a priori* entities. Additionally, the idea of cultural relativity, which was originally intended as an antidote to universalist beliefs about civilization (Boas, 1896/1940), is being extended into the extreme position that all cultures should essentially be treated as sovereign worldviews. This combination of reification and separatism is a formula for paradoxical paralysis. If we must respect all cultures, and if part of that respect is that no culture should impose its worldview on another, and if we cannot suspend our cultural category (because it has been reified), then we are all locked into a descending spiral of first-order power struggles for social control. The contribution of intercultural communication has been to provide a way out of this first-order paralysis with the possibility of second-order coordination. In that view, our cultural categories are constructed, our affiliations with them are chosen, and our collective worldviews are therefore mutable. Only with this second-order assumption are we able to take each other's perspective sufficiently to coordinate mutual adaptation. This capability is probably central to our continued survival in the social world we have created.

> Once one accepts the view that all knowledge is a cognizing subject's construction, that subject regains such autonomy as it can find within the constraints of an unknowable world. And with autonomy comes responsibility. What we know, largely determines how we act. Consequently, if we want to act responsibly, we shall have to take responsibility also for the way we see the world. (von Glasersfeld, 2010, p. 20)

References

Aman, R. (2018). *Decolonising intercultural education: Colonial differences, the geopolitics of knowledge, and inter-epistemic dialogue.* Routledge.

Bateson, G. (1972). *Steps to an ecology of mind: Collected essays in anthropology, psychiatry, evolution, and epistemology.* Chandler.

Benedict, R. (1934). *Patterns of culture.* Houghton Mifflin.

Benedict, R. (1946). *The chrysanthemum and the sword.* Houghton Mifflin.

Bennett, M. (1977). Forming feeling process: The communication of boundaries and the perception of patterns. Unpublished Ph. D. dissertation, University of Minnesota, Twin Cities.

Bennett, M. (1986). A developmental approach to training intercultural sensitivity. In J. Martin (Guest Ed.), Special Issue on Intercultural Training, *International Journal of Intercultural Relations*, 10(2), 179–186.

Bennett, M. (2013a). *Basic concepts of intercultural communication: Paradigms, principles, & practices.* Intercultural Press.

Bennett, M. (2013b). Intercultural constructivism. In C. E. Cortés (Ed.),

Multicultural America: A multimedia encyclopedia (pp.577-581). Sage.

Bennett, M. (2016a). A constructivist epistemology of hate. In E. Dunbar, A. Blanco, & D. A. Crèvecoeur-MacPhail (Eds.), *The psychology of hate crimes as domestic terrorism: US and global issues* (Vol.1, pp.317-350). Praeger.

Bennett, M. (2016b). The value of cultural diversity: Rhetoric and reality. *Springer Plus*, 5: 897. https://doi.org/10.1186/s40064-016-2456-2

Bennett, M. (2017a). Constructivist approach to intercultural communication. In Y. Y. Kim (Ed.), *The international encyclopedia of intercultural communication*. Wiley.

Bennett, M. (2017b). Development model of intercultural sensitivity. In Y. Y. Kim (Ed.), *The international encyclopedia of intercultural communication*. Wiley.

Bennett, M. (2020). A constructivist approach to assessing intercultural communication competence. In G. Rings & S. Rasinger (Eds.), *The Cambridge handbook of intercultural communication* (pp.521-535). Cambridge University Press.

Bennett, M. (2021). The *Intercultural Viability Indicator*: Constructivist assessment of organizational intercultural competence. *Journal of Intercultural Communication and Interactions Research*, 1(1), 55-82.

Bennett, M. (2025). A short conceptual history of intercultural learning in study abroad. In M. Steppat & S. J. Kulich (Eds.), *Historical intersections of intercultural studies: Tracing genealogies, trajectories, diversifications*. Intercultural Research 12. Shanghai Foreign Language Education Press. Originally published (2010) in Hoffa, B., & DePaul, S. (Eds.), *A history of US study abroad: 1965 – present*. Special Issue of *Frontiers: The Interdisciplinary Journal of Study Abroad*. The Forum for Study Abroad (pp.214-242).

Bennett, M., & Castiglioni, I. (2004). Embodied ethnocentrism and the feeling of culture: A key to training for intercultural competence. In D. Landis, J. Bennett, & M. Bennett (Eds.), *The handbook of intercultural training* (3rd ed., pp.249-265). Sage.

Berger, P., & Luckmann, T. (1967). *The social construction of reality: A treatise in the sociology of knowledge*. Anchor.

Bjerregaard, J., Lauring, J., & Klitmøller, A. (2009). A critical analysis of intercultural communication research in cross-cultural management: Introducing newer developments in anthropology. *Critical Perspectives on International Business*, 5(3), 207-228.

Blumer, H. (1969). *Symbolic interactionism: Perspective and method*. Prentice Hall.

Boas, F. (1940). The limitations of the comparative method of anthropology. In Boas, F., *Race, language and culture* (pp.270-280). Macmillan. (Originally published 1896)

Briggs, J., & Peat, F. (1984). *The looking glass universe: The emerging science of wholeness*. Simon & Schuster.

Brown, G. S. (1972). *Laws of form*. Bantam.

Buber, M. (1970). *I and thou*. Charles Scribner's Sons.

Busemeyer, J. R., & Bruza, P. D. (2012). *Quantum models of cognition and decision*. Cambridge University Press.

Butterworth, G., & Harris, M. (1994). *Developmental psychology*. Lawrence Erlbaum Associates.

Chomsky, N. (1957). *Syntactic structures*. Mouton.

Chomsky, N. (1959). A review of B. F. Skinner's *Verbal Behavior*. *Language*, *35*(1), 26–58.

Craig, R. (1999). Communication theory as a field. *Communication Theory*, *9*(2), 119–166.

Delia, J. G., Crockett, W. H., & Gonyea, A. H. (1970). Cognitive complexity and the effects of schemas on the learning of social structures. *Proceedings of the 78th Annual Convention of the American Psychological Association*, *5*, 373–374.

Delia, J., O'Keefe, B. J., & O'Keefe, D. J. (1982). *The constructivist approach to communication*. In F. E. X. Dance (Ed.), *Human communication theory: Comparative essays* (pp. 147–191). Harper & Row.

Derrida, J. (2007). *Psyche: Inventions of the Other* (Vol. 1, P. Kamuf & E. G. Rottenberg, Eds.). Stanford University Press.

Dewey, J. (1960). *The quest for certainty*. Capricorn.

Fantini, A. (2012). Language: An essential component of intercultural communicative competence. In J. Jackson (Ed.), *The Routledge handbook of intercultural communication*. Routledge.

Foerster, H. von (1979). Cybernetics of cybernetics. In K. Krippendorff (Ed.), *Communication and control* (pp. 5–8). Gordon & Breach.

Foerster, H. von (1984). On constructing a reality. In P. Watzlawick (Ed.), *The invented reality: Contributions to constructivism* (pp. 41–61). Norton.

Foucault, M. (1984). *The Foucault reader* (P. Rabinow, Ed.). Pantheon.

Glasersfeld, E. von (1984). An introduction to radical constructivism. In P. Watzlawick (Ed.), *The invented reality* (pp. 17–40). W. W. Norton.

Glasersfeld, E. von (1995). *Radical constructivism: A way of knowing and learning*. Routledge.

Glasersfeld, E. von (2002). Cybernetics and the theory of knowledge. *UNESCO Encyclopedia*. Section on System Science 255 and Cybernetics.

Glasersfeld, E. von (2007). Aspects of constructivism: Vico, Berkeley, Piaget. In E. von Glasersfeld (Ed.), *Key works in constructivism* (pp. 91–99). Sense.

Glasersfeld, E. von (2010). Why people dislike radical constructivism. *Constructivist Foundations*, *6*(1), 19–21.

Goffman, E. (1974). *Frame analysis: An essay on the organization of experience*. Harvard University Press.

Gould, S. (2002). *The structure of evolutionary theory*. Harvard University Press.

Gregory, R. (1966). *Eye and brain: The psychology of seeing*. Weidenfeld & Nicolson.

Hall, E. T. (1959). *The silent language*. Doubleday.

Hofstede, G., & Hofstede, G. J. (2005). *Cultures and organizations: Software of the mind*. McGraw-Hill.

Jaynes, J. (1976). *The origin of consciousness in the breakdown of the bicameral mind*. Houghton Mifflin.

Kelly, G. (1963). *Personal construct theory*. Norton.

Kelly, G. (2017). A brief introduction to personal construct theory. *Costruttivismi*, *4*, 3–25.

Kuhn, T. (1967). *The structure of scientific revolutions*. University of Chicago Press.

Kulich, S., Weng, L., Tong, R., & DuBois, G. (2020). Interdisciplinary history of intercultural communication studies: From roots to research and praxis. In D. Landis & D. P. S. Bhawuk (Eds.), *The Cambridge handbook of intercultural training* (4th ed., pp. 60-163). Cambridge University Press.

Lakoff, G. (1987). *Women, fire, and other dangerous things: What categories reveal about the mind*. University of Chicago Press.

Lakoff, G., & Johnson, M. (1980). *Metaphors we live by*. University of Chicago Press.

Lakoff, G., & Johnson, M. (1999). *Philosophy in the flesh: The embodied mind and its challenge to Western thought*. Basic Books.

Lange, D. L., & Paige, R. M. (Eds.). (2003). *Culture as the core: Perspectives on culture in second language learning*. Research in Second Language Learning. Information Age Publishing.

Littlejohn, J., Foss, K., & Oetzel, J. (2021). *Theories of human communication*. Waveland Press.

Lord, R., Dinh, J., & Hoffman, E. (2015). A quantum approach to time and organizational change. *Academy of Management Review*, *40*(2), 263-290.

Matsumoto, D. (2010). *APA handbook of intercultural communication*. American Psychological Association. https://doi.org/10.2307/j.ctv1chs0s5

Maturana, H. (1988). Reality: The search for objectivity or the quest for a compelling argument. *The Irish Journal of Psychology*, *9*(1), 25-82.

Maturana, H., & Varela, F. (1992). *The tree of knowledge: The biological roots of human understanding* (Revised edition). Shambhala.

McLeod, S. (2018). Jean Piaget's theory of cognitive development. *Simply Psychology*.

Mead, G. H. (2015). *Mind, self and society* (C. W. Morris, Ed., annotated ed. by D. R. Huebner & H. Joas). University of Chicago Press. (Originally published 1934)

Mead, M. (1968). The cybernetics of cybernetics. In H. von Foerster, J. White, L. Peterson, & J. Russell (Eds.), *Purposive systems* (pp. 1-11). Spartan Books.

Papert, S., & Harel, I. (1991). Situating constructionism. In S. Papert & I. Harel (Eds.), *Constructionism* (Chapter 1). Ablex Publishing Corporation.

Pearce, B. (2005). The Coordinated Management of Meaning (CMM). In W. B. Gudykunst (Ed.), *Theorizing about intercultural communication* (pp. 35-54). Sage.

Penrose, R., Hammeroff, F., & Kak, S. (Eds.). (2017). *Consciousness and the universe: Quantum physics, evolution, brain & mind*. Cosmology Science Publishers. (Originally published 2009)

Phillips, D. D. (1995). The good, the bad, and the ugly: The many faces of constructivism. *Educational Researcher*, *24*(7), 5-12.

Piaget, J. (1957). *The construction of reality in the child*. Routledge & Kegan Paul.

Pinker, S. (1994). *The language instinct*. Morrow.

Pusch, M. (2004). Intercultural training in historical perspective. In D. Landis, J. Bennett, & M. Bennett (Eds.), *Handbook of intercultural training* (3rd ed., pp. 13-36). Sage.

Rogers, C. (1961). *On becoming a person: A therapist's view of psychotherapy*. Constable.

Rogers, E., & Hart, W. (1998). Edward T. Hall and the origins of the field of intercultural communication. Paper presented at the National Communication Association, International and Intercultural Communication Division, New

York, 21–24 November 1998.

Rogers, E., Hart, W., & Yoshitaka, M. (2002). Edward T. Hall and the history of intercultural communication: The United States and Japan. *Keio Communication Review*, *24*, 3–26.

Rovelli, C. (2017). *Reality is not what it seems: The journey to quantum gravity*. Riverhead.

Rovelli, C. (2018). *The order of time*. Riverhead.

Rovelli, C. (2021). *Hegoland*. Riverhead.

Russell, B. (1948). *Human knowledge: Its scope and limits*. Allen & Unwin.

Shannon, C., & Weaver, W. (1948). *The mathematical theory of communication*. University of Illinois Press.

SIT (2021) — School for International Training.

Skinner, B. F. (1957). *Verbal behavior*. Appleton-Century-Crofts.

Stewart, E., & Bennett, M. (1991). *American cultural patterns: A cross-cultural approach* (Revised ed.). Intercultural Press. (Originally published 1972)

Tannen, D. (1990). *You just don't understand: Women and men in conversation*. Ballantine.

Thelen, E., & Smith, L. B. (1994). *A dynamic systems approach to the development of cognition and action*. MIT Press.

Vanderstraeten, R., & Biesta, G. (1998). Constructivism, education, and John Dewey. Paper delivered at the 20th World Congress of Philosophy, Boston, MA. *The Paideia Archive*, *2*, 34–39.

Vygotsky, L. (1986). *Thought and language*. MIT Press.

Watzlawick, P. (Ed.). (1984). *The invented reality: Contributions to constructivism*. Norton.

Watzlawick, P., Bavelas, J. B., Beavin, J. H., & Jackson, D. D. A. (1967). *Pragmatics of human communication: A study of interactional patterns, pathologies and paradoxes*. Norton.

Wheatley, M. (2006). *Leadership and the new science: Discovering order in a chaotic world* (3rd ed.). Berrett Koehler.

Whorf, B. (1956). *Language, thought and reality: Selected writings of Benjamin Lee Whorf* (J. Carol, Ed.). John Wiley.

Wittgenstein, L. (1922). *Tractatus logico-philosophicus*. Kegan Paul.

Wittgenstein, L. (2009). *Philosophical investigations* (4th ed., P. M. S. Hacker & J. Schulte, Trans.). Blackwell. (Originally published 1953)

Wolinsky, S. (1993). *Quantum consciousness: The guide to experiencing quantum psychology*. Bramble.

Zimbardo, P. (2007). *The Lucifer effect: Understanding how good people turn evil*. Random House.

Zohar, D. (2016). *The quantum leader: A revolution in business thinking and practice*. Prometheus.

2

Historical and Conceptual Roots of the Theory of Sociocultural Models

Valery CHIRKOV
University of Saskatchewan

Summary: In this chapter, the author addresses the historical and conceptual origins of the theory of sociocultural models (TSCM) that aims at explaining mechanisms of *intra*cultural relations and communication. The author treats intracultural relations as a baseline from which the examination of *inter*cultural relations should start. The chapter has three sections which examine German, French, and Anglo-American scholars' contributions to understanding the psycho-socio-cultural regulation of people's intracultural relations. Each section targets four aspects of this type of regulation:

(1) the regulatory processes that exist within the communal space;
(2) the corresponding mental correlates that are formed in the minds of members of the community under the influence of the processes (1);
(3) the mechanisms of interactions of (1) and (2); and
(4) functions of the emergent synthesis of (1) and (2) and the modes of their execution.

The chapter ends with a summary that highlights the consilience of the reviewed ideas. That consilience validates the TSCM, which aims at merging the examined thoughts in a way that allows cultural psychology and intercultural relations scholars to use it as a theoretical background for their research.

Introduction

Intra- and *inter-cultural relations* constitute the essence of people's social functioning. Many scholars are interested in *inter*cultural relations and communication because of their practical importance in many domains of people's lives (Bennett, 2013; Landis & Bhawuk, 2020). However, it is essential to first understand *intra*cultural relations, which form the baseline for any intercultural interactions. Intracultural interactions are the relationships among members of the same cultural community — the people who identify with this community and who care about its well-being and sustainability (Abi-Hashem & Peterson, 2013b). Intracultural relations are regulated by sociocultural mechanisms, which are therefore important to uncover and examine. In turn, intercultural relations happen when members of different cultural communities come together to communicate, work, and cooperate with each other (Abi-Hashem & Peterson, 2013a). When members of different cultural communities interact, it is obvious that the habitual mechanisms of interactions for each of them are disrupted, and special efforts must be made to restore the flow of communication. Thus, it is logical to start the investigation of intercultural dynamics by analyzing the mechanisms of intracultural relationships and then progressing to the analysis of the disruption of these mechanisms during intercultural interactions.

The purpose of this chapter is to trace the historical and conceptual roots of understanding the sociocultural mechanisms of regulating people's intracultural relationships and interactions (on a history of intercultural relations see Kulich et al., 2020). One of the current understandings of these mechanisms has been conceptualized as the Theory of Sociocultural Models (TSCM) (Chirkov, 2020). This theory has been developed on a theoretically rich ground. Its ideas and propositions have their origins in conceptualizations elaborated upon at different times, in different countries, and by representatives of different disciplines. A concise review of these ideas has been presented in Chirkov (2020). In the current chapter, I extend this analysis, predominantly by examining the conceptual and theoretical ideas of various scholars on the issue of the social regulation of people's actions. The analysis will also serve the purpose of validating the TSCM. Many scholars and researchers from different times, countries, intellectual traditions, and disciplines have come to similar conclusions about the nature of the mechanisms under investigation. Thus, it is highly probable that because of the *consilience* of these ideas (Wilson, 1999), they reflect the real processes that unfold within the phenomenon of inquiry. In this way, the consilience of ideas about sociocultural mechanisms will confirm their validity.

People's social relations and interactions together with scripts, dynamics and the constituents of these interactions are not their individual creations. These relations and interactions emerge within and are regulated by the communal prescriptions that have been developed and have existed long before the modern interacting individuals were even born. Such pre-existing knowledge, scripts, and practices of relations and interactions have been conventionally attributed to *culture*; hence, we can examine the *cultural regulation* of human interactions and relations through *sociocultural models*. The adjective *sociocultural* highlights that social interactions and their meanings are mutually constitutive. Culture assigns meaning to various actions and makes them meaningful for the actors involved with them. Subsequently, these meanings are maintained through people's social interactions.

This historical and conceptual account of the sociocultural mechanisms of human relations is grouped in three sections based on geographical locations: German heritage, French tradition, and Anglo-American tradition together with recent anthropological accounts in the USA. I will analyze scholars within each group along with four primary components of sociocultural regulation:

(1) the regulatory processes that exist within the communal/public/externalized/social space;
(2) the corresponding mental structures and processes that are formed and that function in the minds of members of the community under the influence of the regulatory processes outlined in (1);
(3) the mechanisms of interactions between (1) and (2);
(4) the functions of the emergent synthesis of (1) and (2) and the modes of their execution.

Not all these components are represented in the analyzed groups; therefore, the completeness of their accounts will differ from one representative to the next.

After examining these traditions regarding these components, I will present an overview that sums up the analyzed ideas and concepts with consideration of the way they have contributed to the understanding of the mechanisms of the psychosociocultural regulation of people's actions and practices and form the essence of the TSCM.

The German Tradition

German scholars have a long history of thinking about, conceptualizing, and understanding the sociocultural contexts of people's lives and their roles in regulating people's actions. This history can be traced back to the 18th and 19th centuries, in the works of scholars such as Johann Gottfried Herder (1744–1803), Wilhelm von Humboldt (1767–1835), Johann Friedrich Herbart (1776–1841), Adolf Bastian (1826–1905), and some others (see more in Berlin, 1976; Jahoda, 1992; Kalmar, 1987; Klautke, 2013b; Koepping, 1983). Moreover, German scholars were among the first in the Western countries to develop a conceptual framework for such analysis. For this section, I will extract and examine two ideas: *objektiver Geist* and *Volksgeist*. [1]

Objektiver Geist. This concept was introduced by Georg Wilhelm Friedrich Hegel (1770–1831). Philosophers continue debating about the meaning of this idea in Hegel's writings (Pinkard, 2019). For our sociopsychological investigation, it is enough to accept that *objektiver Geist* represents the externalized social mind that stands in contrast to the subjective individual minds of people (Boldyrev & Herrmann-Pillath, 2013). One of the scholars who borrowed this concept and applied it to try to understand the mechanisms of sociocultural regulation of people's actions was Wilhelm Dilthey.

Wilhelm Dilthey (1833 – 1911) aimed to identify the bases of knowledge for human sciences and to develop a methodology for this

---

[1] Both these concepts have nearly the same meaning of *collective mind*. *Geist* (German) literally means 'ghost,' 'spirit,' or, less literally, 'mind' or 'mentality.' *Objektiver* means 'objective' or outside of the subjectivities of individuals (the subjective minds). Therefore, the first concept means 'objective mentality/mind.' In turn, *Volks-* stands for 'people.' Thus, *Volksgeist* can be translated as the collective mentality of the community of the people. Referring to Herder's use of this term, Jahoda (1992) wrote that "A *Volk* is characterized by shared language and historical tradition which shape the mentality [*Volksgeist*] of its members" (p. 76). In addition to these terms, German scholars also used notions of *Völkerseele* (the soul of the people) and *Volkscharacter* (people's collective character). These concepts reflect ideas similar to the mental commonality of the collectivity of people. Later, *Volksgeist* was replaced by the notion of *Kultur* (German) and then *culture* (Jahoda, 1992; Kalmar, 1987).

domain of scientific inquiry by studying people's *life-expressions* (de Mul, 2004). He used the term *objektiver Geist* to address both of these objectives (Dilthey, 1994). According to Dilthey, members of the community objectify the mental states and processes they have in common (their collective thoughts, values, behavioral intention, affects, etc.) "in the world of senses" (p.155); hence, creating the *objektiver Geist*② or objective mind. According to Dilthey, the domain of the objective mind

> extends from the style of life and the forms of social intercourse to the system of purposes which society has created for itself and to custom, law, state, religion, art, science and philosophy. [...] It is the medium in which the understanding of other persons and their life-expressions takes place. [...] For everything in which the mind has been objectified contains something held in common by the I and the Thou. (p.155)

Thus, the objective mind is the repository of collective values and norms that are shared by members of the community. In turn, these members of the community use this knowledge to their advantage. In addition, through this sharedness, people understand each other and unambiguously communicate with their fellow citizens.

The objective mind is the product of the history and development of the community. Therefore, it represents an enduring extension of the past into the present — "in this objective mind, the past is a permanently enduring present for us" (p. 155). This makes people and their everyday lives the products of their history.

Dilthey paid special attention to the role objective spirit plays in enculturating children:

> From this world of objective mind the self receives sustenance from earliest childhood. [...] The child grows up within the order and customs of the family which he shares with the other members and his mother's orders are accepted in this context. Before it learns to talk, it is already completely immersed in that common medium. It learns to understand gestures and facial expressions, movements and exclamations, words and sentences, only because it encounters

---

② [Editor's note] "Dilthey employs Hegel's term *objektiver Geist* to denote the intersubjective products and creations of human culture as constituted by the systems of law or economics, political and social institutions or natural languages. Dilthey introduced the term in his treatise 'The Construction of the Historical World in the Human Sciences' of 1910" (Dilthey, 1994, p.164).

> them always in the same form and in the same relation to that they mean and express. Thus, the individual orients himself in the world of objective mind. (p. 155)

This indicates another important function of objective spirit: to be the source for developing the self and making the child a full-fledged member of its community.

The objective mind opens "the possibility of knowledge in the human studies" (p. 155) and provides the context for understanding individual life-expressions. Specifically, every life-expression — such as cognitive schemes, routinely executed actions, verbal expressions, everyday conversations, culturally contingent arrangements and decorations of spaces, and many other forms — is placed into "the articulated order in the objective mind" (p. 155), such as law or religion. Therefore, to understand these expressions and their meaning, the human sciences researcher must consider to what common sphere of the objective mind this expression belongs, and interpret them against a background of the structured common features of that common sphere (p. 155). Dilthey uses greetings as an example. Greetings have different meanings in different situations. Structured and prescribed by the objective mind, the order of handshakes and bows while greeting another person signifies "a certain mental attitude to other people" (p. 156). The objective mind prescribes what form of greeting (and corresponding meaning) is appropriate for a particular context and situation. To understand what a person conveys by this or that form of salutation, it is necessary to know the order and meaning of acknowledgment prescribed by the objective mind. Therefore, the objective mind stands between the expression and what is expressed, and should be the starting point in an investigation of various life expressions.

Volksgeist. The emergence of the concept of *Volksgeist* is traced to Johann Gottfried Herder (Smith, 2005). It corresponds to Hegel's notion of the objective mind. Herder together with Wilhelm von Humboldt applied the idea of *Volksgeist* to societal and nation-building issues (Berlin, 1976; Jahoda, 1992). However, it was philosopher and psychologist Moritz Lazarus (1824–1903) and his colleague philologist and philosopher Heymann Steinthal (1823–1899) who (re)introduced this concept into the social sciences, including psychology, to examine what later will be identified as the sociocultural regulation of people's actions and the relationship between culture and people's minds. These scholars also introduced *Völkerpsychologie*, the discipline that aims at studying *Volksgeist*. Subsequently, Wilhelm Wundt (1832–1920) elaborated his version of *Völkerpsychologie* and presented it as one of the sub-disciplines of the science of psychology that should complement physiological (experimental) psychology. Later, *Völkerpsychologie* was reincarnated in the forms of cultural anthropology, ethnopsychology, cultural psychology, and psychological and cognitive anthropology (Danziger, 1983; Diriwächter, 2004, 2012).

Near the end of the 19th century, many German scholars were deeply dissatisfied with the individualistic nature of the emerging science of psychology — the approach that is still prevalent in 21st-century psychology. According to this conceptualization, the person is treated as an isolated monad that acts upon his or her individual motives, cognitions, and affects. Simultaneously with such individualistic thinking, some scholars in Germany and later in other countries have treated the individual as a part of the larger social universe. This means that they consider that people act not only based on their individual and idiosyncratic inclinations but more so because of the social and cultural prescriptions that exist in their communities. These prescriptions and the conditions of their development should be the primary targets for psychologists and other human and social sciences researchers to understand the driving forces behind people's actions and experiences. The social universe and the related prescriptions, values, skills, and knowledge of each cultural community, among other things, constitute the *Volksgeist/* collective mentality that belongs to and is the expression of its members' individual mentalities. This collective mentality exists independently of the individual mentalities, but it is also embedded in each of them. Therefore, according to Lazarus and Steinthal, to fully understand human psychology, researchers must examine the content of the corresponding *Volksgeist*. In addition to forming human mentalities, *Volksgeist* unites the corresponding communities and brings them together in coherent societies and nations. Therefore, this collective mind should constitute the primary object for historical, moral, and social sciences, including psychology. Thus, the goal of these sciences should be to discover the "laws of the development of the folk spirit" (Klautke, 2013b, p.297).

According to many interpreters of *Volksgeist* studies (Allolio-Näcke, 2014; Diriwächter, 2012; Jahoda, 1992; Kalmar, 1987; Smith, 2005), Lazarus, Steinthal, and their followers struggled to unambiguously define and reconcile two parts of the idea: its ideational component that resides in the minds of members of the community and their behaviors along with its objectified elements that are present in the life-expression of these people, such as books, art forms, law, religion, architecture, and other material and symbolic objects. Therefore, Lazarus and Steinthal wrote about the psychological features of *Volksgeist*, stating that it is "a system [...] of opinions, concepts, understandings, and ideas " that are "embedded" in people's "ever developing activity" (as cited in Kalmar, 1987, p. 676). Consequently, "the group *Geist* in its various manifestations [...] was 'simply the law-governed behavior and development of inner activity'" (p. 675).

On the other hand, Lazarus and Steinthal included the following topics to be studied by *Völkerpsychologie*: "language, mythology, religion, cult, oral literature (*Volksdichtung*), writing, and art forms [...] and customs (*Sitte*), written law, labor, and occupations (*Beschäftigung*), and home and family life as part of 'practical life'" (as cited in Kalmar, 1987, p. 674). [3] Thus, the collective mentality was also conceptualized as having externalized/objective elements, but their demarcation from the behavioral and mental ones was not clearly identified.

Ultimately, Jahoda (1992) summarized the dual nature of *Volksgeist* the following way:

> The *Volksgeist*, or 'objective spirit', exists in two modes: one is intrapsychic and consists of thoughts, sentiments and dispositions; the other represents its material embodiment in books, works of art, monuments, industrial products, means of transport and exchange, weapons of war, and toys. [...] Thus the *Volksgeist* is part of the individual — not, of course, as an organism, but as a historical being living in society; moreover, the *Volksgeist*, being all-pervasive, also surrounds the individual in material or organizational form. (p. 148)

Following such an understanding, most commentators agree that *Volksgeist* is a precursor to the notion of *Kultur* and, later, of the modern idea of *culture* in its formative (shaping mentalities of people) and regulative (regulating the mental and behavioral activities of people) functions.

Lazarus and Steinthal did not directly address how and through

---

③　See on elements of *Volksgeist* also Jahoda (1992, pp. 149–150).

what medium the two parts of *Volksgeist* constitute each other. In turn, Wundt (1916), who also believed that the object of *Völkerpsychologie* is *Volksgeist*, connected the collective mind to "those mental products which are created by a community of human life and are, therefore, inexplicable in terms merely of individual consciousness, since they presuppose the reciprocal action of many" (p. 3). Thus, the collective mind is created through the interactions among the *Volk*, or members of the cultural community. Moreover, these communal mental products are irreducible to the individual mentalities of these people; they are supra-individual and broader and larger than the individual minds. The same idea of the systemic, interactionist, and dialogical nature of *Volksgeist* was expressed by Lazarus and Steinthal. They considered *Volksgeist* not as the substance with a particular content, but as an activity (*Thätigkeit*) (Kalmar, 1987, p. 681). These ideas have important implications for understanding the ontology of *Volksgeist*. It is rooted in never-ending everyday activities and interactions of members of communities, and it exists as long as these *Volk* members perform their actions under the guidance of their collective mind.

Volksgeist has several functions. First, its existence promotes the unity and harmony of collective functioning (Jahoda, 1992, p. 148). Second, as Kalmar (1987) noted, "each individual Geist is largely determined by the group Geist to which it belongs" (p. 679). Thus, the socialization of a person into the collective mentality of the community shapes his or her mind, self, cognition, and other mental faculties. German thinkers emphasized the trans-individual character of collective mentality, and continuously highlighted the two-way connections of the collective mind with individual minds. Common features of individual minds are externalized in the collective/ objective mind, which supplies individual minds with order and meanings. Ultimately, the collective/objective mind has both communal and mental components. This mind is maintained through everyday interactions; it has a history, and transmits this history into the present life of the community. The collective/objective mind works as a repository of knowledge and skills accumulated by the communities' older generations that can be used by younger members as the source of wisdom and inspiration; it is also the source of children's socialization and mental development. The concept of the collective/ objective mind has important methodological implications. To understand "life-expressions" of people, human science researchers must examine the collective mentality within which these expressions take place.

They must know the context and history of the regulative devices that manage these expressions. Hence, researchers need to turn their attention to the collective/objective mind.

The French Tradition

In France, social sciences have also had unique trajectories of development (Heilbron, 2004). Many French scholars worked on understanding the nature of the social and cultural phenomena and their relationships to people's mentalities and behaviors. In 1756, François-Marie Arouet Voltaire (1694 – 1778) invented the term *l'esprit des nations* (the spirit of nations), and used it to explore the history of different civilizations and to conduct their cultural comparisons (Voltaire, 1759). The 19th-century French human and social sciences scholars were aware of German conceptual innovations in the domains of culture, sociology, social philosophy, and corresponding disciplines. Many of them followed the developments of *Volksgeist* and *Völkerpsychologie* and implemented them in France (Klautke, 2013a). Klautke states that the French "founding father" of modern sociology, Émile Durkheim (1858 – 1917), was well informed about these German conceptual advances. From 1885 to 1886, he had a one-year internship in Germany and wrote several reports and reviews of Wundt's works. Ultimately, Durkheim borrowed and translated "what Wundt had called the 'folk soul', often misunderstood as a 'metaphysical' definition of national character,' [and] presented [it] as 'collective representations'" (Klautke, 2013a, p.313).

Durkheim: Social Facts and Collective Representation. Durkheim aimed to establish the science of sociology as an empirical discipline, to articulate the object and units of its inquiry, to differentiate it from other social disciplines, predominantly psychology, and formulate its methodology. Two concepts form the core of Durkheim's theoretical thinking on these issues: *social facts* and *collective representations*. The social fabric of societies is made up of social facts. A social fact "consists of ways of acting, thinking, and feeling external to the individual, and endowed with a power of coercion by reason of which they control him" (Durkheim, 1895/ 1938, p.3). Social facts not only make up the social reality and the object of sociology, but they also regulate people's actions by controlling them. But it remained unclear in Durkheim's theorizing how these facts can control people's behavior. Therefore, Durkheim turned to a psychological concept of *representation*. In 1898, he wrote the article where he coined the term *représentations collectives* or collective representations, ④ and separated it from the concept of individual representations. Collective representations incorporate the factors and mechanisms through which communities exercise their control over people's actions, experiences and cognitions. Durkheim (1924/1974) presented the idea of collective representations in the following way:

> Society has for its substratum the mass of associated individuals. The system which they form by uniting together, and which varies according to their geographical disposition and the nature and number of their channels of communication, is the base from which social life is raised. [...] The representations which form the network of social life arise from the relations between the individuals thus combined. [...] There is nothing surprising in the fact that collective representations, produced by the action and reaction between individual minds that form the society, do not derive directly from the latter and consequently surpass them. (pp. 24 – 25)

Several points in this quote require attention, to examine the idea of the communal regulation of people's behaviors. First, as Durkheim highlighted, a community of associated individuals constitutes the basis of society. Associated members of a community create collective representations through their interactions. Subsequently, these collective mental products override the individual mentalities of the participating individuals. As a sociologist who wanted to differentiate sociology from psychology, in the notion of collective representations Durkheim saw the essence of the social fabric of communities and the object of sociological research that allows researchers to avoid reducing "social" to "mental" or "psychological."

　　Durkheim (1895/1938) eloquently discussed that peoples' actions are regulated through collective representations. People's

---

④ Modern sociologists define *collective representations* as "the ideas, beliefs, and values elaborated by a collectivity and that are not reducible to individual constituents. [...] Collective representations help to order and make sense of the world. [...] [They] inhibit and stimulate social actions. Their force [...] comes from them being within all of us and yet external to the individual" (Scott & Marshall, 2009).

execution of duties and the control of their actions are managed by laws and customs (collective representations) that exist externally to individuals. However, this regulation has a dual nature. Collective representations "are not sociological phenomena in the strict sense of the word. They belong to two realms at once; one could call them sociopsychological. They interest the sociologist without constituting an immediate subject matter of sociology" (pp. 8-9). Thus, collective representations are social and belong to the communal realm, but they are also "sociopsychological" and belong to the psychological realms of individuals.

Durkheim highlighted that collective representations are generated by the actions of and interactions among "individual minds that form the society." Therefore, individual minds are constituents of the collective mind, but the latter "surpasses" them and is larger than a simple aggregate of individual mentalities. In turn, collective representations penetrate individuals' minds and form their mental variants according to societal prescriptions. Durkheim emphasized this dialectic by indicating that "while society transcends us it is immanent in us and we feel it as such. While it surpasses us it is within us, since it can only exist by and through us" (1924/1974, p. 54). In this quotation, Durkheim articulated the fundamental tension between individual and collective representations that exist in their mutual co-constitution.

According to Durkheim, the symbiosis of collective and corresponding individual representations executes several functions:

— Society is interested in order, structure, and uniformity in actions and thoughts across all its members; in turn, collective representations bring cohesion and coherence to the social lives of the members of the community.

— Society is interested in keeping this uniformity intact; therefore, its important function is to regulate people's behaviors. Durkheim discussed that peoples' actions are controlled through collective representations. People's execution of duties and the regulation of their actions are controlled by the laws and customs (collective representations) that exist externally to them. This regulation is executed not only by the direct enforcement of "right and approved" actions, but mostly by generating "collective sentiments" that represent "the voice of the collective." In Durkheim's opinion, because of collective representations, "collective sentiments" have a tone quite different from that of purely individual sentiments. Therefore, the messages of these internalized societal "voices" become imperative for people to execute (Durkheim, 1924/1974, p. 58).

— Elsewhere, Durkheim (1924/1974) called collective representations a "storehouse of intellectual and moral riches" (p. 54). Therefore, collective representations are also a repository of communal knowledge, skills, and technologies that allow new members of the community to learn them and use them for their needs.

— Collective representations form social facts that constitute the social reality where people live. Social reality exists because of people's involvement with it through their thoughts about it and through their actions and interactions aimed at it. This reality exists relatively independently of each member of the group, and it is objectively real for them. It is also real because of its controlling and coercive power, as discussed above.

Moscovici: Social Representations. Serge Moscovici (1925–2014) continued the Durkheimian line of conceptual thinking regarding the societal regulations of people's mentalities and behaviors. As a social psychologist, he was more interested than Durkheim in reconnecting *social* and *mental* without reducing the former to the latter and vice versa. Moscovici is considered to be the founder of a new school of social psychology, the discipline that is built around the concept of *social representations* (Farr, 1998). In 1961, Moscovici published his study focused on the construction of the meaning of psychoanalysis in different segments of French society during the 1950s (Moscovici, 1961/2008). In this study, he coined the concept of *les représentations sociales,* or social representations, that various social groups develop regarding particular social objects (scientific theories, technology, political figures, etc.). Social groups develop social representations to "anchor" (Moscovici's term) these social objects into their existing worldviews (Moscovici discovered that Catholics have different social representations of psychoanalysis compared to Marxists) and to provide tools for communicating about and behaving toward these objects. Moscovici (1973) defined social representations as a

> system of values, ideas and practices with a twofold function; first, to establish an order which will enable individuals to orient themselves in their material and social world and to master it; and secondly to enable communication to take place among the members of a community by providing them with a code for social exchange and a code for naming and classifying unambiguously the

various aspects of their world and their individual and group history.
(p. xiii)

Also, a "social representation" is understood as "the collective elaboration 'of a social object by the community for the purpose of behaving and communicating'" (Moscovici, 1963, p. 251, in Wagner et al., 1999, p. 96). Thus, social representations are a mechanism of societal regulation of individuals' actions.

Moscovici (2001) continuously stressed the dual nature of social representations as having both social and mental elements. Social representations are social because they are "impersonal," in the "sense of belonging to everyone," and because "they are the representation of others, belonging to other people or to another group." Nevertheless, social representations are personal representations because people feel affectively that they belong to their egos (p. 153). In other words, people internalize these representations and experience them as part of their identities. Consequently, Moscovici connected social and mental through social representations, and established their inseparable unity.

According to Moscovici (2001), social representations execute the following functions:

— Social representations constitute or construct social reality. "That is to say that shared representations, their language, penetrate so profoundly into all the interstices of what we call reality that we can say that they *constitute* it" (p. 154).

— Social representations "*conventionalize* the objects, persons, and events we encounter" (p. 22). They categorize objects, giving them definite forms; they model them into particular types that are shared and understood in a similar manner among group members. As a result, social representations create "an 'environment' in relation to the individual or the group" (p. 36). Thus, these representations categorize and typify the social world to make it usable for people.

— Social representations *bring order* to the constructed reality, thus creating existential security for people by making them perceive the world as orderly, stable, and predictable.

— Social representations *prescribe* to people how they should think about and act regarding these constructed objects. "Representations are *prescriptive*, that is they impose themselves upon us with an irresistible force. This force is a combination of a structure which is present before we have even begun to think, and of a tradition which decrees *what* we should think" (p. 22). "Groups create representations so as to filter information derived from the environment and thus control individual behavior. They function, therefore, as a kind of manipulation of thought and of the structure of reality [...]" (p. 37).

— Social representations structure people's *understanding* of their worlds because they have a center of core beliefs around which arrangements of more peripheral beliefs, ideas, and representations are formed. In social representations, "we have an 'encyclopedia' of [...] ideas, metaphors and images which are connected one to another according to the necessity of the kernels, the *core beliefs* [...] stored separately in our collective memory and around which these networks form" (p. 153).

— Social representations penetrate the minds of people and shape their mentalities. "Whilst these representations, which are shared by many, enter into and influence the mind of each, they are not thought by them; rather, to be more precise, they are re-thought, re-cited and re-presented" (p. 23).

— Social representations supply members of a group with "a code for social exchange" (Moscovici, 1973, p. xiii), thus enabling communication among them.

According to Moscovici, the goal of social psychology is to study these social representations in their social and mental components.

Bourdieu: Structure, Habitus, and Practice. To analyze Bourdieu's understanding of the sociocultural regulation of human actions, I need to combine the first three categories suggested for this analysis into one group because my initial categorization fundamentally contradicts the primary theoretical goal of Bourdieu's work, which is to bridge the gap between *objectivism* and *subjectivism* in social theory (Bourdieu, 1977; Bourdieu & Wacquant, 1992; Brubaker, 1985; King, 2000; Postone, LiPuma, & Calboun, 1993). *Objectivism*, which is represented primarily by structuralism and Marxism, considers that social life and human actions are regulated by forces and powers that function independently of the conscious will of agents. This regulation primarily happens through material and economic conditions, social structures and institutions. In turn, *subjectivism*, which is represented by Sartre's existentialism, social phenomenology, and ethnomethodology, emphasizes that social life and the actions of agents are controlled by individuals' desires, beliefs, and judgements that give individuals relative freedom to choose their own life and destiny. According to Bourdieu, such a dichotomization of social regulation does not reflect the reality of social life and, therefore, it cannot serve as the basis for understanding and explaining it. Objectivism discounts human subjectivity as a constituent of social reality; whereas subjectivism overlooks the material and social formation of agents' conceptions, representations, and values, and their inevitable constraints by external conditions and structures (Bourdieu, 1977; Brubaker, 1985, p.750).

Bourdieu proposed that social researchers should consider these objective and subjective constitutive poles of social reality in their dialectical unity, the point at which they continuously co-construct each other. Thus, he does not focus much on what is "out there" in social regulation, but on how what is "out there" is related to what is "in here" — the cognitive and other mental structures within the person's mind and body that consequently guide the individual's perceptions, cognitions, and actions. In turn, he focuses on how these actions and practices reproduce the very conditions that develop agents' subjectivities. Using his own terminology, Bourdieu (1977) focused on *structures*, *habitus*, and *practices*. Social structures are the products of the collective history of a society and include its objective structures, such as language and economy. They also include *social fields* — "the multidimensional space of positions and the position taking of agents" (Postone et al., 1993, p.5) — and objectified *cultural capital*, such as art artifacts, technology, and tools, among other externalized cultural goods. These structures cannot work without individuals who possess the corresponding *habitus*, the mental and embodied generative mechanism that recognizes and interprets those structures and conditions and which produces the corresponding practices. According to Bourdieu, social life and its control are "intrinsically double" (Brubaker, 1985, p. 750). This means that material conditions affect people's behavior only through the mediation by habitus that generates the practices that reproduce those social and material conditions and the structures that engender the habitus.

Therefore, the objective structures of the environment, where people live and function, the ways of their lives, and the means of production define the social structures, conditions, and institutions that produce the habitus that is internalized by individuals. Subsequently, habitus is sensitive and responsive to the conditions that have generated it. When a person gets into certain conditions while pursuing his or her interests, and the corresponding habitus is activated, it generates *practices* that aim at achieving the individual's goals. Properly executed, these practices not only achieve the person's goals, but they also unintentionally reproduce the very conditions that engendered the habitus and, therefore, made these practices happen. Thus, social structure, habitus, and practices are involved in the continuous cycles of production and reproduction of these three elements, and through these cycles, they create the social reality where people live.

The central element of Bourdieu's mechanisms of sociocultural regulation is *habitus*. Habitus refers to the mental dispositions (the "cognitive and motivating structures": Bourdieu, 1977, p. 76) that are determined by the social structures and conditions where people live and that mediate, both mentally and behaviorally, the interactions of these people with the world. Habitus encompasses "categories of perception and appreciation" (Bourdieu & Wacquant, 1992, p. 136) and "schemes of production and interpretation" (Bourdieu, 1977, p. 80). These categories and schemes are responsible for creating the primary functions of habitus: habitus structures people's perception, categorizes their cognition, and works as an interpretative lens that enables members of a community to make sense of the world, other people, and themselves. Habitus also generates actions and practices that connect these interpretations to the existing situation and its conditions, and it secures the person's ability to achieve his or her goals.

Habitus is inculcated by teachers and trainers and then appropriated by the individual. It becomes internalized as a "durable and transposable disposition" (Bourdieu, 1990, p. 52) and a construal of the self. When the child is born in his or her sociocultural community/society, he or she must be socialized and enculturated to become a full-fledged member of this community. In doing this, "the whole group intervenes [...] with a whole universe of ritual practices and also of discourses, sayings, proverbs, all structures in concordance with the principles of corresponding habitus" (Bourdieu, 1977, p. 167). This means that members of the community who possess habitus externalize them during interactions with children, and thus transmit their dispositions to them. Therefore, learning and internalizing the externalized habitus of others become the primary mechanisms of children's socialization.

Bourdieu continuously emphasized that habitus is the product of the history of the community. Because of this, members of the community, the bearers of this habitus, are historical figures that represent the past projected into the present. History produces habitus that generates practices that develop history for future generations. Therefore, habitus carries itself into the future and continues those structures that generated this habitus in the past: "Habitus is embodied history, internalized as a second nature" (Bourdieu, 1990, p. 56).

The system of habitus that is learned and accumulated by the individual throughout his or her life constitutes his or her *embedded cultural capital*. The higher this capital, the more aspects of the world, including various objectified cultural forms (literature, art, philosophy etc.), can be noticed, attended to, understood, and appreciated.

Habitus generates *practical knowledge* of how to act in a particular situation in a way that ensures that this action does not interrupt the existing social order and that produces outcomes desired by the individual. This knowledge is automatic and taken-for-granted. It gives a person a "feel for the game" (Bourdieu, 1990, p. 66) that allows him or her to experience social competence and a sense of reality, without being fully conscious of the determinants of such feelings.

Related to the concept of the sense of the game are the notions of *doxa*⑤ (Bourdieu, 1977) and *doxic experience* (Bourdieu & Eagleton, 1992). According to Bourdieu's understanding, doxa and doxic experience are synonyms that denote a fit between social structures, situations, and the corresponding fields in which an agent finds him- or herself, and the person's habitus or mental structures, which classify and interpret his or her encountered structures and situations. He clarifies that "when there is a quasi-perfect correspondence between the objective order and the subjective principles of organization (as in ancient societies) the natural and social world appears as self-evident. This experience we shall call doxa" (1977, p. 164). For example, when experiencing a conflict with a sales clerk in one's own community, a customer has a doxic experience, knowing what is appropriate to say or do. When traveling abroad, this knowledge is lacking, and the same situation is experienced far differently without any hints of doxa. A doxic

---

⑤ *Doxa* (Greek) means common belief or popular opinion. This term is at the root of terms such as *orthodoxy* (adherence to an accepted, believed to be correct, doctrine or creed, especially in religion) and *heterodoxy* (adherence to beliefs that contradict the accepted orthodoxy).

experience generates "the sense of reality" and "the sense of limits" of what is doable and sayable in particular situations.

Through developing doxa, a person experiences the social world as self-evident and as a valid and unquestionable reality. A doxic experience makes the ontology of the social reality taken-for-granted, obvious, and undeniable. Moreover, such an experience substantiates the existing social order and makes it the order of natural necessity. This means that one knows what the right order to do something is and how it should be done. Using Giddens's terminology, in the ordered world the person experiences *ontological security* (Giddens, 1991) when what is "out there" is the same as what is "in here." At this point, there is no dissonance between them.

The doxic experience is important to maintain the perception of the stability of social reality. Because of this, society is interested in preserving doxa by various means, including discourses (political, ideological, medical, economic, etc.), propaganda, and different ideologies: "The self-evidence of the world is reproduced by the instituted discourses about the world in which the whole group's adherence to that self-evidence is affirmed" (Bourdieu, 1977, p. 177).

This triad of *structure*, *habitus*, and *practice* constitutes the system where these elements continuously interact with each other while co-constructing and reproducing each other and the whole system. This system executes several functions. First, it constructs social reality in its material, structural, and symbolic forms. Second, it takes unsocialized children and develops members of society who are capable of not only freely and successfully functioning in it, but also of reproducing its structures, institutions, and conditions; thus, ultimately, these newly socialized beings continuously maintain the existence of this local sociality and these people's social world. Third, this system ensures that individuals are successful in achieving their goals and satisfying their needs within the existing social order. Ultimately, it regulates the individual and collective activities of the members of the community, and out of these people it makes a coherent and functional society.

Anglo-American Contributions

John Locke and John Stuart Mill are considered the forefathers of the sociocultural movement in English-speaking countries. John Locke (1632–1704) announced the idea of the cultural determinism of human cognition, ways of behavior, and habits of the heart. Speaking to a person born in a different country, he noticed that "the exercise of [mental and behavioral] faculties was bounded within the Ways, Modes, and Notions of his own Country, and never directed to any other, or farther Enquiries [...]" (*An Essay Concerning Human Understanding*, as cited in Jahoda, 1992, p. 18). In turn, John Stuart Mill (1806–1873) was concerned with establishing moral sciences, including psychology. He proposed the discipline of *ethology,* which is based on observing the everyday habits and behaviors of people to understand how their characters are formed. He also concluded that people's characters are strongly determined by national and cultural influences and argued that they need to be accounted for by researchers (Cahan & White, 1992; Jahoda, 1989).

Subsequently, these themes were picked up in the United States of America. I will briefly review the contribution of William Sumner; I will provide an extensive analysis of the contribution of Alfred Schutz, and will conclude this section by examining the works of American cognitive anthropologists Roy D'Andrade and his colleagues and Brad Shore.

In his book *Folkways* (1906/1959), American sociologist William Graham Sumner (1840–1910) provided a conceptualization of what we now label the sociocultural regulation of people's behavior. He introduced the terms *mores*[6] and the *folkways of the in-groups.* According to Sumner, mores produce the societal force that regulates people's actions by producing "habit in the individual and custom in the group" (p. 3). They are developed and function unconsciously, like animal instincts, and regulate every aspect of people's everyday lives. Their purpose is to satisfy people's needs and interests; notably, they do this in ways that community members consider moral and right. Mores are true, and they include not only permissions but also restrictions and taboos; children learn mores at early ages "by traditions, imitation and authority" (p. 3). Sumner explored their nature and made several insightful comments about their systemic nature that is constructed out of individual minds: "It

---

[6] *Mores* are the essential or characteristic customs and conventions of a community (Soanes & Stevenson, 2008). Synonyms: customs, conventions, way of life, traditions, practices, habits.

appears as if there was a 'mind' in the crowd which was different from the minds of the individuals which compose it"; in turn, "it seems as if the crowd had a mystical power in it greater than the sum of the powers of its members" (p. 19). Thus, through Sumner, the insightful ideas of the mind of the crowd and its influence on individual minds were announced in the American social sciences.

Alfred Schutz (1899 – 1959), an Austrian-American phenomenological sociologist, set his scientific goal to investigate the phenomenology of the life-worlds of people and the construction of social reality through people's everyday lives. Part of his inquiry was related to examining the psychosociocultural regulation of people's actions. Inspired by Sumner's concepts of *mores* and *folkways*, Schutz (1944) introduced the term the *cultural pattern of the group life* and proceeded to use this term synonymously with *folkways of the in-group* (Schutz, 1964).

Schutz defined these folkways of the in-group as "socially accepted as the good ways and the right ways for coming to terms with things and fellow-men" (1964, p. 230). Schutz considered these folkways to be "the social heritage" (later, "the stock of knowledge") of the community that is delivered to children who are born into the community by the processes of enculturation and socialization, and to strangers who want to be accepted by the group by the process of acculturation. According to Schutz, these folkways designate "the structure and significance of the elements" of the social world of the community, and they also provide "the scheme of interpretation prevailing in and accepted by in-groups without question" (p. 231). These folkways are taken for granted by members of a group as they are the natural and habitual ways to deal with things. For these folkways to be taken for granted means that members of a group perceive their social world as solid and unchangeable. As such, it will continue to be the same until something dramatic happens (for example, colonization, occupation, or deportation).

The cultural pattern categorizes typical problems of group life (for example, separating men's and women's duties in the home and community, worshiping the divine, keeping one's honor spotless, and many others), and provides solutions to these problems for typical group members. In this case, this pattern works as *the system of typifications*. According to Schutz, this system also typifies and categorizes human individuals and their course-of-action patterns, their motives and goals, as well as the sociocultural products that originated in their actions (1964, p. 232). When confronting a particular problem or situation, a person has his or her motives and goals to deal with it. For example, when a person wants to marry another person, he or she has particular reasons for this aim; thus, this person has his or her unique perception of a potential partner, his or her family, and other important features. Schutz labeled this selectivity of the attention of individuals as *relevance* (Schutz, 1970b). In addition to individuals' idiosyncratic relevances, the group folkways also serve as the *system of relevances* by prescribing to members of the community what aspects of the environment are important and, to continue the example with marriage decision, what features of potential partners they should attend to. Such a system also sets the goals for peoples' communal strivings, and it designates the values and moral codes that justify these goals. Thus, the system of relevances serves as the *social matrix of attention* (Campo, 2015) and the *social matrix of motivation* (Schutz, 1970b).

Other important elements, and correspondently functions, of the group's folkways are a *scheme of interpretation* and a *scheme of expression*. To function smoothly within his or her given social world, a person must construe the elements of this world, other people, their actions, and general situations in a manner that is similar to the perception of other members of the community. Such smoothness can be achieved only if all members of the community have similar rules to interpret their world. Such uniformity is achieved by providing all of them the same communal schemes of interpretation. People in a community use these schemes "for interpreting the social world" (Schutz, 1970a, p. 81) in a unified fashion. After interpreting a situation or phenomenon in a socially prescribed way, the person may act. However, he or she must act in a way that brings to this person his or her desired outcomes and is simultaneously considered acceptable to in-groups. Such purpose is achieved by applying a *scheme of expression*, which, according to Schutz, is a receipt "for handling things and men in order to obtain the best results in every situation with a minimum effort by avoiding undesirable consequences" (Schutz, 1970a, p.81).

The continued interactions among members of the community maintain the sociocultural world and the forces behind social institutions, regulations, sanctions and other prescriptions.⑦ Thus, the analysis of

---

⑦ "Sociality is constituted by communicative acts in which I turns to the others, apprehending them as persons who turn to him, and both know of this fact" (Schutz, 1970a, p.165).

such interactions constituted an important part of Schutz's thinking and writing (Schutz, 1970a).

To understand Schutz's phenomenological approach to "interactional relationships" (or, in our terminology, "intracultural relations"), it is important to consider the concept of *intersubjectivity*[8]. The source of intersubjectivity lies in the fact that all members of the social group have learned and internalized the same folkways of their in-group life with all the systems and schemes that were discussed above. As such, intersubjective intracultural relations unfold within "a communicative common environment" that is characterized by "mutual understanding and consent" (p. 165) among communicating partners. Schutz labeled relational intersubjectivity together with mutual understanding and consent in relationships as the " *We-relationship*"[9](p. 186), which can be defined as the situation when the person is grasping what is going on in his or her partner's mind, and vice versa (p. 32). How does this relationship happen? An agent starts a communicative action using the scheme of expression aimed at receiving a particular answer or action from his or her partner. The agent expects that the partner will understand the agent's intentions and respond accordingly. Such understanding may happen only if the partner is using the scheme of interpretation that is congruent with the agent's scheme of expression — when there is a *reciprocity of understanding*. This congruency may take place if both individuals possess the same folkways of in-group life and share its composition (systems of typification, relevances, schemes of expression, and understanding). If this is the case, then what is happening on the agent's side is reciprocated on the partner's side. Specifically, in this case, Schutz speaks about the *reciprocity of motives* and *reciprocity of positions*. The agent's goal (his or her motivational purpose) is to elicit in his

---

[8] *Intersubjectivity* is a condition of people's everyday lives when the individual "reasons and acts on the self-understood assumption that these others are basically persons like himself, endowed with consciousness and will, desires and emotions" (Schutz, 1970a, p. 319). It is important to add that in this case, "others" have the same assumptions about our agent, and together they all think, desire, and understand their social world in relatively similar ways and everyone knows that this is the case.

[9] *We-relationship* is "the relationship which ensures when two persons, dealing with one another in a face-to-face situation, consider each other reciprocally in a thou orientation" (Schutz, 1970a, p. 323). *Thou orientation* is an attitude toward a communicative partner in a face-to-face situation when an agent is aware of his or her partner and considers this particular individual and his or her body as the field upon which the symptoms of his inner consciousness are played (Schutz, 1970a, p. 184).

or her partner the desired and expected reaction. By using the scheme of understanding that is reciprocal to the agent's scheme of expression, the partner understands the intention of the agent, and uses this intention as the motive for his or her communicative reaction. Then, it is natural that the situation of reciprocity of positions arises. Such reciprocity lies at the core of We-relationships. If our agent becomes a partner to a person who, in our example, initially was a partner, then the dynamics of the relationship and the mutuality of understanding will happen in the same manner despite the change of positions. The new agent will use the internalized scheme of expressions and develop a goal for this interaction. Subsequently, his or her partner will understand the intention by using a congruent scheme of interpretation, grasp the intent of the agent, and become motivated by it. Therefore, the social interaction that had happened in the first episode is reciprocally duplicated in the second one, which results in a smooth and congruent interactional dynamic.

When two individuals from different groups who do not share the same in-group folkways start communicating, then problems, which are identified in our modern language as "challenges and problems of intercultural relations," emerge. Following Schutz's conceptualization, the essence of these challenges lies in the fact that there will be no communicative common environment, mutuality of understanding and consent, We-relationships based on Thou orientations or, correspondently, reciprocity of motivation and positions. Such relationships could hardly proceed. In turn, if they do proceed, they will not be smooth, productive, or satisfying. Schutz well described this situation in his article "The Stranger: An essay in social psychology" (1944). Elsewhere (Chirkov, 2022), I use this article as the basis for analyzing acculturation and intercultural relations problems.

Overall, Alfred Schutz provided an insightful and conceptually rich framework for analyzing the sociocultural regulation of people's everyday lives. The group possesses and correspondently supplies its members with folkways of the in-group life (also described as the cultural pattern of the group life). Members of the group internalize these and then use them to build their relationships, seamlessly interact in their everyday lives and, through these interactions, maintain the social order and social reality of their everyday worlds. The core of Schutz's analysis is the intersubjectivity, mutuality, and reciprocity of the members' categorization, understanding, actions, motivation, and relational positions. This mutuality is the glue for these people's social reality and the context within which their constitutive relationships unfold.

The Ideas of Cultural Models in American Cognitive and Psychological Anthropology

One of the primary postulates of cognitive anthropologists is that human cognition is only partially derived from the individual's experiences, idiosyncratic contemplations, and thinking. They state that human cognition (and the related linguistic furnishings of people's thoughts) is fundamentally cultural (Bender & Beller, 2011, 2013; D'Andrade, 1989, 1995). [10] One approach to studying the cultural content of cognitive representations is the *cultural models school* (Quinn, 2011). This school has been developed by D'Andrade (1992) and his colleagues (D'Andrade & Strauss, 1992; Holland & Quinn, 1987), along with Shore (Shore, 1996) and other anthropologists (Bennardo & de Munck, 2013). This approach is consistent with the cognitive sociology agenda (Zerubavel, 1997) and the cultural sociology focus (Alexander, 2003). The primary proposition of these approaches is that societies and cultures form and then supply their members with cultural schemes, scripts, or models about the world within which these members live. Through these schemes/models, societies provide their citizens with the necessary knowledge about the world, other people, and themselves — recipes for categorizing and understanding the sociocultural environment and then acting in it.

Roy D'Andrade (1931–2016) and his colleagues have been credited for bringing the term *cultural model* into cognitive anthropology and beyond (D'Andrade, 1995; D'Andrade & Strauss, 1992; Holland & Quinn, 1987). Quinn and Holland (1987) articulated the definition of cultural models that has become the staple of this school of thought, and they also brought this idea

---

[10] The same idea was expressed by Schutz in 1953: "Only a very small part of my knowledge of the world originates within my personal experience. The greater part is socially derived, handed down to me by my friends, my parents, my teachers and the teachers of my teachers. I am not only taught how to define the environment (that is, the typical features of the relative natural aspect of the world prevailing in the in-group as the unquestioned but always questionable sum total of things taken for granted until further notice), but also how typical constructs have to be formed in accordance with the system of relevances accepted from the anonymous unified point of view of the in-group. This includes ways of life, how to come to terms with the environment, efficient recipes for the use of typical means for bringing about typical ends in typical situations" (Schutz, 1953, pp.9–10).

beyond cognitive anthropology:

> Cultural models are presupposed, taken-for-granted models of the world that are widely shared (although not necessarily to the exclusion of other, alternative models) by the members of a society and that play an enormous role in their understanding of that world and their behavior in it. (p.4)

Other terms that have been synonymously used in this area of thought are *folk models* (D'Andrade, 1987), *cultural schema* (Nishida, 1999), and *cultural scripts* (Goddar & Wierzbicka, 2004; Wierzbicka, 1996, 2002).

D'Andrade highlighted the *intersubjective* nature of cultural models, the necessity of *internalizing* them to become the regulators of people's experiences and actions, and, correspondingly, their *implicit nature*. Through the term the intersubjectivity of cultural schema, D'Andrade suggests that these schemas are not simply shared by members of the groups, but that "everybody in the group knows the schema, and everybody knows that everyone else knows the schema, and everybody knows that everyone knows that everyone knows the schema" (1987, p.113). In turn, intersubjectivity together with collective intentionality (D'Andrade, 2006) constitute the social ontology of cultural models, cultural schemas, and social institutions. D'Andrade followed the classical understanding of the nature of internalization as the process of making cultural representations, schemas, and models part of one's individual mental organization. Following his mentor Melford Spiro, he suggested that there are several stages of internalization (D'Andrade, 1995, pp. 227-228). This provides an insightful framework for empirical studies on the cultural regulation of human behavior. When cultural models/schemas are internalized, members of the groups act on them without being fully aware of their content. These models exist implicitly, meaning that members of the group successfully use these models, but they "cannot provide a reasonable description" of them (D'Andrade, 1987, pp.113-114).

A colleague of D'Andrade, Naomi Quinn, together with her research collaborators summarized several methods and techniques for extracting and examining cultural models (Quinn, 2005). This book, together with previous publications (D'Andrade, 1992; Holland & Quinn, 1987), provides researchers with guidelines for research methodology for cultural models.

Brad Shore (1945-present) is an American cognitive and psychological anthropologist who developed his version of the cultural models theory that is similar to that of D'Andrade and his colleagues'; however, it has several distinct features that set it apart from that school of thought (Shore, 1996). The primary proposition of his approach is that "a particularly powerful way of thinking about culture: [is] as an extensive and heterogeneous collection of 'models,' models that exist both as public artifacts 'in the world' and as cognitive constructs 'in the mind' of members of a community" (p.44).

The first, and in my mind the most important distinction from D'Andrade's school is that Shore explicitly differentiated the public aspects of cultural models that are "in the world" from the ones that are "'in the mind' of members of a community" (p. 44). He distinguished *public models* that consist of public artifacts and are observable by outsiders and experienced by insiders from *mental models,* which represent the public models in the minds of the group members. According to Shore, the idea of "culture as a stock of conventional models" (p.44) bridges the understanding between culture as an external and objective phenomenon and culture as a collection of knowledge and mental representations in the minds of in-group individuals. Public models are externalized and instantiated in social institutions and cultural products such as "houses, pottery, tools, paintings, songs, dances, [and] types of clothing" (p. 44), among many others. In addition to such material representations, public models exist in less tangible forms; for example, they include communal patterns of greetings, methods of solving conflicts, settling agreements, as well as particular styles of speech or movements.

In turn, Shore distinguishes between *instituted* and *conventional* models, which are subtypes of public models. He equated instituted models with social institutions[1] (pp. 50 – 52). One may say that instituted models are the synthesis of social structures and stable patterns of human activity that are infused with the corresponding meanings of these structures and the sense of purpose of the patterned actions. Sequentially, conventional models are part of the stock of shared cognitive resources of the person's community (p. 47). To say this differently, conventional models are the shared cognitive/mental

---

[1] *Social institution* is "a complex of positions, roles, norms and values lodged in particular types of social structures and organising relatively stable patterns of human activity with respect to fundamental problems in producing life-sustaining resources, in reproducing individuals, and in sustaining viable societal structures within a given environment" (Turner, 1997, p.6).

aspects of instituted models. They are the communal conventions of perceiving, categorizing, evaluating, and interpreting events or people and the scripts of acting upon these interpretations.

The discussion of conventional models leads to another distinction between *special-purpose models* and *foundational schemas*. Special-purpose conventional models regulate the experiences and behaviors of people in specific domains, such as driving, cooking, intimate relations, and many others. Therefore, these models have domain-specific applications. In turn, foundational schemas arrange the special-purpose models and make higher-order structures, which may ultimately lead to a hierarchical system of models. These schemas unite the special-purpose models based on their common overarching purposes for communal life. Examples of foundational schemas include concepts such as individualism and collectivism. These high-order foundational schemes combine and structure many special-purpose models, such as parenting, education, self-development, personhood, and many others; they initiate their effects around the primary tenets of the foundational schemas. These schemas either emphasize the individual and his or her unique features, interests, and aspirations (as in individualism) or they focus on the well-being of the community, where individuals are considered to serve the collective goals and purposes (as in collectivism). Communities may differ in terms of the number of these schemas they have and the tightness of the special models within the corresponding schemas. As Shore noted, these networks of various level models and schemas have never been examined by anthropologists.

Another important conceptualization concerns mental models. Shore distinguishes *personal mental models* from *conventional mental models*. Each person has his or her unique life history and related personal experiences of various events, environments, and people. These experiences are stored in the minds of people, and they serve as their personal mental models. These models comprise these people's biographies, personal narratives, and schemas for their idiosyncratic interpretation of the world. These models belong only to particular individuals. In addition to these models, every member of cultural communities learns and internalizes the communal conventional models that become their conventional mental models. These are the internalized communal recipes for experiencing the world and acting on it. These models are personalized cognitive resources that have been extracted from the communal stock of knowledge. They are not individuals' creations; rather, they are public pieces of knowledge that are borrowed for individual use. These models constrain individuals' attention, prescribe what should be attended to, categorize events, bring sense to them and, eventually, guide people in their actions. Together, personal and conventional mental models constitute the intrasubjective world of an individual mental life. An important feature of cultural models is that they are implicit, meaning that people are usually not aware of them.

According to Shore's conceptualization, systems of cultural models constitute a crucial mechanism for regulating people's cognition, behaviors, and experiences. To summarize, this mechanism executes several functions. Cultural models are the repository of communal knowledge, skills, practices, and scripts for regulating people's communal and personal lives. This knowledge is stored in externalized and instituted forms, such as libraries, books, museums, works of art, and architecture, and also as social conventions for diverse behaviors including dating, marrying, parenting, teaching, and many other practices. It also exists as the values and moral codes that people live by. Children learn and internalize these models and make them the internalized regulators of their lives, actions, and experiences. These internalized models categorize the world and regulate the attention and cognitions of the individual; they interpret everything that happens around the person; they prescribe what motivation to execute in a situation and what emotion to experience and display in another. Finally, they provide the repertoire of appropriate actions and scripts for their execution. D'Andrade's and especially Shore's ideas about cultural models strongly influenced the content and structure of the Theory of Sociocultural Models.

Similar ideas about cultural models and their functions have been expressed by cultural anthropologist Richard Shweder (1996), linguistic anthropologist David Kronenfeld (2018), and sociolinguist James Gee (1992).

Conclusion

The consilience of the examined perspectives on the sociocultural regulation of people's intracultural relations indicates that systems of such regulation exist: they are the real and powerful forces that determine and guide people's conduct. Although each of the scholars analyzed above used their own terms and had various emphases within these systems, they all expressed nearly the same understanding of the sociocultural regulation and the nature of the sociocultural reality that executes control of people's conduct. The conducted analysis unpacked more than just the mechanisms of regulation. It also tackled the ontology of the social and cultural fabric of the niche where people live.

Starting with inquiries in the 19th century, scholars highlighted the systemic nature of such mechanisms of regulation. This means that the systems of control acquire qualities (emergent properties) that are not reduced to the attributes of these systems' constituents[12](Capra & Luisi, 2014; Mingers, 2014). Systems of sociocultural regulation are trans-situational, trans-individual, and are not reducible to the sum of individuals' mental regulatory structures. The collectively intentional and intersubjective nature of the social regulative systems is their emergent property that evolved out of the continued relationships and interactions of human individuals.

The stock of sociocultural regulatory systems comprises the communal society and culture, and has been labeled by many scholars as *social* or *sociocultural reality*. It is real because it exists independently of the cognition and will of individuals; it exists independently of what these people know about this reality and even whether or not they accept it. Finally, social reality is real because it has a strong causal potential to direct and control people's actions, cognitions, and experiences.

Sociocultural regulatory systems are products of communal history and can be understood in their human-made, anti-reifying nature through conducting a historical analysis. These systems bring the past to the present and, by being maintained in the present, they also determine the future of communities. Therefore, time-based (historical) and space-focused (geographical) analyses of these systems should be used to examine these models. [13]

Unanimously, the reviewed thinkers stated that the sociocultural regulative systems are the repository of the communal language,

---

[12] "Emergent properties are the novel properties [of systems] that arise when a higher level of complexity is reached by putting together components of lower complexity. The properties are novel in the sense that they are not present in the parts: they emerge from the specific relationships and interactions among the parts in the organized ensemble" (Capra & Luisi, 2014, pp. 154–155).

[13] Refer to works of Michel Foucault on the archeology of knowledge (1972) for his approach to the historical analysis of imprisonment (1995), insanity (1973/1995, 2006), and sexuality (1980). He demonstrated the emergence of these social institutions from a historical perspective, and analyzed the powers that shaped their existing forms.

knowledge, habits, technologies, customs, values, moral norms, styles of thinking, appropriate emotions and motivations, styles of communication, and many other communal achievements. Having this heritage at hand eliminates the need for every member to invent his or her way of cooking, parenting, or doing anything else; rather, they borrow such prescriptions from the wisdom of their ancestors and successfully use them. Later, they may improve these instructions; the cumulative nature of culture makes it possible for it to develop and change.

All the reviewed scholars agree that the social mechanisms are uploaded into members' minds and this happens during the socialization and enculturation of children. It is an important function of every cultural community to carefully monitor the process of the transmission of the communal stock of knowledge and the regulative mechanisms to new members. As a result of this enculturation, children's identities are developed, and their sense of self and personhood is built.

Sociocultural regulative systems exist through the continuous flow of people's everyday interactions and relationships. Members of communities co-construct these systems through their everyday lives; in turn, these systems govern the actions and experiences of members. This is the fundamental dialectics of sociocultural reality; it is maintained through people's coordinated actions, which themselves are managed by the realities they are co-creating. The emphasis of this dialectic is Bourdieu's seminal argument against the bipolar thinking in either objectivist or subjectivist terms. Such a constitution of the sociocultural world makes its ontology different from the ontology of the natural world.

Because social regulative systems form and supply content to individual mentalities, recognizing them has important methodological implications. To understand the individual's mind and to inquire into why people do, think, and feel the way they do, researchers must consider the embeddedness of individual minds within their corresponding sociocultural realities. This means that before inquiring into people's behavioral and mental peculiarities, psychologists must consider the *collective mind/collective representations/social representations/ cultural patterns of the group life/cultural models* within which these minds were formed and now function. This focus on the sociocultural environment of people's functioning constitutes the fundamental proposition of the sociocultural movement in psychology (Kirschner & Martin, 2010; Rosa & Valsiner, 2018; Valsiner &

Rosa, 2007).

Almost all the analyzed scholars, to differing extents, acknowledged the existence of mental representations of the external regulatory mechanisms. Bourdieu explicitly articulated the role and importance of *habitus*, understood as mental dispositions of different natures, in making social regulation work. Schutz and Shore also conceptualized the mental component of the social regulation. Specifically, the concepts of personal and conventional mental models (by Shore) and the schemas of interpretation and expression (by Schutz) make the understanding of the sociocultural nature of people's psychological worlds more complete. In turn, other scholars used the same terms to represent both the external/communal as well as the internal/mental components of the regulative mechanisms. For example, the terms *Volksgeist*, *collective representations*, *social representations*, and *cultural models* designate both aspects of the sociocultural regulation. It is essential to distinguish between the communal and mental elements of sociocultural regulation to understand the ontology of the social as well as the processes through which the external elements regulate the actions and experiences of agentic individuals.

The majority of the examined scholars paid special attention to the role sociocultural systems play in ensuring that communication among community members is smooth and comprehensible by all and that it requires little effort for community members to express communicative intentions and comprehend them.

Additional functions that the regulative systems and their mental components execute are:

— categorizing the world, other people and oneself; the regulative systems provide the linguistic furnishing of this categorization and create the cultural glossary of terms relevant to various domains of life (Wierzbicka, 1997);
— establishing the relevance and importance of these categories;
— providing the interpretive lenses that guide the extraction of the communal meaning out of the established categories;
— inserting into people's minds values, moral codes, and ethical principles that should regulate their lives and actions;
— prescribing what feelings people should experience and how they express them when diverse events occur in communal life;
— demanding what goals to set in life and what motives should be cultivated to achieve these goals;
— forming and supplying a repertoire of practices that can be used for achieving one's goals;

— assigning a system of sanctions, including rewards and punishments, to control people's behaviors.

The theoretical propositions, assumptions, and functions extracted from this analysis constitute the framework of the TSCM. This theory serves as an "umbrella" conceptual structure that aims at consolidating the essential features of the analyzed regulative mechanisms. This theory assists social and cultural psychologists, in helping them establish interdisciplinary bridges and find their grounding in the sociocultural realities where people live and function.

It is important to note that articulating and examining various sociocultural systems of behavior regulation constitutes an important area of research in modern psychology. This historical review confirms that this direction of psychological thinking has solid and elaborated roots that should be explored further and incorporated into modern psychologists' conceptual and methodological arsenal.

References

Abi-Hashem, N., & Peterson, C. E. (2013a). Intercultural communication. In K. D. Keith (Ed.), *The encyclopedia of cross-cultural psychology*. Wiley-Blackwell.

Abi-Hashem, N., & Peterson, C. E. (2013b). Intracultural communication. In K. D. Keith (Ed.), *The encyclopedia of cross-cultural psychology*. Wiley-Blackwell.

Alexander, J. C. (2003). *The meaning of social life: A cultural sociology*. Oxford University Press.

Allolio-Näcke, L. (2014). Völkerpsychologie. In T. Teo (Ed.), *Encyclopedia of critical psychology*. Springer.

Bender, A., & Beller, S. (2011). The cultural constitution of cognition: Taking the anthropological perspective. *Frontiers in Psychology, 2*(67). doi:10.3389/fpsyg.2011.00067

Bender, A., & Beller, S. (2013). Cognition is ... fundamentally cultural. *Behavioral Sciences, 3*, 42–54. doi:10.3390/bs3010042

Bennardo, G., & de Munck, V. (2013). *Cultural models: Genesis, methods, and experiences*. Oxford University Press.

Bennett, M. J. (Ed.) (2013). *Basic concepts of intercultural communication: Paradigms, principles, and practices* (2nd ed.). Nicholas Brealey.

Berlin, I. (1976). *Vico and Herder: Two studies in the history of ideas*. Viking Press.

Boldyrev, I. A., & Herrmann-Pillath, C. (2013). Hegel's "Objective Spirit," extended mind, and the institutional nature of economic action. *Mind & Society, 12*, 177–202. doi:10.1007/s11299-012-0111-3

Bourdieu, P. (1977). *Outline of a theory of practice* (R. Nice, Trans.). Cambridge University Press.

Bourdieu, P. (1990). *The logic of practice* (R. Nice, Trans.). Stanford University Press.
Bourdieu, P., & Eagleton., T. (1992). Doxa and common life. *New Left Review*, *199*(1), 111-121.
Bourdieu, P., & Wacquant, L. J. D. (1992). *An invitation to reflexive sociology*. The University of Chicago Press.
Brubaker, R. (1985). Rethinking classical theory: The sociological vision of Pierre Bourdieu. *Theory and Society*, *14*(6), 745-775.
Cahan, E. D., & White, S. H. (1992). Proposals for a second psychology. *American Psychologist*, *47*(2), 224-235.
Campo, E. (2015). Relevance as social matrix of attention in Alfred Schutz. *Societa Mutamento Politica*, *6*(12), 117-148. doi:10.13128/SMP-17852
Capra, F., & Luisi, P. L. (2014). *The systems view of life: A unified vision*. Cambridge University Press.
Chirkov, V. (2020). An introduction to the theory of sociocultural models. *Asian Journal of Social Psychology*, *23*(2), 143-162. doi:10.1111/ajsp.12381
Chirkov, V. (2022). Alfred Schutz's "Stranger," the theory of sociocultural models, and mechanisms of acculturation. *Culture & Psychology*, *29*(1), 116-138. doi:10.1177/1354067X221103991
D'Andrade, R. G. (1987). A folk model of the mind. In D. Holland & N. Quinn (Eds.), *Cultural models in language and thought* (pp. 112-148). Cambridge University Press.
D'Andrade, R. G. (1989). Cultural cognition. In M. I. Posner (Ed.), *Foundations of cognitive science* (pp. 795-830). The MIT Press.
D'Andrade, R. G. (1992). Schemas and motivation. In R. G. D'Andrade & C. Strauss (Eds.), *Human motives and cultural models* (pp. 23-44). Cambridge University Press.
D'Andrade, R. G. (1995). *The development of cognitive anthropology*. Cambridge University Press.
D'Andrade, R. G. (2006). Commentary on Searle's "Social ontology: Some basic principles": Culture and institutions. *Anthropological Theory*, *6*(1), 30-39.
D'Andrade, R. G., & Strauss, C. (Eds.). (1992). *Human motives and cultural models*. Cambridge University Press.
Danziger, K. (1983). Origins and basic principles of Wundt's *Völkerpsychologie*. *British Journal of Social Psychology*, *22*, 303-313.
de Mul, J. (2004). *The tragedy of finitude: Dilthey's hermeneutics of life*. Yale University Press.
Dilthey, W. (1994). The hermeneutics of the human sciences. In K. Mueller-Vollmer (Ed.), *The Hermeneutics reader: Texts of the German tradition from the Enlightment to the present* (pp. 148-164). Continuum.
Diriwächter, R. (2004). Völkerpsychologie: The synthesis that never was. *Culture & Psychology*, *10*(1), 85-109. doi:10.1177/1354067X04040930
Diriwächter, R. (2012). Völkerpsychologie. In J. Valsiner (Ed.), *The Oxford handbook of culture and psychology* (pp. 43-57). Oxford University Press.
Durkheim, É. (1895/1938). *The rules of sociological method*. The Free Press.
Durkheim, É. (1898). Represéntations individuelle et représentations collectives. *Review de Metaphysique et de Morale*, *6*, 273-302.
Durkheim, É. (1924/1974). *Sociology and philosophy*. The Free Press.
Farr, R. M. (1998). From collective to social representations: *Aller et retour*. *Culture & Psychology*, *4*(3), 275-296.

Foucault, M. (1972). *The archaeology of knowledge and the discourse on language*. Pantheon.

Foucault, M. (1973/1995). *Madness and civilization: A history of insanity in the age of reason*. Vintage Books.

Foucault, M. (1980). *The history of sexuality*. Vintage Books.

Foucault, M. (1995). *Discipline and punish: The birth of the prison*. Random House.

Foucault, M. (2006). *History of madness*. Routledge.

Gee, J. P. (1992). *The social mind: Language, ideology, and social practice*. Bergin & Garvey.

Giddens, A. (1991). *Modernity and self-identity: Self and society in the late modern age*. Stanford University Press.

Goddar, C., & Wierzbicka, A. (2004). Cultural scripts: What are they and what are they good for? *Intercultural Pragmatics*, *1-2*, 153–166.

Heilbron, J. (2004). The rise of social science disciplines in France. *Revue européenne des sciences sociales*, *42*(129), 145–157.

Holland, D., & Quinn, N. (Eds.). (1987). *Cultural models in language and thought*. Cambridge University Press.

Jahoda, G. (1989). Cross-cultural comparisons. In M. H. Bornstein (Ed.), *Comparative methods in psychology*. Erlbaum.

Jahoda, G. (1992). *Crossroads between culture and mind: Continuities and change in theories of human nature*. Harvester Wheatsheaf.

Kalmar, I. (1987). The *Völkerpsychologie* of Lazarus and Steinthal and the modern concept of culture. *Journal of the History of Ideas*, *48*(4), 671–690.

King, A. (2000). Thinking with Bourdieu against Bourdieu: A "practical" critique of the Habitus. *Sociological Theory*, *18*(3), 417–433.

Kirschner, S. R., & Martin, J. (Eds.). (2010). *The sociocultural turn in psychology: The contextual emergence of mind and self*. Columbia University Press.

Klautke, E. (2013a). The French reception of *völkerpsychologie* and the origins of the social sciences. *Modern Intellectual History*, *10*(2), 293–316.

Klautke, E. (2013b). *The mind of the nation: Völkerpsychologie in Germany, 1851-1900*. Bergham.

Koepping, K.-P. (1983). *Adolf Bastian and the psychic unity of mankind: The foundations of anthropology in nineteenth century Germany*. University of Queensland Press.

Kronenfeld, D. B. (2018). *Culture as a system: How we know the meaning and significance of what we do and say*. Routledge.

Kulich, S. J., Weng, L., Tong, R., & Dubois, G. (2020). Interdisciplinary history of intercultural communication studies: From roots to research and praxis. In D. Landis & D. P. S. Bhawuk (Eds.), *The Cambridge handbook of intercultural training* (4th ed., pp. 39–59). Cambridge University Press.

Landis, D., & Bhawuk, D. P. S. (Eds.). (2020). *The Cambridge handbook of intercultural training* (4th ed.). Cambridge University Press.

Mingers, J. (2014). *Systems thinking, critical realism and philosophy: A confluence of ideas*. Routledge.

Moscovici, S. (1961/2008). *Psychoanalysis: Its image and its public*. Polity Press.

Moscovici, S. (1973). Foreword. In C. Herzlich (Ed.), *Health and illness: A social psychological analysis* (pp. ix–xiv). Academic Press.

Moscovici, S. (2001). *Social representations: Explorations in social psychology*.

New York University Press.

Nishida, H. (1999). Cultural schema theory. In W. B. Gudykunst (Ed.), *Theorizing about Intercultural Communication* (pp. 401–408). Sage.

Pinkard, T. (2019). Objective spirit: the pulse of self-consciousness. In M. F. Bykova (Ed.), *Hegel's philosophy of spirit: A critical guide* (pp. 147–163). Cambridge University Press.

Postone, M., LiPuma, E., & Calboun, C. (1993). Introduction: Bourdieu and social theory. In C. Calboun, E. LiPuma, & M. Postone (Eds.), *Bourdieu: Critical perspectives*. (pp. 1–13). The University of Chicago Press.

Quinn, N. (Ed.) (2005). *Finding culture in talk: A collection of methods*. Palgrave Macmillan.

Quinn, N. (2011). The history of the cultural models school reconsidered: A paradigm shift in cognitive anthropology. In D. B. Kronenfeld, G. Bennardo, V. de Munck, & M. D. Fischer (Eds.), *A companion to cognitive anthropology* (pp. 30–46). Wiley-Blackwell.

Quinn, N., & Holland, D. (1987). Culture and cognition. In D. Holland & N. Quinn (Eds.), *Cultural models in language and thought* (pp. 3–42). Cambridge University Press.

Rosa, A., & Valsiner, J. (Eds.). (2018). *The Cambridge handbook of sociocultural psychology* (2nd ed.). Cambridge University Press.

Schutz, A. (1944). The stranger: An essay in social psychology. *American Journal of sociology*, *49*(6), 499–507.

Schutz, A. (1953). Common-sense and scientific interpretation of human action. *Philosophy and Phenomenological Research*, *14*(1), 1–38.

Schutz, A. (1964). Equality and the meaning structure of the social world. In A. Schutz & A. Brodersen (Eds.), *Collected papers* (Vol. 2, pp. 226–273). Martinus Nijhoff.

Schutz, A. (1970a). *On phenomenology and social relations: Selected writings*. The University of Chicago Press.

Schutz, A. (1970b). *Reflections on the problem of relevance*. Yale University Press.

Scott, J., & Marshall, G. (2009). *A dictionary of sociology (online version)*. (3rd ed.). Oxford University Press.

Shore, B. (1996). *Culture in mind: Cognition, culture, and the problem of meaning*. Oxford University Press.

Shweder, R. A. (1996). True ethnography: The lore, the law, and the lure. In R. Jessor, A. Colby, & R. Shweder (Eds.), *Ethnography and human development: Context and meaning in social inquiry* (pp. 15–52). The University of Chicago Press.

Smith, W. D. (2005). Volksgeist. In M. C. Horowitz (Ed.), *New dictionary of the history of ideas* (Vol. 6, pp. 2441–2443). Thomson.

Soanes, C., & Stevenson, A. (Eds.). (2008). *Concise Oxford English dictionary* (11th ed.). Oxford University Press.

Sumner, W. G. (1906/1959). *Folkways*. Dover Publications.

Turner, J. (1997). *The institutional order*. Longman.

Valsiner, J., & Rosa, A. (Eds.). (2007). *The Cambridge handbook of sociocultural psychology*. Cambridge University Press.

Voltaire, F.-M. A. (1759). *An essay on universal history, the manners, and spirit of nations: From the reign of Charlemaign to the age of Lewis XIV*.

Wagner, W., Duveen, G., Farr, R., Jovchelovitch, S., Lorenzi-Cioldi, F.,

Marková, I., & Rose, D. (1999). Theory and method of social representations. *Asian Journal of Social Psychology*, *2* (1), 95–125. doi: 10. 1111/1467–839X. 00028

Wierzbicka, A. (1996). Japanese cultural scripts: Cultural psychology and "cultural grammar." *Ethos*, *24* (3), 527–555.

Wierzbicka, A. (1997). *Understanding culture through their key words: English, Russian, Polish, German and Japanese.* Oxford University Press.

Wierzbicka, A. (2002). Russian cultural scripts: The theory of cultural scripts and its applications. *Ethos*, *30* (4), 401–432.

Wilson, E. O. (1999). *Consilience: The unity of knowledge.* Vintage Books.

Wundt, W. (1916). *Elements of folk psychology: Outline of a psychological history of the development of mankind [electronic resource].* Project Gutenberg Literary Archive Foundation.

Zerubavel, E. (1997). *Social mindscapes: An invitation to cognitive sociology.* Harvard University Press.

2A

A Synopsis of the Theory of Sociocultural Models and Its Application to Intercultural Relations Research (Chirkov, 2020, 2022)

Valery CHIRKOV

- To successfully function, every *cultural community* develops a system of regulatory mechanisms to organize the behaviours and experiences of its members. A cultural community is a group of people who identify themselves as being part of this group, care about its well-being, and are committed to ensure that their community operates effectively. These communities may have physical locations and boundaries — for example, villages of ethnically distinct tribes — or these boundaries can be imagined, where members of communities are dispersed across locations but are still connected through common identity and other common features — for example, virtual communities, communities based on sex, age, and other demographics, or communities grounded in physical or mental attributes.
- To make the community sustainable and coherent, its members need to act relatively uniformly and in a coordinated fashion. This uniformity should be the result of their mutual understanding of the goals and means for communal life. Therefore, their behaviours must be identically regulated. These regulatory mechanisms are called *sociocultural models* (SCMs). SCMs are the mostly unspoken, taken-for-granted rules and prescriptions that allow members to interpret various events and aspects of their community and the

scripts for acting based on these interpretations.

- SCMs are hierarchically organized; there are high-order *foundational models* and, subordinate to them, *special-purpose models* (as defined by Shore). This system of interconnected models constitutes a *culture of the community*. The foundational models are the overarching systems of a community's values and worldviews. They unite and provide meaning to the special-purpose models. Communities create special-purpose SCMs for each domain of their lives, including family, parenting, education, health care, governance, communication, and many others. These models are interconnected among themselves and with the foundational models; thus, anyone who wants to learn the culture of a community cannot just learn the isolated models. Researchers must understand their interconnectedness together with the overarching foundational models that unite the specialized models into a coherent system of communal life regulation.
- Special-purpose SCMs have components that make their functioning possible. These include the *categorization* and *verbal furnishing* of the domains that the model regulates: what elements and categories the domain consists of and how to label these elements. In addition, SCMs include systems of *values* and *moral beliefs* that belong to a particular domain (special-purpose models) but may also apply to wider areas of communal life (foundational models). SCMs have a *repertoire of practices* that members are required to perform in that domain together with providing these members with the *motivation* to execute these actions (*schemes of expression*, by Schutz). Central components of any SCM are the *schemes for interpretation* (by Schutz). These schemes allow members of the community to make sense of things and events, other people around them, and themselves and to interpret these items in relatively uniform ways. SCMs provide structure through *controlling tools* and *sanctions* to reward or punish particular practices if people obey or, conversely, violate the prescribed communal order. Through this structure, SCMs supply community members with uniform regulatory mechanisms; in turn, their internalization makes the behaviours and experiences of people similar and coherent.
- SCMs are products of a community's history. They have evolved under the influence of various ecological, economic, political, and social forces. These models bring the past to the present and, after they are internalized by members of the community, they are projected into the future. Tracing the historical background of these models constitutes an important piece of sociocultural work as

it allows researchers to understand the sociocultural world where a particular group of people live.

- SCMs accumulate communal knowledge, skills, and values. They provide typical solutions to typical problems for an average member of a community. By learning and internalizing SCMs, members of the community gain access to this *repository of their community's wisdom* and, in turn, they can use it to resolve various problems in their lives.

- SCMs simultaneously exist in the public communal domain and in the minds of the people of the community. Thus, each model has *public/communal* as well as *internalized/mental aspects*. These two inseparable poles continuously interact and co-produce each other.

- The public aspects of the models are represented in the communal domain in *material forms* (architecture, technologies, tools, furniture, space arrangements), in the forms of *institutionalized models* (formally accepted written documents and instructions that govern the social institutions in the community), and as *conventional models* (shared mental aspects of institutionalized models) (based on Shore). For example, teachers are provided with numerous directives and instructions about teaching; these are institutionalized models because these documents exist in the public domain and they are taken as the formal and accepted ways of conducting the pedagogical activities of educators. On the other hand, the teachers at a school have their collective interpretations of these normative documents and use these shared interpretations to manage their pedagogical activities on site. These shared, often unspoken agreements about teaching are conventional models.

- New members of the community are born into the existing SCMs. The manner in which their parents, relatives, educators, and other community members behave toward these children is driven by these models. These models are communicated to children explicitly, through direct instructions and teaching, and implicitly, through verbal, nonverbal, and subconscious clues. Through enculturation and socialization, children learn and internalize SCMs and become full-fledged members of the community who understand what is going on and how to react to the happenings of diverse situations.

- Internalized SCMs are experienced by community members as *automatic, subconscious,* and *taken-for-granted prescriptions for life*. Members of the community do not think or discuss these taken-for-granted experiences; they live them without putting forth too much reflection: "This is how we do things; this is how we live our lives; this is who we are." These experiences form members' collective identities. The taken-for-grantedness of SCMs presents a serious challenge in researching them.

• SCMs are unevenly distributed among the members of the community. Members from different walks of life may develop their divergent sub-models and selectively learn and internalize them. Children are exposed to the SCMs through the interpretations provided by their family members and other socializing agents. Often, children are intrinsically selective in accepting various models and their parts; as such, they endorse particular elements and reject others. Therefore, upon becoming adult members of a society, people from the same community may differ in terms of the levels to which they endorse the communal SCMs.

• The *internalized aspects of SCMs* constitute an important part of people's mental worlds. In addition to these aspects, people's mentalities have *idiosyncratic components*, which are based on their unique life experiences. Considering the selectivity of people's SCMs internalization and the presence of the idiosyncratic components of their mental worlds, people from the same community may have diverse and distinct mentalities. Therefore, it is important to note that the internalization of SCMs does not make the mentalities of people mirror copies of these models.

• The internalization of SCMs forms a person's *self*; in turn, the self becomes the coordinator of one's SCM-governed and idiosyncratic activities. The human self is socially developed through a person's interactions with others. Through continuously experiencing actions, attitudes, and positions of others toward one's self, a member of the community forms his or her understanding of this self and develops an ability to reflect on it. The developed mature self gives individuals the power to be relatively free from the influence of internalized SCMs.

• When a person's behaviour is governed by a model, he or she unintentionally reproduces it and, thus, maintains this model's existence. When a person gets into a situation governed by a particular model, the corresponding internalized aspects of the model (*habitus*, by Bourdieu) is actualized and a strong congruence between what is "out there" (the public aspect of SCMs) and what is "in here" (the mental aspect of SCMs) is established. As a result of this congruence, the feeling of *doxa* (by Bourdieu) is experienced. This *doxic experience* makes people feel immersed in their world, and to them, this world feels predictable and secure.

Such a world is felt as being ontologically real.

• In doing cultural and sociocultural research in cultural communities, it is important to know SCMs of that community. To understand why people do, feel, and think the way they do, researchers must investigate the content of and relationships among the SCMs that govern these people's activities and experiences. Without understanding these models, scholars cannot fully comprehend the cultures of the communities or the mentalities of the people.

• An important function of SCMs is to regulate people's *intra*cultural relations and communication. Internalizing the same SCMs of communication makes in-group relations predictable and does not require unnecessary explanations and elaborations about what should be done or said or why this is the case. This smoothness is based on the *reciprocity* and *interchangeability of the schemes of interpretation* and *schemes of expression* (by Schutz). On one side of the interaction, there are the schemes of expression and communicative intentions; subsequently, on the other side, there are congruent schemes of interpretation. As the communication proceeds, the partners continuously change their communicative positions. The reciprocity of the schemes allows the flow of community members' communications to occur uninterrupted.

• In contrast, this reciprocity of positions is disrupted when people from different communities try to communicate with one another. Their schemes of expression and interpretation during *inter*cultural relationships are not congruent. Thus, when a person initiates an interaction, his or her partner may interpret his or her actions differently from one's initial communicative intentions. In turn, misunderstanding and confusion may develop.

• The theory of sociocultural models invites intercultural relation researchers to study various SCMs, including specialized models for communication and relationships among people in different situations as well as the models that relate to specific domains of communal life. It calls these researchers to examine the histories of these models and the factors that determine their existing forms. Moreover, this theory enables researchers to investigate how these models work in the everyday lives of people, how they experience these models, and how they use them to solve their problems.

References

Chirkov, V. (2020). An introduction to the theory of sociocultural models. *Asian Journal of Social Psychology*, *23*(2), 143–162. doi:10.1111/ajsp.12381

Chirkov, V. (2020). The sociocultural movement in psychology, the role of theories in sociocultural inquiries, and the theory of sociocultural models. *Asian Journal of Social Psychology*, *23*(2), 119–134. doi:10.1111/ajsp.12409

Chirkov, V. (2022). Alfred Schutz's "Stranger," the theory of sociocultural models, and mechanisms of acculturation. *Culture & Psychology*, *29*(1), 116–138. doi:10.1177/1354067X221103991

3

Whiteness Centered and Unnamed: History of Whiteness Theory in Intercultural Communication Research

Thomas K. NAKAYAMA
Northeastern University
Judith N. MARTIN
Arizona State University

Summary: This chapter responds to recent calls for interrogating the history and development of research and theory in intercultural communication. The rise of the hashtag # CommunicationSoWhite and subsequent publications point to the underlying power of whiteness in the construction of communication itself. In intercultural communication, Kulich et al. (2020) note that the intercultural field(s) is/ are more diverse and nuanced than "we" might think, and acknowledging the ambiguity — who is the "we" in tracing the history of intercultural communication? — they call for further detailed analysis of early documents and lines of publication to clarify the strength and breadth of our field. Thus, we interrogate the absence of whiteness theory/studies in our field, as attention to absences in the development of a field of study can be instructive in clarifying the "we," as well as how intercultural communication was shaped in whose interests and goals.

We begin by exploring the political and social contexts in which the field of intercultural communication was established (the FSI and the influence of E. T. Hall). We demonstrate how these contexts and characteristics of influential interdisciplinary scholars specifically impacted the subsequent research trajectories, including topics, methods, and theory development that ultimately shaped intercultural communication to serve primarily the interests of whiteness in various roles — as foreign service workers, sojourners, business people and more. We discuss the implications of whiteness as an unnamed force in shaping the interests of intercultural communication and what's at stake here. Finally, we conclude with some challenges facing the future of intercultural communication.

Introduction

As others have noted, the history of our field is diverse and complicated, and reflects an over-emphasis on U.S. American and English-speaking histories (Baldwin, 2016; Szkudlarek, 2009; Szkudlarek & Romani, 2017), and is typically told "through Western eyes" or from "ideologically mainstream positions and assumptions" (Gorski, 2008, cited in Kulich et al., 2020; Martin, Nakayama, & Carbaugh, 2012; Piller, 2017). Kulich et al. (2020) attempt to remedy this limitation by providing a comprehensive examination of our *interdisciplinary* history, including some of the "bypassed lines of thinking." Our chapter builds on this attempt by interrogating a set of heretofore unreflected assumptions about the tradition(s) and historical foundations of intercultural communication studies, to present a more realistic understanding of our past to ultimately better address future theoretical and applied challenges.

We start with the question of why intercultural communication theory and research, at its inception in the 1940s in the United States, ignored the role of whites in intercultural interactions or, when included in study, why that role was largely unnamed. It is only in the past few decades that the study of white identity, white practices, and whites' role in interactions has been incorporated into intercultural communication scholarship (See Holling & Moon, 2015; Moon & Holling, 2015; Nakayama & Krizek, 1995). Some of the reasons for the absence are known and well documented. Others, more subtle, have not been discussed in detail. The next section explores the history of the field and the obvious and less obvious reasons for this absence.

Political and Social Contexts in Which the Field of Intercultural Communication Was Established

The "birth" of the field of intercultural communication studies in the 1940s in the United States has been well documented and described. As Wendy Leeds-Hurwitz (1990, 2010) and others (Baldwin, 2016; Frohnmayer, 2017; Rogers & Hart, 2002) have described, the field emerged from the U.S. State Department's Foreign Service Institute training, designed by anthropologist E. T. Hall and other interdisciplinary scholars for largely white U.S. American government workers (Rogers, 1999). Thus, at its inception, the training (and study) focused on "cultural others" in international contexts by mostly U.S. white male scholars. Before turning attention to the specifics of the training, the trainers and trainees, it is worth exploring the global and domestic political and social contexts in which this training was developed and implemented. The contexts reflect the dominant twin attitudes of white supremacy/racism and global engagement in U.S. contexts.

The U.S in the 1940s and the post-WWII era can be characterized by intentional and rampant demonization of and discrimination against Japanese, Japanese-Americans, and other persons of Asian descent. Historian John Dower, in *War without Mercy*, identifies WWII as a "race war," and describes in excruciating detail, as Harry Kitano observes, the extent of anti-Japanese racism (in contrast to attitudes toward Germans) propagandized by the U.S. government in "songs, slogans, propaganda reports, secret documents, Hollywood movies, the mass media and quotes from soldiers, leader and politicians" (Kitano, 1986). Dower documents how a kind of "normalcy" of viewpoints was re-established, and also the destructive real-world impacts of this racism. For example, many U.S. Americans were in favor of dropping even more bombs on the Japanese with a goal of eventually exterminating Japan (Dower, 1986). In addition, the government incarcerated Japanese Americans during the war, but not German Americans, even though there were close ties between Germans and German Americans and Hitler had been a threat for a very long time. The U.S. government also maintained highly restrictive anti-Asian immigration policies and favored European immigration.

White supremacy reigned in the U.S. with anti-black racism and segregation according to the law of the land — prior to voting rights, anti-housing discrimination legislation, and the Brown vs Board of Education ruling. Data recently made public of survey results of 300,000 U.S. American WWII soldiers reveal the rampant and deeply held racist attitudes that counter the squeaky-clean image of "The Greatest Generation" (Ruane, 2021). The results revealed that 75 percent of soldiers from the North and 85 percent of soldiers from the South thought Blacks and Whites should train and serve separately. Some of the harshest language came from white soldiers commenting on the segregated army. One soldier commented:

> White supremacy must be maintained. [...] I'll fight if necessary to prevent racial equality. I'll never salute a negro officer and I'll not take orders from a negroe. I'm sick of the army's method of treating [Black soldiers] as if they were human. Segregation of the races must continue.

Another soldier wrote: "God has placed between us a barrier of color ... We must accept this barrier and live, fight, and play separately" (Ruane, 2021).

This racism specifically extended to the exclusion of African Americans in global politics. Scholars have highlighted the discrepancy between the Cold War foreign policy rhetoric emphasizing freedom, justice, and equality and the reality of racism that "had so long been ingrained in what many referred to as the lily-white Department of State" (Krenn, 1999). According to Ledwidge (2006), while there was an active African American Foreign Affairs Community (AAFAC) attempting to engage with foreign service policies, the U.S. foreign service establishment was not interested in recruiting African-Americans to engage in formulating foreign policy. He points to the absence of blacks in the state department and executive branch:

> irrespective of AAFAC's actions, U.S. racism conditioned the American elite [...] [to] justify the exclusion of blacks from the corridors of power and guaranteed the institutionalization of white hegemony in government generally and in relation to foreign policy. (p.221)

In fact, Ledwidge asserts that the maintenance of white hegemony was part of the western nations' political agenda, e.g., the Versailles Peace Conference participants were almost exclusively white nations, whose actions supported the racialized international status quo:
"European and Euro-American early twentieth century politics

were determined by a complex web of political and economic factors, and the belief in the cultural and racial supremacy of western nations" (Ledwidge, 2006, p. 227).

In addition to the contexts of domestic and international racism, any hint of prewar national isolationism was gone as the U.S. engaged in global leadership (Blower, 2014; Chalberg, 1995; Foertsch, 2008), with a great deal of business and diplomatic efforts engaged in Marshall plans for rebuilding Germany and Japan. Apparently, initial efforts of U.S. personnel in these rebuilding and diplomatic efforts were less than successful (Pusch, 2004), and it was thus in these political/economic social contexts that Congress passed the Foreign Service Act, establishing the Foreign Service Institute (FSI), charged with training businessmen and diplomats to work more effectively overseas. It is useful to know that earlier legislation, the 1924 Rogers Act, merged the State Department and Foreign Service and instituted an exam — one allegedly biased against women and ethnic minorities, helping to maintain the white supremacy of the State Department and Foreign Service. In 1924 then Under Secretary Joseph Grew expressed his general views of women, the examinations, and the Foreign Service:

> In the case of Miss Field who enters [the Foreign Service] subsequent to the passage of the Rogers Act, we shall probably send her first to a consulate where she will have rough and tumble work to perform and see if she can get away with it. If she fails, it will be an indication that no woman is capable of carrying out all the duties of a Foreign Service officer and this would probably make it more difficult for women to pass in the future. (Calkin, 1978, p. 73)

While the 1946 Foreign Service Act included language to "insure that the officers and employees of the Foreign Service are broadly representative of the American people" (Part B Objectives), the Congress that enacted that law had only 11 white women and two black men in a House of 435 members; in the Senate, every one of the 96 members was a white male. And the FSI was similar in upholding the reigning white supremacy norm. A 1936 photographic register of all 701 officers of the U.S. Foreign Service shows 700 white men and one white woman. An occasional racial slur was common, e. g., a 1937 eulogy of the late American minister to Finland included "praise for his 'rich repertory of Southern negro stories', one of which the author gratuitously repeats. In its social attitudes and behavior, the Foreign Service has always been a follower, not a leader" (Kopp, 2019).

It also appears that Congress wasn't bothered that the Foreign Service lacked women or minorities — its concern was "a surfeit of Ivy Leaguers" (Kopp, 2019), and, unfortunately, the description of the State Department as "pale, male and Yale" is as accurate today as it was in the 1950's (Ahmed, 2021; Jakes, 2020; Whittington, 2020). It's still a continuing issue (see Bettinger-Lopez & Turkington, 2020; Whittington, 2020).

Who were the FSI trainers and trainees? As described in the intercultural communication literature, the FSI trainers were an interdisciplinary team of prominent social scientists, including anthropologist E. T. Hall, the noted "father of intercultural communication," and linguist George Trager who, along the way, established a new interdisciplinary field of intercultural communication by applying linguistic concepts and models to nonverbal communication. Like most other government and business leaders, these scholars were all male and white as were the trainees — the diplomats/businesspeople sent abroad to represent the United States. While building positive relationships among diverse people of the United States was a later training focus (Pusch, 2004), the early training was certainly not designed to help African American, Asian American, Native American, or Latinx government workers communicate more effectively in intercultural settings. Further, prior to the passage of the 1946 Act, the (all white male) State Department staff was surveyed as to what was needed in the new FSI — they all stressed the need for language training (Leeds-Hurwitz, 1990). Would this needs assessment outcome have been different if women and ethnic/racial groups had been included in the assessment?

It is clear that this early development of intercultural communication as a theoretical and applied field was in service of elite, white men. The training focused on understanding how the communication patterns of white Americans differed from those of other nationalities, and ways to help these white Americans communicate more effectively in overseas settings. Thus, issues of race and white privilege in particular were ignored or silenced and the absence has had tremendous implications for theory development, research, and pedagogy in intercultural communication.

The Consequences of the Centering of Whiteness

This section describes the consequences of the centering of whiteness in the very establishment of intercultural communication studies in the United States. A close review of literature over the decades reveals the impact of centering on subsequent research trajectories, on topics studied, research methods employed, and theory development. Much has been written describing how the "standpoint" (the cultural and research background/beliefs) of scholars, and of people in power, comprehensively influences their work, and often says more about them than about their subject matter or their "subjects" (Rosaldo, 1989). This connection is easy to see historically; Gould (1993) describes the 19th-century scholarly research when leaders and intellectuals "did not doubt the propriety of racial thinking, with Indians below whites, and blacks below everyone else" (p. 85), e. g., European scholars' racist characterizations of African cultures (Brantlinger, 1986). But that is also true in the 20th and 21st centuries: e. g., intercultural scholars note the racist consequences of white, elite western researchers' misunderstanding or inaccurately describing the cultural and communication patterns of "others" (Kim, 2012; Lu & Gatua, 2014), e. g., Tuhiwai Smith's (1999) critique of white scholars' racist characterizations of Maori people. Thus, we must acknowledge that all academic knowledge is "historically contingent and a contextual production" (Mendoza & Kinefuchi, 2016, p. 275).

The academic knowledge generated as the ICC field developed was no exception, also "historically contingent and contextual." Leeds-Hurwitz (1987, 1990) describes the training at the FSI as a marriage between Anthropology and Linguistics — anthropology was known as the study of culture, and linguistics necessary for the important language training curriculum. In addition, Linguistics was viewed as the most scientific of the "soft" sciences. E. T. Hall and his Linguistics colleagues, Birdwhistell and Trager, designed and implemented the training — applying Linguistics models to the stuff of culture. Examining the then current research practices in these two disciplines in conjunction with the centering of whiteness helps us better understand the nature and the limitations of the FSI training. Anthropological methods were focused on studying "culture at a distance" (Benedict, 1934; Mead & Metraux, 1953), sometimes described as "the veranda approach" (Eckl, 2008; Eramian, 2018), and Linguistics focused on the micro analysis of language, linguistic elements and language teaching. Scholars in both disciplines ignored issues of power, colonialism, and larger social and political contexts.

FSI trainees complained that the anthropological concepts were too abstract, and Hall noted that the linguists were more successful in teaching the trainees language than the anthropologists were at teaching "culture" (Leeds-Hurwitz, 1987). Hall saw the problem as stemming from the "out of consciousness" nature of culture — the nonverbal "microculture" patterns. So trainers developed a systematic study of cultural nonverbal patterns — applying linguistic models/ terms to nonverbal communication (chronemics, kinemics, etc.). What might have been included in the training had there been ethnic, racial, and gender diversity of trainees and trainers? For instance, perhaps a discussion of the "unconscious" elements of cultural communication might have included discussions of stereotypes, prejudice, implicit bias etc., and discussion of postcolonial intercultural communication.

By considering the role of whiteness in intercultural communication, we can highlight some of the ways that whiteness, as a hidden assumption, can productively help us move forward in enriching our understanding of intercultural interaction. Here we turn to three examples: cultural communication patterns, sojourning, and questions of method.

Cultural Communication Patterns: Kulich et al. (2020) point out that E. T. Hall consistently viewed culture as based on smaller cultural (racial/ethnic) units, demonstrated in his studies of Navajo/ Pueblo/ Anglo relations in the 1930s, Black/White racial issues in Denver in the 1940s, or military relations on the island of Truk, as far as the 1960's and 70's. While some scholars continued researching/theorizing interethnic and interracial communication within U.S. domestic contexts (see Daniel, 1970; Daniel & Smitherman, 1976; Smith, 1973 [aka Molefi Asante]), a larger movement away from this way of thinking about "cultures" developed (Moon, 1996). So, in Hall's later and other colleagues' work contrasting communication patterns of international cultural groups, these distinctions and the heterogeneity of U.S. Americans were ignored, wiped out. There were dozens of studies contrasting "American" communication patterns with those of other countries, e. g., Japan. In these studies, culture was conflated with and assumed to be determined by nationality. Each nation reflected a particular culture, so that Germany and German culture were unitary, just like France and French culture, Russia and Russian culture, and so forth. This approach has been critiqued from a number of angles (e.g., Ono, 2010), but our interest here is how whiteness is inadvertently centered but unnamed.

This framework erases cultural differences within nations that can be more or less significant depending on the nation. For example, Belgium, Canada, and South Africa are easily recognizable as multicultural nations. However, much intercultural communication research has erased the multicultural character of many nations in its studies. For the United States, in particular, this has meant that "American" culture has been conflated with white American culture. White American cultural patterns become representative of all of American culture, without explicitly saying so. The relationship between nation-states and culture is analyzed in a wider context by Rongtian Tong in the present volume.

Sojourning: While the concept of the sojourner is defined as short-term, voluntary movement between cultures, most of the studies in this area have focused on white American students on study-abroad programs or other similar programs. There have been some studies of international students in the United States, but it is conceptualized as a largely white-centered activity in the U.S.

Studies on international students in the U.S. have most often taken the nation-culture approach. This has resulted in the sojourner experience being largely understood through the lens of the white American university students, without explicit acknowledgement. This has meant that the frameworks that have emerged from the experiences of white Americans have been universalized to make claims about the sojourner experience.

This approach has created blind spots in the sojourner literature. It assumes, for example, that the experiences of a white American in another country are generalized, and it doesn't capture the potentially differential experiences of non-white students in that same country. Do African American students, for example, have other experiences — related to racism, exoticism, stereotypes, racial aggression, racial fetishization — that are not experienced by white Americans in their acculturation? Do the experiences of white Americans capture the complexities of many others as sojourners? These are important questions that are overlooked in assuming that the experiences of white Americans are universal.

<u>Methods of Study</u>: Quantitative social science methods influenced by social psychology became the dominant approaches used to study intercultural communication. While E. T. Hall and others at the Foreign Service Institute came from Anthropology and Linguistics, among other fields, the development of intercultural communication shifted from its multidisciplinary roots to finding a home in the communication field (Leeds-Hurwitz, 1987, 1990, 2010). Part of the reason for this move was a desire to find academic respectability by borrowing methods from more respectable fields, i. e., science. Anthropology, for example, was seen as too "soft" and too abstract. Social psychology offered more rigorous methods that were replicable and more concrete in its research findings.

This turn toward quantitative social science approaches aligned well with the interests and assumptions of whiteness. The conflation between nation and culture, for example, is easily deployed by using nation as a variable to make comparisons with other nations. This method erases cultural, linguistic, and racial diversity within nations. For a nation like the United States (in which white identity is the dominant racial group), whiteness as a cultural practice and value system becomes the same as "American" cultural practices and values. When white American culture becomes American culture, other cultural groups are erased. This erasure has meant that intercultural communication has largely been in the service of white Americans. We (Nakayama & Martin, 2007) earlier identified three specific ways in which the centering of whiteness influenced and distorted intercultural communication research/theory: (1) "Americans" and hegemonic whiteness; (2) Americans and diasporic relations; and (3) overlooking "other" voices and experiences.

We can see how the dominant research methods in intercultural communication can reinforce hegemonic whiteness in defining and characterizing American culture. However, as a part of these research methods, there is little attention to diasporic relations that influence intercultural contact and interaction. Many people of various cultural backgrounds desire to travel to their families' places of origin. While they may have some cultural knowledge about these cultures, these diasporic relationships are often erased in studying sojourners or other intercultural migrants. The rigidity of the use of variables that conflate nation with culture erases these relationships and the ways that people travel. This is one way that "other" voices and experiences are erased. The conflation of culture and nation erases other non-dominant cultures in a myriad of ways that need more exploration.

Future Challenges for Intercultural Communication Studies

In the mid 1990's intercultural communication scholars, influenced by interdisciplinary work in whiteness studies, ethnic studies, critical theory, and critical race theory, began exploring the role of power as an implicit force in driving the field in theorizing and praxis. Nakayama and Martin (1999) argued that whiteness, like other social and cultural identities, is productively understood as a communication phenomenon, and they challenged the ways that whiteness functions in the many facets of everyday life, noting that whiteness must be understood before it can be undone. Whiteness was identified as a key element in the construction of "others," and to understand and make visible the frequent invisibility and normativity of white supremacy/privilege and its influence on intercultural encounters (Collier et al., 2002), scholars provided theoretical directions for research and praxis (Alley-Young, 2008; Cooks, 2003; Moon, 2010; Shome, 2000).

In the larger field of communication studies, scholars also began to examine issues of race and white supremacy in communication theorizing, and pointed to the underlying power of whiteness in the construction of communication itself and of praxis — leading to the hashtag, #CommunicationSoWhite (Chakravartty et al., 2018). A number of publications have interrogated communication theorizing, undergraduate and graduate curricula, and editorial policies describing heavy reliance on white, male, European scholars (theoretically and methodologically) from past eras, written from white and Western standpoints (Calvente et al., 2020; Chakravartty et al., 2018; Chakravartty & Jackson, 2020; Martin & Nakayama, 2006), some blaming the field's quest for legitimacy by relying on/accepting racist foundations of other disciplines (McCann et al., 2020), others exploring how often the study of whiteness itself *recenters* whiteness (Washington, 2020).

Recent work in intercultural communication explores the intersections of whiteness with gender, class, sexuality, nation/ality, and so on, e.g., McIntosh et al. (2019), and the ways in which whiteness works around the world and its impact on intercultural communication, e.g., Steyn & Conway (2010). Steyn (2007) has made the point that in South Africa whiteness has never had the quality of invisibility that is implied in the "standard" whiteness literature, and in post-apartheid South Africa white South Africans cannot assume the same privileges with such ease, when state power is overtly committed to breaking down racial privilege.

The pattern that emerges is that quantitative social science does not account for history. History can be a huge influence in understanding cultures and cultural practices and values. History also explains why some cultural groups come into contact more often with other cultural groups. The emergence of Dutch-Indo people reflects the history of colonialism by the Netherlands in Indonesia; the mixed race heritage of Richard Branson reflects the history of British colonialism in India. The history of colonialism has created many cultural combinations that are not random but a product of history. This hybridity brings together various cultures that are reflected in many aspects of any culture. Hybridity is not new (Kraidy, 2005), but attention to the complexity of cultures and cultural interaction is often overlooked in the focus on cultural differences.

As we look forward to the future of intercultural communication, we believe it is imperative that we think about the hidden assumptions in our scholarship and who is served by the approaches, assumptions, and directions of our research. While we may not often see how intercultural communication studies largely shed light on the interactions of some people over others, it is imperative that we are self-reflexive in our scholarship. In this chapter, we urge a serious reconsideration of the ways that intercultural communication scholarship has been complicit with whiteness and its impact on those who are "other."

References

Ahmed, A. S. (2021, 13 May). "Pale, male & Yale": Can the State Department be fixed? *huffpost*.

Alley-Young, G. (2008). Articulating identity: Refining Postcolonial and Whiteness perspectives on race within communication studies. *The Review of Communication*, *8*(3), 307–321.

Baldwin, J. R. (2016). Murky waters: The histories of intercultural communication research. In L. Chen (Ed.), *Handbook of intercultural communication* (Vol. 9, pp. 19–43). Mouton de Gruyter.

Benedict, R. (1934). *Patterns of culture*. Houghton Mifflin.

Bettinger-Lopez, C., & Turkington, R. (2020, June 8). Gender representation and diversity in the foreign affairs community. *Council on Foreign Relations*.

Blower, B. L. (2014). From isolationism to neutrality: A new framework for understanding American political culture, 1919 – 1941. *Diplomatic History*,

38(2), 345-376.

Brantlinger, P. (1986). Victorians and Africans: The genealogy of the myth of the dark continent. In H. L. Gates, Jr. (Ed.), *"Race,"* writing and difference (pp.185-222). University of Chicago Press. (Original work published in 1985)

Calkin, H. L. (1978). Women in the Department of State: Their role in American foreign affairs. Department of State, Superintendent of Documents, U.S. Government Printing Office.

Calvente, L. B. Y., Calafell, B. M., & Chávez, K. R. (2020). Here is something you can't understand: The suffocating whiteness of communication studies. *Communication and Critical/Cultural Studies*, *17*(2), 202-209.

Chakravartty, P., & Jackson, S. J. (2020). The disavowal of race in communication theory. *Communication and Critical/Cultural Studies*, *17*(2), 210-219.

Chakravartty, P., Kuo, R., Grubbs, V., & McIlwain, C. (2018). # CommunicationSoWhite. *Journal of Communication*, *68*(2), 254-266.

Chalberg, J. C. (1995). *Isolationism: Opposing viewpoints*. Gale Publishing.

Christian, M. (2019). A global critical race and racism framework: Racial entanglements and deep and malleable whiteness. *Sociology of Race and Ethnicity*, *5*(2), 169-185.

Collier, M. J., Hegde, R. S., Lee, W. S., Nakayama, T. K., & Yep. G. A. (2002). Dialogue on the edges: Ferment in communication and culture. In M. J. Collier (Ed.), *Transforming communication about culture* (pp.219-280). Sage.

Cooks, L. (2003). Pedagogy, performance, and positionality: Teaching about Whiteness in interracial communication. *Communication Education*, *52*(3-4), 245-257.

Daniel, J. (1970). The facilitation of white-black communication. *Journal of Communication*, *20*, 134-141.

Daniel, J. L., & Smitherman, G. (1976). How I got over: Communication dynamics in the Black community. *Quarterly Journal of Speech*, *62*, 26-39.

Dower, J. W. (1986). *War without mercy: Race and power in the Pacific War*. Knopf Doubleday Publishing Group.

Eckl, J. (2008). Responsible scholarship after leaving the veranda: Normative issues faced by field researchers — and armchair scientists. *International Political Sociology*, *2*(3), 185-203.

Eramian, L. (2018). Participant observation. In H. Callan & S. Coleman (Eds.), *International Encyclopedia of Anthropology*. Wiley online library. https://doi.org/10.1002/9781118924396.wbiea1357

Foertsch, J. (2008). *American culture in the 1940's*. Edinburgh University Press.

Foreign Service Act (1946). Public Law 724, 79th Congress, As amended to Dec. 1, 1956. Government Printing Office.

Frohnmayer, R. (2017, Fall). A case for intercultural communication training. *americanambassdors.org*. Council of American Ambassadors: Review article.

Gorski, P. C. (2008). Good intentions are not enough: A decolonizing intercultural education. *Intercultural Education*, *19*(6), 515-525.

Gould, S. J. (1993). American polygeny and craniometry before Darwin: Blacks and Indians as separate, inferior species. In S. Harding (Ed.), *The "racial" economy of science: Toward a democratic future* (pp. 84-115). Indiana University Press. (Original work published in 1981)

Holling, M. A., & Moon, D. G. (2015). Continuing a politic of disruption: Race(ing) intercultural communication. *Journal of International and Intercultural Communication*, *8*(2), 81–85.

Jakes, L. (2020, June 27). A reckoning with race to ensure diversity for America's face abroad. *nytimes*.

Kim, M-S. (2012). World peace through intercultural research: From culture of war to a research culture of peace. *International Journal of Intercultural Relations*, *36*(1), 1–16.

Kitano, H. H. L. (1986, 25 May). War without mercy. *latimes*.

Kopp, H. W. (2019). Diversity and inclusion in the U.S. Foreign Service: A primer. *American Foreign Service Association*.

Kraidy, M. W. (2005). *Hybridity, or the cultural logic of globalization*. Temple University Press.

Krenn, M. L. (1999). *Black diplomacy: African Americans and the State Department 1945–1969*. Routledge.

Kulich, S. J., Weng, L., Tong, R., & DuBois, D. (2020). Interdisciplinary history of intercultural communication studies: From roots to research and praxis. In D. Landis & D. P. S. Bhawuk (Eds.), *Cambridge handbook of intercultural training* (4th ed., pp. 60–163). Cambridge University Press.

Ledwidge, M. (2006). Race, African-Americans & U.S. foreign policy. Ph. D. thesis, Politics in School of Social Science, Faculty of Humanities, University of Manchester.

Leeds-Hurwitz, W. (1987). Intercultural Communication and Anthropology: Understanding their common history. *Practicing Anthropology*, *9*(3), 4–11.

Leeds-Hurwitz, W. (1990). Notes in the history of intercultural communication: The Foreign Service Institute and the mandate for intercultural training. *Quarterly Journal of Speech*, *76*, 262–281.

Leeds-Hurwitz, W. (2010). Writing the intellectual history of intercultural communication. In R. T. Halualani & T. K. Nakayama (Eds.), *Handbook of critical intercultural communication* (pp. 21–33). Blackwell Publishing.

Lu, Y., & Gatua, M. W. (2014). Methodological considerations for qualitative research with immigrant populations: Lessons from two studies. *The Qualitative Report*, *19*, 1–16.

Martin, J. N., & Nakayama, T. K. (2006). Communication as raced. In G. Shepard, J. St. John, & T. Striphas (Eds.), *Communication as … : Stances on theory* (pp. 75–83). Sage.

Martin, J. N., Nakayama, T. K., & Carbaugh, D. (2012). The history and development of the study of intercultural communication and applied linguistics. In J. Jackson (Ed.), *The Routledge handbook of language and intercultural communication* (pp. 17–37). Routledge.

McCann, B. J., Mack, A. N., & Self, R. (2020). Communication's quest for whiteness: The racial politics of disciplinary legitimacy. *Communication and Critical/Cultural Studies*, *17*(2), 243–252.

McIntosh, D. M., Moon, D. G., & Nakayama, T. K. (Eds.). (2019). *Interrogating the communicative power of whiteness*. Routledge.

Mead, M., & Metraux, R. (Eds.). (1953). *The study of culture at a distance*. University of Chicago Press.

Mendoza, S. L., & Kinefuchi, E. (2016). Two stories, one vision: A plea for an ecological turn in intercultural communication. *Journal of International and Intercultural Communication*, *9*(4), 275–294.

Moon, D. G. (1996). Concepts of "culture": Implications for intercultural communication research. *Communication Quarterly*, *44*(1), 70–84.

Moon, D. G. (2010). Critical reflections on culture and critical intercultural communication. In T. K. Nakayama & R. T. Halualani (Eds.), *The handbook of critical intercultural communication* (pp. 34–52). Wiley-Blackwell.

Moon, D. G., & Holling, M. A. (2015). A politic of disruption: Race(ing) intercultural communication. *Journal of International & Intercultural Communication*, *8*(1), 1–6.

Nakayama, T. K., & Krizek, R. L. (1995). Whiteness: A strategic rhetoric. *The Quarterly Journal of Speech*, *81*(3), 291–309.

Nakayama, T. K., & Martin, J. N. (Eds.). (1999). *Whiteness: The communication of social identity*. Sage.

Nakayama, T. K., & Martin, J. N. (2007). The "White problem" in intercultural communication research and pedagogy. In L. M. Cooks & J. S. Simpson (Eds.), *Whiteness, pedagogy and performance: Dis/placing race*. Lexington Books.

Ono, K. A. (2010). Reflections on "Problematizing 'nation'" in intercultural communication research." In T. K. Nakayama & R. T. Halualani (Eds.), The *handbook of critical intercultural communication* (pp. 84–97). Wiley-Blackwell.

Piller, I. (2017). *Intercultural communication: A critical introduction* (2nd ed.). Edinburgh University Press.

Pusch, M. D. (2004). Intercultural training in historical perspective. In D. Landis, J. M. Bennett, & M. J. Bennett (Eds.), *Handbook of intercultural training* (3rd ed., pp. 13–37). Sage.

Rogers, E. M. (1999). Georg Simmel's concept of the stranger and intercultural communication research. *Communication Theory*, *9*(1), 58–74.

Rogers, E. M., & Hart, W. B. (2002). The histories of intercultural, international, and development communication. In W. B. Gudykunst & B. Mody (Eds.) *Handbook of international and intercultural communication* (2nd ed., pp. 1–18). Sage.

Rosaldo, R. (1989). *Culture and truth: The remaking of social analysis*. Beacon Press.

Ruane, M. E. (2021, 20 Dec.). "Greatest Generation" survey on race, sex and combat during World War Ⅱ runs counter to its wholesome image. *The Washington Post*.

Shome, R. (2000). Outing whiteness. *Critical Studies in Media Communication*, *17*(3), 366–372.

Smith, A. (aka Molefi Asante) (1973). *Transracial communication*. Prentice Hall.

Smith, L. T. (1999). *Decolonizing methodologies: Research and indigenous peoples*. St. Martin's Press.

Steyn, M. (2007). As the postcolonial moment deepens: A response to Green, Sonn, and Matsebula. *South African Journal of Psychology*, *37*(3), 420–424.

Steyn, M., & Conway, D. (2010). Introduction: Intersecting whiteness, interdisciplinary debates. *Ethnicities*, *10*(3), 283–291.

Szkudlarek, B. (2009). Through Western eyes: Insights into the intercultural training field. *Organization Studies*, *30*(9), 975–986.

Szkudlarek, B., & Romani, L. (2017, July). From an imperialist to a responsible agenda: Going beyond the limitations of cross-cultural training models. Paper presented at the 59th Annual Meeting of the Academy of International Business AIB, Dubai, United Arab Emirates.

Washington, M. (2020). Woke skin, white masks: Race and communication studies. *Communication and Critical/Cultural Studies*, *17*(2), 261–266.

Whittington, K. (2020, July 30). The color of diplomacy: A U.S. diplomat on race and the foreign service. *warontherocks*.

4

Paradigms of Intercultural Communication: A Comparative Survey of Universal and Relational Traditions of Thought

Gesine Lenore SCHIEWER
University of Bayreuth, Germany

Summary: In this chapter, concepts that are common in intercultural communication research and practice are traced back to two general paradigms. One of the two paradigms can be found in prominent approaches of the so-called "dialogue of cultures," but also for example in intercultural education research. It refers to approaches of philosophy in the tradition of Descartesian universalism and rationalism. The other paradigm is associated with the culture-relative or relational thinking of Johann Gottfried Herder, Wilhelm von Humboldt, and others. Both paradigms were explicitly or implicitly taken up in the twentieth century in communication studies, which was now forming as an independent field of research. The two lines of tradition are here presented in outline. Finally, the explanation of the historical dimensions concludes with an overview of the strengths and weaknesses of the two paradigms.

Introduction

In the course of the 18th century, a concept of language was developed in the philosophy of the time, in which basic problems of the sign-theoretical considerations of the 17th century were taken up. The development of a semiotic concept of knowledge from basic anthropological assumptions can therefore be traced back to the first impulses in the thinking of René Descartes and its gradual formulation especially by Gottfried Wilhelm Leibniz, Étienne Bonnot de Condillac, Johann Heinrich Lambert, and Johann Gottfried Herder. Since the 18th century at the latest, then, one can speak of two general paradigms that are of considerable persistence and have a formative influence on 20th-century approaches to communication theory. The aim of the overview in this chapter is to trace the development of these paradigms and to outline their significance for communication theory, especially regarding intercultural communication and international dialogue, as the paradigms represent interdisciplinary connections that have rarely been considered so far.

1. Philosophy of Language and Epistemology in the 17th and 18th Centuries

In the 17th century, the main concern was to clarify the significance of signs for human thought. In the background was the question of the relationship between body and mind, and great importance was attached to the whole topic for a number of concerns. ① These included, first of all, the discussion of the function of artificial sign systems for the "ars inveniendi" and the "ars iudicandi," i.e., for new approaches to thinking and their evaluation. The discussion of logic and calculi was also based on the approach of optimizing human thought and cognitive processes through skillful sign selection and operations. Furthermore, the considerations on the creation of a "grammatica rationis" or a rational grammar were motivated by the idea of making the truth of statements verifiable by means of a semantically unambiguous and systematically regular system of signs. The quest for a common language that all people could learn without difficulty and that would facilitate communication was the basis of the search for a "lingua universalis," for which Leibniz in particular also demanded a logical-philosophical basis. Equally, however, the question of the use of natural language in a scientific context and the

---

① The explanations in Section 1 adapt the more extensive analyses offered in Schiewer (2005). Adapted by permission from Springer Nature (Leonore Schiewer, *Deutsche Vierteljahresschrift für Literaturwissenschaft und Geistesgeschichte*, 2005).

consideration of the suitability of German as a scientific language were prompted by reflection on the role of the linguistic sign in human thought.

1.1 René Descartes's Idea of a Universal Language˙

These themes are already partly laid out in Descartes's works. For example, in his well-known letter to the mathematician Marin Mersenne of November 20, 1629, he outlines the concept of a "langue vniuerselle," whereas he criticizes the idea of a "nouuelle langue" because, in Descartes's view, it is ultimately only a primitive grammar (Descartes, 1897, pp. 76–82). The achievement of a "langue vniuerselle" could, however, as Descartes hopes, consist in arriving at practically error-free judgements on the basis of sign operations. The prerequisite, however, is that it is first possible to establish an order "entre toutes les pensées qui peuuent entrer en l'esprit humain" (Descartes, 1897, p. 80). Here Descartes presents the assumption, also formulated in his *Meditationes de Prima Philosophia* (first published in 1641), of a substantial difference between body and soul and thus of the independence of the intellect from the sign, which is only subsequently assigned to the ideas, primarily for communication purposes (cf. Descartes, 1959, pp. 129 ff.).

In addition to "intellectio," the young Descartes cites "imaginatio," i. e., the power of imagination, as a second faculty. As Lüder Gäbe has pointed out, Descartes illustrates the difference between these powers in the *Meditationes de Prima Philosophia* using the example of a thousand-sided polygon (cf. Gäbe, 1972, pp. 80 ff.). According to Descartes, the intellectual comprehension of a thousand-sided triangle is possible in the same way as that of a simple triangle. A pictorial-imaginative conception through the "imaginatio," on the other hand, is limited to the latter, since the human imagination is overstrained in the case of a complex polygon (cf. Gäbe, 1972, pp. 80 ff.). This means that complex objects can only be penetrated intellectually, while simple ones can also be subjected to "imaginatio." Therefore, memory as an aid to understanding must be supported by the use of signs, as Descartes states in the sixteenth of the *Regulae ad Directionem Ingenii* (cf. Descartes, 1908, p. 454). On the level of "imaginatio," signs thus ensure compensation for the "capacity weakness of the human mind" (translated from Gäbe, 1972, p. 82).

1.2 The Idea of Feature Semantics in Gottfried Wilhelm Leibniz's Work

It is precisely this example of the polygon that Leibniz draws on in 1684 in the treatise *Meditationes de Cognitione, Veritate et Ideis* for his account of the different forms of human cognition. Leibniz emphasizes that the nature of a complex object is usually not immediately obvious, so that the corresponding concept requires a longer analysis in order to be raised to the level of a "cognitio adaequata." In this form of cognition, every component that enters into a "notio distincta" with clearly delimitable characteristics is also clearly recognized. As a result of the impossibility of recognizing complex objects directly, signs, whose meaning must be clear in principle, but not situationally, would have to take the place of the ideas in question:

> [...] ita cum Chiliogonum seu Polygonum mille aequalium laterum cogito, non semper naturam lateris et aequalitatis et millenarii (seu cubi a denario) considero, sed vocabulis istis (quorum sensus obscure saltem atque imperfecte menti obversatur) in animo utor loco idearum quas de iis habeo, quoniam memini me significationem istorum vocabulorum habere, explicationem autem nunc judico necessariam non esse. [...] (Leibniz, 1978, p.423)

It has been pointed out by Ulrich Ricken that Leibniz, unlike Descartes, grants the sign an indispensable function for thinking (cf. Ricken, 1990, pp. 29f.). In fact, in the *Meditationes de Cognitione, Veritate et Ideis*, the use of signs is described as "cognitio symbolica," and the significance of this symbol-dependent form of cognition, although it is "blind," is placed in the hierarchy of all human forms of cognition immediately after the highest rank, which is occupied by both "adequate" and "intuitive" cognition. According to Leibniz, the cognition of the ideas of complex objects basically takes place by means of the "cognitio symbolica," since the capacity of the human visual imagination is limited. Only the "notionis distinctae primitivae" are exclusively accessible to the "cognitio intuitiva" and thus not dependent on representation by a sign (cf. Leibniz, 1978, p.423).

Whereas for Descartes the sign is to a certain extent a second-order aid, namely a relief and support for memory, which in turn is a subordinate aid of the intellect, Leibniz's design assigns to the sign a constitutive role for the actualization and handling of certain concepts of humanity. The assessment of the sign as a means of compensating for humanity's insufficiently developed power of imagination is thus subject to a reassessment due to a changed conception of the faculty of knowledge. Descartes regards the intellect as a purely abstract faculty of knowledge, which is only supplemented at a second level by certain functions of the sign (cf. Gäbe, 1972, pp. 74f. and 80ff.). Leibniz, on the other hand, concedes to the sign a role in the thought processes themselves, which directly establish human cognition. The sign and explicitly also the natural languages of humanity are thus clearly upgraded by Leibniz in their significance for the human cognitive processes of the so-called upper cognitive faculties. However, their task remains limited to the function of actualizing complex ideas, and their value in comparison with pure conceptual operations does not go beyond that of a secondary form of cognition.

This view is the essential basis of all reflections on language and sign theory in Leibniz's work. The project of a "characteristica universalis," first formulated in the 1660s, the reflections on the "grammatica rationis," the "lingua universalis" and the logical calculus, as well as the programmatic reflections on natural language and on German, are based on the assumption, theoretically formulated in the *Meditationes de Cognitione, Veritate et Ideis*, of the fundamental importance of the sign for concept formation. Descartes developed the idea of artificial sign systems on the one hand and natural language use on the other in his early writings *Dissertatio de Arte Combinatoria* (1666) and *Dissertatio Praeliminaris de Alienorum Operum Editione, de Scopo Operis, de Philosophica Dictione, de Lapsibus Nizolii* (1670). In the *Preface* to *Des Marius Nizolius Vier Bücher Anti-Barbarus*, Leibniz emphasizes that in this treatise language is accorded a central importance for the philosophical establishment of truth, and the adequate use of natural language in a scientific context is fundamentally discussed. It is about a "natural method of speaking" based on the principles of simplicity, clarity, intelligibility, appropriateness, and unadornment. Only then could language be a support for memory without impairing the power of judgement (cf. Leibniz, 1978, pp. 138 and 3). With this reasoning, Leibniz still closely follows Descartes's argumentation (cf. Descartes, 1908, pp. 144ff.). However, on the basis of his general criteria of good language use, namely "claritas," "veritas," and "elegantia," Leibniz derives a principle of the certainty of philosophical language, which states: the truth of a sentence can only be distinctly clarified if the meaning of the individual words is known (cf. Leibniz, 1978, pp. 138 and 3). Although Leibniz emphasizes that the way words are put together in a sentence also has an influence on the clarity of a sentence, he considers this aspect negligible, since dark constructions are more likely to be found among orators and poets than among philosophers anyway, which is why he can concentrate on the clarity of words in his investigation (cf. Leibniz, 1978, pp. 139 and 4f.).

For the use of language in a scientific context, recourse should be made to the current meaning, provided that this is not in itself unclear or contradictory. If, however, the current meaning of a word is ambiguous, then either a formal meaning must be determined by abstraction, which encompasses all of the meanings, or — if this is not possible — a word meaning must be determined from which the other present ones can be derived, just as they in turn have emerged from a common origin (cf. Leibniz, 1978, pp. 140 and 6). The meaning thus established must finally be set forth and consistently maintained in a definition, which in turn must be both true and clear (cf. Leibniz, 1978, pp. 140 and 6f.). The central idea of Leibniz's explanations is thus the problem of how the truth content of a statement can be made verifiable by way of establishing semantic unambiguity.

The use of natural language in philosophical-scientific contexts thus requires exact explanations and definitions of meaning. This laborious step would not be necessary in the creation of the alphabet of an artificial "characteristica universalis," since here the signs do not represent complex content, as is the case with the words of natural language, but semantically simple basic elements that then allow logical conclusions with reliable knowledge gain. Accordingly, Leibniz's famous encyclopedia project is about presenting a basic inventory of human knowledge in a clear and orderly manner, which can have the status of necessary and *a priori* valid axioms as well as that of only probable and consequently conditionally valid hypotheses. However, Leibniz did not succeed in actually conceiving an artificial "characteristica universalis."

1.3 The Epistemological Upgrading of Language in Étienne Bonnot de Condillac

That Leibniz's work, and in particular his *Monadologie* of 1714, played a significant role in the thinking of the French philosopher Condillac has been undisputed since Laurence L. Bongie identified his *Monadologie* in 1980. The linguistic and sign-theoretical aspects of Condillac's philosophy also show an orientation toward the Leibniz-

Wolff tradition, although Condillac accentuated psychological viewpoints and contributed significantly to Herder's initiation of an anthropological approach to human cognitive processes. This position with references to both paradigms makes his work so significant.

According to Condillac, in the context of human cognitive faculties, language assumes the status of an instrument that enables the dissection and ordering of simultaneous thought complexes. Its significance for human cognition is supposed to consist in examining complex thoughts or "pensée" for the constitutive "idées distinctes," thus establishing reflected and clear knowledge. Condillac thus assumes that, just like sensory perception, thoughts initially represent a confused conglomerate that only attains clarity on the basis of a sign-based process of analysis. According to Condillac, the analytical method to be applied is based on the entire "ars inveniendi": "[...] ce qu'on nomme méthode d'invention n'est autre chose que l'analyse" (Condillac, 1948, 2: 378). Condillac's approach corresponds to Leibniz's conception in his *Meditationes* insofar as, according to Condillac, sensations also cause composite "confused" ideas, which in turn only become "clear" ideas through the detailed investigation of the relevant features. The role attributed to language in this procedure by both authors is comparable: according to both Leibniz's and Condillac's conception, sophisticated analytical procedures are only possible at all by means of language or other signs, while "confused" cognition can also be achieved without linguistic or other signs.

However, the basic epistemological assumptions of Leibniz and Condillac differ strikingly. Whereas Leibniz understands cognition as a pure conceptual analysis, according to Condillac the analysis of even abstract concepts requires a tracing back to the sensory perceptions of humans:

Or, vous avez vu, Monseigneur, qu'une idée abstraite est une idée que nous formons en considérant une qualité séparément des autres qualités auxquelles elle est unie. Il suffit donc d'avoir des sens pour avoir des idées abstraites.

Mais tant que nous n'avons des idées abstraites que par cette voie, elles viennent à nous sans ordre; elles disparoissent quand les objets cessent d'agir sur nos sens: ce ne sont que des connoiss-ances momentanées, et notre vue est encore bien confuse et bien trouble.

Cependant c'est la nature qui commence à nous faire démêler quelque chose dans les impressions que les organes font passer jusqu'à l'ame. Si elle ne commençoit pas, nous ne pourrions pas commencer nous-mêmes. Mais, quand elle a commencè, elle s'arrête; contente de nous avoir mis sur la voie, elle nous laisse, et c'est à nous d'avancer. (Condillac, 1947, 1: 439)

The assumption that all cognition is based on sensory perceptions, which must be brought into a natural order, establishes the basic principles of the methodology advocated by Condillac. Condillac's work *La langue des calculs*, which was only published posthumously, is primarily dedicated to tracing thought back to the respective sensually perceived "germ" (cf. Condillac, 1948, 2: 428f.). The better a language is made, the more precisely the corresponding analyses can be carried out. The first stage of a natural language, he said, is made up of the so-called "langage d'action," i.e., the natural gestures and facial expressions of human beings. The further development of a language and the expansion of its sign inventory take place exclusively through the gradual creation of analogical similarity relationships. A "langue bien faite," such as algebra, is therefore characterized by a maximum of consistent analogies, on the basis of which an object can be viewed in an appropriate manner (cf. Condillac, 1948, 2: 419).

According to Condillac, the only possible path to knowledge is to progress from the known to the unknown, because the unknown is to be found in the known. Precise observation of what is already known is necessary, since knowledge of it is often insufficient. For this reason, all true statements are identical propositions, which are therefore not trivial, but rather extend our knowledge. Condillac answers the question of why a series of identical propositions is necessary for the knowledge of a thing, although in the end the same property of the object in question is thematized in all of them, by referring to the limitations of the human faculty of comprehension (cf. Condillac, 1948, 2: 431f.). Since a property is to be considered from different perspectives, it could only be grasped as a unity if humanity were able to survey the possible different perspectives at the same time. Since this is not the case, however, it represents a sequence of properties for the recognizing human being, which is not given in the thing, but only in the language used for the analysis. In fact, every science could be reduced to a first truth, which would contain all further truths already discovered as well as all those still to be discovered. The prerequisite here, however, would be to speak very simply by means of a well-made language (cf. Condillac, 1948,

2 : 454). It is to be anticipated that these considerations of Condillac's have some parallels with the sociological approaches to knowledge to be outlined below in this chapter. We will return to this below.

In addition to the assumption, already highlighted above as a Leibnizian substrate, that the origin or "germ" of a thought already contains all further aspects and developments, there is a further consistent correspondence with Leibniz's monad theory: the human cognitive faculty does not allow for an all-embracing view of an object, but only its step-by-step dissection. This is supposed to be the difference from God's wisdom. However, Condillac's differentiation between necessary and contingent truths no longer corresponds to Leibniz's, since Condillac regards contingent truths as experiential knowledge mediated by sense perception without further examination, which does not refer to essential properties of things and for this reason is variable. Necessary or eternal truths are gained through abstraction. This is the "reversal of previous methodological thinking" emphasized by Wolfgang Proß, which postulates "a methodological independence and certainty of human knowledge, where until now one could only speak of a probability of the anthropomorphic results of thought" (translated from Herder, 1987, p. 1151). According to Condillac — and Herder —, the knowledge and language of a people correspond to their respective needs and are thus to be regarded as perfect in each case (cf. Condillac, 1947, 1: 434). Human cognition thus experiences a clear revaluation, with which the anthropologically conditioned view receives unrestricted dignity. Connected with this is the recognition of sense perception also for the formation of abstract ideas. Regardless of the ideas' respective scope and their stage of development, the knowledge corresponding to the needs of a linguistic community in Condillac's view has a systemic character. For analysis, which already begins at the level of "langage d'action," leads as such to the formation of a system in the sense of an ordered set of knowledge.

The systemic character of knowledge is related to the systemic character of language: "Puisque les mots sont les signes de nos idées, il faut que le système des langues soit formé sur celui de nos connaissance" (Condillac, 1947, 1: 427). This connection between knowledge and language establishes that cognition can be right or wrong, succeed or fail, and that both true and false systems can be designed (cf. Herder, 1987, pp. 1151f.). Since in the "langue des calculs," in contrast to natural languages, analogy relations are consistently carried out, such an artificial language, according to

Condillac, is to be preferred to any natural language if reliability of cognition is the goal. In principle, the use of natural language is also possible in a scientific context, but a source of error arises in this case, among other things because it requires memory, which is not necessary with a "langue des calculs" (cf. Condillac, 1948, 2: 468). In this argument, then, the view of signs as a support for memory, as also advocated by Descartes and Leibniz, is reintroduced after all. It is precisely from the assumption that everything still unknown is contained in what is already known and the resulting restriction to the method of analysis in Condillac's approach that the deferral of natural languages to the "langue des calculs" arises. For according to this concept, a complex thought ("pensée") contains all distinct ideas which only need to be separated, named, and brought into a logical order.

1.4 The Turn to the Semiotics of Natural Language in Johann Heinrich Lambert's Work

Only with the explicit rejection of the monad theory by Johann Heinrich Lambert in his second major philosophical work, the *Anlage der Architectonic, oder Theorie des Einfachen und des Ersten in der philosophischen und mathematischen Erkenntniß* (1773), is the indispensability of natural language recognized for the attainment of new knowledge. Lambert no longer focuses on the question of the divisibility or non-divisibility of matter, but on force. According to Lambert's approach, forces are not materially manifest, but can act on material things despite their immateriality. Against this background, Leibniz's monad theory is explicitly rejected. To the forces, which are described by Lambert as "spiritual," are attributed the properties of thinking, willing, and acting, thus distinguishing three types of forces. In this way, the concept of force in Lambert's approach takes on central importance for the entire theme of knowledge (cf. Lambert, 1771, p.77).

The above-mentioned three types of forces are also the basis of the system typology that Lambert establishes in the context of his reflections on a general systematology (Lambert, 1988). He distinguishes theoretical systems whose components are connected only by the forces of understanding from those that are based on the "forces of the will" and that represent moral or even political systems, and these in turn from physical systems whose components are held in connection by mechanical forces. The central role of systematology in Lambert's thought is explained by the interweaving of the concept of system with the basic assumptions of his philosophical *oeuvre* as a whole.

According to his empiricist-sensualist approach, all cognition starts from immediate sensory perceptions, which as such should lead to "clear," albeit fleeting concepts. Scientific knowledge, which belongs to the systems of the first type, is founded by Lambert on a complex logic of concepts and characteristics, whereby at the beginning one must always proceed *a posteriori*, since simple concepts must first be determined with recourse to immediate sensation, in order to be able to use them without further consultation of experience. Only in order to check the results obtained is it necessary to apply them to experience again. In addition to investigating how conclusions can be drawn from what is known, it is also a matter of formulating new research questions. Lambert thus includes the search for the known starting from the unknown in the task field of science, and in this way expands its field in comparison to Condillac by a second path of knowledge. This claim is derived from Lambert's basic empiricist-sensualist position, which requires, among other things, that experiences, observations, and experiments be accorded the greatest significance for the knowledge of nature. The *a priori* path, on the other hand, is only possible in a few sciences such as arithmetic and geometry. The importance of experience and sensory perception for scientific knowledge also implies the indispensability of natural language, while the use of artificial sign systems is recognized as a desideratum that can only be realized to a limited extent — even though Lambert, like Leibniz and Condillac, regards artificial, "scientific" sign systems as ideal, while natural language is judged to be deficient in terms of semantic unambiguity and the stability of the relationship between form and content.

Lambert's insight that knowledge of nature is not a rationally finite operation but a principally infinite process causes a considerable tension in his entire approach. Lambert follows patterns of thought of 17th-century philosophical rationalism insofar as he believes that the standards of mathematical evidence and methodology could also be applied in philosophy and natural science (Lambert, 1918). He thus pursues the idea of necessary truth, which a person could achieve in all areas of research. Lambert thus abandons the modesty proclaimed by Leibniz with regard to the contingency of human possibilities of knowledge, and strives for the necessity of knowledge regardless of the object. According to Lambert, however, this truth is no longer a purely logical-apriorical one, but is always based on a ground of experience. Thus, in Lambert's work, a radicalization of the human claim to knowledge is connected with a changed conception of knowledge. Lambert's work thus juxtaposes a rejectionist orientation toward "mathesis universalis" and the time-related theorizing of empirical research on nature.

For Lambert's fundamental reflection on the necessity and performance of signs for human thought, the psychological approaches of the 18th century that take into account the sensuality of human beings gain central importance alongside a Baumgartenian substrate. Since, according to Lambert, "clear concepts" depend on concrete perceptions, the arbitrary visualization of such concepts is only possible by means of the use of linguistic signs, which function, as it were, as a substitute for sensory impressions (cf. Lambert, 1764, pp. 8 – 11). This view is based on Lambert's assumption that analogous conditions prevail in the so-called "bodily world" and the "intellectual world," since bodily-sensory conditions correspond to every operation of the intellect. The bodily-sensory perception could therefore be replaced by the material sign, which thus acquires fundamental importance for the formation of the intellectual faculties of humanity.

1.5 Language in Johann Gottfried Herder's Concept of the Whole Man

The view of scientific knowledge advocated by Lambert in his philosophy of science, which includes both rationalist and empiricist-sensualist components and emphasizes the role of natural language for the activity of understanding and reason, makes Lambert's work an important source for Herder's anthropological foundation of cognition. Indeed, in 1799 Herder based his *Meta-critique of the Critique of Pure Reason* in essential aspects on Lambert's philosophical works and, referring to his concept and in a debate with Leibniz in particular, justified the assumption of the interaction of sensuality, understanding, and reason that he advocated against Kant. Herder anchors his epistemology in a "physiology of the human powers of cognition," and takes a psychological approach (Herder, 1881, 21: 41). He develops a semiotic concept of knowledge with an explanation of the transformation of sensory perception into concepts of understanding and reason through the use of signs, especially language.

This means that at the end of the 18th century — when Kant's Critical Writings had already withdrawn the importance of signs and language for the development and exercise of human cognitive activity — Herder arrived at a psychologically grounded and semiotically supported anthropology. It takes into account the diversity of sign systems with regard to their forms, functions, and performances in the respective temporal and spatial context. Thinking and cognition are regarded as necessarily linguistic-historical, which makes any system design with an absolute claim inadmissible.

The historical dimension is paralleled with systematic considerations in Herder's entire thinking, which is characterized by differentiation and relativization of human cultural products. Herder views the growth of human knowledge in terms of synchronously coexisting forms of knowledge that differ in type and precision. He develops a differentiated approach to different levels of accuracy of knowledge, which takes into account practical everyday knowledge as well as mathematics, and matches the requirements that the sign system to be used has to satisfy to the respective goal of knowledge. The question of truth is consistently linked to an anthropological theory of knowledge (cf. Herder, 1881, 21: 125f., and Schiewer, 1996, pp. 173 – 177). Since, according to Herder, arbitrary signs make human thinking as such possible in the first place, the psychological conditionality of the human being is inherent to it. Nevertheless, due to the process character of human cognitive efforts, a gradual refinement and the achievement of increasing accuracy of knowledge is possible. In the process, errors may very well occur, but in principle these can also be corrected in the further course.

Thus, cognition is no longer to be understood as an "ars inveniendi," but as an integral concept in which epistemology and ontology are programmatically linked. The concept of the system is marginal here against the background of a conception of space and time as conditions of infinite variation, as well as a concept of cognition that describes human cognitive possibilities as an anthropologically conditioned process. Nevertheless, in Herder's epistemological outline, which regards the linguistic sign as a fundamental element of all cultural and knowledge formation, a link to the tradition of the "cognitio symbolica" — with references to Lambert and Leibniz, among others — is unmistakable. Thus, the formation of the historical view of language and knowledge, despite a fundamentally modified epistemology and philosophy of science, can be seen as a consistent further development and application of the theories of the late 17th century and the first half of the 18th century that revolve around this problem.

2. Interdisciplinary References of Philosophy of Language and Communication Theory

It is well known that both linguistics and communication theory in the narrower sense were essentially formed in the 20th century. Philosophical traditions certainly did not play a decisive role in this process, but they were not without influence either. Systematic research on these developments can hardly be seen to date, but numerous individual studies are available. And so, for example, Noam Chomsky's confrontation with Descartes's rationalist conception of the sign can be mentioned, which was presented above in the outline. Wilhelm von Humboldt was also important for linguistic approaches such as linguistic relativity and stimulation for the formation of theories in communication studies. Herder is occasionally acknowledged, for example in the work of Ludwig Jäger, who advocates a cultural-scientific linguistics.

Lambert is almost forgotten today, even in the history of philosophy. However, one of the renowned communication scholars of the 20th century, Gerold Ungeheuer, who unfortunately died young, read Lambert's works intensively. Ungeheuer's interest in Lambert's writings was based on the fact that, in his view, Lambert was the only person in the 18th century who (1) took up the concept of semiotics again, (2) reflected on the communicative aspect of language, (3) addressed a "theory of word disputes," (4) enriched word semantics with a classification of semantic uniqueness and ambiguity, and (5) emphasized the individuality of experiences that every human being has (Ungeheuer, 1980, pp. 87 and 92).

Beyond this immediate reception of Lambert, the fundamental orientations described above, which have developed in the course of the history of philosophy, continue to have an effect across disciplines in theories of communication.

2.1 Paradigms of Universalism and Relativism in Communication Theories Since the 20th Century

The paradigms of the 17th and 18th centuries presented in the first section of this chapter thus remain virulent. Concepts in the tradition of Cartesian rationalism and universalism are competing with those in which individuality of experience, error, semantic unreliability, and the whole human being as a being with desires, memories, and feelings are taken into account.

Since the 20th century, these paradigms have been exemplified by two predominant approaches: on the one hand, there is the communication theory of Jürgen Habermas, which integrates linguistic, language-philosophical, and sociological components and thereby elevates reason and rationality to leading categories (Habermas, 1981). On the other hand, there is Gerold Ungeheuer's anthropologically oriented communication theory, which describes communication in its empirical basis of experience. This includes in particular the individuality of experiences and semantics of communication and the possibilities of communication failure.

2.2 "Dialogue of Cultures" in the Universalist Paradigm

The volume *Crossing the Divide: Dialogue Among Civilizations*, initiated by Kofi Annan and published in 2001, presents a framework concept for the practice of international dialogue at all political, institutional, and social levels. The aim is to take a counter-position to Samuel P. Huntington's thesis of the "Clash of Civilizations," and to see in the dialogue of civilizations as a cultural idea of global understanding the chance for a peaceful future. On the occasion of a round table at the headquarters of the United Nations in 2000, the Secretary General, twelve heads of state and government, as well as the foreign ministers of various countries unanimously declared that, with the help of such a dialogue between cultures, all nations would be able to replace hostility and confrontation with dialogue and understanding. Far-reaching hopes were thus attached to this approach, which also found its way into the discussions of the Global Issues Working Group of Germany's Federal Foreign Office with the Forum on Global Issues, and is discussed, for example, in the documentation of the 6th and 7th Forum on "Globalization and Communication" and the "Dialogue of Cultures." Of course, there is no question that this approach, and with it the theory of communicative action by Jürgen Habermas on which it is decisively based, came into difficulties of explanation as early as 2001 with the attack on the World Trade Center in New York, and must finally be judged as completely unrealistic by 2022 at the latest.

Although the theoretical foundations of the approach are not made explicit, a careful analysis of the concept of dialogue presented reveals that (1) Jürgen Habermas's model of communication theory is central, among other things with its intense emphasis on the acceptance of differences, the prerequisite of mutual understanding, trust, mutual respect, openness, the renunciation of influence, as well as the objective of convincing and not persuading (cf. also on the criticism of this approach Schiewer, 2006). Important are (2) theological perspectives with the concept of the "global ethic" by Hans Küng, who is also one of the authors of the volume initiated by Kofi Annan. The immutable ethical values accentuated by Küng, which are to have global validity, refer to solidarity, non-violence, tolerance, truthfulness, equality, and the partnership of men and women (cf. Küng, 1990, 1997). They are also given a significant position with regard to the outlined concept of the "dialogue of cultures" insofar as the cross-cultural, common, and intersubjective basis of these values is assumed. In other words, as the authors believe, they represent a crucial prerequisite for intercultural dialogue with regard to the integration of diverse perspectives in the field of faith and religions (cf. Schiewer, 2009).

Precisely because of the hoped-for significance of this conception for the work of the UN and the Forum on Global Issues, the author of the present chapter subjected it to a careful analysis a decade and a half ago. This was because Habermas himself was open to critical questioning after the 2001 attacks: "Since September 11, I have often been asked whether or not, in light of this violent phenomenon, the whole conception of "communicative action" I developed in my theory has been brought into disrepute," said Jürgen Habermas in a conversation with Giovanna Borradori (Borradori, 2003, p.35). He problematized his own concept in this way, only to defend it. He acknowledged that the instruments of rational and reason-based argumentation, which he regarded as universal, had to be restricted as the basis of the dialogue of cultures: insofar as interpretations owe a "moment of blindness" to "the traces of forced assimilation to constraints imposed by a superior party," communication is "always ambiguous, suspect of latent violence" (Borradori, 2003, p. 38). However, while Habermas endeavored to minimize this serious concession, the theorization of a dialogue of cultures relevant to political practice must by no means ignore precisely this field of communicative violence and conflict potentials.

That is why the concept of the dialogue of cultures, both from the perspective of communication theory and in its application-oriented dimensions, remains altogether bound to rationalist and universal thinking. Among other things, Habermas's close coupling of communication and consensus to be achieved rationally by means of the "better argument" and his differentiation of rationally accentuated communicative action and strategic action oriented toward subjective interests should be emphasized. Basically comparable concepts of rational discourse ethics have become established in the field of consensus-oriented mediation. Even if Habermas's post-2001 statements do not amount only to a relativization of the universal rationality assumption through the fallibility of reason, the precondition of ideal communication taking place under symmetrical conditions remains (cf. Schiewer, 2009).

In contrast to this, approaches based on anthropological communication theory, socio-semiotics and emotion linguistics are in the general line of the relativistic paradigm. They tend to aim at uncovering semantics of communication, the often factual asymmetries of communicators, power and interest situations, and thus make problems negotiable in the first place. Among others, Gerold Ungeheuer's approach, whose discussion of Johann Heinrich Lambert was outlined above, should be mentioned in this context.

When we speak of an anthropological foundation, we are referring to the fact that communication and international communication processes, as intercultural interaction and dialogue situations, are inseparably linked to the human condition. The basic assumptions that result from this for corresponding communication concepts can be summarized in three points.

(a) *Communication is necessarily perspectival, even when a rational exchange is aimed at.*

The concept of " perspectivity " was already reflected on by the sociologist of knowledge Karl Mannheim in 1924 and 1925 in his study *Eine soziologische Theorie der Kultur und ihrer Erkennbarkeit (Konjunktives und kommunikatives Denken)*. According to Mannheim, "subjunctive experience" or "subjunctive recognition" is characterized by the fact that only one side of the counterpart can be perceived at a time, and this is a perspective that is embedded in the personal dispositions with which one approaches the counterpart. These dispositions include the insights that people generally experience through sense organs, that they are *hic et nunc*, and that the people facing them have a specific meaning for them because of their interests and desires. Thus, according to Mannheim, encounters are fundamentally perspectival and one-sided: " We called this cognition 'perspective' and asked what the similarities were between the concept originating in the field of optical perception and the type of experience of perspectival cognition in question" (translated from Mannheim, 1980 [1924/25], p. 212). The perspectival peculiarity of optical perception is characterized by the fact that in the optical observation of a thing or a landscape, the observer gets a different image of the object from every point in space. But each of these images is an experience of this landscape, even if it is oriented as a "foreshortening" and "displacement" toward the location of the observer. The respective image is determined both by its own location and by what is being looked at. And although — or precisely because — it is perspective, Mannheim describes this location-bound image as true. For landscapes are an object that, in principle, can only be perceived in perspective. If someone wants to experience a landscape, they do not take a map, which is an artificial projection, a fiction of a supra-local objectivity by fixing objective conditions, but must inevitably occupy a place in space themselves (cf. Mannheim, 1980 [1924/25], p.212).

For this reason, communication is always bound to the perspective of the speaker. People can never recognize other people in the way the other person might be "in him-or herself." Everyone knows another only to the extent and in the way that they themselves enter into the common relationship, exist in it, and develop in it. According to Mannheim, this is reflected particularly succinctly in the use of pet names, which occur in children's language and in the language of couples and friends. But of course it must be added that every form of address is an expression of the specific position of the participants to each other (cf. Mannheim, 1980 [1924/25], pp. 212 f.). In addition, according to Mannheim, everyone can also recognize themselves only insofar as they stand in existential relations to others. Mannheim regards social existence as a precondition for self-knowledge for three reasons: firstly, because we can only place ourselves in human existential relationships on the basis of our social existence; secondly, because every person makes another side of our self vibrate; and thirdly, because we see ourselves more easily through the eyes and in the perspective of another than from ourselves.

Mannheim's notion of "perspectivity" thus implies not only the respective encounter of communication partners, but also the particularity of *alter* and *ego* in each of their various encounters. In this context, Mannheim takes into account the emergence of communally borne perspectives in the collective experience, among other things, but these are not solidified structures that could lead to homogeneous cultural, national, or religious collective identities. Mannheim's concept therefore does not meet the frequently held assumption that intercultural communication situations are more difficult than intracultural ones because differences in language, thinking, politics, religion, and thus community identities, among other things, have to be overcome. From this point of view, it is almost astounding that the basic fact described by Mannheim of multiple perspectives that change from encounter to encounter is what makes communication and dialogue possible in the first place. Supra-temporal structures and abstract concepts — somewhat confusingly called "communicative experience" by Mannheim — are of course not denied, but they cannot cancel out the fundamental perspectivity of every encounter, no matter how factually accentuated. If we follow the famous economist Amartya Sen, then this is precisely where the opportunity for a successful dialogue of cultures lies: Sen speaks of

> the odd presumption that the people of the world can be uniquely categorized according to some *singular and overarching* system of partitioning. [...] The illusion of destiny, particularly about some singular identity or other (and their alleged implications), nurtures violence in the world through omissions as well as commissions. We have to see clearly that we have many distinct affiliations and can interact with each other in a great many different ways. [...] (Sen, 2006, pp. xii, xiv)

In the concept of the dialogue of cultures based on Habermas's approach, rationality, commonly shared values, and semantics of unity are considered important, which makes communication processes very presuppositional. In contrast, the basic assumption of perspectivity in the sense outlined here, in orientation toward Karl Mannheim and Amartya Sen, reflects the encounter of the most diverse communication partners. It is precisely these encounters that can be seen as an opportunity for international and intercultural dialogue.

(b) *Perspectivity is linked to the fact that communication partners have different horizons, perceptions, and goals, and are subject to cultural variables.*

If one assumes the subjectivity, individuality, and plural identity of the communication partners, then communication is generally accompanied by more or less latent knowledge asymmetries of the partners involved in the sense of the sociologist of knowledge Thomas Luckmann. Divergences and misunderstandings that occur openly and covertly in communication are thus not unusual. Although the need for agreement seems to be deeply anchored in human beings, so that a "no" or a rejected offer can indeed cloud the atmosphere, dissent is no more to be confused with the failure of communication than consensus is with its real success.

Only when this is recognized is it possible to expose and defuse the often subtle mechanisms that serve to create, if not force, consensus. In particular, the use of latent threats, the mechanism of which has been lucidly analyzed by sociologist Helmut Popitz (cf. Popitz, 1999), is to be thought of here. What is particularly surprising is Popitz's observation that in groups in which the members jointly make decisions that are binding for all — as, it should be noted, in the case of Habermas's discourse ethics — each member is both the threatener and the threatened. Popitz emphasizes in parenthesis that this is a disappointing experience when such groups are formed in the hope that equal decision-making rights will eliminate power structures. The first thing is that the threatener makes it clear that he or she clearly prefers certain actions, reactions, expressions, etc., of the counterpart and does not want others. Thus the action of the threatened is weighed down by the expectations of others; an alternative of docility and reticence emerges (cf. Popitz, 1999, pp. 81 and 87). However, the threatened person decides whether the threatener will be taken at his word. The threatener potentially risks his credibility: "If he cannot honour the threat, he diminishes the effect of any future threat. Whoever threatens not only tries to exercise power, he also risks power" (translated from Popitz, 1999, p. 83). The forms of expression can be extremely diverse and subtle. In the case of "covert threats," non-verbal, gestural-mimic signals or even discreet hints are sufficient. In a conversation among friends, colleagues, party members, etc., the covert threat, for example, depicts the consequences — unwanted by all — of non-conformist behavior. According to Popitz, it can be quite clear that the threatener may trigger possible sanctions. Nevertheless, in this way the "face" of all participants, including that of the "covert compliant," is saved. Threats are particularly effective when compliance can be expected: "They are cheap if the threat is effective. If the threatened person complies, the threatener does not have to do anything" (translated from Popitz, 1999, p. 91). In contrast, promises are expensive in this case because they have to be kept. Every norm-compliant behaviour is thus rewarded, and the actual field of action of threats is where conformity is to be expected: in daily life and in consensus-oriented rational discourse.

With his analysis, Popitz thus uncovers an implicitly concealed power structure even of the dialogue of cultures initiated by Kofi Annan, which — although certainly not intended — is of weight. Jürgen Habermas's consensus-oriented concept of discourse based on speech-act theory represents a rational conception of communication that sets up a repair mechanism on a meta-communicative level that is intended to serve the clarification and resolution of misunderstandings. However, an "ideal speech situation" is postulated here. In contrast, Gerold Ungeheuer's concept of communication is much less "ideal": he emphasizes the impossibility of communicating one's own worlds of experience unbrokenly in language and the asymmetry of every conversational situation (cf. Ungeheuer, 1987). Nevertheless, there is certainly room in this theory for optimizing communicative competence. Considerations of paraphrase as a means of checking understanding as well as the appeal to the assumption of responsibility by the language user are central here. This responsibility refers to not exploiting the possibilities of linguistic and social dominance. Here, efforts to avoid the failure of a dialogue are thus related to the realities of the conversation as such. Awareness is raised of the potential problems of the communication process that can prevent success even with the best of intentions.

(c) *Communication partners are in relationships of cooperation as well as competition.*

Complementary to the striving for cooperation is a second basic human characteristic of pursuing one's own and egoistic interests in competitive situations. This certainly applies to all forms of political-social and organizational communication, indeed it can ultimately apply to almost every communication situation, as the enforcement of consensus by means of latent threats also shows.

Regardless of whether one speaks of "strategy," as in business communication, or of "cunning," as the sinologist Harro von Senger did, and even of the "Brechtian cunning" of large enterprises (Spinner, 1994, p.44), one is dealing with specific forms of rationality which, as "strategic success potential," aim at an advantageous competitive position in a manner guided by interests (cf. Zerfaß, 2006, p.241). The identification of cooperative consensus with rational argument in Habermas's model — with its demarcation from strategic-persuasive and thus non-rationally controlled communication — thus becomes problematic. Finally, it is assumed that interests are to be set aside in favor of the "better argument." Here, universal rationality is identified with cooperation and more or less explicitly played off against the uncontrolled-emotional strategic enforcement of egoistic goals (cf. also the relevant chapter on emotion and economy in Schiewer, 2014, and Schiewer, 2010).

The second paradigm (b) implies the need for well-founded knowledge of different styles of conversation, of culturally shaped forms of dialogue and strategies. In this context, cross-cultural international dialogue constellations require communication-theoretical and practical foundations that correspond to the complex realities of the actual perspective diversity of the present. This requires comparative dialogue and sociolinguistic studies within the framework of intercultural conflict linguistics.

3. "Autonomous Sphere of the Intellectual" ("Autonome Sphäre des Geistigen") vs. "Being-Connectedness of Knowledge" ("Seinsverbundenheit des Wissens"): A Communication-Theoretical Perspective

It has been shown that the relativist paradigm corresponds, among other things, to the sociological assumption of the "being-connectedness of knowledge." Matthias Lemke and Gregor Wiedemann succinctly formulate, albeit in a completely different context, the extent to which this in turn contrasts with the rationalist-universal paradigm: "In the motif of the being-connectedness of knowledge, the idea of a sphere of the intellectual that is autonomous vis-à-vis the materiality of social and the corporeality of human life is rejected as idealistic" (translated from Lemke & Wiedemann, 2016, p. 24). Referring to the concept of "latency observation" introduced by Niklas Luhmann, they make clear the extent to which Karl Mannheim's approach has taken the point out of a fundamental problematic. For of course, in a logic of the children's game "I see something you don't see," the connectedness of being can be turned in such a way that the counterpart (alter) is always arrested in its perspectivity, and is enlightened in a know-it-all way by *ego* about its latencies and criticized for its "epistemologically definitive understanding of the world and itself" (translated from Lemke & Wiedemann, 2016, p. 25). With the concept of "competition in the realm of the intellectual," Mannheim had captured the struggle of different world interpretations for the public interpretation of being, the implications of which Lemke and Wiedemann emphasize:

> The ideology-critical scheme of latency observation functions here as a weapon with which the opponents in the struggle for interpretive hegemony strive to destroy their respective opponents by compromising their respective claims to a true interpretation of the world, i. e., one that is appropriate to political-social reality, by demonstrating perspectival narrowness. (Translated from Lemke & Wiedemann, 2016, p. 27)

Opponents thus accuse each other of the one-sidedness of their view, and each claim for themselves an objective and superior view. Against this backdrop, Mannheim's merit is that he describes knowledge in general as being bound up with being and that "every interpretation of the world is therefore shaped by the particularity of its location," which means that the proof of such a particularity of view *per se* can no longer be seen as criticism (cf. Lemke & Wiedemann, 2016, p. 27).

From the perspective of communication theory, especially with regard to intercultural communication and international dialogue, a relativistic paradigm reflected in this way remains significant into the present and for the future. For the term "lying press," which was already used in the 19th century, and the ubiquitous talk of "fake news" since Donald Trump's presidency, work almost exemplarily with the scheme of latency observation. Even if there is little, if any, reason to hope that the claim to power of the latency observer, which always leads to oppression, violence, and war, can be overcome, an insight into the general connectedness of knowledge to being at least opens up a possible path to "communicative humility," even if only on the condition that there is a willingness to do so.

Conclusion

In this chapter, two general paradigms in the field of communication theory concepts are elaborated, which are presented in their historical developments since the 17th century with a view to philosophical, linguistic-philosophical, semiotic, sociological, and knowledge-sociological foundations. The focus of the chapter is on the theorization processes of the 18th as well as the 20th and 21st centuries. The explanations show that both paradigms, albeit in very different ways, seek to compensate for the bondage of the human being to the human condition. Both paradigms have produced models in the 20th century that also aim quite differently at critically questioning communicative practices that can be described as unenlightened.

However, the prerequisite of readiness for what I have called "communicative humility" remains inescapable, i. e., in the case of the universalist paradigm for rational withdrawal and in the case of the relativist paradigm for the withdrawal of claims to power and domination.

References

Anan, K. (2001). *Brücken in die Zukunft: Ein Manifest für den Dialog der Kulturen. Mit einem Geleitwort von Joschka Fischer*. Fischer.

Borradori, G. (2003). *Philosophy in a time of terror: Dialogues with Jürgen Habermas and Jacques Derrida*. The University of Chicago Press.

Condillac, É. De (1947–1949). *Œuvres philosophiques de Condillac: Texte établie et présenté par Georges Le Roy* (3 Vols.). Presses Universitaires de France.

Condillac, É. De (1980). *Les monades* (L. L. Bongie, Ed.). Taylor Institution. (Original work published 1746)

Descartes, R. (1897). *Œuvres I* (C. Adam & P. Tannery, Eds.). Cerf.

Descartes, R. (1908). *Œuvres X* (C. Adam & Paul Tannery, Eds.). Cerf.

Descartes, R. (1959). *Meditationes de prima philosophia* (L. Gäbe, Ed.). Meiner. (Original work published 1641)

Descartes, R. (1973). *Regulae ad directionem ingenii* (H. Springmeyer, L. Gäbe, & H. G. Zekl, Eds.). Meiner. (Original work begun 1619, not completed)

Gäbe, L. (1972). *Descartes' Selbstkritik: Untersuchungen zur Philosophie des jungen Descartes*. Meiner.

Habermas, J. (1981). *Theorie des kommunikativen Handelns*. Suhrkamp.

Herder, J. G. (1881). *Eine Metakritik zur Kritik der reinen Vernunft*. Vol. 21 of *Sämmtliche Werke* (B. Suphan, Ed.). Weidmannsche Buchhandlung. (Original work published 1799)

Herder, J. G. (1987). *Werke, Vol. 2: Herder und die Anthropologie der Aufklärung* (W. Proß, Ed.). Wissenschaftliche Buchgesellschaft.

Küng, H. (1990). *Projekt Weltethos*. Piper.

Küng, H. (1997). *Weltethos für Weltpolitik und Weltwirtschaft*. Piper.

Lambert, J. H. (1764). *Neues Organon oder Gedanken über die Erforschung und Bezeichnung des Wahren und dessen Unterscheidung vom Irrthum und Schein*. 2 Vols. Wendler. (Reprint of Vols. 1 & 2 = *Schriften I & II*, Georg Olms, 1965.)

Lambert, J. H. (1771). *Anlage zur Architektonik, oder Theorie des Einfachen und des Ersten in der philosophischen und mathematischen Erkenntniß*. 2 Vols. Hartknoch. (Reprint of Vols. 1 & 2 = *Schriften III & IV*, Georg Olms, 1965.)

Lambert, J. H. (1918). *Über die Methode die Metaphysik, Theologie und Moral richtiger zu beweisen* (K. Bopp, Ed.). Kantstudien, Ergänzungshefte No. 42. Berlin. (Posthumous)

Lambert, J. H. (1965 ff.). *Philosophische Schriften* (H. W. Arndt, Ed.).

10 Vols. (Already published: Vols. 1-4, 6, 7, 9.) Olms.

Lambert, J. H. (1988). *Texte zur Systematologie und zur Theorie der wissenschaftlichen Erkenntnis* (G. Siegwart, Ed.). Meiner.

Leibniz, G. W. (1966). *Hauptschriften zur Grundlegung der Philosophie* (3rd ed., A. Buchenau, Trans., E. Cassirer, Ed.). 2 Vols. Meiner.

Leibniz, G. W. (1978). *Die philosophischen Schriften*, Vols. 4 - 7 (C. J. Gerhardt, Ed.). Georg Olms. (Rpt. of edition Berlin, 1880 ff.)

Leibniz, G. W. (1986). *Monadologie* (H. Glockner, Trans.). Reclam. (Original work published 1714)

Lemke, M., & Wiedemann, G. (2016). *Text Mining in den Sozialwissenschaften: Grundlagen und Anwendungen zwischen qualitativer und quantitativer Diskursanalyse*. Springer.

Mannheim, K. (1980). Eine soziologische Theorie der Kultur und ihrer Erkennbarkeit (Konjunktives und kommunikatives Denken). In K. Mannheim (Ed.), *Strukturen des Denkens* (pp. 155 - 322). Suhrkamp. (Original work published 1924-1925)

Popitz, H. (1999). *Phänomene der Macht* (2nd ed.). Mohr.

Ricken, U. (1990). *Sprachtheorie und Weltanschauung in der europäischen Aufklärung: Zur Geschichte der Sprachtheorien des 18. Jahrhunderts und ihrer europäischen Rezeption nach der Französischen Revolution*. Akademie-Verlag.

Schiewer, G. L. (1996). *Cognitio symbolica — Lamberts semiotische Wissenschaft und ihre Diskussion bei Herder, Jean Paul und Novalis*. Niemeyer.

Schiewer, G. L. (1998). "Exakte Wissenschaft" und natürliche Sprache: Zeichentheoretische Konzepte in den sprachphilosophischen Reflexionen Leibniz' und J. H. Lamberts. In L. Danneberg, J. Niederhauser (Eds.), *Darstellungsformen der Wissenschaften im Kontrast* (pp. 455-470). Narr.

Schiewer, G. L. (2005). Die Bedeutung von ars inveniendi und System-Begriff für die Ausbildung einer historisch-genetischen Sprachbetrachtung im 18. Jahrhundert. *Deutsche Vierteljahresschrift für Literaturwissenschaft und Geistesgeschichte, 79*, 29-63.

Schiewer, G. L. (2006). Der "Dialog der Kulturen" als Problem einer interkulturellen Kommunikationskultur: Anmerkungen zur Initiative der Vereinten Nationen. In W. B. Hess-Lüttich (Ed.), *Eco-Semiotics: Umwelt- und Entwicklungskommunikation* (pp. 371-394). Narr.

Schiewer, G. L. (2009). Der "Dialog der Kulturen" als diskurstheoretisches Problem: Zur Kontroverse von Jürgen Habermas und Joseph Kardinal Ratzinger um Wissenschaft und Religion. In S. Wichter & O. Stenschke (Eds.), *Wissenstransfer und Diskurs* (pp. 43-58). Transferwissenschaften Vol. 6. Peter Lang.

Schiewer, G. L. (2010). Der "Dialog der Kulturen" in der Diskussion: Grundlagen und Perspektiven internationaler Kommunikation in nicht-idealer Situation. In P. Hanenberg, I. C. Gil, F. V. Guarda, & F. Clara (Eds.), *Rahmenwechsel Kulturwissenschaften* (pp. 75-84). Königshausen & Neumann.

Schiewer, G. L. (2014). *Studienbuch Emotionsforschung: Theorien, Anwendungsfelder, Perspektiven*. Wissenschaftliche Buchgesellschaft.

Sen, A. (2006). *Identity and violence: The illusion of destiny*. Penguin.

Spinner, H. F. (1994). *Der ganze Rationalismus einer Welt von Gegensätzen: Fallstudien zur Doppelvernunft*. Suhrkamp.

Steck, M. (1977). *Der handschriftliche Nachlass von Johann Heinrich Lambert (1728-1777)*. Universitätsbibliothek Basel.

Ungeheuer, G. (1980). Lamberts semantische Tektonik des Wortschatzes als universales Prinzip. In G. Brettschneider & C. Lehmann (Eds.), *Wege zur Universalienforschung: Sprachwissenschaftliche Beiträge zum 60. Geburtstag von Hansjakob Seiler* (pp. 87–93). Narr.

Ungeheuer, G. (1987). Vor-Urteile über Sprechen, Mitteilen, Verstehen. In: J. G. Juchem (Ed.), *Kommunikationstheoretische Schriften I: Sprechen, Mitteilen, Verstehen* (pp. 129–143). Alano, Rader Verlag.

Zerfaß, A. (2006). *Unternehmensführung und Öffentlichkeitsarbeit: Grundlegung einer Theorie der Unternehmenskommunikation und Public Relations* (2nd ed.). VS Verlag für Sozialwissenschaften.

Conceptual and Thematic
Developments 2:

From African Interactions to "Where We're Going"

5

The Shadow Play of Intercultural Interactions in Africa: A Historical Perspective

Wim M. J. VAN BINSBERGEN
African Studies Centre, University of Leiden;
Erasmus University, Rotterdam

Summary: The concept of interculturality has often been used to denote the encounter or combination of more than one culture. Much of the anthropology of social organization since the 1960s has been preoccupied with a form of deconstruction of identity and ethnicity, "tribe," or "nation." For anthropologists (and for some historians of African ethnicity), African tribes, although dominating the societal thought of African actors, are recently invented traditions, impositions by bureaucrats, White entrepreneurs, missionaries, and European researchers. For analysts who bring to their work a different regional perspective than that of the North Atlantic region, such an approach often amounts to a self-sacrifice. Classic anthropology, with its genesis in a context of North Atlantic discovery, mercantilism, imperialism, and colonialism, and its preference during most of its existence for remote abodes of "otherness," has been predicated on a more or less absolute distinction between the researcher and the researched, reflected in that between emic and etic. Here an aporia arises, which standard social-science methodologies cannot solve and which makes the conceptualization of interculturality difficult. The chapter argues that cultural patterning typically addresses specific facets and spheres of a person's total life, and each of these orientations may have a different history and provenance: a person is usually at home in more than a handful of such orientations, and these are usually neither internally fully integrated nor mutually finely attuned. In Western thought, it is only recently that such post-structuralist concepts as *différance* and *differend*, and the elaboration of ternary and multi-value logics, have created a context where we can think beyond binary logic, to affirm interpersonal encounter despite different cultural orientations—where we can bring about interculturality.

Though I speak with the tongues of men and of angels, and have not charity, I am become as sounding brass, or a tinkling cymbal. (*1 Corinthians* 13: 1)

PART I. THEORY

1. Culture and Interculturality

1.1 A Few African Approaches to Interculturality

To approach the possibility of a dialogue among all cultures, let us listen to one of the most authoritative voices to speak of intercultural philosophy[①] from Africa, that of the celebrated Ghanaian philosopher Kwasi Wiredu:

Philosophical universalism means at least three things. First, philosophical theses are, as a matter of semantic fact, of a universal significance. Second, irrespective of their place of enunciation, they can, in principle, be understood and assessed by people in any part of the world provided, that they have the interest and the requisite abstract abilities. Third, philosophical dialogue is possible among the inhabitants of all cultures, and can be fruitful both intellectually and practically. (Wiredu, 1998, p.155)

---

① *Intercultural philosophy* is a relatively late scion on the tree of intercultural reflection. Somewhat older is comparative philosophy, which is a much more straightforward and unproblematic — but admittedly also less forward-looking — undertaking, in that it takes for granted the accepted corpora of regional philosophy (Indian, Chinese, Islamic, Western, African etc.) without seeking to transcend their difference or to amalgamate them. Cf. Bahm, 1977; Larson & Deutsch, 1989; Masson-Oursel, 1923; Radhakrishnan & Raju, 1960; Wiredu, 1984.

Yet Wiredu's immensely optimistic claim here is rather contentious. He defines philosophy as necessarily universal, hence philosophy's universal significance, communicability, and capability of being dialogued world-wide follows not as a claim to be ascertained (or possibly spurious), but *per definitionem*, hence *ipso facto* true. The refuge to universalism without stopping to consider the foundations for such universalism is, however, common among philosophers; it is also for instance manifest (and chided by me) in the work of the Congolese/American philosopher and novelist Valentin Mudimbe (cf. Van Binsbergen, 2005). We should carefully scrutinize the dimension of universalism, and that will be one of our concerns in this chapter.

Wiredu continues:

> I am not, however, predisposed to any wishful thinking regarding the prospects of interculturalism in philosophy. Although there are heart-warming signs of mounting interest in intercultural discourse in philosophy today [...], the enormity of the factors that hinder genuine intercultural dialogue is impossible to ignore or diminish. Even if we set aside moralistic considerations, such as the apparent tardiness of the West to accord dialogic charity and respect to Africa, there are conceptual confusions deriving from the imposition of Western categories of thought on African thought materials [...] Still, much is going to depend on how persuasive we, African philosophers, are going to be in presenting the African philosophic case for the edification of our own people as well as others. Such an enterprise cannot consist of just disseminating narratives of how various African peoples think but also developing arguments for the soundness or profundity of appropriate elements of the thought of our ancestors. That is the first part of the African philosophic task. The second part must consist of a synthesis of insights from all accessible cultural sources. That is an eminently intercultural project. (Wiredu, 1998, pp. 164–165)

I fear that such "a synthesis of insights from all accessible cultural sources" will be an unrealistic pipe-dream — without adducing any explicit grounds, it assumes uniformity and the possibility of mutual accommodation between the format and categories of human thought of all times and places, even if we confine "human" to "anatomically modern humans" — the variety that appeared on earth only 200,000 years ago and to which all humans living today belong.[2] Yet Wiredu's point concerning "conceptual confusions deriving from the imposition of Western categories of thought on African thought materials" is certainly well taken. That is not so rare among intercultural philosophers, from Placide Tempels trying[3] to capture the Luba (Congo and Zambia, South Central Africa) worldview through global philosophical discourse, to the more recent *Ubuntu* philosophers of Southern Africa,[4] who, highly trained in the North Atlantic academic philosophical tradition and no longer involved in any practical, day-to-day manner in a traditional African life-world, under the pretension of committed to writing a time-honored and all-encompassing oral philosophy of African village life, in fact nostalgically present a constructive social and ethical philosophy of their own invention (see Van Binsbergen, 2003).

1.2　The Recent Routinization of the Concept of Culture

How could I possibly resist and defy the common present-day belief that cultures exist to such an extent that interculturality is a matter of course? I have begun to suspect that, with the adoption into general and common language use, world-wide, "culture" has become a global and collective representation, supported by a widespread communicative network of ideological connections which have allowed the concept of culture to function as an ideological state apparatus (Althusser,

---

[2]　In recent decades, I have given much attention to the reconstruction of Anatomically Modern Humans' ancient modes of thought, initially through web page, later also in book publications (Van Binsbergen, 2009–2010, 2018, 2021a, 2022; Van Binsbergen & Woudhuizen, 2011). I have found these modes to comprise, among others, "range semantics," triadic thought, and cyclical element transformation. The central puzzle for these modes of thought appears to lie in the difficulty (also manifest in the Greek Pre-socratic philosophers, for whom we have extensive textual documentation, e. g., De Raedemaeker, 1953; Diels, 1964) of thinking unity and difference, or immutability and change, at the same time.

[3]　With considerable success, I would say — not only because of the persuasive internal consistence of *Bantoe-filosofie* (1946) but also because I am intimately familiar with an African worldview — that of the Nkoya of Zambia — that is closely akin (both in contents and in linguistic expression) to that of the Luba who were Tempels's interlocutors. I attribute the success to Tempels's intercultural knowledge and talent, especially if one considers that he was far from a trained philosoper and merely derived a superficial impression of Thomist philosophy from his education as a Roman Catholic priest.

[4]　For instance, Bewaji & Ramose, 2003; Bhengu, 1996; Boele van Hensbroek, 2001; Murithi, 2006; Ramose, 1999; and Samkange and Samkange, 1980.

1976; Geschiere, 1986; Gramsci, 1985) facilitating citizens' acquiescence vis-à-vis the state and its power elite. This is, of course, Karl Marx's juvenile adage in 1844: "Religion is the sigh of the oppressed creature, the heart of a heartless world and the soul of soulless conditions. It is the opium of the people" (1970, p.131).

An effort to deny the reality of cultures (not: of *culture*, singular, in the sense of cultural programming of individuals through a process of social communication) could be taken as a form of hubris of iconoclasm, rejecting a collective representation, therefore inviting strongly negative sanctions. In principle, similarly sacrosanct were once:

- The belief in God,
- The belief in the immutability and absolute nature of sexual difference,
- The belief in women's subservience and reproductive tasks,
- The belief in Black people's inability to invent on their own impetus, and to fully participate in White culture,
- The belief in Black people's inability at self-government, etc.

All these collective representations, once at the heart of a substantial body of then respectable writing, have now largely been rejected: in some cases (e.g., the belief in God) at considerable costs for societal normative integrating and for individual mental health, perhaps even doing violence to the truth, but at least upholding the relentless rationality that has formed the backbone of North Atlantic thought ever since the Enlightenment of the 18th century. ⑤

Although today raised to the status of a self-evident, universal

---

⑤ In my recent book *Sangoma Science* (2021) I remind the reader that such rationality is eminently predicated on the Aristotelian doctrine of the excluded third ("where P, there not not-P"), which is merely one of the many different types of logic possible. If one adopts an alternative position, notably one to the effect that all Being constantly oscillates between existence and non-existence (like a proverbial crew member beamed up successfully and integrally, or not, into a space craft — as in the TV series and motion picture *StarTrek* initiated by Gene Roddenberry), then the denial that God exists becomes just as meaningless as the affirmation of His existence. It may be possible, on such a basis, to design a wisdom philosophy (for first sketches, cf. Van Binsbergen, 2009, 2020a) which may also serve to accommodate and transcend the formal incompatibilities between rival cultural orientations. This train of thought is highly relevant in the present context of exploring African interculturality, since it was prompted by my own situation of finding myself caught between the incompatibilities of my habitus as both a North Atlantic scientist and a Southern African diviner-healer.

human given, yet the concept of culture in the sense of everything one learns as a member of one's society (Tylor, 1871, 1: 1) is a relatively recent[6] product of North Atlantic elite academic contexts, and as such it is likely to have built-in limitations, for instance hegemonic implications.

Classic, structural-functionally inclined anthropology (cf. Kroeber & Kluckhohn, 1952) produced a concept of culture (as bounded, integrated, conscious, coinciding with a population group and a language, reflecting a shared history, etc.) that has since been generally received, first in North Atlantic educated society, then worldwide, and today it is part of the standard conceptual toolkit of ordinary social participants. This has consequences for the continued viability of the term culture and for interculturality as a theoretical and academic concept. The concept of interculturality has often been implicitly predicated on such a naïve concept of culture, and is used to simply denote the encounter or the combination of more than one culture.

Much of the anthropology of social organization since the 1960s has been preoccupied with a form of deconstruction of identity and ethnicity, "tribe," or "nation" (cf. Helm, 1968) — my own skepsis vis-à-vis the concept of interculturality has been largely informed by the anthropological position. I have personally made significant contributions to that endeavor (Van Binsbergen, 1981, 1985a, 1997b, 2008), and that background has informed my reluctance to see interculturality as the interactions between *cultures*, plural. For anthropologists (and for some historians of African ethnicity), African tribes, although emphatically dominating the societal thought of African actors, are recently invented traditions, impositions by bureaucrats, White entrepreneurs, missionaries, and European researchers; hence little more than reified forms of *false consciousness*[7] meant to create imaginary token identities that should divide Africans and keep them from developing a unifying class consciousness. The standard example would be South Africa under apartheid, where the White-dominated, racialist state did everything, including the creation of pseudo-states in the form of Bantustans, in order to reinforce the divisive tribal illusion — which is still the scourge of a majority-ruled South Africa thirty years later.

---

[6]   For a very condensed overview of the history of the concept of culture, cf. Perpeet, 1976; Van Binsbergen, 2003, pp.472–473 (and references cited there).

[7]   Friedrich Engels, Letter to F. Mehring, in Marx and Engels (1949, 2: 451).

For analysts who bring to their work a different regional perspective than that of the North Atlantic region, such a distancing approach to accepted African identities is sometimes impossible, or rather unaffordable. Thus, among my African Ph. D. students, Dr. Julie Ndaya-Duran, a Congolese student of the Congolese women's Christian prayer group "Le Combat Spirituel," despite my insistence could not bring herself to totally distance herself from the emic position (to be discussed below), even though her research amply brought to light the occasionally manipulative, exploitative, and ideological aspects of that group (Ndaya Tshiteku, 2008). By the same token Dr. Pascal Touoyem, a Cameroonian studying ethnicity in Africa and himself strongly identifying with the Bamileke ethnic group, could not be persuaded to adopt the deconstructive model for his approach to African ethnicity, and as a result created considerable difficulties for himself in the supervision and defense of his Ph. D. thesis (2014). For these African colleagues, yielding (in what was effectively, given the hierarchical organization of academia, a situation of unequal interculturality) to the North Atlantic scholarly pressure toward deconstruction of collective representations that they perceived as eminently African and with which they identified, would have amounted to open and public betrayal of their own conscious identity, and that price they understandably found too high to pay.

Nor was it necessary to pay that price. As we shall see, the etic (implicitly *othering*) perspective in transcontinental knowledge formation is only one side of the medal: it must be complemented by the emic perspective which (because of the assumption of a fundamental, underlying unity of humankind) implicitly contains the promise of mutual understanding and accommodation, even without going to the extreme of self-sacrifice through existential betrayal. It is remarkable that many aspects of interculturality are not consciously perceived by the actors involved. This is a large difference from ethnicity, which exists on the basis of these actors' conscious distinctions, "naming and framing."

Streamlining in nostalgic representation is also part of the artificial creation of culture. Performativity and virtuality are closely related (cf. Van Binsbergen, 1997a, 1998, 2001, 2015 [Ch. 1]). As already referred to above, a common thread connects the early attempts at systematization and codification of African thought by Tempels (1946) and the Rwandan philosopher, Kagame (1955), via codifications of African socialism by the African state presidents

Kaunda (1971) and Nyerere (1962), to Ubuntu philosophy. The process is as inspiring as it is alienating from whatever authentic tradition and practice has ever existed on African soil.

If we wish to create clarity about the concept of interculturality, we have no option but to offer a formal definition of culture. Also, on that basis we can attempt to delineate the difference between culture and ethnicity. In that connection, we can think of:

- a cultural orientation,
- acquired by a social communicative process (in other words, it is not innate, not genetically determined), [8]
- so deeply programmed into the human person that it is almost impossible to shed or to negotiate, and resulting in such perceptions of the world (or rather, such world-creating perceptions) as, to the actor involved, are self-evidently true,
- yet of limited scope, and situational, therefore an individual may combine several such orientations through life, often even in the course of one day;
- situationality, which means that culture (in the sense of cultural orientation) is only partial; as a result culture is not closed into itself, not bounded, not integrated, not easy to determine, nor does it coincide with the conscious distinctions which the actor herself makes about her life world and its central concepts.

In other words: historically influenced *cultural orientations* may exist, may be piled one on top of the other, may interact; but (as a refrain to which we shall gradually develop a counterpoint as the present argument proceeds) *cultures* do not exist. [9]

---

[8] Some cultural contents (e. g. lithic techniques in the Palaeolithic and basic narrative complexes as reconstructed by comparative mythology) have been found to display surprisingly large intertia, in other words, they stay more or less unaltered, recognizable across millennia, even tens of millennia. This is surprising because one might expect them to have been victims of cultural drift and free variation, changing them beyond recognition within a few centuries. The psychoanalyst Carl Gustav Jung claims that their inertia has a hereditary basis in the so-called collective unconscious, but this explanation is highly contentious, especially in anthropology, which is predicated on the tenet of the learned nature of all cultural orientations. Cf. Van Binsbergen, 2022, #11.3.

[9] This was the state of my thinking, and the title of my Rotterdam inaugural address, in 1999, when (having so far mainly identified as a social scientist with a sprinkling of linguistics, religious studies, history, and archaeology, and a fair helping of poetry) I had just exchanged my Amsterdam chair in the anthropology of ethnicity (see next page)

2. The Anthropological Approach

A number of features characterize modern anthropology, with its historical dimension, as a mode of knowledge formation:

1. An accepted tradition of coherent theory, which is so deeply ingrained in the beginning student that it is hard to shed later in one's career[⑩]
2. Fieldwork as the principal method of intercultural knowledge construction
3. The distinction between emic and etic (with the underlying implication of an absolute difference between the researcher and the researched).

It is points 2 and 3 for which a separate discussion follows.

2.1 Fieldwork as a Form of Intercultural Knowledge Construction

Much has been written on fieldwork as the privileged anthropological mode of intercultural knowledge construction. [⑪] What is often overlooked is that, beyond the one-way observation, interview, and eavesdropping in which the researcher's sense form is the active instrument, fieldwork also encompasses a unique two-way validation, in which the researcher humbly submits to the host community:

> The more the fieldworker is defenceless, the more devoid of personal and state-supported North Atlantic hegemonic protection, the more isolated from her home background, the stronger the social control that the participants can exert on her, and the

---

(continued)for the Rotterdam chair of Foundations of Intercultural Philosophy. I can now substantially qualify the adage "cultures do not exist." If (as I propose in my 2021 book on Sangoma science, and in my various shorter texts on wisdom (2009, 2020a)) everything constantly oscillates between Being and Non-Being, even cultures may yet exist despite their theoretical undesirability; so do tribes, nations, etc.

⑩ Cf. "Half a century ago I received a very long and intensive training as an empirical social scientist"; since then I have grown aware that "in the last analysis the conceptual and interpretative initiative lies, not with the anthropologist, but with the competent local socio-cultural actor" (Van Binsbergen, 2015, p.38).

⑪ A blatantly arbitrary selection may include for instance De Lame, 1997; Devisch, 2006; Epstein, 1965; Jongmans & Gutkind, 1967; Kamler & Threadgold, 2003; Van Binsbergen, 2003.

more massive the flow of information. [...] (Van Binsbergen, 2003, pp.496-497)

2.2   Emic and Etic

The distinction as proposed by Kenneth Pike between "an internal structuring of a cultural orientation such as is found in the consciousness of its bearers, on the one hand, and, on the other, a structuring that is imposed from the outside" has enabled a codification of "the two-stage analytical stance (both *etic* and *emic*) of the classic anthropology that had emerged in the second quarter of the twentieth century with such proponents as Malinowski, Evans-Pritchard, Fortes, Griaule and Leiris" (Van Binsbergen, 2003, pp.22-23).

For the analyst, notably the intercultural philosopher, one of the crucial issues is: to what extent can we adopt the emic perspective of modern world citizens and consider cultures and their boundaries as real and given — and to what extent must we adopt a distancing, etic view, which deconstructs culture (and interculturality), and seeks to expose it as a nostalgic construct essentially serving the status quo? In the last few decades, a number of approaches (attracted by the lure of a promise of harmony, non-violence, non-exclusion, and equality) have proceeded to discuss interculturality without considering this question.

Classic anthropology, with its genesis in a context of North Atlantic ages of discovery, mercantilism, imperialism, and colonialism, and its preference (during most of its existence prior to the last half century) for remote abodes of (conceptual, cultural, identitary, linguistic, religious) "otherness," has been predicated on the more or less absolute distinction between the researcher and the researched. This distinction is also reflected in the distinction between emic and etic. Here an aporia arises, which standard social-science methodologies and binary logic have not been able to solve — so that interculturality appears theoretically impossible. Let us take a closer look at this aporia.

2.3   An Epistemological Approach to Interculturality

Underlying the question as to the possibility or impossibility of interculturality is a fundamental consideration of epistemology, to which we shall now briefly turn. As we have seen, culture may be defined as a person's sense of (largely conscious) conceptual, linguistic and motoric orientation, which (through interpersonal processes of communicative learning especially prior to adolescence) has been programmed so deeply and so effectively that it is usually very hard for that person to ignore or relinguish such an orientation. On the other hand, the general rhetoric according to which "a" culture contains "a total way of life" enabling one to live one's entire lifespan within it from the cradle to the grave tends to be grossly exaggerating, even essentially wrong: cultural patterning typically addresses specific facets and spheres of a person's total life, and each of these orientations may have a different history and provenance. A person is usually at home in far more than a handful of such orientations, and these are usually neither internally fully integrated nor mutually finely attuned.

For instance, the cultural orientation toward tenderness, altruism, generalized reciprocal exchange and non-violence that in many societies is expected to attend the domain of close kin relations may be very well combined with violence, cruelty, and insensitivity in dealings with non-kin, within a formal organization or in cash economy, etc., and yet may exist side-by-side in the person of a soldier, a cattle-raider, or a *mafioso*. Joseph Stalin was reputedly a tender father; Adolf Hitler was famously courteous to German women classified as Aryan, but sent 3 million Jewish women to their (usually unmarked and collective) graves. And even Barack Obama, in most respects the opposite of Hitler, and himself the deserving role model of billions of Black and post-colonial peoples, and in general of well-intending world citizens *tout court*, despite being a champion of the democratic rule of law, yet allowed Osama bin Laden to be summarily executed on the spot without the slightest form of trial.

Nor is this contradiction peculiar to statal politics in the modern world. It has a counterpart among the Nkoya people of Zambia and other African contexts. Among the Nkoya, the ideal of intimate, caring, generous relationships between close kinsmen at the village level absolutely prohibits all overt expressions of violence (usually people take the way out of resorting to invisible, immaterial violence, viz., to magic). With the many occasions for rivalry and friction owing to diminishing resources from the soil and the forest yet sky-rocketing prices for commodities, school fees, transport and other present-day requirements, the village headman's main task of peace-keeping is rendered even more difficult because he lacks all formal sanctions. In compensation, Nkoya life has traditionally comprised several domains in which violence could be manifested:

not only the covert forms of magical violence, but also intergroup violence between clans and especially between kingdoms; detection and lynching of witches as intra-group enemies; and, focusing on royal capitals, the institution of slavery, originally of a somewhat mild nature (as pawnship after manslaughter, whereas at the annual royal harvest festivals slaves would be immolated) — then from the 18th century CE (with the penetration of mercantilist long-distance trade including slave trade) the Nkoya notions of kinship would be so much eroded that royals would sell their very own sister's sons into slavery.

Another example: urban society, in Africa and elsewhere, contains numerous people from numerous different ethnic backgrounds who may each believe themselves to represent a different ethnic culture. Yet that is only a very partial culture, attending to family life, life crisis ceremonies, evaluations in the personal sphere, and selected token ethnic markers such as circumcision, facial tattoos, and the like. Outside the sphere of the family, urbanites, regardless of their ethnic cultural background, share a common cultural urban orientation. This allows them to cross the street safely, take a bus, use money and credit cards, shop in a supermarket, operate a bureaucracy, operate the Internet, a cell phone, a TV set, a motor car — and by and large, despite the predictable emphasis on their being different, to the extent to which they are urban they are monocultural instead of multi-or intercultural.

What a cultural orientation does is create a sense of self-evident reality (we might as well say: create a self-evident reality, *tout court*) in which a person's perceptions, evaluations, and actions no longer have to be shaped by her or him from scratch and in full deliberative consciousness, but may comfortably become ready-made, automated, and beyond moral censure. Thus a person is, among other things, a rough bundle of scarcely integrated or accommodated cultural orientations; and so are her friends and neighbors, in such a way that the greater the social, demographic, and geographic distance between two persons, the greater the likelihood that their respective bundle of cultural orientations has a strikingly different composition, and is also perceived as different. By a rather confusing usage, which is responsible for a proliferation of unjustified claims in terms of interculturality, modern discourse speaks of " a culture " (e.g., North Atlantic urban culture, Yanamamo culture, or Nkoya culture, as distinct from "culture" in the sense of cultural orientation) in reference to a social domain in which a significant portion of most individual persons' respective cultural orientations tends to converge. Since such "a culture" has largely a statistical and ephemeral, situational existence, to conceptualize their interaction as "interculturality" would be rather unconvincing.

As professor of intercultural philosophy (Rotterdam, 1998 – 2006, and until 2011 as far as doctorates were concerned), I interpreted my task primarily as *investigation of the possibility of interculturality*. This proved a major challenge in its own right, and my answer was largely negative. Examined merely at the abstractly theoretical level, I found interculturality to be a nostalgic, hegemonic, and politically suspect illusion. I summarized the epistemological reasoning that led me to this position in terms of the definition of knowledge as "justified true belief."[12] But if we think that this definition offers us a criterion to distinguish between valid knowledge and its deceptively spurious rivals, we are mistaken. All three criteria in the above knowledge definition, "justified," "true," and "belief," are merely cultural, whose applicability in concrete cases cannot be determined from first principles alone (as in some universal logical or mathematical rules) but must be evaluated by the specific application of the cultural orientation the person in question happens to be following as a result of the socio-cultural communicative processes to which she has been subjected throughout her lifetime. In other words, what a cultural orientation does is to create specific truth provinces, each peculiar to a particular cultural orientation. Within this truth province, a particular propositional claim may be justifiably found to be true, but between two such truth provinces, each constructed by a different cultural orientation, a commonality of truth may be neither established nor expected. Strictly speaking, interculturality is, from this perspective, a mere illusion, an impossibility.

If each cultural orientation then appears to create its own universe constituting its own truth province — outside of which truth cannot exist and cannot be transmitted nor appreciated — culture would seem to be fundamentally incommunicable.

2.4 The Myth of the Excluded Third and of Logical Consistency

The myth which this heading specifies goes back to Aristotle (*Metaphysica* IV.4, 1006b and following; IV.7, 1011b), as far as the Western tradition is concerned. In many ways Aristotelian rationality allows

---

[12] For this, see Austin, 1988; Gettier, 1963; Lehrer, 1979; Lowy, 1978; Moser, 1993; and Müller, 1889.

us to respond adequately and pragmatically in our interaction with the non-human world (which therefore can be argued to display a structure similar to that of our binary logic, most of the time and at the meso[13]-level of our conscious human interaction with it). Yet we cannot close our eyes to the fact that, in the interaction between human individuals and between human groups, the same logic incessantly creates intransigent positions of recognized and emphasized difference which cannot come to an agreement since both sides, by their own logic, are justified to consider themselves right, whereas their respective truths are mutually incompatible and in conflict.

The main conflicts in our globalizing world of today (e. g., those between North Atlantic military capitalism on the one hand, and militant Islam on the other hand, as rival paths through modernity; those between economic short-term maximizing globalism and a future-orientated ecological responsibility; those between consumption on the one hand, and integrity and global solidarity on the other hand; between state-monopolized, protective socio-political order and organized crime) remind us of the potentially paralysing and destructive implication of such consistency. In Western thought, it is only recently that such post-structuralist concepts as *différance* and *differend* (Derrida, 1967, 1974), and the elaboration of ternary and multi-value logics, have created a context where we can think *beyond* binary logic, can affirm interpersonal encounter despite blatantly different cultural orientations on either side — in other words, where we can bring about *interculturality*.

Thus we meet an aporia which we cannot overcome in the context of anthropology alone: if cultures do not exist, and if the differences between rival, confronting cultural orientations have to be approached with an intransigent Aristotelian logic of non-compromise, there is no conceptual space left within which interculturality might be confidently situated. Yet many millions of people in the world today believe in interculturality and expect the world from it — fortunately, for without an understanding between warring constituent groups at the

---

[13] I take the meso-level of phenomena to be that of our normal Galilei-Newton world, at the order of magnitude of the human body: i. e., 100^0 (= 1) metres. At very much higher and very much lower orders of magnitude (galaxies, elementary particles), the self-evidences of our Galilei-Newton world dissolve, and the apparent paradoxes and wonders of the theories of relativity and quantum mechanics replace the (appearance of the) transparent logical structure and the object-subject distinction of the meso-level world, bringing out the restrictive boundary conditions of the latter.

local, regional, and global level, humanity would be rapidly heading for extinction. Obviously the way out lies in taking a relative view of the anthropological heritage, even if we are not prepared to give up that discipline's accomplishments so easily.

2.5 How to Overcome the Aporia Which Has Arisen?

Explicitly, deliberately, and exclusively adopting the etic perspective may be considered a form of *analytical violence*. The very act of fieldwork consists, even for a die-hard anthropologist, of blending both emic and etic perspectives. For the historian (especially relevant for our topic focus) the situation looks less bleak, so that the task at hand appears to be manageable and capable of being accomplished.

The interlocking, often heterogeneous and usually scarcely integrated strands of cultural orientations that make up a person's (or a group's) life world need not be articulated by the actors in terms of distinct, consciously constructed, and consciously maintained boundaries. Usually these strands are not named, and their boundaries are fluid and fluffy. Nonetheless, the socio-political space in which people live their life world tends to consciously perceived by the actors as an internally structured space — structured in terms of explicitly named and demarcated constituent parts (even though such demarcation is not always totally consensual among the people involved, nor totally consistent). It is illuminating to call the constituent parts "ethnic groups," and their explicit definition and structural accommodation in space and time, "ethnicization."

In this perspective, ethnicity is simply the structuring of the largest socio-political space (the international order, sometimes just the nation-state) in terms of explicitly named and more or less consensually distinguished constituent parts. In post-colonial Africa, ethnicization has been the dominant form for the articulation of higher-level structural units, and hence the major form the expression of identity has taken. Articulating the higher-order political space, situating individuals and groups there, and justifying such distinctions often by reference to history or to some invented tradition has been the major form of political ideology in modern Africa, where distinctions in terms of class have remained weakly developed. Religious affiliation tends to be linked to regional origin since missionary bodies, in Christianity especially, have tended to concentrate on particular geographic spots in the wider socio-political space, expressing such articulation through the use of a particular local language for intra-group communication and for the translation of sacred texts. Framing and naming are thus recognized as among the principal mechanisms of ethnicization.

With the rise of the (or rather, "a" — notably, a highly manipulable, strategic, and exploitatble) concept of "culture" to prominence, not only in the world of social science but even in the local and regional emic discourse (as part of the world-wide response to major processes taking place during the last few decades: globalization, massive transcontinental migration, and the installation of a multicultural ideology in the North Atlantic region), many have tended to conflate "ethnic group" and "culture." This process was aided, in modern Africa, by the fact that the same type of conflation was at work in post-Enlightenment Europe of the 18th and 19th centuries CE, when a particular mystique of "the people" (*das Volk /le peuple, die Nation/la nation*) was claiming a "natural" coincidence between territory, language, identity, the sense of a shared collective past, the possession of a specific historical destiny, and... *culture* (supposed to converge for all adults living in the extended socio-political space in question). In this perspective, one can understand how *intercultural* increasingly became an ideological, mobilizing, and nostalgic blanket term for the accommodation of cultural aspects of more than one nation.

It would seem, then, that our aporia cannot be overcome in an anthropological perspective alone, as long as this presupposes the extreme *othering* of the other about whom we seek intercultural knowledge. But there are other possibilities.

While widely adopted among anthropologists, the distinction between emic and etic (and much of the theoretical framework that has informed it) is habitually shunned by modern historians, precisely in order to avoid the *othering* that lies at the root of emic/etic, and in order to create some kind of fusion between researcher and the researched.[14] Whereas anthropology is predicated on an implied absolute distinction between the researcher and the researched, each with their own conceptions and implied worldview, the hallmark of the historian, on the other hand, is to try to operate at the interface between the here and now (when and where the historiography takes place), and in the researched context of historical action and belief. In the hands of the historian, concepts that are being used by the historical actors (such as "state," "witchcraft,"

---

[14] I have advocated a similar fusion for the study of myth (Van Binsbergen, 2022, Ch.3).

"god," "justice") are not translated into some purportedly cultureless and abstract *etic* term, but are taken on organically, in the endeavor to produce a historiographic text that blends *etic* and *emic*. For sub-Saharan Africa, I can think of no better examples than the work of the late lamented Terry Ranger, whose impressive powers of imagination, evocation, and political identification with the African peoples as well as his inimitable writing style allowed him to write excellent African historiography (Ranger, 1967, 1970, 1972, 1975, 1985) even if he did not command a single African language (beyond his own native English), and was incomparably more at home in university departments and at Christian mission stations than in African villages.

The anthropologist turning to the analysis of interculturality emphatically considers it a handicap when she finds out that "cultural" and "intercultural" have become emic concepts consciously and explicitly used by the actors themselves. However, for the historian, such a finding would be a blessing, a confirmation that the historical research is on the right track.

What then is the experience of fieldwork? After often cumbersome and even desperate beginnings, most fieldwork projects, if persevered in, ultimately seem to yield valuable knowledge across the boundaries of the research host's and the researcher's respective cultural orientations. A number of significant insights come to the fore here:

- Unity and continuity, even if impossible to achieve with verbal means because of the acquired academic inclination to apply a binary Aristotelian logic, may yet be found at the level of *action*, when unity of purpose may overrule discord of theoretical position.
- It is possible to live an alien truth even if (at the conscious level) the person involved may be emphatically conscious that subjectively, and against that person's original cultural orientation, that alien truth is very likely just an untruth. ⑮

---

⑮ This has often been my experience as a religious anthropologist, ever since my first fieldwork (on popular Islam in North-western Tunisia, whose experiential aspects I have described in Van Binsbergen, 2003, Ch. 1, and my novel of 1988), right through to my work on urban Christian churches especially in Lusaka (1972-1973); on the *Bituma* cult of the Zambian Nkoya people (1972-present); on oracular shrines and local ethnopsychiatry among the Manjacos of Guinea-Bissau, West Africa (1981-1983); and on the *Sangoma* cult in Francistown, Botswana (1988-present). In the field, the flow of information and insight is largely dependent on the research hosts' perception of the fieldworker's wholehearted engagement, so that as I rule I acted as I had been told by my teachers of anthropological fieldwork and danced, (see next page)

- For the approach to interculturality we need a special, non-binary logic, otherwise we cannot even temporarily reconcile contrasting truth provinces.

Under specific conditions, might different truth provinces yet be accommodated, and tolerate each other to exist side by side, even to interpenetrate? I would suggest two:

- When verbalization (which is highly culture-specific and group-specific) is kept at a minimum, as in music, silence, or prayer.
- When there is a strong positive sanction favoring cultivated tolerance, and against the articulation of difference.

In my passionately personal study of ecstatic religion (Van Binsbergen, 2021b) I have explored some of the conditions under which conceptions of reality and truth totally different from Western mainstream academic thought could be entertained, especially a rejection of Aristotle's logic of the excluded third (= "where P there not not-P"). I would stress the need and the possibility of "epistemological charity" (Lepore, 1993; Malpas, 1988; McGinn, 1977), which means: coming to a realization of the effect of "who am I to reject this belief which to many others is not only plausible, but absolutely true?" It is

---

(continued) sang, prayed, sacrificed, killed animals, received and ultimately gave oracles, displayed at least the outward signs of trance — in short, went through the motions with increasing expertise, so that finally at the level of publicly perceptible behavior I could hardly be distinguished any more from the locals. Initially I was very much aware that I was merely pretending to be a believer in the local collective representations, and I hated myself for my professional lack of integrity. Over the decades, however, this antagonistic "othering" attitude on my part gave way to a more accommodating stance, when I realized that

- various forms and levels of skepticism may also have been the covert conviction of some of the local actors themselves (as they did occasionally intimate to me);
- the level of unanimity and agreement among these actors only needed to be limited to whatever beliefs they would articulate publicly, while behind that public façade enormous variations in conceptions, images, and even in acceptance were to be suspected (and sometimes even manifested in private interviews);
- even in my conscious mind I would not remain so deeply convinced of the non-existence of the invisible beings locally venerated as collective representations — speaking and thinking gradually about them became an idiom, a shorthand mediating my implicit intercultural adaptation — to such an extent that after half a century I am still observing the cult of one Tunisian saint, and sacrificing on my personal *Sangoma* altar on my home premises in the Netherlands.

time to incorporate this more lenient and less antagonistic perspective in the conception of interculturality which I would endorse.

The possibility and desirability of interculturality are widely posited, and my own lifelong experience as a fieldworker is that, at the subjective and personal level, intercultural knowledge formation is possible without any doubt.

2.6 My Personal Path Through Interculturality

To my embarrassment, I must admit that, whatever my theoretical distrust of the concept of interculturality, I personally seem to be the very embodiment of the possibility of at least some form of interculturality. As outlined in an earlier manner (Van Binsbergen, 2015, p.428), I was trained at the Municipal University of my home town in the Netherlands as an anthropologist specializing in religion. From my first fieldwork (1968), when I investigated saint worship and the ecstatic cult in rural North Africa, I have struggled with the problem of *the truth of the others' belief* — which I am inclined to consider as the central problem of interculturality. With gusto I participated in rituals, yet in my ethnography I reduced the same people to numerical values. I gradually began to realize that I loathed the cynical professional attitude of anthropology, and I had increasing difficulty sustaining that attitude. In Guinea-Bissau in 1983 (again as outlined earlier in Van Binsbergen, 2015), I did not remain the mere observer of the oracular priests but I became their patient — as nearly all the born members of the local society were. In Francistown, Botswana, from 1988, under circumstances which I have discussed at length elsewhere (Van Binsbergen, 2021b), the usual professional routine for fieldwork became so insupportable to me that I had to throw overboard all methodological considerations. I became not only the patient of local diviner-priests (*Sangoma*s), but at the end of a long local therapy course I ended up as one of them, and thus as, officially and publicly at least, a believer in the local collective representations.

At the time (1990, the very year when the South African freedom fighter Nelson Mandela was released after decades of incarceration) I primarily justified my "Becoming a Sangoma" (Van Binsbergen, 1991) as a political deed, for me as a White man in an area which had been disrupted by monopoly capitalism and by nearby South African *apartheid*. Later I came to realize that it was also and primarily an epistemological position-taking — a revolt against a professional hypocrisy in the hegemonic perspective of anthropology. It was a position which created the conditions for the step which I made when occupying my chair in intercultural philosophy.

Beyond the subjective and necessarily limited lessons of such a strictly personal and, admittedly, exceptional account, we should consider a number of more systematic reasons to regain trust in the possibility and factuality of interculturality.

- In the first place, the intransigence of the Aristotelian rule of the excluded third does not constitute the only logic that is possible. Ternary, multiple, fuzzy, and wisdom logics have been proposed and may give us tools to strike a viable, sociable, and peaceful compromise between the (non-)truth of the other and the (non-)truth of ourselves. At the back of the problematic of interculturality, with its historical dimension, stands not only the concept of culture but also the notion of " inter ": this has been subjected to several discussions in recent postmodern writing, as in the work of the Dutch intercultural and aesthetic philosopher/"ecosophist" Henk Oosterling (2003, 2004, 2005).

- In the second place we may mention the claim of the fundamental unity of humankind, which I have elaborated in other contexts (as in Van Binsbergen, 2015, pp. 8-9). The logical irreconcilability of specific and rival cultural orientations, hence the enormous difficulty of transmitting truth across historically evolved cultural boundaries, may be abstractly argued, yet we may be confident that deep down we all share, as humans, or at least as Anatomically Modern Humans, a commonality that ultimately makes it possible to recognize each other as fellow human beings with similar emotions, thoughts, vulnerabilities, and strengths. The same body (perhaps to be usefully distinguished as male and female for a minority of situations and contexts) means that we can recognize and feel empathy with suffering, physical effort, illness, physical strength, endurance, concupiscence, and take a sometimes profound interest in each other.

- Then, in the third place, we may find inspiration in the critique of logocentricity, which has been a particularly valuable contribution from post-modern philosophy (Derrida, 1967, 1974). Although words are the scholar's main tools, and in general the writer's, the poet's, the myth-maker's, the diviner-healer's, the prophet's — yet words, like alcoholic drink, have the tendency to destroy more than they can heal or conceal. In significant ways, explicit and articulate language is the enemy of interculturality. Why should it be that in prayer, music, [16] the visual arts, or architecture, the apparent cultural boundaries seem to fade more easily than in verbal communication, while true interculturality seems to lie around the corner? An illuminating consideration could be that there is not a single human product that is so utterly patterned, structured, and sanctioned (at the price of unintelligibility, or evident marking as incompetent outsider — in other words exclusion) as language is, hence non-verbality has a great advantage when it comes to crossing cultural boundaries.

• As a fourth consideration: while I have often feared fieldwork as the most oppressive, most difficult thing in my life's experience, yet I have always engaged in it with gusto and a sense of great fulfillment — as if the sheer Promethean attempt to cross boundaries in the pursuit of intercultural knowledge allows me to fulfill the destiny of being human. [17] Fieldwork is actually very dear to me as an inveterate, multiple, and practically world-wide practitioner; I should mention the effort criterion as a touchstone of genuine interculturality. As I outlined in an earlier manner, some work in intercultural philosophy has appeared as being little more than North Atlantic navel-gazing, as when "a European philosopher ignorant of the practice and texts of Buddhism in Japanese, Chinese, Pali etc." comments in a Western language on "the English-language paraphrases of Zen Buddhism as available in the American writings of Daisetz Teitaro Suzuki [1870–1966]" (Van Binsbergen, 2015, p.45).

My earlier conclusion, then, that interculturality is impossible because it rests on the popularization of an ill-taken concept of culture is in itself premature, myopic, hegemonic, desperate, and (if it ran any chance of being taken seriously) potentially destructive

---

[16]   Hebert, 2001; Van Binsbergen, 2015. In my piece on Islam (1999b) I reverse the perspective, and see present Islam as a vehicle for the articulation, transmission, and even the creation of African traditions as in the musical domain.

[17]   My late lamented friend Renaat Devisch has touched on this point in a moving article on the psychoanalysis of the intercultural encounter in fieldwork (Devisch, 2006). However, the psychoanalytic dimension in anthropological fieldwork also has another side. As I have pointed out in reflections on my own fieldwork in Botswana (Van Binsbergen, 2003, 2021b), the researcher, however determined to be objective and scientific, is likely to occasionally succumb to personal projections in which the unresolved conflicts in her own psyche (usually springing from childhood trauma) attach themselves to the field experiences at hand.

of humanity's future. [18]

We have only implicitly considered what would have been a fifth consideration: the anti-hegemonic orientation of true interculturality. The East Asian writer Hwa Yol Jung has sought to capture this element in the concept of transversality, which counters ethnocentrisms and thus turns against Eurocentric universalism: "The intellectual propensity of Western modernity legitimizes itself as the privileged epicenter of the historical telos of the entire globe" (Jung, 2011, p.8).

The social science of Africa, given its 19th-century origin, has been hegemonic, even implicitly racialist, and we should take care to prevent it from reverting to that condition. Let us loosely define hegemony as the frame of mind, and the resulting practices and institutions, which take for granted and seek to perpetuate and to reinforce the existing geopolitical inequalities in the world. Profoundly aware of the historically hegemonic and globalizing tendencies in the Early Modern and more recent history of his motherland, Fernando Ainsa (University of Zaragoza) offers an inspiring approach to hegemony and globalization:

> Beyond the initial excesses that occur in all conquests, the colonization of America introduced innovative variety and unexpected adaptations and metamorphoses to the inequalities and asymmetries that separated the conquerors from the conquered. (Ainsa, 2006, p.40)

Recalling the "brutal experience of world-ization embodied by Spain's conquest and colonization of America" as well as the ensuing

---

[18] From 2005 I have frequented Cameroon, and there (in addition to the Western Grassfields and the wider Burea region) especially the Université Yaounde I. In 2006, at the invitation and under the chairmanship of my friend and colleague Dr. Godfrey Tangwa, I offered a seminar in the Department of Philosophy on the epistemology of intercultural philosophy, in which essentially the same reasoning on the basis of the standard definition of knowledge formed the core of an argument as to the impossibility of interculturality. I am grateful to Dr. Tangwa for pointing out the inadequacy of that argument. I take this opportunity to express my debt also to my dear colleague and friend Sanya Osha, who from the early 2000s has been an inspiring critic of my work; to my dear former student Pius Mosima, who has developed a most illuminating critical light on my work; and to my wife Patricia van Binsbergen-Saegerman, who shared my research and writing struggles and triumphs over the past 39 years and who was my sparring partner in many conversations preparatory to the present argument. It is fitting that I should also mention my first wife, the late lamented Henny van Rijn, who contributed much to our first spell of Nkoya fieldwork (1972-1974) and to my scientific thinking in the first phase of my career, as well as our daughter Nezjma.

"*mestizo* phenomenon and the birth and evolution of new cultures" enables us, for our time, to envision "an intensified intercultural dialogue and new forms of cultural interchange" (Ainsa, 2006, pp. 40, 42).

This is a perspective rather in line with the approach in my present argument: interculturality lies not only in the interaction between people and groups in the present-day world, it also points to a particularly fertile context of continuity, hybridization, innovation, and transformation which typically arises as a result of historical processes leading toward globalization, and in which not purity but hybridity, and not firm boundaries but porous ones, as well as continuities and boundary crossing take precedence.

Even if we accept the possibility that fieldwork might be a valid and reliable mode of intercultural knowledge production, the above considerations (especially the effort principle, but also the trap of hegemonic Eurocentrism) make it necessary to try to identify the specific conditions under which fieldwork might be particularly successful at yielding intercultural knowledge. But even if an entire discipline pretending to cater for intercultural knowledge is built on such a methodology, we must still ask (a) whether its claim to constitute a form of interculturality is well founded, and (b) if so, under which conditions such interculturality in fieldwork may be achieved. These conditions are not exactly secret:

- A broad and profound general and practical knowledge of the socio-cultural situation at hand, built up over many months of personal exposure;
- Considerable mastery of the local language(s);
- Probably most important, extensive and sufficiently empowered feed-back mechanisms in the contact between the researcher and representative members of the community at hand, so that the local and competent cultural owners can exercise a fair measure of control over the representations that are committed in writing by the ethnographer, and the latter while in the field cultivates a receptive humility. ⑲

---

⑲　I have explained above how anthropological fieldwork in itself is predicated on the principle of daily, extensive feedback from the host community, but that in itself is not sufficient to satisfy the requirement of informant empowerment. It was not among the formal fieldwork lessons I received at Amsterdam University in the (see next page)

The overwhelming characteristic of successful attempts at intercultural knowledge construction through fieldwork is that they require a great and prolonged personal, existential effort on the part of the fieldworker.[20] Valid intercultural knowledge cannot be had cheaply nor superficially. The trouble with many purportedly intercultural claims today, worldwide, is that they are made too facilely, shunning the hard work of interculturality (or letting someone else do that work). Philosophers who have engaged in the codifying of so-called "sage philosophy" in Africa (e.g., Oruka, 1990; for a critical treatment see Mosima, 2016) often try to do so without stopping to consider the methodological requirements for fieldwork as a valid and reliable strategy of intercultural knowledge acquisition. European philosophers approaching Japanese Zen Buddhism, African notions of time, or the West African Dogon worldview not on the basis of personal and extended exposure and participation but through mere library study, and who yet make claim to being intercultural philosophers, have not engaged in an intercultural, but in a Eurocentric and hegemonic exercise, and their claims may do damage to the very cause of interculturality.

In the work of interculturality, boundaries are created and affirmed at the same time as they are being transcended. Interculturality is not

---

(continued)1960s, and by consequence did not play a role in my writings on North Africa. The condition can hardly be met in the common situation ("There And Back Again" — the title which Tolkien invented for Bilbo Balins's book on his travels in Middle Earth, and which I put to good use in my 1979 polemics on fieldwork with Sjaak van der Geest, a. k. a. Wolf Bleek) when the fieldworker returns to her distant home after one major spell of fieldwork, writes her ethnographic publications, and is never seen in the host society ever after. Cultivating an enduring, increasingly close relationship with the Nkoya people across over half a century has enabled me to organize the informant feedback condition in a rather fortuitous manner: in the years when I was writing my book *Tears of Rain* (published 1992), I was in constant epistolary contact (e-mail was not yet an option) with an active group of educated Nkoya, who checked the details (including English translations) of my texts and steered them in the right direction. Of course, such involvement came at a certain price: the members of my local reading committee themselves had obvious interests in regional ethnic dynamics and their textual representation. Yet juggling between conflicting local partisanships is a ubiquitous aspect of fieldwork anyway.

[20] Remotely, we are reminded here of Freud's (1940) emphasis on "dream-work" as the central transformation that produces dream images out of the processing of (especially sub-conscious) experiences and the conflicts they have left. But in intercultural work, the vector is different: the culture worker is working consciously, facing the contradictions between cultural orientations and seeking to overcome them selectively in compromise.

about the absence of boundaries, but about the charitable negotiation of boundaries.

At this point, most of the theoretical baggage which we need for a pathway through interculturality in Africa may be considered to be in place. It is time to proceed to Part Ⅱ. Here the approach will be as eclectic and selective as it has been in Part I, as massive aspects of the descriptive phenomena at hand will necessarily remain outside our scope. I will simplify the complex situation (complex also because of the tangle of theoretical and methodological dimensions indicated in Part I and also by the dangers of Eurocentrism and hegemonism) by assuming that between Africans themselves, especially in the national socio-political space, what we mainly see is interethnic exchanges; these are rarely intercultural because largely the same or converging cultural orientations may be assumed to underlie much of African social life, especially within the socio-political space of present-day nation-states. Likewise, in the consideration of such transcontinental influences as could be said to amount to interculturality in Africa, I simplify matters by paying attention only to one-to-one interactions (African-European, African-Mediterranean, African-Indian, and others), without venturing into a consideration of the obvious extensions of this pattern where all the various elements of interaction criss-cross one another on African soil. My perspective on African life is overwhelmingly from the local, African-centred situations which I have gotten to know through prolonged personal fieldwork, and while I do not deny the importance of other possible considerations, I lack the data to discuss them with any degree of authority and detail.

PART Ⅱ. GLIMPSES OF INTERCULTURALITY IN THE AFRICAN CONTEXT

1. Focus on Africa

The conceptualization of the overarching socio-political space is a prime task in the study of interculturality, especially regarding Africa. The effort, over the past sixty years, to understand and deconstruct African emic conceptions of socio-political space in terms of tribe, ethnic group, and culture, has been part of that task. Here I find it important to proceed from an essentializing approach to African ethnicity (in the sense that tribes are taken to be the present-day remnants of once viable, pre-conquest major socio-political units)[20] toward a more sociological one: in post-independent African states, the widest socio-political space is emically though consensually divided up into a relatively small number of sub-national, named, bounded units, and these are called "tribes" or ethnic groups. They may constitute a context for the continued, but now encapsulated, exercise of traditional leadership in the hands of chiefs — once more or less independent kings.

> While theorists of cultural pluralism have generally supported tribal sovereignty to protect threatened Native cultures, they fail to address adequately cultural conflicts between Native and non-Native communities, especially when tribal sovereignty facilitates illiberal or undemocratic practices. (James, 1999, p.57)

Michael James then argues that the subaltern institutions of tribal sovereignty contribute to "the fair discursive conditions required for mutual learning and mutual critique in an intercultural public sphere" (James, 1999, p.57). That sphere needs further scrutiny.

With our focus on interculturality in Africa, we can only cast faint light on the study of African post-conquest transformations since the late 19th century — a roller-coaster of social and political change whose study and documentation have filled entire libraries and have been the specialist province of African studies, with thousands of researchers world-wide and its own specialized scientific journals, associations, and research institutions. Partly because of huge theoretical and methodological advances booked in adjacent fields of study (e.g., the study of urban society, globalization, migration, and ethnicity), we have progressed considerably since the second quarter of the 20th century, when most of Africa was still under European-dominated colonial rule and the study of "culture contact in Africa" was the overarching term in which most of the Africanists of the first hour (including Mair, 1938; Malinowski, as in 1939, 1943; and others) made their mark. Given the bureaucratic format of the colonial state, it imparted the basic assumptions of its territorial organization to lower-level institutions in Africa, and these received ample attention from researchers from the beginning.

As an example of the structuring of socio-political space against the background of local cultural, identitary, and linguistic inputs, I

---

[20] This contention was already contested, rightly, by Colson (1968); see also Abolurin & Owolabi (2003).

will now present a case study of a rural area in Western Zambia —
the region of the Nkoya people with whom I have been closely
associated for the past 50 years. It is to reinforce my repeated
assertion, above, that ethnic and linguistic fragmentation at least in
Zambia (but to my understanding much further afield, throughout
South Central Africa and possibly throughout sub-Saharan Africa)
does mean emic classification but not interculturality in a strict
sense, because the units thus emically distinguished basically all share
in the same cultural orientations.

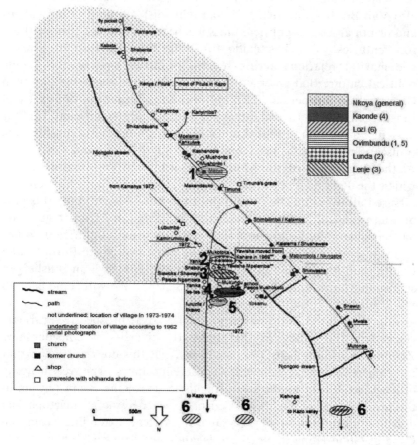

Figure 1

Linguistic-ethnic diversity in the valley of Njonjolo,
Kaoma District, Zambia, 1973–1974
(Originally published in: Van Binsbergen, 2021a, p.210;
courtesy of Shikanda Press)

2. Ethnic Diversity and Aspects of Tradition

2.1 Linguistic Micro-diversity, Ethnic Fragmentation, and Underlying Continuity of Culture: The Njonjolo Valley

As explained similarly in a previous study (see Van Binsbergen, 2021a, pp.209-211 for the following account), the Njonjolo valley in Western Zambia has been one of my principal fieldwork sites (see also Van Binsbergen, 1981). Geographic displacement of individuals and of kin and socio-political units has been a dominant feature there for centuries. This has made for a far-flung pattern of kinship and marital relations across several countries sharing the Lunda political culture that emerged in the course of the second millennium CE (cf. Van Binsbergen, 1992a). As I have argued previously (Van Binsbergen, 2020a), and as appears especially significant for our present discussion, the Lunda complex displays considerable transcontinental influence from South, South East, and East Asia. As the target area of the south-bound vector of the cross-model by which the Pelasgian substrate complex from the Mediterranean was diffused all over the Old World since the Late Bronze Age, this part of South Central Africa, like much of sub-Saharan Africa in general, has considerable socio-cultural continuity with significant other regions, especially the Mediterranean, West and North Europe, and Central and East Asia (see Van Binsbergen, 2011b; Van Binsbergen & Woudhuizen, 2011, Ch.28.9, pp.373-374). We will come back to this, below.

In the later 20th century, non-Nkoya prospective farmers flocked to the valley so that linguistic diversity is considerable. Zambia as a whole boasts 72 languages, yet this does not mean that for Zambia we must reckon with 72 different cultures. The great majority of languages belong to the same linguistic stock (the Bantu phylum as the main branch of the Niger-Congo or Niger-Kordofan macrophylum which comprises most of sub-Saharan Africa, extending from the Cape of Good Hope to Northern Uganda and Senegal), even though they are often not mutually understandable. Their basic lexicon (including their kinship terms and the 100 words of the basic Swadesh list) is convergent, and the historically informed socio-cultural and religious life is informed largely by a common Niger-Congo cosmology centering on horticulture, small-scale animal husbandry, puberty initiation, kingship, ancestor veneration, spirits of the wild, and belief in sorcery. It would be misleading to equate linguistic or ethnic diversity with cultural diversity.

Although specifically selected cultural traits (such as language use, circumcision, specific musical and dancing forms, and style of kingship) may be stressed by the local actors as public markers of their diversity (for which they scarcely distinguish, at the explicit and conscious level, between linguistic, ethnic, and cultural diversity), it is true to say that Zambia, and by extension South Central, Southern, and Central Africa may be considered one huge cultural area — in which interculturality manifests itself, not so much in the interethnic exchanges between Africans, but in transcontinental cultural orientations as largely brought by mercantilism, colonialism, and globalization.

2.2 European/African Interculturality in a Cultic Context

Continuing our eclectic exploration of interculturality in Africa, we might discuss the effect of urbanization as one of the most significant transformations over the past century. Here of course the study of formal organizations (including churches and ethnic associations as the main forms of African self-organization), ethnicity, the rise of formal and especially informal commercial enterprise, the growth and contestation of urban norms, of "urbanism as a way of life" (Wirth, 1938), and of virtualization of the relations with the rural village home and its productive and reproductive concerns (Van Binsbergen, 2015, Ch. 1; also 1997a, 1998) has received ample attention from researchers. As a focus of interculturality we could briefly consider a rural cult of affliction, which I have studied from 1972 onwards both among the Nkoya urban migrant minority in Lusaka, and in the Nkoya area of origin, 400 kms west of Lusaka.

2.3 Tradition and Western Propriety

While South Central African women have historically honored a custom of approaching a sacred site with bare breasts, a custom prevalent in rural areas in the early 1970s, in towns by this time women had grown conscious of people not belonging to their own ethnic group and region and would call out " Zikomo, Bambo/ khalani chete/tikupemphera pano" (Please sir, be quiet, we are praying here). Non-traditional codes of propriety, imposed by Western education, had thus grown into a basic rule of urban life as in Zambia (for this description, see Van Binsbergen, 2021b, p.202).

2.4   Tradition Goes Underground

In the mid-1970s, my ethnographic research in Lusaka was partly conducted in response to a remark in 1969 by Elizabeth Colson (for decades the grand old lady of Zambian anthropology, succeeding Audrey Richards) in passing that, given their originally rural locus, cults of affliction (dealing with occurrences of affliction such as disease)[22] were not being performed in the Zambian cities. However, when one and a half decades later I shifted my research site to the booming city of Francistown, Botswana, I did encounter a situation as claimed by Colson: a city full of Africans most of whom had been born in neighboring villages, but who had apparently not bothered to bring their rural religious practices (and beliefs) into town. Although I was an experienced anthropologist of religion, and living with my family in the midst of a popular African compound, all I could see was Black urbanites going to their work, their shopping malls, their churches — but apparently not engaging in any time-honored local religious tradition. Yet patience, the trust of some of our research hosts,[23] and our good fortune enabled us to cross the strong boundaries

---

[22]   A cult of affliction (for which see Carter, 1972; Turner, 1968; Van Binsbergen, 1981 with extensive references) is a ritual and doctrinal complex in which new adepts are recruited through diagnosis and healing, gradually proceeding from novice adepts to leadership. Coming from the Indian Ocean region, ultimately at home perhaps in South East Asia, such cults have rapidly spread all over South Central Africa from the 19th century onward. In ways beyond our present scope, in the Nkoya versions of these cults all sorts of transcontinental resonances are manifest, e. g., Buddhism and Sunda expansion.

[23]   When in the mid-1980s, as head of political science and history at the Leiden African Studies Centre, I had launched a departmental research program with focus on Southern Africa (rendered topical by the imminent transition to majority rule), it had been obvious for me to heed the invitation of my close friend and colleague Richard Werbner, Manchester, and to shift my personal fieldwork site from Zambia to Francistown, Botswana. Richard had done extensive rural fieldwork among the Kalanga people of Zimbabwe and Botswana, had become an authority on the region's dominant Mwali cult, and we had collaborated on the wider study of regional cults (see Werbner, 1977). His former research assistant, Timon Mongwa, had made the grade as entrepreneur and as mayor of Francistown, and greatly facilitated our family's stay and my research. But none of this, not even Werbner's personal visit to Francistown in spring 1989, helped to break through the veil of dissimulation surrounding rural religious traditions in town. The *Sangoma* cult, which my wife joined eight months after our arrival, only to be followed by me within a year, formed a different case for this as it was locally perceived as an alien, recent introduction mainly from Nguni-speaking regions, not continuous with current village cults in the immediate surroundings of Francistown.

surrounding the domain of local traditional cults in town. I have interpreted such cults' initial invisibility in town as an inhibition interculturally imposed by the cultural dominance of nearby White, still apartheid-based, South African society.

3. Transcontinental Continuities

3.1 Interculturality in Botswana: A Culturally Contested Space

As described in an earlier context (Van Binsbergen, 2015, p.101), in Francistown, Botswana's second largest city with a population of well over 60,000 Botswana nationals of Black African background and a few thousand Whites, there are a large number of different African Christian churches at work (see also Van Binsbergen, 1990). Ancestral spirits would be mediated to the globally informed church environment in very muted form, and a public production of African cultural tradition is usually anathema within the urban environment so that traditional culture has gone underground. The population is massively involved in healing churches, yet rival therapeutic institutions are available (herbalists and spirit mediums); ethnicity plays a role in this, since the Kalanga minority constitutes a challenge to Tswana majority hegemony. Yet many churches are bilingual or trilingual in their ritual practice, and apart from ethnic overtones in inter-church conflicts many services have simultaneous translation into Tswana, Kalanga, Ndebele, and other relevant regional languages.

3.2 The Musical Sphere as a Context for Interculturality

In the theoretical discussion of Part I, I have briefly indicated how non-verbality as in the musical sphere may be capable of braving cultural boundaries which at the verbal level cannot be surmounted. The musical sphere is the domain of widely recognized excellence of the Nkoya people. Interculturality here works in a number of ways: it breaches the otherwise rather impenetrable ethnic and linguistic opposition between the Nkoya and the Lozi people during the past hundred years, but it also testifies to the unexpectedly rich and diverse transcontinental past of Nkoya music, a past that seems to be the principal key to understanding the continued dominance of Nkoya music in the region.

The following developments have been described in an earlier manner, now adapted for this chapter (see Van Binsbergen, 2015, pp. 159 – 160). For the larger part of the past 150 years, the dominant Lozi (a. k. a. Barotse and Luyi) were the ethnic group in control of the Barotseland traditional administration, with the Nkoya subaltern and subservient. Up to the 1980s the latter were considered a despised minority also in the Zambian towns.[24] Yet supposedly "Lozi" court music, its song lyrics and its very performers, have been of Nkoya origin. This development cannot be adequately accounted for from regional and historical dynamics within South Central Africa, and my research during the past two decades into sub-Saharan Africa's transcontinental continuities (Van Binsbergen, 2017) is able to offer an answer.

The Lunda cluster of states to which the Nkoya and the Lozi belong, commonly held to have come into being in the mid-2nd millennium CE, appear to originate in a South Asian-derived, largely Buddhist-informed state system that exercised a greater or lesser degree of control in South Central Africa in the late 1st and early 2nd millennium. An influence on this South Central African state complex appears to have been "Shivaite Chola princes taking refuge when their South Asian empire collapsed" by the 14th century (Van Binsbergen, 2015, p. 160); these princes had elaborate orchestras. This musical tradition has given legitimacy to the South Central African state system and its rulers. A number of Nkoya names such as Shikanda,[25] Mangala, Kola, the word *mukupele* for "hourglass drum," and others are closely comparable to South Asian languages (see Van Binsbergen, 2015, p. 160). A study of mythology, moreover, yields evidence of South Asian and specifically Buddhist, Hindu, and Chola influence upon South Central Africa in the 1st and

---

[24] I have elsewhere described the process by which the Nkoya after initial rejection have gradually responded favorably to state penetration and opted to participate in the state's and the ruling party's representative and legistlative institutions (cf. Doornbos & Van Binsbergen, 2017; Van Binsbergen, 1986).

[25] Shikanda, from Skanda/Karttikeya/Murugan/Subrahmanya, the South Asian war god whose name is often associated with that of the Macedonian king Alexander the Great/Iskander, who — in the legendary footsteps of the Greek god Dionysos and pharaoh Sesostris/Senwosret (I / Ⅲ) — reached India in the late 4th century BCE. Like (a) the Ancient Egyptian gods 𓅃 Horus, 𓏏𓆑 Tefnut, and 𓈙𓅱 Shu and (b) like humanity as a whole in the Zulu cosmogony (Colenso, 1855b, pp.239–240; see also 1855a), Skanda was reputedly born in a thicket of reeds (hence the epithet *Saravanabhava*), and his name has the same meaning in Sanskrit, "soaring high," as that of the legendary Nkoya prince Luhamba in Nkoya. Yet the name Shikanda can also be given a local etymology, "pertaining to the Mukanda male puberty/circumcision rite" (cf. Crowley, 1982; Turner, 1967, pp.151–279; Van Binsbergen, 1993).

early 2nd millennium CE (see Van Binsbergen, 2022, pp.555-556). Beyond this, it has turned out to be possible to find remarkable parallels between Chinese traditional (i.e., Taoist) pharmacopoeia and that of "diviner-healers in Southern Africa"; evidence has also been explored for African influences on East Asia under the Tang dynasty and again in the Early Modern period (recorded in Van Binsbergen, 2017, pp.370, 393).

3.3 Ethnicization, Streamlining, Virtualization in Africa Does Not Preclude Cultural Identity

What took relatively long to register with European researchers, and to be problematized as a major form of innovation on African soil, was the increasing dominance of formal organization also outside the governmental sphere in the narrower sense. The ubiquity of the formal organization in Africa (as in the North Atlantic region from the beginning of the Common Era and especially from Early Modern times) in such major spheres as the state, the economy, formal education, religion, medical care and recreation means an incessant element of interculturality between Africa and the North Atlantic region since Early Modern times (cf. Van Binsbergen, 1985b, 1993). In this connection we should pay attention to the many forms of *hybridization*[26] which are characteristic regarding this point, and which in the last few decades have often been discussed under the heading of *globalization*.

As part of my sustained study of the Nkoya people and their ethnicization, I have repeatedly (1992a, 1997b, 1999a, 2003, 2011a, 2015: Ch.1) looked at the process of transformation brought about by the framing of Nkoya cultural orientations in the context of the Kazanga Cultural Association. That organization had been founded by a Nkoya elite of relatively affluent town dwellers in Lusaka, and elsewhere in the urbanized region called the Line of Rail in central Zambia, for what they have nostalgically cherished (but largely without their personal participation and continued belief) as "our traditional culture." The format, inspiration, goals, priorities, and forms of leadership were all products of interculturality,

---

[26] So-called corruption, i.e., the instrumental use of roles and prerogatives within modern formal organizations for personal or parochial group purposes that have not been stipulated by that formal organization (but that often have been inspired by more local and time-honoured values, goals, and roles, such as kin obligations), forms a relatively well-studied aspect of such hybridization.

and made for a radical format change underneath which the original cultural orientations could scarcely be recognized. Yet the villagers eagerly and massively participating in the annual Kazanga Cultural Ceremony at the heart of Nkoyaland did not mind the transformation (if they noticed it at all consciously), and celebrated the diluted and greatly transformed results as if these were the real thing. The explicit purpose of the festival is intercultural: to present Nkoya identity to the non-Nkoya majority of Zambians and thus to gain political recognition and access by an eminently modern strategy of multicultural politics (for which see Taylor, 1992). The performative repertoire of the Cultural Ceremony is not commodified, so that there is little reason to be cynical about "the globalising erosion of the symbolic and ethnic domain" (Van Binsbergen, 2015, p. 165).

3.4 Format Change Toward Interculturality: The Globalizing Virtualization of Nkoya Spirituality

Above I have spoken of cults of affliction being staged in the 1970 urban environment of Zambia, where their performance is considerably informed by ultimately European norms of propriety as mediated interculturally. When we shift the focus to rural Nkoyaland, and inspect the entire time-honored local religious sphere, the accommodation to transcontinental intercultural conditions becomes even more manifest (for the following, see Van Binsbergen, 2015, p. 277). While traditional spiritual complexes make up the religious life world of the Nkoya people, many who now identify as Nkoya have undergone considerable Christian influence; what is more, in the 18th and 19th centuries Islamic Swahili long-distance traders left some cultural traces. [27]

---

[27] For a discussion of these traces, see Van Binsbergen (2015, pp. 277 – 278). They are mainly to be found in the so-called "material culture" — use of cast-iron cauldrons, muzzle-loading guns, and calico textiles — the latter especially as ancestral offerings at graves. Over the decades, I have detected no overt traces of Islamic influence; before the 20th century part of the Nkoya did practice male genital mutilation ("circumcision": Van Binsbergen, 1993), but not as a result of recent Swahili Islamic influence. Yet some individuals, like many other Bantu-speakers, show an aversion to eating pork, which may be related. Meanwhile, from 1900 on this trait has become a distinctive ethnic marker by which the non-circumcising Nkoya distinguish themselves from the circumcising but otherwise rather closely related neighboring ethnic groups such as the Luvale, Munda, Lunda, and Chokwe. The originally Islamic/West Asian geomantic divination (originally known as ʿilm al-raml, "sand science," which on the wings of Islam spread all over Southern and South Central Africa, also penetrated to Western Zambia, but I have never seen it practiced among the Nkoya.

In terms of the Cultural Ceremony as already discussed above, its globally derived format is non-local and hence devoid of its localizing exclusivity; all people attending are forced into a vicarious cultural insidership. The essence of the virtualization is that original insiders are turned collectively into outsiders, banned from the original spiritual scenario. ⊗

3.5 A Long-Range, Global Perspective as a Possible Background to Interculturality

While cults of affliction largely appear to be a relatively recent, 19th-century phenomenon (see also White, 1949), female puberty rites (as thematized in Van Binsbergen, 2021b, pp.187–188) have a global distribution that goes back to prehistoric times. In this context we can compare the 1972 work of Americanist Morris Opler on Apache girls' puberty rites. Such rites thus offer a case of long-range interculturality which comes close to affirming the fundamental unity of humankind, testifies to all kinds of intercultural continuities and exchanges, and allows us to regard Africa and its inhabitants as very much part of a wider world. The Apache female puberty rites are very similar to those found in South Central Africa (see Van Binsbergen, 2009–2010, pp.260–261). Such parallels may be merely coincidental, though they can be traced also for matters of divination, myth, gaming, basketry, and fishing techniques; yet we should bear in mind the phenomenon that in the Upper Palaeolithic of Central to East Asia the peripheral branches of Proto-Austric, Proto-Amerind, and Proto-African languages existed side by side sharing, to a considerable extent, a common culture of hunting and gathering. Cultural transfer across the seas, in this case the Atlantic, has been rejected (see Ortiz de Montellano, 2000); nonetheless it may yet turn out to constitute an explanation for these African-North-American continuities.

3.6 Forms of Interculturality between Southern and South Central Africa and the Ancient Mediterranean

Our final descriptive piece suggestive of long-range interculturality

---

⊗ Such as was fully accessible to me during prolonged field-work in the 1970s, long before the initiation of the Kazanga Cultural Society with its re-invented Kazanga Festival and the attending virtualization discussed above, when the Nkoya musical and dancing repertoire was still in place and informed rituals and celebrations often on a weekly basis.

focuses again on ritual forms in South Central and Southern Africa, especially the ecstatic *Sangoma* cult into which I was initiated in 1990 and which has given me privileged access, as a fieldworker and as a colleague, to otherwise sheltered information. Here again we see the most extensive lines of intercultural continuities across virtually the entire Old World, since at least the beginning of the Common Era.

Until the 19th century, the main sources of information on occult phenomena outside the North Atlantic were traveler's accounts, and particularly the writings from and concerning Graeco-Roman antiquity. On the latter we are extensively informed (for instance Dodds, 1951). Only since the early 19th century did Bronze-Age accounts of Ancient Egyptian and Mesopotamian "magic" come to broaden the scope of our insight into occult beliefs and practices of the Western "Old" World.

The topic is too broad to do justice to in mere passing, but a few pointers may suffice to indicate its importance. A crucial factor is that, in Africa, many magical and occult practices have a more or less acknowledged background (Becker, 1913) in Islamic secret sciences which, flourishing in West and South Asia in the late 1st and early 2nd millennium CE, were in fact highly continuous with Graeco-Roman approaches, and often preserved these in Arabic versions when the original Greek texts had gone lost. But there are also indications of even older connections. The pathbreaking work of Dierk Lange (2004, 2011, 2012) has proved beyond doubt the cultural and demographic continuity between Ancient Mesopotamia (especially the Assyrian empire of the 7th–6th centuries BCE) and West Africa. Other suggestions of continuity between the Ancient Near East (including Egypt) and sub-Saharan Africa may be found in the aftermath of the Sea Peoples episode, which by the end of the Bronze Age in the Mediterranean (ca. 1300 BCE) brought a wide variety of peoples on the move, some of which passed via Egypt into the Sahara and West Africa — constituting the southbound branch of the "cross model" identified for the Pelasgian demographic and cultural extension (Van Binsbergen, 2011b; Van Binsbergen & Woudhuizen, 2011, with extensive references). Other indications are few and far between, yet well worth considering. When describing in unique detail the traditional pantheon of the Tswana people of today's Botswana and South Africa (local knowledge of which had otherwise been largely eroded and disappeared by the turn of the 20th century), the missionary J. T. Brown in 1926 sketched a detailed array of deities which displays parallels with ancient Graeco-Roman religion, Yoruba religion in West Africa, and perhaps even more strikingly with the religion of the ancient Near East.

The god of divination turns out to be Nape — we can compare the ancient Mesopotamian god of wisdom ✳ ⊁⧻ Nabu, which is the etymon of the standard word for prophet in Hebrew and Arabic *nabī*, but which also seems to surface in western West Africa as the term *napene* for oracular priest (Van Binsbergen, 2017, p. 288). Turning to a setting with which I have considerable direct experience: even though the far more extensive South and East Asian continuities in the present-day *Sangoma* cult are rather more conspicuous (see Van Binsbergen, 2003, 2020b, 2021b), yet the *Sangoma*s also display two traits by which they are reminiscent of late Graeco-Roman antiquity:

- Especially in private conversations among themselves (accessible to me through participant observation), they consider themselves to be "gods" (Tswana: *badimo*) — a trait detected in ritual leaders of South Asian Hinduism (Van der Veer, 1988), but also in Hermeticism: "equal yourself to god" (cf. Ferguson, 2003; Quispel, 1992).
- *Sangoma*s (and other magical practitioners in South Central *and* Southern Africa) seek to entrap spirit familiars — for instance by luring and locking them into honey-covered containers placed near fresh graves — so as to make them their magical servants in the execution of their occult transgressions. These are greatly feared practices which have been discussed under the heading of necromancy (e.g., Van Binsbergen & Wiggermann, 1999).

The Pelasgian hypothesis (Van Binsbergen, 2011b; Van Binsbergen & Woudhuizen, 2011), with its claim of dispersion of a specific cultural package from the Late-Bronze-Age Mediterranean in all directions including across the Sahara, offers a potential mechanism by which such transcontinental continuities may be explained, even though they go against the grain of transcontinental *othering* characteristic of mainstream geopolitical thinking since the 19th century.

4. Conclusion

With these extensive examples of interculturality in the African context, we might hark back to a principle that crucially and arguably informs all interculturality: the fundamental unity of humankind (see also Monroe, 1996). If we question "the subordinating nature of North-South knowledge formation" (Van Binsbergen, 2020b, p. 24), we will be inclined to pay attention to African philosopher Kwasi Wiredu, who has been weighing the issue of cultural universals against particulars (1996; see also Eze, 2001 on a post-racial future). This has a strong historical significance:

> In philosophy the idea of humanity and the theoretical and conceptual elaboration of its unity has received extensive attention. With St. Paul, and again prompted by the mounting proto-globalisation in the Roman Empire in the first century CE, Christianity took a radical distance from the parochialism of Judaism. [...] The Paulinian idea did inspire Western philosophy with the idea of the fundamental unity of humankind, which [...] was elaborated especially from Johann Gottfried Herder on. (Van Binsbergen, 2020b, pp. 35 – 36)

References

Abolurin, J. A., & Owolabi, K. A. (2003). Fictional tribes and tribal fictions: Ethnicity, ethnocentrism, and the problem of the "other" in Africa. *Identity, Culture and Politics: An Afro-Asian Dialogue*, 4(1), 85–108.

Ainsa, F. (2006). The destiny of utopia as an intercultural and mestizo phenomenon. *Diogenes*, 53(1), 31–43.

Althusser, L. (1976). *Positions*. Editions Sociales. (Originally published 1970)

Aristotle (1831). *Aristoteles Graece*, I-V (I. Bekker, Ed.). Berlin: Reimer.

Austin, D. (Ed.). (1988). *Essays presented to Edmund Gettier*. Kluwer.

Bahm, A. J. (1977). *Comparative philosophy: Western, Indian and Chinese philosophies compared*. University of New Mexico Press.

Becker, C. H. (1913). Neue Literatur zur Geschichte Afrikas. *Der Islam*, 4, 303–312.

Bewaji, T. J. A. I., & Ramose, M. B. (2003). The Bewaji, van Binsbergen and Ramose debate on ubuntu. *South African Journal of Philosophy*, 22(4), 378–415.

Bhengu, M. J. (1996). *Ubuntu: The essence of democracy*. Novalis.

Boele van Hensbroek, P. (Ed.). (2001). African Renaissance and ubuntu philosophy. Special issue of *Quest: An African Journal of Philosophy*, 15.

Brown, J. T. (1926). *Among the Bantu nomads: A record of forty years spent among the Bechuana, a numerous & famous branch of the Central South African Bantu, with the first full description of their ancient customs, manners & beliefs*. Seeley, Service & Co.

Carter, M. (1972). Origin and diffusion of Central African cults of affliction.

Paper read at the conference on "The History of Central African Religious Systems," Lusaka.

Colenso, J. W. (1855a). Elementary grammar of the Zulu-Kafir language. London: Richard Clay.

Colenso, J. W. (1855b). Ten weeks in Natal: A journal of a first tour of visitation among the colonists and Zulu Kafirs of Natal. London: Macmillan.

Colson, E. (1968). Contemporary tribes and the development of nationalism. In J. Helm (Ed.), Essays on the problem of tribe: Proceedings of the 1967 annual spring meeting of the American Ethnological Society (pp. 201–206). University of Washington Press.

Crowley, D. J. (1982). Mukanda: Religion, art and ethnicity in West Central Africa. In S. Ottenberg (Ed.), African religious groups and beliefs: Papers in honor of William R. Bascom (pp. 206–221). Archana Publications for Folklore Institute.

De Lame, D. (1997). L'étude anthropologique comme rencontre interculturelle: Une expérience rwandaise. Bulletin des Séances. Académie royale des Sciences Outre-Mer (Belgium), 43, 495–510.

De Raedemaeker, F. (1953). De philosophie der Voorsocratici. Standaard.

Derrida, J. (1967). L'écriture et la différence. Editions du Seuil.

Derrida, J. (1974). Of grammatology (G. C. Spivak, Trans.) Johns Hopkins University Press. (Originally published 1967)

Devisch, R. (2006). A psychoanalytic revisiting of the fieldwork and intercultural borderlinking. In J. Mimica (Ed.), Explorations in psychoanalytic ethnography, Theme issue Social analysis, 50(2), 121–147.

Diels, H. (1964). Die Fragmente der Vorsokratiker, Griechisch und Deutsch. Vol. 1. Weidmannsche Verlagsbuchandlung.

Dodds, E. R. (1951). The Greeks and the irrational. University of California Press.

Doornbos, M. R., & van Binsbergen, W. M. J. (2017). Researching power and identity in African state formation. UNISA Press.

Epstein, A. L. (Ed.). (1965). The craft of social anthropology. Social Science Paperback/Tavistock.

Eze, E. C. (2001). Achieving our humanity: The idea of the postracial future. Routledge.

Ferguson, E. (2003). Backgrounds of early Christianity. Wm. B. Eerdmans.

Freud, S. (1940). Traumdeutung. In A. Freud et al. (Eds.), Gesammelte Werke: Chronologisch geordnet (Vols. 2/3, pp. 1–642). S. Fischer. (Originally published 1899)

Geschiere, Peter L. (1986). Hegemonic regimes and popular protest: Bayart, Gramsci and the state in Cameroon. In W. M. J. Van Binsbergen, F. Reijntjens, & G. Hesseling (Eds.), State and local community in Africa (pp. 309–347). Cahiers du CEDAF, 2–4.

Gettier, E. (1963). Is justified true belief knowledge? Analysis, 23, 121–123.

Gramsci, A. (1985). Selections from cultural writings (D. Forgacs & G. Nowell-Smith, Eds). Harvard University Press.

Hebert, D. G. (2001). The Tokyo Kosei wind orchestra: A case study of intercultural music transmission. Journal of Research in Music Education, 49(3), 212–226.

Helm, J. (Ed.). (1968). Essays on the problem of tribe: Proceedings of the 1967 spring meeting of the American Ethnological Society. University of Washington Press.

James, M. R. (1999). Tribal sovereignty and the intercultural public sphere. *Philosophy & Social Criticism*, *25*(5), 57–86.

Jongmans, D. G., & Gutkind, P. C. W. (Eds.). (1967). *Anthropologists in the field*. Van Gorcum.

Jung, H. Y. (2011). *Transversal rationality and intercultural texts: Essays in phenomenology and comparative philosophy*. Ohio University Press.

Kagame, A. (1955). *La philosophie bantu-rwandaise de l'être*. Académie royale des sciences coloniales.

Kamler, B., & Threadgold, T. (2003). Translating difference: Questions of representation in cross-cultural research encounters. *Journal of Intercultural Studies*, *24*, 137–151.

Kaunda, K. D. (1971). *Humanism in Zambia and a guide to its implementation*. Zambia information services.

Kroeber, A. L., & Kluckhohn, C. (1952). *Culture: A critical review of concepts and definitions*. *Peabody Museum of Archaeology & Ethnology, Harvard University* (*47*, 1).

Lange, D. (2004). *Ancient kingdoms of West Africa: Africa-centred and Canaanite-Israelite perspectives*. Röll.

Lange, D. (2011). Origin of the Yoruba and "The Lost Tribes of Israel." *Anthropos*, *106*, 579–595.

Lange, D. (2012). The Assyrian factor in Central West African history: The reshaping of ancient Near Eastern traditions in sub-Saharan Africa. Paper presented at the International Conference "Rethinking Africa's transcontinental continuities in pre-and protohistory," African Studies Centre, Leiden University, April 12–13, 2012.

Larson, G. J., & Deutsch, E. (Eds.). (1989). *Interpreting across boundaries: New essays in comparative philosophy*. Motilal Banarsidass.

Lehrer, K. (1979). The Gettier problem and the analysis of knowledge. In G. Pappas (Ed.), *Justification and knowledge* (pp. 65–78). D. Reidel.

Lepore, E. (1993). Principle of charity. In J. Dancy & E. Sosa (Eds.), *A companion to epistemology* (pp. 365–366). Blackwell.

Lowy, C. (1978). Gettier's notion of justification. *Mind*, *87*(345), 105–108.

Mair, L. P. (Ed.). (1938). *Methods of study of culture contact in Africa*. Memorandum 15. International Institute of African Languages and Cultures.

Malinowski, B. (1939). The present state of studies in culture contact: Some comments on an American approach. *Africa*, *12*(1), 27–48.

Malinowski, B. (1943). The Pan-African problem of culture contact. *American Journal of Sociology*, *48*(6), 649–655.

Malpas, J. E. (1988). The nature of interpretative charity. *Dialectica*, *42*, 17–36.

Marx, K. (1970). *Critique of Hegel's "Philosophy of Right"* (A. Jolin & J. O'Malley, Trans.). Cambridge University Press. (Originally published 1844)

Marx, K., & Engels, F. (1949). *Selected works in two volumes*. Vol. 2. Foreign Languages Publishing House.

Masson-Oursel, P. (1923). *La philosophie comparée*. F. Alcan.

McGinn, C. (1977). Charity, interpretation and belief. *Journal of Philosophy*, *74*, 521–535.

Monroe, K. R. (1996). *The heart of altruism: Perceptions of a common humanity*. Princeton University Press.

Moser, P. K. (1993). Gettier problem. In J. Dancy & E. Sosa (Eds.), *A* companion to epistemology (pp. 157–159). Blackwell.

Mosima, P. M. (2016). Philosophic sagacity and intercultural philosophy: Beyond Henry Odera Oruka. Ph.D. Thesis, Tilburg University. Leiden: African Studies Centre (2017).

Müller, F. M. (1889). *Natural religion: The Gifford lectures delivered before the University of Glasgow in 1888*. London: Longmans, Green, & Co.

Murithi, T. (2006). Practical peacemaking wisdom from Africa: Reflections on ubuntu. *Journal of Pan African Studies*, *1*(4), 25–37.

Ndaya Tshiteku, J. (2008). Prendre le bic: Le Combat Spiritual congolais et les transformations sociales. Ph.D. Thesis, Erasmus University Rotterdam. Leiden: African Studies Centre.

Nyerere, J. K. (1962). *Ujamaa: The basis of African socialism*. Dar es Salaam.

Oosterling, H. (2003). Sensable intermediality and interesse: Toward an ontology of the in-between. *Intermédialités: histoire et théorie des arts, des lettres et des techniques*, *1*, 29–46.

Oosterling, H. (2004). Radikale Mediokrität oder revolutionäre Akte? Über fundamentales Inter-esse.

Oosterling, H. (2005). From interests to inter-esse: Jean-Luc Nancy on deglobalization and sovereignty. *SubStance*, *34*(1), 81–103.

Opler, M. E. (1972). Cause and effect in Apachean agriculture, division of labor, residence patterns, and girls' puberty rites. *American Anthropologist*, *74*(5), 1133–1146.

Ortiz de Montellano, B. (2000). "Black warrior dynasts": L'Afrocentrisme et le nouveau monde. In F.-X. Fauvelle-Aymar, J.-P. Chrétien, & C.-H. Perrot (Eds.), *Afrocentrismes: L'histoire des Africains entre Égypte et Amérique* (pp. 249–273). Karthala.

Oruka, H. O. (1990). *Sage philosophy: Indigenous thinkers and modern debate on African philosophy*. Brill.

Perpeet, W. (1976). Kultur, Kulturphilosophie. In J. Ritter (Ed.), *Historisches Wörterbuch der Philosophie* (Vol. 4, cols. 1309–1324). Schwabe.

Quispel, G. (1992). Hermes Trismegistus and the origins of gnosticism. *Vigiliae christianae*, *46*, 1–19.

Radhakrishnan, S., & Raju, R. T. (Eds.). (1960). *The concept of man: A study in comparative philosophy*. George Allen & Unwin.

Ramose, M. B. (1999). *African philosophy through ubuntu*. Mond.

Ranger, T. O. (1967). *Revolt in Southern Rhodesia 1896–1897*. Heinemann.

Ranger, T. O. (1970). *The African voice in Southern Rhodesia*. Heinemann.

Ranger, T. O. (1972). Mcape. Paper read at the conference on the History of Central African Religious Systems, Lusaka, organized by the University of Zambia/University of California Los Angeles, 30 Aug. — 8 Sept. 1972.

Ranger, T. O. (1975.) *Dance and society in eastern Africa, 1890–1970*. Heinemann.

Ranger, T. O. (1985). *Peasant consciousness and guerilla war in Zimbabwe*. James Currey.

Samkange, S., & Samkange, T. M. (1980). *Hunhuism or ubuntuism: A Zimbabwe indigenous political philosophy*. Graham.

Taylor, C. (1992). *Multiculturalism and the politics of recognition: An essay by Charles Taylor with commentary by Amy Gutman, Steven C. Rockefeller, Michael Walzer, and Susan Wolf* (A. Gutman, Ed.). Princeton University Press.

Tempels, P. (1946). *Bantoe-filosofie*. De Sikkel.

Touoyem, P. (2014). *Dynamiques de l'ethnicité en Afrique: Eléments pour une théorie de l'état multinational*. Centre d'Etudes Africaines.

Turner, V. W. (1967). *The forest of symbols: Aspects of Ndembu ritual*. Cornell University Press.

Turner, V. W. (1968). *The drums of affliction: A study of religious processes among the Ndembu*. Clarendon Press.

Tylor, E. B. (1871). *Primitive culture*. 2 vols. London: Murray.

Van Binsbergen, W. M. J. (1979). Anthropological fieldwork: "There and back again." *Human Organization*, 38(2), 205–220.

Van Binsbergen, W. M. J. (1981). The unit of study and the interpretation of ethnicity: Studying the Nkoya of Western Zambia. *Journal of Southern African Studies*, 8(1), 51–81.

Van Binsbergen, W. M. J. (1985a). From tribe to ethnicity in western Zambia: The unit of study as an ideological problem. In W. M. J. van Binsbergen & P. Geschiere (Eds.), *Old modes of production and capitalist encroachment: Anthropological explorations in Africa* (pp.181–234). Kegan Paul International.

Van Binsbergen, W. M. J. (1985b). Samenlevingen en culturen in zwart Afrika: Honderd jaar na de wedloop. Struktuurveranderingen op kontinentale schaal. *Tijdschrift voor Ontwikkelingssamenwerking, special issue on "Africa hundred years after the Berlin Conference,"* 10(2), 30–43.

Van Binsbergen, W. M. J. (1986). The post-colonial state, "state penetration" and the Nkoya experience in Central Western Zambia. In G. S. C. M. Hesseling, W. M. J. Van Binsbergen, & F. Reyntjens (Eds.), *Aspects of modern state penetration in Africa* (pp.31–63). African Studies Centre.

Van Binsbergen, W. M. J. (1988). *Een buik openen*. In de Knipscheer.

Van Binsbergen, W. M. J. (1990). The state and African independent churches in Botswana: A statistical and qualitative analysis of the application of the 1972 Societies Act. Paper presented at the conference on Power and Prayer, Institute for the Study of Politics and religion, Free University Amsterdam, 10–14 December 1990.

Van Binsbergen, W. M. J. (1992a). Kazanga: Etniciteit in Afrika tussen staat en traditie. Inaugural lecture, Amsterdam Vrije Universiteit. (1994, The Kazanga festival: Ethnicity as cultural mediation and transformation in central western Zambia, *African Studies*, 53(2), 92–125)

Van Binsbergen, W. M. J. (1992b). *Tears of rain: Ethnicity and history in western central Zambia*. Kegan Paul International.

Van Binsbergen, W. M. J. (1993). Mukanda: Toward a history of circumcision rites in western Zambia, 18th-20th century. In J.-P. Chrétien, C.-H. Perrot, G. Prunier, & D. Raison-Jourde (Eds.), *L'invention religieuse en Afrique: Histoire et religion en Afrique noire* (pp. 49 – 103). Agence de Culture et de Coopération Technique/Karthala.

Van Binsbergen, W. M. J. (1997a). Virtuality as a key concept in the study of globalisation: Aspects of the symbolic transformation of contemporary Africa. Netherlands Foundation for Tropical Research: Working papers on globalization and the construction of communal identity, 3.

Van Binsbergen, W. M. J. (1997b). Ideology of ethnicity in Central Africa. In J. M. Middleton (Ed.), *Encyclopaedia of Africa south of the Sahara* (Vol. 2, pp.91–99). Scribners.

Van Binsbergen, W. M. J. (1998). Globalization and virtuality: Analytical problems posed by the contemporary transformation of African societies. In B. Meyer & P. Geschiere (Eds.), *Globalization and identity: Dialectics of flows* and closures, special issue *Development and Change*, *29*(4), 873–903.

Van Binsbergen, W. M. J. (1999a). Nkoya royal chiefs and the Kazanga Cultural Association in western central Zambia today: Resilience, decline, or folklorisation? In E. A. B. van Rouveroy van Nieuwaal & R. van Dijk (Eds.), *African chieftaincy in a new socio-political landscape* (pp.97–133). LIT.

Van Binsbergen, W. M. J. (1999b). Islam as a constitutive factor in so-called African traditional religion and culture: The evidence from geomantic divination, mankala board games, ecstatic religion, and musical instruments. Paper for the conference on Transformation processes and Islam in Africa, African Studies Centre and Institute for the Study of Islam in the Modern World, Leiden, October 15, 1999.

Van Binsbergen, W. M. J. (2001). Ubuntu and the globalisation of Southern African thought and society. In P. Boele van Hensbroek (Ed.), *African Renaissance and ubuntu philosophy, special issue of Quest: An African Journal of Philosophy*, *15*(1–2), 53–89.

Van Binsbergen, W. M. J. (2003). *Intercultural encounters: African and anthropological lessons toward a philosophy of interculturality.* LIT.

Van Binsbergen, W. M. J. (2005). "An incomprehensible miracle": Central African clerical intellectualism versus African historic religion. A close reading of Valentin Mudimbe's Tales of Faith. In K. Kresse (Ed.), *Reading Mudimbe, special issue of the Journal of African Cultural Studies*, *17*(1), 11–65.

Van Binsbergen, W. M. J. (2008). Ideology of ethnicity in Central Africa. In J. M. Middleton & J. Miller (Eds.), *New encyclopedia of Africa* (Vol.2, pp.319–328). Scribner's/Gale.

Van Binsbergen, W. M. J. (2009). Expressions of traditional wisdom from Africa and beyond: An exploration in intercultural epistemology. Royal Academy of Overseas Sciences/Academie Royale des Sciences d'Outre-mer, Classes des Sciences morales et politiques, Mémoire in-8°, Nouvelle Série, Tome 53, fasc. 4.

Van Binsbergen, W. M. J. (2009 – 2010). Before the Presocratics: Cyclicity, transformation, and element cosmology. *QUEST: An African Journal of Philosophy, Special issue*, *23–24* (1–2), 1–398.

Van Binsbergen, W. M. J. (2011a). The Kazanga ceremony, Kaoma district, and the University of Zambia: Provisional report on a fieldtrip to Zambia, July 2011.

Van Binsbergen, W. M. J. (2011b). The limits of the Black Athena thesis and of Afrocentricity as empirical explanatory models. In W. M. J. van Binsbergen (Ed.), *Black Athena comes of age* (pp. 297 – 338). LIT. (The chapter has copyright 2010, the whole book 2011)

Van Binsbergen, W. M. J. (2015). *Vicarious reflections: African explorations in empirically-grounded intercultural philosophy.* PIP-TraCS: Papers in intercultural philosophy and transcontinental comparative Studies 17.

Van Binsbergen, W. M. J. (2017). *Religion as a social construct: African, Asian, comparative and theoretical excursions.* Shikanda Press.

Van Binsbergen, W. M. J. (2018). *Confronting the sacred: Durkheim vindicated through philosophical analysis, ethnography, archaeology, long-range linguistics, and comparative mythology.* Shikanda Press.

Van Binsbergen, W. M. J. (2020a). Grappling with the ineffable in three African situations: An ethnographic approach. In P. Y. Kao & J. S. Alter (Eds.), *Capturing the ineffable: An anthropology of wisdom* (pp. 179 – 242).

University of Toronto Press.

Van Binsbergen, W. M. J. (2020b). Notes on the fundamental unity of humankind. *Culture and Dialogue*, *8*, 23–42.

Van Binsbergen, W. M. J. (2021a). *Joseph Karst as a pioneer of long-range approaches to Mediterranean Bronze-Age ethnicity: A study in the history of ideas*. Shikanda Press, Papers in Intercultural Philosophy/Transcontinental Comparative Studies No. 12.

Van Binsbergen, W. M. J. (2021b). *Sangoma science: From ethnography to intercultural ontology. A poetics of African spiritualities*. Shikanda Press, Papers in Intercultural Philosophy/Transcontinental Comparative Studies No. 20.

Van Binsbergen, W. M. J. (2022). *Pandora's box prised open: Studies in comparative mythology*. Shikanda Press, Papers in Intercultural Philosophy/Transcontinental Comparative Studies No. 26.

Van Binsbergen, W. M. J., & Wiggermann, F. A. M. (1999). Magic in history: A theoretical perspective and its application to ancient Mesopotamia. In T. Abusch & K. van der Toorn (Eds.), *Mesopotamian magic* (pp. 3–34). Styx.

Van Binsbergen, W. M. J., & Woudhuizen, F. C. (2011). Ethnicity in Mediterranean protohistory. British Archaeological Reports (BAR) International Series No. 2256. Archaeopress.

Van der Veer, P. (1988). *Gods on earth: The management of religious experience and identity in a North Indian pilgrimage centre*. Bloomsbury Academic.

Werbner, R. P. (Ed.). (1977). *Regional cults*. Academic Press.

White, C. M. N. (1949). Stratification and modern changes in an ancestral cult. *Africa*, *19*, 324–331.

Wiredu, K. (1984). How not to compare African thought with Western thought. In R. A. Wright (Ed.), *African philosophy: An introduction* (3rd ed., pp. 149–162). University Press of America.

Wiredu, K. (1996). *Cultural universals and particulars: An African perspective*. Indiana University Press.

Wiredu, K. (1998). Can philosophy be intercultural?: An African viewpoint. *Diogenes*, *46*(184), 147–167.

Wirth, L. (1938). Urbanism as a way of life. *American Journal of Sociology*, *44*, 1–24.

6

Intercultural Communication: Concepts of Personhood and Community

Keyan G. Tomaselli
University of Johannesburg
Paul Z. Tembe
Zhejiang Normal University & University of South Africa

Summary: Communitarianism between three different societies is the topic of this chapter. The comparative analysis of Confucianism (China), *ubuntu* (Southern Africa) and *jantelagen* (Sweden) maps their respective contours in relation to their host societies. Claims to exceptionalism are questioned. The analysis rather explains why communitarianism works in some societies but less so in some others (mostly African). The comparison opens the door to a more sophisticated analysis than has been the case to date with regard to *ubuntu*, and how communitarianism can benefit national economies and distribution of social resources when it moves from being simply ethnic rhetoric to actual implementation through social structures. Both authors have worked in three societies under analysis, so they do bring their lived experiences to bear, if implicitly in this case.

Introduction

A brief historical overview of different intercultural communication (IC) paradigms explains how IC has been adopted and adapted within different national contexts. Our analysis involves the polar concepts of individualism and communitarianism. Prior work has argued that conventional IC paradigms account for only part of the picture, in that they largely ignore non-material dimensions of life, religion, and the unexplainable (Tomaselli, 2020). IC has been also examined in how it has been very differently elaborated and elevated through Chinese scholars drawing on Jacques Derrida and British cultural studies to address global issues (Tomaselli & Du, 2021).

Our comparison highlights Paul Z. Tembe's discussion of the sub-Saharan African concept/code of conduct/social practice of *ubuntu* (communitarianism) within a transnational context that goes beyond "voiding" of the concept which is often applied by its apostles to everything and anything, including justifications for crime and corruption. In short, Tembe elaborates on a type of IC that takes into cognizance comparative lived experiences of different people and their cultures. His work distances itself from colonialism, whose mission was to discover and assimilate those outside the European cultural realm. He deliberately distances his analysis of *ubuntu* from the hierarchical type of IC that aimed to establish and promote cognitive and social cultural superiority toward non-Western cultures (Tembe, 2020, p. 22).

It is in the differences and similarities of the lived experiences to be described that the intercultural dimensions reside. Our African example will apply the Rwandan scholar Alexis Kagame's (1956) linguistic categories of "personhood" in a comparative analysis that will include *Jantelagen* in Sweden and Confucianism in China. The existence of a plurality of ontological referents in African languages is based on the notion of *ntu* (be-ing). This root word stems from Bantu languages, connoting a sense of "personhood," and acknowledging humanity of the individual. Kagame expanded on the notion of Being that French linguist Placide Frans Tempels had detected in African languages. According to Tempels, the bantu conception is in accordance with the "beings-forces" of the universe in relationships in which nothing moves without influencing other forces by its movement: "The world of forces is held like a spider's web of which no single thread can be caused to vibrate without shaking the whole network" (1959, p. 52). By drawing on Aristotle's *Physics*, Kagame identified a four-level grid upon which the Bantu language verbal root *ntu* could be described. Reality is ordered by Kagame into levels of influence between the concepts of *Muntu* (being with intelligence), where the South African scholarly notion of indigenous knowledge systems (IKS) might be located, *Kintu* (being without intelligence), *Hantu* (location in space and time), and

Kuntu (roughly, modality, the way in which something happens and is experienced).

A Quick History

Communication Research Trends (Biernatzki, 1986, 1995), a journal that summarizes other research, reports that intercultural communication as a field of study arose in the West during the 1960s within the domains of diplomacy and peace studies. This occurred in the context of "the ugly American" because the Western academic enterprise tended to constitute minorities as "fodder for a national melting pot" (Biernatzki, 1986, p. 1). Rooted in explorer, trader, soldier, missionary, and adventurer tales of the exotic, early anthropologists sometimes proffered systematic forms of knowledge that enabled the training of colonial administrators.

World War II and its globally restructuring aftermath required very intensive intercultural understanding as new geopolitical configurations emerged from its ashes across the Soviet Union, Europe, China, the Koreas, and Japan. The demand for intercultural communication was global:

> Japanese businesspeople were just as puzzled about the strange ways of Americans and Germans as were Westerners about the ways of the Orient. And, their interests were no longer academic, but had price tags in the billions of yen, dollars and Deutschmarks. (Biernatzki, 1995, p.3)

China experienced quasi-similar colonial histories to those experienced within Africa, and communitarianism is a feature of both (Tembe, 2020, p.21).

A decade later, with a much more nuanced approach, Edward Hall (e.g., 1976) amongst others trained American businessmen and development agents on cross-cultural interactions between different nations located differently along the individualist-communitarian axis. His approach included ritual, non-verbal, less rational and poetic dimensions of life and living that needed to be understood in any intercultural encounter. The mechanistic Pavlovian sender-receiver, stimulus-response modeling that had typified early mechanistic intercultural communication studies and practices was not for Hall a principal method or theory. For Hall, grammar and vocabulary interrelate with gesture, proxemics, emotions, tone of voice, rhythms of time, facial expression, and so on. These are components of primary-level culture that could not be accounted for by transmission theories of communication that mechanistically and mistakenly equated signal with content. As Tembe (2020, p. 120) points out on the post-millennium context, cross-cultural communication strategies have, in the wake of public diplomacy, soft power, diversified global trends and a multipolar world, become a central pillar for strategic positioning in regional and international affairs involving both kinds of societies in a new global order. For example, Sweden's meshing of mercantile systems and communitarianism have positioned this society as a global success story without the need to impose the neoliberal ideal (Tembe, 2020, p. 121). Similarly, China in recent decades has offered a lived space not totally committed to creating a sole locus for the production of capital (2020, p. 121) to the exclusion of cultural and human aspects.

Another seminal Western scholar who came onto the scene during the later Hall era was Geert Hofstede (2001). His cultural dimensions theory — using the metaphor of "software of the mind" — describes the effects of a society's cultures and the values of its subjects, and *how* these values relate to behavior. Hofstede's original theory proposed six dimensions along which cultural values could be analyzed: individualism-collectivism; uncertainty avoidance; power distance (i. e., strength of social hierarchy), and masculinity-femininity (i. e., task orientation versus person-orientation). A fifth dimension, long-term orientation, accounts for values not discussed in the original model. Indulgence versus self-restraint was also added. Hofstede established a major research tradition in cross-cultural psychology that has been drawn upon by researchers and consultants in many fields relating to international business and communication (Hofstede & Hofstede 2005). For the individualism-collectivism contrast of values, see also Triandis (2014).

While Hofstede explains how communitarianism emphasizes the connection between the individual and the community, he neglects what happens when a communitarian society relies on models borrowed from individualistic societies for the production of knowledge for running economies and governments (Tembe, 2020, p. 99). The result might be a state of arrested development regarding claims to be decolonized while, ironically, continuing to rely on neo-colonial blueprints, which emphasize individual accumulation often at the expense of communal development. As we argue below with reference to Robert St. Clair's work, the communal foundation via which individual success is achieved is often silenced in what Edward Hall calls "low-context" societies which ignore the communal, class, and bureaucratic networks that underpin anyone's "rise to the top. "

A Socio-Linguistic, Transdisciplinary Intercultural Communication

Robert St. Clair (2015; see also Vaagen, 2016) was founding director of the Institute for Intercultural Communication, University of Louisville. St. Clair devised a systems framework for cultural theory and cultural metaphors that transcend social network analysis. In systems theory, as in Kagame's schema, everything interlinks with a larger network of connections. St. Clair was instrumental in the establishment of the China Association for Intercultural Communication (CAFIC) where his ideas took root. Conventional IC scholars neglected the evidence that a human and non-human system differ significantly, and that in business, advertising, and mass media, these two kinds of systems are inappropriately conflated. Cultural network theory, he argues, views culture as a system and describes interactions of components within that system. In addition, some systems are creative and proliferate into new systems. This aspect is true of both human and non-human systems (the second generation of systems theory).

St. Clair, a transdisciplinary linguist, spoke 29 languages. He is thus something of a cross-over artist in that he was as comfortable in both conventional positivist IC and the anti-positivist cultural studies paradigms. Unlike campus-bound scholars, he actually lived his quotidian intercultural encounters in many places amongst different communities, and different ontological worlds. IC for him was thus not a textbook experience, but an intensively experiential one, as we will demonstrate also with regard to some African manifestations.

In a most revealing interview with Meng-yu Li (2011), St. Clair observed that Westerners myopically imagine themselves to be self-made individuals, a form of mental blindness sourced from hyper-individuated Western philosophy. As St. Clair reminds us, supporting every successful person anywhere are multiple layers of other people who play significant roles in enabling that individual to become successful. This view of life is obvious in Asia, observes St. Clair. Most Asians imbue a social self, while the individual self is inevitably involved in a matrix of relationships with many others. Harmony, a key component of both Chinese and African value systems, always incorporates the role that the individual self plays in wider social contexts. In the USA, the unique Chicago School of Sociology similarly provided a model of the social self in American culture. Irving Goffman (1956) also provided models of the dramaturgical self (the ego-centrical self) within modernity. Related to this research was the model taken by the New School for Social Research in Frankfurt, Germany, in which it was argued that the self is socially constructed, as picked up later by British cultural studies (Stuart Hall, 1996). Missing from such models, St. Clair observed, is a lack of detailed systemic architecture of such social structures. For St. Clair, how reality is socially constructed and distributed needs to be studied in relation to other kinds of social and linguistic patterns. This is what we attempt in this chapter.

Our intention is not to critique these approaches, but to briefly signpost them within the global history that spans the explorer age, colonialism, post-colonialism, and globality. St. Clair's cultural networks and systems approach is far more historicized, multi-dimensional, and transdisciplinary than conventional IC, drawing as he does on Michel Foucault, and a whole swathe of social theories that are usually missing from technical IC training and statistical applications. His analysis, like Tembe's, also admits that communitarianism is a characteristic of many societies. Communitarianism is not exceptional to Africa, as is so often claimed by its often essentialist scholars. Linguistics and language in St. Clair's approach are crucial, as are biological impulses and physiological ways of reading signs.

Communitarianism Beyond Sub-Saharan Africa

We emphasize the significance of understanding fundamentals of local "knowledge of the game" of a given culture in order for successful IC engagements to occur. Such knowledge will help in understanding salient values that impact or apply as a template for local frames of reference. It is only with such knowledge that one may be able to understand and draw comparisons between an array of local, regional, or national value systems as is the case with St. Clair, Tempels, Tembe, and Kagame. In applying the works of Tempels (1959), Kagame became the subject of criticism from one-dimensional Afrocentric analysts. He was criticized for over-borrowing from European perspectives of defining and understanding philosophy.

It is imperative that one appreciates the era and conditions under which Kagame lived. His analysis of levels for understanding the "individual" in society by reading Kinyarwanda grammar and meanings of basic lexical representation ought to be commended. Current and contemporary scholarship should not preoccupy itself with proving that there is in fact a uniquely African philosophy. Neither does it need to prove that such a philosophy is at par with that of West European origins. Instead, current scholarship ought to examine all philosophers in order to avoid current Afro-eccentric scholars from entering into a decolonization cul-de-sac. Such perspectives that are founded on the notion of decolonization may tend to be misinterpreted to mean that African identities and their performances are grounded in the existence of encounters with European explorers, slave traders, colonialists, and architects of globalization. Tembe dispels the myth of African agency that is founded on encounters with the rollout of the 16th-century European colonial project into the African continent.

The type of African agency that Tembe's work dispels is that which is founded on a reaction to colonial encounters on the African continent. Such agency tends to be reactive and regressive in nature. In the end, such type of agency fails to deliver on African freedoms as it manifests as a remedial measure to post-colonial ills in Africa. It is as if Africans have neither identity nor social systems. It is a type of agency that lacks a type of performance aimed toward delivery of public goods. It is as if African identities and their cultural and social beings stem from a reaction to the presence of colonialism in Africa. It is a type of agency that promotes essentialist Afrocentrism. It is in countering the vague post-colonial African agency that this work proposes a holistic framework of *Isintu*, *Ubuntu*, and *Umuntu* for African agency. In his analysis of *ubuntu* Kagame emphasizes the role of indigenous African proverbs, idioms, and aphorisms such as *umuntu ngumuntu ngabantu* (I am part of my community or I belong to my community).

In drawing on such analysis, Tembe highlights the origins of the African performative agency founded in local linguistic structures that predate slavery and colonialism. He digs into fundamental patterns of behavior, "those that set the rules of the game" for sub-Saharan people with the aim to highlight the independence of local value systems that reflect African culture as founded on "practice philosophy" rather than any which are based on abstraction for abstraction's sake.

Kagame and St. Clair come to a similar conclusion that an "individual" in society is subject to the existence and dictates of society. An "individual" serves and exists for the good of society. In short, for an "individual" to persist, it needs to perpetually prove itself to society. As already mentioned above, beyond a mere physical existence an "individual" needs constant validation from society.

An "individual" may be defined as a "social utility criterion" which is to serve society at all times. In using the Nguni meaning of this above-suggested structure, it would read as follows: *umuntu*, the "individual" is a temporary state in the act of becoming *abantu*, "the people." This would justify the aphorism *umuntu ngumuntu ngabantu*, i.e., "I am because you/we are." However, added to that existence is the duty and perpetual performance, strife, and will for *umuntu* to become *abantu* in order for her/him to gain validation as central to society and its dictates. Such an understanding brings forth the fact that an *umuntu* "individual" is not a subject of society, rather society is a product of the constant movement of being between the illusive state of *umuntu* "individual" and *abantu* as "the people" or society.

Read from the grammar of sub-Saharan language groups to explain the above phenomenon (use of the ever-evasive *ntu* as a central entity in the formation of a cultural paradigm), one can highlight internal processes that define salient communal values that drive communitarian African societies. However, such an analysis would remain Afrocentric and essentialist like those that claim humanism as a construct solely manifesting among indigenous African societies. The emphasis is different in Asante's study of African communication, which speaks of the need for an interface between Asia and Africa (2010, p. 154).

In making a case for an existence of a communitarian society elsewhere, Tembe (2020; see also Tembe & Gumede, 2020) draws examples from China and Sweden, highlighting salient factors that reflect the manifestation of value systems founded on communitarianism in those societies. Tembe offers a comparison of sub-Saharan Africa, China, and Sweden in an effort to demonstrate that all three societies define and place the "individual" away from processes of individuation toward those that set her/him as an agent or axis of the "social utility criterion."

In the case of China and Sweden, similar to tendencies observed in sub-Saharan Africa, language and grammar play a central role in the definition and practices of an "individual" in society. All three abstract, rationalize, conceptualize, and implement processes where all "individuals" serve as mere instruments of the "social utility criterion" — where the aim is to build a coherent communitarian social system. Embedded in these communitarian societies is a language and grammar that perpetuate a cultural system that is responsible for production, implementation, and transmission of values, norms, and codes from the present to the next generations. For a partly related concept, that of Sociocultural Models, see the chapter by Valery Chirkov in the present volume.

Changes in productive forces signify a fundamental change in societal relations and power. While the West has managed to maintain its foundational social stratum and distribution of goods, all other societies that have maintained colonial production models have been stressed from pressures of market failures or successes. Some failures result from systems borrowed from European and North American production systems, which have led to economic successes over those economies, but which have tended to dismally fail in the African continent. Such failures result from reliance on foreign grammars of rationalization and implementation. One such recent example is that of the International Monetary Fund's (IMF) "structural adjustments" during the 1980s in sub-Saharan Africa.

Tembe (2020, p. 98) argues that there is clear evidence of a direct relationship between the growth in gross domestic product (GDP) and the level of impact of borrowed value systems in any given nation. The higher the impact of foreign and borrowed value systems, including language and grammar, the lower the GDP growth. However, in nations that subdue modernity to adopt or manifest local value systems, GDP growth increases. So, those who design their governance and production mechanisms in accordance with indigenous value systems tend to enjoy higher levels of growth and relative prosperity compared to those who rely on borrowed cultures and models for running society and their economies.

While sub-Saharan Africa may be regarded as a victim of the above-mentioned reliance on borrowed social and production systems, both China and Sweden seem to have survived the perennial menace that impact most developing markets. These nations have tended to rely on local value systems in production and distribution with the aim of establishing and maintaining a uniform societal, cultural, political (including economic) distribution of capital.

The Case of Southern Africa

In Southern Africa, the intercultural communication approach is indigenized via the notion of *ubuntu* (Zulu: "we are people through other people"). *Ubuntu* is usually offered as a supposedly unique African concept that promotes the communitarian idea of human interconnectedness (see Kamwangamalu, 1999; Mbigi, 1997). *Ubuntu* is self-referential, it contains its own authority that cannot be disputed, as there is no external record against which to test the authenticity of its claims about identity, belonging, and ethnicity. That's why it is essentialist and prone to misuse in justifying corruption by individuals claiming communitarian members and allegiance (Tomaselli, 2016). As Piet Naudé (n. d.) observes of its misuse in South Africa, "Our ancestors turn in their graves. Never was *ubuntu* meant as blind emotional endorsement of corrupt behaviour that would allow one individual to gain unjustly to the direct detriment of the welfare of the community."

In reclaiming African roots from the above-mentioned travesty, Tembe (2020, pp. 22–23) identifies three kinds of *ubuntu* "that have wrestled for space and prominence, within the corridors of power, the public eye and international communities." The first embraces forgiveness and harmony; the second reflects norms and traditions, spoken language, respect for elders, and kindness. Thirdly, in embracing modernity, there is a fluid *ubuntu* that transcends race and language, one that celebrates diversity. This third type, rarely discussed in the published literature, epitomizes the aphorism *umuntu* (individual, performer) *ngmuntu ngabuntu* (Tembe, 2020, p. 24), which exceeds the very limiting "I am because you are" formulation. This phrase is not merely an ontological reflection of the self, "but is representative of the ability to deliver good to the communal table to continue being regarded as part of *abantu* (community)" (Tembe, 2020, p. 53). As in China, it refers to collective responsibilities (which are often lost in the individuated race to wealth and power).

Ubuntu is similar to altruism in that individuals interact with many others within multiple social layers. *Ubuntu*, argues Tembe (2020, p. 27), is the software that possesses capabilities extending beyond "the signification of identities." But in liberated South Africa, sloganeering *ubuntu* discourses boast of the hardware capabilities of society in the absence of a value system that can read and apply the associated software that mobilizes individual capability in addressing social problems.

Ubuntu can accommodate both inclusion and exclusion, bearing in mind Stuart Hall's (1996) observation that every inclusion is simultaneously an exclusion. Power, often absent from IC discussion with both social and business practices, is here injected into the analysis. Both contemporary *ubuntu* and intercultural communication are rooted in who controls resources, who regulates access to communication networks, and who writes the *ubuntu* software (metaphorically speaking) that through a "social utility criterion" (Tembe, 2020, p. 30) shapes the nature of meaning-making that enables cultural continuity from pre-to post-modern conditions.

Inherited international intercultural communication theory exemplifies old thinking. Missing, however, from intercultural models were intuition, empathy, religion, and cultural sensitivity. South African scholars during apartheid (1948 – 1990), for example, had developed models, instruction manuals, and theories on how interactions with people of different colors could best be managed (Du Preez, 1987; Groenewald, 1988). The idea of *ubuntu* was one of the concepts then appropriated for "domestication" purposes as apartheid began to unravel during the late 1980s. Language planning and reification of indigenous African terms into apartheid discourse was a feature of semantic engineering designed to make labor relations more efficient, but not necessarily more humanistic (Tomaselli, Louw, & Tomaselli, 1990).

Further legitimation of this unique, idiosyncratic, and instrumentalist intercultural modeling was based on ontological "African" difference enabled by Edward Hall's (1976) theory of high and low context cultures. Holistic and relational forms of communication apply in Hall's theory to high context (communitarian) Asian cultures, whereas low context Western business interactions tend to be individualistic, logocentric, and goal orientated. While during the 1980s in South Africa race, culture, and language remained as intractable ethnic signifiers, the claim for differentiating "blacks" (as subjects of "high context culture," e.g., *ubuntu*) from "whites" (as more individuated Western-type subjects of "low context culture") provided a new conceptual template that now took indigenous African ontology into account by admitting that blacks were the same but different. The shift was geared toward a model that enabled the setting in place of a discursive structure for political negotiation at the end of the 1980s.

Having revised their interpretations of Western intercultural theory in the 1990s during the post-apartheid transition, the IC discipline as then practiced in South Africa was explicitly morphed into a new indigenized discourse that needed to be talked through, as political power shifted from one (white) racial boot to the (black) other foot. The discourse of *ubuntu* is positive, but its lack of practice and materialization into social and public institutions is the problem in South Africa, as it remains an ideal rather than a practice.

From Intercultural Communication to *Ubuntu*

Ubuntu during the post-apartheid transition was being applied, across business disciplines, in any context (see Broodryk, 2007; van Niekerk, 2013). However, only a few have taken a *critical* approach (see, e.g., Fourie, 2007; Ngcoya, 2009; Swanson, 2007) or offer comparative analysis (Tembe, 2020).

Below, we will hence pursue a different international IC schema that examines *ubuntu* in relation to other concepts and practices. The populist, post-apartheid auto-centric "black" ideological discourse promotes *ubuntu*, claiming pan-African exceptionalism, disregarding all other humanist and relational systems (and so-called races) that claim similar traits — like Zhong Dao. As we shall show, other societies like Sweden and China do incorporate similar ideas and associated actual behavior that are manifested within their social, political, and economic institutions.

Much discussion of *ubuntu* assumes an ahistorical framework in a nostalgic, imagined pre-modern utopian society where subjects of the practice are presumed to behave morally and without consciousness of class relations, modes and relations of production, or social formations. The problem with the idealized discussion is that it refuses to examine power relations and offer class analysis, and address social problems. It is discursively mobilized as a rhetorical handle to suggest that all is well — when it is not (Tembe, 2020, p. 24). Yet it is power, securing the moral high ground, and legitimate personhood, that underpin the political and populist discussion, and often the academic discussion also. Who wields the discursive power of *ubuntu* for what purposes, with what effect? Who is included and who is excluded? Who benefits from applications of power concealed by the populist discourse of *ubuntu*?

African communities, as Thaddeus Metz (2011) argues, consider it apt to answer criminality with a particular expectation: Africans trying to cope with a crime, traditionally, would seek to appease angry ancestors (supernaturalism), thereby protecting the living community from their wrath, or to mend a broken relationship between the offender, his victim, and the community. This approach is usually credited with suggesting a restorative rather than punitive response to apartheid-era political crimes (Gade, 2011; Metz, 2011; Ovens, 2003).

Much of the uncritical work on *ubuntu* homogenizes the myriad of disparate cultures found in Africa under the catchphrases "African experience," "African culture" (singular), or "African values," all essentialist Afrocentric expressions. This homogenization is then placed within a dichotomy between "Western ontologies" — Cartesian, rational and objective — and "African psychology," taken to be racially unique and largely unknowable to non-Africans. Metz, in contrast, has searched for the commonalities, especially between *ubuntu* and Confucianism, albeit in a rather idealized way, as a solution rather than as an ethnic prescription.

Modernization is often argued by modernized African scholars to have "corrupted" or despoiled the pre-modern morality of the true and pure African. The idea of a quintessential Africanness that has been marred by Western influence ignores the fact that cultures are dynamic, always in a process of becoming. Cultures are actually constantly moving targets, always being hybridized from both within and without. The mobilization of holistic constructs such as "Africa" or "Asia" or "Latin America" as the sites of presumably organic cultural value systems forgets that these entities were themselves the products of the (Western) geographical imagination; they are not "natural" areas of cultural sameness.

The Case of China

In China, intercultural communication studies straddles the need to establish a united, harmonious and hierarchy-abiding society and the need to communicate with a greater world that relies on a bottom-up form of governance. A construct for such a rationale and societal system is founded on Confucian postulates, as founded on the notion of being aware of one's station in life (hierarchy) and the pursuit of filial piety (harmony). A language and grammar that are born of such a system will for obvious reasons speak and foster a society that adheres to hierarchies and harmony set in place as a rule of practice for all members of society. In other words, the striving for "individuals" to become "people or society" is highly manifest in practice in China, similar to tendencies observed in the adherence to *ubuntu* values salient in sub-Saharan Africa where the ideal is, however, not found in the consistent implementation.

Such an observation is founded neither on an idea of local value-system essentialism and populism nor on attempts at exorcizing a colonial past. Instead, these are observations that come forth as one engages in analysis of factors responsible for performances founded on salient local value systems. The difference between China and sub-Saharan Africa is that such values are manifest across the board in the former, and offer foundation for the entire social system from production, distribution, and consumption of public goods. These "central" and salient communitarian values are relegated to the periphery of social and political (including economic) capitals in the latter. While the three kinds of *ubuntu* have wrestled for space and prominence within the corridors of power, the public eye, and international communities in sub-Saharan Africa, in China Confucianism with its emphasis on harmony and hierarchies founded on a family rationale consists of a guideline for all practice in society.

While *ubuntu* may be regarded as the software that possesses capabilities extending beyond "the signification of identities" in the form of *inhlonipho* (respect), *isithunzi somuntu* (human dignity), *uzwelo* (compassion), *ubumbano* (solidarity), and *ukuvumelana* (consensus), all consisting of salient rules of practice in sub-Saharan Africa, Confucianism is a *de facto* societal guide for conduct in China, and it manifests as a template for social, cultural, political, and economic production in the nation. Such an understanding demonstrates that China has its local value system as a rationale for development and thus a *de facto* guide for practice in society.

In short, identity production and performances in China are aligned to local value systems across the board, while local sub-Saharan value systems continue to remain an ideal that resides at the periphery of corridors of power, production of knowledge, and all other types of capitals sought by the peoples of the region. Our analysis of *isintu* (Xhosa: tradition) is an attempt at unleashing the performative force of *ubuntu*, with the hope that it will help tap into hidden talents to create spaces for social cohesion and for production of a variety of capitals aimed at empowering all members of society in the language and grammar that are understood by all members.

How does an understanding of the underlying local value systems help in the practice of intercultural communication? In dealings with China, one needs to take into consideration that respect and understanding of their culture underpin a foundation of any successful negotiations and relations. Such consideration is not unique to China, it is a universal phenomenon. However, there have been tendencies to regard patterns of intercultural communication founded on hierarchies around Western encounters and its hegemonic hold on other nations beyond the European realm. An understanding of how a specific value system functions in its own locality beyond political and economic frameworks imposed by hierarchies of developed, developing, and underdeveloped worlds firstly arms locals with a better rationale of themselves and their place in the world. Secondly, it helps those who interact with a given society to partake in the productions of various capitals without being a detriment to the locals and the spaces upon which they produce their daily living.

The Case of Sweden

China and Sweden rely on communitarianism as a bedrock for their respective social systems and as a guide for practice. Both nations give preference and priority to the public good over that of an individual. In common, both nations have managed to subdue modernity to their respective value systems.

While China relies on Confucian postulates for organizing and developing society, for Sweden it is *Jantelagen*. *Jantelagen* is founded on an allegorical novel titled *En Flykting Korsar Sitt Spår* (A Fugitive Crosses His Tracks) by the Danish-Norwegian writer Aksel Sandemose, written in 1933. The novel consists of rules on how to establish and run a sustainable stable, equal, and uniform society.

Despite apparent differences in the implementation of systems that keep communitarian values and success in place, China and Sweden are a proof that rationalization founded in one's value system supersedes the rationale of reliance on borrowed systems founded on foreign languages and performative grammars. The use of local idioms and traditions, as highlighted in the works of Astrid Lindgren, seems to be the norm among the Nordic communitarian societies (see Steene, 2007), a trait that is also witnessed among South East Asian nations. Into that group of communitarian societies, although the majority no longer rely on their value systems for social cohesion, we would include sub-Saharan African people.

There is an ironic paradox between South African and Swedish social practices. While South Africans tend to evade their value system being "politically correct" by using phrases such as "in accordance with the law" or "according to our Constitution," Swedes adhere to their value system by using that same expression in the form of *lagom*. Etymologically and in accordance with the old Swedish language, "*lagom* or *laghum*" means "according to law." Although South Africa and Sweden seem to share common communitarian values, they are different in that the former has abandoned the original framework of their value systems, while the latter has built its entire social system and modernity based on its local value systems.

Such a paradox reveals a Swedish society that has managed, through the ages, to subdue modernity and the legal system beneath its traditions and culture, which comprise their value system. Sweden relies on laws based on establishing and maintaining a uniform society. Laws concerning human rights, land use and distribution, and education are all based on the adages and allegories such as those by Sandemose and Astrid Lindgren. These are laws based on communitarianism with strong regard for personal freedom, self-reliance, and privacy. In South Africa, we have tended to give primacy to modernity and Roman-Dutch law, which stand for values and a way of life that are inconsistent with the value systems of the majority of South Africans. South Africa is today battling to sort out differences between its written laws and realities that face its majority black population. One such conflict may be witnessed in the use of land and distribution. Laws in place have failed to transition from written legislation into practices that aim to benefit society. Such conflicts occur as a result of the legislation in place being alien and distant from local frames of reference that constitute such local value systems. These disparities result in a society that is dependent on handouts from the government and lack of personal initiative. The root evil of these conflicts is the lack of intercultural communication among cultures and peoples that constitute South Africa.

> *Si duo dicunt idem non est idem.*
> (If two languages say the same thing, it is not the same thing.)
> Proverbial; translation by J. Stone, 2006

It is not the foreign grammar *per se* that is the devil in the attempts at formulating a feasible and successful social system. It is the lack of local aspects, as in the language and grammar of practice in specific areas, that are foundational for knowledge and capital production in a nation. Foreign language and grammar may express favorable ideals for local populations, but if these are not understood within the premises of local value systems, that is, if they lack expressions founded on local value systems and reflective of local frames of reference, these ideals will fail to deliver the necessary public goods.

How does an understanding of the underlying local value systems help in the practice of intercultural communication? Sweden has had an advantage of having lived in peace with its neighbors for the last century and a half without any war, oppression, and exploitation. It is for that reason that the rationale upon which its citizenry is manifested can simply be read from the *En Flykting Korsar Sitt Spår* allegory. The allegory saliently encapsulates what may be compared to hierarchies or lack thereof as witnessed in the Chinese system: harmony, a prerequisite in place as a template for members of society to avoid individualistic tendencies and greed; and social uniformity, preventing wide disparity in access to public goods and opportunities toward production of knowledge, as social, cultural, and economic capitals.

It is only under conditions where local citizens fully understand the processes and the practice of their identities that it is possible for them to have full representation in both local and international spaces. The occurrence of a balanced recognition of the self and representation beyond one's own borders and region allow for a coherent and productive form of intercultural relations. This occurs because, firstly, locals understand themselves in full and are allowed spaces upon which to practice their identities both at home and abroad. Secondly, strangers and potential partner nations are given ·a chance to understand one's nation and thus engage according to the local "knowledge of the game" or "rules of the game" that consists of local value systems. It may seem as if an understanding of "knowledge of the game" or "rules of the game" is a prerequisite for a successful practice of intercultural communication.

Toward a Synthesis

Why is it that China and Sweden enjoy success in social and economic development while much of Africa is locked in perennial strife and impasses of underdevelopment? Furthermore, is it then possible to formulate and practice successful intercultural communication in societies that suffer from arrested development, whether they consist of the individualistic or communitarian type of social system?

The answer may be present in a (fictional but useful) dialogue between Kagame's four-level theory of personhood and Tembe's call for *isintu* as a rationale for performance and practice, or as a path toward "knowledge of the game" among sub-Saharan societies. In short, the discussion seeks to address the gap between propositions set forth by the two scholars. The dialogue that tackles the alleged conceptual gap does not imply a contradiction. On the contrary, it is complementary, and helps in the search for a missing piece in the puzzle of contemporary sub-Saharan identity production and practice — or limitations that in turn impact on attempts of a coherent and gainful practice of intercultural communications.

Kagame points out that in sub-Saharan society personhood is ordered by levels of influence between the concepts of *Muntu* (being with intelligence), where the South African notion of indigenous knowledge systems might be located, *Kintu* (being without intelligence), *Hantu* (location in space and time), and *Kuntu* (roughly, modality, the way in which something happens and is experienced).

Tembe (2020, p. 15) argues that *ubuntu* consists of three integral parts: firstly *amasiko*, which consists of traditions, norms, and customs; secondly *isintu* as rituals, performances, and practices that help with the embodiment of *ubuntu*; and thirdly *umuntu*, the performer and practitioner of *isintu* and bearer of the *ubuntu* value system as a state of being and identity.

It is lack of space to practice the *isintu* (rules of the game) of *ubuntu* that leads to limited production and practices of sub-Saharan identities, which in turn results in the prevalence of schizophrenic states of existence for the region's citizens. In turn, persistence of unfulfilled identities leads to limited participation in the spaces that are fundamental for production, distribution, and implementation of knowledge. Such conditions result in a society that has limited knowledge of the self, limited production opportunities, and limited access to types of capitals that are necessary for the production of full citizenry and social development.

The shortcomings caused by lack of *isintu* practices, in spaces of production of a variety of capitals beyond limitations of identity production, also lead to limitations in the formulation of premises for coherent and gainful intercultural practices.

The greatest contribution by Kagame in the outline of his four-level grid of personhood may be found in his definition of *Hantu*, as a space and time wherein persons exist and practice their personhood in relation to processes of being *umuntu*. It may seem as if, beyond influences from Tempels and Aristotle's *Physics*, Kagame may have taken a page from Marxist definitions of time and space, where "altering of the qualities of space-time and the relationship between space and time" is "a consequence of the expansion of capital" (Harvey, 1990, p.418).

Hantu as defined by Kagame is a statement that in the sub-Saharan cultures of *ubuntu* there will be no progress or "expansion of capital" given the conditions of limited spaces afforded by colonialism, oppression, discrimination, and exploitation of spaces of social and economic production. Beyond pointing out lack of spaces and time, i. e ., *Hantu* to practice sub-Saharan rules of the game, Tembe's (2020) inquiry seeks to find out the reason or justification for such a lack in post-colonial Africa.

In a globalized paradigm shift from human to machine dependency of the 4th Industrial Revolution, spaces to practice local value systems have become a primary resource for the unleashing of diverse knowledge systems, including those dormant within a variety of indigenous knowledge systems the world. Opening up spaces for full practices of local value systems will make possible a coherent and gainful process of intercultural communication. Successful practices of intercultural communication the world over will prevent yet another era of cultural hierarchies, which resulted in contemporary hegemonies and their ills to humankind. However, this time around it would be oppression, discrimination, exploitation by design — and not by an accidental historical process born of the 16th-century developments in Europe.

The Failure of Intercultural Concepts

Where there was almost no criticism of intercultural communication theory, the growing debate around *ubuntu* is livelier. The approaches in each case are, however, prescriptive and work off *a priori* assumptions about race, morality, and integrity. Metz (2011), however, is addressing larger questions in the context of offering pro-active ways of harnessing *ubuntu* toward democratic ends. Yet the situation is much more complex — scientific approaches may be able to develop cultural sensitivity scales, but they do not easily measure semantic engineering, regressive language planning, or how cultural self-concepts might result in what David Coplan describes as "an auto-cannibalistic disorder" (2009, p. 81). This phraseology resonates especially with regard to the ways in which *ubuntu* has been uncritically appropriated by idealist academic authors to mean anything and everything, and by business to exploit new forms of labor relations. It is our impression that many Asians critically negotiate these discursive rapids by generating a trajectory of cultural studies that draw specifically on critical discourse analysis and cultural studies "readings" on TV and other media as a means to negotiate Chinese "culture" (e. g., roles of motherhood, family obligation, business practices) in relation to Western social and business practices.

A second cognate strand, translation theory, has become the means for the empirically-minded to achieve this. The study of Western brands and linguistic communities evident in social media are indicators of academic internationalization. A Chinese ethnocentrism was not much in evidence at the Chinese conferences and seminars in which Tomaselli participated (2015-2019) as similarities were discussed in relation to differences, unlike highly theorized and over-generalized cultural studies approaches. These discourse analyses are valuable as markers of academic intercultural negotiation. Such studies are indicators of Chinese and Asian scholarship that, unlike the South African ethnocentric and exclusive instances, want to enter the global world, and *not* claim total difference or separation from it. As Juliane House (2015, pp. 95-96) so effectively observes, owing to its inherent reflective nature, translation has great potential for intercultural communication and intercultural understanding.

Conclusion

Our argument is for a post-Africanist approach to intercultural communication, rooted in pragmatism. Such an approach advocates for the "learning of the world's best practices," irrespective of whether they are African, Eastern, or Western (Ekpo, 2010, p. 184), looking to the period of the "post-" as a way out of a suffocating Afro-ethnocentrism. By incorporating our two very different ethnic, racial, linguistic, and lived experiences, our discursive orbits interact in living ways that have brought them into a harmonic dialogue. Where Paul Tembe's "lived" and ordinary experiences within South Africa, China, and Sweden were initially considered "unscientific" by his academic peers (Tembe, 2020, p. 32), Keyan Tomaselli's cultural encounters were heavily influenced by one of his students, Ngaire Blankenberg (1999), an albino from South Africa who had studied in North America, and who brought to bear a critical analysis that drew on W. E. B. de Bois, an African American philosopher, in examining the contradiction that communitarianism created between two kinds of tyrannies, that between the individual and the community. This critique has now been moderated by Tembe (2020), who implicitly responds to the Blankenberg critique.

The grammars of African languages may be understood to ascribe greater *agency* to more than the (sometimes radically) materialistic objects enshrined in the languages of historically industrialized nations. The formers' grammar has a place for qualifying an existent in terms of its *subjective* relatedness to the other things, persons, and animals around it. Subject and Object thus become interchangeable, in much the same way as occurred in the medieval Scholastic realism of pre-modern Europe. In thus retaining spaces for the authority of the spirits and the ancestors, for example, these grammatical syntheses also permit speakers to ascribe some measure of reality to the powerful influence of the memory of the spoken word. It seems that some essentialist strands of the IKS paradigm are embedded in these kinds of relations. In South Africa especially, these IKS threads draw on a number of so-called *a priori* African values, of which the most commonly cited is *ubuntu* (Tavanaro-Haidarian, 2018). This concept of shared and lived relations is mostly discussed in the academic literature as self-evident, Africanist, and contemporarily relevant. It is presented as a series of propositions, as a kind of analytical philosophy, that exists in and of itself — no matter the mayhem of many of the African societies in which this idealist set of prescriptions occur. Critiques of this framework, which assumes an African exceptionalism and which can result in the tyranny of the individual over the community, are few and far between. Nkonko Kamwangamalu's (1999) pan-African linguistic analysis stands almost alone as a basis for the concept claiming a communitarian ontology.

References

Asante, M. K. (2010). Oro-La: Communicating the person in an African cultural sense. In X. Dai and S. J. Kulich (Eds.), *Identity and intercultural communication (I): Theoretical and contextual construction* (pp. 151 – 160). Intercultural Research Vol. 2. Shanghai Foreign Language Education Press.

Biernatzki, W. E. (Ed.). (1986, 1995). Intercultural communication. *Communication Research Trends*, *7*(3) (1986), *15*(4) (1995). Theme issues.

Blankenberg, N. (1999). In search of a real freedom: *Ubuntu* and the media. *Critical Arts*, *13*(2), 42–65.

Broodryk, J. (2007). *Understanding South Africa: The uBuntu way of living*. Pretoria: uBuntu School of Philosophy.

Coplan, D. (2009). Innocent violence: Social exclusion, identity, and the press in an African democracy. *Critical Arts*, *23*(1), 64–83.

Du Preez, H. (1987). Intercultural communication in South African organisations. *Communicatio: South African Journal for Communication Theory and Research*, *13*(1), 8–15.

Ekpo, D. (2010). From Négritude to Post Africanism. *Third Text*, *24* (2), 177–187.

Fourie, P. J. (2007). Moral philosophy as the foundation of normative media theory: The case of African Ubuntuism. *Communications*, *32*(1), 1–29.

Gade, C. B. N. (2011). The historical development of the written discourses on *Ubuntu*. *South African Journal of Philosophy*, *30*(3), 303–329.

Gade, C. B. N. (2012). What is *Ubuntu*? Different interpretations among South Africans of African descent. *South African Journal of Philosophy*, *31* (3), 493–503.

Goffman, I. (1956). *The presentation of self in everyday life*. Doubleday.

Groenewald, H. J. (1988). Communication in South African society: A perspective on the future. In H. C. Marais (Ed.), *South Africa: Perspectives on the future*. Owen Burgess.

Hall, E. T. (1976). *Beyond culture*. Doubleday.

Hall, S. (1981). Cultural studies and the centre: Some problematics and problems. In S. Hall, D. Hobson, A. Lowe, & P. Willis (Eds.), *Culture, media and language: Working papers in cultural studies, 1972 – 79*. Unwin Hyman.

Hall, S. (1996). Who needs identity? In S. Hall & P. du Gay (Eds.), *Questions of identity* (pp. 1–17). Sage.

Harvey, D. (1990). Between space and time: Reflections on the geographical imagination. *Annals of the Association of American Geographers*, *80* (3), 418–434.

Hofstede, G. (2001). *Culture's consequences: Comparing values, behaviors, institutions, and organizations across nations* (2nd ed.). Sage.

Hofstede, G., & Hofstede, G. J. (2005). *Cultures and organizations: Software of the mind* (Revised & expanded 2nd ed.). McGraw-Hill.

House, J. (2015). *Translation quality assessment: Past and present*. Routledge.

Kagame, A. (1956). *La philosophie Bantu-rwandaise de l'être*. Académie Royale des Sciences Coloniales.

Kamwangamalu, N. (1999). Ubuntu in South Africa: A sociolinguistic perspective to a pan-African concept. *Critical Arts*, *13*(2), 24-41.

Kant, I. (1989). *Critique of pure reason*. Palgrave. (Originally published 1781)

Li, M. (2011). An interview with Robert N. St. Clair on culture, language and communication. *The Free Library* (China Media Research), 1 January.

Mbigi, L. (1997). *Ubuntu: The African dream in management*. Knowledge Resources.

Metz, T. (2011). Ubuntu as a moral theory and human rights in South Africa. *African Human Rights Law Journal*, *11*(2), 532-559.

Naudé, P. (N. d.). The arrogant misuse of Ubuntu. *MBA. co. za*. Accessed 19 May 2015.

Ngcoya, M. (2009). *Ubuntu, globalization, accommodation and contestation in South Africa*. Diss. American University.

Nicolaides, A. (2014). Utilizing Ubuntu to inform Chief Executive Officer (CEO) thinking on Corporate Social Responsibility (CSR) and codes of ethics in business. *Journal of Social Science*, *41*(1), 17-25.

Ovens, M. (2003). A criminological approach to crime in South Africa. *Acta Criminologica*, *16*(3), 67-80.

Oyowe, A. O. (2013). Strange bedfellows: Rethinking *ubuntu* and human rights in South Africa. *African Human Rights Law Journal*, *13*(1), 103-124.

Sandemose, A. (1933). *En Flykting Korsar Sitt Spår*. Gyldendal.

St. Clair, R. N. (2015). The stratification of cultural networks. *Intercultural Communication Studies*, *24*(1), 1-22.

Steene, B. (2007, 14 Nov.). Astrid Lindgren's legacy. *Opendemocracy*.

Swanson, D. (2007). Ubuntu: An African contribution to (re)search for/with humble togetherness. *Journal of Contemporary Issues in Education*, *2* (2), 53-67.

Tavanaro-Haidarian, L. T. (2018). *A relational model of public discourse: The African philosophy of Ubuntu*. Routledge.

Tembe, P. Z. (2020). *Ubuntu beyond identities*. Real African Publishers.

Tembe, P. Z., and Gumede, V. (Eds.). (2020). *Culture, identities, ideologies in Africa-China cooperation*. Africa World Press.

Tempels, P. (1959). *Bantu philosophy*. Présence Africaine 28.

Tomaselli, K. G. (1992). The role of the mass media in promoting intercultural communication in South Africa. *Communicatio: South African Journal for Communication Theory and Research*, *18*(1), 60-68.

Tomaselli, K. G. (1999). Misappropriating discourses: Intercultural communication theory in South Africa, 1980-1995. *Communal/Plural: Journal of Transnational and Cross-cultural Studies*, *7*(2), 137-158.

Tomaselli, K. G. (2016). Ubuntu and intercultural communication: Power, inclusion and exclusion. *Intercultural Communication Studies*, *25*(2), 1-13.

Tomaselli, K. G. (2020). Intercultural communication: A southern view on the way ahead: culture, terrorism and spirituality. *Annals of the International Communication Association*, *44* (1), 19 - 33. https://doi. org/10. 1080/23808985.2019.1595696

Tomaselli, K. G., & Du, Y. (2021). Identity, *différance*, and global cultural studies: China going abroad. In M. Steppat & S. Kulich (Eds.), *Literature and interculturality (3): From cultural junctions to globalization* (pp. 231 - 262). Intercultural Research Vol. 10. Shanghai Foreign Language Education Press.

Tomaselli, K. G., Louw, E., & Tomaselli, R. (1990). Communication, language and the crisis of hegemony in South Africa. In S. Thomas & W. A. Evans

(Eds.), *Communication and culture 4* (pp. 1-17). Ablex.

Triandis, H. (2014). Dynamics of individualism and collectivism across cultures. In S. J. Kulich, L. Weng, & M. H. Prosser (Eds.), *Value dimensions and their contextual dynamics across cultures* (pp. 61 - 82). Intercultural Research Vol. 5. Shanghai Foreign Language Education Press.

Vaagen, R. W. (2016). Communication across cultures, time and space: A Festschrift in honor of Professor Robert N. St. Clair, President IAICS, 2013 - 2015. *Intercultural Communication Studies*, 25(1), 1-16.

van Niekerk, J. (2013). Ubuntu and moral value. Unpublished Doctoral thesis. University of the Witwatersrand.

7

The Cultural Perception of Space: Expanding the Legacy of Edward T. Hall

Richard HARRIS
Chukyo University, Japan

Summary: In 1963, Edward T. Hall coined the term *proxemics* to describe what he then termed "the interrelated observations and theories of humans' use of space as a specialized elaboration of culture" (Hall, 1966, p. 1). Expanding on this theme in his book *The Hidden Dimension*, Hall inspired a generation of scholars to look more closely at the myriad ways in which people perceived and interacted with each other and with the physical environments, natural and built, in which they found themselves.

Hall's focus, however, was mainly on interpersonal space, looking for instance at differences in social distance compared across cultures, and on how these differences were reflected in such phenomena as conversations, queueing, or seating arrangements. As the world globalizes, however, and people from different cultural backgrounds come more frequently and significantly into contact with each other, particularly in urban environments, other aspects of proxemics have become more salient. It is too often assumed that any two or more people in a certain setting, irrespective of cultural background, will tend to perceive their surroundings in similar ways and, to a large extent, share similar cognitive and emotional experiences. Consequently, there is a focus on the *content* of the interaction, with a corresponding neglect of the physical and cultural *context*. In this chapter I expand Hall's pioneering insights by suggesting a model that considers a wider range of intercultural perceptions and responses.

Introduction

> *We do not see things as they are;*
> *we see them as we are.* (Anaïs Nin)

Edward Twitchell Hall (1914–2009) can fairly be thought of as one of the principal founders of the academic field of intercultural communication, introducing many concepts that are still routinely used by scholars today. Many of his books, starting with *The Silent Language* (Hall, 1959), have been continuously in print, and his influence on research and practice has been immense, perhaps particularly in the study of what has become known as the anthropology of space. [1] Hall's original investigations into the responses of humans in different cultures to personal space and concepts of crowding, a study for which he coined the term *proxemics*, were revolutionary for their time and have proved to be of lasting value (see also the analysis in Altman & Vinsel, 1977). Over the last half-century, however, various factors including migration (voluntary and involuntary), mass tourism, and urbanization[2] have increasingly brought people from very different cultural backgrounds together, exposing wide variations in cultural values and perceptual responses to the environment that can bring about confusion, misunderstanding, and even conflict. In this sense, the topic of different responses to physical space, both naturally occurring and humanly constructed, is no longer of merely academic interest but has become an issue of vital importance, necessitating further study.

Possibly influenced by Hall's multidisciplinary work, attempts have been made, not only from anthropology but from the sociocultural, psychological, and philosophical traditions, to categorize different

---

[1] See, for instance, the comprehensively edited volume by Low & Lawrence-Zúñiga (2003).

[2] Since 2008, according to the United Nations, for the first time in history more than fifty percent of the world's 8 billion people now live in urban areas — a proportion significantly higher in developed countries (see data at population.un.org).

aspects of space and its effects on human interaction, most notably perhaps Edward W. Soja's concept of "first space" (Soja, 1996) as a physical, recognizable entity. An example might be the U. S.-Mexico border fence; although many national boundaries are to a large extent abstract or non-material, the fence is an observable reality, a first space, albeit with important non-physical associations. A further exploration of the cultural interpretation of space is Homi K. Bhabha's third-space theory (Bhabha, 2004), in which the space in focus can either be a physical space, such as a classroom or a coffee shop, or an abstract concept implying a context within which individuals form unique yet hybridized identities. So deeply ingrained are these attitudes and responses that their influence is often not seen as culturally contingent, but as universal "common sense." As Julian Baggini has written, "assumptions about the nature of self, ethics, sources of knowledge, the goals of life, are deeply embedded in our cultures and frame our thinking without our being aware of them" (Baggini, 2018, pp. xiii-xiv).

Hall, like most anthropologists since the conceptual revolution initiated by Boas, Benedict, and Mead in the early 20th century (King, 2019), paid more attention and respect to the diversity of human cultures than to any supposed commonality, and this has been a core tenet of the intercultural field from its inception. Nevertheless, the attitude that all humans are basically "the same under the skin," characterized by Milton Bennett as "minimization" (Bennett, 1998), still has its adherents, and attempts to demonstrate a universal cognitive and perceptive core to humanity, however flawed, have had a long and enduring influence. The well-known hierarchy of human needs postulated by the psychologist Abraham Maslow (Maslow, 1943) is a case in point. Uncontroversial in its description of a base level of physiological needs — all animals need air, food, and water in order to survive — the respectively ascending levels of safety, belonging, esteem, and self-actualization are defined and expressed so differently across cultures as to render them virtually meaningless in any supposed universal sense. Similarly, many of the items in anthropologist Donald Brown's list of traits asserted to be found in all human societies, even prompting his coining of the term "universal people" (Brown, 1991), are either biologically banal (childhood fear of loud noises, wariness around snakes, pain), distinctly questionable (collective decision-making, envy), or incomprehensively vague (false beliefs, intention). Brown's views have been enthusiastically endorsed by many, however, including evolutionary psychologist Steven Pinker, who is an eloquent advocate for the universalist influence of nature in human activity relative to that of its supposed culturally contingent rival, nurture (Pinker, 2002). Cross-cultural psychologists such as Richard Nisbett, however, arguing for the pervasive influence of learned patterns of behavior, have found significant differences in cognitive and perceptual processes across cultures (Nisbett, 2003). The United Nations Universal Declaration of Human Rights (1948) attempts, with the noblest of intentions, to formulate a universalist moral code to which all societies could adhere, but has been criticized as fundamentally Eurocentric[3] in its assumptions, and so ambiguous as to be open to a wide and contradictory range of interpretation — and has not been made legally binding in any country. [4]

Given the enduring appeal of universalism, and as an example of the lack of cultural awareness alluded to by Baggini above, it is often assumed that perception of the environment is a kind of biological universal since, with few exceptions and some degree of individual variation, all humans are physiologically similar in that they receive information about the external world by means of their five senses of sight, hearing, touch, taste, and smell. Illustrative of this attitude are oft-heard quotidian appeals to "human nature," "common sense," or the "obvious." The philosopher John Searle has noted, with regard to this view:

> There is a common-sense conception of visual perception that is demonstrably false. It is the conception according to which vision is a matter of the passive reception of stimuli and the production of visual experiences by the neurobiological apparatus. (Searle, 2015, p.70)

That is, while the fact of sensory reception of physical stimuli may be unobjectionable, the *perception* of such stimuli is far more complex, involving processes of selection, organization, and interpretation that are far from universal. By means of these perceptive processes, humans shape the wealth of stimuli that constantly flood their senses

---

③ Kwame Anthony Appiah's arresting phrase in this regard is "Eurocentric hegemony *posing* as universalism" (Appiah, 1992, p.58). Nevertheless, it is notable that many non-European nations enthusiastically endorsed the document.

④ It is worth noting that anthropologist Melville Herskovits, president of the American Anthropological Association at the time of the declaration's drafting, argued passionately but unsuccessfully for it to be based on the principle of cultural relativity rather than universality — which would have made it a very different document.

into a coherent whole that becomes for them veridical, albeit constructed, reality. Such meaningful coherence, though, is without doubt culturally contingent; our backgrounds — social, environmental, economic, religious, familial, educational — predispose us to focus on certain aspects of the environment to the exclusion of others, to assign these selections to certain socially sanctioned mental categories, and to interpret them according to culturally defined meanings. [5]

A dramatic illustration of Searle's point has been offered by anthropologist Colin Turnbull, from his experience of living with the Mbuti people in the dense rain forests of the Congo. Kenge, a man raised in the forest who had excellent eyesight superbly adapted to his environment, proved, on first exposure to the open savannah, to have no robust sense of depth perception, the awareness that objects in the visual field appear to diminish in size with distance. Accordingly, Kenge mistook a far-off herd of buffalo — animals with which he was very familiar — for a swarm of insects (Turnbull, 1961). In analogous fashion, immigrants moving from rural to urban settlements are likely to have culturally-formed reactions to the sights, smells, and sounds of the new environment that will be fundamentally different from those of the lifelong urban residents who are their new neighbors. And according to Julian Baggini, the built environment itself embodies to a certain extent the values of its inhabitants, which are "embedded in the fabric of the world's great monuments, which can be read like living books, expressions of the philosophies of the people who built them. " Elaborating this point, he goes on to claim:

> The Forbidden City in Beijing is constructed on Confucian principles, the Alhambra in Granada is infused with Islamic thought, while even the cafés of the Parisian *rive gauche* testify to the existentialist vision of philosophy as a personal, everyday pursuit. (Baggini, 2018, p. xiv)

Both Searle's comment and Turnbull's anecdote above are concerned with visual perception, but the point made regarding cultural impact is clearly applicable to the other four senses as well. The unexpected smell of a clove cigarette in a foreign setting will transport the Indonesian expatriate back to his homeland just as powerfully as the taste of Proust's madeleine unlocked previously lost memories of his Combray childhood — both reactions inaccessible and

---

[5] See Berger & Luckmann (1966) for the classic treatment of this theme.

to a certain extent incomprehensible to anyone without those cultural or individual references. Certain sounds, such as the Muslim call to prayer, carry very different meanings, cognitive and emotional, depending on the religious background of the hearer, and the significance of texture to the blind cannot be fully appreciated by those with sight.

For the purposes of this chapter I shall be concentrating mostly on visual perception, but shall mention the other senses when appropriate. I shall also be considering three other aspects of perception than the sensory: cognitive, emotional, and moral. By cognitive perception I am referring to the interpretation of the sensory stimulus according to the knowledge, experience, memory, and cultural bias of the perceiver — an interpretation which may not, of course, be shared by others. Emotional perception concerns the affective response to a stimulus: is it pleasant or unpleasant? Does it make the perceiver anxious or relaxed? Happy, sad, or indifferent? By moral perception I am alluding to an evaluative reaction: is the perception of a sensory experience judged to be right or wrong, good or bad, normal or abnormal? Obviously, these distinctions are to a certain degree arbitrary, and clearly overlap, but I believe that considering them somewhat separately in this manner helps to navigate the complexity of culturally inflected reactions to a scene or experience. Finally, I need to mention that one aspect of space perception that I shall unfortunately not be discussing in this chapter is that of the ubiquity and influence of computer-mediated social networks. As Pankaj Mishra has written: "Today's colossal exodus of human lives into cyberspace is ever more dramatically transforming old notions of time, space, knowledge, values, identities, and social relations" (Mishra, 2017, p.335). Not only is it probably too early to assess fully the effects of the transformations described by Mishra, it is a theme of vital and growing importance requiring a detailed treatment in its own right, and falls outside the parameters of this chapter.

Given the complexity of the concept of cultural influences on the perception of physical space, it is necessary to construct some kind of structure, however artificial and incomplete, in order to facilitate discussion of the theme. I am therefore proposing a six-part framework of different kinds of space perception that, while having little or no discrete physical reality, nevertheless enables a manageable analysis of an otherwise amorphous mass of information. My first category I have termed *cosmological*, referring to understandings and assumptions as to the nature of the earth and the universe, both physical and metaphysical. Under the *geographical* frame I consider different ideas about the people of the world and their views regarding the regions they and others inhabit on the earth's surface. *Environmental* deals with the effects of the physical landscape, both naturally occurring and humanly constructed, on perception and interaction, while *communal* refers to issues such as settlement patterns, boundaries, and differing conceptions of public and private space. Under the heading of *residential* I discuss the relationship between human perception and houses or dwelling places, with some reference also to workplaces; and in my final category, *personal*, topics such as interpersonal distance, body language, and other aspects of non-verbal communication are addressed. Clearly, these six frames are to a certain extent arbitrary, and overlap considerably, yet they do constitute an approach, however flawed, to what may otherwise seem an impenetrable tangle.

Cosmological Perception

The way in which individuals think of the wider cosmos may at first appear to have little to do with everyday life, and on first consideration the cosmological frame may appear to be the most abstract of the six; yet its influence pervades, often implicitly, all aspects of human existence. All cultures and all individuals imbue the world as they experience it with systems of symbolic meaning, often influenced by their religion, to the extent that their conception of the world they inhabit, their literal worldview, is based on much more than sensory experience. In fact, emotional and moral perceptions through this cosmological lens tend to be more salient than any conclusions arrived at by means of the senses. Edward Hall, with his long and intimate experience of the lives of his Pueblo and Navajo friends and neighbors in New Mexico, was well aware of this essentially spiritual dimension to perception (Hall, 1994). For cultures and individuals whose governing paradigm is a religious one, the existence of a reality beyond the rationally explicable — a soul, spirit, or the supernatural — is an accepted aspect of life, but is an attitude rejected in much of the developed world, where the dominant scientific paradigm posits an entirely materialist basis for existence. "The mystery is not about why the Universe has some very particular properties rather than others," states physicist Anthony

Aguirre, "but about the connection between those properties and our very existence as living, conscious beings contemplating those properties" (Aguirre, 2019, p. xii).

Connected to the difference in outlook between science and religion is the fundamental issue of the degree of freedom that humans have in their lives; that is, to what extent are humans in control of, or controlled by external forces. There is a continuum of thought in this respect featuring, at one end, the post-Enlightenment, Utopian confidence that science and rationality will eventually enable humans to understand and manipulate all aspects of the world and their lives. At the other end of the scale is the belief that the universe is inherently mysterious, unknowable, and unpredictable. Between these two poles lies the multifarious range of human responses to existence, displaying a mixture of scientific and metaphysical elements. "The worldview in which most of us were tacitly brought up holds that we are spectators and actors in a universe that would be pretty much the same without us," claims David Park, before going on to make the highly questionable generalization that "in the East, that possibility is almost unimaginable" (Park, 2005, p. 17). Most religions in fact occupy a middle position on this continuum, conceiving of a cosmos inhabited by supernatural forces that are either indifferent to humanity, benign, or malevolent, requiring some form of propitiation by ritual or intercession. Others may rely on sacred texts or human representatives claiming some kind of supernatural mandate, challenges to or even inquiry into which may be termed sacrilege, with legal, social, and personal consequences.

Although the prevailing liberal attitude in the developed world is that people are in principle free to believe in and practice what they like, emotional and moral reactions to "other" religion-inflected thought and behavior can lead to serious conflict. Secular France, for instance, along with many other European jurisdictions, in a policy move widely interpreted as targeting Muslim women, has banned the open display of religious symbols such as headscarves in public institutions including state schools and government offices. A similar law in Quebec has recently sparked outrage at the dismissal of a Muslim teacher for wearing a *hijab*, contrary to the law's prohibition against the wearing of religious symbols by public servants. [6] (It is true that the law applies equally to crucifixes, but these can be worn

---

[6] See Cecco (2021).

beneath clothing without contravening the law.) Such bans are usually defended as upholding tradition, but as immigration and cultural mixing increase these measures can be seen as discrimination and even persecution, or at the very least as a failure to appreciate the subtleties of a different cultural reality.

A particularly salient example of the influence of cosmological perception is the concept of sacred space, the notion that certain locations either on the earth's surface or elsewhere in the cosmos are imbued with a spiritual essence absent from the profane residuum of the material universe. Secular societies today have almost entirely dispensed with this concept, yet as Carlos Eire writes of pre-Reformation Europe, "specific earthly points [...] were believed to be closer to heaven. [...] [S]pace itself assumed a hierarchical order in Catholic piety" (Eire, 2016, p. 30). Even the great mediaeval cathedrals were often built on sites held in pre-Christian times to hold some kind of numinous power. Etiolated vestiges of this belief remain for Catholics in the form of particular shrines or holy sites, but in general the paradigm shift[7] brought about by such factors as the heliocentric theory of the solar system, the Protestant Reformation, and the rise of scientific thinking based on rigorous observation and measurement have led in the developed West at least to what Max Weber famously termed "the desacralization of the world" (*die Entzauberung der Welt*) — a development with wide-ranging ramifications (see Sheldrake, 1990). In many cultures, however, the idea of sacred space is an ever-present reality, involving the veneration of mountains, groves, springs, grottoes, and other features of the landscape that can be all too easily profaned by unwitting trespassers such as tourists or migrants. Rituals to placate the spirits of the land prior to construction are regularly performed in many places, including developed and largely secular Japan. In Hong Kong, China, even the mighty Disney corporation was obliged to redesign its hitherto unchangeable theme park layout in the face of pressure from local *feng shui* experts.[8]

A further aspect to the range of cultural differences in cosmological

---

[7] "Paradigm shift" is the term given by Thomas Kuhn to a fundamental change in understanding such that it is no longer possible to revert to the former model. Other examples from those given in the text would be the germ theory of disease and Einsteinian relativity (Kuhn, 1996).

[8] Hong Kong, China provides many examples of the clash between secular and spiritual cosmological worldviews.

perception can be seen in the attitude of people to the whole earth itself, not just specific sites on its surface. For many Christians, among others, for instance, the earth is a temporary, fallen abode of the flesh, an inferior prelude to eternal life in a non-physical, *post-mortem* realm. The contrast with belief systems such as those of native Americans, and many pre-industrial societies, who tend to view the whole earth as a sacred space, the Great Mother, is dramatic, and secular humanists also may have a more reverential, custodial perspective toward the planet (see Berry, 2009). Other cosmological conceptions would include the Buddhist belief in six different realms of existence into one of which the individual is reincarnated after death, the Hindu notion of very long cycles of cosmic creation, decay, destruction, and rebirth, or the Taoist view of the essential unity of heaven and humanity.

Even recent debates over the reality of and the appropriate response to climate change may also owe something to differing cosmological perspectives. As it becomes ever clearer, however, environmental problems such as deforestation, fossil fuel usage, pollution, and the associated effects of climate change are global in nature and can only be solved by people from all cultures and nations working together. It is to be hoped that the urgency of the situation will encourage and accelerate this process. The stunning photographs taken of the earth by the Apollo astronauts between 1968 and 1972, the most reproduced images in history,[9] were epiphanic to many people irrespective of religious outlook, and possibly influenced such developments as the annual Earth Day celebration, the favorable response to James Lovelock's Gaia Hypothesis (Lovelock, 2006), and the increase in membership of environmental groups. Difficult though our own cosmological assumptions may be to recognize, their fundamental importance as a source of cultural misunderstanding and conflict can hardly be in question.[10]

---

[9] The wide-ranging influence of these images, along with other pictorial depictions of the cosmos, is discussed in fascinating detail in Cosgrove (2001).

[10] The enduring conflict over the status of Jerusalem is a tragic example of the incompatibility of differing cosmological conceptions, perceptions of the city being almost entirely emotional, inaccessible to rational debate.

Geographical Perception

In 1976 the illustrator Saul Steinberg produced a cover for the *New Yorker* magazine that has since spawned countless imitations in cities around the world. Titled "View of the World from 9th Avenue," the drawing shows the area between that thoroughfare and the Hudson River in meticulous detail familiar to most New Yorkers. Beyond the river, however, a featureless brown strip is labelled "New Jersey" and the remaining entirety of the continental United States is sporadically and approximately indicated by the names of five cities, three states, and a few random, unnamed rocks. The Pacific Ocean looks hardly wider than the Hudson, and three indistinct land masses on the horizon beyond are roughly designated "Russia," "China," and "Japan." At one level, of course, the cover refers to the stereotype of New Yorkers as intensely parochial and self-absorbed, but the image's enduring popularity, demonstrated by its transposition to so many other cities around the globe, suggests a deeper relevance: the historical and ubiquitous tendency of people to see themselves and their place of residence as the center of the world, their knowledge of and interest in other regions diminishing rapidly with distance. [11] Examples abound at both regional and national levels; China has always thought of itself as the "Middle Kingdom," and the arbitrary agreement in 1884 to locate the prime meridian in London, England, has doubtless reinforced the already robust conviction on the part of that city's (and country's) inhabitants that they occupy the world's central location. [12] As the world globalizes and urbanizes, such literally ethnocentric perceptions, with all their emotional force, can hardly fail to be a source of confusion and resentment.

For the majority of people, ideas about the shape of the world and the disposition of its landmasses and its peoples come from maps, and the information derived from them is usually internalized as objective truth, rather than maps being understood as being the highly selective, often politicized constructions of compromise and convention that they in fact are. There is no entirely satisfactory method of representing the curved surface of the

---

[11] For a wide-ranging discussion of this fascinating theme, see Michell (1994).

[12] An apocryphal but nevertheless instructive insight can be gleaned from the alleged 20th-century London newspaper headline: "Heavy fog in the English Channel: Europe cut off."

earth on a flat sheet of paper, and the chosen projection reflects the intentions, benign or manipulative, of the cartographer. Thus the familiar Mercator projection, devised in the 16th century when European nations were energetically exploring and colonizing the world, considerably facilitated navigation by rendering the meridians parallel, which enabled ships' courses to be plotted on straight-line compass bearings. While being of undeniable convenience and benefit to sailors, however, this projection inevitably distorts the shape and size of countries closer to the poles, making Greenland, for instance, appear twice the size of the whole of South America, whereas its area is in fact only slightly larger than that of Mexico. Conversely, land masses in the tropics, including the enormous continent of Africa, appear much smaller than their actual size, and correspondingly less significant than the developed, temperate countries of Europe. The particular features of the Mercator map, then, should have led to its being recognized as an invaluable tool for navigation, but a seriously flawed representation of the actual world. Unfortunately, however, it became the standard map used in classrooms in the developed world for centuries until its political implications were exposed in the 1970s by the German historian Arno Peters, who promoted an equal-area projection as being "fairer" to developing countries near the equator.[13] Even a cursory comparison of this projection to a three-dimensional globe, however, shows that it pays a heavy price for this egalitarian treatment with respect to area, in that it severely distorts the *shape* of the earth's landmasses. The "Peters map" is therefore neither more nor less accurate than the Mercator projection; it merely suggests a different perception.

Rather than relying on any one, necessarily imperfect, depiction then, a range of maps making use of different projections and conventions would be a far better way of representing the complexity of the earth and its countries. Maps centred on the zero meridian, for instance, a convention determined by an international committee in 1884, give great visual prominence to the countries of Europe and North America. Those commonly found in Asia, however, tend to be centred on the 180-degree meridian, dramatically exposing the scale of the Pacific Ocean and restoring many smaller islands to a prominence denied them by Eurocentric versions. Area cartograms offer yet a

---

[13] The so-called "Peters map" was used on the cover of the 1980 Brandt report on global inequality, making clear the connection between cartographic misrepresentation and economic disadvantage.

different perspective by deliberately distorting the size of countries in order to highlight such factors as population, economic strength, literacy rates, military spending, and infant mortality — unconventional but equally valid perceptions of the world. [14] And no map is inherently obliged to adhere to the convention of placing north at the top, a point eloquently made by *McArthur's Universal Corrective Map of the World*, a popular Australian representation with south (and therefore Australia) at the top, the position of status and honor. For similar reasons, mediaeval European maps showed east at the top (thereby giving rise to the original, literal meaning of *orientation*), as that was the direction of the Christian holy land and thus deserving of special status and worth. It is perhaps noteworthy that the "top" having this connotation is itself a cosmological perception, possibly deriving from the popular Christian conception of heaven as above, up therefore being the direction of good.

So entrenched are some cartographical conventions that the shock of seeing them controverted can either be welcomed as constructive or rejected as subversive. At the very least, their exposure as mere convention can shine a light on the deliberate distortions of ideologically motivated cartography. The delineation of national frontiers in Africa and the Middle East without regard for historical or cultural boundaries remains a source of intense conflict, and the gerrymandered maps of electoral districts in the United States and other countries prioritize political benefit over physical and social reality. "To those who have strength in the world," states Brian Harley, "shall be added strength in the map" (Harley, 2001, p. 158). [15] For most people, of course, maps serve the primarily utilitarian purpose of facilitating navigation from one place to another, but even the humblest road map inevitably involves an often unregarded compromise in its selection, in translating from what exists on the ground to screen or paper, of what to include and what to omit. Attention is therefore focused on some aspects of the landscape to the exclusion of others, thus replicating in some measure the experience of the Steinberg cartoon described above. GPS systems such as aircraft in-flight displays are particularly prone to this kind of editing, showing only the sketchiest information about the ground beneath. A notable exception is that of airlines

---

[14] Smith (2021) is a wonderful collection of these area cartograms, covering an impressively wide range of important topics.

[15] An excellent recent overview of this topic is offered by Aspen Pflughoeft (2021).

based in Islamic countries, which routinely display the location of Mecca, enabling Muslims to face the correct direction for their prayers, just as arrows on the ceilings of Middle Eastern hotel rooms similarly help believers to align themselves with this spiritually important focus.

The naming of places and geographic features has always been a contested topic.[16] Korean visitors to Japan tend to resent their hosts' conviction that the body of water dividing their two countries is the Sea of Japan, just as many French sensibilities are offended at having to cross the English Channel on their way to London — only to be further irritated, no doubt, by their train's arrival at Waterloo Station. Is it correct to talk of Burma or Myanmar, Bombay or Mumbai, Mount McKinley or Denali?[17] Without direct experience or local contact we are obliged to rely on external sources for much of this kind of geographical information, and those sources may themselves be inaccurate or biased. We form our perceptions of the world we have not visited and its inhabitants we have not met through exposure to various kinds of media, including maps, none of which has an unassailable claim to objective truth. Based on this selective exposure, however, we form firm images and associations which in many cases may be no more than stereotypes, with all their attendant dangers. Both news and entertainment media, in so far as they can be distinguished, tend to focus on the dramatic, so it is hard to hear mention of Columbia without immediate connotations of drug cartels. The potential for intercultural offense, albeit unintentional, through reliance on such one-dimensional generalizations is obvious.

Environmental Perception

From their earliest beginnings on the grasslands of Africa, in a very short space of time in evolutionary terms, human beings have spread around the globe adapting to an astonishingly diverse range of physical environments, from almost waterless deserts to humid rainforests, to frozen tundra. Their behavioral and psychological

---

[16] This issue is discussed with humor and insight by Monmonier (2006).

[17] In a recent book Simon Winder discusses this English carelessness in the naming of places and the tendency to over-generalize, citing "the Victorian tradition in English ships that all European sailors were simply 'Dutchmen' even if they actually came from Sweden or Italy or wherever" (Winder, 2019, p. xv).

responses to this variety of landscapes have influenced the formation of an equally diverse range of cultures. Polynesian sailors navigate confidently across vast swathes of open ocean, responding to subtle variations in tide, current, and water color imperceptible to outsiders, just as the Inuit of the arctic circle find their way through regions of apparently featureless snow and ice, and the San people of the Kalahari, like the Australian aborigines, have the ability to locate food and water in the most ostensibly inhospitable surroundings. Since there appear to be no significant neurobiological or genetic differences among humans from such widely separated habitats, societies must have developed distinct yet environmentally appropriate cultural responses and culturally specific ways of accommodating to the world around them. Human beings, that is, are influenced by their cultures, not their biology, to pay close attention to certain features of their particular landscape and to develop a survival-enabling sensitivity to its most subtle variations. [18]

It follows from the above that people from different cultural backgrounds will have very different perceptions — sensory, cognitive, emotional, and moral — of the same scene or experience, and what may be too easily assumed to be the one correct way of viewing or interpreting a scene may justifiably be seen in an entirely dissimilar manner by someone who, by virtue of his or her background, is paying attention to an alternative selection of elements in the environment and correspondingly ignoring others. One attempt to categorize the possible range of reactions to an ostensibly unchanging scene has been made by D. W. Meinig, who has suggested ten plausible "readings" of a landscape depending on the attitude of the perceiver — artists, farmers, property developers, for instance, will all be seeing the same mountain but experiencing very different thoughts and emotions (Meinig, 1979). Obviously far from comprehensive, Meinig's taxonomy nevertheless demonstrates very clearly how the cultural background of an individual observer influences what is experienced and how it is interpreted, a necessary reminder of the highly contextual and contingent nature of our reactions with regard to the perception of space. In the post-Romantic West, the appreciation of mountains as sublime and magnificent — "nature's cathedrals" — is unlikely to be shared by villagers living in the shadow of an active

---

[18] Ethnographic literature offers a wealth of examples in support of this assertion, including the episode described by Colin Turnbull as cited in the introduction to this chapter.

volcano, or in daily fear of unpredictable landslide, or who view the wilderness as the home of dangerous animals or malevolent spirits. Even in the case of an unequivocally benign phenomenon, the Tikopia islanders with whom Raymond Firth lived were bemused by his rapturous appreciation of a multicolored sunset, an event they regarded with complete indifference (Firth, 1957).

The psychological mechanism of habituation is the ability of human beings to focus on selected aspects of an environment while keeping the background constant. Thus it is that longtime city dwellers learn to "tune out" the constant noise of traffic, and office workers are not conscious of the hum of air conditioners or the tapping of keyboards. Country dwellers will sleep happily through the chattering and buzzing of animals and insects, or the flow of a river, yet will wake instantly at an unfamiliar or threatening sound, even at a lower volume. As urbanization and migration accelerate, however, increasing numbers of people are finding themselves in an environment that is not only unfamiliar but heavily mediated, in which they are technologically insulated from the effects of weather, darkness, and natural smells and sounds. People from more organic cultural backgrounds may well experience the city as a locus of sensory deprivation, cut off from the "real" world to which they were formerly accustomed. Edward Hall noted in a famous study that many Arab visitors were uncomfortable in U.S. houses, finding them "tomb-like" in that they lacked the access to light and air that characterized traditional Middle Eastern architecture (Hall, 1966). Central air conditioning, an increasingly common feature of architecture in the developed world, is still rare in many regions, where natural cooling is the norm or where the inhabitants have learned to adapt, sartorially and psychologically, to fluctuations in temperature and humidity. The general increase in temperature associated with global climate change is likely to accelerate this tendency further, and it has been suggested that there may be both individual and social effects from this rise in the availability of or need for air conditioning, as humans become less willing or less able to adapt to climatic changes, and may therefore be less likely to mingle with neighbors at outdoor gatherings on summer evenings, as has long been traditional in Mediterranean and many other cultures (Cox, 2012).

Finally in this section, mention must be made of the contentious and nowadays largely discredited theory of environmental determinism. Drawing on data that seem to suggest that a society's economic success correlates with its distance from the equator, the specious and perniciously racist argument has been made that, since they have to plan ahead, store food, and prepare in other ways for the winter, people from the temperate latitudes are "naturally" more hardworking, productive, and intelligent than their counterparts in the tropics (Huntington, 1915).[19] This "equatorial effect" is generally held nowadays to be an historical accident, in many cases an outcome of the distorting effects of European colonization, although Jared Diamond has advanced a persuasive and far less offensive argument that the physical geography of the Eurasian landmass enabled easier latitudinal communication, commerce, and technology exchange, developments further facilitated by that area's disproportionate number of domesticable animals and edible crop species compared to the equatorial regions (Diamond, 1997). The enduring appeal of the environmental determinist idea, however, is such that prejudicial stereotypes can still be found among inhabitants of the temperate zones, even within the same country — the ingenious, industrious Yankee being compared favorably to the indolent Southerner, while workers in the north of Italy and even Germany may hold derogatory opinions regarding the work ethic and character of their southern compatriots. In the southern hemisphere similar attitudes obtain, but in the reverse direction, so that enterprising Australians from Melbourne, for example, may hold a dim view of tropical Queenslanders. Proximity to the equator has all too often been interpreted as a climatic determinant, producing people and cultures all too happy to lie in the sun picking fruit from trees without going to the trouble of cultivating them. Consequently, it may then seem right and natural that the hardworking people from temperate latitudes have come to dominate the world economically, politically, and culturally. Such attitudes are often unconscious, but the implicit bias they suggest is tellingly embedded in thoughtless jokes and lazy stereotypes; their continuing existence can only impede intercultural understanding and communication.

Communal Perception

Human beings are, with some rare exceptions, social animals living

---

[19] The apparent counter-example of tropical yet successful Singapore is explained by the fact that the city-state's population is 80% Chinese from more temperate regions.

in groups of differing sizes. Across the world, in an impressive diversity of environments discussed in the last section, they live and interact in settlements that vary widely in scope, shape, and character, sharing space and resources according to the culturally determined rules and traditions of the community. So effectively are these rules and traditions internalized, however, that over time they can ossify into virtually immutable values, inflexible codes, and moral imperatives with regard to the use of space and the concomitant rights and responsibilities of the community's members. These indurate perspectives thus appear to those members as universal common sense, rather than the culturally contingent constructs that they are. Within a settled culture these patterns of thought and behavior are widely, albeit tacitly, understood, and rarely challenged; it is only when outsiders holding different values and assumptions break or contest them, either intentionally or unknowingly, that misunderstanding and conflict can arise. How do we distinguish, for instance, public space from private, and what are the appropriate or permissible behaviors connected to each? Failure to appreciate these conceptual subtleties has led to tragic outcomes, as in the 1992 case of the Japanese exchange student who was fatally shot because he was unaware that, unlike in Japan, a Louisiana householder's private property extends to the sidewalk, along with his or her right to repel perceived trespass with lethal force. The "zero tolerance" policies with regard to graffiti of many U.S. and European cities would perplex visitors from parts of India, where even the outside walls of houses are considered public space, freely used for advertising or political slogans without any need for the residents' consent. How do newcomers to a city recognize "safe" areas and distinguish them from potentially dangerous "no go" zones? Whose responsibility is it to clean the shared walkway used by many families in an apartment block? What is the correct response to the neighbor's incessantly barking dog? Who has the authority to adjudicate in disputes over parking spaces?

As the numbers of migrants to cities increase, so people all across the world find themselves unmoored from the old, traditional certainties of communal life, trying to adapt to physically and socially ambiguous environments where, all too often, interactions with neighbors take the form of conflict over differing communal expectations and assumptions. Too few of the rapidly growing urban settlements make committed attempts to replicate the traditional seasonal festivals or other gatherings of rural communities that provide residents with convivial and amicable interaction, strengthening relationships and building new communities.

A useful starting point for any discussion of settlement patterns and their influence on attitudes to space and communication is the distinction made by the German sociologist Ferdinand Tönnies in the late 19th century. Tönnies identified two distinct types of human association that he termed *Gemeinschaft* and *Gesellschaft*.[20] (This formulation was to prove of immediate utility, quickly taken up and elaborated by scholars such as Max Weber and, in critical mode, Emile Durkheim.) Often translated simply as "community," the concept of *Gemeinschaft* for Tönnies implies a loose, organic, essentially unplanned organization, to which members are committed as much as, or more than, any individual considerations. *Gesellschaft*, in contrast, denotes a structured, purposive form of association maintained by individuals acting teleologically in their own interest. The term means "company" or "corporation" in contemporary German, but is also used to describe the structure of civic society, in which explicit planning and control are seen to be necessary. The model for a *Gemeinschaft* type of organization is the family, but any form of association based on shared beliefs and values, such as a religious group, would qualify. Agricultural villagers may well feel an allegiance to extended family and locality far stronger than to employers or to civil society at large. A modern business enterprise, on the other hand, or a planned housing development, may be more of a *Gesellschaft*, in which individuals are linked less by tradition or shared values and more by relative self-interest, such as the need to make a living or the desire for a more comfortable house. In reality, of course, most human associations exhibit elements of both of these types, but the attitudes of individuals to such ideas as responsibilities, rights, authority, autonomy, and boundaries may be strongly influenced by their previous exposure to predominantly *Gemeinschaft* or *Gesellschaft* environments. The organic, unplanned layout of settlements in the developing world and older European cities offer a stark contrast to the relentlessly grid-planned towns and housing developments seen in more modern developments.[21] The

---

[20]　Tönnies was originally a scholar of Thomas Hobbes, and it is likely that he based his categories on Hobbes's concepts of "concord" and "union."

[21]　An example is the Indian city of Chandigarh, designed to be the post-independence capital of Punjab by the western architects Mayer, Nowicki, and Le Corbusier, and owing little to the vernacular architecture and traditional settlement patterns of the region.

historian Eric Hobsbawm has discussed these concepts, expanding their reference and applying them imaginatively to a range of contemporary issues, concluding that globalization is impelling the entire planet towards an increasingly remote form of *Gesellschaft* (Hobsbawm, 2007), and the Marxist theorist Fredric Jameson has written of the ambivalent postmodern nostalgia, even envy, evinced by *Gesellschaft* dwellers for a romanticized *Gemeinschaft* past (Hardt & Weeks, 2000). Mention must also be made, although a thorough discussion lies outside the scope of this essay, of the theory of "imagined communities" advanced by Benedict Anderson (Anderson, 1991). In his work, Anderson emphasized the influence of various media on the formation of a community mindset, including not only print and broadcast media, but also institutional media such as schools, maps, and museums. (His inclusion of maps as a major factor relates back to their discussion in the Geographical section above; one way in which a community could be defined would be its collective allegiance to a particular map.)

The tendency noted by Hobsbawm and Jameson for *Gemeinschaft* institutions to be eroded from within by *Gesellschaft* attitudes has famously been illustrated by Garrett Hardin in his essay on the "tragedy of the commons" (Hardin, 1968). Basically, Hardin argues that the ancient *Gemeinschaft* idea of public common land, to which each stockholding villager has equal grazing rights, will inevitably be compromised, since there will always be some who take economically rational advantage of this unregulated access by grazing more of their own animals on the land until the resource is depleted for all. Obvious contemporary parallels to this depressing analysis exist at every social scale, from industrial abuses of environmental resources through pollution, overfishing, or deforestation, through the greed of financiers responsible for global economic crises, to the individual who fills his or her giant coffee flask at the office coffee machine. In each case, short-term self-interest prevails over considerations of communal wellbeing.

Hardin's conclusions, like those of Hobsbawm and Jameson, may prove to be overly pessimistic, but there is little doubt that expanding populations, dwindling resources, growing inequality, and accelerating urbanization are exposing serious rifts in attitudes to the use and control of space. Attempted migration from poorer to richer nations prompts the latter to reinforce their borders, either through legislative means backed up by the threat of force, or by the erection of physical barriers such as the wall forming the barrier between the

United States and Mexico.[22] Even within a nation's borders, gated housing developments (often ironically called "communities"), socioeconomically homogeneous and protected against intruders by armed private security forces, are expressions of a similar impulse: to maintain what is essentially a class divide (Diener & Hagen, 2012). Some writers, however, maintain that gated settlements are no longer the preserve of the rich; David Frye, for instance, insists: "Gated communities are found among every class and ethnic group" across the world (Frye, 2018, p. 245). Other motivations for physical separation exist. In Israel, a security fence has been erected to protect settlements built on occupied land from the former Palestinian occupants, who have been forcibly evicted. From an international perspective these settlements, and the security fence, are illegal, but the Israeli view is the cosmological one that the land in question was promised to them by their god more than three thousand years ago. Comparably questionable historical arguments are routinely used to justify the annexation of territory.

Spatial arrangements communicate — or, as Edward Hall pithily expressed the thought, "Space speaks" (Hall, 1959, p. 158) — and the messages received from gated housing developments, dilapidated urban slums or ghettoes, discriminatory legislation, and security barriers are hardly conducive to the creation of stable communities, which have been defined by Peter Block as "human systems given form by conversations that build relatedness" (Block, 2008, p. 29), a formulation that usefully emphasizes the complementary ideas of communication and connection. These concepts are also at the heart of Robert Putnam's notion of social capital, which he defines as "social networks, norms of reciprocity, mutual assistance, and trustworthiness" (Putnam, 2000, p. 19). Crucially though, Putnam goes on to distinguish two types of social capital that he terms bonding or bridging. Bonding social capital tends to be inward-looking, connecting people who already share similar worldviews, such as would be found in a gated development or an isolationist nation. Bridging social capital, on the other hand, is outward-looking, seeking to bring together people of differing perspectives and experience. Any society or organization that concentrates on the bonding type will tend to polarize into mutually exclusive or even hostile camps, creating the potential for conflict over competition

---

[22] A recent book by geographer Tim Marshall (2018) shows how widespread this phenomenon of barrier-building has become.

for resources or political agendas. The multicultural community that globalization is necessarily bringing about therefore needs to build and encourage systems that develop bridging capital, enabling it to incorporate difference, not just peaceably, but productively. [23]

Residential Perception

Property developers, construction companies, and residential sales agents routinely claim to be building "homes" rather than just "houses," appealing to the positive, if subliminal, connotation of the former term, to which images of cosiness, warmth, and tranquility are readily attached. Such conflation has certainly encouraged, if not engendered, a convergence of meaning in popular usage such that the two terms are virtually interchangeable, thus obscuring a distinction that remains vital in many cultures. The idea of "going home" for most Japanese, for instance, means a great deal more than merely returning from work to the (increasingly) urban or suburban structure shared with a nuclear family. Instead, it refers to an emotionally significant journey made usually twice a year, at New Year and during the summer festival, back to one's roots, typically in the countryside, the location where one was born, where one's ancestors are buried, and where the family funerary monument is maintained and venerated. [24] (Such an attachment to origin may well be related to the fact that the average Japanese changes domicile two or three times during his or her lifetime, whereas a U.S. American typically changes residence eleven or twelve times. [25])

Many other examples could be given, but the general point is that concepts of house or home vary widely across cultures, and Amos Rapoport defines the house usefully as "an institution, not just a structure, created for a complex set of purposes" (Rapoport, 1969, p.28). So culturally normalized is our idea of the house (or home), however, that the purposes to which Rapoport alludes are often

---

[23] Creative approaches to building community along these lines can be found in the work of such scholars as sociologist Amitai Etzioni (1993) or urban planner Peter Katz (2000).

[24] In China, the vast numbers of people who travel back to their home towns from their places of work in the new industrial cities at Chinese New Year have led to this journey being called the greatest voluntary human migration in the world.

[25] For the U. S., see *Calculating migration expectancy* (2024). For Japan, see Shoji (2020).

assumed to be globally valid, driven by basic and universal human needs (like those identified by Abraham Maslow referenced in our introduction), for shelter, security, and comfort. Notably, the architect Christopher Alexander together with his colleagues has compiled a detailed list of structural features (such as alcoves and liminal spaces) which are said to characterize all aspirational human dwellings (Alexander, Ishikawa, & Silverstein, 1977). In fact, though, notwithstanding the differences deriving from such factors as climatic conditions, socioeconomic conditions, availability of materials, levels of technology, and other physical determinants, the most salient factor in forming the concept of the house is that of cultural values.

Among the values that influence perception of our places of residence are the related themes of security, privacy, status, and aesthetics. The issue of security has two main aspects: in the first place a dwelling constitutes a physical barrier against a potentially hostile environment, a necessity in extreme climates such as the arctic, but a question of individual choice, guided by notions of comfort and cultural conditioning in more temperature regions. The second aspect of the security factor, however, is perhaps more important in that the house can represent a safe haven from animal and human predation. The anthropologist Robert Ardrey popularized the idea that territoriality, the need aggressively to protect property was a basic human drive (Ardrey, 1966), and city planners such as Oscar Newman introduced influential ideas of defensible space to urban design (Newman, 1973). Such theories have helped to foster an attitude among many property owners in the developed world in which outsiders, especially those perceived to be from another culture, are unwelcome, and potentially dangerous. Armed response warning notices, gated housing developments, and private security forces can be seen as disturbing phenomena to those cultures with more hospitable traditions and values. The 2001 attack on the U.S. and terrorist incidents throughout the developed world have no doubt exacerbated this degree of suspicion, sometimes bordering on paranoia, fostering an even greater perceived need for security and protection. The fact that such perceptions may not be rationally or statistically justifiable, of course, does not render them any less emotionally compelling.

Culturally specific notions of privacy are notoriously difficult to analyze or explicate, but the potential for inadvertent transgression by those with different internalized codes or expectations is almost limitless. The "American Dream"-inspired desire for a freestanding house on its own land would seem to indicate a strong need for privacy, yet visitors from other parts of the world are often surprised by the unfenced front lawns and large picture windows common to U.S. suburbia — especially in their apparent contradiction of the security concerns discussed above. Such features seem to invite the passer-by to look within, a practice discouraged in much of Europe by blinds or net curtains. Visitors from some Muslim countries, where women are strictly concealed within the house, may be particularly troubled by the perceived moral laxity of such openness. At the same time, the external accessibility of the U.S. house may be in strong contrast to the division of the interior space, in which each member of the family tends to have his or her own space — father's den, teenagers' rooms, mother's kitchen — including obscure (to an outsider) rules as to who is allowed where and when. This arrangement is almost perfectly reversed in Japan, where exterior privacy is highly valued, houses often being screened by trees or walls, but interior privacy is traditionally minimal, spaces being used by all members of the household, in former times even sleeping on the floor in the same room, still a common practice in Japanese inns. For Robert Carter, the moveable screens used in Japanese homes to temporarily separate spaces symbolize a pervasive cultural feature, "division within unity," based on "mutual trust and the lack of a strong need for division" (Carter, 2013, p.131). ㉖

Other than its utilitarian roles, the house also functions as a symbol of status in many cultures. Home ownership may be seen as a visible sign of worldly success, and the bigger the house the greater the signified achievement. Social worth and standing are indicated, often pejoratively, by house-related expressions such as "starter home," the "wrong side of the tracks," or the particularly offensive "trailer trash." The sales agent's mantra of "location, location, location" has at least as much to do with the social desirability of the neighborhood as with purely geographical factors. Of course, for many people home ownership actually involves paying large sums each month to a bank or a mortgage company, who are the real owners of the house. Immigrants from cultures less prone to perceiving the house as a status symbol, and where the size of a dwelling is more commensurate with the number of people living in it, are often astonished at the scale of houses in their new living

---

㉖　For the architectural space representation in China, see Yan (2012).

environments, as well as at the financial commitment of many householders to their residences. They may also be bemused by the European and U.S. social custom of entertaining at home; few Japanese, for instance, would invite friends for dinner at their house, such social occasions tending to take place at restaurants, the house being viewed as a private, exclusively family domain. [27] The western focus on dining at home perhaps helps to explain the fact, curious to many outsiders who see them as rather intimate and functional spaces, that bathrooms and kitchens are showpieces and major selling points in U.S. houses. This particular cultural feature has been wittily and memorably spoofed by the anthropologist Horace Miner in his essay "Body Ritual Among the Nacirema" (Miner, 1956). Written in the sober, scholarly style of an ethnographic field report of an exotic culture, the article pokes serious fun at the oddity and contingency of contemporary American (*Nacirema* backwards) cultural patterns with regard to bathrooms. An interesting recent addition to this topic has been made by sociologist Ray Oldenburg, who has described the positive function of community amenities such as cafés, bathhouses, and pubs, examples of what he terms the "third place," distinct from both home and work, such that the house itself is reserved for non-social activities such as sleeping and family intimacy (Oldenburg, 1989).

The external appearance of houses, their aesthetic appeal, is not a significant factor in many parts of the world, where vernacular architecture produces dwellings that vary only slightly from a traditional, culturally acceptable model that changes slowly over time (Oliver, 2003). In such cultures, residences designed by specialists in specific response to client requirements are exceptional, the prerogative of the very rich and increasingly influenced by globally mediated images of what constitutes prestige. [28] By contrast, in much of the developed world the idea of a vernacular style in the sense of a building pattern that has evolved over time to suit the needs of a community and in which residents participate has largely disappeared, a development doubtless linked to much higher rates of mobility and the concomitant weakening of community bonds, as discussed in the previous section.

---

[27] Indeed, there are cultural traditions, as in some regions of Cambodia, where the presence of anyone but a relative, or a very close friend, inside the house would be all but unthinkable.

[28] It was estimated decades ago that only five percent of the world's houses are architect-designed — most of them in rich countries. But see Conroy (2007).

Such traditional buildings that do remain are often seen as "heritage" objects, maintained for purposes of historical education, nostalgia, and tourism, although aesthetic considerations are also applicable (see Tung, 2001). In the place of a true vernacular style has arisen a kind of "imposed vernacular," in the form of speculative tract housing projects of similar design with no popular input, embodying *Gesellschaft* values of efficiency, planning, and profit. Often marketed as ready-made communities, these developments yet possess few qualities that immigrants from truly communal cultures would recognize. A common reaction is that, although the houses look as though they belong together, there are no signs of street life suggestive of a collective commitment to the neighborhood, and no obvious way to become part of the society. The convivial front porch has largely vanished, to be replaced by a multi-car garage with direct access into the house, and zoning codes mean that residents can no longer walk to local shops and markets, resulting in the loss of opportunities for informal neighborly encounters. Such perceptions on the part of immigrants from *Gemeinschaft* backgrounds naturally engender feelings of exclusion, rendering the transition to a new way of life even more difficult. As philosopher A. C. Grayling observes, "in a bigger and more diverse world the interactions of individuals who are no longer embedded in tight webs of family and community relationships [...] might easily have a more transient and superficial quality" (Grayling, 2013, pp. 103–104).

Personal Perception

In 1963 Edward Hall coined the term *proxemics* to describe what he then called "the interrelated observations and theories of man's use of space as a specialized elaboration of culture" (Hall, 1966, p. 1). In his analysis, he defined four spatial "zones" recognized in all cultures, although varying in specific dimensions: the intimate, for expressing love or comfort; the personal, for casual conversation and friendly encounters; the social, for business meetings and formal conversations; and the public, for lectures, speeches, and large-scale addresses. Of course, the very cultural specificity of the distances appropriate to each zone provides ample opportunity for inadvertent violation and misunderstanding, and Stella Ting-Toomey has written that "[i]ntercultural irritations most often occur in defining what constitutes intimate space as opposed to personal space" (Ting-

Toomey, 1999, p. 128).

Many writers have used the image of an invisible bubble to describe this intimate-personal boundary, the area beyond the physical outline of the body that people nevertheless feel to be his or her private domain. Globalization and urbanization have inevitably increased the frequency of encounters between individuals with bubbles of different dimensions, and responses to the Covid-19 pandemic have further complicated the issue, such that adapting to context may be more difficult. Most of us recognize the need to reduce the size of our bubbles when riding on the subway in rush hour, but if we are the only person on a bus and the next person to board takes the seat next to us — a common, sociable occurrence in the Philippines, for example — we may experience a visceral sense of intrusion, if not threat. Many U.S. Americans, Northern Europeans, and Japanese can experience excruciating discomfort, if not actual alarm, when interacting with people from Latin cultures, where tactile communication is a normal part of conversation, or with many Arab men, who traditionally expect to feel the other person's breath on their cheek during a friendly conversation.

The bubble metaphor may also extend to other features of the environment to which we feel a personal connection: my chair, my desk, my parking space. There are few aspects of our lives that do not exhibit a proxemic implication, and the emotional and moral reactions we have to perceived transgressions may be no less severe for being below the level of conscious awareness. How far from another person do we stand during a conversation? What is the appropriate distance for a third person to approach without intruding? What is the acceptable distance between people in a ticket office queue? How do we interact with someone speaking on the telephone? What is the polite protocol for receiving mobile telephone calls in a social situation? Do lowered voices during a conversation imply respect for others nearby or furtiveness? Does poking a head around an office door signify politeness or trespass? Under what circumstances is it appropriate to touch another person, or make eye contact? How are any of these situations affected by such factors as age, gender, or status?

From the above examples it is clear that proxemics in the sense of propinquity with regard to other people is just one code among many non-verbal behaviours that communicate without recourse to verbal language. Indeed, it has been estimated that over two-thirds of information is exchanged by non-verbal communication channels (see Mehrabian, 1971). Not, of course, that the message intended to be sent is necessarily identical to that received. On a state visit to Japan in 2009, U.S. President Barack Obama simultaneously charmed his hosts and offended a sizeable number of his compatriots by bowing to the Japanese Emperor as well as shaking hands. Media outrage in the U.S. ranged from jingoistic rhetoric about the President not having to bow to anybody, to spurious analysis as to whether the bow was of appropriate depth or the handshake was redundant. In Japan, meanwhile, Obama's gesture clearly delighted the imperial couple along with the vast majority of the population, who interpreted it as culturally sensitive rather than a sign of submissiveness. Interestingly, the U.S. reaction on this occasion was almost the precise reverse of that to the incident that took place at a gathering of world leaders at St. Petersburg in 2006, when President George W. Bush gave German Chancellor Angela Merkel a spontaneous and clearly unwelcome neck massage. An action that may have been seen as friendly gesture in Crawford, Texas was viewed as highly inappropriate in Germany. On this occasion, though, most U.S. commentators could not see what the Germans were making a fuss about.

Along with proxemics, then, other non-verbal communication codes must be considered as elements of personal space perception, including: gesture and body language; dress, appearance, and artefacts; facial expression; paralinguistics (volume, tone, silence, phatic expressions); haptics (touch); olfactics (smell); chronemics (use of and attitudes to time). Of course, these codes cannot be kept entirely separate from proxemics; a person has to be close to another to touch them, to smell them, and to be aware of subtle changes in facial expression or posture. Given the range, the variety, and the ubiquity of these influences, then, for the remainder of this section I shall briefly consider (in reverse order) personal perception in the contexts of the five perceptive frames I have discussed so far, demonstrating their inextricably interrelated nature, as well as their perhaps ultimate dependence on personal perception as the basic foundation from which all our communication strategies are derived — an approach that I believe Edward Hall would have endorsed.

Residential spaces demonstrate clearly many examples of the way personal bubbles expand to accommodate other aspects of the environment, as noted in the last section. For many Westerners the house, along with its contents, is very much an extension of the self, a reflection of the occupant's worth and character (see Marcus,

1995). It may be a place to entertain and impress friends, but only within carefully (often mysteriously, to outsiders) circumscribed limits. Certain areas of the house are out of bounds, even to other members of the family, without an explicit invitation; parents are strongly discouraged from entering teenagers' rooms, and children may be excluded from the parents' bedroom or father's study. The very fact that certain rooms are designated for specific purposes, unlike Japanese houses or Hopi dwellings, where the space stays constant and accessible, but the activities that take place within it change according to need, serves to demonstrate conceptual and behavioral differences with regard to the relationship of individuals to the spaces they inhabit. The cultural patterns learned from growing up in a nuclear family in a detached house will inevitably be divergent from the personal space attitudes developed through an upbringing in an extended family or, to take an extreme case, from a childhood in a Sarawak longhouse, in which several families live together with little sense of personal privacy.

Like the residential effect of the longhouse, communal space, the physical shape of the society in which an individual learns his or her cultural norms and values, is a major influence on a sense of individual boundaries. The unplanned, organic form (*Gemeinschaft*) of older, mixed-use settlements may inculcate in its residents a mindset with regard to privacy and personal space very different to that of those brought up in the rule-bound, rectilinear grid of a planned suburb or a gated development of more or less identical structures (*Gesellschaft*). Of course, this is not to say that there are no rules in the former type of community; they may in fact be abundant and inflexible. They are more likely, however, to be implicit, tacitly understood by long-term residents, rendering them hard to recognize and adhere to by newcomers. In a small, traditional village or town there may well be less privacy than in a large city with a transient, shifting population; on the other hand, the higher population density of the city means that personal space is more frequently, if inadvertently, invaded, with personal boundaries harder to maintain. The common urban interaction strategy of avoiding eye contact, seeming so unfriendly to many immigrants, is doubtless a response to this conundrum.

The connections between the perceptions of environmental space and personal space are manifold. It is often said in Japan that U.S. Americans seem to "take up more space," even after allowance is made for their generally larger body size. Their voices are louder, gestures are broader, postures more voluminous — all of which may be related to an unconscious American sense of coming from a huge country with ample space to spread out, as opposed to the physical restraint felt to be appropriate to inhabiting a mountainous, highly urbanized archipelago the size of California but with four times the population. Other environmental factors may also influence personal worldviews with regard to space perception. An upbringing in a land prone to frequent natural disasters such as earthquakes, volcanic eruptions, floods, or famines may engender a different attitude to risk and personal fragility compared to people from a more predictably hospitable environment. Seasonal affective disorder can have unanticipated and debilitating effects on anyone moving to a temperate location from a consistently sunny homeland, and the dense sensory environment of a large city, with its noise, smells, and physical proximity to others may well be perceived as an intrusion into personal space (see Gallagher, 1993).

With regard to geographical perception, everyone has a mental and emotional image of the shape of the world, together with his or her place (usually central) in it. These subjective maps are formed through exposure to various influences, including education, the media, religious teaching, and our own necessarily limited experience of people and places. The generalizations that constitute these images need have little or no relationship to geographical reality for them to affect our actions and attitudes, often condescending, with regard to others. We tend to interact with others from outside our normal social *milieu*, that is, from a position of often unconscious ethnocentrism, arrogating to ourselves a set of rights and beliefs that, from our assumed position of privilege in the world, license us to act in ways that can easily be perceived by others as violations of personal space. The growth of global tourism has exacerbated this tendency, travelers seeing themselves as not just socioeconomically but culturally and personally superior to the "others" among whom they are sojourning (see Abram, Waldren, & Macleod, 1997; V. L. Smith, 1989). Our bodies, and the ways in which we use, display, and adorn them are products of a highly specific cultural geography, and outside of this familiar context, even with the most innocent of intentions, a total avoidance of offense is probably impossible.

In my admittedly arbitrary structure, cosmological perception and personal perception appear to be the furthest apart, yet in fact the two concepts complete a circle. Notions about the physical body inevitably reflect metaphysical beliefs, and connections between personal microcosm and universal macrocosm, though taking different forms, are found in cultures all over the world, whether humans are thought to be created by a supernatural entity or are the result of as yet imperfectly understood cosmic forces. As Carlos Eire writes: "Three essential reconfigurations of reality stand out most starkly [...] first, how matter relates to spirit; second, how the natural relates to the supernatural; and third, how the living relate to the dead" (Eire, 2016, p. 748). The longevity and ubiquity of systems purporting to link the individual body to the wider cosmos, from Chinese *feng shui*, to western zodiacal horoscopes, to a widely divergent range of religious doctrines clearly indicate the enduring appeal of such beliefs. Equally significant are opposing convictions about the body itself, whether it is essentially sacred or profane and who has control over it, and such differences exist even in cultures that appear in many other ways similar. Jehovah's Witnesses, Christian Scientists, Roman Catholics, and professed atheists may all reside in the same community and speak the same language, but their widely divergent beliefs with regard to such topics as abortion, gay marriage, or capital punishment reveal deep divisions in their perception of personal autonomy.

Conclusion

We "cannot *not* communicate," as Paul Watzlawick famously asserted (Watzlawick et al., 1967, p. 30), but the spaces within which we interact, from more or less natural environments to the constructed city, have their own unique communicative power. Too often we assume that reactions, orientations, and attitudes to these spaces are, to a large extent, universal givens, arising from our common sensory apparatus and varying only in fairly insignificant ways. When our expectations that other people see the world largely as we do, then, are violated, as I hope to have shown can happen all too easily in an increasingly globalized world, we tend to react viscerally rather than rationally to this perceived infraction of common sense. For most westerners, for instance, if someone pushes in front of them in a queue, the initial response is unlikely to be the empathetic one that the person is acting in accordance with his or her cultural norms. There is, of course, no single, universally applicable strategy for avoiding or dealing with the misunderstanding, tension, and conflict that differences in space perception can produce, but certain attitudes and habits of mind on the part of both host and visitor, long-term resident and migrant, may help to mitigate their worst effects. The crucial first step, repeatedly emphasized by Edward Hall, is to become aware of our own cultural conditioning with regard to the interpretation of a situation, and to be prepared to identify and question our basic assumptions, recognizing their essential contingency.

From this recognition we can move to an attitude of not just understanding, but respect for alternative cultural perspectives, seeing them as equally justifiable as our own. In accordance with the ideal progression advocated by the management scholar Fons Trompenaars, attaining the two stages of recognition and respect makes possible the desired outcome of reconciliation, in which neither cultural system is validated above the other, and a way is found for them to co-exist without conflict (Trompenaars & Hampden-Turner, 1998). Vital to this process is an insatiable curiosity about the world and its diversity, a desire to expand our understanding beyond merely that necessary to function within our own culture. Julian Baggini believes that the western value of individualism hampers intercultural understanding, encouraging ethnocentric attitudes and a reluctance to consider alternative perceptions. He is nevertheless optimistic that these obstacles can, with goodwill, be overcome, leading to a stronger sense of global community: "Greater intimacy or belonging can be created [...] if local and regional identities can be more expressed without excluding outsiders, if common values can be asserted and shared" (Baggini, 2018, p. 216). At the same time, we must accept that our knowledge, values, and abilities will always be partial and contingent, and we need to constantly recalibrate and modify our perceptions through respectful dialogue and questioning. Reaction and opposition are inevitable, but the multicultural, globalized world is the future, and it is in all our interests to ensure that it is as free of conflict and misunderstanding as possible.

It is the author's hope that the model presented here may serve to inspire other scholars to investigate further the fascinatingly complex and important topic of diverse cultural reactions to space. Hall's groundbreaking work on proxemics remains an essential starting point, but there is more to explore. As the world continues to globalize, potentially contentious interactions between individuals who see (and hear, and feel, and smell, and taste) the world differently can only increase. Given the scope of the model, it can be seen that few interactions will be unaffected by concepts of spatial perception in one or more of its aspects, and an awareness of their influence can help to foster intercultural understanding and mutually respectful dialogue. [29]

References

Abram, S., Waldren, J., & Macleod, D. V. L. (Eds.). (1997). *Tourists and tourism: Identifying with people and places*. Berg.

Aguirre, A. (2019). *Cosmological Koans: A journey to the heart of physical reality*. W. W. Norton.

Alexander, C., Ishikawa, S., & Silverstein, M. (1977). *A pattern language: Towns, buildings, construction*. Oxford University Press.

Altman, I., & Vinsel, A. M. (1977). Personal space: An analysis of E. T. Hall's proxemics framework. In I. Altman & J. F. Wohlwill (Eds.), *Human behavior and environment* (vol. 2, pp. 181–259). Plenum Press.

Anderson, B. (1991). *Imagined communities: Reflections on the origin and spread of nationalism*. Verso.

Appiah, K. A. (1992). *In my father's house: Africa in the philosophy of culture*. Oxford University Press.

Ardrey, R. (1966). *The territorial imperative: A personal inquiry into the animal origins of property and nations*. Atheneum.

Baggini, J. (2018). *How the world thinks: A global history of philosophy*. Granta.

Bennett, M. J. (Ed.) (1998). *Basic concepts of intercultural communication*. Intercultural Press.

Berger, P. L., & Luckmann, T. (1966). *The social construction of reality: A treatise in the sociology of knowledge*. Anchor Books.

Berry, T. (2009). *The sacred universe: Earth, spirituality, and religion in the twenty-first century*. Columbia University Press.

Bhabha, H. K. (2004). *The location of culture*. Routledge.

Block, P. (2008). *Community: The structure of belonging*. Barrett-Koehler.

Brown, D. E. (1991). *Human universals*. McGraw-Hill.

Calculating migration expectancy using ACS data. (2024). United States Census Bureau, 22 Aug.

Carter, R. E. (2013). *The Kyoto School: An introduction*. SUNY Press.

Cecco, L. (2021). Outrage as Quebec teacher removed from classroom for wearing hijab. *The Guardian*, 13 Dec.

Conroy, S. C. (2007). The 98 percent solution. *Architect*, 7 May.

Cosgrove, D. (2001). *Apollo's eye: A cartographic genealogy of the earth in the western imagination*. Johns Hopkins University Press.

Cox, S. (2012). *Losing our cool: Uncomfortable truths about our air-conditioned world (and finding new ways to get through the summer)*. New Press.

Diamond, J. (1997). *Guns, germs, and steel: The fates of human societies*. W. W. Norton.

Diener, A. C., & Hagen, J. (2012). *Borders: A very short introduction*. Oxford University Press.

Eire, C. M. N. (2016). *Reformations: The early modern world 1450–1650*. Yale

---

[29] A shorter version of this chapter appeared in the *Journal of Intercultural Communication & Interactions Research* (Peter Lang) 2(1), 2023, pp. 135–150.

University Press.

Etzioni, A. (1993). *The spirit of community: Rights, responsibilities, and the communitarian agenda*. Crown Publishers.

Firth, R. (1957). *We, the Tikopia: A sociological study of kinship in primitive Polynesia* (2nd ed.). Beacon Press.

Frye, D. (2018). *Walls: A History of Civilization in Blood and Brick*. Scribner.

Gallagher, W. (1993). *The power of place: How our surroundings shape our thoughts, emotions, and actions*. Poseidon Press.

Grayling, A. C. (2013). *Friendship*. Yale University Press.

Hall, E. T. (1959). *The silent language*. Doubleday.

Hall, E. T. (1963). A system for the notation of proxemic behavior. *American Anthropologist, 65*(5), 1003–1026.

Hall, E. T. (1966). *The hidden dimension*. Doubleday.

Hall, E. T. (1994). *West of the thirties: Discoveries among the Navajo and Hopi*. Doubleday.

Hardin, G. (1968). The tragedy of the commons. *Science, 162* (13 Dec.), 1243–1248.

Hardt, M., & Weeks, K. (Eds.). (2000). *The Jameson reader*. Blackwell.

Harley, J. B. (2001). *The new nature of maps: Essays in the history of cartography*. Johns Hopkins University Press.

Hobsbawm, E. (2007). *Globalization, democracy and terror*. Little Brown.

Huntington, E. (1915). *Civilization and climate*. Yale University Press.

Katz, P. (2000). *The new urbanism: Toward an architecture of community*. McGraw-Hill.

King, C. (2019). *Gods of the upper air: How a circle of renegade anthropologists reinvented race, sex, and gender in the twentieth century*. Doubleday.

Kuhn, T. S. (1996). *The structure of scientific revolutions* (3rd ed.). University of Chicago Press.

Lovelock, J. (2006). *The revenge of Gaia: Why the earth is fighting back — and how we can still save humanity*. Allen Lane.

Low, S. M., & Lawrence-Zúñiga, D. (Eds.). (2003). *The anthropology of space and place: Locating culture*. Blackwell.

Marcus, C. C. (1995). *House as a mirror of self: Exploring the deeper meaning of home*. Conari Press.

Marshall, T. (2018). *The age of walls: How barriers between nations are changing our world*. Scribner.

Maslow, A. H. (1943). A theory of human motivation. *Psychological Review, 50*(4), 370–396.

Mehrabian, A. (1971). *Silent messages*. Wadsworth.

Meinig, D. W. (1979). The beholding eye: Ten versions of the same scene. In D. W. Meinig (Ed.), *The interpretation of ordinary landscapes: Geographical essays* (pp. 33–48). Oxford University Press.

Michell, J. (1994). *At the centre of the world: Polar symbolism discovered in Celtic, Norse and other ritualized landscapes*. Thames & Hudson.

Miner, H. (1956). Body ritual among the Nacirema. *American Anthropologist, 58*(3), 503–507.

Mishra, P. (2017). *Age of anger: A history of the present*. Farrar, Straus & Giroux.

Monmonier, M. (2006). *From Squaw Tit to Whorehouse Meadow: How maps name, claim, and inflame*. University of Chicago Press.

Newman, O. (1973). *Defensible space: Crime prevention through urban design*.

Collier Books.

Nisbett, R. E. (2003). *The geography of thought: How Asians and Westerners think differently ... and why*. Free Press.

Oldenburg, R. (1989). *The great good place: Cafés, coffee shops, bookstores, bars, hair salons, and other hangouts at the heart of a community*. Paragon.

Oliver, P. (2003). *Dwellings: The vernacular house world wide*. Phaidon.

Park, D. (2005). *The grand contraption: The world as myth, number, and chance*. Princeton University Press.

Pflughoeft, A. (2021). The world probably doesn't look like you think it does — and that matters, a lot. *Deseret News*, 2 July.

Pinker, S. (2002). *The blank slate: The modern denial of human nature*. Allen Lane.

Putnam, R. D. (2000). *Bowling alone: The collapse and revival of American community*. Simon & Schuster.

Rapoport, A. (1969). *House form and culture*. Prentice-Hall.

Searle, J. R. (2015). *Seeing things as they are: A theory of perception*. Oxford University Press.

Sheldrake, R. (1990). *The rebirth of nature: The greening of science and God*. Century.

Shoji, K. (2020). Can't find tissues? Get some towels, it's moving time. *The Japan Times*, 24 Mar.

Smith, D. (2021). *Penguin state of the world atlas* (10th ed.). Penguin.

Smith, V. L. (Ed.) (1989). *Hosts and guests: The anthropology of tourism*. University of Pennsylvania Press.

Soja, E. W. (1996). *Thirdspace: Journeys to Los Angeles and other real-and-imagined places*. Wiley-Blackwell.

Ting-Toomey, S. (1999). *Communicating across cultures*. Guilford.

Trompenaars, F., & Hampden-Turner, C. (1998). *Riding the waves of culture: Understanding cultural diversity in global business*. McGraw-Hill.

Tung, A. M. (2001). *Preserving the world's great cities: The destruction and renewal of the historic metropolis*. Clarkson Potter.

Turnbull, C. M. (1961). *The forest people*. Simon & Schuster.

Watzlawick, P., Bavelas, J. B., Beavin, J. H., & Jackson, D. D. A. (1967). *Pragmatics of human communication: A study of interactional patterns, pathologies and paradoxes*. W. W. Norton.

Winder, S. (2019). *Lotharingia: A personal history of Europe's lost country*. Farrar, Straus & Giroux.

Yan, X. (2012). Harmony and orderliness: The architectural space representation of Chinese culture. In SISU Intercultural Institute (Ed.), *Identity and intercultural communication (Ⅱ): Conceptual and contextual applications* (pp. 179 – 197). Intercultural Research Vol. 3. Shanghai Foreign Language Education Press.

8

Intercultural Communication: Where We've Been, Where We're Going, and Issues We Face — Revisited

Stephen M. CROUCHER

*Massey University (New Zealand) and Higher
School of Economics (Russia)*

Summary: This chapter reviews the evolution of research literature on intercultural communication. This review has four purposes. First, this review summarizes the development of the discipline from the traditional United States perspective, with a focus on the work of Edward T. Hall, while also recognizing the work of others. Second, this review discusses the discipline's theorizing period of expansion. Third, the review briefly explores how the discipline has grown outside of the traditional U.S. perspective, focusing especially on China, Australia, South Africa, and South America. Finally, the review offers a perception of opportunities, issues, and directions for development of the discipline.

Introduction

In Edward T. Hall's (1959) book *The Silent Language,* Hall used the phrase "intercultural communication." Hall is largely credited as the founder of the field of intercultural communication (Leeds-Hurwitz, 1990). The formalized field of intercultural communication has grown exponentially since Hall's reference in 1959. As the field has grown, so has its complexity. In 2015, Croucher, Sommier, and Rahmani argued it was impossible to deny the complexity of the term "intercultural." Countless analyses and reviews have been written over the years about "intercultural" and intercultural communication. What all these writings share is a desire to understand and expand the discipline. Today the discipline includes more theories than ever before, is increasingly international in scope, and researchers and practitioners who identify as intercultural communication specialists abound globally. However, there is still a lot to learn about this bourgeoning field. To this end, this chapter presents a critical overview of the state of the intercultural communication discipline. Specifically, the purpose of this chapter is four-fold:

- *first*, it discusses the influence of Hall and his contemporaries, recognizing those who came before (and who are often forgotten or lesser known) ;
- *second*, it reviews the theoretical expansion of the discipline;
- *third*, it describes the development of the discipline outside of the United States; and
- *finally*, it identifies crucial questions and challenges, and discusses where to go from here with the discipline. ①

1. The Development of "Intercultural Communication"

While Hall is often credited as the "founder" of the intercultural communication discipline, the term "intercultural" is *much* older than Hall. Archibald Baker (1929) in his analysis of religions examined the relationships between intercultural relations and the modern world. William Ernest Hocking (1934) explored intercultural contacts between faiths. German philosopher Edmund Husserl used the term "interkulturell" as an adjective in his work on intersubjectivity (1931/1973). In the 1930s, Rachel Davis DuBois

---

①   Stephen M. Croucher is a Professor and Head of School of Communication, Journalism, and Marketing at Massey University, New Zealand. He is also a Lead Research Fellow at the National Research University (Higher School of Economics), Russia. Address: Private Bag 756, School of Communication, Journalism, and Marketing, Massey University, Wellington 6022, New Zealand: s.croucher@massey. ac. nz. The present study builds off and expands on the statements in Croucher, Sommier, and Rahmani (2015).

developed a series of intercultural education courses at New York University and began to theorize on how intercultural education and training could improve competence and awareness (see Kulich, 2019). In 1935 she first used the term "intercultural education." Her work (1934, 1939, 1943, 1950) on intercultural education, conflict resolution, communication, and intergroup relations predated that of Hall and others more commonly credited with "founding" intercultural communication. For a more in-depth review of Davis DuBois and her contribution to the development of intercultural communication, see Davis DuBois and Okoradudu (1984).

In the years leading up to the publishing of *The Silent Language*, Hall was influenced by researchers from cultural anthropology, linguistics, and Freudian psychoanalytic theory. In cultural anthropology, the works of Franz Boas, Ruth Benedict, Margaret Mead, and Raymond Birdwhistell shaped Hall by showing the connections between culture and communication (Rogers, Hart, & Miike, 2002). From linguistics, George L. Trager's work with Native American languages (like Hall's interests) further amplified Hall's interest in the links between language, communication, and culture. Edward Sapir and Benjamin Lee Whorf's (1940/1956) work in linguistics and on linguistic relativity were critical to the development of the field of intercultural communication. The notion that language influences human thought and meaning shaped how Hall and his predecessors understood, conceptualized, and operationalized intercultural communication. While at the Foreign Service Institute (FSI), Hall worked closely with Harry Stack Sullivan and Frieda Fromm-Reichmann to explore psychoanalytic theory, particularly non-verbal and unconscious aspects of human behavior and communication.

Turning to the work of Hall (1914 – 2009), his intercultural communication work took shape at the FSI. Hall was the Director of the Point IV Training Program at the FSI in Washington DC from 1950 through 1955. In the wake of World War II, the U.S. government recognized it must better train its diplomatic corps, as the government recognized that few of its corps were proficient in foreign languages or the customs of their countries of assignment. The FSI, within the Department of State, offered training to foreign service officers. Along with linguistic training, Hall implemented cultural awareness training and training in intercultural communication. In fact, about half of the courses at the FSI were devoted to intercultural communication. It is during this time that Hall compiled all his ideas on "intercultural communication." In 1959, with the publishing of *The Silent Language,* Hall unknowingly laid out the new academic field of "intercultural communication."

Through his work at the FSI and in *The Silent Language,* Hall outlined six key elements of the study of intercultural communication (Rogers et al., 2002):

- *First,* researchers at the FSI focused on intercultural communication and not broad macro-level issues (anthropology, linguistics). The key became the intercultural elements of communication.
- *Second,* nonverbal communication became an integral line of research.
- *Third,* emphasis was placed on the unconscious aspects of communication, particularly in nonverbal communication.
- *Fourth,* the study of intercultural communication accepted and appreciated cultural differences without judgment.
- *Fifth,* participatory training methods were encouraged.
- *Sixth,* intercultural communication was seen as a highly practical field of study.

With the concept of "intercultural communication" out for consumption, researchers, practitioners, and academics began to take hold of the new concept as a field of inquiry. University classes in intercultural communication were first offered in the late 1960s at the University of Pittsburgh (Gudykunst & Nishida, 1978). Alfred Smith published his book *Communication and Culture* in 1966, which further outlined the concept of intercultural communication. As the discipline developed, associations like the International Communication Association (ICA) in 1970 and the Speech Communication Association (now the National Communication Association/NCA) in 1975 formed intercultural divisions. Such formations recognize the stability of the field. In 1972, Samovar and Porter published the first edited book on intercultural communication, followed in 1973 by Harms' textbook, in 1974 by the publication of the first *International and Intercultural Communication Annuals,* then in 1977 with the establishment of the *International Journal of Intercultural Relations.* These were all key steps in developing the field and establishing it within communication as a discipline. After the late 1970's, building off the work of Hall and many others, came a period of theoretical expansion. [2] Today, intercultural communication is generally defined as the study of communication between individuals from different cultures. A closely linked field is

---

[2] For a further discussion of Hall and the FSI, see Leeds-Hurwitz (1990).

cross-cultural communication, or the comparison of communication across cultures (Croucher, 2017).

2. Theoretical Expansion of the Discipline

As the intercultural communication discipline came into the 1970s and 1980s, a key question was the place of theory within the discipline. From 1976 through 1983, various intercultural communication researchers compiled reviews of theory within the discipline (Asante, 1980; Asante & Newark, 1976; Gudykunst, 1983; Howell, 1979; Prosser, 1978; Saral, 1977, 1979). Largely within the pages of the ICA's *Communication yearbook*, these pieces framed the new discipline and outlined the challenges it faced moving forward. The primary challenge outlined was the development of uniquely intercultural theories, which is still a challenge for the discipline today. Kulich et al. (2020) outlined eight theoretical themes that are consistently explored by intercultural communication researchers: identity, perceptual bias/prejudice, language, values or belief systems, culture learning/schema-based adaptation, effectiveness/competence, speech codes, and conflict. Six of these themes are briefly reviewed below.

Identity

Two concepts for the study of identity in intercultural communication have been identified, the modern and the traditional (Banks & Banks, 1995). The *traditional* supposes that communication can be understood as an inward source of identity stress in which a communication partner attempts to diminish anxiety (Hall, 1992). We negotiate our identity until we achieve agreement with each other about our identity (Ting-Toomey, 1993). The *modern* paradigm, on the other hand, posits that identity is dynamic and dependent on time as well as the context of society (Hoffman, 1989). Within these two paradigms, researchers have proposed various identity-related theories. One of the most prominent identity-related theories is Face Negotiation Theory (FNT). Ting-Toomey and Kurogi defined face as "a claimed sense of favorable social self-worth that a person wants others to have of her or him" (1998, p. 187). When interacting with others, we risk losing face as our self-worth is potentially challenged. FNT describes how we manage these conflicts through facework. Ting-Toomey (2005) argued that face and facework are universal. FNT has been employed in the domains of health (Kirschbaum, 2012), interculturality (Ting-Toomey, 2005; Zhang, Ting-Toomey, & Oetzel, 2014), online media (Lim et al., 2012), and other areas of study.

Perceptual Bias/Prejudice

Perceptual bias/prejudice is a second area of theory development in intercultural communication. While largely coming from sociology and psychology, intercultural and cross-cultural researchers are increasingly exploring perceptual bias/prejudice. Allport defined prejudice as "an aversive or hostile attitude towards a person who belongs to a group, simply because he belongs to that group, and is therefore presumed to have the objectionable qualities ascribed to the group" (1954, p. 7). Numerous theories have been proposed to understand prejudice (mostly sociological or psychological): realistic group conflict theory (Sherif, 1966), symbolic racism theory (Kinder & Sears, 1981), integrated threat theory (ITT) (Croucher, 2013b; Stephan & Stephan, 1996), intercultural communication apprehension (ICA) (Neuliep & McCroskey, 1997b), and generalized ethnocentrism (Neuliep & McCroskey, 1997a). ICA is the fear or anxiety individuals experience when interacting with those from another culture. Researchers have found a positive relationship between ICA and general ethnocentrism (Lin & Rancer, 2003; Neuliep & McCroskey, 1997b; Wrench et al., 2003).

Language

Ferdinand de Saussure stated that language was the ordered arrangement of signs. A sign consists of the signifier (outward symbol), and the signified (inward mental image of what the signifier means) (de Saussure & Baskin, 1959). When exploring language from an intercultural perspective, researchers have shown that while language might be universal, how it is understood is culturally defined (Hall, 1959; Kroskrity, 2000; Silverstein, 1995). Integrating language and computer-mediated communication (CMC), Walther (1992, 2012) developed the Social Information Processing Theory (SIPT). When looking at the effects of CMC on language, Walther argued that CMC was not inferior to face-to-face communication, given that certain conditions were met. SIPT provides a way to examine the effects of CMC on language use in different cultural contexts.

Values or Belief Systems

Primarily coming out of psychology and cross-cultural studies, the examination of values and cultural dimensions is prominent in intercultural and cross-cultural communication. Research by Hofstede (2001) and Schwartz (1999) has expanded our understanding of how culturally based values/dimensions affect communication. Hofstede's (2001) cultural dimensions have had a profound effect on intercultural and cross-cultural communication. Dimensions such as individualism/ collectivism, masculinity/femininity, power distance, and uncertainty avoidance have been extensively researched and used as foundations for cultural comparisons, while researchers have criticized these dimensions (see Croucher, 2013a; McSweeney, 2002). [3]

Culture Learning/Schema-Based Adaptation

There is an extensive body of literature examining cultural adaptation, assimilation, and cultural integration issues. In intercultural communication, acculturation strategies (Berry, 2003), the cross-cultural adaptation model (Kim, 2001), and the cultural fusion model (Croucher & Kramer, 2017; Kramer, 2000) have garnered the most attention. Berry's model (2003) proposes four main strategies between which a migrant can make a selection when they engage with a new culture: separation, marginalization, integration, or assimilation. While research has shown this model to be applicable in a variety of settings (see Krause, 2019; Sam & Berry, 2006), researchers have criticized the model for a rigid set of categories, testing migrant samples *a priori*, and for asserting that immigrants would be willing to "lose" their cultural belonging (Del Pilar & Udasco, 2004; Giang & Wittig, 2006; Phinney et al., 2001). Kim's cross-cultural adaptation model has received the most attention in intercultural communication. Her multi-step process includes deculturation, enculturation, and acculturation. While some research contributions have vindicated this model (McKay-Semmler & Kim, 2014), other researchers have criticized the theory for numerous reasons: restructuring a psyche's composition, lack of support, Darwinism, etc. (Croucher, 2011; Kramer, 2000). Croucher and Kramer's (2017) cultural fusion model has offered an alternative to adaptation. Fusion describes how newcomers blend elements of their native with the new culture and how this

---

③ For further discussions of these critiques of Hofstede's dimensions, see Baskerville (2003) and Signorini, Wiesemes, and Murphy (2009).

blending also impacts the host culture.

Effectiveness/Competence

A sixth key theoretical theme in intercultural communication is intercultural competence. Spitzberg defined competence as "interaction that is perceived as affective in fulfilling certain rewarding objectives in a way that is also appropriate to the context in which the interaction occurs" (1988, p. 68). Intercultural competence has four major elements: situational, psychomotor, affective, and knowledge (Spitzberg & Cupach, 1984). Competence is a critical aspect of every communicative interaction, particularly intercultural interactions. Competence is linked with various communication theories: anxiety/uncertainty management (AUM) (Gudykunst, 1993), identity management theory (Cupach & Imahori, 1993), and FNT, to name a few.

While the field has various theoretical areas/themes, what is less known about the field is its development, significance, and position outside of the United States. The following section reviews the development and position of intercultural communication outside of the U.S. context, with particular emphasis on China, Australia, South Africa, and South America. These four contexts have been chosen for inclusion in this chapter to represent the diversity of the discipline.

3. Development Outside of the United States

China

Intercultural communication (or communication between cultures) in the Chinese context is trans-disciplinary and involves linguistics, international relations, and communication studies. Linguistic researchers tend to define intercultural communication as "jiao ji" [in Chinese "交际"], which emphasizes the interactions of people meeting from different cultures. As for international relations researchers, they tend to define intercultural communication as "jiao liu" [in Chinese "交流"], emphasizing communication on a state/national level. Researchers from communication studies tend to use "chuan bo" [in Chinese "传播"], which emphasizes the flow of information (Fei, 2017; Guan, 1996). After Hall's (1959) work and the development of the formal discipline of intercultural communication in the U.S., it took a few decades for the discipline to take hold as an established discipline in China. In the early 2000s, the field of communication (and intercultural communication) became more established in Chinese universities. Increasingly Chinese academics began to publish more peer-reviewed articles (Guan, 2006), intercultural readers appeared in Mandarin (Yu, 2006), key intercultural communication concepts were interpreted and applied in the Chinese context (Fei, 2017), and new concepts and research paradigms grounded in Chinese culture began to emerge. For example, Li (2008) described how the concept of "cultural antibody" emerged to describe the Chinese counter-power against Western modernity. As more Chinese academics and universities began to interact with "Western" academics researching intercultural communication, national congresses, journals, edited volumes, and associations devoted to intercultural communication emerged. Today the discipline is taught at numerous universities throughout the country.

Australia

When tracing the development of intercultural communication as a formal discipline, it's essential to consider the context in which academic events occur. The FSI was founded in the aftermath of WW Ⅱ, when politically, economically, militarily, and socially there was a significant need for the U.S. government to understand the "other." In other nations, such as Australia, context has played a significant part in the development and position of intercultural communication. Flew asserted "a distinctively Australian perspective on intercultural communication arises from consideration of the nation's history, geography, demography, social policy, and political economy" (2017, p. 58). He delineated three phases of intercultural communication in the Australian context. The first is the colonial/early nation period. In this stage, the European monoculture was promoted, often excluding all other cultures via force and through policies such as the White Australia Policy. In the second stage (1945-1975), Australia became more diverse with migration. However, there was still significant resistance to this diversity. While multiculturalism policies were first proposed in the 1970s, such policies were more to promote cohesion and not for diversity (Pakulski, 2014). The final phase (1975-present) represents a period of more active recognition of Australia's cultural diversity. While multiculturalism, a recognition of indigenous rights, and openness to immigration are encouraged, such recognitions are not universally accepted. Due to Australia's close economic and political ties with

Asia, and the need to recognize indigenous rights, the nation and its universities are increasingly having to address intercultural issues and communication.

South Africa

The study of intercultural communication in South Africa is influenced by its colonial, apartheid, and post-apartheid periods. During the colonial era there were four races: White, Indian, Black, and Colored. Within each of these races were distinct ethnic groups. Relations among these groups were marred with tension, conflict, and war. The Apartheid era (1948–1994) officially legalized the separation of the races in all aspects of South African life. In 1994, with the end of Apartheid, South Africa began what was known as the Rainbow Nation, an era symbolizing unity in diversity (Habib, 1997). As new laws were enacted and old ones repealed, different races and ethnic groups found themselves, and still do, coming together more in South Africa. The purpose of intercultural communication became an attempt to unite the diverse groups under one South Africa and create shared identity and meaning for the nation. Moola and Sibango (2017) explain that while inequities, racism, and segregation remain, intercultural communication is used to help promote a united cultural understanding of what it means to be "South African."

South America

Protzel explains that intercultural communication in the South American context can be seen as "an anthropologist's task, a foreigner's (and maybe national) experience of local exoticism, or as the living result of biological miscegenation, i.e., the blend of different biological phenotypes (races) through human reproduction" (2017, p. 14). With South America's diversity of languages, races, indigenous populations, and environmental, political, and economic systems, it is no surprise that communication schools and departments have flourished on the continent since the 1970s. The study of intercultural communication in South America is distinct from other parts of the world in two ways. First, one of its primary academic and practical focuses is on building mutual understanding between modern society and indigenous groups within the same countries. Second, extensive attention is spent on understanding and challenging linguistic and racial segregation and environmental concerns. For example, researchers increasingly explore the influence of culture on environmental decisions.

4. Challenges, Issues, and Areas for Development

In 2015, we asserted that the intersections of intercultural communication and health and social media were areas of growth for the discipline (Croucher et al., 2015). I stand by this assertion. What I would like to emphasize at this time is the critical link between intercultural communication and health. As the global COVID-19 pandemic rages in 2021 (when this chapter was written), the importance of intercultural communication cannot be over-stated. Researchers are increasingly showing that with rising case numbers, scapegoating, prejudice, xenophobia, discrimination, hate speech, hate crimes, and violence are common toward minorities blamed for the spread of COVID-19 (Croucher, Nguyen, & Rahmani, 2020; Croucher, Permyakova, & Turdubaeva, 2021; Croucher et al., 2021; Girardelli, Croucher, & Nguyen, 2021; Meleady, Hodson, & Earle, 2021; Nguyen et al., 2021; Rzymski & Nowicki, 2020; Zeng, Wang, & Zhang, 2020). Effective intercultural communication will be one way to stem the tide of rising prejudice and negative sentiment toward minorities. In addition, as nations push to reach vaccine targets, many governments are finding that culture is impeding vaccine uptick. In New Zealand for example, as of October 2021, Māori and Pacific Islanders have the highest rates of COVID-19 vaccine hesitancy (Brown, 2021). The government is working with local groups and *iwi* (roughly translated as tribe, but also means social units/groups) to increase vaccine awareness and improve vaccination rates. The importance of outreach and culturally appropriate education and interaction over the vaccine has been critical to reaching this community. Intercultural communication is the key.

Alexander et al. (2014) presented various challenges, urgencies, and issues facing intercultural communication. Four issues were also presented by Croucher et al. (2015). It is two of these issues that I would like to return to, as I see them as still critical to the future of the discipline, and ones that are not yet resolved: debate over terminology, and the spread of research to less studied cultures.

Firstly, the very definition of intercultural communication is still an unresolved issue. As a reader goes through this volume, they will encounter (I imagine) many definitions of "intercultural communication." While this may not be a bad thing, as it does show the depth and breadth of the discipline, we members of this discipline should think about whether a more unified definition is appropriate.

In addition, when one scans the literature, the journals, edited volumes, and other publication forms, and reads what is "intercultural communication," one should ask whether it is *really* "intercultural communication." I assert that an extensive body of literature that is labeled "intercultural communication" is in fact "cross-cultural communication" or "intergroup communication." Studies comparing phenomena across groups or within groups would not fit the definition of "intercultural communication." There is nothing inherently wrong with this. However, it is critical that the discipline reflect on what is *really* intercultural.

Secondly, researchers within intercultural communication must continue to explore less-studied cultures. Intercultural communication remains highly U.S.- and East-Asian-centric. Strides are being made to globalize the discipline, with more work coming out of Europe, Australasia, and other regions. However, a majority of the theories and scales used are still primarily developed in the U.S. It's still common to have editors and reviewers ask for justification for why a study on nation X is important but not ask for the same justification when exploring the U.S. As a discipline we need to continue moving beyond the U.S.-Asian-centric views on theory, method, and context, in order to gain more knowledge about insufficiently studied cultural experiences.

Conclusion

As an established discipline, intercultural communication is relatively new. However, as a philosophical, sociological, linguistic, and anthropological endeavor the study of the intercultural in communication has what we might call a storied history. The future trajectories of this discipline are vast. As we look to the myriad theoretical approaches, and the diverse global development, we can see a discipline that has come a long way since Hall's early musing in *The Silent Language*.

References

Alexander, B. K., Arasaratnam, L. A., Durham, A., Flores, L., Leeds-Hurwitz, W., Mendoza, S. L., Oetzel, J., Osland, J., Tsuda, Y., Yin, J., & Halualani,

R. (2014). Identifying key intercultural urgencies, issues, and challenges in today's world: Connecting our scholarship to dynamic contexts and historical moments. *Journal of International and Intercultural Communication*, 7, 38–67. doi: 10.1080/17513057.2014.869527

Allport, G. (1954). *The nature of prejudice*. Addison-Wesley.

Asante, M. K. (1980). Intercultural communication: An inquiry into research directions. In D. Nimmo (Ed.), *Communication Yearbook 4* (pp. 401–411). ICA-Transaction Books.

Asante, M. K., & Newmark, E. (Eds.). (1976). *Intercultural communication: Theory into practice*. Speech Communication Association.

Baker, A. G. (1929). How shall we relate Christianity to other religions? *The Journal of Religion*, 9(3), 478–480.

Banks, A., & Banks, S. R. (1995). Cultural identity, resistance, and "good theory": Implications for intercultural communication theory from Gypsy culture. *Howard Journal of Communication*, 6(2), 146–163. doi: 10.1080/10646179509361693

Baskerville, R. F. (2003). Hofstede never studied culture. *Accounting, Organizations and Society*, 28, 1–14.

Berry, J. W. (2003). Conceptual approaches to acculturation. In K. M. Chun, P. Balls Organista, & G. Martin (Eds.), *Acculturation: Advances in theory, measurement, and applied research* (pp. 17–37). American Psychological Association.

Brown, T. (2021, October 4). Covid-19 vaccine uptake among Māori 2/3 of general population. *RNZ*.

Croucher, S. M. (2011). Social networking and cultural adaptation: A theoretical model. *Journal of International and Intercultural Communication*, 4, 259–264. doi:10.1080/17513057.2011.598046

Croucher, S. M. (2013a). Communication apprehension, self-perceived communication competence, and willingness to communicate: A French analysis. *Journal of International and Intercultural Communication*, 6(4), 298–316.

Croucher, S. M. (2013b). Integrated threat theory and acceptance of immigrant assimilation: An analysis of Muslim immigration in Western Europe. *Communication Monographs*, 80(1), 46–62. doi: 10.1080/03637751.2012.739704

Croucher, S. M. (Ed.). (2017). *Global perspectives on intercultural communication*. Routledge.

Croucher, S. M., & Kramer, E. M. (2017). Cultural fusion theory: An alternative to acculturation. *Journal of International & Intercultural Communication*, 10(1), 97–114. doi: 10.1080/17513057.2016.1229498

Croucher, S. M., Nguyen, T., Pearson, E., Murray, N., Feekery, A., Spencer, A., Gomez, O., Girardelli, D., & Kelly, S. (2021). A comparative analysis of Covid-19 related prejudice: The United States, Spain, Italy, and New Zealand. *Communication Research Reports*, 38, 78–89. doi: 10.1080/08824096.2021.1885371

Croucher, S. M., Nguyen, T., & Rahmani, D. (2020). Prejudice toward Asian-Americans in the Covid-19 pandemic: The effects of social media use in the United States. *Frontiers in Health Communication*. doi: 10.3389/fcomm.2020.00039

Croucher, S. M., Permyakova, T., & Turdubaeva, E. (2021 in press). Prejudice toward Asians and migrants during the COVID-19 pandemic in Russia and Kyrgyzstan. *Russian Journal of Communication.* doi: 10.1080/19409419.2021. 1958697

Croucher, S. M ., Sommier, M ., & Rahmani, D. (2015). Intercultural communication: Where we've been, where we're going, issues we face. *Communication Research and Practice*, *1* (1), 71-87. doi:10.1080/22041451. 2015.1042422

Cupach, W. R ., & Imahori, T. T. (1993). Identity management theory: Communication competence in intercultural episodes and relationships. In R. L. Wiseman & J. Koester (Eds.), *Intercultural communication competence* (pp. 112-131). Sage.

Davis DuBois, R. (1934). *Changing attitudes toward other races and nations.* Service Bureau for Education in Human Relations.

Davis DuBois, R. (1939). *Out of the many — one: A plan for intercultural education.* Service Bureau for Intercultural Education.

Davis DuBois, R. (1943). *Get together Americans: Friendly approaches to racial and cultural conflicts through the neighborhood-home festival.* Harper & Brothers.

Davis DuBois, R. (1950). *Neighbors in action: A manual for local leaders in intergroup relations.* Harper.

Davis DuBois, R ., & Okoradudu, C. (1984). *All this and something more: Pioneering in intercultural education. An autobiography.* Dorrance.

Del Pilar, J. A ., & Udasco, J. O. (2004). Marginality theory: The lack of construct validity. *Hispanic Journal of Behavioral Sciences*, *26*, 3-15. doi:10. 1177/0739986303261813

de Saussure, F ., & Baskin, W. (1959). *Course in general linguistics.* McGraw Hill.

Fei, J. (2017). Intercultural communication: A Chinese perspective. In S. Croucher (Ed.), *Global perspectives on intercultural communication* (pp. 40-46). Routledge.

Flew, T. (2017). Intercultural communication: An Australian perspective. In S. Croucher (Ed.), *Global perspectives on intercultural communication* (pp. 58-61). Routledge.

Giang, M. T., & Wittig, M. A. (2006). Implications of adolescents' acculturation strategies for personal and collective self-esteem. *Cultural Diversity and Ethnic Minority Psychology*, *12*, 725-739. doi:10.1037/1099-9809.12.4.725

Girardelli, D., Croucher, S. M., & Nguyen, T. (2021). La pandemia COVID-19, la sinofobia e il ruolo dei social media in Italia. *Mondi Migranti*, 85-104. doi: 10.3280/MM2021-001005

Guan, S. J. (1996). *Intercultural communication: A field help to promote international communication skills* [跨文化交流学:提高涉外交流能力的学问]. Peking University Press.

Guan, S. J. (2006). A review of intercultural communication studies in China in the last decade. *International Communication*, *12*, 32-36.

Gudykunst, W. B. (Ed.). (1983). *International and intercultural communication annual* (Vol. Ⅶ). Sage.

Gudykunst, W. B. (Ed.). (1993). Toward a theory of effective interpersonal and intergroup communication: An anxiety/uncertainty management (AUM) perspective. In R. L. Wiseman & J. Koester (Eds.), *Intercultural communication theory* (pp.33-71). Sage.

Gudykunst, W. B., & Nishida, T. (1978). The intercultural communication workshop: Foundations, development and affects. *Communication*, 7, 72–92.

Habib, A. (1997). South Africa: The Rainbow Nation and prospects for consolidating democracy. *African Journal of Political Science*, 2(2), 15–37.

Hall, B. J. (1992). Theories of culture and communication. *Communication Theory*, 2(1), 50–70. doi:10.1111/j.1468-2885.1992.tb00028.x

Hall, E. T. (1959). *The silent language*. Doubleday.

Harms, L. S. (1973). *Intercultural communication*. Harper & Row.

Hocking, W. E. (1934). Christianity and intercultural contacts. *The Journal of Religion*, 14(2), 127–138.

Hoffman, D. M. (1989). Self and culture revisited: Culture acquisition among Iranians in the United States. *Ethos*, 17(1), 32–49. doi:10.1525.eth.1989.17.1.02.a00020

Hofstede, G. (2001). *Culture's consequences: Comparing values, behaviors, institutions and organizations across nations* (2nd ed.). Sage.

Howell, W. S. (1979). Theoretical foundations for intercultural communication. In M. K. Asante, E. Newmark, & C. A. Blake (Eds.), *Handbook of intercultural communication* (pp.23–42). Sage.

Husserl, E. (1973). *Zur Phänomenologie der Intersubjektivität* (1931). *Texte aus dem Nachlass, dritter Teil: 1929–1935* (I. Kern, Ed.). Martinus Nijhoff.

Kim, Y. Y. (2001). *Becoming intercultural: An integrative theory of communication and cross-cultural adaptation*. Sage.

Kinder, D., & Sears, D. (1981). Negative attitudes and politics: Symbolic racism versus racial threats to the good life. *Journal of Personality and Social Psychology*, 40, 414–431.

Kirschbaum, K. (2012). Physician communication in the operating room: Expanding application of face-negotiation theory to the health communication context. *Health Communication*, 27, 292–301. doi:10.1080/10410236.2011.585449

Kramer, E. M. (2000). Cultural fusion and the defense of difference. In M. K. Asante & E. Min (Eds.), *Socio-cultural conflict between African Americans and Korean Americans* (pp.183–230). University Press of America.

Krause, M. (2019). Tasting interculturality: Culinary visions of America in Elif Shafak's *The Bastard of Istanbul*. In M. Steppat & S. J. Kulich (Eds.), *Literature and interculturality (1): Concepts, applications, interactions* (pp. 243–266). Intercultural Research Vol.8. Shanghai Foreign Language Education Press.

Kroskrity, P. V. (2000). Regimenting languages: Language ideological perspectives. In P. V. Kroskrity (Ed.), *Regimes of language: Ideologies, polities, and identities* (pp.1–34). School of American Research Press.

Kulich, S. J. (2019). Reconsidering intercultural narratives: Prologue to research on Rachel Davis DuBois and early textual approaches to interculturality. In M. Steppat & S. J. Kulich (Eds.), *Literature and interculturality (1): Concepts, applications, interactions* (pp.1–13). Intercultural Research Vol.8. Shanghai Foreign Language Education Press.

Kulich, S., Weng, L., Tong, R., & DuBois, G. (2020). Interdisciplinary history of intercultural communication studies: From roots to research and praxis. In D. Landis & D. P. S. Bhawuk (Eds.), *The Cambridge handbook of intercultural training* (pp.60–163). Cambridge University Press.

Leeds-Hurwitz, W. (1990). Notes in the history of intercultural communication:

The Foreign Service Institute and the mandate for intercultural training. *Quarterly Journal of Speech*, *76*(3), 262-281. doi:10.1080/08838151.2012. 705198

Li, S. W. (2008). Cultural anti-body in intercultural communication: Starbucks event in China Forbidden City as a case [跨文化传播中的文化抗体研究——以故宫星巴克咖啡传媒事件为个案]. *Journal for Journalism and Communication* [新闻与传播研究], *15*(6), 64-71.

Lim, S. S., Vadrevu, S., Chan, Y. H., & Basnyat, I. (2012). Facework on Facebook: The online publicness of juvenile delinquents and youths-at-risk. *Journal of Broadcasting & Electronic Media*, *56*, 346-361. doi:10.1080/ 08838151.2012.705198

Lin, Y., & Rancer, A. S. (2003). Ethnocentrism, intercultural communication apprehension, intercultural willingness-to-communicate, and intentions to participate in an intercultural dialogue program: Testing a proposed model. *Communication Research Reports*, *20*(1), 62-72. doi:10.1080/08824090309 388800

McKay-Semmler, K., & Kim, Y. Y. (2014). Cross-cultural adaptation of Hispanic youth: A study of communication patterns, functional fitness, and psychological health. *Communication Monographs*, *81*, 133-156. doi:10.1080/03637751. 2013.870346

McSweeney, B. (2002). Hofstede's model of national cultural differences and their consequences: A triumph of faith — a failure of analysis. *Human Relations*, *55*(1), 89-118.

Meleady, R., Hodson, G., & Earle, M. (2021). Person and situation effects in predicting outgroup prejudice and avoidance during the COVID-19 pandemic. *Personality and Individual Differences*, *172*, 110593. doi: 10.1016/j.paid. 2020.110593

Moola, S., & Sibango, B. (2017). Intercultural communication in South Africa. In S. Croucher (Ed.), *Global perspectives on intercultural communication* (pp.25-28). Routledge.

Neuliep, J. W., & McCroskey, J. C. (1997a). The development of intercultural and interethnic communication apprehension scales. *Communication Research Reports*, *14*, 145-156.

Neuliep, J. W., & McCroskey, J. C. (1997b). The development of a U.S. and generalized ethnocentrism scale. *Communication Research Reports*, *14*, 385-398.

Nguyen, T., Croucher, S. M., Diers-Lawson, A., & Maydell, E. (2021). Who's to blame for the spread of COVID-19 in New Zealand? Applying attribution theory to understand public stigma. *Communication Research and Practice*, *7*(4), 379-396. doi: 10.1080/22041451.2021.1958635

Pakulski, J. (2014). Confusions about multiculturalism. *Journal of Sociology*, *50*, 23-36.

Phinney, J. S., Horenczyk, G., Liebkind, K., & Vedder, P. (2001). Ethnic identity, immigration, and well-being: An introduction perspective. *Journal of Social Issue*, *75*, 493-510. doi:10.1111/0022-4537.00225

Prosser, M. (1978). Intercultural communication theory and research: An overview of major constructs. In B. D. Rubin (Ed.), *Communication yearbook 2* (pp.335-343). ICA-Transaction Books.

Protzel, J. (2017). Intercultural communication in South America. In S. Croucher (Ed.), *Global perspectives on intercultural communication* (pp.14-

20). Routledge.

Rogers, E. M., Hart, W. B., & Miike, Y. (2002). Edward T. Hall and the history of intercultural communication: The United States and Japan. *Keio Communication Review*, *24*, 3–26.

Rzymski, P., & Nowicki, M. (2020). COVID-19 related prejudice toward Asian medical students: A consequence of SARS-CoV-2 fears in Poland. *Journal of Infection and Public Health*, *13*(6), 873–876. doi: 10.1016/j.jiph.2020.04. 013

Sam, D. L., & Berry, J. W. (Eds.). (2006). *The Cambridge handbook of acculturation psychology*. Cambridge University Press.

Samovar, L. A., & Porter, R. E. (Eds.). (1972). *Intercultural communication: A reader*. Wadsworth Publishing.

Saral, T. B. (1977). Intercultural communication theory and research: An overview. In B. D. Rubin (Ed.), *Communication yearbook 1* (pp. 389–396). ICA-Transaction Books.

Saral, T. B. (1979). Intercultural communication theory and research: An overview of challenges and opportunities. In D. Nimmo (Ed.), *Communication yearbook 3* (pp. 395–406). New Brunswick, NJ: ICA-Transaction Books.

Schwartz, S. (1999). A theory of cultural values and some implications for work. *Applied Psychology: An International Review*, *48*(1), 23–47.

Sherif, M. (1966). *Group conflict and cooperation*. Routledge.

Signorini, P., Wiesemes, R., & Murphy, R. (2009). Developing alternative frameworks for exploring intercultural learning: A critique of Hofstede's cultural difference model. *Teaching in Higher Education*, *14*, 253–274.

Silverstein, M. (1995). Language and the culture of gender. In B. G. Blount (Ed.), *Language, culture, and society: A book of readings* (pp. 513 – 550). Waveland Press.

Smith, A. G. (1966). *Communication and culture: Readings in the codes of human interaction*. Holt, Rinehart & Winston.

Spitzberg, B. H. (1988). Communication competence: Measures of perceived effectiveness. In C. Tardy (Ed.), *A handbook for the study of human communication* (pp. 67–105). Ablex.

Spitzberg, B. H., & Cupach, W. R. (1984). *Interpersonal communication competence*. Sage.

Stephan, W. G., & Stephan, C. W. (1996). Predicting prejudice. *International Journal of Intercultural Relations*, *20*, 409–426.

Ting-Toomey, S. (1993). Communicative resourcefulness: An identity negotiation perspective. In R. L. Wiseman & J. Koester (Eds.), *Intercultural communication competence* (pp. 72–111). Sage.

Ting-Toomey, S. (2005). Identity negotiation theory: Crossing cultural boundaries. In W. B. Gudykunst (Ed.), *Theorizing about intercultural communication* (pp. 211–233). Sage.

Ting-Toomey, S., & Kurogi, A. (1998). Facework competence in intercultural conflict: An updated face-negotiation theory. *International Journal of Intercultural Relations*, *22*, 187–225. doi:10.1016/S0147-1767(98)00004-2

Trager, G. L. (1946). An outline of Taos grammar. In C. Osgood (Ed.), *Linguistic structures in North America* (pp. 184–221). Wenner-Green Foundation for Anthropological Research.

Walther, J. B. (1992). Interpersonal effects in computer-mediated interaction: A relational perspective. *Communication Research*, *19*(1), 52 – 90. doi: 10.

1177/009365092019001003

Walther, J. B. (2012). Interaction through technological lenses: Computer-mediated communication and language. *Journal of Language and Social Psychology*, *31*, 397-414. doi:10.1177/0261927X12446610

Whorf, B. L. (1940/1956). *Language, thought and reality: Selected writings of Benjamin Lee Whorf.* (J. B. Carroll, Ed.). MIT Press.

Wrench, J. S., Corrigan, M. W., McCroskey, J. C., & Punyanunt-Carter, N. M. (2003). Religious fundamentalism and intercultural communication: The relationships among ethnocentrism, intercultural communication apprehension, religious fundamentalism, homonegativity, and tolerance for religious disagreements. *Journal of Intercultural Communication Research*, *35* (1), 23 - 44. doi: 10.1080/17475740600739198

Yu, W. H. (Ed.). (2006). *Intercultural research reader* [跨文化研究读本]. Wuhan University Press.

Zeng, G., Wang, L., & Zhang, Z. (2020). Prejudice and xenophobia in COVID-19 research manuscripts. *Nature Human Behaviour*, *4*(9), 879. doi: 10.1038/s41562-020-00948-y

Zhang, Q., Ting-Toomey, S., & Oetzel, J. G. (2014). Linking emotion to the conflict face-negotiation theory: A U.S.-China investigation of the mediating effects of anger, compassion and guilt in interpersonal conflict. *Human Communication Research*, *40*, 373-395. doi:10.1111/hcre.2014.40.issue-3

Cross-Cultural Encounter

9

The Culture of Cultural Encounter

Rolf ELBERFELD
University of Hildesheim

Summary: It was only a little more than a century after the uncountable noun "culture" played an important role in Herder's new version of the history of humanity that the plural form "cultures" was first introduced into the language of the humanities by Jacob Burckhardt and then picked up and disseminated by Friedrich Nietzsche. The plural form has permanently changed the manner in which not only the present but also the past is described. Thus there has been a longer period of development that has enabled us today to speak of a "culture of cultural encounter." This chapter recalls the concepts of culture and cultures offered by four thinkers — Johann Gottfried Herder, Wilhelm von Humboldt, Jacob Burckhardt, and Friedrich Nietzsche — through whom such a perspective has become possible. This historical inquiry lays ground for interpreting the creative work of two composers, one Japanese and one German, as a "culture of cultural encounter." We should ask whether it is not high time to develop a "culture of cultural encounter" in the context of general education, beyond the opposition between a mere cultural relativism and the universalism of a single progressive culture.

Introduction

The formation of new words is the rule rather than the exception in the history of natural languages. That is because, as Wilhelm von

Humboldt has remarked, "[t]he *vocabulary* of a language can in no way be regarded as an *inert completed mass*" (1999, p. 93). Newly generated words either soon disappear from language use, or they unfold an eventful and often inconsistent life, as in the case of the word "culture." Today, far more than two hundred years after the word "culture" became familiar in German and many other languages, it possesses a timeliness it rarely enjoyed previously. When it was introduced into the German language about the mid-18th century it was felt to be a foreign word. Thus Moses Mendelssohn wrote in 1784:

> The terms intellectual improvement, or enlightening the mind, cultivation [Cultur], and civilization, are as yet scarcely naturalized in the German language. Their use is almost confined to books. By the majority of mankind they are scarcely known or understood. (1800, p. 39)

It has developed from a foreign word suited to academic circles to being a key word for the self-description of humanity, one also used in everyday speech as the merest matter of course. Yet in the discussions surrounding the word "culture," a small but extremely effective differentiation has hardly ever been considered. Only a little more than a century after the uncountable noun "culture" played an important role in Herder's new version of the history of humanity was the plural form "cultures" first introduced into the language of the humanities by Jacob Burckhardt and then picked up and disseminated by Friedrich Nietzsche.

Thus there has been a longer period of development that has enabled us today to speak of a "culture of cultural encounter." In the following I would like to recall the concepts of culture and cultures offered by four thinkers — Johann Gottfried Herder, Wilhelm von Humboldt, Jacob Burckhardt, and Friedrich Nietzsche — through whom this perspective has become possible. In my last part, I will interpret the creative work of two composers, one Japanese and one German, as a "culture of cultural encounter."

1. The Uncountable Noun "Culture" in Herder's Work

Herder's use of the word "culture" refers especially to different degrees and stages of the cultivation and education of whole peoples. He speaks of "educated" and "cultivated" peoples and nations which have left their "savageness" behind and thus set themselves more and more apart from "nature." For Herder, the positive aim of "humanity" is closely connected to the cultivation of peoples. ① His interpretation consistently suggests that a teleology is at work in history, one that features different degrees:

> Whether we name this second genesis of man *cultivation* from the culture of the ground, or *enlightening* from the action of light, is of little import; the chain of light and cultivation reaches to the end of the Earth. Even the inhabitant of California or Tierra del Fuego learns to make and use the bow and arrow: he has language and ideas, practices and arts, which he learned, as we learn them: so far, therefore, he is actually cultivated and enlightened, though in the lowest order. Thus the difference between enlightened and unenlightened, cultivated and uncultivated nations, is not specific; it is only in degree. (Herder, 1803, 1: 410)

In Herder's concept of culture, all human beings possess "culture," though of different grades. From a modern perspective, that all human beings possess "culture" appears as a fact to be taken absolutely for granted. By contrast, in Herder's time it was rather uncommon to attribute "culture" to all human beings, since in the European imagination of the time people from many ethnicities seemed to be closer to animals. Herder's concept of culture describes humanity as a community based on culture and cultivation, through which every person becomes a human being in a free and diverse manner, in the sense of a "second genesis." Yet the unified aim which becomes apparent in the quoted passage is the highest possible cultivation and enlightenment of all humanity as an indication of "humanity." At the same time this is a basic perspective which was connected in the eighteenth century with the uncountable noun "culture." In Herder's concept of culture the dimension is created in which we can nowadays speak of a "culture of cultural encounter."

---

① "The progress of history shows, that, as true humanity has increased, the destructive demons of the human race have diminished in number; and this from the inherent natural laws of a self-enlightening reason and policy" [Herder, 1803, 2: 281].

2. "Ideal of Humanity" and "Contrasting Diversity" in Wilhelm von Humboldt's Work

The efforts of Wilhelm von Humboldt point in a very similar direction. It is chiefly one of his early drafts which, as an aid and indication, we can use from a present-day perspective to develop further the idea of a "culture of cultural encounter." Even before Humboldt in a comprehensive way made the diversity of languages philosophically fruitful, in 1795 he drafted the "plan for a comparative anthropology," which was designed to set side by side and assess comparatively the moral character of the diverse human ethnicities (*"die Eigenthümlichkeiten des moralischen Charakters der verschiedenen Menschengattungen neben einander aufstellen und vergleichend beurtheilen"*: Humboldt, 1960, p. 337). Humboldt assumes that the character of an individual nation cannot be grasped without including its contrasting diversity as against the others ("contrastierende Verschiedenheit": 1960, p. 339). He understands the comparative procedure not only as something external but as essential for the realization of the ideal of humanity: this ideal of humanity, as he writes, represents as many varied forms as are compatible with one another; therefore it can never appear otherwise than in the totality of individuals.[2] The ideal does not exist as an abstract and formal concept, it rather appears only in an individualized manner. It is always real only in an individuated, concrete, and historical form. According to Humboldt, however, this is not a disadvantage; the diversity of the ideal's individual forms is rather to be stimulated and extended, as it can only be realized and kept alive in this way. It is not enough, as Humboldt writes, that a comparative anthropology teaches a knowledge of the diversity of human characters; in itself it also contributes to expanding it and to manage the actually existing one more appropriately.[3]

This procedure results in the concept of the human being and of

---

[2] "Das Ideal der Menschheit aber stellt so viele und mannigfaltige Formen dar, als nur immer mit einander verträglich sind. Daher kann es nie anders, als in der Totalität der Individuen erscheinen" (Humboldt, 1960, p. 340).

[3] "Nicht genug, dass eine vergleichende Anthropologie die Verschiedenheit menschlicher Charaktere kennen lehrt; sie trägt auch selber dazu bei, eine grössere hervorzubringen, und die schon wirklich vorhandene zweckmässiger zu leiten" (Humboldt, 1960, p. 345).

humanity remaining bound, by the comparison, to the respective historical process. The concept of the human being does not exist prior to its individual and historical realization in the timeless space of rationality. Instead, its individual and historical formation is, at the same time, the production of new possibilities of being human. The possibility of the human does not precede its actuality; rather its actuality brings forth new possibilities. ④

According to Humboldt, comparative anthropology is concerned with the extension and differentiation of the concept of humanity in the context of the world's individual and historical formations of culture. The extension and differentiation process itself, however, is bound to the individual and historical conditions of its own emergence. Accordingly, the more an individual form is able by comparison to create a reference to other historical formations, enhancing itself in its individual form, the more comprehensive the ideal appears to be in each respectively individual shape. It is precisely not a comprehensive *synthesis* of all differences that Humboldt is calling for, but rather an enhancement of individuality by making differences fruitful, since they emerge and are changed and formed especially in comparison. Humboldt is not yet using the plural "cultures," although his ideas point in this direction. The plural form "cultures" is first used by Jacob Burckhardt, whose innovation cannot, however, be understood without his predecessors Herder and Humboldt.

3. The Plural "Cultures" in the Work of Jacob Burckhardt

Jacob Burckhardt is likely to be the first to develop the plural form "cultures" as a term in the language of the humanities. He uses the plural for the first time in his manuscripts for the lecture *Reflections on History* in the year 1868, at a prominent place in the triad of "State, Religion, Culture" (1943, especially pp. 62 ff.). ⑤ Without dwelling on the details of Burckhardt's culture concept and the doctrine of three powers (state, religion, culture), I would like to point to a short but significant quotation which characterizes his use of the plural "cultures": "If we turn now to the culture of the

---

④ Cf. Borsche (1990, p.114).

⑤ This lecture only became famous in 1905 under the title *Reflections on History* ("Weltgeschichtliche Betrachtungen") in a compilation by Jacob Oeri. See also Elberfeld (2008, p.118).

nineteenth century, we find it in possession of the traditions of all times, peoples and cultures [...]" (Burckhardt, 1943, p. 64). ⑥ This sentence characterizes the nineteenth century's "culture" as a particular culture which possesses and utilizes all the world's other traditions and "cultures." What Goethe suggested in speaking of "world literature" appears to be already put into effect in this description. The time's cultural development itself gives rise to the plural form "cultures" and its productive application in this period. If not even earlier, then since the "World Exhibitions" — the first of which took place in London in 1851 — people at least in Paris and London received an increasingly concrete impression of other "cultures." The plural form permanently changed the manner in which not only the present but also the past was described. People increasingly spoke of the different "cultures" of the present and past. Classical studies now treated the "ancient civilizations" in the plural, and the present-day cultures were likewise differentiated. Because the use of the plural initially appeared only in a lecture and was not directly used in a book and thus published, it took others to introduce the plural "cultures" into the German language more intensively in the context of books, and to expand its use.

4. The Plural "Cultures" in the Work of Friedrich Nietzsche

In the winter semester of 1870/71 Friedrich Nietzsche heard Burckhardt's lecture, as spoken of above, in Basel, and adopted the plural "cultures" in his own language use. At first he associated it with negative connotations which appear especially in his famous work *The Birth of Tragedy From the Spirit of Music* (1872). Only from 1876 on did he increasingly see the plurality of cultures as an opportunity for the shaping of future history (see also Elberfeld, 2008, pp. 124 – 125). The actual breakthrough toward a positive appraisal of the plural is found in his book *Human All-Too-Human*

---

⑥   With this interpretation, one's own culture as well as other cultures are relativized. In this sense Burckhardt writes: "We must grant the nineteenth century a special faculty for appreciating greatness of all times and kinds. For by the exchange and interconnection of all our literatures, by the increase of traffic, by the spread of European humanity over all the oceans, by the expansion and deepening of all our studies, our culture has attained a high degree of general receptivity, which is its essential characteristic. We have a standpoint for everything and strive to do justice even to the things that seem to us most strange and terrible" (1943, p. 174).

(1878), aphorism 23:

> The Age of Comparison. — The less men are fettered by tradition, the greater becomes the inward activity of their motives; the greater, again, in proportion thereto, the outward restlessness, the confused flux of mankind, the polyphony of strivings. For whom is there still an absolute compulsion to bind himself and his descendants to one place? For whom is there still anything strictly compulsory? As all styles of arts are imitated simultaneously, so also are all grades and kinds of morality, of customs, of cultures. Such an age obtains its importance because in it the various views of the world, customs, and cultures can be compared and experienced simultaneously, — which was formerly not possible with the always localised sway of every culture, corresponding to the rooting of all artistic styles in place and time. (1910, 1: 38)

When Nietzsche here speaks of a "confused flux" and a "polyphony of strivings," this tellingly describes, more than at any other time, the current situation of cultures, at least in many regions of Europe. Nietzsche is struggling to cope with this "polyphony of strivings," and he sees comparison as the central procedure — which he does not understand in a strict and external sense but rather imagines as a "simultaneous experience" of different cultures and customs. Living one's own life becomes in itself a comparison in which very different things come to be heard.

Already in the preliminary studies for Nietzsche's *Human All-Too-Human*, we can glimpse the insight that a person can live through different cultures and that this can signify a form of growing for the individual. In his Notebooks we read that capable persons will experience the stage of maturity several times when they live through different cultures and thus achieve a culmination once in understanding each of these; persons can feel in advance within themselves the content of whole centuries, because the course they are taking through the different cultures is the same that several generations take consecutively. [7] In Nietzsche's statements a plurality appears not only in the context of cultures apart from individual

---

[7] "Der gut befähigte Mensch erlebt mehrenmal den Zustand der *Reife*, insofern er verschiedene Culturen durchlebt und im Verstehen und Erfassen jeder einzelnen einmal einen Höhepunkt erreicht: und so kann ein Mensch in sich den Inhalt von ganzen Jahrhunderten vorausfühlen: weil der Gang, den er durch die verschiedenen Culturen macht, derselbe ist, welchen mehrere Generationen hinter einander machen" (Nietzsche, 1967, p. 551). See also Elberfeld (2008, p. 135).

persons, rather plurality penetrates the very subject and its identity to become the central medium of its "education." When persons live through different cultures, they become internally more plural and polyphonic in their views, judgments, thoughts, and feelings. Thus Nietzsche interprets the I which lives through these experiences in itself as a "polyphonic subject."

Based on Herder, Wilhelm von Humboldt, Burckhardt, and Nietzsche we can now grasp clearly and distinctly what a "culture of cultural encounter" can mean today. In the last part, this will be illustrated with the example of two contemporary composers.

5. *Culture* of Encounter Between *Cultures* in the Present Time

Against the background of the reflections developed above, I would like to present the hypothesis that cultural encounter nowadays takes place especially *within individual persons and not between "cultures"* which in some way can be understood as wholes and can be "represented" by individual persons. In this reorientation, the purpose is to direct our attention to the concrete experience of cultural encounter within individual persons who have *educated* themselves by considering different cultures and historical contexts. This formulation suggests two different levels of possible experience regarding cultural encounter.

For one thing, it is possible for individual persons to live in different cultures by either dwelling in different places or belonging to different social groups by means of bi- and trilingualism. For another, it is possible to absorb different cultures in oneself by studying ancient cultures from books or concrete illustrative materials.

Both forms of cultural encounter can be found especially in artists' biographies, where both forms do not exclude each other but are actually interdependent and mutually fruitful. That is because when a person begins living in another culture and learning a foreign language, that culture's historical dimension will increasingly kindle their interest. In the same manner it often happens that, motivated by reading books about foreign cultures, an individual will decide to live for some time in another culture. This "polyphony of aspirations," which for individuals grows out of such forms of experience and stimulation, has been increasing in strength in various cultures since the nineteenth century.

In the manner just described, the formula "cultural encounter" as a way of living sounds rather harmless. Yet in most non-European cultures, especially in those which were colonized by European powers, what often happened was an *enforced* encounter with other cultures, which was and is consistently felt to be a destruction of a respective tradition. In the twentieth century this is increasingly the situation of migrants, who for various reasons were and still are coerced to find a living far away from their home. All these people have been forced to undergo a "cultural encounter" in foreign cultures within themselves. ⑧

Unlike these, people who voluntarily and maybe with artistic or philosophical motivations attempt (and have attempted) to "live through different cultures" are surely a minority. In these cases we can observe again and again how living through different cultures, be it in relation to the present or the past, evokes new ways of creating and thinking. In Nietzsche's sense, they become "polyphonic subjects" in whom diverse cultural practices and ways of thinking become effective as a network of new and unpredictable interactions.

From these descriptions it should become clear that cultural encounter is not so much an abstract formula but rather is itself capable of being a *cultural practice*. "Cultural encounter" can then mean allowing diversity and difference to take effect within oneself. In this sense, the aim should be to develop a comprehensive "*culture* of cultural encounter" which opens new perspectives especially within individuals but also (for that very reason) between individuals. In the last part, I will illustrate this new culture of cultural encounters in the case of two composers.

5.1 Toshio Hosokawa

The Japanese composer Toshio Hosokawa (born in 1955), who has been working at the Institute for Advanced Study (*Wissenschaftskolleg*) in Berlin, studied composition in Germany from 1976 through 1986 with the Korean composer Isang Yun in Berlin and the German Klaus Huber and the Briton Brian Ferneyhough in Freiburg. But before he came to Germany, Hosokawa was mainly interested in classical European music: "At that time [1968-1969], I was deeply

---

⑧　This form of cultural encounter is described especially by Homi Bhabha: "I have lived that moment of the scattering of the people that in other times and other places, in the nations of others, becomes a time of gathering. Gatherings of exiles and émigrés and refugees [...] Also the gathering of people in the diaspora: indentured, migrant, interned; the gathering of incriminatory statistics, educational performance, legal statutes, immigration status [...]" (1994, pp. 199-200).

absorbed in listening to the likes of Beethoven and Mozart, but I also encountered the music of Toru Takemitsu. [...] It was at such a time that I heard your [i. e., Pierre Boulez's] ' Improvisation sur Mallarmé Ⅱ , ' and was astounded and deeply affected by it" (2006, p. 9). Even at the present time, average Japanese will identify European music with Beethoven and Mozart. By now these composers' music has become connected with Japanese culture in such a manner that some Japanese could take them to be a Japanese cultural heritage item. When the Japanese began rapidly absorbing European culture in 1868, this amounted to a rupture which characterizes Japanese culture to the present day. After almost 140 years of a reception of European and North American culture, almost all of the adopted elements have become so deeply merged with Japanese culture that it is often difficult to identify their cultural origins clearly. [9] This also includes the cultivation of a certain image characterized by clichés.

Thus Hosokawa in his youth initially becomes acquainted with an image of European music that is characterized by the Japanese cliché of Europe but seems, as music, to be closer to him than his own ancient musical traditions, which at first played no role in his musical interests. What appeared to be "culturally foreign" from a certain perspective eventually became a part of his "own" culture, although, as will be seen later, Japanese traditional music too remained influential in the background (and underground). When Hosokawa heard Pierre Boulez's music, he began to sense that beyond the clichés there appeared to be a quite different musical Europe. Thus at this time, to simplify a little, there was a mingling in Hosokawa's life of a clichéd Europe, Japanese culture as background, and present-day Europe.

When he came to Germany the intercultural complexity grew in strength, as he began his studies in Berlin with the Korean composer Isang Yun. Having already become an "intercultural person" for his part by his life history, Yun could become a model for taking recourse to ancient Japanese traditions in the context of the then current compositional work. With his first work "Jo-Ha-Kyū" in 1980 for flute, violin, viola and violoncello, whose title refers to an ancient procedural form of theatrical works in Japan, Hosokawa won the composition contest "Valentino Bucchi" in Rome. Soon afterwards there followed compositions also for Japanese instruments, as in

---

[9] For this reception process and its philosophical significance, cf. Elberfeld (1999).

"Nocturne for jūshichigen" (1982), on which he wrote a commentary explaining that this is his first composition for a traditional Japanese musical instrument, when he was studying with Isang Yun, and that he wrote it under the impression of the *koto* play of Kazue Sawai, which he had heard in a Berlin concert. (Kazue Sawai presented this ca. 12-minute work on November 12, 1982 in Tokyo.) Hosokawa goes on to explain that he was familiar with *koto* music from an early age because his mother played *koto*, yet it seemed boring to him compared to Western music; it was only when he heard Kazue Sawai playing that he first sensed what a highly interesting instrument *koto* is. Hosokawa tells us that his actual encounter not only with *koto* but also with various other traditional Japanese instruments took place during his studies in Berlin.[⑩] With this new turn, the old impressions of his childhood arose again and assumed their place next to the impressions from his studies in Japan and in Germany. The various motives that were now able to take effect next to and through each other until the present show, in Hosokawa's creative work, how a variety of cultural traditions can take effect in a person so that an intercultural character comes into being. It goes without saying that by itself this is not yet a sign of quality, but in a certain way it can become the starting point for one.

Hosokawa's experience can be understood as representative of many composers who have come from East Asia to Europe or the USA to study, in the past and at present. Each of these is challenged anew to transform their constellation of diverse cultures within themselves into art, as aesthetically designed experience.

5.2 Hans Zender

The composer Hans Zender (1936-2019) may illustrate an experience

---

[⑩] "Dieses Werk habe ich 1982 in Berlin geschrieben. Es ist meine erste Komposition für ein traditionelles japanisches Musikinstrument. Damals war ich Schüler von Isang Yun, und dieses Werk war auch eine meiner frühen Kompositionen. Ich habe sie unter dem Eindruck des koto-Spiels von Kazue Sawai geschrieben, die ich in einem Konzert in Berlin hörte. Da meine Mutter koto spielte, war mir koto-Musik seit frühester Jugend durchaus vertraut. Doch verglichen mit westlicher Musik erschien sie mir langweilig, und ich konnte mich für sie nicht begeistern. Als ich dann in Berlin das Spiel von Kazue Sawai hörte, dämmerte mir zum ersten Mal, was für ein hochinteressantes Musikinstrument die koto ist. Meine eigentliche Begegnung nicht nur mit der koto, sondern auch mit verschiedenen anderen traditionellen japanischen Musikinstrumenten hatte ich während meiner Studienzeit in Berlin" (*Der fremde Klang*, 1999, p. 124).

originating in Europe, one that was perhaps first formulated by Burckhardt and Nietzsche and is thus intricately connected to the development of the European concept of culture. In 1977, Zender wrote in a text titled *On Isan Yun* about the perspectives of the future culture of humankind that our spirit now nourishes itself from the sap of ancient and new cultural grounds. Zender argues that there is only one possibility for the future, and that is a universal human culture because the sources of one's own country are no longer enough. We must hence integrate, a long process which can no longer be mastered by instinct. Our consciousness has received a new function for all forms of culture, including the arts. At the same time that our own folklore dies out we become fascinated by other modes, and it is in Asia that we find the greatest contrast to our Western thinking about forms. We can learn the most from our anti-pole; if we manage to integrate the essence of this gigantic culture without surrendering ourselves or succumbing to schizophrenia, we can discover new dimensions. Yet what will happen when we, initially as listeners, open ourselves to the antipodal art forms of this newly discovered counterpart? Something will change within us, something new will begin to take shape without our noticing. When the infantile period of naïve and external imitation, which seems to be inevitable, is overcome, perhaps a process of intellectual examination whose results cannot yet be anticipated can begin. ⑪ This, then, is Zender's reflection.

Having made a mark already at the beginning of the 1970s as a conductor and composer, Hans Zender took part in this process of

---

⑪ "Unser Geist nährt sich heute aus den Säften alter und neuer Kulturböden. Es gibt nur eine Möglichkeit für die Zukunft: eine universale Menschheitskultur; die Quellen des eigenen Landes genügen nicht mehr. Wir müssen integrieren — und das ist ein langer Prozess, den wir nicht mehr nur mit dem Instinkt bewältigen können; das Bewusstsein hat eine neue Funktion für alle Kulturformen erhalten, auch in Bezug auf die Kunst. Uns faszinieren im gleichen Augenblick, in dem unsere eigene Folklore abgestorben ist, deren andersartige Ausprägungen; und wo fänden wir die größeren Kontraste zu unserem westlichen Formdenken als in Asien? Wir können am meisten von unserem Gegenpol lernen; schaffen wir es, die Essenz dieser Riesenkultur zu integrieren, ohne uns aufzugeben oder in Schizophrenie zu verfallen, so können wir neue Dimensionen entdecken. [...] Aber was geschieht, wenn wir uns, zunächst als Hörer, den antipodischen Kunstformen unseres neuentdeckten Gegenüber öffnen? Irgendetwas verändert sich in uns, etwas Neues bildet sich unmerklich aus. Und wenn die infantile Periode der naiven, äußerlichen Imitation, die anscheinend unumgänglich ist, überwunden ist, kann vielleicht ein Prozess der Auseinandersetzung beginnen, der in seinen Ergebnissen noch gar nicht anzusehen ist" (Zender, 2004, p. 11).

intellectual examination since his visit to Japan in 1972, if not earlier. The deep impressions which he had received in encountering Japanese culture brought about a sustained intercultural perspective in his work which continues to be effective and which is reflected in the quoted passage. In 1975 his intercultural experience found expression in his first "Japanese piece" titled "Muji no kyō" (or Song of the empty script, see Zender, 2004, p. 315) for voice, flute, violin, and piano with synthesizer and *tutti* instruments. This piece cannot be understood without the deep impression which, as he says, he gained during his first visit to Japan from ancient Japanese culture, when Europe's intellectualism and technology, the hectic pace and noise of modern life, appeared to him more questionable than ever. [12]

After this piece, he also begins to adopt the ancient Chinese tradition of contemplation on music, as reflected in his Lo-Shu pieces of which the first was composed in 1977. In these pieces he especially picks up an "idea of form" from ancient China (see Zender, 2004, p. 317). [13] The two pieces just spoken of are just the beginning of an interculturally oriented composition process which at the same time originates, clearly and with rich associations, in a European tradition. What is consistently important for Zender is to allow his own foundations to be reflected in new ways, in order to transform his own limitations and prejudices.

In Hans Zender's life a culture of cultural encounter has established itself which is representative, in a certain manner, of the procedure of many European artists. Since the end of the nineteenth century, creative minds in Europe and also the USA again and again reached new artistic pathways also in encountering especially the Asian cultures and artistic traditions. Here in the context of the arts an intercultural way of living becomes apparent which hitherto has been mostly characterized and guided by biographical coincidence.

---

[12] "Das Stück ist sicherlich nicht denkbar ohne den tiefen Eindruck, den ich auf meiner ersten Japanreise von der alten japanischen Kultur empfing; der Intellektualismus Europas, Technologie, die Hektik und Lärmentfaltung des heutigen Daseins, all das erschien mir so fragwürdig wie nie" (Zender, 2004, p. 314).

[13] In a text on the Twelve-Tone Scale of Ancient China: A Contribution to the Question of Micro-Intervals ("Betrachtung der Zwölftonleiter des alten China: Ein Beitrag zur Frage der Mikrointervalle"), Zander mintains that evidently the Chinese system provokes a wholly new kind of harmonious thinking (2004, p. 21: "Es ist evident, dass das chinesische System eine völlig neue Art des harmonischen Denkens provoziert").

Conclusion

To conclude these considerations, we could ask whether it is not high time to develop a "culture of cultural encounter" in the context of *general education*, beyond the opposition between a mere cultural relativism and the universalism of a single progressive culture. People — and that means not only artists — nowadays are increasingly called upon to develop forms of cultural encounter in themselves, in order to become able to transform different cultures into fruitful and "polyphonic" mobilities in their life. The aim cannot be an external joining together of cultural differences, but rather a *cultivation* of new forms of intercultural experience which unfold their full potential in the life of each individual person.

The newly created Humboldt Forum in central Berlin can be understood as a place where this diversity can be cultivated within individual persons, making use of different museums and events of various formats. It is especially in bringing together European and non-European collections that a unique chance arises to allow one's own "polyphony" to be enriched and grow fruitful in unexpected encounters. In order to interpret these newly and continuously evolving interconnections between the most diverse cultures in individual persons, it would be necessary to develop a historical resonance theory capable of offering a crucial perspective for cultivating a living mobility of diversity and unity within and between people. If we follow Wilhelm von Humboldt, the Humboldt Forum's central objective could thus be to shape and extend the "ideal of humanity" through the fruitful diversity in each single person. Humanity always remains dependent on those people who allow it to unfold within themselves.

References

Bhabha, H. K. (1994). *The location of culture*. Routledge.
Borsche, T. (1990). Die Säkularisierung des *Tertium comparationis*: Eine philosophische Erörterung der Ursprünge des vergleichenden Sprachstudiums bei Leibniz und Humboldt. In T. de Mauro & L. Formigari (Eds.), *Leibniz, Humboldt, and the origin of comparativism* (pp.103–118). John Benjamins.
Burckhardt, J. (1943). *Reflections on history*. George Allen & Unwin. (Original work published 1868)
Der fremde Klang: Tradition und Avantgarde in der Musik Ostasiens (26–30 Mai

1999). Biennale, Neue Musik Hannover. (Catalogue)

Elberfeld, R. (1999). *Kitarō Nishida (1870-1945): Das Verstehen der Kulturen. Moderne japanische Philosophie und die Frage nach der Interkulturalität.* Rodopi.

Elberfeld, R. (2008). Durchbruch zum Plural: Der Begriff der Kulturen bei Nietzsche. *Nietzsche-Studien*, *37*(1), 115-142.

Herder, J. G. von (1803). *Outlines of a philosophy of the history of man* (T. Churchill, Trans., 2nd ed.). 2 vols. London. (Original work published 1784-1791)

Hosokawa, T. (2006). *Birds fragments* (CD). Alter ego.

Humboldt, W. von (1960). Plan einer vergleichenden Anthropologie. In A. Flitner & K. Giel (Eds.), *Werke in fünf Bänden* (Vol. 1, Schriften zur Anthropologie und Geschichte, pp. 337 - 375). Wissenschaftliche Buchgesellschaft. (Original work published 1797)

Humboldt, W. von (1999). *On language* (M. Losonsky, Ed., P. Heath, Trans.). Cambridge University Press. (Original work published 1836)

Mendelsohn, M. (1800). On enlightening the mind. *The German museum, or monthly repository of the Literature of Germany, the North and the Continent in general* (pp.39-42). London.

Nietzsche, F. (1910). *Human all-too-human: A book for free spirits, Part 1* (H. Zimmern, Trans.). T. N. Foulis. (Original work published 1878)

Nietzsche, F. (1967). *Werke: Kritische Gesamtausgabe* (G. Colli & M. Montinari, Eds.). Vierte Abteilung Zweiter Band. Walter de Gruyter.

Zender, Z. (2004). *Die Sinne denken: Texte zur Musik 1975-2003* (J. P. Hiekel, Ed.). Breitkopf & Härtel.

10

Creating and Changing Corporate Cultures in Japanese and U.S. Subsidiaries

Clifford H. CLARKE
University of Hawai'i (Ret.)

Summary: In the context of developing corporate and host-national managers of U.S. and Japanese subsidiaries, many scholars and trainers have expressed skepticism about the effectiveness of training initiatives. Intercultural training program designs and evaluations infrequently consider the measurable benefits to corporate clients. In the 1960s and 1970s, training goals have focused on individual assessments of (a) increased cultural knowledge, (b) changing attitudes toward overseas assignments, and (c) demonstrating intercultural communication skills on the last day of training.

This chapter traces the history of an intercultural management consulting/training firm with dozens of professionals serving dozens of global clients in long-term contracts throughout thirty years (1980–2010). They shifted intercultural training paradigms by collaboratively engaging corporate leaders, selected researchers from universities, and managers of foreign subsidiaries anticipating new assignees. This firm approached clients seeking collaboration in (a) assessing the individual assignees and the sending and receiving organizations, (b) designing training that integrated assessment data with theories that could guide intercultural learning processes, (c) creating multicultural and interactive team-training approaches, and (d) assessing the performance of new skills, as demonstrated in training and in the workplace, that met corporate standards of function-specific performance in the workplace.

The chapter includes a case study of the firm's International Management Development Program, which sustained dozens of other client initiatives. Results indicated increased productivity and profits in multicultural workforces with transformative bicultural leadership capable of creating synergies within their subsidiaries' workforces. The integration of researcher-consultant-trainer roles into corporate subsidiaries in long-term embedded positions was one of the unique elements of this history.

1. Early Intercultural Training for Global Businesses

When the intercultural communication field began spreading off campuses in the early 1970s, a few individuals turned toward intercultural business research, consulting, training, and ultimately executive coaching. They encountered many problems that needed to be understood and overcome. Ten of these were:

(a) The translation of intercultural academic jargon into business language and style. For example, trainers' goals are in terms of competency and effectiveness whereas businesses were aiming for higher performance and productivity.

(b) The paradigms of the intercultural field initially attracted businesses, but then produced no measurable performance results due to a lack of collaboration with client management in designing program evaluations. Paradigms in intercultural training had to evolve to meet businesses' operational requirements, e. g., with collaborative training designs aligned to headquarters and subsidiary needs. Corporations also appreciated collaboration on the processes of evaluating outcomes to see increases in productivity result on the job (OTJ).

(c) Personalization of cultural knowledge in training created challenges because manager-trainees raised their defenses with the hint of personal changes necessary for success abroad. Trainers needed to learn about changing cultures in a way that motivated trainees to accept the challenges as necessary. Client assignees for assignment abroad were often filled with confidence because of their perceived competencies, which they felt was why they were selected.

(d) Manager-trainees learned quickly that training based on

personal needs assessments alone did not enable trainers to understand their business context, since trainers had little to no experience in business. Such training was focused on the vendor's expert knowledge rather than designing training for the trainee's performance on the job, beyond just focusing on improved communications across cultures. Trainees' contexts were unknown to trainers. The trainee's intended role, functions, and tasks were often not brought into the design or training. Research was needed on their sending and receiving organizations at home and abroad.

(e) Corporations were hesitant to give much meaning to evaluations that only rated conceptual competencies, trainee satisfaction, and a few generic intercultural skills. Intercultural training program designs and evaluations rarely considered the concrete benefits to corporate clients due to inadequate research and client collaboration. Trainers employed few measurements of managers' performance in their business context. Traditional intercultural training goals focused on individual assessments of increased cultural knowledge, changing attitudes toward overseas assignments, and demonstrating generic intercultural communication skills at the end of training. Cost-benefit analysis was not applied to determine return-on-investment measurements.

(f) "Results" was another key word in business vocabulary (a core value at Intel Japan). Nevertheless, intercultural competency training has enabled improved communication skills and friendships across cultures, which are sorely needed in the business world. Primary objectives that prioritized performance results in the workplace were required to be successful in training global businesses. Performance results needed to demonstrate higher productivity measures and progress toward business goals of increased profit margins. When measurable performance results were not mentioned in proposals and reports by trainers or consultants to clients, I saw them directly tossed into the trash basket as useless as soon as the vendors left the room (P&G Japan and Motorola Japan).

(g) Initial intercultural training efforts, other than second-language training, focused largely on cognitive knowledge about culture as in culture-general training. "Culture-specific training" and "culture-comparative training" were the dominant approaches that developed. Trainers found in training business managers that a focus on cultural information about assignment cultures was not easily applied in their business roles on their assignments. A "culture-interactive" training design (George Renwick, in personal conversation) was preferred by businesses, especially in the context of their new roles and functions abroad.

(h) Trainees required a more comprehensive training design that engaged their thoughts, attitudes, and actions in integrated ways. These required interactions in role-playing with their other-culture business partners. This necessitated intercultural trainers to investigate each trainee's new business context including the expectations and standards of their new business management team on assignment and those of their home office. These were the all-important sending and receiving managers upon whom each assignee's welfare and career depended. Their expectations were the bases upon which the assignee's performance was evaluated at home and abroad.

(i) To design training and assess measurable training results, the trainer must have understood the assigned goal, role, functions, tasks, and required competencies as explained by the home office and the management team abroad. These were needed in addition to trainees' personal goals and those of his or her family (if included on the assignment).

(j) Trainers often had difficulty knowing why an approach or methods were successful or failed because training designs were not grounded in theory. If trainers did not understand how and why it was successful or failed, they could engage in research to find those theories that applied, which was my intention in returning to my graduate program in Interdisciplinary Studies in the Social Sciences at Stanford University in 1977 to 1983. It was naturally from that era's social science theories that I drew upon for the foundations of our intercultural consulting and training. These ten issues in intercultural business consulting and training in the seventies and beyond required interdisciplinary research approaches to be understood holistically as they are in the intercultural workplace. They required new paradigms and knowledge to change their assumptions about intercultural work in global businesses. I was fortunate to have had prior employment experience in Japan under Japanese management, as one "foreigner" among 1,100 Japanese employees.

2. Historical Foundations and Shifting Intercultural Training Paradigms in Global Businesses

Historical Overview

This overview of one consulting firm's dive into integrating research and training in its initial two-year client project, 1980 – 1982, is designed to provide context for the balance of this chapter. I founded an intercultural management consulting and training firm in 1980 while directing the fifth year of the Stanford Institute for Intercultural Communication (SIIC). I committed the firm to utilizing social science theories of the era by applying them in the designs of multiple intercultural training models and consulting interventions with the firm's clients. My first client accepted my need to utilize the experience as the context for my dissertation research. Mitch Hammer and I published that research a few years later (Clarke & Hammer, 1995). The first name of our organization was the Intercultural Relations Institute, a non-profit organization. The switch to a new name, The Clarke Consulting Group (CCG), took place in 1985 when the organization lost its NPO status. I will use this CCG name throughout the chapter.

Our first ten full-time associates in May 1980 were selected from sixty-six applicants from Japan and the USA. These ten associates were strangers to each other when assigned to CCG's first $500,000 contract for 18 months with the Procter and Gamble Company (P&G) on-site at P&G's plant in Modesto, California, in a diapers manufacturing plant. They learned how to make Pampers! For this project there were 2 management and organization development consultants, 3 English language and culture trainers, 2 Japanese language and culture trainers, 2 spousal trainers, 1 staff assistant, and me as executive coach and project managing director. Our services with P&G were to support a technology transfer project by facilitating multiple approaches in simultaneous programs, i. e., to fulfill every foreseeable client need vis-à-vis intercultural integration in the context of the binational organization's development around the technology transfer project. There were 72 P&G managers and technicians assigned to the project. Our goal was to contribute significantly to the development of a culturally synergistic new subsidiary plant culture in Kobe, Japan. Two weeks into the project we were told that our approach was too academic and irrelevant to their work. We were threatened with termination if we failed to change our approach. P&G gave us one paid week off to get our act together and become relevant. We returned after the week to engage the project as embedded ethnographic researchers at multiple stages of production in the P&G plant. We all lived and worked in the temporary trailers next door to the plant, in which technology training and weekly group meetings occurred. We dedicated our efforts to constantly customize our interventions to the client's requirements because we had not begun with adequate attention and collaboration on understanding the client's needs. We began to discover their organizational culture during the re-orientation stage of our work. Our client appreciated our watching and listening. We were given access to all the planning and execution of elements of their project, including P&G's management and technology manuals. These we adapted for CCG's consulting and training purposes throughout the entire first 18 months. It was an intensive and comprehensive training and intercultural organizational development project operating 16 hours a day. We were expected to commit to the same pressure since our staff had moved to live locally in Modesto.

CCG provided:

(a) Texts and learning methods for 18 months of two languages and bicultural training that included intercultural communication and elements of P&G's corporate culture.

(b) Nine months of intercultural management functions development focused on the client's ten managerial functions.

(c) On-going organization developmental initiatives including facilitation of management meeting facilitation, team building, and intercultural issues resolution (problems and conflicts). However, the P&G management training program on "proactive conflict resolution" was rejected by the Japanese, who said they do not have conflicts. We changed the design to call it "issues."

(d) On-call context-based executive and management coaching, and

(e) Full-time spousal support programs.

All material aids, such as manuals, were developed in collaboration with the clients of both cultures and were integrated with the client's language in technology training classes. Three CCG trainers served as intercultural facilitators. CCG also created and facilitated the management development programs with a process that valued each culture's standards, functional procedures, assumptions, and expectations as expressed by each person of both intracultural teams. Each team was coached to become the cultural informants (Tremblay, 1957) for the other culture's team members. Team building sessions were facilitated through issues with culture-equitable discussion assured by mutually acceptable ground rules that respected cultures and enabled facilitated explanations of the different assumptions, expectations, and values of desired processes and procedures. The changing roles and functions we were asked to provide continued expanding without limits. Requirements exceeded our training assumptions and expectations.

After the client's first cost-benefit analysis 18 months into the project, they cut their U.S. management/technician team by six who did not move to Japan. They credited CCG for supporting this cost-saving decision by achieving better than expected results. The Japanese counterparts for those six had adequately fulfilled their learning objectives so that their American partners were no longer required in Japan. Four CCG associates transferred to Kobe, Japan, with the P&G's team of twelve. The project continued in Japan for six months until the start-up of the new plant for the four of us who were engaged in daily coaching with those in box-jobs, resolving conflicts, facilitating intercultural management team meetings, and executive coaching. We left the project in Japan after six months to continue serving P&G with new projects for 18 years, until mid-1998.

These first two years' results with P&G alone provided a complete platform upon which a thriving intercultural management consulting business grew rapidly, entirely by word-of-mouth and extensive news media coverage in both countries. P&G was spreading the word and our telephone began ringing with new clients expressing their needs for assistance. Our clients grew to over 300 global corporations that benefitted from CCG's services for twenty years. CCG's 20 years of services, 1980–2000, were possible because a total of 226 outstanding associates collectively billed $ 50 million for the company all together. By the end of the nineties, CCG maintained 60 full-time associates split between the U.S. and Japan. These associates held post-graduate degrees (87%) in different fields of study (49). They had employment experience in 24 countries and 23 languages, with employment in 121 companies. Thirty Americans had worked for 5 years' average in Japan and 8 Japanese in the U.S. for 4 years' average. The primary area of our work was with joint Japan-US businesses in both countries. However, we also had specialists for other initiatives for global clients in or from 25 countries around the world. Our clients were mostly Fortune 500 international companies primarily from Japan and the U.S.

CCG as intercultural specialists worked in the following general areas of services:

(a) The intensive IMD (intercultural management development) long-term integrated English language, intercultural communication, and corporate culture training programs at CCG's head office in the U.S.

(b) The CES (client embedded support) teams served long-term in clients' operations in Japan, the U.S., and Russia, as trainers and coaches for client's IMD program graduates and other employees at all levels.

(c) The COD (consulting and organization development) team served clients in organizational culture research, development, or as culture change specialists, and the RDT (research and development) team supported and followed up on their work products. These consultants worked at CCG's head office in northern California, in clients' subsidiaries abroad on short and long-term assignments, and as intercultural facilitators of regional team meetings or of transitional leadership alignment projects.

(d) The LWX (living and working in "X" country) teams trained clients generally for one to four weeks each, to prepare for assignments abroad in East and Southeast Asian countries.

The less traveled support groups included:

(1) the MCD (marketing and client development) team,

(2) the MPT (materials production team) for research, training, reports material production, plus marketing materials, and eventual placement of our research instruments online,

(3) the F&A (finance and administration) team, including finance, human resources, and contracted legal advisors, and

(4) the RIS (resources and information systems) team who helped us organize and access CCG's resources.

Some members served in more than one team. There were ultimately 24 designed training programs and 6 types of client consulting projects offered to clients throughout the two decades, and CCG's client-focused research approach to clients provided the foundations for them all.

Finally, there were multiple project-based academic researchers that were engaged in on-site research efforts (the clients' location). Many came for our Train-the-Trainer programs. These were Drs. Mitch Hammer, Michael Paige, Todd Imahori, Harumi Befu, Muneo Yoshikawa, Judith Martin, Sheila Ramsey, George Renwick, and Kline Harrison (Clarke, 2008). Three of these worked with us for one to five years. These gave CCG highly valued contributions which significantly increased our quality of services and provided the scholars with opportunities to experience the applied field and to publish their research in academic journals. This overview of CCG's organization, associates, and services provides a partial history of one firm's early efforts to integrate theory into practice that engaged researchers and practitioners working together on assessment, design, development, execution, and evaluation of short and long-term projects for global business clients around the world.

Paradigm Changes

Several paradigm changes enabled the planning and execution of the first two years of intercultural consulting and training in direct response to our client's requirements. Paradigms were the collection of beliefs, theories, concepts, assumptions, and framework or mindset from which we see the world of work every day. However, paradigms were also barriers that slowed progress toward better understanding of encounters across cultures in multiple contexts. We were fortunate to begin with one intense and demanding client that necessitated those changes. P&G brought to CCG their vision of a dynamic bicultural manufacturing organization in Japan. Our first misguided assumptions were that we would provide a program for them to benefit individuals by enabling them to communicate with each other interculturally and productively. We had not conceived that our role would be to build or change organizational cultures collaboratively with clients. CCG's approach seemed like common sense to 16 companies such as P&G, IBM, Rohm & Haas, Baxter International, DuPont, Motorola, Intel, and others who became long-term clients in the following decades. Simultaneously, CCG's commitment to the integration of theories and practices had great influence on our designs of training and other interventions. With CCG's approach to the investigation into individual trainees' workplace circumstances, their expected goals, roles, and functions, and their sending organization's expectations and standards, we were able to tailor the standard elements of their short-term programs to be more person-focused on the trainees' expected assignment's roles, functions of their work, and assumed organization contexts abroad in their assignments.

The most hidden and dangerous paradigms in businesses were about assumptions, expectations, and standards, which were hidden behind individual judgments. They were evident in any performance assessment in business organizations. "Standards" in business operations were not considered to be one of McKinsey & Company's "Seven S" model of organizational characteristics (Pascale & Althos, 1981). The unveiling of paradigms was necessary for trainers to reveal those hidden standards behind assumptions and expectations in our roles in society so that trainees would understand upon what standards they were being evaluated in performance appraisals. Paradigm shifts occurred as we listened deeply in our exploratory process in ethnographic interviews (Spradley, 1979) of multiple clients in preparation for intercultural training in the anticipated trainee's organization.

Paradigm shifts on CCG's first project in 1980 were learned from reflections on the history of assumptions about training for intercultural effectiveness. Initially, those in the field explored *culture-general training* principles, which were believed appropriate across any differences of culture to training and are based on significant research. Too often, culture-general training is thought of as a dependable training model for the future because of the stereotyping in other methods (Gary Fontaine and Paul Pedersen, in personal conversation). Another problem concerned *culture-specific training*, which was attacked by trainees as being based on stereotypes or was simply not applicable to their anticipated roles abroad.

The training paradigm continued to evolve into *culture-comparative training*, which was effective in conveying a comparison of how two cultures behaved in certain situations and how they valued certain principles. One problem with this assumption was that it provided trainees the material with which to look for similarities and deny differences. Trainers could go beyond comparing differences into applying them in the workplace, in order to develop pathways toward resolving those differences in instructive ways that enable behavioral changes in training and in the workplace of the assignment.

Integrated *culture-interactive training* was introduced to the business world by George Renwick, and it integrated the values of earlier training models. At CCG, trainers facilitated trainees in intercultural interactions in exploring their awareness of their cultural differences, reaching an understanding of each with the other, accepting the other's perspectives as valuable, exploring their adaptability with synergistic solutions, and integrating these solutions into their challenges of creating a binational organization with common goals and processes. They learned from each other how their standards, expectations, and assumptions impacted performance of certain tasks in business. They were building solutions together that resolved conflicting processes in business operations. Training designs and processes engaged trainees in learning in the contexts of their work roles and functions abroad. Roleplays were based on organizational knowledge of anticipated roles and functions discovered through our research in the client's organization. Adding to the goal of communicative competency, training objectives for performance improvements on-line evolved of necessity in training for businesses. Trainees from IBM made very clear to CCG trainers that educational goals were irrelevant for business trainees and they would not participate until they were informed of applicable training objectives.

Another paradigm shift among trainers in business in the seventies and eighties was the assumptions about the objectives of their work. Preventing trainees from returning home early due to their personal difficulties in performing effectively abroad was the existing approach to clients (Nessa Loewenthal, in personal conversation). Research presented evidence of financial costs of early return for client organizations. Trainers assumed that client savings by reducing those costs of replacement would serve to motivate clients into training programs. The problem with this paradigm was that corporations often interpreted it as a negative view of their strengths. It suggested that their selected assignees were weak or disrespected. Trainees themselves felt they would never fail abroad because they were experts. CCG's paradigm shift was to approach intercultural training and other interventions for the client by empowering assignees to actually come home early ahead of contract because they would successfully fulfill or exceed their goals. Thereby, training could save the company the extra costs of an unnecessary year or more of the budget. The first paradigm was to solve the problem, the second was to prevent the problem, which in business is "proactive" thinking. P&G collected evidence that the company gained 32 times ROI (return-on-investment) with costs of $550,000 and savings of $18 million. They gave CCG the credit. Eleven of the first dozen assignees who transferred to Japan after 18 months in California came home a year ahead of schedule, and the remaining one was assigned there permanently to maintain a liaison role to the home offices. In addition, they exceeded their goals by having the fastest start-up, the lowest scrap, the highest quality, and the safest start-up in history (productivity measurements), better than their six other paper products plants in the world. Those were manufacturing goals that can be counted in dollars and weighed against training costs to reveal the ROI. Groups in the six other manufacturing plants around the world did not receive such training.

There was a shift in CCG's intercultural trainers' perceived roles in training. P&G required our shifting into a strategic organizational developer role on top of training. In the early 1980s George Renwick, our consultant, asked CCG trainers, "What roles do you play in your work with clients?" He wrote on the whiteboard for the next 20 minutes until the whiteboard was filled with at least thirty words in response from the room full of associates. A few of these in addition to training were researcher, consultant, counselor, facilitator, coach, problem-solver, conflict resolver, listener, evaluator, and many more. None of them had expected all of these responsibilities that developed because of CCG's complex approach to serving clients and clients' needs for interculturalist trainers and consultants. Our paradigm shifting had changed ours and our clients' lives. Full collaboration with clients and development of their trust was essential since a great deal of proprietary information had to be revealed. However, such trust was in their own interest of designing customized interventions (Yuki et al., 2005). CCG assured clients of collaboration along every step of our interventions. In summary, paradigm shifting is the only route to survival when trained intercultural consultants and trainers engage global clients in transitions across cultures. "Role flexibility" (Ruben, 1976; Ruben & Kealey, 1979) from theoretical research on intercultural competency was one key to client satisfaction. Paradigm shifts between the sixties and nineties in intercultural training are discussed in Clarke (2017).

3. An Overview of Theories Applied to Training by CCG

This section demonstrates the interdisciplinary sources of theories applied by CCG from the 1980's onward. Our purpose is to provide an overview of the theories that we found useful in the design and execution of comprehensive and context-based interventions on behalf of CCG's clients in Japan and the U.S.A. Our work was supported by interdisciplinary approaches to researching, consulting, and training. This section is not intended to be a traditional review of literature in an academic sense. Its purpose is to assist the reader in understanding the theoretical background that CCG brought into practices that enabled us to assist in creating and changing corporate cultures, improving team effectiveness, and increasing individual productivity.

A number of years ago I wrote "Practicing the Integration of Discipline and Compassion" (Clarke, 2008) and explored the benefits of integrating theoretical researchers and applied practitioners. CCG gained great competitive advantage by engaging the theory builders with the intercultural relationship builders directly in our work. These researchers and those professors from nearby Stanford University were from the disciplines of cultural anthropology (including group identity change theories), cognitive psychology (especially maturation, cognitive dissonate theories, and identity development), behavioral psychology (emphasizing behavioral change and role-modelling theory), social psychology (with attributions theories), organizational behavior (particularly culture building and motivation theories), sociology (focusing on expectation states and status equalization theories), social linguistics (particularly non-verbal and turn-taking theories), communications (intercultural, interpersonal, and organizational theories), and Japanese studies (in organizational and interpersonal/intracultural communication areas). I discussed (in Clarke, 2008) how some of these contributed to our work and to their publications on the results of our work. What we found was that integration of researcher and practitioner in client projects served to improve the process and the results of designed interventions. An integration of our strengths inspired mutual respect and trust from which clients benefitted with creative solutions and increased productivity.

My studies with and support from Stanford University professors provided explanations of the success of the Intercultural Communication Workshop (ICW) that I initiated in 1967 with international students in multicultural workshop groups at Cornell University (Clarke, 1971; Clarke & Hoopes, 1975). We had observed and tracked in our workshops (1967–1971) a developmental team process through seven stages of engaging with diversity. Those stages of development toward a multicultural identity were facilitated by the trained ICW facilitators at Cornell. These stages were:

(a) The *denial stage*, which was usually expressed by those from the U.S. only because to the half who were from other countries differences were so obvious. Quickly the non-U.S. group persuaded most of the U.S. students to move on and accept their feelings of differences they so eloquently revealed.

(b) The *stage of awareness* of the reality of cultural differences in perceptions, values, and communication styles. This process engaged contrast-culture stories from represented cultures' group members and culture-comparative diagrams created by group members.

(c) The *stage of mutual respect* began when they expressed their commitment to interact, to understand and support the diversity within the group. They learned that judgments across cultures had no place without knowledge of the other culture's premises, assumptions, expectations, and standards. The ICW facilitator at some point in the process would ask the group for that commitment if they were ready to express it. Further into the workshop, students' increasing interest in exploring each other's experiences suggested that they were benefitting from the ethnographic methodology of inquisitively relying on cultural informants and deep listening.

(d) They would next reach the *fourth stage of understanding* and would express their understanding for each other's perspectives, values, feelings, and behaviors. On occasion facilitators would work outside of the groups during breaks with a couple of participants who were having difficulty, bridging their respective opinions or interpretations of the other's experiences.

(e) By the time relationships were developing among the group members they entered the *fifth stage of appreciation*, with shared expressions of appreciation for learning from each other. Such appreciation was characterized as the attribution of worth or value to the other. This was often expressed as one's feelings of admiration for the other's perspective. A distinct in-group atmosphere became obvious with characteristic in-group joking.

(f) Their *sixth stage of adaptation* was marked by curiosity and interest in adopting different values or norms in their own lives, to "try it out" or to "see what it feels like to do that." Some would even begin role-playing a new behavior within the group.

(g) Lastly, before the end of the workshop or perhaps during the evaluation discussions that ended the workshop, some participants would express the *seventh stage of integration*, the conviction to actually integrate a newly understood perception, value, or behavior into their own lives. Some who were already practicing integration in their lives would share their stories of their most embarrassing moments across cultures from which they learned. Those who grew up in different cultures would express their sense of being in the final stage of integration.

It would be a mistake to assume that integration rarely happens, is statistically insignificant, or should not be valued because so few people reach it. Those who have integrated multiple cultural perceptions, values, and behaviors into themselves have the highest potential of becoming bridge persons that this world sorely needs to work toward peace. Those who question that potential will not be the facilitating role-models the world sorely needs. The question in 1980 was, could the ICW experience transfer to Japanese and American business managers and technicians in the Akashi Project? (This was the name P&G gave to the two-year technology training project including six months in Japan due to the start-up plant being in Akashi, Kobe.) From the outset, I believed and acted on the assumption that our new CCG team could transfer our training methods to bring similar results at the personal level to members of the Akashi Project. I had new confidence with the guidance of Amir's (1969) and Ruben and Kealey's (1979) findings. Our consulting group's diversity was designed to provide a role model for our clients (Bandura, 1976), in that we too were from all over the U.S. and Japan with multiple graduate degrees, two nationalities, languages, genders, and a wide variety of intercultural and professional experiences.

Once engaged with P&G on our two-year project, I searched for the theories that could provide the foundations of our work. In retrospect, the facilitators of ICWs a decade earlier (1967–1971) had observed and tracked a developmental team process of seven stages of engaging with diversity, which I reviewed above. Because of that history and my studies at Stanford I understood how *attribution theories* of *internal-external locus of control effects* (Rotter, 1966) and *cultural democracy theories* (Ramirez & Castañeda, 1974), from their studies in psychological differentiation effects, would be salient factors in building feelings of equity among team members who began their journey with a high status awareness (Berger, Cohen, & Zelditch, 1972), quick attributions as actors or observers of events in each other's culture (Jones & Davis, 1965), culturally influenced assumptions about their abilities to exercise control (Rotter, 1966), and need for a sense of equity between cultures, a natural national pride that demands respect (Ramirez & Castañeda, 1974). This was a challenge due to the Japanese expressing assumptions of inferiority as new hires associating with old-time members of a U.S.-owned subsidiary.

More generally, from our participant observations and ethnographic interviews (Spradley & McCurdy, 1980) with many hundreds of business managers of both cultures, Japanese observers usually attribute causes of difficulties to be the expat leadership's personal competencies, whereas U.S. expatriates generally attribute causes of failure to the local manager's personal trait competencies. We coached several expatriate leaders into revealing to their Japanese managers the limitations of authority that they had due to headquarters policies. This turned around his Japanese managers' attitudes. They began to act with more sympathy. The theories of *the Actor-Observer effect* (Jones & Davis, 1965; Jones & Nesbitt, 1971) supported practitioners' understanding of attributions between expatriate leaders and local managers.

Status Differentiation and Expectation States Theories of Berger, Cohen, and Zelditch (1972) were definitely impacting the workplace by generating an assumption of a vertical structure among members, which new hires are expecting in any business culture. When we shared with them that both cultural team members were in language, communication style, and corporate culture training it sparked a jubilant sense of competitiveness. They raced to become first in mastering each other's language. The Japanese began with the assumption that they were the only trainees. CCG's first intervention was supporting the top U.S. manager's decision to create systemic equity by eliminating role assignments until the second year of training. We treated opportunities where we could demonstrate respect for both teams' members. Inevitably the *Social Comparison Theory* of Festinger (1954) operating between members showing *In-Group favoritism and Out-Group discrimination* (Tajfel, 1978), researched in the intercultural field by Triandis et al. (1988), applied to CCG's work because members of each in-group succumbed to feelings of *Relative Deprivation* (Tajfel, 1978). The Japanese felt handicapped because the technical training was all in English. The U.S. managers felt handicapped because the Japanese knew intimately the cultures of Japan and would be comfortable when they returned home. Another factor for both cultures was the differences in style of communication (see Yoshikawa & Clarke, in Figure 1).

The lack of initiative with questions in the technology classrooms was an enigma for the U.S. trainers, while the expectations regarding U.S. managers who were taking no responsibility for following up or coaching after their delegation of tasks, while eternally waiting for the Japanese to come to report on progress, were a bothersome enigma for the Japanese. Sources of the confusion could be explained in research by sociolinguists when we analyzed the patterns of language behavior and the differences of the language function itself. CCG's trainers were aided by Duncan and Niederehe (1974), Duncan and Fiske (1977), Duncan, Brunner, and Fiske (1979), and Gumpertz (1982a, 1982b), and in exploring the cultural differences among project members by observation and interviews of their interactions. Especially, in intercultural meeting facilitation communication was improved by recognizing the non-verbal and linguistic cues, which often lead to opening new doors to deeper meanings. Communication patterns alignment to shared norms without violating or imposing strangeness in the process was a task for facilitators and team members to create equity of contributions through awareness and facilitation of turn-taking patterns. Characteristics of face-to-face interactions with the top manager were more formal with the Japanese, which is why many of them would not report to his office voluntarily. The U.S. nature of showing immediate friendliness was

——COMMUNICATION STYLES CONTINUA——

Yoshikawa, M. & Clarke, C. H. (1972) ©

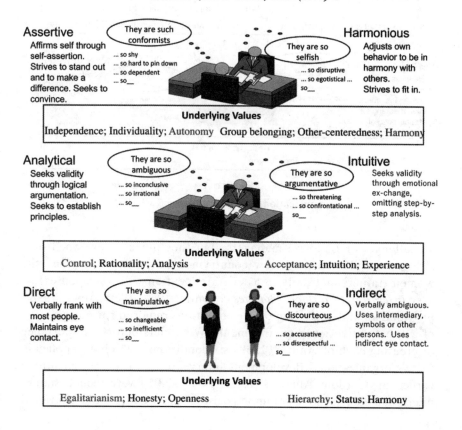

Assertive
Affirms self through
self-assertion.
Strives to stand out
and to make a
difference. Seeks to
convince.

They are such
conformists
... so shy
... so hard to pin down
... so dependent
... so__

They are so
selfish
... so disruptive
... so egotistical ...
so__

Harmonious
Adjusts own
behavior to be in
harmony with
others.
Strives to fit in.

Underlying Values
Independence; Individuality; Autonomy   Group belonging; Other-centeredness; Harmony

Analytical
Seeks validity
through logical
argumentation.
Seeks to establish
principles.

They are so
ambiguous
... so inconclusive
... so irrational
... so__

They are so
argumentative
... so threatening
... so confrontational ...
so__

Intuitive
Seeks validity
through emotional
ex-change,
omitting step-by-
step analysis.

Underlying Values
Control; Rationality; Analysis   Acceptance; Intuition; Experience

Direct
Verbally frank with
most people.
Maintains eye
contact.

They are so
manipulative
... so changeable
... so inefficient
... so__

They are so
discourteous
... so accusative
... so disrespectful ...
so__

Indirect
Verbally ambiguous.
Uses intermediary,
symbols or other
persons. Uses
indirect eye contact.

Underlying Values
Egalitarianism; Honesty; Openness   Hierarchy; Status; Harmony

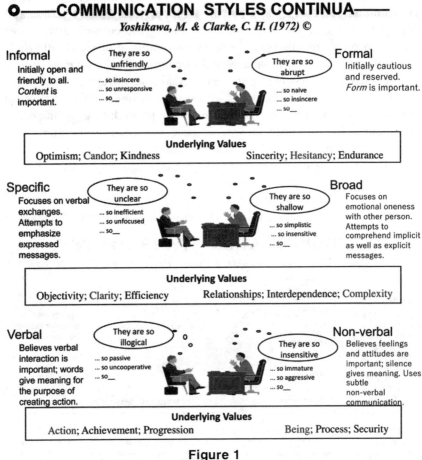

○————COMMUNICATION STYLES CONTINUA————
Yoshikawa, M. & Clarke, C. H. (1972) ©

Informal
Initially open and friendly to all. *Content* is important.

They are so unfriendly
... so insincere
... so unresponsive
... so___

They are so abrupt
... so naive
... so insincere
... so___

Formal
Initially cautious and reserved. *Form* is important.

Underlying Values
Optimism; Candor; Kindness   Sincerity; Hesitancy; Endurance

Specific
Focuses on verbal exchanges. Attempts to emphasize expressed messages.

They are so unclear
... so inefficient
... so unfocused
... so___

They are so shallow
... so simplistic
... so insensitive
... so___

Broad
Focuses on emotional oneness with other person. Attempts to comprehend implicit as well as explicit messages.

Underlying Values
Objectivity; Clarity; Efficiency   Relationships; Interdependence; Complexity

Verbal
Believes verbal interaction is important; words give meaning for the purpose of creating action.

They are so illogical
... so passive
... so uncooperative
... so___

They are so insensitive
... so immature
... so aggressive
... so___

Non-verbal
Believes feelings and attitudes are important; silence gives meaning. Uses subtle non-verbal communication.

Underlying Values
Action; Achievement; Progression   Being; Process; Security

Figure 1
Communication Styles (Yoshikawa & Clarke)
-In two parts-

a challenge for Japanese managers, but they quickly developed such an openness with their fellow countrymen (they were all men; the women trainers met daily in a separate location with the spouses).

Intergroup Contact Theories (Amir, 1969; Pettigrew, 1998) provided an understanding of the conditions required for our creation of a constructive work environment. We understood the importance of creating each of Amir's (1969) six conditions, which we applied in CCG's organizational development interventions. The four identified earlier in Gordon Allport's research (1958) were equal status, intergroup cooperation, common goals, and support from institutional authorities. The project design had already commenced with common project goals, interaction intensity and duration, a supportive organization, and facilitative leadership. Equal status and cooperative, pleasurable activities required creative operational development. Equal status was the most difficult. But besides delaying role assignments for one year, every Japanese was learning technical procedures in the nine stages of production. U.S. technical trainers were learning how to train Japanese technicians. After classroom training seemed to be increasingly ineffective, they learned that the Japanese preferred to learn on the manufacturing line by watching the line operate and then being coached by the technical trainers on-the-spot and upon return to the classroom. In this manner they caught up with their training schedule.

U.S. managers required individual test taking. Japanese learned better when they would take tests together so that they could learn in the process from each other. They asked the U.S. trainers to allow this variation and achieved great results in their preferred method. Learning styles are indeed different. CCG's trainers facilitated these solutions through facilitating cultural informants within both cultural team members. Many other speaking modifications for the U.S. technology trainers were part of their learning from the Japanese technicians. (CCG developed an *English for Intercultural Communications* card for their shirt pockets with 10 tips for monitoring English expressions.) In developing managerial functions development, both cultures' teams were given equal respect and valued for their contributions to the formation of processes and standards that were included or excluded. Their process consisted of mutually understanding stories of how they each first learned their preferred process for each managerial function. The process was guided by that of the ICW developmental process but aimed for a goal of creating a "third culture" organization (Casmir, 1993). They achieved a truly bicultural synergy (Harris & Moran, 1979) of eight functions of management that took them nine months to formulate in sessions of four hours two days a week. We celebrated with a cross-culturally competitive baseball game, Japanese vs. Americans. The major insight from this match was when, every inning, the Japanese rotated positions and the Americans all remained in their original choice of positions. But wait, Japanese were supposed to be the hierarchical and Americans were the equality culture. So why did the Americans have only one pitcher, who was the top manager of the project?

We were tasked with changing the cultures of members of two

Membership Groups (Hyman & Singer, 1968; Hyman et al., 1970), the groups to which individuals were born and felt comfortable in, and *Referent Groups*, which are new groups that form around shared values and customs, like the Akashi Project could become. Members of the groups were also either steeped in either of Hall's (1976) *Low Context* or *High Context* cultures. Perceptions either reflected a cognizance of the complexities that abound in the social environments (high context) or reflected perceptions with more focus on one thing at a time (low context). Further, Hayashi (1994; Hayashi & Jolley, 2002) taught us about analogue and digital styles of communication and how they applied to intercultural business communications, in linear and circular fashions. Insight was also provided by Yoshikawa & Clarke's six Communication Style Continua affecting Japan-U.S. persons' interactions (see Figure 1). In the nine-month process, CCG interculturalists facilitated each cultural group member to commit to a new *Reference Group* moving from their original *Membership Groups*, in the process of creating a joint culture for the P&G's Akashi Plant. The goal was a new integrated and "synergistic" organizational culture (Adler, 1986; Rhinesmith, 1992; and Harris & Moran, 1979), in other words, a "third culture" organization that evolved with their efforts over the term of the project.

This task required considerable work through understanding *Cognitive Style Differences* (Cole, 1976), *Cognitive Dissonance Theories* (Festinger, 1957; Mischel & Baker, 1975), *Communication Theories* (Barnlund, 1976), *Ethnography of Communications* (Hymes, 1964), and *Psychological Differentiation Theories* (Witkin et al., 1977). Field-dependent and field-independent cognitive styles (Witkin et al., 1977) were visible among the teams. Modifications in identities, attitudes, behaviors, values, assumptions, and expectations occurred in the project on an on-going basis. CCG interculturalists were on-site to intervene and/or facilitate individuals and groups through these changes. These perspectives and skills were necessary in moving forward by building bridges to resolve new perceptions and commitments to work toward a shared new organization culture. Understanding *Cultural Adjustment Theories* from John Berry (1992) helped us understand individuals in various stages of adjustment to differences. *Communication Competency Theories* from Ruben and Kealey (1979) guided us in developing clients' skills to effectively interact with each other, to facilitate progress in their adjustment to goals of working in a bicultural organization. These were a part of every aspect of our interventions, but particularly in facilitation of the bicultural meetings. *Culture Shock Theory* from Oberg (1960) was also essential in recognizing and managing productively, sometimes through counseling but preferably in the moment of choice at the bottom of the curve. One Japanese spouse locked down in her home and her husband had to take time off to attend to her. One of CCG's associates went to her home to counsel her in dealing with her culture shock. Some others like the two Japanese Americans had fewer difficulties interacting with the Japanese.

Many researchers have questioned the Culture Shock Theory due to the lack of quantitative evidence, but that may be because they have not worked for two years or more within a technology transfer and plant start-up project of two very distinctly different cultures or engaged with expatriate managers who find themselves in a downward spiral of negative feedback from local managers. It's a totally different set of subjects than a small group of international students or tourists spending some time in a strange country. The pattern CCG found repeatedly once the U.S. managers began work at the plant in Akashi, Kobe, had 13 steps:

(a) In sequence from the outset, the managers began showing signs of pressure and stress.

(b) Their judgments about their surroundings were defensive and based upon old norms at home being absent.

(c) They began taking independent action in an effort to "do it my way."

(d) Intracultural feedback began to circulate within their same-culture team.

(e) They joined in together using humor against the other culture's team.

(f) Collectively they attempted to rely on their previous behavioral norms as though they had no training for the experience of intercultural work together.

(g) When decisions were obviously wrong, they began to express frustration and question their effectiveness, productivity, identities and commitments were questioned. (At this point, it would have been a disaster for anyone to return home early. We responded by helping them remember the new behavioral norms that the joint team had created laboriously in California).

(h) They then began to reach out to their Japanese colleagues with shared memories of the joint norms.

(i) Before long they were joking with each other, coping by using appropriate humor.

(j) Feedback loops began opening across cultures.

(k) The joint team began acting with decisions made together.

(l) They returned to their joint team norms and processes, and

(m) Ultimately, they met or exceeded their start-up objectives.

This was our trainees' "U-curve" experience, the metaphor used in discussions of culture shock. Most expatriates make it around the curve toward the recovery direction and succeed with resiliency. CCG's role was to assist hundreds of expat managers in identifying their personal resources and goals for turning around their personal U-curve with resiliency and new approaches. Our research question is, what is the motivation for an expatriate manager to turn the U-Curve around and succeed in their assignments? This needs to be further understood through research. Practitioners and assignees do not benefit from disagreements about whether the U-Curve exists or not. A qualitative approach taken by anthropologists, as participant observers and ethnographic interviewers (Spradley, 1979, 1980), with members of a group of dozens including members of both cultures may yield new evidence of this phenomenon.

We further observed that situational solutions are not always transferred to other situations. Social comparisons (Festinger, 1954) with relative deprivation feelings (Tajfel, 1978) continued as an issue when each of the Japanese members discovered in Japan that the U.S. members lived high up the mountain in expensive "expatriate housing" while they lived nearby in the plant and communities of *burakumin*, the discriminated-against minority Korean Japanese. They had forgotten that in California they themselves were given nice homes, as expatriates anywhere of any culture are given better than local average housing. In Japan, though, the U.S. managers returned every night to their families in the hills of Kobe at precisely 6:00 p. m. after a long commute, while the Japanese worked until 10:00 p. m. because their families lived close-by. The consequence was that each intracultural team attacked the other. U.S. managers claimed the Japanese managers did not love their families as much as they. Japanese claimed the U.S. managers were early quitters and hen-pecked by their wives. Anger flared for hours the next day to such an extent that the Japanese Associate Plant Manager called for a work stoppage and a meeting for all Japanese managers after he had found red paint on the men's bathroom mirrors "Yankee Go Home" (Clarke & Takashiro, 2019). (I remembered such signs in 1950 growing up in Kyoto when I was ten years old, and I knew what it implied.) The meeting lasted one afternoon for four hours. He chose to facilitate the meeting himself in Japanese. He severely scolded them for most of the time and ordered them in a very forceful way to stop such behavior and change their attitudes. He then explained to them exactly the rationale behind the decisions that he helped to make. He asked them to share responsibility for those decisions and their current reality. After considerable discussion they accepted his explanation and request. This was not the only cross-cultural incident in those six months, but his actions did resolve the issue and operations returned to the normal fast pace and intensity (Clarke & Takashiro, 2019). Perhaps more studies on the U-Curve need to be initiated with managers in businesses that work under high pressures, in addition to all those with student subjects where most previous research interests have been focused.

Often CCG was called into almost-failed situations. To summarize those non-trained expatriate managers' experiences, I found a similar U-Curve, the *Expatriate Failure Syndrome*, while coaching the executive on a *Pathway to Successful Cultural Leadership*. Most of the outcomes were successful so that managers continued performing the company's mission abroad.

A predictable path of an overseas assignee is:

(a) Begin the journey without cultural discipline,

(b) Form premature judgments from misinterpreting behavior,

(c) Quickly execute many changes top-down,

(d) Receive negative feedback and see no results,

(e) Create defenses to avoid repetition of events,

(f) Justify behavior by good intentions and the " right [corporate] way,"

(g) Try again with more control under pressure from head-quarters,

(h) Create hostilities, breakdowns of communication, and eroding trust,

(i) Give up, become a distant manager, delegate, go home.

The costs for this path are great:

(a) Loss of customers who don't feel adequately served,

(b) Lower morale with time lost complaining and in attendance at work,

(c) Decreased productivity in the workplace,

(d) Sabotage & violations of standards,

(e) Human capital escapes to better opportunities with competitors,

(f) Replacement costs for recruiting,

(g) Lawsuits & proprietary information loss,

(h) Increased waste with quality breakdowns,

(i) Longer time to make decisions & mistakes,

(j) Circumvented channels with dual structures (local and corporate).

The new expatriate roles are Intercultural Mediator, Local Manager Developer, and Organizational Culture Facilitator:

(a) Reach out for a cultural interpreter with a concerned and open mind to learn,

(b) Approach staff with humility and desire to understand culture in the local workplace,

(c) Teach your management team H. Q.'s expectations and your own limitations,

(d) Collaborate in facilitating synergistic solutions to managerial differences and conflicts.

With wise upper management at home, all will be forgiven for charting a new path for the subsidiary to succeed.

The benefits from expatriate adaptations are greater:

(a) Development of a synergistic corporate culture through continual mediation,

(b) Leadership with the tools and the role model to enable bridging of cultures,

(c) Leadership with passion and an ability to inspire an organization with changes,

(d) Development of managers and employees with intercultural competencies,

(e) Development of culture as the core of business operations, successes, and failures,

(f) Measurement of results of performance and measure savings with cost-benefit analyses,

(g) Promotion of added value over time with continual improvements from staff, while rewarding whole teams rather than individual contributors, except for promotions of course.

(h) Facilitation of mutual respect and trust that lead to increases in productivity.

This was CCG's supportive regimen for executive expatriates and it motivated changes for achievement of personal and corporate goals on assignment (McClelland, Atkinson, & Lowell, 1953).

Expatriates abroad have three choices (failure, mediocrity, or success), and they are strongly motivated by personal achievement of corporate goals (McClelland, Atkinson, & Lowell, 1953). However, authority once given can easily be taken away. Expatriates find that achievements abroad do not necessarily lead to bigger opportunities at home. Some of our manager trainees have returned home to be fired, despite extraordinary achievements abroad. These had simply lost touch with any career-protectors at home. Some went on to higher positions in regional management positions. Others chose to leave the company and stay in Japan with other employers because of their finesse in the Japan business. Some of these even found places in Japanese-owned companies. The research on re-entry shock and our experiences led CCG into providing re-entry training and coaching for expatriates and their families from 1982 (Austin, 1986; Black, Gregersen, & Mendenhall, 1992; Clarke, 1972, 1990, 1991; Tung, 1998). These CCG services were offered in Japan or after they returned to the U.S. In a summary of our training approaches near the end of our 18 months in California, the P&G Human Resources Manager of the Akashi Project, Michael J. Copeland (personal conversation), in 1982 attributed these seven characteristics to CCG's work: research grounded, competence driven, business integration, holistic designs, intercultural interactions, participatory learning, and performance evaluations with reports to each client.

4. Integrating Training Designs with Company Goals and Standards

Integrated training design and development through researching client organizations

First, an overview of CCG's integrated training designs provides a review of how training skills can be aligned with company goals and properly assessed as critical outcomes of achievements. Measurements of training results provide data for the corporate client's evaluation at

Levels 3, 4, and 5 below. Level 1 assists the trainers in modifying the design or delivery. Level 2 builds confidence in the trainees that excel. It is critical for trainers and trainees to understand these five levels of evaluation in order to aim for the deepest level of achievement possible, delivering results and benefits to the client organization and the individual trainees, as well as to the vender firm's quality in the process.

The five levels below are based on Phillips (1997) and Kirkpatrick (1975):

• Level 1: The evaluation of the participants' satisfaction with a course. It measures things like the material, the pace of delivery, the relevance of the material, the balance of teaching and discussions, and the teacher's or trainer's style. (Reasonable as Formative Evaluations)

• Level 2: The evaluation of the participants' abilities to perform the objectives of the training course or to achieve the outcomes designed for the course, usually by being tested at the end of the course on the desired knowledge or skills. (Formative and Summative Evaluations)

• Level 3: The evaluation of the participants' abilities to understand the learning objectives and how they fit into broader work responsibilities, by being tested after training and 6 months later to test for retention and application in the workplace. (Formative and Summative)

• Level 4: The evaluation of the participants' abilities to demonstrate the new performance objectives in daily work responsibilities and environments, by observation of trainees in their workplace by trainer of supervisor, who would need to be trained on what to observe. (Summative Evaluations)

• Level 5: The evaluation of organizational or institutional benefits or effects in terms relative to the costs of investment that supported the learning activities for the participants. (By client and trainer's analysis of the impact of the investment on internal goal achievements; Summative Project Evaluations).

Clarke's client projects garnered support for Level 3–5 evaluations from 1980 onward because our first client demanded it. It required total collaboration with the corporate client in the project design from the proposal writing onward through the program's conclusion, follow-up in the workplace, and project report to the client. This approach to training designs and assessments for evaluation became our entry point of any training projects for our global corporation clients.

CCG's performance-based research design and training design process linked training to business goals. Our approach to understanding these begins with in-depth interviews with sending and receiving managers of the candidates for foreign subsidiary assignments. We found a simplified inquiry process very supported by client managers:

(a) Inquire into the *business goals* for the assignee once on assignment, for the individual, team, department, or organization as a whole,

(b) Identify the assignee's *key roles* abroad and the reporting structure abroad and to home offices,

(c) Identify the *principal functions* required to perform each of those functions,

(d) Identify the *key tasks* required or expected for each of the functions,

(e) Identify the *core competencies* required for success in a particular job task, including comprehensive knowledge, skill sets, and attitude standards,

(f) Identify the *specific skills* required to meet the performance standards to be used as performance objectives, and

(g) Identify the measurable *behavioral indicators* of each skill's performance as the training objective.

Our *performance-based training* is a systematic format of instruction in which skills or competencies to be learned are clearly defined for the trainee and are designed to reflect the skills required to ultimately achieve business goals. Effective trainers usually state the skill mastery requirements for each task prior to the beginning of training. *Criterion-referenced evaluations* are evaluation instruments or tasks designed to measure the exact objective and the specific behaviors required to accomplish a particular task. *Measurements* are observable behavioral indicators that give us information about the achievement of the Level 3 type of evaluation indicators, and the Level 4 type of evaluation indicators of measurable improvement in business results that provide data about the company's internal productivity measurements. It is from these that we are able to assist the client in Level 5 evaluations, i. e ., cost-benefit-analyses for return-on-investment benefits. Following this, a firm has all it needs to satisfy potential clients with data that encourages new client contracts.

4.a. Key Research Processes in Organizational Culture Change Projects

CCG's approach to understanding corporate cultures within the human relations and interpersonal and intercultural aspects included an ethnographic research engagement for a designated time as limited as the client would provide. We relied on methodologies that we adapted to gathering data by a four-step process, as below, engaging client employees and managers from up to seven sites (Motorola) and as few as two (IBM). For multiple clients we executed all four steps, including 3M-Sumitomo, AT&T, Baxter International, Boston Scientific, DuPont, Eastman Kodak, Federated Department Stores, Fuji-Xerox, Hitachi America, Honda R & D, Intel, Kawasaki-Armco Steel, Monsanto, Procter & Gamble, and Rohm & Haas. These four data gathering steps were necessary to engage with clients in their change initiatives that yielded valuable data for the client to reflect upon in the planning stages of corporate culture change initiatives, as they were called in businesses. These four steps were based in part on the methods discussed in Spradley (1979, 1980) and Spradley & McCurdy (1980), and they included:

• *Artifacts analyses* of the client's corporate documents for both external and internal distributions. There were 18 varieties of documents, some of which were confidential. We spent a day in IBM's library archives examining manuals, executive presentations, and documents, such as training manuals for new-hires, supervisors, and managers for each of their managerial functions including decision making, motivating, team building, evaluating, and more. Based on the readings of such artifacts, the team was ready for the second stage.

• *Observation*. Teams or CCG's "participant observers" attended or participated in up to 12 areas of observable client interactions, including manager meetings, lunchroom engagements, departmental and team meetings, performance appraisal discussions, new-hire orientations, and project reporting to superiors. Actually, at Rohm & Haas we were told that decisions were made in hallways between managers, so we observed hallway activities. CCG researchers used an 18-item "observation checklist" and observed as unobtrusively as possible. Based on the notes from all observations, the team was ready for the third stage.

• *In-depth interviews* with members of multiple departments and divisions, multiple levels from worker to management, including the top leadership, both genders, and members with varieties of longevity at the company. Interviewees were selected with strict representative and sampling guidelines which required supporters and dissenters of the organization's culture. Numbers interviewed varied from 50 to hundreds at multiple sites in Japan and the U.S., as with Motorola. Cultural interpretations and implications derived from the answers to the exploratory (spiraling) questions with deep listening skills can clarify the extent to which cultural diversity plays a role in each of the 8Ss. This interview process revealed the degree to which cultural perceptions and expectations impact performance in the "8Ss."

• *Surveys* were developed based upon analyses of intensive interview notes from each client's database. Content analyses and Q-sorting each client's results led to the identification of common experiences. We adapted the names of McKinsey's 7S's categories of organizations characteristics (Pascale & Althos, 1981), and modified this to the human interaction elements using our interview data that focused on items where culture played a significant role in altering perceptions, assumptions, expectations, and standards or norms of behavior. We added an 8th characteristic, "Standards," which was evident in the data but omitted from McKinsey's list of seven. The 8S's titles began with an action verb, in order to convey that interaction was the birthplace of intercultural issues over differences. The 8S's were:

(a) Creating *Shared* Corporate Vision, Values and Goals,
(b) Aligning Business and Resource *Strategies*,
(c) Designing Organizational *Structure* and Role Functions,
(d) Developing *Staffing* Policies and Demography,
(e) Installing Operational and Human Resource *Systems*,
(f) Determining Individual and Team Performance *Standards*,
(g) Aligning Leadership and Management *Styles*, including developing intercultural competencies at the levels required for effective intercultural interactions, and
(h) Developing *Skills*, including Functional and Technical Competence.

Indicators in each "S" were selected from our client interview data by multiple raters and placed into 10 evident sub-divisions for each "S", each with 5 indicators. The survey thus had 8 sections with 50 items in each, 400 in total. This total was similar in size to other culture surveys that we had seen, i.e., Johnson & Johnson. It could be taken at one time or at eight different times, depending on the subject's available time. We indicated that returns were due within two weeks. Corporate managers were fully cooperative in requiring participation, hence with each administration there were close to 100% returned surveys. After the survey draft was developed, tested for validity and reliability with pilot groups, and modified, if necessary, it was ready for utilization with clients.

Surveys were collected from entire company populations or smaller sample groups, such as management teams or one department or another depending on the interests of our clients and the terms of CCG's contract. Based on the analyses of corporate culture surveys, the team was ready to prepare for the fifth stage of reports. Nine additional instruments were developed and utilized over the years with CCG's clients for exploring different management functions within corporate organizations where there could have been intercultural issues such as teambuilding, leadership assessments, intercultural decision making, intercultural communication competency analysis, and four others. A subject's personal information and demographics were also collected, but personal information sources were not shared with the client. Confidentiality was assured in the survey instructions. Clients were able to choose which demographics they wanted to examine in CCG's client survey report.

• *Reports on survey results* were presented in print and on Powerpoint to CCG's client with recommendations for actions. CCG asked each client to select their project SAT (Strategic Advisory Team) members using five criteria. Without an SAT, corporate culture change projects had little chance of success. These criteria were:

(a) *Authority* to commit resources and lead or manage change,

(b) *Accountability* for measuring and getting results from each department,

(c) *Authenticity* in monitoring data, standards, setting directions and goals, thereby conveying to all employees that this process was monitored by the SAT for accuracy,

(d) *Affiliation* with and accessible representation of all employees in each department, and

(e) *Assurance* of follow through and continuity of the culture change in SAT's project commitment.

The project goals were to create a unified corporate culture for empowering employees, developing teamwork within and between local and global organizations, integrating conflicting people, systems and cultures, and building a more competitive position of the company in their marketplace. There was a good deal of research on management and employee engagement (Baumruk, 2006; Gibbons, 2006; Kahn, 1990; Luthans & Peterson, 2002; Saks, 2006). CCG focused on its tactical approach with the SAT to engage the project leaders with the authority and responsibility to achieve the project's objectives. Our approach relied upon deep engagement with SAT project leadership in its execution. Without such engagement in all aspects of a project, it would mean accepting high risks of failure from the leadership's position that the project was led by the external consulting vendor. In collaboration with the SAT, the research data allowed us to identify the ideal performance standards and current gaps in our regular meetings. We analyzed with the SAT the root causes of existing gaps in performance. We prioritized with the SAT the key issues, action plans, and goals for changes in organizational culture. Sometimes this involved meeting with department managers and executives to resolve strategic level issues identified in the SAT-led workshops. Thereby, mid-level managers were engaged in resolving tactical level issues in action planning workshops led by upper-level management.

We used the format of a "key issues worksheet" to clarify each issue, cause, impact, goal, benefit, barrier, supporter, and to prioritize action plans. Before initiating the action plans, we jointly designed monitoring systems for measuring changes. One action plan was for CCG to provide skills training and systems modifications with SAT support, where necessary, to achieve desired performance goals. For this we depended on departmental managers to authorize and engage employees. Results of interventions were reported to the SAT. We also encouraged SAT leaders to recognize and reward successful achievements of performance targets of managers and teams when they occurred throughout the company, and to celebrate their work periodically.

4.b. Facilitating the Creation of Synergistic Standards for a Managerial System

CCG's approach to building new synergistic standards for eight managerial functions was discussed in detail in Clarke & Takashiro (2019). Below is a summary of that developmental program. In that process, facilitating diversity into a synergistic merging of cultures for a jointly developed system of eight managerial functions (decision making, leading, motivating, training, evaluating, conflict resolving, negotiating, and managing meetings) was grounded in theories and very complex circumstances. The participants were half Japanese and half from the U.S.; there was diversity among each cultural group in age, industry, ethnicity, geography, education, and intercultural experience; two from the U.S. were Japanese Americans from Hawai'i with prior Japanese language and cultural training. Because English is taught in Japan, the Japanese all had different levels of comprehension that required multileveled classes. Most within and between groups were strangers. Prior industrial experience was diverse. Six shipbuilders were going to be manufacturers of Pampers diapers. Commonalities were that they were all male, all married, most with children, all studying each other's language, and all anticipating assignment to boxed positions, each with one of the other. Another commonality was that each had committed for the next two years to be working 16-hour days in very intense circumstances.

Our work in developing a managerial system began in the second month of the project and continued for a total of 288 hours over nine months (Clarke & Takashiro, 2019). Two other CCG trainers and I became facilitators of our COD work (consulting and organization development) by initiating the processes for building an organization with a synergistic organizational culture. This shift of paradigm in the trainer's role was new to CCG's associates. We designed a process that gradually facilitated a change from multiple membership groups to a single new reference group (Hyman, 1942; Hyman & Singer, 1968) to be known as the Akashi Plant culture. We began collaboratively developing the managerial standards by applying a focused ethnographic interviewing approach (Spradley, 1979) of storytelling for each function, one each month. In the first month their stories were about how they learned their personally preferred steps in the process of decision making. Individuals wrote their stories as homework for others to read in their respective cultural groups of Americans or Japanese. With 18 stories in each cultural group in their own language, they were able to explore the detailed assumptions, meanings, causes, and values behind each story for each function. They worked together intraculturally to identify the sequential steps necessary to the process of their preferred decision-making process. Their next step was to rank order steps in the process of decision-making by consensus. This process enabled them to learn about each other and begin building the two cultural teams. They also developed their own acceptable story for each function, rather than allowing stereotypes about Japanese or American management processes to be represented. In an intercultural session on another day, they shared their story with the other cultural group. They met for four hours every Tuesday and Thursday. Intercultural learning in depth about each other's expectations was the objective.

When they shared their rank ordering step-by-step, they discovered differences to work on and similarities to celebrate. Fortunately, across cultures there were 75% similarities and 25% differences on average. However, they found that the 25%, the most important steps, had all floated to the top of each list. These differences had to be acknowledged, respected, understood, appreciated, adapted, and integrated (Clarke, 1971; Clarke & Takashiro, 2019) into the final document for each managerial function. In this process, we relied upon the ethnographic "cultural informant" role (Tremblay, 1957) that each member of one group played with the other group. They thereby practiced spiraling inquiry skills for exploring an individual cultural informant's perceptions, interpretations, and values reflected in behaviors. Such a person had to interact at that mutually trusting level to be in a bicultural box position when work roles were assigned at the end of the first year of training. There would be two people in the same position starting in the second year, one American and one Japanese, where each could hopefully become the other's cultural informant before leaving for Japan together. During the process of facilitating this highly focused learning activity on developing an integrated managerial culture, we were assessing progress along the intercultural identity development scale that was first developed in ICWs at Cornell (Clarke, 1971; Clarke & Hoopes, 1975).

From our understanding of the importance of building trust between groups and individuals across cultures, found later by Nishishiba and Richie (2000), Yuki et al. (2005), and Clarke and Takashiro (2021), we found that respect (Wiley & Kowske, 2012) and trust (Lewis, 1999) led directly to increased productivity. Lack of trust was an impediment to progress in intercultural interactions. Building common commitments to a new team and an expanded identity also required time, personal investment, and strong support by project authorities, who established clear common goals for the project. It required demonstrated status equality across cultures in intense interactions to create structures and roles. It also required cooperation and pleasurable activities. Finally, effectiveness required facilitative leadership, which CCG provided, and P&G

strategically anticipated. All of these requirements fulfilled Amir's (1969) conditions for effective intercultural interactions among groups. These were the guidelines guiding our planning and execution. Additionally, identification of intercultural competencies (Ruben, 1976; Ruben & Kealey, 1979) were instrumental in CCG's facilitation of the group members' interactions. It was imperative that members held no unfounded judgments against other members and that they developed new understandings of presumptions, perceptions, and interpretations of other's behaviors as just their personal thoughts or feelings, without presuming they were universally shared by others. If cultural premises of opinions are not yet known, how could judgments across cultures be valid? It was also necessary for all members to communicate with respect for and empathy with the other by showing reciprocal concern. Since roles were not assigned until the end of the first year, it was necessary to demonstrate role flexibility, as we did with constantly increasing role assignments. Lastly among Ruben and Kealey's (1979) intercultural competency standards, everyone needed to demonstrate tolerance in our unsettled and changing circumstances. From the conditions surrounding our project and with these interaction competencies, trust increasingly became a natural outcome.

A CCG objective in on-going facilitation of the managerial functions' standardization processes was to reduce uncertainties during intercultural encounters (Berger & Calabrese, 1975; Gudykunst, 1985), which we did by establishing processes with which members could identify cultural informants (Tremblay, 1957) about the managerial role function, behavioral norms and underlying values as they had earlier learned from prior employment. Naturally, many conflicts were inevitable, and we approached them with our conflict-resolution process (Clarke & Lipp, 1998) that evolved through the experiences with P&G and other clients for two decades. Further, as explained in detail in Clarke and Takashiro (2020), through the process of analyzing critical incidents (CI) (Flanagan, 1954), to explore differences between culture team members in our conflict resolution process we ultimately created the P&G Akashi Plant's culture assimilator (CA) (Fiedler et al., 1971) based upon an average of six CI in each of the eight managerial functions as above. Each cultural group's CA was based upon 48 CI, all created by the 36 members of the Akashi Project. CCG utilized the CI as a final exam that revealed the Akashi team's ability to isomorphically interpret each other's behavior. Finally, CCG also relied upon our understanding of Bandura's role modeling method in his social learning theory (Bandura, 1976). CCG's associates were coached to role model Ruben and Kealey's (1979) competencies and to support the development of Amir's (1969) conditions in the Akashi Project's learning, working, and living environment at the Modesto P&G plant and community. Through facilitating an understanding of these competencies, and role modeling them, our goal was to train the Akashi team members to practice and facilitate each other's demonstration of them in their interactions. We also encouraged them to be inspired by P&G's support of Amir's conditions, which all permeated their environment.

4.c. Intercultural Management Meeting Process Facilitation

Throughout CCG's work beginning with P&G, the clients have requested our support in facilitating intercultural meetings. Requests were usually for managerial and executive level support in the organizations. It occurred in monocultural meetings as well. For example, at the ATD (formerly American Society for Training and Development) board meetings, I was asked to play a contrast-culture role to awaken board members to each time they would speak from an ethnocentric perspective. Their theme at that time was "Going Global." In meetings I role-modeled the skill of thinking globally and highlighting their personal ethnocentric expressions by contrasting their thought with a challenge from a global perspective with a different assumption. They felt the process was an enlightening and pleasurable experience each time, in part because they were all learning together. They stopped to discuss each of my interventions and to analyze each of their expressions from another cultural perspective that I would represent. They very patiently allowed for every intervention and expressed their appreciation with laughing and ribbing their neighbors, and also directly to me in a more serious manner. In Clarke and Takashiro (2019) we elaborated on the roles of the intercultural communication facilitators in the context of the bicultural management development process at the Akashi Project context. We also explained the TIID (Transformative Intercultural Identity Development; Clarke & Takashiro, 2019), as a derivative from the original ICW process at Cornell (explained in Clarke, 1971, and Clarke & Hoopes, 1975). Below is a summary of those procedures with our supportive theories.

In this application, our focus was on the actual roles and functions involved when facilitating intercultural managerial meetings, such as the plant manager's weekly meetings at P&G Japan for three hours every Monday morning for six months. The theories supporting these roles and functions gave us assurance of effectiveness in the interest of the clients. These meetings were bicultural but conducted largely in English with side expressions in Japanese permitted. The intercultural meeting facilitator's (IMF) role was always secondary to the Group Manager's leadership role. He clearly explained our facilitator roles to all members, in both languages, before the first meeting or for invited members of the plant. The purpose of the IMF roles was to assure cross-cultural understanding of the discussion content and communication processes, including the cultural norms established in the Akashi Project in California such as equitable turn-taking, deep listening, and explaining otherwise hidden assumptions. IMFs sometimes explained non-verbal or paralinguistic behavior when the other culture's members seemed confused. IMFs enabled the members of each group to feel respected and to develop trust in their counterparts. The IMFs provided a process for resolving any additional problems that resulted from the cultural diversity. We developed eight IMF role functions, which were:

(a) *Preparing Interactions*. Prior to each meeting, we monitored the distribution of each meeting's agenda and documents to be read before the meeting. As the meeting began, the leader would clarify his role in guiding the content of discussion and the facilitator's role in aiding the process of communication and documenting key decisions after seeking clarification of them from members. The IMF assisted in developing the ground rules for participating in meeting discussions, including clarifying assumptions and expectations underlying members' ideas and questions, allowing equal time for all to contribute, maintaining a respectful nature of meeting discussions, allowing time for brief, intracultural, clarifying side conversations in first languages, and monitoring quick judgments from ethnocentric perspectives. Although the members had all been in the California Akashi Project, these IMF actions were all necessary to set the conditions for the most effective and productive meetings. Our theoretical foundations for these process clarifications were from Amir's (1969) contact hypothesis research outlined previously. Our first objective was to assure these conditions for management team meetings.

(b) *Clarifying Meaning*. As discussions on the agenda began, our core functions began with assuring that interpretations influenced by culture were explained clearly to established common understandings among the members. Methods for doing this included checking on a speaker's perception and/or interpretation of what was heard just before, verbally asking about participants' non-verbal behaviors, questioning unclear assumptions and expectations, and attending to sociolinguistic differences or language interpretation differences. Theoretical understandings that enabled these interventions were Barnlund's (1976) Interpersonal Meaning elements of perception orientations + system of values + communication styles, Casse's (1980, 1982) four reasoning and/or negotiating styles (logical, normative, intuitive, and emotional), Cole's (1976, also Cole & Means, 1981) cultural variations in cognition, Gumpertz's (1982a) elements of discourse, Hall's (1976) significant insights into low-high context cultures, Jones and Davis's (1965) actor-observer effects, Ramirez and Castañeda's (1974) cultural democracy stemming from field-sensitive to field-independent research, and Rotter's (1966) locus of control studies. Some of these apply to subsequent functions below as well.

(c) *Interpreting Cultures*. This function in Japanese and Americans' meetings required a keen awareness of the deep cultures of each. Knowledge of those predominant variations within each culture were useful, but all cultures have people along multiple continua of cultural variations. Critical in understanding variables among Japanese was awareness of status relationships between its members and also between departments, between age groupings, between degrees of experience in foreign companies in Japan, and between genders. Cultural factors are often seen in communication styles, in depths of disclosure, in usage of rational or emotional expressions, in presumed levels of authority, in the degree of integration between values and behaviors, and in the "proper place" for attending to harmony or honesty in interactions, both of which are valued as paths to integrity for Japan and the U.S. respectively. Of all the differences, this has had the most impact on the effectiveness and productivity of management meetings in both countries. This facilitator function in intercultural meeting interactions emphasizes skills in intervening for cultural clarifications in a way that enables others to explain their own biases and preferences of style that, without explanation, can create misunderstandings. Another guideline for meeting interactions has been to have the leader give every member the responsibility to explain their cultural assumptions that may lead to misunderstandings. That makes the facilitator more accepted for their role and not risk being the "cultural expert." Facilitation was best received as enablement of the meeting's members to openly express their opinions without fear of reprisal when they were more open about their thoughts. In other words, IMFs respond to diversity by understanding, accepting, and appreciating its fresh perspective. The theoretical support we had for facilitating these interactive interventions came from Clarke and Lipp's (1998) steps toward intercultural conflict resolutions, Doi's (1981) study of interdependency and independency, Gudykunst's (1985) reduction of uncertainties, Hall's (1976, 1987) context orientation, Kohls's (1981) concepts of deep culture awareness, Ruben's (1976) and Ruben and Kealey's (1979) intercultural competencies, and Yoshikawa and Clarke's Communication Style Continua (see Figure 1).

(d) *Identifying Problems*. The roots of intercultural communication problems are found in hidden premises, assumptions, and expectations that interfere with cognitive processing of meaning. Inflexible mindsets mired in the petrified values of ancestors present themselves as defenses against changes and the challenges of the modern world, always in transition with an increasingly rapid pace. Gaining employment in Japan or the U.S. with a foreign-investment company precludes the maintenance of business-as-usual for members of either culture. The new-hire manuals are filled with previously unheard expectations, even down to the usual 3 to 6 company values. Among new-hire Americans in U.S. Japanese subsidiaries or new-hire Japanese in Japan's foreign-owned companies, there is a period of euphoria followed by a downward spiral toward total confusion. The strongest manage the ride for a variety of reasons, but they all go through the challenges unless they are corporate transplants from other such companies. By the time they arrive at or near the top, most have adjusted, except for those corporate transplants of first timers in a *gaishikei* (foreign-owned company in Japan). Therefore, there are usually some meeting members who bring experience to the table. Their helpfulness depends upon their attitude toward their experiences. The ones with positive attitudes and openmindedness make excellent cultural informants for their less experienced associates. They usually participate when given the role of senior assistant facilitator. They see the problems before they occur because they have transversed those muddy waters before. They are experienced in cultural problem-resolution processes. They understand the cultural differences of the "width of the track" or the "pace of decision making" which their comrades are frequently accused by Americans of violating. Problems arise from cultural variables in assumptions about teamwork. The American members assume that each person must above all "do their part" whereas the Japanese members value "reaching in" to help all other members. This was one of six company values/standards at Honda R. & D. in the U.S. Assumptions about being proactive versus reactive, or thinking strategically or tactically, have been causes for being in the in-group or the out-group, which often determines a member's career trajectory or next promotion (P&G). Hidden expectations about these matters are often causes of problems. Such problems are often resolved when facilitators seek out individuals after meetings. Theoretical foundations for searching for such potential problems were found in Rohlen's (1974) discussion of Japanese white-collar organizations, Tajfel's (1978) intergroup differentiations, Triandis et al. 's (1988) reflections on individualism and collectivism effects on relationships, Wuerth's (1974) actor and observer biases, and transitions from membership-reference-membership groups (Bernard J. Siegel, in personal conversation) in the company depending on interactions around the meeting. Bernard J. Siegel was Professor of Cultural Anthropology at Stanford University.

(e) *Monitoring Process*. Our focus in monitoring communication processes in meetings is to assess the effectiveness of meeting progress toward reaching its goals for each meeting and to identify and resolve stumbling blocks between its members. Therefore, we analyze interaction skills such as turn-taking, the balance of statements and questions, domination of speaking, equity of cultures, distribution of questions and statements, patterns of inclusion and exclusion, reliance on and ignorance of non-verbal and paralinguistic utterances, status consciousness, and patterns of communication styles employed. Theories that informed our methods of analyses were from sociolinguistics, anthropology, sociology, and social psychology of groups. Primary resources were Berger, Cohen, & Zelditch (1972) on the effects of status differentiation and expectation states; Clarke and Kanatani's (1979) analysis of turn-taking in small group communication between Japanese and American professionals; and Yoshikawa and Clarke's Communication Style Continua of six culture-comparative communication styles of Japanese and Americans (see Figure 1); Duncan and Niederehe's (1974) analysis of turn-taking; Duncan et. al. 's (1979) study of strategic signals in face-to-face interactions; Festinger (1957) on the developmental effects of cognitive dissonance; Gumpertz's (1982) work on code-switching and on discourse analysis in research; Rogers (1962) on developing change agents through the diffusion of innovation methods; Scalzi and Spring (1975) on intercultural workshop group dynamics; and Spradley's (1980) participant observation skills.

(f) *Suggesting Directions*. Our function of suggesting directions was certainly not in terms of the operational subject matter of members' discussions. That was the role of the leader. However, if we thought that a change in the process of communication would facilitate more effective communication, we would make such suggestions for changes. Noting the five functions above, we were continually learning about each group member's difficulties, and suggested changes to reduce such noted barriers. Theories that supported these activities in addition to those above were Bandura's (1976) methods of role modeling to effect changes; Barnlund's (1976) model for the integrated pathway toward meaning; Casse's (1980) four reasoning styles; Yoshikawa and Clarke's communication style differences between Japanese and Americans (see Figure 1); Ruben and Kealey's (1979) intercultural competencies as effective guides for a more ideal communication process; Trompenaars & Hampden-Turner's (1997) useful approach to understanding business misunderstandings and resolving conflicts across cultures, and other resources above (in (e), Monitoring Process).

(g) *Summarizing Decisions*. In summarizing decisions made in the group meeting, as intercultural facilitators we were sometimes called upon to wordsmith the thoughts expressed in members' decisions from the whiteboard after each agenda item was finished because of their need for clarity in a way that both cultures could understand and support. We also had to represent the opinions expressed in broken English or Japanese, for a more general understanding. We were charged with monitoring the communication and distribution processes by supporting the meeting leader's staff assistant. Careful attention to the process was required to support the meeting's decision-making process because of the influence of culture on assumptions of the "one best way" (a P&G saying). In intercultural meetings in binational businesses, we have observed about clients that there were five variations of the process of making decisions: authoritative, democratic, consensus, alignment with external restrictions or requirements, and ownership. In certain ways these were influenced by bases of social power, e. g., ascription (owner or status), attribution (assigned or assumed by others), achievement (expert or top performer), or affiliation (to an external referent or higher goal) (French & Raven, 1959). Clarification of the decision-making process from the outset and with each decision was made, to check for consistency, especially if the process was decided at the beginning by consensus. Mutual understanding of these variations of decision-making processes is critical for members to understand and agree with the chosen process. Theoretical support for some of these functional skills were found in Berger, Cohen, and Zelditch's (1972) status and expectation states; Casse's (1980) four variations of reasoning patterns; Duncan and Fiske's (1977) structure and strategies of interactions; Fisher's (1980, 1988) study of international negotiations at the United Nations and the role of culture and perceptions in mindsets across cultures; French and Raven's (1959) bases of power and authority to make or influence decision-making; and Gumpertz's (1982a) discourse strategies and interaction analysis. The facilitator's last two roles were always done after consultation with the group leader.

(h) *Debriefing Interactions.* This last item on the agenda focused on members' thoughts about the meeting's communication process and its impact on the quality of decisions. We also asked them for feedback on the facilitator's role functions, and often called them out one-by-one for input in their native language. Finally, we shared our summary of decisions written on the whiteboard and asked for any needed changes. When all members were contented, the leader closed the meeting. Afterwards we would seek out one-to-one follow-ups to assure that no one was unfinished or had unexpressed thoughts in the meeting about the content or the process. Any critical input from the follow-ups were shared with the meeting leader. The follow-ups yielded some subjective perceptions that the members thought were not relevant to the group (the "width of track" issue). The IMFs throughout each meeting were guided primarily by theories from Amir (1969) and intercultural competency researchers, especially Ruben and Kealey (1979), backed up with discourse analysis methods from Gumpertz (1982) as well as work by Clarke and Kanatani (1979), Duncan and Fiske (1977), Nishida (1985), Scalzi and Spring (1975), Spradley (1980), and Yoshikawa and Clarke (see Figure 1). These principal functions of IMFs' roles in meetings were integrated with the IMF behavioral skill sets detailed in Clarke and Takashiro (2019). After this meeting facilitative process was instituted for several weeks, members' productivity soared from being able to make decisions on one to three of the items on their agenda to being able to develop resolutions on all eight to ten items each Monday in the same three-hour period. The top management

IMF role expanded into CCG's role in developing intercultural teams in other business contexts that engaged Japanese, American, and other Southeast Asian employees or managers together in one team of 5 to 15 members.

4.d. Building Intercultural Business Teams

Based upon in-depth ethnographic interviews of members in our early clients, CCG developed an instrument for data gathering and analysis of a team's effectiveness and productivity. We found eight characteristics that determined teams' effectiveness in achieving goals. Below are the characteristics and a few of the questions that guided our interviews to solicit participants' thoughts and feelings:

• *Vision and Strategy*: What is your team vision? What is your strategy that will determine your directions and drive your decisions regarding how you will achieve your vision?

• *Goal Achievement*: What are your team goals? How are you going to meet your deadlines in order to achieve the team's goals? What qualities should be in a "job description" that will enable your team roles to be performed effectively?

• *Communication and Information Sharing*: What are your expectations for team communications and information sharing, i. e., initiative, frequency, style, types of info, and channels of communication? Please write down the salient features of your expectations.

• *Meeting Productivity*: What are your desired behavioral norms for communicating in your team meetings and what are any guidelines you can agree to as a team building exercise? How could meeting times be more efficient and productive than normal?

• *Decision Making*: How will your team assure that decisions are made in a way that respects all members' opinions? Please write down the salient features of your team's best decision-making process for all to acknowledge commitment.

• *Problem Solving*: By what kind of process will your team resolve problems, should they occur, i. e., when one member may not be keeping up with the schedule; when a schism develops within the team on the strategy for achieving team goals; or when you cannot agree on the content or style of the report or presentation? Please write down the salient features of your team decision-making process for all to acknowledge commitment.

• *Team Members' Relations*: What are your members' expectations for implementing some of the values you wish to hold as a team regarding the way you build team member relations, i. e., trust, reliability, inquisitiveness, selflessness, punctuality, accountability, flexibility, and hard work?

• *Cultural Synergy*: What are your cultural assumptions about team processes that may be held by all members given their different cultures and value systems (see Figure 2)? How can the team support a win-win approach to recognizing and incorporating those differences in your teamwork?

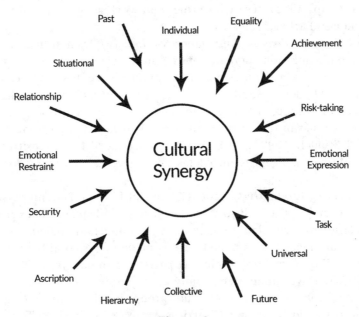

Cultural Value Assumptions
Integrate toward Cultural Synergy

Figure 2

Cultural Values and Synergy

Based on works by Edward Hall, Geert Hofstede, Fons Trompenaars, and Talcott Parsons.

© (Form) 1990. Clifford H. Clarke, Global Integration Strategies, LLC

CCG also researched the literature to find prior studies in these team characteristics. These are the contributions in the eight categories found in the literature in the 1980s and 1990s. The following are examples of items used in each of the eight team characteristics followed by its literature source:

• *Vision and Strategy*: (a) A globally inspiring mission, a global corporate vision, and global information sources and systems (Rhinesmith, 1992). (b) Team members have a shared global vision and values and develop an "International Spirit" in their work environment (Barham & Oates, 1991). (c) Corporate strategy includes a pluralism of values, which is inspirational, consistent, reinforced, and rewarded (Rhinesmith, 1992).

• *Goal Achievement*: (a) Team efforts are appropriately directed toward satisfying the needs of local, host country customers (Bedward & Anderson, 1992). (b) All team members are aware of the global needs and priorities of the company and are working for its global benefit (Yip, 1992). (c) Clear roles and work assignments are fairly distributed (Parker, 1990).

• *Communication and Information Sharing*: (a) Team members adjust their communication styles appropriately when interacting with members of other cultures in order to maximize team productivity (Neale & Mindel, 1992). (b) The team offers opportunities for speakers of various languages to talk privately with one another during meetings in their native language (Bedward & Anderson, 1992; Neale & Mindel, 1992). (c) Team members need to be sensitive and aware of their colleagues' problems and concerns (Harris & Moran, 1991).

• *Meeting Productivity* (client, Michael J. Copeland, in personal conversation): (a) Prior to meetings, adequate background information is provided to members on important agenda topics. (b) In team meetings, adequate use is made of visual aids to ensure understanding of meeting topics. (c) After team meetings, key ideas and decisions are summarized orally and recorded in writing.

• *Decision Making*: (a) Full group involvement and group consensus should be sought (Harris & Moran, 1991). (b) The team has a decision-making process that is accepted by all team members (Stewart, 1985). (c) Authority and responsibility are delegated to team members in a manner that promotes maximum effectiveness (Neale & Mindel, 1992).

• *Problem Solving*: (a) The team should attempt to spell out things within the limits of the cultural differences involved and delimit the mystery level by directness and openness (Ratiu, 1993). (b) Team members know when it is necessary to consult top management in reaching a decision (Michael J. Copeland, in personal conversation). (c) The team discusses several alternatives before decisions are reached on important issues (Oetzel, 1995).

• *Team Members' Relations*: (a) Create an atmosphere of mutual trust and cooperation (Neale & Mindel, 1992). (b) Establish an informal, comfortable and relaxed climate (Parker, 1990). (c) Maintain a formal leader and shift the leadership functions according to the changing needs, skills, and circumstances of the team (Parker, 1990).

• *Cultural Synergy* (see Figure 3): (a) Team members demonstrate respect for the cultural values and behavior of other members (Barham & Oates, 1991; Fontaine, 1986). (b) When differences in opinion arise, team members incorporate culturally different ways of thinking, values, and practices (Adler, 1991) according to the cultural roots of their different opinions. (c) A team incorporates culturally different ways of thinking, which maximize individual members' contributions to team goals (Casse, 1982; Harris & Moran, 1991).

Researching Corporate Cultural Synergy

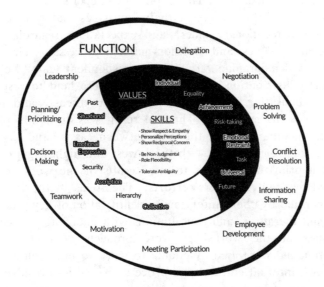

Figure 3
Corporate Cultural Synergy: Research Challenges
© 2002 Clifford H. Clarke

The purpose of this instrument, the GTI (Global Team Inventory), was to create a profile of how effectively the members of the business team are functioning that could be measured by clients' assessment of their productivity goals for the team. It was designed to assess the strengths and weaknesses of a multicultural team, to identify the most significant gaps in the team's productivity indicators, to prioritize issues that require action plans to raise productivity levels, and to create the clarity required for effective interactions and planning. The GTI had 50 behavioral descriptions as indicators in the aforementioned eight teamwork characteristics. The instrument first asked respondents to rate their "current" perception of the current status of each item. The GTI's second question on the same items asked for the respondent's personal preferences of the ideal behaviors in their best-of-teams scenario. Both questions used a scale of six measures, which enabled an assessment of the gaps in the team's current and ideal performance. The gaps of significance were in the report.

The client team's profile report highlighted strengths and areas needing alignment. The results identified opportunities for improvement through a quantified gap analysis process. Reports included graphic representation of the sources of their key issues that were based on varieties of perceptions, values, and expectations regarding, i. e., communication styles and decision-making processes. These were presented by demographic variables in a respondent team. Following the report's distribution, team workshops were held to respond to questions about the team profile results, to discuss, and to plan activities with its members. The end result was an action plan for each team member to close the gaps between "as is" and "as should be" indicators for the ones with the lowest and highest gaps, which were then prioritized by the team. Results of the workshop were generated by team members' efforts. The items in the instrument were generated by client interviews, identification of key processes in the relevant literature, and consultations with intercultural specialists. The results of the workshops were products of each member's contribution and were used by clients to work together on clarifying their teams' internal cultural and process difficulties, resolve them, and move on with new process criteria that contributed to their team's success. A CCG intercultural meeting facilitator joined each client's team workshop.

The client's key benefits from the process were:

(a) A comprehensive picture of current team effectiveness,
(b) Improved joint problem-solving skills,

(c) Increased understanding of expectations of other team members,

(d) Open exchange of key information,

(e) Strategic and tactical input from all team members,

(f) Ability to resolve cultural issues within the team,

(g) Deeper trust between multicultural team members,

(h) Setting of shared goals and real commitment from team members,

(i) Process guidelines for team interactions,

(j) Prioritized global teamwork issues with an individualized action plan to accomplish each.

When team members attend to the potential cultural differences within them, they developed greater respect and trust in their team members. Greater respect and trust in teams enabled higher productivity results. Increasing intercultural team productivity was one of CCG's key client services to multiple clients.

5. An IMD Case Study of Developing Leaders for Multicultural Organizations

Among CCG's earlier products that integrated research and training was the IMD (International Management Development) program, which ultimately engaged other global clients. However, P&G contracts continued for the next 16 years with two to three each year. The program was highly collaborative with the client in creative ways because the client was committed to their investment in developing future leaders of the company in Japan. CCG's associates involved with this program were our IMD program staff and our CES members embedded in the client's subsidiary in Japan. This research project on the IMD's effectiveness was directed by our associates in our research team led by Dr. Mitch Hammer. Executing the IMD and PDOT (pre-departure onsite training) programs were respectively our IMD trainers and our CES associates embedded in the company's subsidiary in Japan. PDOT and the IMD programs were completely integrated with the client's full collaboration. The trainees' PDOT program was executed first, followed by the IMD program at CCG's main office in Foster City, CA. The program was initiated following the plant start-up in 1982 and closed in 1998 with two to three programs per year that varied between 9 to 18 weeks in durations determined by status in the subsidiary, manager level or new hires.

5.a. The IMD Program's Objectives and Design Elements

The overall program objectives were: (a) to demonstrate professional intercultural business communication skills required for subsidiary employees upon return to Japan, (b) to demonstrate effectiveness in on-the-job assignments in the U.S., (c) to advance into leadership positions in their multicultural organizations upon return home, (d) to increase future P&G assignments abroad, which was the strategy for ultimately strengthening leadership at home.

Two separate although similar programs were designed for 18-week and 9-week trainees. IMD's 18-week programs were aimed at *professional* development of new hires into P&G Japan who qualified with above-450 entry TOEFL scores. New-hire recruitment soared after this opportunity for new hires was announced in Japan. Each training program was limited to 12 participants. The 18-week trainees' program elements were: (a) Pre-departure on-site training (PDOT), (b) 1-day PDOT comprehensive training in EBP (English for Business Purposes), CCC (Client's Corporate Culture), and IBS (Intercultural Business Skills), (c) Weekly reviews, (d) Extensive training in community activities (increased knowledge acquisition, skills development, skill application at various sites nearby), (e) Increased supervisor support (by engaging P&G Japan-bound manager trainees), and (f) Culture shock counseling support (provided with program associates).

The IMD 9-week program was aimed at *leadership* development for 12 middle manager candidates with minimal-550 entry TOEFL scores. Supplemental aspects of the 9-week program for managers were: (a) individualized training projects, (b) scheduled community activities, (c) pre-mid-final assessments with video-tape-recorder (VTR) based reviews of performance, and (d) client management pre-post program engagement. The 9-week trainees' program elements were: (a) PDOT: 35 hours total over 5 weeks (plus 4-day off-site training before departure), (b) Targeted training in EBP, CCC, and IBS, (c) All three skill sets introduced quickly, then spiraled daily, (d) Intensive training (with application in community interactions and individual targeting reduced), (e) Limited opportunities for supervisor support, (f) Culture shock counseling support (provided with program associates).

5.b. The IMD Program's Three Integrated Training Modules

Each program was designed with three thoroughly integrated modules (see Figure 4).

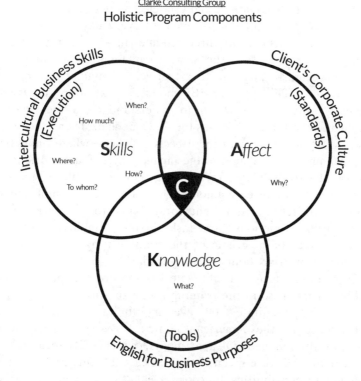

International Management Development
Clarke Consulting Group
Holistic Program Components

C = Competence, the masterful integration of all three
Skills, Affect, & Knowledge; Entwined and Inseparable
Figure 4
Integrated Program Components

Program Module 1, English for Business Purposes: (a) Foundation: Grammar, Vocabulary, Pronunciation, (b) Productive Skills: Speaking and Writing, and (c) Receptive Skills: Listening and Reading.

Program Module 2, Client's Corporate Culture (CCC): (a) American/Japanese Client's Cultural Values, (b) Trainees' Own Cultural Values, (c) Client's Corporate Culture, (d) Communication Style Switching Skill, and (e) Miscommunication Analysis and

Resolution.

Program Module 3, Intercultural Business Skills (IBS): (a) Listening and Clarifying, (b) Building Relationships, (c) Leading and Participating (in discussions and team meetings), (d) Summarizing and Presenting Information, (e) Giving and Receiving Critical Feedback, (f) Debating and Persuading, (g) Problem Solving, (h) Managing Tasks and Projects, (i) Negotiating, and (j) Teleconferencing.

These three modules were engaged every day in a spiraling of the day's topic through all three modules in an integrated fashion. Trainees understood that the same topic required learning of the applicable English language to effectively communicate, regarding "what to say." This was the EBP module. Next, they discussed the aspect of "why" to say it, or to understand the values that were implicit in each topic. This was the CCC module. Then, they learned "how" to say it, along with the aspects of when, where, how much, and to whom to speak, akin to the Japanese high context orientation. This was the IBS module. In so doing they were able to master the competency in all three elements which holistically employed their cognitive, affective, and behavioral skills for performing their assigned roles, functions, and tasks in their employer's company. The immersive characteristic of the training program was sustained for a minimum of six hours every workday.

Two other program characteristics were: a prohibition of speaking in Japanese in the training rooms or with each other in the evenings. To facilitate the evening limitations and to learn independence in the American context, P&G assigned them to geographically independent apartments, which CCG secured before their arrival. All were given their own car, TV set, and maintained individual responsibilities to cook, clean, shop, and pay personal utility bills from their per diem, which required personal bank accounts with checkbooks (not used in Japan). For each word of English in the training center, trainees had to toss a quarter ($0.25) into a pot for trainees' special events, e. g., graduation parties. The English as a Second Language training tapes enabled the trainers to employ our "Take Two" (VTR-based) training method, which was a useful tool for trainees to personalize their learning and see their results. After years of use, CCG released a VTR with multiple scenarios of this methodology to TESOL CA (Teaching English to Speakers of Other Languages, California), so that teachers other than CCGs could benefit from it. In addition, the tapes were used to demonstrate how much the trainees had learned when corporate visitors came to see their progress, which brought tears to one Human Resource Manager's eyes.

5.c. The IMD's Twenty-Step Theory-Integrated Learning Process

When IMD trainers followed these learning steps, the client trainees' needs were satisfied and trainees (a) felt respected, accepted, and appreciated by their trainers, (b) were motivated by the learning process, including their peers' support, (c) were inspired by their real managers, who were sent to support their subordinates, and (d) accepted the challenge to achieve higher success than they or CCG had expected.

Our Twenty-Learning-Step process is presented here in sequence with associated theories and constructs. Trainees were guided and supported:

1. *To make a personal commitment to their organization's goals* for the training based upon motivation theory, expectancy principles, goal incentives, and self-esteem (Weiner, 1985); locus of causation and control (Rotter, 1966) were foundations for assuring desired results. Trainees initially sought extrinsic rewards in the company, since IMD graduates had achieved a significantly higher promotion rate than non-IMD graduates after some time at home (Hammer, 1995).

2. *To feel one's current situation and feelings were well understood* based upon trainers' acknowledgement and the learnings from Clarke and Hoopes' (1975) ICW identity development stages, and Rogers' (1951) client-centered counseling theory that suggested rapport building is essential to developing trust in relationships. Rapport building is accomplished by facilitators' demonstration of empathy and by repeating the speaker's meaning in the facilitator's own words to convey understanding and acceptance.

3. *To feel that one's current style and skills were valued*: Respect and trust are what employees want and what companies need in order to win (Lewis, 1999; Wiley & Kowske, 2012). Building respect (Wiley & Kowske, 2012) and trust (Lewis, 1999) were both fundamental in increasing productivity in technology transfers and plant start-ups (Hammer, 1995). this goes together with attribution theory (Weiner, 1985), particularly a focus on the emotional prerequisites to motivation.

4. *To see the consequences of one's current behavior* as role-played by an assignment-culture trainer was supported by Cole's (1976) multiple cultural perceptions theory and Barnlund's (1976) Interpersonal Meaning construct: Ipm = f [PO + SV + CS] (i.e.,

perception orientation, system of values, and communication style). Trainees who denied negative consequences of their behavior in videoed " Take One " could see their behavior reaction more accurately from their videotaped role-play (Bandura, 1970, 1976). Trainees were then ready to see the trainer's positive consequences of their adaptive behavior in "Take Two. "

5. *To identify the causes of those consequences*: Following "Take One" and "Take Two, " trainees interviewed their assignment-culture partner with appreciative inquiry skills (Cooperrider & Srivastva, 1987), in order to seek an understanding of their perceptions and interpretations of the trainee's behavior. Assignment-culture partners were either trained CCG associates or employees coached in LWJ (living and working in Japan) training simultaneously at CCG. Knowledge Acquisition Theory (Cole, 1976), Behavior Modification Theory (Bandura, 1969), and Deep Culture Inquiry (Kohls & Knight, 1981) were very supportive of this step.

6. *To feel the implications of those consequences*: Trainees discussed their feelings of "what if I would have gone to Japan without knowing that? I would have looked like a fool. " Also, they answered the question, "How does it feel to know what behavior will achieve your objectives in that situation?" (Berger & Calabrese, 1975; Berger & Gudykunst, 1991; Gudykunst, 1998) and learned about self-fulfilling prophecies (Merton, 1968).

7. *To feel motivated to solve the resulting problem of inappropriate behavior*: The trainers' objective in processing the trainee through "Take One" and "Take Two" was to motivate the trainee to want to resolve his or her own communication problem after seeing the negative consequences of "Take One" behavior revealed. Trainers of the trainee's culture offered appropriate role-play behavior in each context when they reached Step 10, in order to increase the expectation of success and thereby motivation. Motivation theory (Weiner, 1985) and social learning theory (Bandura, 1977) provided strong underlying theory for this step.

8. *To feel the need to change one's attitude or behavior*: At the emotional level, the trainers' objective was to give the trainee enough time to express his or her real feeling about the possibilities of failure and success in intercultural interactions presented in the role-plays. This allowed each trainee the time to work out any cognitive dissonance (Festinger, 1957) that usually resulted from the original feedback, and to determine causalities and design how to take responsibility (Rotter, 1966) for adapting behavior in order to

play the role appropriately.

9. *To set achievable and measurable objectives*: IBM trainees in the mid-1980's taught CCG trainers how important it was for them to be given clear and achievable objectives that they could understand and enable them to believe in their eventual success. While studying under Lee Cronbach in 1979 at Stanford, Clarke learned that having behaviorally measurable objectives was essential in the evaluation of training (Bandura, 1977; Weiner, 1985). It was essential in securing the P&G contracts as well.

10. *To see role-modeled appropriate behavior*: Role plays in CCG training programs were extracted from client organizational research data, and trainers learned the behavioral, attitudinal aspects of each as well as how the actual players in each incident interpreted the described interactions. As such, the role plays were authentically representative of real-time events that had occurred in the trainees' companies and played with trainees of the target culture after observing a trainer from the trainee's culture demonstrate the appropriate behavior. Role-plays were sometimes fun but were not played lightly. There were no games played at CCG except the baseball games in the Akashi project in Modesto, California (Bandura, 1976; Byrne & Griffit, 1973; Byrne & Nelson, 1965).

11. *To identify the roots and rationale for the new behavior*: During this training step, appreciative inquiry of research subjects in the trainees' organizations, including the trainees, revealed the deeper reasons for certain desired behaviors in their organizations, based on the values and norms of the companies in which they worked (Hayes & Allinson, 1988; Kealey, 1989; Ratiu, 1993). This was also one methodology in CCG's organizational research (Cooperrider & Srivastva, 1987).

12. *To practice the alternative behaviors*: This is the focus of each of the "Take Two" videotaped role-plays with the trainees. Alternative behaviors were identified through the research in client organizations. Sometimes a trainee would do a "Take Three" or more, in order to master the behavior. Then they were given opportunities to demonstrate the behavior spontaneously over dinner or during an on-the-job training daytrip to their client's local branch or a store where the client's product was sold (Bandura, 1976; Clarke & Hammer, 1995; Clarke & Hoopes, 1975).

13. *To receive constructive feedback* for one's efforts in trying the new behavior. In intercultural interactions, so much of the feedback that is given and received is negative, due to the lack of

shared premises of individuals from different cultures who are involved. That is one of the reasons for culture shock (Oberg, 1960). Therefore, a dedicated effort is required to first establish common premises through learning about each other's cultural perceptions, values, and communication style (Barnlund, 1976) before feedback can be given constructively. Sometimes, e. g., from a boss, negative feedback can serve to motivate employees by fear, but in CCG's training, feedback was always constructive when given by the trainers, who also served as role models for trainees in receiving constructive feedback. Japanese trainees adapted to this process once they saw how much they could learn and benefit from it (Bandura, 1977; Fishbach, Eyal, & Finkelstein, 2010; Weiner, 1985).

14. *To receive measurements of one's new performance*: Trainees sought to be measured against clear standards so that they could know how much more they had to practice before they mastered each skill. It is measurement against hidden standards that provide a disservice to the trainees or to employees in a workplace. This approach began with Drucker's Management By Objectives (MBO) theory (Drucker, 1954; Odiorne, 1965).

15. *To feel intrinsic rewards for demonstrating new skills*: Trainees were eager for intrinsic rewards that would give them confidence and self-esteem from their accomplishments. Built into the program were regular visits from headquarters and Japan subsidiary managers, whose primary role was to give them strong support, praise, and to boost their expectations of success using self-determination theory (Deci & Ryan, 1985; Ryan & Deci, 2000).

16. *To receive extrinsic rewards for demonstrating new skills*: Trainees were eager for the extrinsic rewards that they felt would come upon returning home a success, such as promotions, which they had observed among other IMD graduates before them. They demonstrated strong achievement motivation and self-determination to achieve excellence, and they did so with an average 262 gain on TOEIC (Test of English for International Communication) scores during the course of training. They were also assured of an extended OJT (on-the-job training) experience in the U.S. at their corporate headquarters (Deci & Ryan, 1985; McClelland, 1985; McClelland et al., 1953, 1976).

17. *To see results of applying new skills in real work situations*: During the training program, the trainees went on day-trip OJT experiences in nearby locations associated with their businesses,

where they were instructed to apply their new communication skills. CCG trainers accompanied them to these sites to coach them in inconspicuous ways, thereby assuring them of success in their efforts (Bandura, 1977; McClelland et al., 1976; Weiner, 1985).

18. *To have reflection-integration time to appreciate the new skills*: Time was set aside near the end of the training program for trainees to reflect on the gains that they had made. Trainers edited videotapes of "Take One" and final "Take Two" tapes to demonstrate the significant growth the trainees had achieved. They reflected on their growth and discussed their respective feelings about their experience in the training. Time was also given to focus on the transitions to their upcoming OJT assignments. Supervisors from those locations were invited to come to the training center in California, to give the trainees an orientation and begin building new relationships that would ease their transition to those sites. A buddy system was developed to begin transitions to a new group (Rohlen, 1974).

19. *To have positive feedback from the organization,* the members' new reference group: During the graduation week of training, managers from the subsidiary in Japan were present to praise and assure them of leadership roles and the support of other IMD graduates at home (Hyman, 1960; Hyman, Levine, & Wright, 1970; Hyman & Singer, 1968).

20. *To feel receptivity from one's home cultural environment*: Upon return to their home workplaces, the trainees were supported by CCG in-house associates and all of the IMD alumni who had become a substantial group. These provided continuity for belonging to a reference group within their larger P&G Japan membership group, a key factor for long-term effectiveness of the training. Also, their managers welcomed them home with ever increasing responsibilities (Hyman, Levine, & Wright, 1970; Hyman & Singer, 1968).

CCG applied these Twenty Learning Steps in all of its IMD and PDOT programs in CCG California and our CES associates in client subsidiaries in Japan for 16 years. The IMD program methodology's success was in part because of these theories that undergirded the practices in these two CCG programs. New CCG trainers were trained in the methodology with the theoretical explanations as to why it was effective and should never be overlooked as a curriculum process guide and problem analysis tool if trainees were not achieving their potential performance.

5.d. The Case Study Research Report

In 1994 CCG initiated a research project that investigated the overall contribution of eight years of the IMD program to the success of the managers and organization of its major client. The uniqueness of this study was that in addition to training results in California it integrated self, focus groups, and supervisor ratings in Japan up to eight years after the participants were in training. It further utilized Human Resources information to assess both program graduates and comparison groups in over 20 dimensions critical to organizational productivity. The research study was named the "Organizational Effects Study, 1984-1985."

The Study Participants were the two groups of graduates and two groups of comparison sample groups (CSG) for the 9-week and the 18-week IMDs included 33 9-week graduates with 32 CSGs and for the 18-week IMDs included 38 graduates with 26 CSGs. In addition, subjects that provided data on the graduates and CSGs were the client's Human Resource professionals who oversaw the development of the managers and employees, as well as the 33 supervisors who were international managers and regional international managers to whom each IMD graduate and CSG member reported.

Criteria for Selection of Participant Groups
Program Graduates: These were all individuals who participated in the program from 1986 through 1993 for both 18-week and 9-week program graduates.
Comparison Groups: (a) Recruited in the same years as the graduates, (b) Recruited on the same level as the graduates, (c) Having the same educational background (in degree attained and institution attended), (d) Having similar international experience and similar experience working with a U.S. company, and upper-level executives.
Supervisors: (a) Individuals with direct knowledge of the daily performance of both participant groups over an extended period of time, and (b) largely, but not exclusively, Americans (and Japanese supervisors with extensive and successful experience working in the U.S.).

The Assessment Methods utilized with the graduates and the CSG members were self-report surveys and six focus group interviews. Methods used with the HR office were gathering data from pre-post training TOEIC scores, and survey reports on promotion rates and overseas assignments. Methods used with higher-level managers were two focus group interviews and survey reports on organizational productivity, intercultural management, and communication skills.

The three dimensions of research that provided data for the study enabled the assessment of the program's objectives, which were: (a) to demonstrate professional intercultural business communication skills required for subsidiary employees upon return to Japan, (b) to demonstrate effectiveness in on-the-job assignments in the U. S ., (c) to advance into leadership positions in their multicultural organizations upon return home, (d) to increase future P&G assignments abroad, which was the strategy for ultimately strengthening leadership at home, and (e) to increase employee loyalty to the company as reflected in employee commitment, job satisfaction, and effectiveness.

Research Dimension 1: Productivity data contributed to our understanding of success in terms of objectives (c) and (d) regarding intercultural management competency, promotion rates, and overseas assignments. *Examples* of items measured in these areas were: (a) Assumes appropriate leadership roles in multicultural groups, (b) Gives effective performance feedback when working with people from other cultures, and (c) Number of overseas assignments of 3 months or more in the last 2 years and based on an understanding of their cultural values.

Research Dimension 2: Organizational Climate data contributed to our understanding of success in terms of objective (e) regarding organizational commitment, job satisfaction, and organizational effectiveness. Examples of items measured in these areas were: (a) Satisfaction with pay and benefits, (b) Loyalty to the organization, (c) Production of high-quality results on the job, (d) Ability to adjust quickly to changes in work goals and practices, (e) Satisfaction with promotion rate, (f) Ability to anticipate problems and minimize negative effects, and (g) Sense of commitment to the organization.

Research Dimension 3: Intercultural Competency data contributed to our understanding of objectives (a) and (b) regarding particularly the results of the IBS module in the IMD program: *(a) General Intercultural Skills, (b) Giving & Receiving Feedback, (c) Meeting Management Skills, (d) Listening Skills, (e) TOEIC scores, (f) Negotiation Skills, (g) Persuasion Skills, (h) Problem Solving Skills, (i) Interacting Skills,*

(j) Speaking Skills, (k) Intercultural Skills (Supervisor's Ratings), (l) Relationship Building Skills, and *(m) Writing Skills.* Examples of items measured in these areas were: (a) Demonstrates flexibility about culturally different ideas, (b) Adjusts to different ways of communicating, (c) Resolves conflicts with persons from other cultures in culturally appropriate ways, (d) Clarifies meaning of statements not understood, (e) Initiates conversation with persons from other cultures, and (f) Provides adequate background information prior to meetings with persons from other cultures.

Research Summary. Overall, the program gave a *measured competitive edge* to participants vs. comparable peers on both program objectives, for both 9- and 18-week program graduate groups. Effects of the training program were measured in the areas of: (a) productivity measures (management sourced), (b) organizational climate (participant sourced), and (c) intercultural competency (program sourced).

Program Graduates vs. CSG Employees Comparisons were done to measure levels of success of IMD 9- and 18-week graduates compared to their respective comparative sample groups (CSG) who never participated in the IMD program. (All objectives and their indicators in the research study were determined as elements of success of the program in collaboration with client representatives responsible for engaging CCG for the IMD and CES programs for 16 consecutive years.)

(a) Productivity:
Of these 3 skill sets, the graduates of the 18-week program scored substantially higher in all three of them compared to their CSG members. Outstanding indicators for the 18-week program graduates were: number of overseas assignments, promotion rate, and intercultural management skills. The graduates of the 9-week program scored substantially higher in only one of them compared to their CSG members, the number of overseas assignments.
(b) Organizational Climate:
Of these 3 skill sets, the graduates of the 18-week program scored substantially higher in two of them compared to their CSG members. Outstanding indicators for the 18-week program graduates were job satisfaction and organizational commitment, but not organizational effectiveness. The graduates of the 9-week program scored substantially

higher in only one of them compared to their CSG members.

(c) Intercultural Competency:
Of these 13 skill sets, the graduates of the 18-week program scored substantially higher than their CSG members in 12 of them. The only unimpressive rating indicator for the 18-week program graduates was interacting skills. The graduates of the 9-week program scored substantially higher in only three of the sets compared to their CSG members. The only three substantially higher ratings for the 9-week IMD graduates were TOEIC scores, listening skills, and persuasion skills.

These results were substantially higher than we expected, and clearly demonstrated increases in employee performance measurements directly related to IMD training participation in the past one to eight years and demonstrated a sustained impact on graduates' work productivity, with more promotions and assignments overseas, and suggested a greater long-term value of 18- vs. 9-week training programs. Intercultural skills for working in a business organization are complex, challenging, and require substantial investments of money and time. Results also demonstrated a higher-than-expected rating on the organization's productivity, employees' job satisfaction, and employees' commitment to the company. The client had invested a lot of financial resources into the development of their employees over the years, and this study clearly demonstrated to them an adequate return on their investment. The study produced results worthy of the client's investment. The study fulfilled the second through fifth levels of evaluation, in that the client had already indicated satisfaction on ROI (return-on-investment) by contracting CCG for 16 years of ongoing IMD programs as well as CES members from CCG embedded in the organization in Japan.

5.e. Summary of Themes Presented by Interview Data

Interview Themes on Productivity Measures:

(a) Program Graduates can manage more global projects than CSG members:
"I still use the program as a key decision step. I am having trouble giving responsibility to my non-program graduates." — A Manager
(b) Program Graduates can work more smoothly with non-Japanese:
"The training helped eliminate mental barriers in working with non-Japanese, and English language barriers when working with other

cultures. " — A Manager
(c) Program Graduates have a better network particularly within the U.S., but productivity depends on job assignment after returning from the IMD program (plus OJT):
"If assigned to a non-Japanese supervisor, then the skills learned will be kept for a long term, but if not, then the skills will diminish. — A Manager.

Interview Themes on Organizational Climate:

(a) Program Graduates show organizational leadership through greater understanding, appreciation, and skills as a cultural liaison in the multicultural organization:
"You have to be a cultural bridge in this company ... The program helps you become that bridge. " — A Graduate
(b) Program Graduates contribute to greater organizational effectiveness in regard to (b1) better business vision (beyond the Japanese perspective) and (b2) integrated business strategies:
"The Graduates have been more open to negotiating the time of the project without the push from higher up in the hierarchy. I think they are more able to do what is right for the business. " — A Manager
(c) Program Graduates contribute to greater willingness to take initiative:
"I became able to take initiative and do things voluntarily. Upon return from the program, people thought my personality had changed. " — A Graduate.

Interview Themes on Intercultural Competency:

(a) Dealing with cross-cultural differences and stress in general (U.S., European, and Asia Pacific):
"Graduates can compare differences between Japanese and Western style, going out and visiting homes, customers, etc. It is a shock at first, but very helpful. " — A Manager
(b) More confidence on overseas trips and assignments:
"One person a year ago could not be doing what she is doing today if she didn't get this training, e. g., communicating across cultures internally and externally, giving presentations, meeting skills, clarification skills for projects and meetings. " — A Manager
(c) Giving and receiving feedback:
"I use interactive listening skills regularly in my job, e. g., clarification skills to avoid cross-cultural misunderstandings and asking direct questions and giving appropriate feedback. " — A Graduate

(d) Meeting management skills:
(Participation) "Although I may not stop the meeting to say what I want, I make sure I express my ideas before the meeting is over." — A Graduate
(e) Leadership:
"Setting up agendas early, facilitating meetings, building the team, resolving issues, staying on task, reaching decisions on time ... I'm comfortable with it all." — A Graduate.

5.f. The Case Study Conclusion

The IMD Case Study was ongoing, on the whole, from 1982 to 1998. This early 8-year (1986-1993) study provided evidence that intercultural training is able to impact business performance directly, even years after the training program. At that time, it was the clients' proprietary information that could not be released to the public due to their desire to maintain a "competitor advantage." There have been excessive discussions about the effectiveness of what was called by some "cross-cultural training," and this was perhaps because early training in organizations was limited to culture-specific and culture-comparative training. Even though culture-interactive training was called intercultural training from the early eighties (even earlier in the university context) with global businesses, as late as 2000 a researcher published an article suggesting that interactive training began in 2000 with her study (my apologies for not revealing much earlier that the paradigm had already shifted). Nevertheless, in the practical world of trainers, hundreds of corporate human resource managers had heard and contracted to employ this new approach and training method long before the century's end. There should be no question whether generic intercultural training for multiple cultures is more effective than interactive integrated training in the workplace context of specific global organizations. It is not. Unfortunately, as the age of instant everything and reduction of internal costs of businesses came upon us with the 21st century, this interactive approach and method grounded in theory and client contexts has not found many committed businesses to even consider a large investment in their management trainees for long-term assignments abroad. We have arrived back at the beginning, when assumptions of excellence abound to the point of overconfidence in the strengths of selected assignees to adapt or to win over the subsidiary with demonstrations of high integrity with non-existent universal behaviors.

Nevertheless, intercultural training can be effective with regard to what P&G brought to CCG's attention, the seven characteristics of our training and other interventions: (a) Research grounded, (b) competence driven, (c) business integrated, (d) holistic designs, (e) intercultural interactions, (f) participatory learning, and (g) performance evaluations with regular reports to each client.

With these foundations and significant corporate investment, intercultural training has demonstrated to yield one client 36 times a return on their investment (ROI) in the first two years. Investments for human resource development cost money and take time, but they also yield measurable exponential gains if intercultural interventions are "best-in-class" or "best practices" (our client's words). Successful interculturalists in the business world first listen deeply to their client's long-term perceived needs and goals for a subsidiary abroad, so that training can be delivered to fill those needs and achieve those goals for productivity gains that can be measured by the client as having value for their operations abroad. Client collaboration is essential to success. Two vital cultural informants, one a client insider and the other an academically trained researcher, can contribute significantly to designing, guiding, and researching the results of an intercultural intervention in global businesses.

6. Discussion

Paradigms of training as cognitive, affective, and behavioral (CAB) are less effective and less focused on the real issues of dealing with intercultural experiences in the client's context. Managers work in very fast-paced businesses. They deserve all seven of the "best practices" and support we can offer them. Applicable theories behind training designs increase trainers' effectiveness, but clients generally do not wish to hear about the theories. Nevertheless, they give the trainers better designs and more confidence that their training will be effective. Paradigms found earlier in intercultural training can be changed to integrate culture-interactive facilitated models that yield task resolution and increased productivity in the context of different roles and organizations. Being in the context of real-time activities of those working together with in-the-moment interventions that facilitate the expression of insights and alternatives can provide clarity, focused discussion, and emic-derived resolutions within an intercultural context that lead to more immediate and more lasting solutions. They also create naturally synergistic, acceptable processes, norms, and objectives which support a group's diversity of values and status equity and can be a memorable pleasurable experience.

The IMD is the model for training off-site with best practices thoroughly integrated with the client organization by various means, such as executive visits, with designed interactions with trainees that meet their emotional, informational, and skill needs. On-site intercultural specialists in the client organizations support long-term utilization of new learnings as well as the evolutionary changes required for an organization's culture. Corporate cultures can be created from scratch and/or modified innovatively, to recognize the added values that subsidiary employees bring to work daily. Such changes through the interventions focused on in this chapter result in personal and interpersonal effectiveness in intercultural teams, departmental meetings, and other training or facilitative processes.

The need to build synergies in operations, in order to support and to be enlightened by cultural diversities, can be occurring along with efforts to facilitate individual and team learning in that intercultural context. Rather than the old fight between two "one best way" belief systems, this new paradigm incorporates multiple perspectives, models, assumptions, and expectations in peoples from diverse cultures. This paradigm also recognizes and supports the reality that there is every alternative of knowledge, attitude, and behavior existing within every culture. One cannot say that one approach will or will not work if the societies being engaged are an individualist and a collectivist together in one reality. A vision of an organization that supports and thrives upon clarifying alternatives existing in the fullness of diversity within and between cultures has proven to create better solutions in exploring and constructing shared values, strategies, structures, systems, standards, styles, and skills for processes that engage leaders, managers, teams, and individual contributors in multicultural organizations.

Due to the rapid changes in societies that are touched by globalization, a fully integrated approach to offering facilitated intercultural insights and alternative paths toward developing synergies in communities is a proven, effective methodology to support personal, team, and organizational goals and objectives. Integrated theories from multiple disciplines, integrated paradigms from multiple cultures, and integrated models from alternative intervention designs all work together to yield highly productive resolutions to intercultural issues in multicultural organizations. Off-site training room designs and models that rely on off-the-shelf tools, games, simulations, and exercises are no substitute for engaging in the day-to-day organizational operations of real-time interactions between members of different cultures within an organization, with skills to facilitate genuine exploratory, inquisitive, respectful, and empathetic relationships.

1. Implications for Research from the IMD Case Study:
(a) Significance of finding predictive elements of a global leadership development program,
(b) Significance of jointly designed research projects by global business and intercultural consulting firm,
(c) Significance of collaboration in identifying corporate training and organizational effectiveness criteria,
(d) Significance of integrating three core elements in research design: corporate culture alignment, intercultural business skills, and second language for business purposes, and
(e) Significance of evaluation research on all five levels of measuring program and organizational effectiveness (Kirkpatrick, 1994; Phillips, 1997).

2. Implications for Practitioners from the IMD Case Study:
(a) Value of pre-intervention organizational research in designing customized interventions,
(b) Demonstrated corporate investment in long-term leadership development brings returns,
(c) Holistic and integrated training with achievable objectives for individual and organizational competencies increases motivation and results,
(d) Interculturally interactive learning within the organizational context brings reality to training, and
(e) Commitment to performance evaluation of individual and organization shows effectiveness.

3. Applications for Organizations from the IMD Case Study:
(a) For integrated leadership development programs jointly designed by institutions and organizations,
(b) For multicultural organizations that require effective leadership in the creative integration of diverse values, norms of role behavior, and communication styles,
(c) For firms with resources to commit to long-term, highly customized methods of leadership development, bringing a high

return on their investment (ROI), a Level 5 evaluation method (Kirkpatrick, 1994; Phillips, 1997), and finally

(d) For governments, businesses, non-profits, educational institutions, and other multicultural organizations.

7. Conclusion

Business clients respond well to those consultants and trainers who practice "serving the client" rather than "selling the client." Securing a new client relationship is the first step of the journey. Therefore, I would like to close with the guiding principles that have undergirded my lifetime of efforts in the intercultural field, especially with global business leaders. Implicit in my conclusions are sprinkled implicit recommendations for improvements in our field.

My guidelines for intercultural trainers and consultants are my 5Cs: to build *credibility*, demonstrate *competence*, *commitment*, *compassion*, and inspire *confidence* in the relationship. We can do this by:

(a) *Demonstrating real interest in the client's situation* by seeking, through exploratory means and genuine curiosity, the client's understanding of all the circumstances of the client's business situation. Question and listen affirmatively for some time before stating your opinions or responding in any other way.

(b) *Demonstrate understanding of the client's situation* by summarizing the client's situation in a way that convinces the client that you have heard, understood, and empathize with the client's situation. The goal may be achieved by referencing your prior experiences that relate to the client's current situation, including the constructive ways you intervened.

(c) *Respond to questions about benchmarks and best practices* by sharing from your experiences, in order to demonstrate your knowledge and resourcefulness. This may be initiated without the client's questions if deemed appropriate, but without the selling tone.

(d) *Highlight the failures and success you have experienced personally* in order to demonstrate your integrity, openness, and humility. Building trust is most important in building confidence in the relationship.

(e) *Consistently check the relevance of your comments to the client's situation*. Move on from thoughts that are not direct responses to the client's comments. This will demonstrate your commitment to align with the client's direction and serve the clients in the most useful manner.

(f) *Explore any topic to reveal the client's perception of the situation, the client's interpretation of it, including causal factors, the client's assessment of others, and the client's description of the more ideal situation.* In other words, the cognitive, affective and behavioral elements of each situation he/she describes will give a more comprehensive understanding of the situation to the consultant.

(g) *Seek to identify behavioral descriptions of incidents* that the client shares as illustrations that demonstrate accurate understanding of the sources of misunderstandings.

(h) *Seek to identify structural relationships of key actors in situations*, in order to explore the context of behavior and the feelings of all involved, i. e., by identifying "top-performer profiles."

(i) *Seek a multilevel and multicultural approach to questioning* as it is the most appropriate for understanding issues in their complexity, i. e.,

(1) The macro perspective of the business's interactions within its marketplace, including customers, competitors, and suppliers,

(2) The fundamental values, goals, and strategies of the business leadership with their perspective on the historical and current performance of the organization,

(3) The operational characteristics of structure, staffing, systems, and standards,

(4) The behavioral capacities and competencies of individuals, teams, and technical or functional groups.

I once heard from Steven Rhinesmith years ago (1992, personal conversation) that success in intercultural business relationships was dependent on one thing, the consultant's personal character. It was from that conversation that I began thinking about the 5Cs above. I believe there is a necessity of clarifying what kind of character is required of closely held consultants. As is said, the first impression may be the only one because second chances rarely come one's way. Their instinct rules in most decisions, especially those regarding personnel. Without any one of the 5Cs the pathway may be more difficult to find. Integrity is the key to many I've met, i. e., Motorola, but to me genuine compassion is the most unique in the business world because it builds trust.

The conclusions on CCG's history of intercultural training in business in the eighties and nineties have reminded me of six factors in this profession that add tremendous significance to our practical survival as a part of the field and to the quality of our contribution to the business world's repetitive cycle of sending new corporate assignees into countries around the world without adequate preparation. I offer them as recommendations to intercultural professionals. Those business managers who go to run the business, train the technicians, develop its managers, open a new division, kick off a new product, even on short trips designed to set directions, monitor progress, or simply leave an impression of the values of the company, could all benefit from a customized learning experience before they depart and/or after arriving in the country. The following are my six recommendations:

1. Invite *collaboration with scholars* in various roles essential to developing and evaluating the quality of program interventions. These roles can be from a full-time director of research to a contracted part-time resource on training design or program evaluator. It may also be a "trainer-of-trainers," or a researcher embedded in a project in any country to investigate and publish outcomes in the interest of the scholar and/or the practitioner. In any case, engaging in long-term meaningful and productive escapades abroad into an unfamiliar culture is a high-risk proposition for anyone. It is simply not true when an expatriate says, "my experience in many other countries will see me through any country." How could experience bouncing around on many European subsidiaries inform an expatriate how to be successful in Japan? Perhaps only in personal responses to culture shock. Efforts to maximize results of intercultural engagements, if facilitated by trained cultural informants as consultants or trainers, will help to build the competencies to improve the chances of success locally while abroad. Investments in such support have been proven to bring added value to the organization and the individual.

This is why SIETARs around the world and IAIR would attract more members to serve the intercultural field, I believe, if they were to maintain more of a balance of scholars and practitioners among their memberships (this observation fits in parts of the whole but perhaps not in others). More importantly, it would facilitate more interactions between scholars and practitioners if both of these groups were willing to engage. We otherwise accomplish limited, unique results from not integrating, and we limit our strategic objectives to benefit our complex societies, from our clients' perspectives (Clarke, 2008). Our engagements at CCG integrating scholars and practitioners were characterized as intercultural interaction because the first difficulties we face are language, style, frameworks, mindsets, and disciplines. These are truly cultural barriers in essence, and mostly hidden. The challenge of intercultural interactions among colleagues may be our greatest challenge in the future, unless we learn from the past, from history.

2. Invite *clients' collaboration* in activities that enable their sojourning managers and technicians to succeed in another culture by practicing the 5Cs at every step, to build important collaborative relationships with clients and to execute projects and initiatives successfully. Collaboration with clients is critical to clients' ownership of intercultural projects and to assuring the best quality of intercultural interventions. (Businesses use the term "initiatives" because it is their role to initiate with authority and take responsibility for the outcomes. "Intervention" implies that a project is the outside vendors' responsibility. P&G referred to the insider who supports the initiative as the "project champion.") Of course, the interculturalist should be responsible for adhering to "Best Practices," but success may not be the result if the client is not invested and deeply involved. Earlier, I referred to the SAT's role (strategic advisory team) in leading culture change initiatives with their commitment to the five key responsibilities of being SAT members. Without a client's SAT leadership of intercultural initiatives, projects of any length face higher risks of failure. With the 5As, they commit to responsibility with the consulting team.

3. An *integrated interactive approach* based on research, for intercultural interventions in businesses, has been demonstrated to assure success. P&G called it the "Best Practices" that CCG brought to support their activities for 18 years. The seven elements (*research grounded, competence driven, business integration, holistic designs, intercultural interactions, participatory learning,* and *performance evaluations with reports to each client*) were demonstrably critical in the achievement of new opportunities in intercultural training and consulting opportunities with many of CCG's client organizations.

4. "*Systems Thinking*" (Senge & Sterman, 1992) insight was essential, because it suggests an understanding of the client's complex

and realistic point of view. CCG learned from our first engagement with P&G in 1980 that intercultural training seldom engaged in the client's point of view and relied more on transferring general or specific knowledge and skills to the trainees (George Renwick, personal conversation). Systems thinking is how P&G took us into multiple roles in providing their intercultural support. Three of us even learned how to make Pampers! When clients receive training, their first thoughts are "How is this good for me in my job?" Their performance must be tied to company results, and if they do not see the connection to the concrete objectives of their roles, they will ask "so what?". With our interventions, we need to be able to respond with systems thinking so as to identify how our objectives are their objectives. This can be accomplished by utilizing CCG's progressive inquiry model of investigating, in sequence, these aspects of trainees' work requirements (see Section 4) and act on the data in these three ways:

(a) Design training programs utilizing interactive experiential learning methods with measurable performance objectives,

(b) Deliver training to achieve measurable performance objectives that are observable on "Take One" and "Take Two" recordings throughout the training; and

(c) Collaboratively assess observable outcomes in the workplace at intervals, by relying on embedded associates and/or supervisors and managers to gather data on identified quantifiable standards of desired outcomes. This process is based on systems thinking.

5. Designing and facilitating *synergistic processes and goals* are deeply appreciated and motivating to trainees in intercultural training. In part, this is because it overcomes the assumption barrier of trainees resenting having to adapt to the corporate culture of headquarters in their subsidiary. If the training design can incorporate mutual learning for the supervisors and managers of the trainees at home and abroad, the trainees and the company will be more motivated to cooperate in building an environment that enables top performance. In an organization committed to benefitting from diversity, there is no better pathway that that of building synergies at every point of intercultural interaction at home and abroad.

6. Finally, expand the trainer's focus by planning the evaluation before designing the training. It is instructive to know the client's

desired end results before we begin designing how it is that we will arrive at the intended destination. Business is not the place for wondering along an unknown path. Training results and lasting outcomes must directly relate to the client's (organizational, departmental, team, and personal) goals. Otherwise, "so what?" — as the IBM trainees taught CCG. Evaluations that demonstrate achieved goals benefit from data and from observable performance objectives on Levels 2 through 5 of evaluations. Level 1 is for trainers' feedback from trainees. A few client organizations might have interest in their trainees' perceptions of their training program, but more frequently reports without Levels 3–5 were tossed into the trash can, in CCG's experience.

Acknowledgment: Rongtian Tong has provided valuable help with the graphic design of several Figures.

References

Adler, N. J. (1986). International dimensions of organizational behavior (and 2nd ed., 1991). PWS-KENT Publishing.

Allport, G. W. (1958). The nature of prejudice. Doubleday Anchor Books.

Amir, Y. (1969). Contact hypothesis in ethnic relations. Psychological Bulletin, 71(5), 319–342.

Austin, C. N. (1986). Cross-cultural reentry: A book of readings. Abilene Christian University Press.

Bandura, A. (1969). Principles of behavior modification. Holt, Rinehart & Winston.

Bandura, A. (1970). Modeling theory: Some traditions, trends, and disputes. In W. Sahakian (Ed.), Psychology of learning: Systems, models, and theories. Markham.

Bandura, A. (1976). Effecting change through participant modeling. In J. D. Krumboltz & C. E. Thoresen (Eds.), Counseling methods (pp. 245–268). Holt, Rinehart & Winston.

Bandura, A. (1977). Social learning theory. Prentice-Hall.

Barham, K., & Oates, D. (1991). The international manager: Creating successful international companies. Random House.

Barnlund, D. C. (1976, July 26). A meaning-centered philosophy and a model for interpersonal meaning [Keynote address]. Stanford Institute for Intercultural Communication. Stanford, CA.

Baumruk, R. (2006). Why managers are crucial to increasing engagement: Identifying steps managers can take to engage their workforce. Strategic HR Review, 5(2), 24–27. https://doi.org/10.1108/14754390680000863

Bedward, M. W., & Anderson, M. V. (1992). Growing your business internationally: How to form profitable overseas partnerships, alliances and joint *ventures*. Probus.

Berger, C. R., & Calabrese, R. J. (1975). Some explorations in initial interaction and beyond: Toward a developmental theory of interpersonal communication. *Human Communication Theory*, *1*, 99–112.

Berger, C. R., & Gudykunst, W. B. (1991). Uncertainty and communication. In B. Dervin, B. & M. Voight (Eds.), *Progress in communication sciences* (pp. 164–192). Norwood.

Berger, J., Cohen, B. P., & Zelditch, M., Jr. (1972). Status characteristics and social interaction. *American Sociological Review*, *37*, 241–255.

Berry, J. W. (1992). Acculturation and adaptation in a new society. *International Migration*, *30*(1), 69–85. https://doi.org/10.1111/j.1468-2435.1992.tb00776.x

Black, J. S., Gregersen, H. B., & Mendenhall, M. E. (1992). Toward a theoretical framework of repatriation adjustment. *Journal of International Business Studies*, *23*(4), 737–760.

Byrne, D., & Griffit, W. (1973). Interpersonal attraction. *Annual Review of Psychology*, *24*, 317–336.

Byrne, D., & Nelson, D. (1965). Attraction as a linear function of proportion of positive reinforcements. *Journal of Personality and Social Psychology*, *1*(6), 659–663.

Casmir, F. L. (1993). Third-culture building: A paradigm shift for international and intercultural communication. *Annals of the International Communication Association*, *16*(1), 407–428. http://doi.10.1080/23808985.1993.11678861

Casse, P. (1980). *Training for the cross-cultural mind: A handbook for cross-cultural trainers and consultants*. Society for Intercultural Education, Training, and Research.

Casse, P. (1982). *Training for the multicultural manager: A practical and cross-cultural approach to the management of people*. Society for Intercultural Education, Training, and Research.

Clarke, C. H. (1971). Intercultural communication workshops. In D. S. Hoopes (Ed.), *Readings in intercultural communication*, *1* (1st ed., pp. 73–79). The Society for Intercultural Education, Training, and Research.

Clarke, C. H. (1972, July 16). *The reentry experience*. [Conference session]. Intercultural Communication: Contrast & Conflict. Tokyo, Japan.

Clarke, C. H. (1990). An organizational model for supporting expatriates, Part 1. *Innovations in international compensation*, *16*(4), Organization Resources Counselors.

Clarke, C. H. (1991). An organizational model for supporting expatriates, Part 2, *Innovations in international compensation*, *17*(1), Organization Resources Counselors.

Clarke, C. H. (2008). Practicing the integration of discipline and compassion. *Journal of Intercultural Communication*, *11*, 1–21.

Clarke, C. H. (2014, October 23). *Developing leaders for multicultural organizations*. [Conference session]. Doshisha University Global Resources Management Program Conference. Kyoto, Japan.

Clarke, C. H. (2017). Reflections from history: How shifting paradigms created intercultural innovations. *Journal of Intercultural Communication*, *20*, 1–26.

Clarke, C. H., & Hammer, M. R. (1995). Predictors of Japanese & American managers' job success, personal adjustment, and intercultural interaction effectiveness. *Management International Review*, *35*(2), 153–170.

Clarke, C. H., & Hoopes, D. S. (1975). Goals and leadership in the intercultural communication workshop. In D. S. Hoopes (Ed.), *Readings in intercultural communication*, 1 (2nd ed., pp. 60–67). The Intercultural Network.

Clarke, C. H., & Kanatani, K. (1979). Turn-taking no shikumi [*The Structure of Turn-Taking*]. *Language, Education and Technology*, 17, 12–24.

Clarke, C. H., & Lipp, G. D. (1998). Conflict resolution for contrasting cultures. *Training and Development*, ASTD, February.

Clarke, C. H., & Takashiro, N. (2019). Transforming shame to collective pride and social equity in bicultural organizations in Japan. In C.-H. Mayer & E. Vanderheiden (Eds.), *The bright side of shame* (pp. 267–282). Springer.

Clarke, C. H., & Takashiro, N. (2020). Turning bicultural critical incidents into inclusive bicultural identities and organizations in US subsidiaries in Japan. In E. Vanderheiden & C.-H. Mayer (Eds.), *Mistakes, errors, and failures* (pp. 565–586). Springer.

Clarke, C. H., & Takashiro, N. (2021). Sustaining love and building bicultural marriages between Japanese and Americans in Japan. In C.-H. Mayer & E. Vanderheiden (Eds.), *International handbook of love* (pp. 975–993). Transcultural & Transdisciplinary Perspectives. Springer.

Cole, M. (1976). An ethnographic psychology of cognition. In R. W. Brislin, S. Bochner, & W. J. Lonner (Eds.), *Cross-cultural perspectives on learning* (pp. 157–175). Halsted Press.

Cole, M., & Means, B. (1981). *Comparative studies of how people think: An introduction*. Harvard University Press.

Cooperrider, D. L., & Srivastva, S. (1987). Appreciative inquiry in organizational life. In W. Pasmore & R. Woodman (Eds.), *Research in organization change and development* (pp. 129–169). JAI Press.

Deci, E. L., & Ryan, R. M. (1985). *Intrinsic motivation and self-determination in human behavior*. Plenum.

Doi, T. (1981). *The anatomy of dependence* (J. Bester, Trans.). Kodansha International.

Drucker, P. F. (1954). *The practice of management*. Harper Business.

Duncan, S., Brunner, L. J., & Fiske, D. W. (1979). Strategy signals in face-to-face interaction. *Journal of Personality and Social Psychology*, 37(2): 301–313.

Duncan, S., & Fiske, D. W. (1977). *Face-to-face interaction: Research, methods, and theory*. Routledge. https://doi.org/10.4324/9781315660998

Duncan, S., & Niederehe, G. (1974). On signaling that it's your turn to speak. *Journal of Experimental Social Psychology*, 13, 234–247.

Festinger, L. (1954). A theory of social comparison processes. *Human Relations*, 7, 117–140. https://doi.org/10.1177/001872675400700202

Festinger, L. (1957). *A theory of cognitive dissonance*. Stanford University Press.

Fiedler, F. E., Mitchell, T., & Triandis, H. C. (1971). The culture assimilator: An approach to cross-cultural training. *Journal of Applied Psychology*, 55(2), 95–102.

Fishbach, A., Eyal, T., & Finkelstein, S. R. (2010). How positive and negative feedback motivate goal pursuit. *Social and Personality Psychology Compass*, 4(8), 517–530. https://doi.org/10.1111/j.1751-9004.2010.00285.x

Fisher, G. (1980). *International negotiation: A cross-cultural perspective*. Intercultural Press.

Fisher, G. (1988). *Mindsets: The role of culture and perception in international relations*. Intercultural Press.

Flanagan, J. C. (1954). The critical incident technique. *Psychological Bulletin*, *15*(4), 327–358.

Fontaine, G. (1986). Roles of social support systems in overseas relocation: Implications for intercultural training. *International Journal of Intercultural Relations*, *10*(3), 361–378.

French, J. R. P., & Raven, B. (1959). The bases of social power. In D. Cartwright & A. Zander (Eds.), *Group dynamics* (pp. 150–167). University of Michigan.

Gibbons, J. M. (2006). *Employee engagement: A review of current research and its implications*. The Conference Board.

Gudykunst, W. B. (1985). A model of uncertainty reduction in intercultural encounters. *Journal of Language and Social Psychology*, *4*(2), 79–98.

Gudykunst, W. B. (1998). Applying anxiety/uncertainty management theory to intercultural adjustment training. *International Journal of Intercultural Research*, *22*(2), 227–250.

Gumpertz, J. J. (1982a). *Discourse strategies: Introduction*. Cambridge University Press.

Gumpertz, J. J. (1982b). *Language and social identity*. Cambridge University Press.

Hall, E. T. (1976). *Beyond culture*. Doubleday.

Hall, E. T., & Hall, M. R. (1987). *Hidden differences: Doing business with the Japanese*. Anchor Press.

Hammer, M. R. (1995, 14–17 May). Organizational effects study [Conference session]. *Society for Intercultural Education, Training, and Research Conference*. Phoenix, AZ.

Harris, P. R., & Moran, R. T. (1979). *Managing cultural differences* (also 3rd ed., 1991). Gulf Publishing.

Hayashi, K. (1994). *Ibunka Interface Keiei* [Cross-Cultural interface of corporate management]. Nihon Keizai Shimbun Shuppansha.

Hayashi, K., & Jolley, G. (2002). Two thoughts on analog and digital language. *The Aoyama Journal of International Politics, Economics and Business*, *58*, 179–196.

Hayes, J., & Allinson, C. W. (1988). Cultural differences in the learning styles of managers. *Management International Review*, *28*, 75–80.

Hyman, H. H. (1942). The psychology of status. *Archives of Psychology (Columbia University)*, *269*, 94.

Hyman, H. H. (1960). Reflections on reference groups. *Public Opinion Quarterly*, *24*(3), 383–396. https://doi.org/10.1086/266959

Hyman, H. H., Levine, G. N., & Wright, C. R. (1970). Introducing social change in developing countries. *Development Digest*, *8*(2), 107–119.

Hyman, H. H., & Singer, E. (Eds.). (1968). *Readings in reference group theory and research*. The Free Press.

Hymes, D. H. (1964). Introduction: Toward ethnographies of communication. *American Anthropologist*, *66*(2), Part 2, 1–34.

Hymes, D. H. (1974). *Foundations in sociolinguistics: An ethnographic approach*. University of Pennsylvania Press.

Jones, E. E., & Davis, K. E. (1965). From acts to dispositions: The attribution process in person perception. *Advances in Experimental Social Psychology*, *2*, 219–266.

Jones, E. E., & Nesbitt, R. (1971). *The actor and the observer: Divergent perceptions of the causes of behaviour*. General Learning Press.

Kahn, W. A. (1990). Psychological conditions of personal engagement and disengagement at work. *Academy of Management Journal*, *33* (4), 692-724. https://doi.org/10.2307/256287

Kealey, D. J. (1989). A study of cross-cultural effectiveness. *International Journal for Intercultural Research*, *13*, 387-428.

Kirkpatrick, D. L. (1975). Techniques for evaluating training programs. In D. L. Kirkpatrick (Ed.), *Evaluating training programs* (pp.1-17). ASTD Press.

Kirkpatrick, D. L. (1994). *Evaluating training programs: The four levels*. Berrett-Koehler.

Kohls, L. R. (1981). *Developing intercultural awareness*. International Society for Intercultural Education, Training, and Research.

Kohls, L. R., & Knight, J. M. (1981). *Developing intercultural awareness: A Cross-cultural training handbook*. Intercultural Press.

Lewis, J. D. (1999). *Trusted partners: How companies build mutual trust and win together*. The Free Press.

Luthans, F., & Peterson, S. J. (2002). Employee engagement and manager self-efficacy. *Journal of Management Development*, *21*(5), 376-387. https://doi.org/10.1108/02621710210426864

McClelland, D. C. (1985). How motives, skills, and values determine what people do. *American Psychologist, 40*(7), 812-825. https://doi.org/10.1037/0003-066X.40.7.812

McClelland, D. C., Atkinson, J. W., & Lowell, E. L. (1953). *The achievement motive*. Appleton-Century-Crofts.

McClelland, D. C., Lowell, E. L., Atkinson, J. W., & Clark, R. A. (1976). *The achievement motive*. Irvington Publications.

Merton, R. K. (1968). *Social theory and social structure* (2nd ed., pp.475-490). The Free Press.

Mischel, W., & Baker, N. (1975). Cognitive appraisals and transformations in delay behavior. *Journal of Personality and Social Psychology*, *31*(2), 254-261.

Moran, R. T., & Harris, P. H. (1982). *Managing cultural synergy*. Gulf Publishing.

Neale, R., & Mindel, R. (1992). Rigging up multicultural teamworking. *Personnel Management*, *1*, 36-39.

Nishida, H. (1985). Japanese intercultural communication competence and cross-cultural adjustment. *International Journal of Intercultural Research*, *9*, 247-269.

Nishishiba, M., & Richie, L. D. (2000). The concept of trustworthiness: A cross-cultural comparison between Japanese and U.S. businesspeople. *Journal of Applied Communication Research*, *28*(4), 347-367.

Oberg, K. (1960). Cultural shock: Adjustment to new cultural environments. *Practical Anthropology*, *7*, 177-182.

Odiorne, G. S. (1965). *Management by objectives: A system of managerial leadership*. Pitman Publishing.

Oetzel, J. G. (1995). *Intercultural small groups: An effective decision-making theory*. Sage.

Parker, G. M. (1990). *Team players and teamwork: New strategies for developing successful collaboration* (2nd ed). John Wiley & Sons.

Pascale, R. T., & Althos, A. (1981). *The art of Japanese management*. Simon & Schuster.

Pettigrew, T. E. (1998). Intergroup contact theory. *Annual Review of Psychology*, *49*, 65-85.

Phillips, J. J. (1997). *Return on investment in training and performance improvement programs*. Butterworth-Heinemann.

Ramirez, M ., & Castañeda, A. (1974). *Cultural democracy, bicognitive development, and education*. Academic Press.

Ratiu, I. (1993). Thinking internationally: A comparison of how international executives learn. *International Studies of Management and Organization*, *13*(1-2), 139-150.

Rhinesmith, S. H. (1992). Global mindsets for global managers. *Training & Development*, *46*(10), 63-69.

Rogers, C. R. (1951). *Client-centered therapy: Its current practice, implications, and theory*. Houghton Mifflin.

Rogers, E. M. (1962). *Diffusion of innovation*. The Free Press.

Rohlen, T. P. (1974). *For harmony and strength: Japanese white-collar organization in anthropological perspective*. University of California Press.

Rotter, J. B. (1966). Generalized expectancies for internal versus external control of reinforcement. *Psychological monographs*, *80*(1), 1-28.

Ruben, B. D. (1976). Assessing communication competency for intercultural adaptation. *Group and Organization Studies*, *1*(3), 334-354.

Ruben, B. D., & Kealey, D. J. (1979). Behavioral assessment of communication competency and the prediction of cross-cultural adaptation. *International Journal for Intercultural Research*, *3*(1), 15-47.

Ryan, R. M., & Deci, E. L. (2000). Intrinsic and extrinsic motivations: Classic definitions and new directions. *Contemporary Educational Psychology*, *25*, 54-67.

Saks, A. M. (2006). Antecedents and consequences of employee engagement. *Journal of Managerial Psychology*, *21* (7), 600 - 619. https://doi. org/10. 1108/02683940610690169

Scalzi, D. V ., & Spring, C. (1975). Value of the intercultural communication workshop on campus. In D. S. Hoopes (Ed.), *Readings in intercultural communication* (1, pp.54-59). The Intercultural Communications Network.

Senge, P. M. (1990). *The fifth discipline: The art and practice of the learning organization*. Century Business.

Senge, P. M., & Sterman, J. D. (1992). Systems thinking and organizational learning: Acting locally and thinking globally in the organization of the future. *European Journal of Operational Research*, *59*(1), 137-150.

Spradley, J. P. (1979). *The ethnographic interview*. Waveland Press.

Spradley, J. P. (1980). *Participant observation*. Waveland Press.

Spradley, J. P., & McCurdy, D. (1980). *Anthropology: The cultural perspective*. Waveland Press.

Stewart, E. D. (1985). *American cultural patterns: Cross-cultural perspective*. Intercultural Press.

Tajfel, H. (1978). *Differentiation between social groups studies in the social psychology of intergroup relations*. Academy Press.

Tremblay, M. A. (1957). The key informant technique: A nonethographic application. *American Anthropologist*, *59*, 688-701.

Triandis, H. C., Brislin, R., Hui, C. H. (1988). Cross-cultural training across the individualism-collectivism divide. *International Journal of Intercultural Relations*, *12*, 269-289.

Trompenaars, F., & Hampden-Turner, C. (1997). *Riding the waves of culture: Understanding cultural diversity in business*. Nicholas Brealey.

Tung, R. L. (1998). A contingency framework of selection and training of expatriates revisited. *Human Resource Management Review*, *8*(1), 23–37.

Weiner, B. (1985). An attributional theory of achievement motivation and emotion. *Psychological Review*, *92*(4), 548–573.

Wiley, J., & Kowske, B. (2012). *Respect: Delivering results by giving employees what they really want*. Jossey-Bass.

Witkin, H. A., Goodenough, D. R., & Oltman, P. K. (1977). Psychological differential: Current status. *ETS Research Bulletin Series 77-16*, 1–44. https://doi.org/10.1002/j.2333-8504.1977.tb01142.x

Witkin, H. A., Moore, C. A., Goodenough, D. R., & Cox, P. W. (1977). Field-dependent and field-independent cognitive styles and their educational implications. *Review of Educational Research*, *47*(1), 1–64.

Wuerth, P. W. (1974). *The actor and observer bias in causal attribution: The effects of consistency and perspective* [Master's Thesis]. Loyola University Chicago, Loyola eCommons.

Yip, G. S. (1992). *Total global strategy managing for worldwide competitive advantage*. Prentice Hall.

Yuki, M., Maddux, W. W., Brewer, M. B., & Takemura, K. (2005). Cross-cultural differences in relationship and group-based trust. *Personality and Social Psychology Bulletin*, *31*(1), 48–62. https://doi.org/10.1177/0146167204271305

Countries — Nations — Nation-States

11

Media and Multiple Identities: Robert E. Park as Precursor to Intercultural Communication Theory and Research

Filipa SUBTIL
ESCS-Escola Superior de Comunicação Social, Instituto
Politécnico de Lisboa and ICNova
José Luís GARCIA
Instituto de Ciências Sociais da Universidade de Lisboa
Wendy LEEDS-HURWITZ
University of Wisconsin-Parkside

Summary: Robert E. Park's early study of foreign-language newspapers in urban centers hosting multiple immigrant groups deserves recognition as an important precursor to several current assumptions within intercultural communication, especially the move away from equating cultures with nations, and the possibility of simultaneously holding multiple identities. Park's research on the media's influence on identity construction contains theoretical contributions that remain highly relevant to a world increasingly configured by global media: in particular, on accepting complexity and the fact that individuals may and do simultaneously hold multiple and conflicting identities. Hence, beyond the nation-state, the appropriate unit of analysis became the ethnic group.

Introduction

Sociologist Robert E. Park was one of the intellectual leaders of the Chicago School of social thought, developed within the Department of Sociology and Anthropology of the University of Chicago between 1915 and 1935 (see Raushenbush, 1979, for the larger context of Park's work; Bulmer, 1986, on the Chicago School specifically). He studied urban life, the media, ethnic relations, and migration. Park's writings did not directly influence intercultural communication theory or research, yet his work serves as a precursor to several current assumptions, especially the questioning of the monolithic view of identity in the modern world, the move away from equating cultures with nations, and the multiple character of subject identity. To use Rogers' vocabulary, Park (along with others he discussed) was a "forerunner" rather than a "founder" (1994, p. xii); to use Jansen's term, he is part of one of our "forgotten histories" (2010, p. 127). Park's work has garnered new readings that are fruitful for discussions of the conflict between cultures, the multidimensional structure of identity, and the problems of intercultural communication (Goldberg, 2017; Kivisto, 2017; Magubane, 2014; Ruwet, 2017; Subtil & Garcia, 2010).

Park graduated in 1887 from the University of Michigan, where he was strongly influenced by John Dewey, then worked as a journalist in several U.S. cities for over a decade until, in 1899, earning an M. A. from Harvard University. Between 1899 and 1900 he attended the classes of sociologist Georg Simmel in Berlin, and in 1903 received his Ph. D. in Philosophy from Heidelberg under the supervision of Wilhelm Windelband and Alfred Hettner. After returning to the U.S. in 1904, he was Assistant Professor of Philosophy at Harvard University for two years. Until he entered the University of Chicago in 1914, he worked at the American Congo Reform Association (ACRA) as a secretary/publicity agent, and later at Tuskegee Institute as Booker T. Washington's researcher, ghostwriter, and co-author. During these years, he learned about the problems of Black Americans, racism, colonialism, and racial conflict. At the University of Chicago, he began by teaching a course exclusively focused on race relations and black identity and social problems, titled *The Negro in America*. Park was especially prepared to address the issues of cultural antagonism because of his experience at ACRA and the Tuskegee Institute, his knowledge of Simmel's ideas of "the stranger," and also sociologist and activist Black leader W. E. B. Du Bois' writings on "double consciousness." These influenced his research on migration and his thinking about the intersecting nature of modern subject identity. With other colleagues at the University of Chicago, he pursued a research program on urban life and the notion of human ecology, investigating the relationship between human beings and their natural and social environments. He embedded these studies with reflections on ethnic and cultural differences, between 1923 and 1935 publishing extensively on this topic (Hughes et al., 1950) in the context — following the end of World War I and the early 1920s — of the development of Pan-Africanist movements and racial clashes, most notably in the Red Summer of 1919. After Park's retirement from the University of Chicago, he taught from 1936 to 1943 at Fisk University (the HBCU in Nashville, Tennessee), where he continued to think about and analyze, more than any modern social scientist, race relations and cultural contacts. His vast experience as a journalist gave him a special competence to understand the importance of communication and media in society and in the construction of culture and identities, being today considered the first media sociologist in the U.S. (Berganza Conde, 2000; Subtil & Garcia, 2010).

Incorporating Park's vast reflections, analyses, and concepts on cultural and racial conflict, without losing a contextualized and critical look, seems to us an important task for discussions of intercultural communication. However, we cannot be exhaustive here, so this chapter emphasizes his innovative work on the role of the foreign-language press in the interaction between cultures of individuals living simultaneously in more than one world. Given its importance to intercultural communication, we specifically focus on Park's book *Immigrant Press and its Control,* which brings together the issues of the media, immigrant communities, and cultural differences.

This chapter reaches beyond a historical perspective on Park's ideas by seeking to extract those of his original contributions that retain relevance in a world ever more configured by technologies and the abundance of complex communication flows now circulating on a fully global scale. By granting importance to language as a tool uniting each community, and by showing how the strength of foreign languages expressed itself through the immigrant press, Park demonstrates that the latter produces a more ambivalent phenomenon than simply the assimilation of immigrants. On the one hand, the immigrant press served as a connecting force, driven by the desire to preserve the mother tongue and culture while at the same time awakening national sentiments that had, until then, remained diffuse. Yet, on the other hand, it facilitated the adjustment of immigrants to the American context. As a result, Park's work contributes to our understanding of a particular liminal moment inherent within many intercultural contexts, the space between *emigrant* identity (emphasizing the country of origin, or homeland) and *immigrant* identity (emphasizing the newly adopted country, or hostland). [1] In the process, he documents the ways in which recent immigrants can hold multiple cultural identities simultaneously, providing a valuable precursor to current research on hybrid identities. As well, Park provides an early model for the shift away from assuming the nation-state as the obvious unit of analysis. [2] Instead, he emphasized smaller ethnic communities (just as many intercultural scholars today do). As with the study of multiple selves, he is not typically cited as a precursor in this theoretical move, but clearly his research provides an early exemplar. Given that Park's work has not yet been granted attention by intercultural communication scholars, it seems unlikely that most readers will already be familiar with his arguments, so details documenting his original arguments seem necessary. [3]

Media and the Role of the Foreign Press

Robert E. Park was an insightful thinker about the world of the press and modern journalism (Hardt, 1989; Muhlmann, 2010; Muhlmann & Plenel, 2008; Phillips, 1976; Subtil & Garcia, 2010). [4] One of

---

[1]   Cooks (2001) also approaches this liminal space, although from a different perspective, and with a different result, discussing the importance of "understanding the places created by borders, as well as the spaces betwixt and between — those (inter)cultural spaces" (p. 346). Others have called this the "third space" (recently in Kramsch & Uryu, 2020, or Zhou & Pilcher, 2019).

[2]   This approach was termed "methodological nationalism" (Amelina et al., 2012; Beck, 2000; Chernilo, 2006a, 2006b; Martins, 1974; Wimmer & Schiller, 2002).

[3]   While intercultural communication has not yet considered Park at any length, scholars in history of sociology and even history of media communication certainly have. Given their number, it is beyond the scope of this discussion to list relevant references for the former group, but significant citations for the latter include Berganza Conde (2000), Buxton (2008), Carey (1996), Czitrom (1982), Peters (1989), Pooley (2007), Pooley & Katz (2008), and Subtil & Garcia (2010).

[4]   Hardt (1989) points out how even those who study the history of the American press have ignored Park's groundbreaking work, and Phillips (1976), quoting Park on the potential of the press to turn ideas into action, says "Today, Park's vision remains just a vision" (p. 87), so that it is not only those within intercultural communication who have overlooked the potential of his contributions.

his most brilliant and oft-cited papers, "The natural history of the newspaper" (Park,1923), is dedicated to an examination of the role of newspapers in social life. The title and some of the premises developed in this text resonate with a social Darwinist perspective, at least regarding the struggle for survival and adaptation to the environment. For Park, newspapers had a *natural history*: that is, like an individual in society, a newspaper was conceptualized as a living organism engaged in a continuous process of adaptation to the social needs of individuals and groups within an increasingly urbanized society. The struggle for survival, in the case of the newspaper, would refer to the struggle to increase (or at least maintain) circulation, since readers are essential to a newspaper's very survival.

The use of the kind of assumptions and language just mentioned can be traced to the influence of Herbert Spencer's Social Darwinism on the first generation of American social theorists. However, Park, much like John Dewey and Charles H. Cooley, withdrew from the main Spencerian thesis on social life. In fact, the topic of communication appears as a key issue in the rupture between the first generation of American social theorists and Spencer. For Spencer, the social order is constructed through a set of individuals involved in a permanent and evolutionary process of individual, free and spontaneous competition, whereas Dewey, Cooley, and Park regarded society as a much more complex and sophisticated organism, in which the communicational-cultural dimension is privileged. In their drawing away from Social Darwinism, these theorists saw communication as the central process of construction of human identity, social organization, and the bond between the individual and the larger society (Cooley, 1920; Coser, 1977 [1971]; Czitrom, 1982; Peters, 1989; Quandt, 1970).

Although Park speaks of a natural history of the newspaper, this is only a metaphor; his approach to the press is fundamentally cultural. For Park, the press is a cultural form articulated with the surrounding social context: the press as the expression of, and acting upon, the collective culture. The world of the metropolis in accelerating growth triggered by the process of industrialization, fed by influxes of large numbers of migrants (internal migrations from the countryside to the city as well as those between nation-states), provides the cultural context necessary to understanding the press. Influenced by Georg Simmel's famous 1903 essay on the city (published in English in 1950), [5] Park considers the press as a fundamental dimension of everyday life in the modern city.

In the large modern metropolis of the time, according to Park, the newspaper could be defined in many ways:

1) As a disseminator of knowledge: "What the popular teachers did for Athens in the period of Socrates and Plato the press has done in modern times for the common man";
2) As a business enterprise whose product is news: "(The editor is the philosopher turned merchant)";
3) As the medium that allows information about our common life to become accessible to the common citizen on a reduced price, contributing to recuperating a certain kind of democracy;
4) As a medium that creates "advertising values", i.e., a space for selling advertising; and
5) As a vehicle of common transportation, like the postal services or the railway (Park, 1923, pp.275–276).

The press is a corollary to the transformations of the urban world, yet simultaneously one of the main drivers of public life. The role of the newspaper is to contribute to transforming the city into a civic universe, i.e., to enable the promotion of consensus, to unify populations, to be the common denominator of the inhabitants of growing metropolises. It is thus possible to say that, for Park, the press and the modern city were intimately correlated and through the press one could see the changes in the world of industrial society's new metropolises.

The type of newspaper drawing Park's attention was not the so-called "elite" press, directed at small groups of readers having ideological, cultural, and religious similarities; rather, it was the "modern newspaper," to use his phrase, from the industrial stage of the press, the one which is read by all the literate population, thus a newspaper for all. As opposed to rural communities, where reading was a luxury only accessible to certain social groups, in the city, with everything in a state of constant becoming, reading the newspaper became necessary for the entire population. This is one of the reasons that explain, from Park's perspective, the existence of such

---

[5] The essay being referred to is "Die Großstädte und das Geistesleben" (1903, not translated into English until 1950). An important German sociologist, Simmel had substantial influence on Chicago sociologists in that period (Levine et al., 1976). For discussion of Simmel within intercultural communication, see Carbaugh & Berry (2001); Coffey (2013); Cooks (2001); Kulich et al. (2020); and Rogers (1994, 1999).

a high number of foreign-language publications in the U.S. Members of immigrant communities not only read their own newspapers, but were also soon attracted by the mainstream American newspapers in English, which they saw as a window open to the external world beyond the circle of their own communities. Park argues that the significant increase in the number of readers of American newspapers in the beginning of the twentieth century was due, to a large extent, to these immigrant readers, using as an example the *New York Evening Journal*, William Randolph Hearst's most successful paper. In the 1920s, NYEJ attracted a new body of subscribers every six years, a group of readers largely composed of recent immigrants. The increasing consumption of newspapers by immigrants would have, according to Park, a profound influence on the character of American newspapers (Park, 1923).

Park's *The Immigrant Press and its Control*, published in 1922, is only one of ten books making up a wider project entitled *Americanization Studies*. Subtitled *The Acculturation of Immigrant Groups into American Society*, this series was dedicated to the so-called "methods of Americanization" in the 1920s. This project was coordinated by Allen T. Burns and financed by the Carnegie Corporation following World War I , when migration to the U.S. reached its highest numbers. The project resulted from the constant appeals made to Carnegie to help the work of several public and private American social institutions involved in teaching new citizens how government worked and their obligations to it. Employing a paradigm of assimilation, *Americanization* is defined in the introductory note by the publisher

> [...] as the union of native and foreign born in all the most fundamental relationships and activities of our national life. For Americanization is the uniting of new with native-born Americans in fuller common understanding and appreciation to secure by means of self-government the highest welfare of all. (Park, 1922, p. xix)

The various studies describe in detail the most important aspects of the life of different immigrant groups, in order to understand relevant distinctions in their Americanization process, how this process took place, and which American institutions were involved. The information collected was considered an important contribution for understanding and managing the problems of Americanization. The topics chosen were intended to represent institutions or social forces vital to the assimilation of immigrants: schools, neighborhoods, immigrant heritage, agriculture, health, family life, the foreign-language press, politics and citizenship, the courts, and industry.

The Influence of Media on Identity Construction and the End of Univocal Identities

The Immigrant Press and its Control asks how reading the foreign-language press can favor the integration of new arrivals (emigrants who become immigrants) into American social and political life. To achieve this goal, the book is mainly dedicated to the social context of the immigrant press, to its contents, and the forms of control it undergoes.[6] Park builds on the realization that the U.S. at the time comprised multiple language communities, resulting from immigrant flows drawn from different countries. This situation was due to sharing the same means of communication: common languages and dialects bring together members of any foreign population, simultaneously separating them from other communities. In 1918, Park lists 43 (or 44)[7] languages and dialects being spoken by the immigrant communities in the U.S. Each linguistic and cultural enclave was strongly committed to cooperation and mutual help to allow the maintenance of a communal existence separate from everyday life in large cities. In general, these communities had a church, a school, a theatre, and almost always a newspaper.

Park emphasizes the role of the newspaper as one of the social institutions contributing the most to maintaining a communal existence. The foreign-language press satisfied the immigrant's natural desire to express ideas in the native language. The example given is New York: in that period, it seemed that each linguistic group, however small, published a printed newspaper or some sort of publication for the benefit of its own members. However, Park's analysis explains not only the press of the large cities, but also the provincial press, as well as the press of the political parties linked to the workers' struggle and the socialist cause (the "radical press"). Park suggests that more foreign-language newspapers were being published and

---

[6] Park presented some notes on this topic in a prior paper (Park, 1920).

[7] Park notes the difficulty in making a clear distinction between languages and dialects since certain forms of discourse can be considered either dialects or separate languages. (That the distinction between a dialect and a language owes much to political considerations is well accepted today.)

read in the U.S. than in the immigrants' countries of origin. Several reasons are presented for such popularity: many of the immigrants did not have permission to read in their native languages (or dialects) in their countries of origin, and many only had the opportunity to learn how to read in the U.S.; those who already had the habit of reading newspapers in their countries of origin did not find them interesting or intelligible; it was common for the oppressed and dependent people of Europe not to have permission to publish in their own languages; those who, in their countries of origin, had been committed to fighting for the right to print and publish in their native languages felt strong empathy and connection to the American press; and, lastly, immigrants tended to read more in the host country because there were more things about which it was necessary to gain knowledge (which was often not immediately available through personal connections).

The immigrant population that came to the U.S. mostly originated from small villages and isolated towns, where customs and traditions were enough to satisfy the demands of everyday life. Once in the U.S., they became blue collar workers required to participate in the cosmopolitan life of large industrial cities. There simply was more news, urgent information that individuals required in their everyday lives to adjust to the new context, to alter old habits, and to forge new points of view. In a context of permanent change and transformation, immigrants needed to abandon existing habits and acquire new ideas. Park thinks that the press performed this precise role, turning into an institution of speech by and for each immigrant group.

In Park's perspective, the press, accompanied by local associations and the church, was fundamental to the preservation of languages. Had it not been so, they would have disintegrated and transformed into migrant dialects mixed with English. However, the press, the associations, and the church were also crucial to reinforcing the sense of belonging to the nation of origin for most of the population, which had never previously experienced nationalism. The strangeness of the new surrounding context intensified the bond between those who had left and those who stayed in the countries of origin. While in the home country, those who would leave it often seemed different from others (for if they had primarily identified as core group members, they more likely would have stayed rather than migrating); but upon arrival in the U.S., with so many people having various cultural backgrounds, suddenly they were identified (by themselves and others) primarily as members of the group they had just left.

Park demonstrates that this effect becomes stronger as the members of a particular racial or ethnic group try to gain public recognition. This is the reason why several nationalist movements first manifested themselves in exile, even gaining financial support in the new country. Nationalist tendencies found expression and strong encouragement in the press, in local associations, and in churches built in the new host country. Through these entities, immigrants felt the strengthening of bonds with their origins, they felt in touch with the political struggle in the countries of origin, and they were even given the opportunity to participate in them. According to Park, consciously or unconsciously, these institutions played a decisive role in the preservation of national sentiment, in addition to promoting a tight relationship between the will to preserve national identity and the mother tongue in written form. This sentiment was heightened among members of oppressed groups who identified their struggle for political recognition with the struggle for the existence of the press itself. A free press, Park tells us, is a fundamental condition for the effective existence of nationalist sentiment, for "nationalism is never in effective existence without a free press" (1922, p. 55). Park believes that the foreign-language newspapers in America were inspired by nationalist claims and that the editors themselves deliberately used their newspapers to delay assimilation of new arrivals.

The immigrant press, although ignored by the intellectual elites due to its perceived triviality, created its own reading public. Nationalistically inclined editors sought to use the press to keep their readers' interests and activities focused on their countries of origin. Yet, as stated by Park, under its conditions of existence, the immigrant press met the requirements for being a factor of promotion rather than obstruction in the movement towards mainstream America. This process of Americanization through contact was detected, for example, in the changes introduced in the vocabulary of immigrants. Even in rural communities, which preserved the foreign language for a longer time, the press tended to Americanize itself (Park, 1922).

Park's next task was to establish the role of the foreign-language press in the process of assimilation. He showed that the foreign-language press had an ambivalent role. While for some editors it constituted a means of segregation and isolation of foreign communities, for others it helped the new immigrants, especially the first generation, to find their way in the American context and to participate in the intellectual, political, and social life of their new country. Living and working in the U.S. stimulated the immigrants' curiosity as to the difference between old and new, and led them to become interested in the events, customs, and ideas of the host country, rather than clinging to those of the country of origin. Hence, the foreign-language press found itself obligated to divulge news about the broader American context to satisfy the demands of its readers, therefore accelerating assimilation. The editors that shared this stance claimed that their press was not merely a news outlet introducing the migrant to the surrounding environment, but also a means of translating and transmitting the American way and American ideas.

The Inter-racial Council, founded in 1919 and chaired by T. Coleman Du Pont, played a key role in that process. Together with the Foreign Language Bureau (Department of Civilian Relief of the American Red Cross), it was one of the two independent agencies promoting relationships established during World War I between the government and the immigrant press. The goal of the Council was to continue the task of Americanization carried out during the war under the command of Secretary of the Interior, Franklin Knight Lane, and Commissioner of Education, Philander Claxton. Their goal was to contribute to something more consistent and definitive than previously available through governmental programs. Therefore, the Council served as a mediator between the native employers, the immigrant workers, and labor organizations. In this respect, Park gave special emphasis to the fact that, for the Council, the foreign-language press could be regarded as a promoter of interaction with the immigrants, thereby providing incentives to American businessmen to buy advertising in these newspapers: "Practical Americanization is the use of American things, and by using them getting our foreign people to like them and prefer them to other things" (Du Pont, 1919, pp. 1–2, as quoted in Park, 1922, p. 87).

Park's research shows that the foreign-language press, regardless of what the editors wanted, facilitated the adjustment of immigrants to the American environment, thus leading to the formation of an identity which, while *not* American by previous standards, yet also was not exactly foreign, that is, following existing European models. Park's reflection shows the influence of Simmel's brief article, "The stranger" (1971 [1908]), [8] whose perspective is now considered of undeniable importance for intercultural communication (Rogers, 1999). The

---

[8] This essay was translated into English for the first time by Park in 1921, one year before the publication of *The Immigrant Press and Its Control*, so it could be included in the *Introduction to the Science of Sociology*.

German sociologist addresses the issue of how spatial forms (e. g., borders or migration movements) structure social interactions and pondered how social interactions manifest themselves in space (e. g., the empty field as an expression of neutrality). Like the traveler, the stranger is also an outsider, but in a different way than guests among their hosts, with whom they share no common history or culture. The stranger is ambivalent, alternating between two groups without completely belonging to either of them. This condition produces feelings of closeness and distance, rupture and belonging, alterity (otherness) and precariousness in relation to the host society. The stranger embraces ideas and commodities drawn from both the community of origin and the host community. Park clearly incorporated Simmel's insights into his approach to immigration, the immigrant press, and cultural contact in American society. Building from the communicational and symbolic experiences of the immigrants, Park sees them as cultural hybrids living simultaneously in two worlds. Originally, Simmel's archetype of the stranger was the Jews; Park did not confine the concept exclusively to Jews, but encompassed all immigrants. His work with the American black community had already moved him away from the premise of a single affiliation. Park was familiar with another view akin to Simmel's on psychosocial conflict which Du Bois had included in *The Souls of Black Folk* (1903), the notion of "double consciousness." In this book, Du Bois argues that the black American has a dual feeling: on the one hand, a communal (black) consciousness and, on the other, a national consciousness. This double consciousness was derived not from heredity but from social situation, an idea that was certainly fundamental to Park when he elaborated on the concept of the marginal man (Goldberg, 2017; Kharlamov, 2012; Marotta, 2006, 2016).

This theoretical backdrop allows a better understanding of the problem presented in Park's study regarding the possibility of incorporating immigrants into national life. This was also a key issue for the Chicago School of social thought influenced by John Dewey. From these works, in which it is already possible to glimpse a complex perspective on immigrant identity, we highlight the pioneering research of William I. Thomas and Florian Znaniecki, *The Polish Peasant in Europe and America* (1984 [1918-1920]), as well as several works by Park and his disciples. These scholars tended to see modern communication, and the press in particular, as a catalyst for conversation and public debate, and thus committed to civil society, community and democracy. For it is participation, more than submission or conformity, that turns immigrants into Americans. Through this process, the American cultural mosaic was changing. Seeking to understand the participation of immigrants in civic life, Park moves into a detailed analysis of the contents of the immigrant press in Part Ⅱ of the book (1922, pp.113–247).

The Move Away from Equating Cultures with Nations and the Phenomenon of Multiple Identities

Park writes that "[r]eading some of these foreign papers is like looking through a keyhole into a lighted room" (1922, p.113). Five topics are covered in his study of the content of the immigrant press: "advertising," "the provincial press," "the cosmopolitan press," "the cosmopolitan press and the war," and "the class war." Park's analysis revealed that the content of the typical immigrant paper was not homogeneous. Diversity was provided by differences in ethnicity, class, and culture, depending on the distinct minorities. However, at the same time he did not find the immigrant press to be very stimulating, except in the case of religious and/or political radicalism, due to the immigrants' low levels of literacy. Almost all the knowledge immigrants had about political, social, and industrial life was gained indirectly from articles in their local press. ⑨

Park draws specific attention to advertising, since it reveals the organization of an immigrant community even more than the rest of the newspaper, providing insight into how much each immigrant group has adapted to the American way of life, or not. Immigrant businesses tend to flourish with recent immigration and resulting segregation, whereas associations and cultural organizations are established more slowly and persist over a longer time. Regarding the first trend, Park provides the example of Syrian newspapers in New York, filled with ads for house rentals, grocery stores, restaurants, and clothing shops, thus serving as a sign of the recent arrival of new Syrian immigrants. The same applies to the newspapers of the Italian community, with ads for groceries and olive oil importers, doctors, lawyers, solicitors, and work agencies. As to the second trend, Park

---

⑨ This issue stems from the educational project developed by Dewey and other Chicago sociologists between 1910 – 1935, such as the Polish-American sociologist Florian Znaniecki (1940).

uses the case of *Abendpost*, the largest newspaper of the oldest German community in Chicago, containing few ads for German businesses. Park saw this as sign of support of this community for American tradesmen. But even in the *Abendpost* it was possible to find ads placed by German doctors, lawyers, and organizations.

When Park refers to "provincial" newspapers, he is talking about the press of the first generations of immigrants. For this audience, the most interesting news concerned the people and places with which they were familiar. The content of provincial newspapers for the oldest generation of immigrants thus was directed toward the homeland they missed. They displayed a strong desire to keep in touch with others sharing the same memories. Park states that "[t]he discovery of a mutual acquaintance is a bond of steel" (1922, p. 137). They appreciated sharing old points of reference and the use of their native tongue was predominantly religious, representing the religious forms practiced by the first generations, remaining almost untouched by the customs and ideas of the cosmopolitan city. This press revealed some mistrust regarding new religious forms, condemning the frivolous ways of the younger generations. Letters have an important place in this kind of press and the letter writers revealed a simple life, with interests mainly in the crops and the weather.

Park shows the content of the cosmopolitan press to be very different from the provincial press. The cosmopolitan press was read by the immigrant industrial workers and by groups more distant from American daily life. The readers of this press lived in a big city but separate from the native-born Americans. They coexisted in a complex world filled with their own group's events, and therefore they needed newspapers in their own language to learn about what was happening around them. In these newspapers, crime and the dramatic aspects of everyday life substituted for the religious and personal news present in the provincial press (Park, 1922).

The coverage of World War I provided Park an opportunity to address the content of the cosmopolitan press. The armed conflict was a topic of particular interest in the immigrant press, more even than in the mainstream American press. National sentiments on the part of the immigrant communities were revived by the war and the role played by the press. Park demonstrates how old European antagonisms resurfaced because these rivalries were a heritage of immigrant populations, despite not being shared by native-born Americans. In certain cases, war provided for many peoples the possibility of realizing their national hopes. In addition, Germany and Austria sought to gain control over the sentiments and the conduct of their immigrants in the U.S., even resorting to threats. Despite this, Park claims that, in most cases, the attempt to force loyalty among opposing or indifferent nationals was largely not successful. Being the editor of a foreign-language newspaper in the U.S. during, and shortly after, World War I was thus not an easy task. The foreign-language newspaper was frequently an intermediary between various communities, seeking to relay ideas from all. In this regard, Park highlights once more the phenomenon of multiple identities.

Park notes that the turmoil of war brought new life to old memories and long neglected, or even forgotten, feelings of loyalty. This created in many immigrant populations a sense of divided allegiance, for which editors could not find any appropriate formulas. The options in editorial policies expressed this instability. It was difficult to find an editor able to follow a coherent editorial policy, or to satisfy both the demands of his readers and governmental censorship. Many wrote one day to satisfy a wider American public and, on the next, appealed to the narrower loyalty of their immigrant readers. In addition, foreign-language newspapers often played the part of intermediary between different communities by transmitting ideas from one to another. In this way multiple, rather than single, identities were emphasized, with the immigrant press presenting itself simultaneously as distant and committed. On some occasions, these newspapers tackled both positions in the same issue, writing one opinion in English, yet taking a very different approach in the native language.

Park's acute insight regarding the phenomenon of liminality in immigrants becomes particularly clear when he addresses the content of the radical press, committed to socialist ideals and the working class. He turns his focus to the effects of the class divide as well as the perception of the U.S. as the home of capitalism. Park argues that the content of the radical press, even in the context of World War I, did not blind it to the other war lying at the heart of its interests — the class war. The radical press tried to make its readers aware of their class condition. The Russian Revolution heightened these circumstances, given that the radical press finally had news at its disposal that seemed to confirm the ideals it spread. This new situation, Park tells us, drove many radical immigrants to feel that a new society was finally coming to pass.

Yet, according to Park, the content of radical newspapers was diverse, including accusations against capitalism and the American people based on facts concerning the hardships of the working class and revolutionary prophecies. The suffering of the proletariat was, in Park's view, the most powerful propaganda weapon at the service of the radicals. The accusations regarding capitalism were made through concrete examples of martyred citizens willing to suffer for their radical ideals. While before World War I such martyrs mainly belonged to the group Industrial Workers of the World (IWW), after the conflict they were joined by the editors of the foreign-language newspapers themselves. The allegations against American society are very clear in these publications, reaching their climax in the anarchist press. By systematically publishing news on the hardships of workers, the radical press sought to promote action among its followers. The suffering endured by men and women while serving the radical cause provides valuable examples given visibility. One last aspect noted by Park concerns what he designates as the racial character of the radical press, i. e., the fact that although the topics of this press were, generally speaking, the same across the country, their forms of expression varied according to their racial (today more typically called ethnic) origin. The quotes Park draws from German, Russian, Finnish, Italian, and Spanish radical newspapers illustrate the differences in these peoples' forms of expression (1922).

A Liminal Moment between Emigrant and Immigrant Identities

Park's final chapter in this study is dedicated to ways of controlling the immigrant press. According to his analysis, there is a high probability that a substantial number of foreign-language newspapers only survived due to advertisers, the alternative to becoming the mouthpiece of societies, parties, or factions. This analysis allows Park to emphasize the powerful contribution of newspapers to change sentiment and attitude toward the countries of origin and the U.S. The publications in their mother tongue gave members of various immigrant groups a unique opportunity to keep in touch and communicate. At the same time, these groups were able to preserve their national organizations, common traditions, and languages. According to content of a particular article, the foreign-language press could orient their interests to the country of origin or introduce the U.S. to immigrants, nurturing reader interest and affection for their new country.

The issue of the control of the press is a very sensitive topic in

American democracy. Although viewing the idea of such control as always repugnant, Park does not take a naïve stance. He argues that any newspaper is always susceptible to multiple influences, since it is obvious that the press is not a completely free agent. He presents two reasons why it is important to identify those influences as well as their relative strengths. First, several agencies and interests have successfully controlled the immigrant press, particularly with hostile purposes regarding the U.S. Second, understanding the influences of the immigrant press may keep an immigrant editor from being led onto dangerous paths. Park identifies three modes of controlling the press: "the levers of control," "enemy propaganda and government intervention," and "control through alliance."

Park first addresses the newspapers' sources of income: subscriptions, advertising, and subventions, each of which has significance for control. Briefly, the distinction is based on the degree of arbitrary control any individual or group exerts on the sources of income, and the increase of dependency on a source of income. For example, the income of "subsidized" and "mendicant" journals stems from political parties and other fraternal or religious organizations since there are few self-sustaining propagandist newspapers. Most radical, socialist, and labor publications are mendicant, meaning they are supported by the parties and societies they represent, or they appeal to the generosity of group members to survive (Park, 1922).

"Independent" newspapers — those in which the editor's views are neither limited by the demands of the interests of parties or institutions, nor predetermined by party doctrine — obtain their primary income from advertising. In the first two decades of the twentieth century, advertising grew steadily, as opposed to subscriptions. ⑩ However, as Park notes, there is a significant difference between the proportion of income and circulation in foreign-language vs. English-language newspapers. Generally speaking, immigrant newspapers were similar in organization and content to English newspapers of the late 19th century; that is, they were not business institutions at the same level of professionalism as contemporary English-language papers.

Park considers circulation to be the only source of revenue for newspapers that can be controlled by individuals or groups due to the

---

⑩   Park notes that this is a significant change in the American press in English, which in the 1860s was mainly dependent on its subscribers, who typically paid five cents a copy.

lack of organization among the public assuring the livelihood of the newspaper, particularly independent newspapers. When circulation guaranteed the subsistence of the newspaper, the press was able to remain relatively independent from advertisers. However, the struggle for circulation provoked a constant decrease in selling prices. The lower the selling price, the larger the circulation required for survival, resulting in increased revenue needed from advertising. In this respect, Park mentions the increasing influence of advertisers, representing the capitalist class, as a recurrent topic in contemporary debates about the press as a threat to democracy. In this sense, the value of advertising in newspapers is a result of circulation. If circulation represents the interests and wishes of the public, while advertising represents commercial interests, then these two forces are interdependent.

Park demonstrates how the immigrant press turned into the main advertising medium for entire communities, including local dealers, foreign-language bookstores, banks, and steamship agencies, as well as professionals such as lawyers and doctors. He finds no evidence of the local or classified ads being used to influence or control the press. He claims that this form of advertising "appeals to the public and not to any organized group capable of exercising arbitrary control over the policies of the paper in which their advertisements are published" (1922, p. 369). However, this is not the case for the potential control held by national advertising. The pioneers in national advertising were patent-medicine manufacturers. The foreign-language newspapers have always published advertising dedicated to medical topics, and these ads occupied much available advertising space.

Park gives particular emphasis to the American Association of Foreign Language Newspapers (AAFLN), led by Louis N. Hammerling, as an example of excessive influence over the foreign-language press through the control of advertising (1922). The most important activities of AAFLN involved political advertising. American politicians were quick to understand the potential of the foreign-language press, even given minimal knowledge of operational details. Bluntly put, "[t]hey realized that it pays to advertise" (1922, p. 382). Hammerling, described as a master of intrigue, acted as middleman between the foreign-language press and the American business world at a time when both parties, due to lack of knowledge, needed a mediator for successful negotiations. According to Park, Hammerling's fast social and political rise resulted from his pioneer efforts in taking a business approach to putting advertising in foreign-language newspapers.

For Park, during World War I the fight of the American government against enemy propaganda led to the first serious attempt to control the immigrant press. This attempt was fundamental to the development of the foreign-language press as an assimilation instrument. For the first time, propaganda was deemed part of the war strategy. When the conflict erupted, American society offered clear opportunities for enemy propaganda. The authorities were skeptical of the U.S.'s ability to act as a unified nation due to the division in popular sentiment and the heterogeneity of the population. Each ethnic group had its own specific interest in the conflict and interpreted this country's participation in the war from the point of view of its own national interest. As Park states, "Some of our immigrant peoples did not regard this country as a nation. It was merely a place in which people lived, like the Austrian Empire — a geographical expression" (1922, p. 413). Besides the different ethnic groups, there were also political factions (socialists, World War I pacifists, and anarchists) who opposed the war based on principle. Except for pacifism, all these ideological perspectives could be found in immigrant communities — and in their newspapers.

Keenly aware of the diversity of viewpoints, German politicians soon recognized the power of propaganda. Well before the beginning of World War I , Germany actively established cultural colonies wherever German emigrants settled. The Deutsch Amerikanischer Bund (German American Alliance) was delegated the task of keeping the German spirit alive and, insofar as possible, turning the U.S. into a German cultural colony. In 1907, this association had achieved influence on a national level. Before the war, it had already established 6, 500 local societies "held together in the bonds of Germanism" (Park, 1922, p. 414), to use the expression Park translates from a German publication. The declaration of war would turn these societies into centers of German propaganda. According to Park, it was not uncommon for immigrant associations to strive to perpetuate the traditions and culture of their home countries. Yet the German case was distinctive because such endeavor so clearly resembled a separatist movement.

The last form of control Park presents is control through alliance. In his view, the desire to control the native-born American has a logical ground that exceeds American mistrust regarding all things foreign or difficult to understand. The cultural heritage of some of the immigrant communities is so different from those born in America that its presence in the press may suggest actions contrary to national aims, or even meddling in the U.S.'s social machinery.

As a result, in American society, there is legitimacy in working to prevent this kind of discord. However, as Park demonstrates, Americans took their Americanization even further, by inviting immigrants to cooperate and use their own institutions to this end. The promotion of independent agencies encouraging the foreign-language press to highlight common cultural heritage between immigrants and locals, making the U.S. seem friendlier, turned the immigrant press into an instrument of Americanization. By publishing U.S. news, or advertising U.S.-produced goods, the foreign-language press itself became an Americanizing influence. This led Park to argue that the foreign-language press would end up becoming an even more important vehicle for Americanization than agencies created specifically for that purpose. In addition, since immigrants proved willing to use their own language and press in the attempt to find a place in the new country, "[t]he foreign-language press, if it preserves old memories, is at the same time the gateway to new experiences" (Park, 1922, p.449).

Generally speaking, the history and sociology of newspapers assert the generic thesis that they, like schools, function as a foundation of national society — a nation would be a society of readers who share reading material and thus ideas and assumptions. But Park's analysis of the immigrant press introduces the argument that this medium has the power to transport the culture of the Other into the host country. This raises two fundamental issues: the existence of the Other in the host society, and the relationship of the host society to the Other. The immigrant newspaper is an ambivalent entity promoting closeness to what is distant and the singularity that what is (geographically) close is actually (culturally) distant. It is thus simultaneously inside and outside. The immigrant press serves as a vehicle of multi-presence, of multiculturality, and of multiple identities, for while the immigrant becomes part of the culture of the U.S., American culture, in turn, becomes accepted by the immigrant, all while reading a newspaper in a language other than English, supporting an identity other than American. Through the newspaper, those who traveled to the U.S. physically were simultaneously able to remain psychologically at home in their nations of origin, though doubtless differently from how they would have been if they had stayed at home. The cultures of the immigrants (Greek, Chinese, Ukrainian, etc.) now existed inside America, a fact made possible through foreign-language newspapers. Park's work contributes to our understanding of a particular pause inherent within intercultural contexts, the space between emigrant identity (emphasizing the country of origin) and immigrant identity (emphasizing the newly adopted country). His work examines the liminal moment when an individual stands between conflicting identities, not yet having fully left the first, not yet having fully taken on the second. This simultaneous support of a double identity (as a member of both the old country and the new one) for even a brief time presaged current interest in multiple identities within intercultural communication.

Conclusion

Park's early study of the role of foreign-language newspapers in urban centers hosting multiple immigrant groups thus provides an important precursor to later work emphasizing the influence of media on community construction (e. g., Anderson, 2006 [1983]; Coyer, 2011; Hollander et al., 2008; Jankowski, 2002; Olorunnisola, 2002; Wilkin, et al., 2007), where he is frequently acknowledged as an influence. But his ideas equally presaged research and theorizing within intercultural communication on identity, immigration, incorporation, cultural pluralism, and cosmopolitanism (e.g., Akindes, 2001; Cheng, 2008; Croucher, 2008; Drzewiecka, 2002; Kim, 2007, Kivisto, 2017; MacDonald & O'Regan, 2012), where he has typically been neither acknowledged nor recognized.

Park's work points to a moment of liminal balance, the moment when an individual pauses between identities, not yet having fully left the first behind, not yet having fully taken on the second. This concurrent support of a double identity (as a member of both the old country and the new one) for even a brief time presaged current interest in multiple identities, cross identities, and nested identities within intercultural communication. Again, his work has not been recognized as relevant by current studies in this area (e.g., Bailey, 2007; Collier, 1998, 2009; Hecht, 1993; Herakova, 2009; Mendoza et al., 2002; Toomey et al., 2013; Witteborn, 2007), but that fact does not reduce its role as a first effort to outline a few major concepts that intercultural researchers take for granted today.

In the process of these moves, Park also provides an early example of the shift away from equating culture and identity with a nation-state, given his willingness to consider ethnic identity as a primary category of analysis. Thus, Park puts forth the combination of an *old national* identity that becomes a *new ethnic* identity (any of the now typically hyphenated identities, such as German-American or Irish-American), with a *new national* identity (as American). In the process, Park demonstrates the value of giving up the equation of culture and identity with nationality long before most others were willing to do so (at least until the 1970s, most of those studying cultural behavior assumed the only and obvious unit of measure was a country — and too many scholars still make this assumption today). Thus, Park provides an early example of the significance of accepting complexity: people can and do have multiple identities simultaneously; countries can be home to multiple cultural groups simultaneously; and understanding how individuals move between their various identities, or how members of different communities manage their interactions, provide valuable topics of study. In the process, Park emphasizes the importance of understanding that media and interaction are intertwined, rather than separate entities: newspapers (and we can add books, poetry, films, etc.) shape their readers' understanding of their own identities. In all these ways, Park was far ahead of his time, and has much to offer current scholars of intercultural communication.

References

Akindes, F. (2001). Sudden rush: *Na mele paleoleo* (Hawaiian rap) as liberatory discourse. *Discourse, 21*(3), 82-98.

Amelina, A., Nergiz, D. D., Faist, T., & Schiller, N. G. (2012). *Beyond methodological nationalism: Research methodologies for cross-border studies.* Routledge.

Anderson, B. (2006 [1983]). *Imagined communities: Reflection on the origin and spread of nationalism* (Rev. ed). Verso.

Bailey, B. (2007). Shifting negotiations of identity in a Dominican American community. *Latino Studies, 5*, 157-181.

Beck, U. (2000). The cosmopolitan perspective: Sociology of the second age of modernity. *British Journal of Sociology, 51*, 79-105.

Berganza Conde, M. R. (2000). *Comunicación, opinión pública y prensa en la sociología de Robert E. Park* [*Communication, public opinion and press in Robert E. Park's sociology*]. Madrid: CIS.

Bhabha, H. K. (2004). *The location of culture.* Routledge.

Bulmer, M. (1986). *The Chicago school of sociology: Institutionalization, diversity, and the rise of sociological research.* University of Chicago Press.

Buxton, W. J. (2008). From Park to Cressey: Chicago sociology's engagement with media and mass culture. In J. Pooley & D. Park (Eds.), *The history of media and communication research: Contested memories* (pp. 345-362). Peter Lang.

Carbaugh, D., & Berry, M. (2001). Communicating history, Finnish and American discourses: An ethnographic contribution to intercultural communication inquiry. *Communication Theory*, *11*(3), 352–366.

Carey, J. W. (1996). The Chicago School and mass communication research. In E. E. Dennis & E. Wartella (Eds.), *American communication research: The remembered history* (pp. 21–38). Lawrence Erlbaum.

Cheng, H. I. (2008). Space making: Chinese transnationalism on the U.S.- Mexican borderlands. *Journal of International and Intercultural Communication*, *1*(3), 244–263.

Chernilo, D. (2006a). Social theory's methodological nationalism: Myth and reality. *European Journal of Social Theory*, *9*, 5–22.

Chernilo, D. (2006b). Methodological nationalism and its critique. In G. Delanty & K. Kumar (Eds.), *The Sage handbook of nations and nationalism* (pp. 129– 139). Sage.

Coffey, S. (2013). Strangerhood and intercultural subjectivity. *Language and Intercultural Communication*, *13*(3), 266–282.

Collier, M. J. (1998). Researching cultural identity: Reconciling interpretive and postcolonial perspectives. In A. Gonzalez & D. Tanno (Eds.), *Communication and identity: International and intercultural communication annual* (pp. 122– 147). Sage.

Collier, M. J. (2009). Contextual negotiation of cultural identifications and relationships: Interview discourse with Palestinian, Israeli, and Palestinian/Israeli young women in a U.S. peace-building program. *Journal of International and Intercultural Communication*, *2*(4), 344–368.

Cooks, L. (2001). From distance and uncertainty to research and pedagogy in the borderlands: Implications for the future of intercultural communication. *Communication Theory*, *11*(3), 339–351.

Cooley, C. H. (1920). Reflections upon the sociology of Herbert Spencer. *American Journal of Sociology*, *26*(2), 129–145.

Coser, L. (1977 [1971]). *Masters of sociological thought: Ideas in historical and social context*. Harcourt Brace Jovanovich.

Coyer, K. (2011). Community media in a globalized world: The relevance and resilience of local radio. In R. Mansell & M. Raboy (Eds.), *The handbook of global media and communication policy* (pp. 166–179). Wiley-Blackwell.

Croucher, S. M. (2008). French-Muslims and the hajib: An analysis of identity and the Islamic veil in France. *Journal of Intercultural Communication Research*, *37*(3), 199–213.

Czitrom, D. J. (1982). *Media and the American mind: From Morse to McLuhan*. University of North Carolina Press.

Drzewiecka, J. A. (2002). Reinventing and contesting identities in constitutive discourses: Between diaspora and its others. *Communication Quarterly*, *50*(1), 1–23.

Du Bois, W. E. B. (1903). *The souls of Black folk: Essays and sketches*. A. C. McClurg.

Du Pont, C. T. (1919). The Interracial Council: What it is and hopes to do. *Advertising and Selling*, *29*(5), 1–2.

Goldberg, C. A. (2017). Robert Park's marginal man: The career of a concept in American sociology. In P. Kivisto (Ed.), *The Anthem companion to Robert Park* (pp. 159–180). Anthem Press.

Hardt, H. (1989). The foreign-language press in American press history. *Journal of Communication*, *39*(2), 114–131.

Hecht, M. (1993). 2002 — A research odyssey: Toward the development of a communication theory of identity. *Communication Monographs*, *60*(1), 76-82.

Herakova, L. L. (2009). Identity, communication, inclusion: The Roma and (new) Europe. *Journal of International and Intercultural Communication*, *2*(4), 279-297.

Hollander, E., Hidayat, D. N., & d'Haenens, L. (2008). Community radio in Indonesia: A reinvention of democratic communication. *Javnost: Journal of the European Institute for Communication and Culture*, *15*(3), 59-74.

Hughes, E. C., Johnson, C. S., Masuoka, J., Redfield, R., & Wirth, L. (Eds.) (1950). *Race and culture: The collected papers of Robert Ezra Park*. Free Press.

Jankowski, N. (2002). Creating community with media: History, theories and scientific investigations. In L. Lievrouw & S. Livingstone (Eds.), *The handbook of new media: Social shaping and the consequences of ICTs* (pp. 34-49). Sage.

Jansen, S. C. (2010). Forgotten histories: Another road not taken — The Charles Merriam-Walter Lippmann correspondence. *Communication Theory*, *20*(2), 127-146.

Kharlamov, N. A. (2012). Boundary zone between cultural worlds or the edge of the dominant culture? Two conceptual metaphors of marginality. *Journal of Intercultural Studies*, *33*(6), 623-638.

Kim, Y. Y. (2007). Ideology, identity, and intercultural communication: An analysis of differing academic conceptions of cultural identity. *Journal of Intercultural Communication Research*, *36*(3), 237-253.

Kivisto, P. (2017). Robert E. Park's theory of assimilation and beyond. In P. Kivisto (Ed.), *The Anthem companion to Robert Park* (pp. 131-157). Anthem Press.

Kramsch, C., & Uryu, M. (2020). Intercultural contact, hybridity, and third space. In J. Jackson (Ed.), *The Routledge handbook of language and intercultural communication* (2nd ed., pp. 204-218). Routledge.

Kulich, S. J., Weng, L., Tong, R., & DuBois, G. (2020). Interdisciplinary history of intercultural communication studies: From roots to research and praxis. In D. Landis & D. P. S. Bhawuk (Eds.), *The Cambridge handbook of intercultural training* (4th ed., pp. 60-163). Cambridge University Press.

Levine, D. N., Carter, E. B., & Gorman, E. M. (1976). Simmel's influence on American sociology. *American Journal of Sociology*, *81*(4), 813-845.

MacDonald, M. N., & O'Regan, J. P. (2012). A global agenda for intercultural communication research and practice. In J. Jackson (Ed.), *The Routledge handbook of language and intercultural communication* (pp. 553-567). Routledge.

Magubane, Z. (2014). Science, reform, and the 'science of reform': Booker T. Washington, Robert Park and the making of a 'science of society.' *Current Sociology*, *62*(4), 568-583.

Marotta, V. (2006). Civilisation, culture and the hybrid self in the work of Robert Ezra Park. *Journal of Intercultural Studies*, *27*(4), 413-433.

Marotta, V. (2016). *Theories of the stranger: Debates on cosmopolitanism, identity and cross-cultural encounters*. Routledge.

Martins, H. (1974). Time and theory in sociology. In J. Rex (Ed.), *Approaches to sociology: An introduction to major trends in British sociology* (pp. 246-294). Routledge and Kegan Paul.

Mendoza, S. L., Halualani, R. T., & Drzewiecka, J. A. (2002). Moving the discourse on identities in intercultural communication: Structure, culture, and resignifications. *Communication Quarterly*, *50*(3/4), 312–327.

Muhlmann, G. (2010). *Journalism for democracy*. Polity.

Muhlmann, G., & Plenel, E. (2008). *Le journaliste et le sociologue* [The journalist and the sociologist]. Paris: Éditions du Seuil.

Olorunnisola, A. A. (2002). Community radio as participatory communication in post-apartheid South Africa. *Journal of Radio Studies*, *9*(1), 126–145.

Park, R. E. (1920). Foreign language press and social progress. *Proceedings of the National Conference of Social Work*, 493–500.

Park, R. E. (1922). *The immigrant press and its control*. Harper & Brothers.

Park, R. E. (1923). The natural history of the newspaper. *American Journal of Sociology*, *29*(3), 273–289.

Peters, J. D. (1989). Satan and the savior: Mass communication in progressive thought. *Critical Studies in Mass Communication*, *6*(3), 247–263.

Phillips, E. B. (1976). Novelty without change. *Journal of Communication*, *26*(4), 87–92.

Pooley, J. (2007). Daniel Czitrom, James W. Carey, and the Chicago School. *Critical Studies in Media Communication*, *24*, 469–472.

Pooley, J., & Katz, E. (2008). Further notes on why American sociology abandoned mass communication research. *Journal of Communication*, *58*, 767–786.

Quandt, J. (1970). *From the small town to the great community: The social thought of progressive intellectuals*. Rutgers University Press.

Raushenbush, W. (1979). *Robert E. Park: Biography of a sociologist*. Duke University Press.

Rogers, E. M. (1994). *A history of communication study: A biographical approach*. Free Press.

Rogers, E. M. (1999). Georg Simmel's concept of the stranger and intercultural communication research. *Communication Theory*, *9*(1), 58–74.

Ruwet, C. (2017). The cities of Robert Ezra Park: Toward a periodization of his conception of the metropolis (1915–39). In P. Kivisto (Ed.), *The Anthem companion to Robert Park* (pp. 201–224). Anthem Press.

Simmel, G. (1950 [1903]). The metropolis and mental life. In K. H. Wolff (Ed.), *The sociology of Georg Simmel* (pp. 409–424). Free Press.

Simmel, G. (1971 [1908]). The stranger. In D. N. Levine (Ed.), *Georg Simmel: On individuality and social forms* (pp. 143–149). University of Chicago Press.

Soja, E. W. (1996). *Thirdspace: Journeys to Los Angeles and other real-and-imagined places*. Wiley-Blackwell.

Subtil, F., & Garcia, J. L. (2010). Communication: An inheritance of the Chicago School of social thought. In C. Hart (Ed.), *Legacy of the Chicago School: A collection of essays in honour of the Chicago School of sociology during the first half of the 20th century* (pp. 216–243). Midrash.

Thomas, W. I., & Znaniecki, F. (1984 [1918–1920]). *The Polish peasant in Europe and America: Monograph of an immigrant group*. University of Chicago Press.

Toomey, A., Dorjee, T., & Ting-Toomey, S. (2013). Bicultural identity negotiation, conflicts, and intergroup communication strategies. *Journal of Intercultural Communication Research*, *42*(2), 112–134.

Wilkin, H. A., Ball-Rokeach, S. J., Matsaganis, M. D., & Cheong, P. H. (2007). Comparing the communication ecologies of geo-ethnic communities: How people stay on top of their community. *Electronic Journal of Communication*, *17* (1 - 2), 387–406.

Wimmer, A., & Schiller, N. G. (2002). Methodological nationalism and beyond: Nation-state building, migration and the social sciences. *Global Networks*, *2* (4), 301–334.

Witteborn, S. (2007). The situated expression of Arab collective identities in the United States. *Journal of Communication*, *57*(3), 556–575.

Zhou, V. X., & Pilcher, N. (2019). Revisiting the 'third space' in language and intercultural studies. *Language and Intercultural Studies*, *19*(1), 1–8.

Znaniecki, F. (1940). *The social role of the man of knowledge*. Columbia University Press.

12

Nation-States, National Cultures, and Intercultural Communication: A Theoretical Inquiry

Rongtian TONG
University of Washington

Summary: The nation-state, as a form of polity, has achieved global dominance (Herzfeld, 2021). Yet within the scope of human history, both the nation-state, as a form of polity, and its dominance are relatively recent phenomena (Burbank & Cooper, 2010). Prior to its ascendancy, the world was filled with a plethora of distinct and unique forms of polities (see Graeber & Wengrow, 2021). How and why, then, did the sweeping transition into a *homogeneous* system of nation-states occur? This chapter aims to review some of the seminal theories — both classical and contemporary — that dissect the rationale behind the formation of the nation-state. It will also explore the historical, philosophical, political, and cultural factors that ultimately led to the arrival of the nation-state as the dominant form of polity.

Understanding the underpinnings of the nation-state is critical to Intercultural Communication, as the field finds its *origins* (see Kulich et al., 2020) in a time and place where the concept of culture both constructed and emerged out of the nation-state. By elucidating the assumptions on which the nation-state is built, perhaps it will lead us to rethink our ideas of culture, how it should be measured, and how it should be analyzed in the future.

1. Introduction

> Nation-states do not exist, simply because the so-called
> "nations" or "peoples" of which the nationalists dream do not exist.
> There are no, or hardly any, homogeneous ethnic groups long
> settled in countries with natural borders.
> — Popper, *Conjectures and Refutations*, 1962

Intercultural Communication (IC) as an academic field studies "how people from different 'cultural' backgrounds interact with each other and negotiate 'cultural' or linguistic differences perceived or made relevant through interactions" (Hua, 2016, p. 27). Are these cultural backgrounds and differences coextensive with nation-states, and with national cultures? Chesebro (1998) revealed a tendency within IC research to adopt the nation-state as a unit of cultural comparison. Similarly, in a critique of Chesebro, Ono (2010) has noted how "comparing nations" is a "defining approach" to IC research (p. 87). This approach has also been extensively practiced by Geert Hofstede and colleagues, who argue that the term "culture" is used for "nations" in political science, sociology, and management. They suggest that societal culture is rooted in "values," which are reflected in "broad tendencies to prefer certain states of affairs over others" (Hofstede, 2012, p. 183) and hence guiding principles. More specifically, this approach goes back to national character study, interpreted by Alex Inkeles and Daniel Levinson since the 1950s as enabling analytic issues focused on "relation to authority," "the individual's concepts of masculinity and femininity," and "primary dilemmas or conflicts, and ways of dealing with them" (Hofstede, 2012, p. 186).

This form of analysis (with a few others) became significant for Hofstede's research, where "nations" are synonymous with "countries," and indeed, "national culture" has been forcefully vindicated as "a meaningful concept" in studying cultural values within "homogeneous national clusters" (Minkov & Hofstede, 2012). As a result, "cultural values" are perceived, rightly or not, to be statistically measurable (Kulich & He, 2012, p. 72). Most recently, Akaliyski et al. (2021) argue that "aggregation" makes it possible to "distill the central cultural tendencies of nations" (p. 1). Yet national character studies are diagnosed by Wendy Leeds-Hurwitz (2010) as having "limited the growth of intercultural communication research, which now sees each country as more heterogeneous" (p. 30). Can both of these sets of assumptions be valid? Or is one problematic, and the other less so?

While there is no doubt that culture is a collective phenomenon, this chapter argues that the focus on nations and nation-states as primary units of cultural analysis and comparison can be problematic for several reasons. For one, it suggests that the population of a nation-state can be represented by a single national culture. While it is true that nation-states play a pivotal role in identity formation — after all, "identification as an individual is scarcely thinkable without categories of collective identity" (Caplan & Torpey, 2002, p. 3) — it is equally important to recognize the nation-state as a social construct (see Ono, 2010). There can be no doubt, of course, that any national culture contains a great variety and diversity of individual personalities (as acknowledged by Hofstede, 2012, p. 191). Nation-states were not formed on the basis of distinct *a priori* ethnic differences — though Barth (1969), and others, take issue with the idea that there is an equivalence between ethnicity and culture as well. Instead, many nation-states were formed as a result of intersecting geopolitical factors, and often through violent and coerced means (see Burbank & Cooper, 2010; Roeder, 2007). Colonialism, for example, has played a paramount role in the establishment of nation-states; indeed, Herzfeld (2021) argues that the modern nation-state is a "child of Victorian evolutionism and of European global colonialism" (p. 4).

This brings us to the second concern: the use of nation-states as units of analysis does not take into consideration the contextual factors that led to each nation-state's creation. By reducing nation-states to uniform and measurable units, it promotes the assumption that nation-states are equal in their creation and can, consequently, equally represent their citizens. That this is not always justified will become clearer later in this chapter. The lack of context also means that the dimensions produced by national scales and measures are often at a superficial level and lack real explanatory value. This is problematic because, as noted by Ono (2010), the portrayal of nation-states "as coherent entities and as stable and fixed formations often serves to reify notions of difference and commonality — rather than putting them into question" (p. 88).

This leads to the third problem: as nation-states are established through the process of connecting the present to the past (Anderson, 2006), this focus on superficial differences and similarities leads to a process of ahistoricism where the past, present, and even future may be misinterpreted or distorted. To elaborate, Hall (1990) provides two definitions of cultural identity, with the first being based on a collective's "shared history and ancestry" (p. 223). Yet Hall's (1990) second definition recognizes that cultural identity is not just a matter of "being," but also "becoming," as cultural identities undergo constant transformations. In other words, no culture throughout history keeps a static and changeless identity. Beugelsdijk and Welzel's (2018) analysis of data from the European Value Studies and World Values Surveys even provides evidence of cultural change at the national level over time. Yet the authors also argue that the relative cultural positions of nation-states remain stable, and that findings using measures such as Hofstede's dimensions "will not be significantly affected by temporal variation, as long as the country scores are interpreted in a relative sense" (p. 1499).

To expand on this notion of relativity and why it may be problematic: a number of Western and Eastern societies, for example, are often compared cross-culturally for their differences regarding dominant values and traits (e.g., Markus & Kitayama, 1991; Nisbett et al., 2001; Triandis, 2014). It should be noted that even if authors did not originally intend for their works to be used to represent societies or used comparatively, successive researchers can reinterpret their works in such a fashion. In any case, a simple distinction between what is taken to be Western individualism and Eastern collectivism would lead to a false understanding of both, especially if Confucianism is believed to be unchanging so that Eastern societies would for this reason continue to be collectivistic. Of course, this is not to say that certain historical processes are not without legacies and do not shape certain culture and values, but as Hsu (2017) points out, "concepts such as collectivism and shame, especially with the support of references to ancient Chinese texts, are presented as essential and timeless keys to unlocking Chinese culture" (p. 104). Hsu (2017) then states that "over-reliance on these perspectives runs the risk of creating a caricatured and anachronistic view of Chinese culture" (p. 104). If we take culture to be "a dynamically fluid concept," we should not neglect considering a temporal dimension of cultural diversity in relation to dominant value frameworks (e.g., Shearman, 2012, pp. 172-173; see also Wu, 2006).

To clarify these concerns, the present chapter consists of three sections:

The next following section seeks to set the theoretical and philosophical framing upon which the nation-state is built. Rather than attempting to trace ideas to their genealogical origins, it focuses specifically on the period of the Enlightenment — as the nation-state, arguably, arose out of the confluence of ideas from this time period. The aim of this section is twofold: (1) to demonstrate the epistemological limits of the time when ideas such as *race*, *culture*, and *nation* were conceived and (2) to demonstrate how the practice of comparing national cultures is rooted in the foundations of IC. Many of the works introduced in this section are not referenced or quoted in their original language, but rather in English renderings.

The section after that aims to explore the theoretical means through which nation-states were established — such as the factors that led to the emergence of nationalism in the early 19th century. It will discuss the theories of Anderson (1983/2006), Foucault (1978/ 1996), and Weber (1922/2019), among others, to explore the intersection of discrete historical circumstances that led to the eventual rise of nation-states, and demonstrate how states endeavored to shape and unify their populations *artificially* through means such as establishing shared heritages, traditions, and collective identities.

The final section details how many nation-states were not formed on the basis of cultural homogeneity or culture, but rather on other exigent factors. It will delve into the elements necessary for new nation-states to emerge, why not all cultural groups can form a state of their own, and how many nation-state projects ultimately end up in failure. Here it should be acknowledged that the chapter cannot claim to account for the larger history of nationhood, nationalism, the nation-state, or forms of government, as the focus is (and keeps returning to) the nexus between nationhood and culture. This section will then contain brief considerations of concepts such as cultural intimacy, multiculturalism, and findings within socio-ecological psychology as further evidence that scrutinizes the limitations of using national cultures as a framework for research.

In a strict sense, a comparative method regarding societies or nations or cultures, which is widely practiced and has offered perceptions of characteristic similarities and differences, hardly belongs within the orbit of intercultural study, the focus of which should be more on interactions (as declared at the outset). Hence a focus on nations and nationhood as such may appear to have only a loose connection to intercultural study and methodology. Nonetheless, the present Intercultural Research book series has repeatedly included a focus on comparative studies of values at the national or country level (for instance Hofstede, 2012; Schwartz, 2012; Shearman, 2012), so that an inquiry into the relation between culture and nation belongs in this thematic context.

2. Defining the Nation-State and Its Theoretical and Philosophical Roots

The term *nation-state* is a conjunction of the terms *nation* and *state*. A *nation*, as defined by Seton-Watson (1977), is a "community of people, whose members are bound together by a sense of solidarity, a common culture, a national consciousness," whereas a *state* is a "legal and political organization, with the power to require obedience and loyalty from its citizens" (p. 1). The emphasis on "a common culture" is significant for our context. These definitions, however, are often open to broader interpretations and frequently used interchangeably (see Akaliyski et al., 2021; Seton-Watson, 1977). Similarly, this confusion extends to the union of these two terms, the nation-state, and the present chapter itself will not be able to escape this indeterminacy entirely in some contexts.

While there isn't a single authoritative definition of the nation-state, many interpretations emphasize homogeneity within a particular polity: "the nation-state assumes that the nation expresses a certain national identity, is founded through the concerted consensus of a nation, and that a certain correspondence exists between the state and the nation" (Butler & Spivak, 2007, p. 30; see also Burbank & Cooper, 2010; Herzfeld, 2021). An exact point of origin for the nation-state is unclear due to its varying definitions and interpretations. However, according to Wimmer and Feinstein (2010), 145 of today's states achieved nation-statehood within the last 200 years. Wimmer and Feinstein (2010) pinpoint the American and French revolutions as the impetus for the nation-state's emergence, as these revolutions provided the ideal of "an independent state with a written constitution, ruled in the name of a nation of equal citizens" (p. 764). Similarly, Roeder (2007) notes how the "American Declaration of Independence and the French Declaration of the Rights of Man and the Citizen ushered in an age of nationalism that led to the conscious creation of nation-states" (p. 5). Thus, we begin with a look at the Enlightenment, as the political philosophies and dialogical conversations of that time led to such appeals and conclusions (see Bailyn, 1967).

During the Enlightenment, many theories on the relationship

between the people and government emerged. Hobbes' *Leviathan* (1651) argues that "the condition of man [...] is a condition of war of every one against every one; in which case every one is governed by his own reason" (1996, p. 86). For Hobbes, *sovereign power* is necessary to achieve societal peace — as sovereignty regulates man's *state of nature*. Hobbes (1651) introduces the term *leviathan* as an analogy for the State or Commonwealth — where the sovereign, as the head, commands and gives life to the *body politic* (1996, see p. 7; for analysis, see Martinich & Hoekstra, 2016). Antithetically, Rousseau refutes Hobbes's beliefs, and argues that Hobbes wrongly attributes the negative qualities of humanity to nature. Instead, Rousseau asserts that it is society that corrupts humanity: "goodness of heart suitable to the pure state of nature by no means was suitable for the new society" (2002, p. 119). Furthermore, Rousseau begins *The Social Contract* (1762) with the statement: "[m]an was born free, and everywhere he is in chains" (2002, p. 156). Yet Rousseau also acknowledges the necessity of society — as the *primitive* state of nature was insufficient for survival: "this primitive condition can no longer subsist, and the human race would perish unless it changed its mode of existence" (2002, p. 163). Rousseau's solution was for individuals to enter a social contract with the community rather than a sovereign: "each of us puts in common his person and all his power under the supreme direction of the general will; and in return each member becomes an indivisible part of the whole" (2002, p. 164). Similarly, Montesquieu's *The Spirit of the Laws* (1748) argues that for government to be effective, political institutions must reflect the social features of the community it represents: "the government most conformable to nature is that which best agrees with the humour and disposition of the people" (1777, p. 7). This view comes close to suggesting the consistency of collective values in a national body. Montesquieu (1748) further argues that government should be relative to climate and geographic conditions, as such conditions shape human behavior (see already Hippocrates's *Of Air, Waters and Places*, chapter 12).

Two assumptions are pertinent here. The first is the emerging belief that government can and should represent the "disposition" or "will" of the people — as expressed by Montesquieu (1748) and Rousseau (1762) respectively. The shifting focus from the sovereign and state to the people becomes the foundational basis of the nation-state, a topic that will be readdressed in the section on Foucault's *governmentality*. The second is the division, designation, and comparison of *primitive* and *modern* forms of civilizations based on differences between peoples and their cultures. As interpreted by Lovejoy (1923), Rousseau's state of nature has multiple connotations, among which it "may be used — and in the eighteenth century was often used — in what may be called a cultural sense, to designate the state in which the arts and sciences — civilization in its non-political clements — had made least progress" (p. 166). Thus, as suggested by Rousseau, some states of nature, or collective being, are considered primitive while others are considered more modern.

There are many potential explanations for the emergence of primitive and modern societal divisions. Graeber and Wengrow (2021) argue that this division was a reaction to indigenous Native American critiques of European society. Specifically, they link Turgot's argument that equality was only possible in primitive societies where households are self-sufficient to the Wendat statesman Kandiaronk's criticisms on European inequality (Graeber & Wengrow, 2021). Graeber and Wengrow (2021) also refer to Gregory Bateson's concept of "schismogenesis," and argue that if national characters do indeed exist, it is the result of the schismogenetic process where societies are defined by their differences (see p. 57). A partly similar explanation is also provided by Said (1978), who traces how European imperial powers aimed to simplify, stereotype, and demean other cultures as a means to dominate the *Orient*.

In any case, this view of a social-Darwinist division between civilizations grew to become accepted and prevalent among many European Enlightment thinkers of the time (e.g., Hume, 1748/ 1987; Kant, 1764/2011), and resulted in further racist *Othering* and stereotyping of civilizations from Asia, Africa, and the Americas. While the notion of *Othering* existed long before the Enlightenment (see Steppat & Tong, 2021, also in Vol. 12), what is unique about the Enlightenment was the "injection" of axiomatic principles found within the natural sciences to the humanities and emerging social sciences — which created a newfound interest and emphasis on *ethnotaxonomy* and the demarcation of different peoples (see Zack, 2017). A basic genealogy of conceptual categorizations (i. e ., species, race, culture) is offered here as such a history of organizing criteria offers insights into how the world is often interpreted and researched today — as the values, norms, beliefs, and experiences of previous generations both directly and indirectly shape our current perspectives and procedures.

Hume in his essay *Of National Characters* (1748) theorizes that *moral causes* shape *national character*. For example, he notes:

> [w]here a number of men are united into one political body, the occasions of their intercourse must be so frequent, for defence, commerce, and government, that, together with the same speech or language, they must acquire a resemblance in their manners, and have a common or national character. (1987, pp. 202–203; see also Martinelli, 2016)

Hume's concept has been influential (see also Caro Baroja, 1970). This idea of *moral causes* proposes an additional dimension to the physical causes (e. g., climate conditions) addressed by Montesquieu (1748). Hume offers some generalizations:

> [t]he common people in Switzerland have probably more honesty than those of the same rank in Ireland. [...] We have reason to expect greater wit and gaiety in a Frenchman than in a Spaniard. [...] An Englishman will naturally be supposed to have more knowledge than a Dane. (1987, pp. 197–198)

Hume's comment on *those of the same rank* is significant: it suggests, without elaborating, that there are character differences across occupational and class roles, thus implying a differentiation regarding the notion of a homogeneous national culture. Nevertheless, these stereotypes also appear to be linked to their respective nations, and this connection is significant notwithstanding the differences based on rank. Potentially, one can trace a thin line from here to the refined methodology of Hofstede, who studied the values evinced by employees in the local subsidiaries of IBM. At the same time, Hume doubts that someone of primitive descent who enters and acclimates to the conditions of a particular modern civilization would attain the national character of that modern civilization. To justify this position, Hume takes a *polygenicist* stance and casts different peoples as entirely different species that, like animals, are incapable of changing their disposition:

> I am apt to suspect the negroes to be naturally inferior to the whites. There scarcely ever was a civilized nation of that complexion, nor even any individual eminent either in action or speculation. No ingenious manufactures amongst them, no arts, no sciences [...]. (1987, p. 208)

Kant (1775), on the other hand, was a *monogenicist* who believed that humans share a singular species origin — through the logic that different peoples can interbreed (Mikkelsen, 2013). However, he similarly argued that environmental factors produced irreversible human traits, and that the demarcation of race (*Rasse*) should be based on inheritable differences between different peoples. It is in Kant's work that we witness the first *scientific* theory of race (Bernasconi & Lott, 2000) — which was influential among German natural scientists of the time (Sandford, 2018). Kant's categorization of race was primarily based on skin pigmentation (e.g., white, black, yellow, and red), and he believed that race had a hierarchical division — arguing that the white race had a higher mental and moral capacity than other races (1764, 1775). There is a body of scholarly work dedicated to parsing out Kant's views on race, the degree to which Kant was concerned with race, and the apparent contradictions between Kant's cosmopolitan philosophy, his universal narrative, and his attitudes toward non-whites (see Eze, 2003; Mikkelsen, 2013; Sandford, 2018). Without getting too much into the weeds, for our purposes, a seminal quote of importance from Kant (1788) is his account of Native Americans: "[...] this race, which is too weak for hard labor, too indifferent for industry and incapable of any culture [...] ranks still far below even the Negro" (2007b, p. 211). Essentially, this quote reveals how culture was interpreted at the time. In what would later be referred to as *high culture* (see Arnold, 1869), the concept of culture during the Enlightenment was largely tied to labor discipline and to intellectual and artistic endeavors, and thus, as demonstrated in both the preceding Hume and Kant quotes, was believed to be limited to certain peoples or classes. Yet for a fair assessment of Kant's racial views, it should be noted in his 1795 essay *Perpetual Peace* (Third Definitive Article), Kant condemns the "injustice" of European commercial states toward the peoples they visit and conquer and the "oppression of the natives" (1903, p. 139).

In terms of Kant's purview of nations, *The Stanford Encyclopedia of Philosophy* notes that when Kant refers to the *right of nations* or a *league of nations*, he is not referring to "nations as peoples but to states as organizations" (Rauscher, 2021, Section 8). Kant (1798) seemingly disapproves of Hume's view on the correspondence between government and character, arguing: "to claim that the kind of character a people will have depends entirely on its form of government is an ungrounded assertion that explains nothing; for from where does the government itself get its particular character?" (2006, p. 215). Instead, Kant (1798) maintains that it is "language, type of occupation, and even type of dress" that "reveal traces of [...] ancestry, and consequently [...] character" (2006, p. 215). Kant (1798) makes a demarcation between innate and artificial characters, speaking of "natural character which, so to speak, lies in the blood mixture of the human being, not characteristics of nations that are acquired and artificial" (2006, p. 222). Kant then provides some innate characters for France, England, Spain, Italy, and Germany based on their ancestry, while stating:

> Russia has not yet developed what is necessary for a definite concept of natural predispositions. [...] Poland is no longer at this stage; and [...] the nationals of European Turkey never have attained and never will attain what is necessary for the acquisition of a definite national character. (2006, pp. 221–222)

By contrast, Herder (1784) contends that all peoples (*Volk/ Völker*) have a culture (*Kultur*). *Outlines of a Philosophy of the History of Man* (1784) begins by agreeing with earlier Enlightenment scholars on how different environments shape different peoples and societies: "[n]ature stretched the rough but firm outline of the history of man and its revolutions [...] hence, according to the circumstances of the place, various modes of life and ultimately kingdoms rose" (Herder, 1800, pp. 18 – 19). Herder explains that "[s]eas, mountains, and rivers, are the most natural boundaries of nations, manners, languages, and kingdoms" (1800, p. 19). Herder (1784) argues that environmental and geographic factors shape the type of society that emerges:

> [o]ne height produced nations of hunters, thus cherishing and rendering necessary a savage state; another, more extended and mild, afforded a field to the shepherd and associated with him inoffensive animals; a third made agriculture easy and necessary; while a fourth led to fishing, to navigation, and at length to trade. (1800, p. 19)

Yet in a departure from some previous assumptions, Herder maintains that societies don't progress in a universal, preordained, or linear *primitive* to *modern* fashion (Cohen & Sheringham, 2016; White, 2005). Herder further states that each *Volk* experiences happiness within their own cultural conditions:

> [t]he very name of happiness implies that man is neither susceptible of pure bliss nor capable of creating felicity for himself, " and he highlights a person's " capacity of enjoyment and the kind and

measure of his joys and sorrows, according to the country, time, organization, and circumstances, in which he lives. (1800, pp. 218-219)

Herder then claims that: "[...] the most natural state therefore is one nation with one national character" (1800, p. 249), with similar arguments elsewhere (see also section 3.2 for language):

[t]heir own mode of representing things is the more deeply imprinted on every nation because it is adapted to themselves, is suitable to their own Earth and sky, springs from their mode of living, and has been handed down to them from father to son. (1800, p. 197)

However, we should note that, while Herder's works are often interpreted and used in the context of reinforcing culturally homogeneous nations — thus appearing to anticipate the methodological assumptions of some modern researchers — his writings also suggest that cultural plurality exists among different communities within nations (see Barnard, 1969; Spencer, 2007). Like Hume (1748), Herder argues that there are occupational divisions within nations that influence individuals: "[t]he shepherd beholds nature with different eyes from those of the fisherman or hunter; and again, in every region these occupations differ as much as the character of the people by whom they are exercised" (1800, p. 199). Unfortunately, this perspective has been largely eclipsed by the emphasis on national cultures, but the indeterminacy is worth clarifying here. Herder also defends the rights of different *Völker* against European chauvinisim:

[n]o Nimrod has yet been able to drive all the inhabitants of the world into one park for himself and his successors; and though it has been for centuries the object of united Europe [...] compelling all the nations of the earth to be happy in her way, this happiness-dispensing deity is yet far from having obtained her end. (1800, p. 224)

Furthermore, Herder opposes the act of states subsuming multiple nations, and writes:

[a] human scepter is far too weak and slender for such incongruous parts to be engrafted upon it; glued together indeed they may be into a fragile machine, termed a machine of state, but destitute of internal vivification and sympathy of parts. (1800, p. 249)

We should not overlook that, much earlier, Vico in *The New Science* (1725) criticizes "the conceit of nations" where each nation believes they "invented the comforts of life" (1948, Section 1.2.125). In terms of historical accuracy, this is overstated, but that need not concern us here. Vico (1725) also notes a tendency for humans to make themselves "the measure of all things" as they judge "distant and unknown things" by what is "familiar at hand" (1948, Sections 1.2.120, 1.2.122). Presumably, these critiques by Vico are directed at Enlightenment writers who judge other cultures as primitive. As Berlin (2013a) interprets Vico, Vico attacked theorists

> who seemed to him to have perpetrated unhistorical anachronisms: like the upholders of theories of natural law or social contract, who credited primitive men with some of the civilised attributes of their own "magnificent" age; and those [...] who [...] assumed the existence of a fixed, unchanging human nature, common to all men, everywhere, at all times. [...] (p.67)

Vico (1725) also writes that "[h]uman choice, by its nature most uncertain, is made certain and determined by the common sense of men with respect to human needs or utilities, which are the two origins of the natural law of nations" (1948, Section 1.2.142). Vico further asserts that "[c]ommon sense is judgment without reflection, shared by an entire class, an entire people, an entire nation, or the whole human race" (1948, Section 1.2.143). According to Marková (2016), Vico's understanding of common sense drew on the Stoic meaning of the term, and is thus "inseparable from moral conduct" and is "accompanied by rhetorical speaking and thinking" (p.47). While Vico does provide discrete categories of shared common sense (e.g., class), the nation being one of those categories suggests that Vico believed in some semblance of a national understanding of morals and rhetoric.

Based on Vico's previously quoted "axioms," Berlin (2013b) claims that

> Vico is the true father both of the modern concept of culture and of what one might call cultural pluralism, according to which each authentic culture has its own unique vision, its own scale of values, which, in the course of development, is superseded by other visions and values, but never wholly so: that is, earlier value-systems do not become unintelligible to succeeding generations. (p.62)

Recent research argues, at any rate, that what Berlin found in Vico was "certain moral norms within all the different cultural forms," so that all nations have some "principles of humanity" in common (Mali, 2012, p. 253). Berlin (2013b) does, however, acknowledge that "Herder may have been the effective discoverer of the nature of this kind of imaginative insight" (p. 62).

Ultimately, it is from Herder's conceptualizations that the idea of a *cultural* nation was concretely formed and later popularized (see Kulich et al., 2020). While Herder did not directly claim that every nation had to have its own state, Patten (2010) notes that it can be inferred through quotes such as: "[a] kingdom consisting of a single nation is a family, a well-regulated household. [...] An empire formed by forcing together a hundred nations and a hundred and fifty provinces is no body politic, but a monster" (Herder, 1800, p. 325). Therefore, Herder's *cultural* nation is not purely cultural, but has political implications as well. His criteria for nations (i. e., culture and language) is believed to serve as a basis and justification for the breakaway and formation of nation-states from other forms of polities (van Benthem van den Bergh, 2018). According to Cohen and Sheringham (2016), "[t]he Herderian legacy created a dominant mind map portraying multiple cultures that served to isolate the people of the world into hermetically sealed caged identities" (p. 27). It is from Herder's concept of *Kultur* — and more broadly the German idealist tradition — where early anthropologists (e. g., Boas, 1911; Tylor, 1871) would later develop their understanding of culture (see Adams, 1998; Kulich et al., 2020; Lentz, 2017). This understanding would then, in turn, be inherited by the field of IC, resulting in a proclivity for examining culture at a national level (see Kulich et al., 2020). For instance, concerning the idea of "national" character, Leeds-Hurwitz (2010) observes: "[n]ational character research is never named in early intercultural communication writings, but it had substantial impact on the assumptions of Edward Hall, who then influenced the assumptions of other, later scholars" (p. 30).

As Leeds-Hurwitz (2010) further notes, in research carried out between the 1930s and 1950s, a "single culture" was often interpreted as "a single country," so that each country was treated as "a monolithic whole" (pp. 25 & 30). Yet while this "made sense" in early research, "the easy match between culture and nation is now out of date" (Leeds-Hurwitz, 2010, p. 30). Hofstede's methodology, accordingly, has been critiqued as "an over-simplified way to categorize cultures," making country scores appear "stereotypical" (as reported by Kulich &

He, 2012, p.73; also Ono, 2010, p.90) — though Hofstede himself warns that national culture scores "should not be used for stereotyping individuals" (2012, p.192). Ultimately, the doubts about matching culture and nation clash with the research methodology used by Hofstede and Minkov, and others, so that the match needs further scrutiny. Can a historical and partly genetic perspective cast light on this conceptual difference?

3. Formation of the Nation-State and Nationalism

3.1 Two Schools of Thought

When we consider the notion of culturally homogeneous nations and nation-states, we should ask how and from what origins they are formed. Analyses explaining this do not necessarily refer to culture, in any specific sense, and tend to go beyond our line of inquiry, but such insights will bring us back to a better understanding of the role of culture in our context. Historically, there are two opposing interpretations of nation formation: *primordialism* and *modernism*. The primordialist tradition traces back to Enlightenment thinkers such as Rousseau and Herder (Bellamy, 2003; Cohen & Sheringham, 2016). Essentially, primordialists view modern nation-states as a continuity from *a priori* ethnic groups that share a common heritage (Bellamy, 2003).

Edward Shils (1957) and Clifford Geertz (1963) are often credited as the founders of the primordialist perspective. Shils (1957) provided a theoretical framework for primordialism by arguing that modern society is "held together by an infinity of" elements such as "primordial affinities" (p.131). Analyzing primary group attachments (see Cooley, 1909), Shils (1957) notes how "the attachment was not merely to the other family member as a person, but as a possessor of certain especially 'significant relational' qualities, which could only be described as primordial" (p.142). Shils (1957) then extends this attachment based on the "tie of blood" to the larger society: "[t]he primordial or ecological basis of Gemeinschaft thus seemed to me to be not merely a precondition of the formation of Gemeinschaft but a very crucial property of the members which greatly influenced their conduct towards each other" (p.142). Shils's (1957) text remains somewhat ambiguous in terms of the connection between primordial attachments and ethnicity — as Shils hardly addresses ethnicity directly. Nevertheless, based on Shils, Geertz (1963) formalized the concept of primordialism by stating "primordial attachment [...] stems from the 'givens' — or, [...] as culture is inevitably involved in such matters, the assumed 'givens' — of social existence" (p. 109). Geertz (1963) then identifies six forms of primordial ties that form the basis of the nation: (1) assumed blood ties, (2) race, (3) language, (4) region, (5) religion, and (6) customs (see pp. 112–113).

By contrast, the modernist approach considers nations and nationalism to be products of modernity. For the most part, primordialism has fallen out of relevance within the humanities and social sciences. As stated by Brubaker (1996): "[n]o serious scholar today holds the view that is routinely attributed to primordialists [...] that nations or ethnic groups are primordial, unchanging entities. Everyone agrees that nations are historically formed constructs [...]" (p. 15).

So how and why did early scholars arrive at the conclusion that is the now defunct primordialist position? As previously mentioned, the broad characterization and categorization of different peoples were in part economically and politically motivated (e.g., Said, 1978). As asserted by JanMohamed (1985), "[t]he perception of racial difference is, in the first place, influenced by economic motives" (p. 61). Prior to the establishment of the triangular trade, "Africans were perceived in a more or less neutral and benign manner" (JanMohamed, 1985, p. 61). A similar process happens with British and American portrayals of China (see Tong, in our companion volume). These categorizations were then further reinforced by limitations in early philosophical postulations of different peoples and societies — which were also influenced by politics. It should be noted that many national academies that were established in the 17th and 18th centuries — such as the Royal Society of London in 1662, the French Academy of Sciences in 1666, and the Prussian Academy of Sciences in 1700 — were "partly founded to support the commercial interests of their respective countries" (Hsia, 1998, pp. 14–15), and furthermore, were closely linked to their respective governments (see Gascoigne, 1999). Moreover, as noted by Foucault (1966), "in any given culture and at any given moment, there is always only one *episteme* that defines the conditions of possibility of all knowledge, whether expressed in a theory or silently invested in a practice" (2001, p. 183).

However, the belief in hermeneutically boxed cultures and nations also emerged from a "spontaneous distillation of a complex 'crossing' of discrete historical forces" (Anderson, 2006, p. 5). These historical forces were largely political, as "European governments gradually came to adopt the idea that every government should properly preside over a population of largely uniform language and culture" in order to claim "a deep territorial lineage" (Graeber & Wengrow, 2021, pp. 29–30 and 168). The following sub-sections take a look at these forces through several notable modernist theories, and is intended to delve into the theoretical means and processes through which the sense of nationalism, and subsequently nation-states and national cultures, were artificially constructed.

3.2 Imagined Communities, Invented Traditions

Benedict Anderson is helpful for our concern when he speaks of "nation-ness" as well as "nationalism" as being "cultural artefacts" (2006, p. 6); "nationalism" comes into being out of and against "large cultural systems," especially "the *religious community* and the *dynastic realm*" (2006, p. 12). As is well known, Anderson defines the nation as an *imagined community*: "[i]t is imagined because the members of even the smallest nation will never know most of their fellow-members, meet them, or even hear of them, yet in the minds of each lives the image of their communion" (p. 6). In other words, despite not having direct physical or proximal connections to most other members of a nation, individuals still relate to and form connections with those fellow-members through shared images. Anderson addresses this "profound emotional legitimacy" (2006, p. 4) of *nationalism* as a process similar to kinship or religion (p. 5). A fuller study of nationalism, in a political and/or ideological sense, is beyond the present scope of inquiry, so that it will only come into focus as it concerns our interest in the culture/nation match.

Several explanations for the rise of *nationalism* are provided by Anderson (1983/2006). Firstly, he posits that toward the end of the 18th century nationalism began to form as a replacement for declining religious sovereignty in Western Europe. It should be noted here that the Enlightenment's return to Greco-Roman intellectual tradition and the secularization of knowledge — which led to the emergence of conceptual categorizations as previously addressed — was also enabled by this decline (see Kulich et al., 2020; Ogunnaike, 2016). As Kent (1995) explains,

the Tridentine form of Roman Catholic theology [...] had reached a
natural limit of usefulness by the mid-seventeenth century. [...]
The gradual revolt of a section of Europe's cultural elites against the
hegemony of Christian world-views was [...] a natural development
as the late-medieval world-order [...] fell apart. (p. 251)

Accordingly, starting with Locke's (1689/1996) rejection of
nativism and promotion of empiricism, the dismissal of Descartes's
innate ideas and the subsequent call for certain unalienable rights
(see Locke, 1689/1980) allowed for the gradual departure from faith
and belief in an immutable divine will to ideas espoused by Rousseau
and others. While Anderson acknowledges that nations had existed
in Europe beforehand, he nevertheless argues that among the first to
adopt the ideals of the Enlightenment and manifest nationalist
movements were the creole elites of the Americas — who revolted
against European rule and established republics in the New World.
Later, as Anderson observes, some European powers would copy and
pirate the Americas model in their own nationalist movements.

Anderson, however, mostly addresses the decline of religiosity in
the context of language. He argues that all great classical civilizations
used sacred languages as a medium to anchor their "superterrestrial
order of power" (Anderson, 2006, p. 13). Thus, the deterioration
of consecrated Latin in Europe necessarily led to the fragmentation,
pluralization, and territorialization of sacred communities (Anderson,
2006, p. 19). We can assume that the process accompanied, if not
enabled, the emergence of city-states as well as in some cases new
imagined nations centered on vernacular languages. Here we can find a
certain analogy with Hofstede's emphasis on national differences in
terms of identity, which features language and religion — "rooted in
history" (Hofstede, Hofstede & Minkov, 2010, pp. 22–23). This
emphasis on language is in line with the conceptual framework
previously offered by Herder (1784), where "[...] every nation is
one people, having its own national form as well as its own
language" (1800, p. 166). In fact, Anderson cites this passage in its
original German during his discussion of language. The nation-language
relation cannot be adequately covered in the present chapter,
significant though it is in itself. However, Anderson explains that the
use of language as a form of demarcation for nations was partly
bolstered by the emergence of "comparative study of languages"
(Anderson, 2006, p. 70), as well as the rise of print-capitalism and
vernacular books. European literati of major languages began to

think of themselves as separate communities, and "language became less of a continuity between an outside power and the human speaker than an internal field created and accomplished by language users among themselves" (Said, 1978, p. 136).

Consequently, language became a form of *simultaneity* that connects the present to the past and the future, the living to the deceased to the unborn. The idea of simultaneity is central to Anderson's argument: "[t]he idea of a sociological organism moving calendrically through homogeneous, empty time is a precise analogue of the idea of the nation, which also is conceived as a solid community moving steadily down (or up) history" (2006, p. 26). We should note here that the temporal dimension of simultaneity may be thought marginal or remote to the concerns of social psychology (and of international management) — yet that is not necessarily the case, as Hofstede argues that "many differences between national cultures" in our time were already discernible in 1700 "if not earlier" (2012, p. 210), without an explanation for the basis of this assumption. Actually, Hofstede devotes a whole chapter to the temporal dimension, outlining "the evolution of cultures" going back to the very beginnings of social history (Hofstede, Hofstede & Minkov, 2010, Chapter 12). However, as we shall see, the political organization in the 18th century greatly differed from modern ones, and perhaps we should not think of them as one continuity (see section 4).

Apart from the question of the origin and rise of nationhood, Herzfeld's (2021) account appears to expand on the notion of simultaneity, while offering a perspective more directly relevant to our inquiry:

> [n]ation-states typically produce official narratives emphasizing cultural, social, economic, and political harmony and unity. They deploy an array of carefully selected, emblematic cultural products, collectively dubbed heritage, as legitimating evidence of the nation's deep past and as a mark of the state's benign tutelage. (p. 1)

Here, we have an understanding of the nation as "producing" or deploying culture, for its own purposes, which can illuminate the notion of a nation/culture identification. Is it the nation that generates its culture, rather than the reverse? This understanding can gain from the research of Hobsbawm and Ranger on *The Invention of Tradition* (1983). Hobsbawm (1983) argues that "'[t]raditions' which appear or claim to be old are often quite recent in origin and sometimes invented" (p. 1). The rationale for inventing traditions or heritage, according to Hobsbawm, is to respond to novel situations through "reference to old situations" (1983, p. 2). That way, the "constant change and innovation of the modern world" is at least partly structured as "unchanging and invariant" (1983, p. 2). This need to structure the modern world as unchanging and invariant is designed to build "emotional resistance to any innovations by people who have become attached to it" (1983, p. 3).

In other words, invented traditions are processes of formalization and ritualization that act as a form of social control, and tether together the population of a society against time. Hobsbawm (1983) claims that invented traditions

> occur more frequently when a rapid transformation of society weakens or destroys the social patterns for which "old" traditions had been designed, producing new ones to which they were not applicable, or when such old traditions and their institutional carriers and promulgators no longer prove sufficiently adaptable and flexible. (pp. 4-5)

Hobsbawm asserts that such changes were a frequent occurrence during the 18th and 19th centuries (though, of course, rapid transformations can be traced in a number of historical periods), and accordingly, he claims that formations of new traditions clustered around this period.

To provide examples of invented traditions, Hobsbawm (1983) offers instances where traditional practices, such as folksongs, are "modified, ritualized and institutionalized for new national purposes" (p. 6). To expand on this idea of national purposes, Hobsbawm notes that the invention of tradition is highly relevant to the construction of the nation and its associated phenomena: "nationalism, the nation-state, national symbols, histories, and the rest" (1983, p. 13). Looking briefly at history, he claims that the state sometimes invokes an ancient past that is "beyond effective historical continuity" in order to justify the creation of new "political institutions, ideological movements and groups" (1983, p. 7). At the same time, Herzfeld (2021) asserts that governments also break "out of the narrative of continuity" by producing "[o]fficial historiography" that "airbrushes inconvenient exceptions" (p. 13). While Herzfeld (2021) in this instance specifically addresses official Thai historiography, the omission or suppression of particular histories has also been practiced elsewhere for purposes of legitimacy, with numerous historical antecedents. The French Renaissance historian Jean Bodin in 1566 (*Methodus ad facilem historiarum cognitionem*), highlighting national characteristics in conjunction with a climate theory, construed a contrast between "strong northerners and weak southerners" in order to stress "French supremacy" — excluding England (Uhlig, 2001, p.92).

In our time, Finnish historiography has been studied for the way a nation's collective scripts are "narratives of exclusion and marginalization in relation to people's experiences" (Kivimäki et al., 2021, p. 16); Finland's history became "a political tool in the making of a civil society" (Haapala, 2021, p. 39). Greece in 2019 officially celebrated the 2,500th anniversary of the Battles of Thermopylae and Salamis against the Persians, associating these with "the new oriental invaders, meaning migrants and border crossers, today": the political justification was that the Battle of Salamis "created the image, for the first time, of a nation, with Greece as its homeland" (Greenberg & Hamilakis, 2022, p.52). In Israel, the prime minister in 2019 claimed that archaeology proved "Palestinians not native to Land of Israel" (a newspaper headline quoted in Greenberg & Hamilakis, 2022, p. 144). It should be noted that highlighting and minimizing specific elements of a history may be especially evident in cases of territorial disputes between nation-states over the historical ownership of land. In the national projects of both Greece and Israel, the modern states were "whitened, at the same time as the ancient pasts which had become their golden ages were Europeanized and racialized" (Greenberg & Hamilakis, 2022, p. 182). In a Japanese context, historiography on the Rape of Nanking, or Japanese aggression during World War Ⅱ in general, is often contested or airbrushed (see Yang, 2001, p.62).

On the whole, we can learn from Hobsbawm that because

> so much of what subjectively makes up the modern "nation" consists of such constructs and is associated with appropriate and, in general, fairly recent symbols or suitably tailored discourse (such as "natural history"), the national phenomenon cannot be adequately investigated without careful attention to the "invention of tradition."
> (1983, p.14)

Perhaps there is something to be gained here from Hobsbawm's theories on tradition for contemporary scientists who study values dimensions, and vice versa. Hobsbawm calls attention to the importance of formalized traditions in modern societies, emphasizing that they are "not confined to so-called 'traditional' societies" (1983, p. 5).

Ultimately, these formalizations can serve ideological and national purposes. Concerning traditional societies, to some degree, Hobsbawm's descriptions of tradition and ritualization may appear to have points of contact with Ronald Inglehart's "traditional" and authority-oriented value dimension (World Values Survey), which in turn corresponds to Hofstede's dimension of "power distance": if a society's power distance score is large, "authority tends to be traditional, sometimes even rooted in religion"; its legitimacy is hardly relevant, while it "gives a sense of security both to those in power and to those lower down" (Hofstede, Hofstede & Minkov, 2010, p. 77). Similarly, research on Hofstede's dimension of individualism and collectivism also suggests that collectivistic societies are more traditional — as they are likely to be large-power-distance societies (Hofstede, Hofstede & Minkov, 2010, pp. 80, 84, 102–103). Furthermore, there is a resemblance between Hobsbawm and Shalom Schwartz's "Tradition" value, which features rites and symbols (2012, pp. 262–263). It appears that these values researchers are not particularly concerned with the provenience or the invented character of tradition, as in non-traditional societies. In any case, the implications of inventing tradition go far beyond folklore, and are related to Hofstede's symbols, heroes, and rituals as practices that manifest culture, for group cohesion or to allow leaders "to assert themselves" (Hofstede, Hofstede & Minkov, 2010, pp. 7–9). This is close to Hobsbawm's understanding of invented tradition as practice "of a ritual or symbolic nature" seeking "to inculcate certain values and norms of behaviour" (1983, p. 1) and to establish or maintain obedience and loyalty of subjects (1983, p. 265).

3.3 Governmentality, Legibility, and Identity

If we return to the question of how nations came into being, apart from how they manifest collective qualities or practices, we should consider the way polities constructed the nation-state, with a greater emphasis on the "state" aspect, through different forms of governance. Can these help to account for a linkage with culture? As the following section will show, concepts in this area tend not to speak of culture, so that they may appear oblique to our main line of questioning. Yet, even if indirectly, they do illuminate our concern with a nation/culture match. To begin with, according to Foucault, in the 15th and 16th centuries there was a "veritable explosion in the art of governing" (1996, pp. 383 – 384). Rather than governing through traditional *sovereign power* as discussed by Hobbes — where a monarch simply ruled over a territory and its inhabitants — new forms of governing gradually emerged, and eventually treated the population as the *subject* to be governed (Foucault, 1996). This becomes highly relevant to explain national identities, as controlled and controllable qualities, whence one could explore an analogy with the invention of traditions, for building resistance to innovations. Foucault refers to the complex population-based form of governing as *governmentality*, and states it as a combination of: *government* and *rationality*. Government refers to "conduct, or an activity meant to shape, guide, or affect the conduct of people," whereas rationality suggests that "before people or things can be controlled or managed, they must first be defined" (Huff, 2020). From *governmentality*, Foucault introduces the concept of bio-power — defined as "the set of mechanisms through which the basic biological features of the human species became the object of a political strategy, of a general strategy of Power" (Foucault, 1996, p.1).

To clarify, bio-power is a form of power that has a normalizing effect by dichotomizing society into categories of "what must live and what must die" (Foucault, 2003, p.254). The population that is referred to in the context of biopower is national (see Foucault, 2003), and therefore biopower is intimately connected to the construction of nation-states (see Painter, 2013). Foucault (1996) further asserts that it is from the 18th century onwards when Western societies "took on board the fundamental biological fact that human beings are a species" (p.1). The manifestation of bio-power came in two distinguishable stages. Initially, bio-power endeavored to *discipline* a population through various state institutions (e.g., schools, prisons, hospitals, etc.). This approach, like sovereign power before it, treats the individual as the object of governance (Foucault, 1995). Foucault (1996) notes how, under disciplinary power, the intention is to build a model of hypothetical perfection. Discipline relates to nationalism and nation-states, as "disciplinary practices of controlling and regulating human lives" are "a precondition for aggregating a population into a single collective body" (Makarychev & Yatsyk, 2017, p. 1). Moreover, as further argued by Makarychev and Yatsyk, "biopolitical instruments of power are indispensable components of discourses and practices of making and shaping national identities" (2017, p.1). Markus and Hamedani (2019) also highlight the role of "current or past institutions in how policies and structures formalize difference, as well as inscribe and maintain a particular social ordering" and incorporate institutions as an integral aspect of how "cultures and psyches make each other up" (pp. 26 – 27; see also Hamedani & Markus, 2019).

As total conformity is unrealistic, however, later bio-power accepts constraints and instead tries to maximize positive elements while minimizing risks and inconveniences — though this is not to say that *disciplinary power* disappears (see Foucault, 1996). This new form of bio-power is referred to by Foucault (1996) as *security*, and endeavors to keep the population's behavior "within socially and economically acceptable limits and around an average that will be considered as optimal for a given social functioning" (p.5). This is not far from Hobsbawm's emphasis on practices "to inculcate certain values and norms of behaviour" (1983, p.1). Security, then, shifts the object of governance from the individual to the population — it disciplines "the population as a whole through managing health, hygiene, nutrition, birth, and sexuality" (Makarychev & Yatsyk, 2017, p.2). The effectiveness of security in disciplining the population lies with how it operates on a "range of factors and elements" that are seemingly external and "far removed from the population itself and its immediate behavior" (Foucault, 1996, p.72). To achieve this, security accumulates and analyzes behavioral data through establishing "profiles, patterns, and probabilities" (Dillon & Lobo-Guerrero, 2008, p. 267). Therefore, central to security and bio-power is the collection and employment of statistics (i. e ., birth rates, death rates, criminal activity). However, early statistics are largely inaccurate as pre-modern states did not have a good grasp on their populations (see Scott, 1998). In order to obtain accurate statistics, territories and their populations need to be first rendered *legible*.

In *Seeing Like a State* (1998), James Scott begins by arguing that, starting in the 19th and 20th centuries, states have endeavored to make society legible "to arrange the population in ways that simplified the classic state functions of taxation, conscription, and prevention of rebellion" (p.2). The pre-modern state, according to Scott, knew little about its subjects. To remedy this, states undertook efforts such as standardizing not only weights and measures, but also languages and legal discourses, establishing cadastral surveys and population registers, and designing cities and transportation to turn "exceptionally complex, illegible, and local social practices" to a "standard grid" whereby everything "could be centrally recorded and monitored" (p.2). Thus, *legibility* is not so much a process of being able to read and understand a population, as it is a process of conforming them to a state of existence where they can then be read and understood. As a result, the act of rendering a state legible further heightens the population's shared sense of communion as institutions within the state become uniform (see section 3.4).

On top of Scott's (1998) examples of state efforts to render a population legible, Caplan and Torpey (2002) similarly provide a mapping of *human legibility* in their exploration of

> the historical constitution and systematization of individual identity and its documentation as a legal and bureaucratic category, the emergence of precise protocols and apparatuses of documentary identification [...] and the intersection of individual and collective systems of registration and identification. (p.4)

This process of identity-construction through legibility is important for our inquiry, seeing that the absence of a common national identity can lead to political instability (see Almagro & Andrés-Cerezo, 2020). Moreover, in the description of the nation-state previously provided by Butler and Spivak (2007), national identity is framed as a central element of the nation-state (see section 2). While Caplan and Torpey (2002) explicitly state that their book focuses on the " history of identification rather than of identities" (p.3), they note several collective identities of importance, "constructed on the basis of religion, nationality, gender, or ethnicity" (p.2). In line with other discrete historical forces addressed in this section, Caplan and Torpey argue that "the 'well-regulated police state'" of late-eighteenth-century Europe generated "a systematic interest in universal means of individual identification" (2002, p. 7). The Enlightenment state no longer selectively identified individuals and groups by external factors, but asserted "a newly comprehensive right of surveillance and identification that applied to all citizens" (2002, p.8). Yet Caplan and Torpey acknowledge that practices of identification were not universal, and assert that further research is necessary "to explain how and why national cultures of identification have differed in their origins, trajectories, and effects" (2002, p. 4). They concede that, while the state's ability in the modern period to "classify, codify, and identify" has grown enormously, "human agency" is still decisive for identification practices, which then tend to bring forth strategies on the part of individuals or groups "to undermine their effectiveness" (Caplan & Torpey, 2002, p.7). This idea will be re-addressed in section 4.3.

3.4 Rationalization, Bureaucratization, and High-Modernization

In *Gemeinschaft und Gesellschaft* (1887/2001), Ferdinand Tönnies reinforces the idea of the nation-state as imaginary by noting:

> the social bond [...] may be conceived either as having real organic life, and that is the essence of Community (*Gemeinschaft*); or else as a purely mechanical construction, existing in the mind, and that is what we think of as Society (*Gesellschaft*). (2001, p.17)

In Tönnies's (1887) typology, originally, rural and peasant communities started out small and its members had interpersonal relationships. However, with modernization and industrialization, communities gradually expanded into societies, and this process weakened the traditional structure of relationships by forcing people to become more rational actors (Tönnies, 1887). In a further summarization provided by Lichtblau (2011), the basic forms of *Gemeinschaft* are "family and kinship together with neighbourliness and friendship," whereas those of *Gesellschaft* are "exchange and contract" (p.457). For Tönnies, therefore, *Gesellschaft* is the epitome of "rational legal relations" and "rational social relations," and people enter it like "alien territory" (Lichtblau, 2011, p.457). The differences between the two ideal types may be a precursor to the cultural dimension of individualism and collectivism, as Triandis (2014) notes how both interlinked terms and their concepts contrast "the centrality of the group" with that "of the individual," and in each case the concepts can be considered "equivalent" (p. 63). Triandis also notes the especially popular character of the contrast between "collectivism and individualism" within modern cultural comparisons (2014, p.62).

Max Weber (1922/2019) explores this process of *rationalization* in *Economy and Society*. While Weber avoids the use of Tönnies's terminology (see Lichtblau, 2011), he conceptualizes similar terms — communalization (*Vergemeinschaftung*) and sociation (*Vergesellschaftung*) — to describe different modes of thinking and actions in the context of social relationships. Under communalization, social actions are more affectual and traditional due to a "mutual sense of belonging among those involved" (Weber, 2019, p.120). By contrast, social actions under sociation are more "rationally motivated" (Weber, 2019, p. 120). Weber in 1917 concedes that most social relationships contain elements of both communalization and sociation, but also hints that the emergence of rationalization has shifted relationships toward the latter: "[t]he fate of our times is characterized by rationalization and intellectualization and, above all, by the 'disenchantment of the world'" (Weber, 1958, p. 155). For Weber, rationalization is defined as the process of replacing *traditionalism* (see Weber, 1905/2001) with a mode of thinking where "one can, in principle, master all things by calculation" (Weber, 1917, in 1958, p. 139). On top of calculability, Weber (1922/2019) provides three additional features of rationalization, whereby societies place greater emphases on: (1) efficiency, (2) predictability, (3) and dehumanization. The dehumanization aspect is relevant to our discussion of culture, as Weber notes how under rationalization, formal-procedural rationality (*Zweckrationalität*) subsumes substantive-value rationality (*Wertrationalität*). In other words, actions that are traditionally based on values are gradually replaced by actions oriented toward ends that justify the means. Weber illustrates the difference in *The Protestant Ethic and Spirit of Capitalism* (1905): "the Puritan wanted to work in a calling; we are forced to do so" (2001, p. 123).

For Weber, bureaucracy is the highest form of formal-procedural rationality (see Weber, 1922/2019). In a manner that appears related to our preceding sub-sections, Weber (1921) notes how the "modern state is absolutely dependent upon a bureaucratic basis. The larger the state, and the more it is or the more it becomes a great power state, the more unconditionally is this the case" (1958, p. 211). Graeber and Wengrow (2021), however, critique this justification for bureaucratization, in which it is claimed that "[a]s society became more complex, it was increasingly necessary for people to create top-down structures of command in order to co-ordinate everything" (p. 360). Graeber and Wengrow (2021) maintain that "[e]vidence of 'social complexity'" shouldn't automatically be "treated as evidence for the existence of some sort of governing apparatus" (p. 360). Nevertheless, the authors concede the pervasiveness of bureaucratization within the modern political *superstructure* (Karl Marx's category). Graeber and Wengrow (2021) list three principles foundational to the modern state: (1) power, (2) bureaucracy, (3) and democracy, yet these principles are not without friction.

In line with Foucault (1978/1996), Graeber and Wengrow note how power is multiplied and enhanced through bureaucracy: "the combination of sovereignty with sophisticated administrative techniques for storying and tabulating information introduces all sorts of threats to individual freedom" (p. 366). The threat to individual freedom is supposedly offset by the third principle, democracy, and indeed Weber notes the connection between bureaucracy and democracy: "[b]ureaucracy inevitably accompanies modern mass democracy in contrast to the democratic self-government of small homogeneous units" (1958, p. 224). Yet Weber (1921) adds the caveat that "'democratization' can be misleading. The demos itself, in the sense of an inarticulate mass, never 'governs' larger associations; rather, it is governed, and its existence only changes the way in which the executive leaders are selected" (1958, p. 225). Whether a Western liberal understanding of democracy is foundational to many modern states is a question that goes beyond the scope of this chapter.

Perhaps we can assume that while homogeneous national cultures did not originally exist, the interests of the state gradually shape a population to become culturally homogeneous through artificial processes — or at least creates the illusion of homogeneity. All of the theories listed in this section point to this conclusion. Ernest Gellner (1983), for example, argues how before industrialization, pre-modern states were internally diverse in terms of culture (see p. 73). However, with industrialization and economic modernization, processes such as education become standardized, which subsequently leads to a unified homogeneous culture (Gellner, 1983). Yet there is also resistance. Returning to *Seeing Like a State* (1998), Scott introduces the concept of *high modernist ideology,* in which governments, as practitioners, are remarkably self-confident about "scientific and technical progress, the expansion of production, the growing satisfaction of human needs, the mastery of nature (including human nature), and, above all, the rational design of social order" (p. 4). Scott (1998) observes how state attempts to act on high modernist designs generally, if not always, end up in failure: "[w]e have repeatedly observed the natural and social failures of thin, formulaic simplifications imposed through the agency of state power" (p. 309). He argues that "[s]implified rules can never generate a functioning community, city, or economy" because formal order is "parasitic on informal processes, which the formal scheme does not recognize, without which it could not exist, and which it alone cannot create or maintain" (p. 310). Informal skills and crafts (Metis), ignored by high modernist ideology, develop within variable contexts and differing environments.

With a similar orientation, Herzfeld (2021) argues that the nation-state is "built on foundations that are antithetical to its design"; though it likes presenting itself as "centralized and unified," "numerous suprafamilial social arrangements [...] threaten its stability from within. [...] Multiple levels of potential and actual factionalism challenge the rhetoric of national unity" (pp. 1 – 2). Seeing that the unified nation is a matter of "rhetoric," can unified country values — or even those of a majority — be plausible and clearly measurable?

4. Global Transitions to the Nation-State

An illustrative case of the building of a nation-state with attention to culture is the German development. The first German nation-state, the *Reich*, was formed in 1871 when the historically German states were united under Prussia (Breuilly, 1996). This was referred to as the *gesamtdeutscher* (whole German) approach, where the new form of state would shift its focus toward one German people. Yet it is noticeable that

> there was very little demand, certainly at popular level, for unification. Germany by 1871 was still an economy dominated by agriculture; sentiments and identities were local or regional in character, the dynasties could still command considerable political loyalty; a broader sense of identity was as, if not more, likely to take a confessional rather than a national form. (Breuilly, 1996, p.10)

The identities and sentiments here are key elements of culture. Such a process of nation-state formation was not confined to Germany, but extended to much of Europe as "the idea that the nation-state was the natural destination of political change was gaining more and more acceptance" (Breuilly, 1996, p. 2). The transition to nation-states as the dominant form of polity did not occur all at once, it was rather segmented and contingent on other historical events. This section will primarily (though not exclusively) focus on the external factors that compelled the formation of nation-states, and how they were not formed on the basis of cultural unity.

4.1 From Empires to Nation-States

Historical research suggests that the emergence of new political ideas from the 18th century "made it possible to imagine a non-empire: a single people sovereign over a single territory" (Burbank & Cooper,

2010, p. 219). However, by the mid-1810s, hardly any autonomous nation-states existed (see Wimmer & Min, 2006). It should be noted here that, as previously mentioned, scholarly definitions of nations and nation-states vary, and the terms are used with more or less precision. For example, Seton-Watson argues that the "old nations of Europe in 1789 were the English, Scots, French, Dutch, Castilians and Portuguese in the west; the Danes and Swedes in the north; and the Hungarians, Poles and Russians in the east" (1977, p. 7). However, Wimmer and Min (2006), on the other hand, claim that whereas France and England were nationally unified bodies by the early modern period, "roughly half of the world's surface was still ruled by empires and half by 'other' political systems" (p. 871). Regardless, the implication here suggests that other external factors are necessary for nation-states to come into existence.

So what exactly are those factors? Wimmer and Min (2006) break the modern transition from empires to nation-states into six different waves, arguing that each was "triggered by the crisis of a major empire and its eventual dissolution" (p. 871). Specifically, they find that (1) the first wave came with the collapse of the Spanish empire; (2) the second wave after World War I with the breakup of the Ottoman and Habsburg empires; (3) the third wave following World War II with decolonization; (4) the fourth wave when the British and French colonial empires could no longer sustain their distant colonies; (5) the fifth wave with the breakup of the Portuguese empire; and (6) the sixth wave with the dissolution of the Soviet Bloc (Wimmer & Min, 2006).

Focusing specifically on the period after World War II, following the intercontinental conflict, the world began to witness the collapse of empires as colonial powers began to decolonize. What emerged from the ashes was the beginning of the current nation-state system. Yet as previously hinted at by Wimmer and Min (2006), it is helpful to be aware that the mid-20th century was

> not a self-propelled movement from empire to nation-state. [...]
> The colonialism that collapsed in Africa and Asia in the 1950s and
> 1960s was not the conservative variant of the interwar decades but
> a colonialism that was interventionist, reformist, and accordingly
> open to challenge. (Burbank & Cooper, 2010, p. 413)

More particularly, the aftermath of WWII left the European powers greatly weakened, and they were left with little choice but to shed their overseas colonies in Asia and Africa. Maintaining colonies by force was no longer viable — in part because of military and economic limitations, but also for moral reasons as the European powers wanted to distance themselves from the inequalities of Nazi ideology (Burbank & Cooper, 2010). Yet the former seems to outweigh the latter, as colonial powers attempted to preserve their modicum of power for as long as possible.

In the context of Asia, European powers such as the French, Dutch, and British attempted to negotiate with their colonies, and convince them to participate in new forms of government where the imperial nations would retain their power, but at the same time provide the colonies with a limited amount of autonomy (Burbank & Cooper, 2010). Alternative polities were attempted, such as the federation and commonwealth, but the British, French, and Dutch lost their colonies across Indochina. It should be noted, however, that while the British lost their authority over the newly independent Asian nation-states, the Commonwealth of Nations did symbolically persist with the British monarch remaining as the head of several newly independent nation-states. The Commonwealth has been acting as a cultural and trade network that granted members trade advantages (see Ukkusuri et al., 2016). On the other hand, France's attempt at this, the *L'Union Française* (French Union), failed disastrously.

For our context, it's especially important to observe that the new nation-states that emerged were not based entirely on cultural communion. Indonesia, for example, has been conspicuously "[s]ewn together out of different islands, kingdoms, languages, and religions," while the Indonesian language was a creation of the colonial era (Burbank & Cooper, 2010, p. 417). Thus the artificiality of the colonial system — where colonial powers arbitrarily drew borders — was inherited by nation-states, and the repercussions of this become even more apparent in the context of Africa.

Following the failures of the imperial powers attempts at maintaining their colonies in Asia, the imperial powers took a different approach to Africa. This new approach would be based on an egalitarian principle of inclusion or investment. However, this too would end in failure as the costs were simply too high, and the European powers figured it would be more cost-effective to maintain post-colonial relationships than to expand efforts to maintain the colonies (Burbank & Cooper, 2010). When Africa decolonized in the 1960s, the new nation-states that emerged retained their former colonial borders — which were artificially carved during the Berlin

Conference in 1884 and subsequent treaties in the 1890s (Michalopoulos & Papaioannou, 2010). Many of these demarcations divided people of one ethnic and cultural origin into separate colonies. The Maasai people, for example, were split between modern-day Kenya and Tanzania; the Anyi between Ghana and the Ivory Coast; and the Chewa between Mozambique, Malawi, and Zimbabwe (Michalopoulos & Papaioannou, 2010). Meanwhile, the arbitrary divisions have also resulted in multiple ethnicities being clustered together.

There appears to be four different levels of ethnic tensions in African nation-states. Deng (1997) argues that only a few nation-states, such as Botswana, have a "high degree of homogeneity or, at least, a relatively inconsequential diversity" (p. 30). For the most part, African nation-states, such as Kenya, "face significant ethnic pluralism," but are "nevertheless containable through an effective system of distribution that upholds the integrity and legitimacy of the state" (Deng, 1997, p. 30). Some African nation-states, such as Zimbabwe and Namibia, however, suffer "racial, ethnic, religious, or cultural divisions severe enough to require special arrangements to be mutually accommodating in an ambivalent form of unity in diversity" (Deng, 1997, p. 30). Lastly, nation-states such as Rwanda or Sudan partially belong in a category of "zero-sum conflict situation," where the state is "embroiled in acute crisis with no collective sense of identification, no shared values, and no common vision for the nation" (Deng, 1997, p. 30).

While some scholars have argued that the ethnic diversity and partitioning of cultural groups within African nation-states undermine the formation of national cultures, others argue that with economic and political modernization, the former parochial ties of pre-colonized polities are reduced (Robinson, 2014). Minkov et al. (2021) explore "the power of nations in the process of cultural homogenization in Africa" vis-a-vis "the power of supranational ethnolinguistic groups" (p. 803). They find that "national culture is a very meaningful concept in Africa" as "nearly all ethnolinguistic groups of a particular country [...] cluster together with the other groups of the same country when compared in terms of approval or rejection of ideologies concerning cultural modernization" (Minkov et al., 2021, p. 816). Describing the nation category as meaningful in these regions for discerning collective values may appear naïve, yet we cannot adequately address this issue in our context. The researchers further maintain that "[a]lthough ethnic culture remains a meaningful concept, as it does account for some significant cultural differences, it is a far weaker group-level discriminant than national culture, and therefore far less relevant" (Minkov et al., 2021, p. 816).

Yet it should be noted that the authors acknowledge several limitations to their study. Specifically, their study analyzes data from the Afrobarometer (afrobarometer. org), which leaves out "countries with significant political unrest, some of which may even be viewed as failed states," as "it is not unlikely that some of those countries have very limited cultural homogeneity" (Minkov et al., 2021, p. 816). Moreover, they note that the Afrobarometer categories "have no other choice but to target relatively educated members of groups of people, living relatively modern lives, and exclude members of marginal groups that have had relatively little contact with modern civilization" (Minkov et al., 2021, p. 816).

This brings up another tangential, but important, issue: the sampling techniques for data collection (see for instance Hofstede, 2012, pp. 187 – 188; Javidan et al., 2006). The issue of sampling invites such questions as: are marginalized groups accessible, and gender differentiations included (Al Anezi & Alansari, 2016)? Who participates and who is omitted or declines? Ultimately, the question of who is represented by studies of national character and values has not been conclusively solved. Furthermore, there is the issue of subjective qualities on the part of both the participant and the researcher. Do all participants treat their respective researchers the same, or are some participants, for example, less trusting of their researchers? Do all researchers conduct their studies in the same way across all samples? Are the questions interpreted similarly across all cultures? A range of such critical issues have been addressed in research. While the earlier quantitative methods employed have been continuously revised, critical analyses of the Hofstede methodology (e. g., Gerlach & Eriksson, 2021; McSweeney, 2002; Moulettes, 2007), as well as of the World Values Survey methodology (e. g., Allison et al., 2021; Haller, 2002; Lundgren, 2015) have been offered. As Allison et al. (2021) acknowledge, quantitative cross-cultural models, notwithstanding their continuous refinement, can only hope to provide "a deeply simplified representation of national social differences." Moreover, it has become clearer that a methodology such as Hofstede's is not well suited to understanding value differences between ethnic groups within nations (see De Mooij & Beniflah, 2017).

4.2 Basis for Nation-State Formation

If one believes "folk wisdom," there may nowadays be 600 – 800 "active nation-state projects" and another 7,000-8,000 "potential projects" (Roeder, 2007, p.3). Yet less than 200 nation-states have been actualized and successfully achieved sovereign status — recognized as independent by the United Nations. This suggests that there are certain necessary conditions required for nation-state projects to achieve independence. The current sub-section takes a look at such conditions and whether nation-states are built on principles of national culture, or other criterion.

Rather than being predicated on culture, according to Roeder (2007), "almost every successful nation-state project has been associated with an existing institution" (p.10). Similarly, Anderson (1983) claims that each of the South American republics that came into being during the 19th century were based on existing administrative units from the 16th to 18th centuries. These administrative units were "arbitrary and fortuitous," but gradually developed "a firmer reality under the influence of geographic, political, and economic factors" (Anderson, 2006, p.52). Anderson goes on to argue that this model of demarcation that was based on administrative units "foreshadowed the new states of Africa and parts of Asia in the mid twentieth century" (2006, p.52). Roeder's (2007) research focuses on a type of administrative unit, the segment-state, which he defines as "smaller territories and populations within the common-state," where the common-state is the entire territory and population (pp. 43-44). The rationale for the creation of segment-states is to provide the common-state with a way "to incorporate within its jurisdiction diverse peoples who did not easily fit within a single nation" (p.43). Yet this is not to say that segment-states were ethnically or culturally homogeneous, as seen in the case of former African colonies.

According to Roeder (2007), of the 177 nation-states that emerged during the 20th century, 153 had formerly been segment-states. Using the USSR as his primary example, Roeder explains how the successful nation-states that emerged following the USSR's collapse were "first-order jurisdictions called union republics, such as Kazakhstan and Ukraine" (2007, p.10). Other nation-state projects, such as Turkestan, Idel-Ural, the Mountain Republic, and Novorossia, that were not segment-states, ultimately failed. In his exploration of Africa, Roeder (2007) finds that the continent had far fewer segment-states than Asia and Europe, and thus why there are few attempts at secession. Thus, as this research demonstrates, the origin of nation-states is not based on "national identity formation, material greed and grievance, nationalist mobilization, or international selection mechanisms" but rather political institutions (Roeder, 2007, p.11). Wimmer and Feinstein (2010) similarly touch on how "the success of nationalist projects is determined by the constellation of power relating nationalist movements and factions to imperial centers, *ancien régimes,* or other factions of the ruling elites [...] when nationalists have had ample time to mobilize the population and delegitimize the old regime or when the established regime is weakened by wars" (p.785). Moreover, Wimmer and Feinstein's (2010) analysis of nation-state formation argues against Gellner and Anderson's classical theories, specifically "that the slow moving forces of economic and cultural modernization did not play a crucial role in the rise of the nation-state across the world" (p.785).

Importantly, this suggests that perhaps not all nation-states came into being through the same process, and therefore, nation-states should have the contexts of their formation examined before comparison. It also implies that most nation-states are not founded on the principle of a shared culture or communion among the people, as the definition of nation-state and nation would suggest. Yet according to Roeder, a precursor to nationalism, political-identity hegemony, emerges within segment-states to enforce a national identity that restricts alternate identities: "[w]hether within an autocratic or a democratic common-state, segment-state leaders can build political-identity hegemony" (2007, p. 149). As with nationalism, this is also achieved through the creation of "research centers that develop and write national histories," the maintenance of "archives, libraries, and museums that preserve and display the monuments of this history" and the establishment of "ministries of education that design curricula for schools and universities to teach a myth of a common origin and a vision of a common future" (Roeder, 2007, pp. 149 – 150). This brings us back to the previous section's discussion on how national identities and cultures are artificially created, and that perhaps it is the nation that produces the culture rather than the other way around. Ultimately, all new states claim a sovereignty deriving from "a nation that is coextensive with the population within its boundaries," so that "most inhabitants at least acquiesce in the status quo" and would neither imagine nor support any "alternative nation-state project to which they would rather belong" (Roeder, 2007, p.348).

Concerning the context of nation-state formation under decolonization, it is worth exploring Partha Chatterjee's seminal work: *The Nation and its Fragments.* Chatterjee states that the newly postcolonial states' economy and polity were "disciplined and normalized under the conceptual rubrics of 'development' and 'modernization'" (p. 3). Chatterjee (1994) describes how "the emancipatory aspects of nationalism were undermined" by private interests, and further claims that "[b]y the 1970s, nationalism had become a matter of ethnic politics" (p. 3). This suggests that, rather than the bottom-up approach initially espoused by Rousseau and Montesquieu, the creation of nation-states was instead a vying for ideological, political, and cultural hegemony that did not represent the will of the people.

Using India as his example, Chatterjee (1994) argues that nation-states that grew out of the colonial experience undergo a distinct form of nationalism, *anticolonial nationalism*, that requires consideration of two cultural domains: the material and the spiritual. The material refers to the "outside" domain, where Western accomplishments had to be "carefully studied and replicated" (Chatterjee, 1994, p. 6), whereas the spiritual refers to the "inner" domain that contains the "'essential' marks of cultural identity" (Chatterjee, 1994, p. 6). Aspects of Western civilization from science to modern statecraft should be imitated in order to modernize. Yet at the same time, the spiritual domain must be preserved and protected from material encroachment. Thus, anticolonial nationalism aspires to "fashion a 'modern' national culture that is nevertheless not Western" (Chatterjee, 1994, p. 6). Yet it's important to ask who constructs this national culture.

According to Chatterjee (1994), anticolonial nationalism "creates its own domain of sovereignty within colonial society" (p. 6). For India, the Calcutta middle class played a decisive role in creating Bengal's "dominant forms of nationalist culture and social institutions" (Chatterjee, 1994, p. 35). Chatterjee (1994) observes how this class was, at the same time, subordinate to the imperial power, and that the "construction of hegemonic ideologies typically involves the cultural effort of classes placed precisely in such situations" (p. 36). Thus, in line with Roeder (2007), a hegemonic national identity that suppresses alternate identities emerges.

One of the ways alternate identities are suppressed is through the classicization of tradition. Chatterjee (1994) observes that nineteenth-century Bengalis could plausibly claim a "cultural ancestry" in the Vedic age (p. 73). The "Hindu" past would form the basis of India's classicization, and while this classicization could accommodate some diverse identities from "Indian tradition," Chatterjee notes the awkward position of Islam, "which could claim, within the same classicizing mode, an alternative classical tradition" (1994, p. 73). Ultimately, Islam would be treated as a "foreign element, domesticated by shearing its own images of a classical past. Popular Islam could then be incorporated in the national culture in the doubly sanitized form of syncretism" (Chatterjee, 1994, p. 74). Chatterjee (1994) also points to a suppression of other potential histories, a process that "raises doubts about the singularity of a history of India" (p. 113).

Importantly for our context, Chatterjee (1994) discerns a dual structure in the nationalist mass movement, with two political domains: the "formally organized political parties and associations [...] seeking to use their representative power over the mass of the people to replace the colonial state by a bourgeois nation-state" and "peasant politics where beliefs and actions did not fit into [...] bourgeois representative politics" (Chatterjee, 1994, p. 159). Chatterjee (1994) observes that the former could not "appropriate its other within a single homogeneous unity," so that there was no "linear development of the consciousness of the peasantry into a new sense of nationhood" (p. 160). The nationalists approached the peasantry in a way similar to the colonizers, and caste practices were kept strategically as a form of domination and subordination. Walia (2021) similarly observes how, since India's state formation in 1947, minority communities have been repressed through Casteism.

To conclude, while nation-states may vary in their creation, it appears that there is nevertheless a universal level of homogenization, or rather domination, that must occur. This suggests that perhaps there is some validity in cultural comparisons at the national level, as alternate histories are erased and minority values marginalized. Yet at the same time, Herzfeld (2021) states that all nation-states require some flexibility and allow for a degree of dissent: "no nation-state can exist for long without that built-in tolerance. Officials often look the other way when minor infractions or unseemly behavior remain relatively discreet but will not countenance anything that too brazenly challenges their moral authority" (p. 2). This will become clearer in the following sub-section.

4.3 Global Ideologies and Cultural Intimacy

Another factor to consider on top of the internal mechanisms required for nation-states to form is the impact of external forces on a nation-state's identity and culture from the global community.

From Chatterjee (1994), we understand that nation-states need to mimic some aspects of the material domain. Yet beyond that, integration and support from other countries are also necessary for nation-states to become sustainable. The integration and support, however, come at a cost. A central idea that can be inferred from Burbank and Cooper's (2010) research is that while empires no longer exist in name, there remains a vertical power dynamic between powerful and weak nation-states — where the weak necessarily succumb to the ideologies of the powerful. This is best exemplified during the Cold War era, where nation-states either aligned themselves with the United States or the Soviet Bloc.

Frantz Fanon's (1963) *The Wretched of the Earth*, for example, argues that the *Third World* — comprising of nation-states that were formerly oppressed and colonized — had to choose between the socialist East or the capitalist West. Similarly, Young (2003) observes how, while former colonies from Asia, Africa, and Latin America were able to achieve independence, it was only a "relatively minor move from direct to indirect rule, a shift from colonial rule and domination to a position not so much of independence as of being in-dependence" (p. 3). Antonio Gramsci (1929–1935) introduces the concept of *cultural hegemony* to address how the ruling elites are able to influence the values, norms, and beliefs of the weak. While Gramsci's original intention may not have been to address nation-states, the concept of cultural hegemony has been applied to the international and world level by political and international relations scholars (see for instance Cox, 1983). Cultural hegemony is exemplified in Daniel Immerwahr's (2019) *How to Hide an Empire*, which explores how, while the United States abandoned its strategy of seizing oversea territories, it nevertheless was able to use its pervasive power — derived from institutions such as capitalism, the military, media, and language — to compel other nation-states to follow its interests.

It should be noted that this ideological domination by the powerful nation-states was not limited to nation-states that were previously colonized either. Herzfeld (2002) notes how Thailand and Greece "had to make major concessions to the European powers in order to maintain any semblance of sovereignty" and "internal cultural regimentation" (p. 907). Herzfeld (2002) uses the term *crypto-colonialism* to refer to those countries that are: "buffer zones between the colonized lands and those as yet untamed" and how crypto-colonies were "compelled to acquire their political independence at the expense of massive economic dependence," with "this relationship being articulated in the iconic guise of aggressively national culture fashioned to suit foreign models" (pp. 900–901). As Herzfeld (2016b) argues in the case of Greece, since the nation-state's declaration of independence in 1821, the Greeks

> were forced to fit their national culture to the antiquarian desires of Western powers. […] The Western powers supported conservative Greek politicians who maintained Greece's status as a 'backward' client state while reproducing the same inequity in the exploitation of their electoral constituents. (p. 10)

Herzfeld (2002) goes on to argue that crypto-colonies actually have it worse than former colonies:

> not only have they suffered many of the economic and political effects of colonialism itself, but they have then found themselves excluded, materially and epistemologically, by the massive forces upholding the binarisms of late-twentieth-century realpolitik. (p. 920)

Yet despite the existence of dominant ideological spheres, the citizens of a nation-state may nevertheless contravene the national culture that is forced upon them. Herzfeld (2016a) introduces the term *cultural intimacy* as "the recognition of those aspects of an officially shared identity that are considered a source of external embarrassment but that nevertheless provide insiders with their assurance of common sociality" (p. 7). Herzfeld uses cultural intimacy "as an antidote to the formalism of cultural nationalism" (2016a, p. 19). Herzfeld also uses the term *disemia* to describe the "formal or coded tension between official self-presentation and what goes on in the privacy of collective introspection" (2016a, p. 19). In his ethnography of a remote Cretan village, Herzfeld (1985) observes how the Cretans occupy an eccentric position within the wider framework of Greek society: "they are often despised and feared outside the island" (p. 9). In contrast to modern Greece, Cretans are often portrayed as primitive goat thieves because they often commit acts that contravene Greece's official code. This includes stealing goats and sheep, abducting brides, owning illegal weapons, and going against language standardization (Herzfeld, 1985). Yet Herzfeld argues that these acts are only perceived as negative because of the penetration of external values — which has gradually eroded the "social significance" of acts that were traditionally "a mark of true manhood" (1985, p. 20). Thus, in a series of anecdotal examples, Herzfeld (1985) explores how practices such as goat theft are actually markers of communal solidarity and an essential part of the villagers' identity.

In a similar vein, Scott's (1985) *Weapons of the Weak* explores everyday forms of peasant resistance within a small Malaysian village, and how the poor resist policies "dreamed up by their would-be superiors in the capital" (xvii). While Scott's ethnography has to do more with class relations than culture, it nevertheless demonstrates an ideological break between the wealthy and poor in Sedaka. Scott (198⁻) notes how histories are interpreted differently based on class differences: "[i]f one asks villagers ab,·ut the impact of double-cropping, what emerges is a core zone of general agreement that gives way to a zone of dispute as weil as a zone of differences in perspective. It is in these last two zones that class is decisive" (p. 148). Specifically, while everyone agrees that some basic living conditions and needs — such as the availability of rice — have improved, the two sides ideologically clash over the use of combine harvesters, access to paddy land, and rituals such as religious charity (Scott, 1985).

Traditionally, Sedaka has "a large variety of ritual ties that lie beyond immediate relations of production and serve both to create and to signify the existence of a community" (Scott, 1985, p. 169). This includes three forms of ritual gift giving: (1) *zakat peribadi*, a form of religious charity that is tied to the harvest that benefits locals within Sedaka; (2) *sedekah/derma*, charitable donations given almost exclusively to the poor for purposes such as paying for funerals; and (3) *kenduri*, ritual feasts for special occasions that are sponsored by both the wealthy and poor (Scott, 1985). Yet Scott (1985) notes how the wealthy moved away from traditional social ties: "[t]hey have had to hire machines in place of village laborers, raise rents, dismiss tenants, and cut back their ceremonial and charitable obligations within the community" (p. 184). Thus, there is a cultural gap where the wealthy attempt to deny their traditions of the past and the morality of the poor, while the poor cling to the moral expectations of "patronage, assistance, consideration, and helpfulness" from the past (Scott, 1985, p. 185).

As argued by Kraus et al. (2011), social class "influences thought, feeling, and action" and therefore "is a cultural identity" (p. 246). Aside from class, other social divisions and identities also form an individual's culture: "[r]ace, gender and class represent the three most powerful organizing principles in the development of cultural identity worldwide" (Belkhir & Barnett, 2001, p. 157). Intersectionality theory also suggests that, and explores how, these varying social identities intersect and overlap to create new and unique identities with attached effects and experiences (see Collins & Sirma, 2020). Hofstede, too, according to Minkov, believed that culture, while applicable to a national society, "applies also to other collectives, such as regions, ethnicities, occupations, organizations, or even age groups and genders" (Minkov, 2013, p. 11). Minkov (2013) even acknowledges the presence of "national subcultures" as a serious argument against the idea of national cultures (p. 26). Yet Minkov (2013) nevertheless justifies the national culture approach by arguing that data from the World Values Survey shows homogeneous cultural clusters at the national level.

4.4 Multiculturalism and Nationalism

Further contradictory to the idea of a singular national culture, as well as nationalism, is the concept of multiculturalism. Multiculturalism is a multi-faceted concept with different attached meanings, a term for "demographic diversity; a political philosophy of equality or justice; a set of policies to recognize and accommodate ethno-racial and religious diversity; or a public discourse recognizing and valorizing pluralism" (Bloemraad & Wright, 2014, p. S292). Psychological research has concentrated on the value dimension to study "the attitudes vis-à-vis the cultural diversity of the population," in particular levels of acceptance and support (Van de Vijver, 2014, p. 167). While ideas of cultural pluralism existed prior to the emergence of nation-states (see Burbank & Cooper, 2010; Steppat & Tong, 2021), in terms of policy, multiculturalism gained momentum in the 1970s. To provide some examples, in the American context, following the civil rights movement reformers proposed to make education "more accessible and supportive to minorities by infusing both the curriculum and the entire educational environment with recognition and respect for 'ethnic diversity'" (Higham, 1993, p. 218). In a Canadian context, a policy of multiculturalism within a bilingual framework was announced in the House of Commons in 1971 (for analysis, see *Multiculturalism @ 50*, 2021). As summarized by Kymlicka (2012), Western nations have introduced a range of multiculturalism policies that endorsed the accommodation of diversity and rejected "earlier ideas of unitary and homogeneous nationhood" (p. 3). Kymlicka (2005) highlights four themes within the Western model of multiculturalism: (1) minority nationalisms,

(2) indigenous peoples, (3) immigrants, and (4) metics.

The first trend, minority nationalisms, involves the treatment of a regional group that "conceives of itself as a nation within a larger state, and mobilizes behind nationalist political parties to achieve recognition of its nationhood, either in the form of an independent state or through territorial autonomy within the larger state" (Kymlicka, 2005, p. 23). Examples of this include Puerto Ricans in the United States, the Scots and Welsh in Great Britain, and the Quebecers in Canada. It should be noted, however, that in the context of Quebec, Handler's (1988) ethnography on Quebec nationalism questions the presupposition that "'a' nation, grounded in history, exists 'in' Quebec," and explores Quebec's *cultural objectification*, where culture is made into "a natural object or entity" that is "bounded and continuous in space and time" and characterizable in terms of traits and properties (pp. 14, 18). Thus, a notion of homogeneous cultures and nations appears highly doubtful, and a national culture and identity which Quebec has claimed for itself have no unitary substance because there are different versions or models of what they are or might be. Kymlicka (2005) notes that while nation-states have in the past attempted to suppress these sub-states by restricting "minority language rights, abolishing traditional forms of regional self-government, and encouraging members of the dominant group to settle in the minority group's homeland," they have come to recognize that these sub-state identities continue to persist, "and that their sense of nationhood and nationalist aspirations must be accommodated in some way or other" (p. 23). Similar to the governmental model that was offered by imperial powers during the decolonization of Asia, this accommodation typically comes in the form of "multinational federalism," which provides the sub-state with a degree of self-governance.

The second trend, indigenous peoples, is related to the treatment of aboriginal populations within a nation-state. As with members of a sub-state, in the past, nation-states had the goal of eliminating these communities through various policies such as "stripping indigenous peoples of their lands, restricting the practice of their traditional culture, language, and religion, and undermining their institutions of self-government" (Kymlicka, 2005, p. 24). However, more recently, as described by Anaya and Williams (2001), the recognition and protection of indigenous peoples has become a focus of contemporary human rights. In 2007, the United Nations General Assembly approved the Declaration on the Rights of Indigenous Peoples (see

Indigenous peoples), which granted such peoples the right to self-determination (i. e., "the right to freely determine their political status and freely pursue their economic, social and cultural development," pp. 4-5).

The third trend, immigrants, consists of migrants who have left one nation-state for another, and under the immigration policy of their new nation-state have the right to become citizens (Kymlicka, 2005). Originally, the expectation for immigrants was that they would assimilate to their new milieu and "become indistinguishable from native-born citizens" (Kymlicka, 2005, p. 25). Yet starting from the late 1960s, this notion of assimilation has become outdated as immigrants from non-European nation-states increase and the idea of a "more 'multicultural' conception of integration" where immigrants "visibly and proudly express their ethnic identity" becomes accepted by public institutions (Kymlicka, 2005, p. 25). Kymlicka (2005) notes that Canada, Australia, and New Zealand all have formal declarations of official multicultural policies by the central government. Furthermore, while the United States does not have a multicultural policy at the federal level, some such policies can be found at the state level. For the American context, important aspects of the cultural policies involved have been examined in Volume 8 of this series (see Kulich, 2019; Steppat, 2019). Clearly, multiculturalism in terms of minorities, indigenous peoples, and immigration has greatly enriched American cultural life (see for instance Hornung, 2007; Lee, 2003).

The final trend, metics, concerns immigrants who according to official laws should not become permanent residents in their new host country, but have nevertheless settled there permanently. This group includes populations such as refugees and illegals. Kymlicka (2005) notes that there is an increasing trend within Western democracies toward "adopting amnesty programs for illegal immigrants, and granting citizenship to long-settled refugees and guest-workers and their children. In effect, long-settled metics are increasingly viewed as if they were legal immigrants" (p. 28).

Aspects of multicultural policies have been challenged and contested. One of the primary criticisms against multiculturalism has been that it does not facilitate a model of integration, but rather separation as "excessive emphasis on diversity reifies differences, undermines collective identity, and hinders common political projects," and in addition, multiculturalism "promotes 'parallel lives' in which minorities live in self-segregated communities" (Bloemraad &

Wright, 2014, p.S303). Prins and Slijper (2002) also identified key themes in arguments against multiculturalism, which included incompatibilities between cultures and the erosion of a national identity. Whether these criticisms are factual and grounded in reality is a discussion that is outside the scope of the current chapter, but it is important to note how multiculturalism has led to the mobilization and growing popularity of far-right political parties and their constituents — who call for the end of multiculturalism. While Kymlicka (2010) argues that the narrative of multiculturalism's end is greatly exaggerated — seeing that multicultural policies for indigenous peoples and national minorities, for example, remain intact — it is also important to be aware that nationalism is "once more emerging as an ideological guiding force for many of those who feel let down, excluded or alienated by current politics" (Knutsen, 2016, p.13).

Here, it is worth exploring the work of Charles Taylor (1994), who addresses the demand for *recognition* by minority and subaltern groups in contemporary politics. Taylor notes the "supposed links between recognition and identity," where "identity is partly shaped by recognition or its absence, often by the misrecognition of others," owing to which a person or group can "suffer real damage" (1994, p. 25). In terms of the politics of recognition, Taylor (1994) makes a distinction between a "politics of equal dignity" and a "politics of difference" (pp. 41 – 42). Focusing on the latter, Taylor (1994) states that a "potential for forming and defining one's own identity," whether as an individual or a culture, is universal, and "must be respected equally in everyone" (p. 42). In other words, under the purview of a politics of difference, different groups must be afforded different treatments based on their respective needs. Taylor (1994) references "reverse discrimination measures" that provide previously unfavored groups a competitive advantage to level the playing field (p. 40). An instance is the Quebec language laws which regulated English-language school attendance to ensure the collective survival of French Quebeckers. Accordingly, Taylor advocates a form of liberalism that respects the identity of minority cultures.

Walia (2021), however, notes how liberal multiculturalism's treatment of racialized communities upholds racial regimes through difference. Walia (2021) identifies far-right mobilizations as a response to multiculturalism, which they perceive as state racism. It should be noted that while calls for nationalism have reemerged, the exact character of nationalism often remains abstract and ambiguous. It is important to recognize that unity does not have to be contingent on a set of shared values or culture, but can be formed through the rejection of what it does not want to be. Walia (2021) observes how far-right leaders utilize concepts such as *ethnonationalism* as a dividing line of difference. Ethnonationalism defines the nation in terms of ethnicity.

In any case, in terms of the significance of multiculturalism for measurements of national cultural values, we should not overlook the attention that *Hofstede Insights* gives to managing cultural diversity in business, highlighting the benefits of "increased innovation, more profitability, teams with better problem solving skills" in recruiting culturally diverse candidates for particular jobs; because "not everyone will see the same situations in the same way," heeding the national value dimensions as offered in Country Comparison (Hofstede Insights) is strongly recommended there. This conceptually limited focus on diversity in connection with national cultural values hardly addresses the scope of multiculturalism and its implications for a necessarily differentiated approach to cultural values.

4.5 Socio-Ecological Psychology

Socio-ecological psychology is "an area within psychology that investigates how mind and behavior are shaped in part by their natural and social habitats (social ecology)" (Oishi, 2013/2014, p.582). In their "Socioecological-Genetic Framework of Culture," Lu, Benet-Martínez, and Wang (2023) posit that "socioecology can influence both culture and personality" (p.366). Returning to the line of thinking from Montesquieu's (or Hippocrates') climatic theory of culture, recent research in socio-ecological psychology has observed intranational cultural differences among members of a nation-state — demarcated by variables such as climate, historical prevalence of pathogens, and historical subsistence styles. For example, while Gelfand et al.'s (2011) original study on tightness-looseness (tolerance for deviance) was conducted on a national level, follow-up studies have applied the construct to intranational contexts. Harrington and Gelfand's (2014) study on tightness-looseness across America, for instance, found a wide variation for the construct at the state level based on ecological and historical factors. Such factors included "natural disaster vulnerabilities, rates of disease, resource availability, and degree of external threat" (Harrington & Gelfand, 2014, p.7990; for further topic foci cf. also Chua et al., 2019, and Talhelm & English, 2020).

It can be argued that even if socio-ecological studies are

conducted on a cross-national basis, they nevertheless affirm the idea that there are cultural differences within a nation-state. This is because, as previously noted, the territorial demarcations of many nation-states are artificially carved and not congruent with the "natural boundaries" espoused by Herder. Thus, as socio-ecological psychology examines how the environment influences behavior and culture, it stands to reason that the theories extend to environmental differences within a nation-state.

This line of reasoning is supported by some socio-ecological studies. Take for instance Van de Vliert's (2013) study on climatic demands. The study uses survey data from both 85 countries and 15 provinces in China, and has shown that cultural disparities exist at both levels. In China, members of provincial communities exposed to the same climate conditions and financial living standards push and pull each other "toward a shared culture" (Van de Vliert, 2013, p. 10). Similarly, Fincher et al.'s (2008) article on pathogen prevalence found a correlation between the prevalence of pathogens and measures of collectivism. While Fincher et al. (2008) primarily used nation-states as their unit of analysis, their argument is that vulnerability to infectious disease leads to psychological mechanisms that influence behavior and culture.

This is especially relevant in a contemporary context, as the global COVID-19 pandemic has disproportionately impacted various communities and regions within nation-states. Based on the pathogen prevalence theory, does this mean that there will be foreseeable cultural differences as a result of COVID-19 in the future?

In a similar vein, Saldanha et al.'s (2021) study on the relationship between information and communication technology (ICT) and culture also "reveals the important role ICT plays in shaping how local environmental or national factors influence innovation" (p. 132). Specifically, they find that "ICT attenuates the negative impact of cultural dimensions related to procedural norms, formality, and structure on innovation" (Saldanha et al., 2021, p. 131).

If we hold these theories to be accurate, even if the government endeavors to homogenize a nation-state's culture for the sake of unity and control, at the same time, enduring cultural differences based on ecological differences as well as discrete historical processes that were experienced by past generations continue to exist. Future research should explore regional level (as in within-a-country) analysis.

5. Conclusions

As addressed in the opening section of this chapter, there is a tendency within intercultural communication to categorize the world into discrete nation-state units when conducting comparative cross-cultural research. Wimmer and Glick Schiller (2002) introduce the term *methodical nationalism* to refer to this "assumption that the nation/state/society is the natural social and political form of the modern world" (p. 301). The authors then demonstrate how methodical nationalism has influenced research on areas such as migration. Yet as evidence from the chapter suggests, such an approach distorts historical and social realities. While no scholars dispute the idea that individual idiosyncrasies exist within a nation-state, ultimately scholars remain divided on whether the concept of national culture is a meaningful unit of analysis and whether members of a nation-state can be accurately represented by a national culture.

The topic of whether nation-states are culturally homogeneous is important for several reasons. For one, the use of nation-states as a unit of cultural analysis may reinforce certain stereotypes as well as reify notions of difference and commonality. Therefore, it becomes crucial to interrogate the validity of the assertion that nation-states are culturally homogeneous and that members of a nation-state can be represented by a national culture. Moreover, an examination of the factors that enforce cultural homogeneity illuminates greater structural processes and conditions that create certain types of cultures. Lastly, current cultural comparisons between nation-states tend to treat all nation-states as equal, without offering additional considerations of relevant differentiation. Future exploration of the degree to which nation-states can be culturally homogeneous based on unique circumstances is required.

Acknowledgements:

I would like to express my sincerest thanks to Dr. Sara Curran, professor at the University of Washington, for introducing me to many of the works cited in this paper, and for being my independent study advisor and helping me think through many of the complex concepts covered. Additionally, I am equally thankful to Dr. Michael Steppat, professor at the University of Bayreuth, for his constant suggestions, feedback, and kind edits throughout my writing of this paper. I am thankful to Dr. Michael Herzfeld, professor emeritus from Harvard University, for reviewing the manuscript near its completion and for suggesting additional readings for areas with which I was unfamiliar. Furthermore, I am grateful to Dr. Dharm Bhawuk, professor at the University of Hawai'i, for taking the time to read and check the chapter after its completion. Lastly, I would like to thank my classmates Nancyrose Houston, Emily Gilroy, Marquis Bullock, Kayla Stevenson, and Juliana Monserrate Arana-Santiago for our many class discussions that ultimately resulted in my writing of this chapter.

References

Adams, W. Y. (1998). *The philosophical roots of anthropology*. The University of Chicago Press.

Akaliyski, P., Welzel, C., Bond, M. H., & Minkov, M. (2021). On "nationology": The gravitational field of national culture. *Journal of Cross-Cultural Psychology*, *52*(8-9), 771-793. https://doi.org/10.1177/00220221211044780

Al Anezi, A., & Alansari, B. (2016). Gender differences in Hofstede's cultural dimensions among a Kuwaiti sample. *European Psychiatry*, *33 Supplement*, S503-S504. https://doi.org/10.1016/j.eurpsy.2016.01.1853

Allison, L., Wang, C., & Kaminsky, J. (2021, January 11). Religiosity, neutrality, fairness, skepticism, and societal tranquility: A data science analysis of the World Values Survey. *PloS ONE*, *16*(1). https://doi.org/10.1371/journal.pone.0245231

Almagro, M., & Andrés-Cerezo, D. (2020). The construction of national identities. *Theoretical Economics*, *15*(2), 763-810.

Anaya, S. J., & Williams, R. A. Jr. (2001). The protection of indigenous peoples' rights over land and natural resources under the Inter-American human rights system. *Harvard Human Rights Journal*, *14*(3), 32-86.

Anderson, B. R. O'G. (2006). *Imagined communities: Reflections on the origin and spread of nationalism*. Rev. ed. Verso. (Originally published 1983)

Arnold, M. (1869). *Culture and anarchy: An essay in political and social criticism*. London: Smith, Elder.

Bailyn, B. (1967). *The ideological origins of the American Revolution*. Harvard University Press.

Barnard, F. M. (1969). *J. G. Herder on social and political culture*. Cambridge University Press.

Barth, F. (Ed.). (1969). *Ethnic groups and boundaries: The social organization of culture difference*. Waveland Press.

Belkhir, J. A., & Barnett, B. M. (2001). Race, gender and class intersectionality. *Race, Gender & Class*, *8*(3), 157-174.

Bellamy, A. J. (2003). *The formation of Croatian national identity*. Manchester University Press.

Berlin, I. (2013a). *Three critics of the Enlightenment: Vico, Hamann, Herder* (2nd ed., H. Hardy, Ed.). Princeton University Press. (Original work published

1960)

Berlin, I. (2013b). *The crooked timber of humanity: Chapters in the history of ideas* (2nd ed., H. Hardy, Ed.). Princeton University Press. (Original work published 1947)

Bernasconi, R., & Lott, T. L. (2000). *The idea of race*. Hackett Publishing.

Beugelsdijk, S., & Welzel, C. (2018). Dimensions and dynamics of national culture: Synthesizing Hofstede with Inglehart. *Journal of Cross-Cultural Psychology*, *49*(10), 1469–1505. https://doi.org/10.1177/0022022118798505

Bloemraad, I., & Wright, M. (2014). "Utter failure" or unity out of diversity? Debating and evaluating policies of multiculturalism. *International Migration Review*, *48*(S1), 292–334.

Boas, F. (1911). *The mind of primitive man*. Macmillan.

Breuilly, J. (1996). *The formation of the first German nation-state, 1800–1871*. Red Globe Press.

Brubaker, R. (1996). *Nationalism reframed: Nationhood and the national question in the new Europe*. Cambridge University Press.

Burbank, J., & Cooper, F. (2010). *Empires in world history: Power and the politics of difference*. Princeton University Press.

Butler, J., & Spivak, G. C. (2007). *Who sings the nation-state?: Language, politics, belonging*. Seagull Books.

Caplan, J., & Torpey, J. C. (2002). *Documenting individual identity: The development of state practices in the modern world*. Princeton University Press.

Caro Baroja, J. (1970). *El mito del caracter nacional: Meditaciones a contrapelo*. Seminarios y Ediciones.

Chatterjee, P. (1994). *The nation and its fragments: Colonial and postcolonial histories*. Princeton University Press.

Chesebro, J. W. (1998). Distinguishing cultural systems: Change as a variable explaining and predicting cross-cultural communication. In D. V. Tanno & A. González (Eds.), *Communication and identity across cultures* (pp. 177–192). Sage.

Chua, R. Y. J., Huang, K. G., & Jin, M. (2019). Mapping cultural tightness and its links to innovation, urbanization, and happiness across 31 provinces in China. *PNAS*, *116*(14), 6720–6725. https://doi.org/10.1073/pnas.181572 311

Cohen, R., & Sheringham, O. (2016). *Encountering difference: Diasporic traces, creolizing spaces*. Polity Press.

Collins, P. H., & Sirma, B. (2020). *Intersectionality* (2nd ed.). Polity Press.

Cooley, C. H. (1909). *Social organization: A study of the larger mind*. Charles Scribner's Sons. https://doi.org/10.1037/14788-000

Cox, R. W. (1983). Gramsci, hegemony and international relations: An essay in method. *Millennium*, *12*(2), 162–175. https://doi.org/10.1177/03058 298830120020701

De Mooij, M., & Beniflah, J. (2017). Measuring cross-cultural differences of ethnic groups within nations: Convergence or divergence of cultural values? The case of the United States. *Journal of International Consumer Marketing*, *29*(1), 1–9.

Deng, F. M. (1997). Ethnicity: An African predicament. *The Brookings Review*, *15*(3), 28–31. https://doi.org/10.2307/20080749

Dillon, M., & Lobo-Guerrero, L. (2008). Biopolitics of security in the 21st century: An introduction. *Review of International Studies*, *34*(2), 265–292.

Eze, E. C. (2003). The color of reason: The idea of race in Kant's anthropology. In P. H. Coetzee & A. P. J. Roux (Eds.), *The African philosophy reader* (pp. 430-456). Routledge.

Fanon, F. (1963). *The wretched of the earth*. Grove Press.

Fincher, C. L., Thornhill, R., Murray, D. R., & Schaller, M. (2008). Pathogen prevalence predicts human cross-cultural variability in individualism/collectivism. *Proceedings of the Royal Society B: Biological Sciences*, https://doi.org/10.1098/rspb.2008.0094

Foucault, M. (1982). The subject and power. *Critical inquiry*, *8*(4), 777-795.

Foucault, M. (1995). *Discipline and punish: The birth of the prison*. 2nd ed. Vintage Books. (Originally published 1975)

Foucault, M. (1996). What is critique? In J. Schmidt (Ed.), *What is enlightenment?: Eighteenth-century answers and twentieth-century questions* (pp. 382-398). University of California Press. (Originally published 1978)

Foucault, M. (2001). *The order of things* (2nd ed.). Routledge. (Originally published 1966)

Foucault, M. (2003). *Society must be defended*. Penguin. (Originally published 1976)

Foucault, M., Senellart, M., Ewald, F., & Fontana, A. (2009). *Security, territory, population: Lectures at the College de France, 1977 - 1978*. Picador/Palgrave Macmillan. (Originally published 1978)

Gascoigne, J. (1999). The Royal Society and the emergence of science as an instrument of state policy. *The British Journal for the History of Science*, *32*(2), 171-184.

Geertz, C. (1963). The integrative revolution: Primordial sentiments and politics in the new states. In C. Geertz (Ed.), *Old societies and new states: The quest for modernity in Asia and Africa* (pp. 105-157). The Free Press of Glencoe & Collier-Macmillan.

Gelfand, M. J., Raver, J. L., Nishii, L., et al. (2011). Differences between tight and loose cultures: A 33-nation study. *Science*, *332*(6033), 1100-1104.

Gellner, E. (2006). *Nations and nationalism*. Blackwell. (Originally published 1983)

Gerlach, P., & Eriksson, K. (2021). Measuring cultural dimensions: External validity and internal consistency of Hofstede's VSM 2013 scales. *Frontiers in Psychology, Cultural Psychology*, *12*:662604. https://doi.org/10.3389/fpsyg.2021.662604

Graeber, D., & Wengrow, D. (2021). *The dawn of everything: A new history of humanity*. Farrar, Straus & Giroux.

Gramsci, A. (1971). *Selections from the prison notebooks* (Q. Hoare & G. N. Smith, Eds.). Alexander Street Press. (Originally written 1929-1935)

Greenberg, R., & Hamilakis, Y. (2022). *Archaeology, nation, and race: Confronting the past, decolonizing the future in Greece and Israel*. Cambridge University Press.

Haapala, P. (2021). Lived historiography: National history as a script to the past. In V. Kivimäki, S. Suodenjoki, & T. Vahtikari (Eds.), *Lived nation as the history of experiences and emotions in Finland, 1800 - 2000* (pp. 29 - 56). Palgrave Macmillan.

Hall, S. (1990). Cultural identity and diaspora. In J. Rutherford (Ed.), *Identity: Community, culture, difference* (pp. 222-237). Lawrence & Wishart.

Haller, M. (2002). Theory and method in the comparative study of values:

Critique and alternative to Inglehart. *European Sociological Review*, *18*(2), 139-158.

Hamedani, M. Y. G., & Markus, H. R. (2019). Understanding culture clashes and catalyzing change: A culture cycle approach. *Frontiers in Psychology*, *10*, art. 700. https://doi.org/10.3389/fpsyg.2019.00700

Handler, R. (1988). *Nationalism and the politics of culture in Quebec*. The University of Wisconsin Press.

Harrington, J. R., & Gelfand, M. J. (2014). Tightness-looseness across the 50 united states. *PNAS*, *111*(22), 7990-7995.

Herder, J. G. (1800). *Outlines of a philosophy of the history of man* (T. Churchill, Trans.). London: Luke Hansard for J. Johnson. (Orignally published 1784)

Herzfeld, M. (1985). *The poetics of manhood: Contest and identity in a Cretan mountain village*. Princeton University Press.

Herzfeld, M. (2002). The absent presence: Discourses of crypto-colonialism. *South Atlantic Quarterly*, *101*(4), 899-926.

Herzfeld, M. (2016a). *Cultural intimacy: Social poetics and the real life of states, societies, and institutions* (3rd ed.). Routledge. (Originally published 2005)

Herzfeld, M. (2016b). The hypocrisy of European moralism: Greece and the politics of cultural aggression. *Anthropology Today*, *32*(1),10-12.

Herzfeld, M. (2021). *Subversive archaism: Troubling traditionalists and the politics of national heritage*. Duke University Press.

Higham, J. (1993). Multiculturalism and universalism: A history and critique. *American Quarterly*, *45*(2), 195-219. https://doi.org/10.2307/2713251

Hippocrates (1881). *Hippocrates on airs, waters, and places* (F. Adams, Trans.). London: Wyman & Sons.

Hobbes, T., & Gaskin, J. C. A. (1996). *Leviathan*. Oxford University Press. (Originally published 1651)

Hobsbawm, E. J., & Ranger, T. O. (1983). *The invention of tradition*. Cambridge University Press.

Hofstede Insights: News (13 Oct. 2021). Why is managing cultural diversity important? (accessed 29 Aug. 2022)

Hofstede, G. (2012). Dimensionalizing cultures: The Hofstede model in context. In SISU Intercultural Institute (Ed.), *Value frameworks at the theoretical crossroads of culture* (pp. 183-216). Intercultural Research Vol. 4. Shanghai Foreign Language Education Press.

Hofstede, G., Hofstede, G. J., & Minkov, M. (2010). *Cultures and organizations: Software of the mind. Intercultural cooperation and its importance for survival* (3rd ed.). McGraw Hill.

Hornung, A. (Ed.). (2007). *Intercultural America*. Universitätsverlag Winter.

Hsia, A. (1998). Historical background: The continental connection. In A. Hsia (Ed.), *The vision of China in the English literature of the seventeenth and eighteenth centuries* (pp.3-28). The Chinese University Press.

Hsu, D. (2017). Searching for meaning in a hybrid and fractured world: Contemporary Chinese cultural identity and its implications for missiology. *Missiology: An International Review*, *45*(1), 103-115. https://doi.org/10.1177/0091829616680647

Hua, Z. (2016). Identifying research paradigms. In Z. Hua (Ed.), *Research methods in intercultural communication* (pp.26-55). Wiley Blackwell.

Huff, R. (2020). Governmentality. *Encyclopedia Britannica*.

Hume, D. (1987). *Essays moral, political, literary* (Revised ed., by E. F. Miller). Liberty Fund. (Originally published 1777; "Of national characters" 1748)

Immerwahr, D. (2019). *How to hide an empire: A history of the greater United States*. Farrar, Straus & Giroux.

Indigenous peoples and the United Nations human rights system (2013). Fact sheet no. 9/Rev. 2.

JanMohamed, A. R. (1985). The economy of Manichean allegory: The function of racial difference in colonialist literature. *Critical Inquiry*, *12*(1), 59–87.

Javidan, M., House, R. J., Dorfman, P. W., Hanges, P. J., & de Luque, M. S. (2006). Conceptualizing and measuring cultures and their consequences: A comparative review of GLOBE's and Hofstede's approaches. *Journal of International Business Studies*, *37*, 897–914.

Kalberg, S. (1980). Max Weber's types of rationality: Cornerstones for the analysis of rationalization processes in history. *American Journal of Sociology*, *85*(5), 1145–1179.

Kant, I. (1903). *Perpetual peace: A philosophical essay* (M. C. Smith, Trans.). Sonnenschein. (Originally published 1795)

Kant, I. (2006). *Anthropology from a pragmatic point of view* (R. B. Louden, Trans.). Cambridge University Press. (Originally published 1798)

Kant, I. (2007a). Of the different races of human beings. In R. Louden & G. Zöller (Eds.), *Anthropology, history, and education* (pp. 82 – 97). The Cambridge edition of the works of Immanuel Kant. Cambridge University Press. doi:10.1017/CBO9780511791925.016 (Originally published 1775)

Kant, I. (2007b). On the use of teleological principles in philosophy. In R. Louden & G. Zöller (Eds.), *Anthropology, history, and education* (pp. 192–218). The Cambridge edition of the works of Immanuel Kant. Cambridge University Press. doi: 10. 1017/CBO9780511791925. 016 (Originally published 1788)

Kant, I. (2011). *Observations on the feeling of the beautiful and sublime and other writings* (P. Frierson & P. Guyer, Eds.). Cambridge University Press. (Originally published 1764)

Kent, J. (1995). The enlightenment. In P. Byrne & L. Houlden (Eds.), *Companion encyclopedia of theology* (pp.251–271). Routledge.

Kivimäki, V., Suodenjoki, S., & Vahtikari, T. (2021). Lived nation: Histories of experience and emotion in understanding nationalism. In V. Kivimäki, S. Suodenjoki, & T. Vahtikari (Eds.), *Lived nation as the history of experiences and emotions in Finland, 1800–2000* (pp.1–28). Palgrave Macmillan.

Knutsen, T. (2016). A re-emergence of nationalism as a political force in Europe? In Y. Peters & M. Tatham (Eds.), *Democratic transformations in Europe: Challenges and opportunities* (pp.13–32). Routledge.

Kraus, M. W., Piff, P. K., & Keltner, D. (2011). Social class as culture: The convergence of resources and rank in the social realm. *Current Directions in Psychological Science*, *20* (4), 246–250. https://doi. org/10. 1177/096372141 1414654

Kulich, S. J. (2019). Reconsidering intercultural narratives: Prologue to research on Rachel Davis DuBois and early textual approaches to interculturality. In M. Steppat & S. J. Kulich (Eds.), *Literature and interculturality I: Concepts, applications, interactions* (pp.1–13). Intercultural Research Vol. 8. Shanghai Foreign Language Education Press.

Kulich, S. J., & He, J. (2012). The empirical foundations of current values research. In SISU Intercultural Institute (Ed.), *Value frameworks at the theoretical crossroads of culture* (pp. 71-102). Intercultural Research Vol. 4. Shanghai Foreign Language Education Press.

Kulich, S. J., Weng, L., Tong, R., & Dubois, G. (2020). An expanded history of intercultural communication studies: From interdisciplinary roots and research to intercultural education and training. In D. Landis & D. P. S. Bhawuk (Eds.), *The handbook of intercultural training* (4th ed., pp. 60-163). Cambridge University Press.

Kymlicka, W. (2005). Liberal multiculturalism: Western models, global trends, and Asian debates. In W. Kymlicka & B. He (Eds.), *Multiculturalism in Asia* (pp. 22-55). Oxford University Press. https://doi. org/10. 1093/0199277621. 001. 0001, accessed 14 Aug. 2022

Kymlicka, W. (2010). The rise and fall of multiculturalism?: New debates on inclusion and accommodation in diverse societies. In S. Vertovec & S. Wessendorf (Eds.), *The multiculturalism backlash: European discourses, policies and practices* (pp. 32-49). Routledge.

Kymlicka, W. (2012). Multiculturalism: Success, failure, and the future. *Migration Policy Institute*.

Lee, A. R. (2003). *Multicultural American literature: Comparative black, native, Latino/a, and Asian American fictions*. University Press of Mississippi.

Leeds-Hurwitz, W. (2010). Writing the intellectual history of intercultural communication. In T. K. Nakayama & R. T. Halualani (Eds.), *The handbook of critical intercultural communication* (pp. 21-33). Wiley-Blackwell.

Lentz, C. (2017). Culture: The making, unmaking and remaking of an anthropological concept. *Zeitschrift Für Ethnologie*, *142*(2), 181-204.

Lichtblau, K. (2011). Vergemeinschaftung and Vergesellschaftung in Max Weber: A reconstruction of his linguistic usage. *History of European Ideas*, *37*(4), 454-465.

Locke, J. (1980). *Second treatise of government* (C. B. Macpherson, Ed.). Hackett Publishing. (Originally published 1689)

Locke, J. (1996). *An essay concerning human understanding* (K. P. Winker, Ed.). Hackett Publishing. (Originally published 1689)

Lovejoy, A. O. (1923). The supposed primitivism of Rousseau's "Discourse on inequality." *Modern Philology*, *21*(2), 165-186.

Lu, J. G., Benet - Martínez, V., & Wang, L. C. (2023). A Socioecological-genetic framework of culture and personality: Their roots, trends, and interplay. *Annual Review of Psychology*, 74, 363-390.

Lundgren, A. (2015). Knowledge production and the World Values Survey: Objective measuring with ethno-centric conclusions. In I. Brandell, M. Carlson, & O. A. Çetrez (Eds.), *Borders and the changing boundaries of knowledge* (pp. 35-52). Swedish Research Institute in Istanbul (Transactions, Vol. 22).

Makarychev, A, & Yatsyk, A. (2017). Biopolitics and national identities: Between liberalism and totalization. *Nationalities Papers*, *45*(1), 1-7. doi: 10. 1080/00905992. 2016. 1225705

Mali, J. (2012). *The legacy of Vico in modern cultural history: From Jules Michelet to Isaiah Berlin*. Cambridge University Press.

Marková, I. (2016). *The dialogical mind: Common sense and ethics*. Cambridge University Press.

Markus, H. R., & Hamedani, M. G. (2019). People are culturally shaped shapers: The psychological science of culture and culture change. In D. Cohen & S. Kitayama (Eds.), *Handbook of cultural psychology* (2nd ed., pp. 11-52). The Guilford Press.

Markus, H. R., & Kitayama, S. (1991). Culture and the self: Implications for cognition, emotion, and motivation. *Psychological Review*, *98*(2), 224-253. https://doi.org/10.1037/0033-295X.98.2.224

Martinelli, R. (2016). On the philosophical significance of national characters: Reflections from Hume and Kant. In G. De Anna & R. Martinelli (Eds.), *Practical rationality in political contexts* (pp. 47-58). EUT Edizioni Università di Trieste.

Martinich, A. P., & Hoekstra, K. (Eds.). (2016). *The Oxford handbook of Hobbes*. Oxford University Press.

McSweeney, B. (2002). Hofstede's model of national cultural differences and their consequences: A triumph of faith — a failure of analysis. *Human Relations*, *55*(1), 89-118.

Michalopoulos, S., & Papaioannou, E. (2010). Divide and rule or the rule of the divided? Evidence from Africa. http://dx.doi.org/10.2139/ssrn.1696195

Mikkelson, J. M. (2013). *Kant and the concept of race*. State University of New York Press.

Minkov, M. (2013). *Cross-cultural analysis: The science and art of comparing the world's modern societies and their cultures*. Sage.

Minkov, M., & Hofstede, G. (2012). Is national culture a meaningful concept?: Cultural values delineate homogeneous national clusters of in-country regions. *Cross-Cultural Research: The Journal of Comparative Social Science*, *46*(2), 133-159. https://doi.org/10.1177/1069397111427262

Minkov, M., Kaasa, A., & Welzel, C. (2021). Economic development and modernization in Africa homogenize national cultures. *Journal of Cross-Cultural Psychology*, *52*(8-9), 801-821. doi:10.1177/00220221211035495

Montesquieu, C. (1777). *Complete works*. Vol. 1: *The spirit of laws*. London: T. Evans. (Originally published 1748)

Moulettes, A. (2007). The absence of women's voices in Hofstede's *Cultural Consequences*: A postcolonial reading. *Women in Management Review*, *22*(6), 443-455.

Muller, B. J. (2017). Governmentality and biopolitics. *Oxford research encyclopedia of international studies*. Oxford University Press. https://doi.org/10.1093/acrefore/9780190846626.013.50

Multiculturalism @50 and the promise of a just society (Fall/Winter 2021). CITC (Canadian Issues).

Nisbett, R. E., Peng, K., Choi, I., & Norenzayan, A. (2001). Culture and systems of thought: Holistic versus analytic cognition. *Psychological Review*, *108*(2), 291-310. https://doi.org/10.1037/0033-295X.108.2.291

Ogunnaike, O. (2016). From heathen to sub-human: A genealogy of the influence of the decline of religion on the rise of modern racism. *Open Theology*, *2*(1). https://doi.org/10.1515/opth-2016-0059

Oishi, S. (2013). Socioecological psychology. *Annual Review of Psychology*, *65*(2014), 581-609. doi: 10.1146/annurev-psych-030413-152156; Epub 2013 (Aug. 26), PMID: 23987114.

Ono, K. A. (2010). Reflections on "problematizing 'nation' in intercultural communication research." In T. K. Nakayama & R. T. Halualani (Eds.), *The *handbook of critical intercultural communication* (pp. 84-97). Wiley-Blackwell. https://doi.org/10.1002/9781444390681.ch6

Painter, J. (2013). Regional biopolitics. *Regional Studies*, *47*, 1235-1248.

Patten, A. (2010). "The most natural state": Herder and nationalism. *History of Political Thought*, *31*(4), 657-689.

Prins, B., & Slijper, B. (2002). Multicultural society under attack: Introduction. *Journal of International Migration and Integration*, *3*, 313-328.

Rauscher, F. (2021). Kant's social and political philosophy. In E. N. Zalta (Ed.), *The Stanford encyclopedia of philosophy* (Summer 2021 Edition).

Robinson, A. (2014). National versus ethnic identification in Africa: Modernization, colonial legacy, and the origins of territorial nationalism. *World Politics*, *66*(4), 709-746. doi:10.1017/S0043887114000239

Roeder, P. (2007). *Where nation-states come from: Institutional change in the age of nationalism*. Princeton University Press. https://doi.org/10.1515/9781400842964

Rousseau, J. (2002). *The social contract and the first and second discourses* (S. Dunn, Ed.). Yale University Press. (*The second discourse* originally published 1755, *The social contract* 1762.)

Said, E. W. (1978). *Orientalism*. Pantheon Books.

Saldanha, T. J. V., John-Mariadoss, B., Wu, M. X., & Mithas, S. (2021). How information and communication technology shapes the influence of culture on innovation: A country-level analysis. *Journal of Management Information Systems*, *38*(1), 108-139. doi: 10.1080/07421222.2021.1870386

Sandford, S. (2018). Kant, race, and natural history. *Philosophy & Social Criticism*, *44*(9), 950-977. https://doi.org/10.1177/0191453718768358

Schwartz, S. H. (2012). Basic human values: Their content and structure across cultures. In SISU Intercultural Institute (Ed.), *Value frameworks at the theoretical crossroads of culture* (pp. 257-294). Intercultural Research Vol. 4. Shanghai Foreign Language Education Press.

Scott, J. C. (1985). *Weapons of the weak: Everyday forms of peasant resistance*. Yale University Press.

Scott, J. C. (1998). *Seeing like a state: How certain schemes to improve the human condition have failed*. Yale University Press.

Seton-Watson, H. (1977). *Nations and states: An enquiry into the origins of nations and the politics of nationalism*. Taylor & Francis.

Shearman, S. M. (2012). Value frameworks across cultures: Hofstede's, Inglehart's, and Schwartz's approaches. In SISU Intercultural Institute (Ed.), *Value frameworks at the theoretical crossroads of culture* (pp. 137-180). Intercultural Research Vol. 4. Shanghai Foreign Language Education Press.

Shils, E. (1957). Primordial, personal, sacred and civil ties: Some particular observations on the relationships of sociological research and theory. *The British Journal of Sociology*, *8*(2), 130-145. https://doi.org/10.2307/587365

Spencer, V. (2007). In defense of Herder on cultural diversity and interaction. *The Review of Politics*, *69*(1), 79-105.

Steppat, M. (2019). "All the races": Reassessing the American community masque. In M. Steppat & S. J. Kulich (Eds.), *Literature and interculturality I: Concepts, applications, interactions* (pp. 339-371). Intercultural Research Vol. 8. Shanghai Foreign Language Education Press.

Steppat, M., & Tong, R. (2021). Prefigurations of intercultural thinking: Explorations in ancient Mediterranean and Chinese sources. *Journal of*

Intercultural Communication & Interactions Research, *1*(1), 101–134.

Talhelm, T., & English, A. S. (2020). Historically rice-farming societies have tighter social norms in China and worldwide. *PNAS*, *117*(33), 19816–19824. https://doi.org/10.1073/pnas.190990911

Taylor, C. (1994). The politics of recognition. In A. Gutmann (Ed.), *Multiculturalism: Examining the politics of recognition* (pp. 25–73). Princeton University Press.

Tönnies, F. (2001). *Community and civil society* (J. Harris, Ed.). Cambridge University Press. (Originally published 1887)

Triandis, H. C. (2014). Dynamics of individualism and collectivism across cultures. In S. J. Kulich, L. Weng, & M. H. Prosser (Eds.), *Value dimensions and their contextual dynamics across cultures* (pp. 61–82). Intercultural Research Vol. 5. Shanghai Foreign Language Education Press.

Tylor, E. B. (1871). *Primitive culture* (Vols. 1 & 2). London: John Murray.

Uhlig, C. (2001). National historiography and cultural identity: The example of the English Renaissance. In H. Grabes (Ed.), *Writing the early modern English nation: The transformation of national identity in sixteenth-and seventeenth-century England* (pp. 89–107). Rodopi.

Ukkusuri, S. V., Mesa-Arango, R., Narayanan, B., Sadri, A. M., & Xian, X. (2016). *Evolution of the Commonwealth trade network: Hubs, criticality and global value chains*. International trade working paper. Commonwealth Secretariat.

Van Benthem van den Bergh, B. G. (2018). Herder and the idea of a nation. *Human Figurations*, *7*(1).

Van de Vijver, F. J. R. (2014). Multiculturalism: Definition and value. In S. J. Kulich, L. Weng, & M. H. Prosser (Eds.), *Value dimensions and their contextual dynamics across cultures* (pp. 165–190). Intercultural Research Vol. 5. Shanghai Foreign Language Education Press.

Van de Vliert, E. (2013). Climato-economic habitats support patterns of human needs, stresses, and freedoms. *Behavioral and Brain Sciences*, *36*(5), 1–57.

Vico, G. (1948). *The new science* (T. G. Bergin & M. H. Fisch, Trans. from 1744 ed.). Cornell University Press. (Original work published 1725)

Walia, H. (2021). *Border and rule: Global migration, capitalism, and the rise of racist nationalism*. Haymarket Books.

Weber, M. (1958). *From Max Weber: Essays in sociology* (H. Gerth & C. W. Mills, Eds.). Oxford University Press. (Lecture "Science as a vocation" originally given 1917, "Bureaucracy" originally published 1921)

Weber, M. (2001). *The protestant ethic and the spirit of capitalism*. Routledge. (Originally published 1905)

Weber, M. (2019). *Economy and society* (K. Tribe, Trans.). Harvard University Press. https://doi.org/10.4159/9780674240827 (Originally published 1922)

White, R. (2005). Herder: On the ethics of nationalism. *Humanitas*, *18*(1), 166–181.

Wimmer, A., & Feinstein, Y. (2010). The rise of the nation-state across the world, 1816 to 2001. *American Sociological Review*, *75*(5), 764–790. https://doi.org/10.1177/0003122410382639

Wimmer, A., & Min, B. (2006). From empire to nation-state: Explaining wars in the modern world, 1816–2001. *American Sociological Review*, *71*(6), 867–897. https://doi.org/10.1177/000312240607100601

Wimmer, A., & Glick Schiller, N. (2002). Methodological nationalism and beyond: Nation-state building, migration and the social sciences. *Global*

Networks, 2(4), 301–334. doi:10.1111/1471–0374.00043

World values survey (2020). Findings and insights.

Wu, M.-Y. (2006). Hofstede's cultural dimensions 30 years later. *Intercultural Communication Studies*, 15(1), 2006, 33–42.

Yang, D. (2001). The malleable and the contested: The Nanjing massacre in postwar China and Japan. In T. Fujitani, G. White & L. Yoneyama (Eds.), *Perilous memories: The Asia-Pacific War(s)* (pp. 50–86). Duke University Press.

Young, R. J. C. (2003). *Postcolonialism: A very short introduction*. Oxford University Press.

Zack, N. (Ed.). (2017). *The Oxford handbook of philosophy and race*. Oxford University Press.

About the Authors

Milton J. Bennett (Ph. D.) founded and directs the *Intercultural Development Research Institute* located in the USA and the EU (idrinstitute.org). He was a tenured associate professor of intercultural communication at Portland State University, where he created its graduate program in that topic. He is currently an adjunct professor in the sociology of cultural processes at the University of Milano Bicocca and an active consultant to corporations, universities, and exchange organizations in Europe, Asia, and the U.S. Dr. Bennett studied physics and cognitive psychology as part of his B. A. degree from Stanford University, has an M. A. in psycholinguistics from San Francisco State University, and holds one of the first Ph. D. 's in intercultural communication (University of Minnesota). His current textbook is *Basic Concepts of Intercultural Communication: Paradigms, Principles, and Practices* (English, Chinese, Italian) and he has current articles in the *Wiley Encyclopedia of Intercultural Communication* (2017), the *Cambridge Handbook of Intercultural Communication* (2020), and the *Cambridge Handbook of Intercultural Training, 4th Edition* (2020). He was a contributing co-editor of the *Sage Handbook of Intercultural Training, 3rd Edition* and is a founding Fellow of the International Academy of Intercultural Research (IAIR), along with being an active member of the European Society for Intercultural Education, Training, and Research (SIETAR).

Valery Chirkov is Professor in the Department of Psychology at the University of Saskatchewan, Canada. He got his Ph. D. degree in social and personality psychology in 2001 from the University of Rochester, Rochester, NY. Before he migrated to North America, Dr. Chirkov worked as an associate professor at Yaroslavl State University, Russia. His research interests lie in examining the mechanisms of sociocultural regulation of people's mental and behavioral activities. Within this line of thinking, Dr. Chirkov has articulated the theory of sociocultural models that was published in 2020 (An introduction to the theory of sociocultural models. *Asian Journal of Social Psychology*). An application of this theory to the understanding of acculturation and intercultural relations was communicated in 2022 (Alfred Schutz's "Stranger," the theory of sociocultural models, and mechanisms of acculturation. *Culture & Psychology*). Dr. Chirkov is also interested in philosophical and methodological aspects of sociocultural psychological research. In 2016, he published the textbook *Fundamentals of research on culture and psychology: Theory and methods*, and he continues this line of methodological thinking by applying critical realism to psychological and cultural psychological studies: (2021) Reflections on an application of realism in psychology. *Theory & Psychology*; co-authored with Anderson, J. (2018) Statistical positivism versus critical scientific realism. A comparison of two paradigms for motivation research: Part 1. A philosophical and empirical analysis of statistical positivism. Part 2. A philosophical and empirical analysis of critical scientific realism.

Clifford H. Clarke's background has been split between Japan and the United States starting with all formative childhood years in Japan. He was stoned at the age of ten by a neighborhood gang of boys and ever since has been studying Japanese and American human relationships. His academic training in Japanese religions, philosophies, anthropology, and psychology have given him insight to the origins of the values and perceptions of Japanese and Americans. His 12 years in intercultural counseling at Stanford and Cornell Universities has informed him of the challenges of bicultural relationships and bicultural identities. His 13 years of teaching in multicultural classrooms at Stanford and the University of Hawai'i has taught him about different culturally influenced learning and teaching styles. His interdisciplinary academic training at Stanford University and 30 years of researching and consulting American and Japanese managers in over 300 global bicultural organizations with Clarke Consulting Group has enabled him to understand the struggles between individual and organizational goals and norms of behavior (Clarke & Hammer, 1995; Clarke & Lipp, 1998).

Stephen M. Croucher (Ph. D., University of Oklahoma, 2006) is the Professor and Head of the School of Communication, Journalism, and Marketing at Massey University. He is also the Wellington Regional Director of the Massey Business School. He is currently a Lead Research Fellow at the National Research University, Higher

School of Economics, Russia. He studies organizational and intercultural communication. He has authored more than 100 peer-reviewed journal articles in journals such as *Scientific Reports, Communication Monographs, Management Communication Quarterly, International Journal of Conflict Management*, and *Mass Communication & Society*. He has authored/co-edited more than 10 books and given keynote addresses in more than 25 nations. He serves on the editorial boards of various journals and served as the editor of the *Journal of Intercultural Communication Research* (2010–2019), *Speaker & Gavel* (2010–2015), and *Frontiers in Communication* (2019–2020). He is the incoming editor of the *Review of Communication*. He has held various leadership positions in the National Communication Association, International Communication Association, and the World Communication Association. He is currently the President of the World Communication Association.

Rolf Elberfeld is Professor of Cultural Philosophy at the University of Hildesheim, Germany. He previously had appointments at universities in Zürich, Innsbruck, and Vienna. He gained his doctorate at the University of Würzburg on the interculturality of Kitarō Nishida; his habilitation thesis was devoted to Dōgen Zenji's phenomenology of time, and Elberfeld was awarded the Straniak prize for philosophy, subsequently the Karl Jaspers prize. His major research areas are phenomenology, intercultural ethics and aesthetics, cultural philosophy, and the philosophy of interculturality and the body. Elberfeld has developed an approach called "transformative phenomenology," as against descriptive and hermeneutic phenomenology, in response to encountering East Asian thought. Elberfeld is directing a nationally funded project on Histories of Philosophy in a Global Perspective. His major book publications include *Kitarō Nishida (1870 – 1945): Das Verstehen der Kulturen* [Nishida: Understanding Cultures] (1999), *Denkansätze zur buddhistischen Philosophie in China* [Approaches to Buddhist Philosophy in China] (2000), *Phänomenologie der Zeit im Buddhismus* [Phenomenology of Time in Buddhism] (2004), *Sprache und Sprachen: Eine philosophische Grundorientierung* [Language and Languages: A Basic Philosophical Orientation] (2012), *Philosophieren in einer globalisierten Welt* [Philosophy in a Globalized World] (2017), and *Zen* (2017).

José Luís Garcia (Ph. D., University of Lisbon, Portugal) is a Senior Research Fellow at the Institute of Social Sciences, University of

Lisbon. His research interests focus mainly on social, communicative, ecological, ethical, and political implications derived from convergence processes between contemporary economy and the technological-scientific field, classical sociological theory, the emergence of new media and their consequences for public life and journalism, social, economic, and moral dilemmas of biotechnologies. He has held a variety of visiting positions at universities in Spain, Brazil, USA, Italy, and France. He is author of dozens of articles and book chapters about communication, information technologies and mass media, social theory, political, social and ethical impacts of technosciences, as well as uncertainty and environmental topics.

Richard Harris was born and raised in London, U.K., and obtained a degree in English Literature from the University of Manchester. He later earned a Master's in Humanities from California State University and a Doctorate in Intercultural Communication from the University of New Mexico. In 1980 he moved to Japan, where he has lived ever since with the exception of two year-long overseas sabbaticals. Harris is Professor of Intercultural Management in the School of Management, Chukyo University, Nagoya. He teaches courses on intercultural communication and management at undergraduate and graduate levels, as well as three seminars on intercultural themes determined by students. He also served two years as Dean of School, an unusual honor for a non-Japanese. Harris's research interests include cultural concepts of the ideal society as reflected in myths of paradise, cultural reactions to physical space, tourism, and the representation of culture in national museums. Currently, he is interested in the theme of cultural relativism and its problems and limitations in an increasingly globalized world. In recent years he has contributed articles on Museums and Tourism to the Sage Encyclopedia of Intercultural Competence, and articles on Acculturation/ Assimilation and Interculturalism to the Sage Encyclopedia of Multiculturalism. His most recent publication (2020) is a book chapter entitled "Perceptions in and of the City: Transformations of Multiculturalism." He has given presentations at many international conferences.

Steve J. Kulich is Distinguished Professor at Shanghai International Studies University, Director of the SISU International Institute, Co-Editor of *Intercultural Research*, and Academic Coordinator for the SISU MBA program. He received his M.A. from the University of

Kansas and his Ph.D. from Humboldt University of Berlin, Germany. In his 40 years in Asia and 26 years in Shanghai, he has pioneered intercultural training courses, M.A. and Ph.D. programs at SISU, and has helped organize ten international Intercultural Communication conferences. With Michael Prosser, he has edited the *International Journal of Intercultural Relations* 2012 (4) " Special Issue: Early American Pioneers of Intercultural Communication." He is on the Editorial Board of the *Intercultural Communication Series*, *Intercultural Communication Research*, and the *Journal of Middle East and Islamic Studies (in Asia)*. Prof. Kulich's work has been published in *Intercultural Communication Studies*, *China Media Research*, *International Management Review*, *China Media Reports Overseas*, *Cross-cultural Psychology Bulletin*, *The International Scope Review*, and by Edgar Elgar Press (in Xu and Bond's *Handbook of Chinese Organizational Behavior*, 2012), Oxford University Press (in Bond's *Handbook of Chinese Psychology*, 2nd ed., 2010), Sage (in Littlejohn's and Foss's *Encyclopedia of Communication Theory*, 2009), Hong Kong University Press, Higher Education Press, FLTRP, SFLEP, and Yunnan People's Press, as well as his 2002 columns in English Salon and Shanghai Scene. He has been honored with a "Special Contribution Award" (CAFIC, 2011) and twice with the Magnolia Award (Silver 2007, Gold 2011) from the Shanghai government, as well as a national "Favorite Foreign Teacher" Award (2014). With his team, he has been chiefly responsible for developing and running China's first international partnership Massive Online Open Course with FutureLearn. He is a former President of the International Academy for Intercultural Research (IAIR).

Wendy Leeds-Hurwitz (Ph.D., University of Pennsylvania, USA) is Director of the Center for Intercultural Dialogue, Professor Emerita of the University of Wisconsin-Parkside (both in the USA), and Associate Faculty at Royal Roads University (Canada). She has held a variety of visiting positions in Paris and Lyon (France), Coimbra (Portugal), Beijing and Macao (China). She has published 13 books, becoming known for work in intercultural communication, social interaction, social construction theory, semiotic theory, ethnography of communication, and disciplinary history.

Judith N. Martin is professor emerita of Intercultural Communication at Arizona State University, USA. She has authored and co-authored many research publications on the topics of cultural adaptation and sojourner communication, intercultural communication competence, ethnic/racial identification and white social identity, as well as interactive media and intercultural communication. Her books include *Intercultural Communication in Contexts*, *Readings in Intercultural Communication: Experiences and Contexts*, *Whiteness: The Communication of Social Identity*, *Intercultural Communication and New Media*, and *Students Abroad, Strangers at Home*.

Thomas K. Nakayama is professor of communication studies at Northeastern University in Boston, Massachusetts, USA. He works in the area of critical intercultural communication. He is the founding editor of the *Journal of International and Intercultural Communication*. He is a former Fulbrighter at the Université de Mons in Belgium. He has been named a Distinguished Scholar by the National Communication Association. He has also been named a Distinguished Research Fellow by the Eastern Communication Association and a Distinguished Scholar by the Western States Communication Association.

Gesine Lenore Schiewer (Ph. D. University of Bern, 1993) is professor and chair of Intercultural German Studies at the University of Bayreuth, Germany. She also holds a position at the University of Bern, and has had visiting professorships in several countries. She is president of the Society for Intercultural German Studies, chairwoman of the Board Institute for International Communication and Foreign Cultural Work in Bayreuth, co-founder and director of the International Research Centre Chamisso Literature, and member of the Advisory Board Bavarian-Togolese Society. Her chief areas of interest are Intercultural German Studies, Linguistics, Literary Studies, Intercultural Communication Research, Emotion and Conflict Research, and International Social Innovation with a focus on participatory communication including educational concepts. Major publications include *Cognitio symbolica: Lambert's semiotic science and its discussion in Herder, Jean Paul, and Novalis* (1996); *Poetische Gestaltkonzepte und Automatentheorie: Arno Holz — Robert Musil — Oswald Wiener* (2004); and *Studienbuch Emotionsforschung* (2014). She has also edited the *Handbook Language and Emotion* (2021/ 2022) and publications on " Theory and Practice of Bilingually Mediated Communication in Discussion, " as well as being editor or co-editor of journals such as *Kodikas/Code* and *Journal for Intercultural German Studies*.

Michael Steppat served as Chair of Literature in English at the University of Bayreuth, Germany, until he achieved Emeritus status in 2015. He also holds a Professorial position of honor in Moscow from the Russian Federation's Ministry of Higher Education and Science. He has been appointed regular visiting professor at Shanghai International Studies University, extending to advisor functions, as well as visiting professor at other Chinese universities. After receiving his Ph.D. from the University of Münster (Germany) and later his 'Habilitation' both from Münster and from Free University of Berlin, he was a Fulbright scholar at the University of Texas at Austin, then research professor at Arizona State University. He has repeatedly been awarded the Myra and Charlton Hinman Fellowship of Amherst College; he has also been granted the position of a Scholar-in-Residence at the John W. Kluge Center of the Library of Congress. He has served as Academic Dean in his Faculty for many years. To move in a new direction, he developed an internationally cooperative graduate program of Intercultural Anglophone Studies. His book publications include *Honor, Face and Violence: Cross-Cultural Literary Representations of Honor Cultures and Face Cultures*; *Americanisms: Discourses of Exception, Exclusion, Exchange*; *Literature and Interculturality* (3 volumes); and a monograph on the early work of St. Augustine of Hippo. A collaborative volume on *Writing Identity: The Construction of National Identity in American Literature* (Moscow City University) extends this range. Spurred by an invitation from the London School of Economics and Political Science in 2011 to organize a workshop, Steppat has increasingly devoted attention to intercultural studies in connection with literature.

Filipa Subtil (Ph.D., Universidade de Lisboa) is Assistant Professor at Escola Superior de Comunicação Social, Instituto Politécnico de Lisboa, and researcher at ICNOVA (Lisbon). She has been visiting scholar at the University of Iowa (2010) and Muhlenberg College (2008) in the USA; at Cardinal Stefan Wyszyński University (2017, 2018) in Poland; and at Universidad de Navarra (2019) in Spain. She was vice-coordinator of the Communication and Politics Section of SOPCOM (Associação Portuguesa de Ciências da Comunicação). Among her research interests are sociology of communication, social theory of the media in the USA and Canada, and frameworks of the media on gender issues. Her published work has appeared in international and national journals and books.

Paul Zilungisele Tembe lectures Mandarin at the University of South Africa and is Associate Professor at the Institute of African Studies at Zhejiang Normal University, Jinhua. He has an M.A. in Kiswahili Studies from Uppsala University, Sweden and a Ph.D. in Chinese Studies from the Chinese University of Hong Kong. He is fluent in English, Kiswahili, Mandarin, Portuguese, Sesotho, Swedish, Xitsonga, and isiZulu.

Keyan Gray Tomaselli is Distinguished Professor, Dean's Office, Faculty of Humanities, University of Johannesburg (UJ). He is also on the board of the UJ Centre for Africa-China Studies, and is an honorary professor in the Centre for Trans-media and Trans-culture, Capital Normal University, Beijing, and a member of the Shanghai University Expert Program. He is also Emeritus Professor and Fellow of the University of KwaZulu-Natal. Co-editor with Qing Cao and Doreen Wu of *Brand China in the Media: Transformation of Identities* (Routledge, 2020), he is also an editorial board member of *Journal of Chinese Film Studies* and *New Techno Humanities*.

Rongtian Tong obtained his undergraduate degree from Washington State University with a major in International Business and minor in Sociology. He has recently worked at Shanghai International Studies University in the field of Intercultural Communication, and he is currently studying for his M.A. at the University of Washington. His publications have appeared in *The Handbook of Intercultural Training* (4th ed.) and *International Journal of Intercultural Relations*.

Wim M. J. van Binsbergen was trained in sociology, anthropology, and general linguistics at Amsterdam University (Municipal). He held professorships in the social sciences at Leiden, Manchester, Durban, Berlin, and Amsterdam (Free University). At the latter institution he took his doctorate (1979) and was the incumbent of the chair of ethnic studies (1990 – 1998), prior to acceding to the chair of Foundations of Intercultural Philosophy, Philosophical Faculty, Erasmus University Rotterdam (1998–2006). Simultaneously, he held senior appointments at the African Studies Centre, University of Leiden (1977 – 2020). Over the decades, he has established himself internationally as a specialist on African ethnicity, African religion, ethnohistory, globalization, intercultural philosophy, comparative mythology, the Mediterranean Bronze Age, and transcontinental continuities between Africa and Asia in pre-and proto-history. He was President of the Netherlands Association of African Studies, 1990 – 1993, President of the Netherlands/Flemish Association for Intercultural Philosophy (1998–2022), and one of the Founding Members/ Directors of the International Association for Comparative Mythology, 2006–2020. From 2002 he has been the Editor of *Quest: An African Journal of Philosophy/Revue Africaine de Philosophie*. His books include *Religious Change in Zambia* (1981), *Tears of Rain* (1992), *Intercultural Encounters* (2003), *Ethnicity in Mediterranean Protohistory* (with Fred Woudhuizen, 2011), *Black Athena Comes of Age* (2011), *Before the Presocratics* (2012), *Vicarious Reflections* (2015), *Religion as a Social Construct* (2017), *Researching Power and Identity in African State Formation* (with Martin Doornbos, 2017), *Confronting the Sacred: Durkheim Vindicated* (2018), *Rethinking Africa's Transcontinental Continuities in Pre-and Proto-history* (ed., 2019), *Sunda: Pre-and Proto-historical Continuities Between Asia and Africa* (2020), *Sangoma Science: From Ethnography to Intercultural Ontology: A Poetics of African Spiritualities* (2021), *Joseph Karst: As a Pioneer of Long-range Approaches to Mediterranean Bronze-Age Ethnicity* (2021), and *Pandora's Box Prised Open: Studies in Comparative Mythology* (2022). His published work is also available from: quest-journal.net/shikanda.

About the Series

The *Intercultural Research* book series of the SISU Intercultural Institute (SII) of Shanghai International Studies University (SISU) aims to be a publication in the tradition of an "annual" with each volume (or pair of volumes) focusing on one important topic or theme central to the historical or ongoing development of intercultural communication. With this goal mind, *Intercultural Research* has and continues to seek to publish seminal, cutting edge chapters on the state of the intercultural field in a specific area.

In seeking to cover and help map out the "state of the art" on the designated domain, each volume (or pair of volumes) aims to include diverse theoretical or applied research from indigenous or comparative cultural, intercultural, or cross-cultural approaches, highlight varied paradigms or investigative methodologies on that subject, and provide pertinent "history and status" overviews that track developments, note or critique trends, and suggest important directions for further research developments. The series thus aims to provide a benchmark reference for assessing the current state of the field and an impetus for stimulating future research development on each specified topic.

While seeking to broadly encompass diverse international approaches to any given topic, because of being published in China, the series seeks to especially consider non-Western perspectives. Each volume aims to incorporate contributions that may have greater relevance to studies in other Asian or Chinese societies. For those domains deemed to merit two volumes, the second companion volume generally includes a focus related to Chinese theories and applications (and some chapters or volumes may on occasion be published in Chinese).

In line with international publishing standards for social science and communication studies, *Intercultural Research* has adopted the editorial policies of the *APA Publication Manual* (6th ed.) or *MLA*

Handbook (8th ed.) (these two volumes on literature) along with specific guidelines developed for the integration of Chinese names and Chinese language publications. These "SII APA Integrated Chinese Editing" standards (two documents) can be found on the web site of the Institute (**http://sii.shisu.edu.cn**) along with model citation, reference, and layout examples. Information on intended future volumes may also be found on the web page. Further inquiries or comments may be addressed to the editors or to the Institute staff at:

icinstitute@shisu.edu.cn

Intercultural Research 跨文化研究

A thematic academic monograph series produced by
the SISU Intercultural Institute (SII) 上外跨文化研究中心

Series Editors: *Steve J. Kulich, Michael H. Prosser*

Volumes in the Series